The Concise Jewish Encyclopedia

The Concise Jewish Encyclopedia

Edited by Cecil Roth

A MERIDIAN BOOK

NEW AMERICAN LIBRARY

TIMES MIRROR

NEW YORK, LONDON AND SCARBOROUGH, ONTARIO

NAL Books are available at quantity discounts when used to promote products or services. For information please write to Premium Marketing Division, The New American Library, Inc., 1633 Broadway, New York, New York 10019.

Library of Congress Cataloging in Publication Data

Main entry under title:

The Concise Jewish encyclopedia.

1. Jews—Dictionaries and encyclopedias. I. Roth, Cecil, 1899–1970.
DS102.8.C66   909'.04924   79–27120
ISBN 0–452–00526–4

Published by arrangement with Massada Press Ltd.

SIGNET, SIGNET CLASSICS, MENTOR, PLUME, MERIDIAN and NAL BOOKS are published *in the United States* by The New American Library, Inc., 1633 Broadway, New York, New York 10019, *in Canada* by The New American Library of Canada Limited, 81 Mack Avenue, Scarborough, Ontario M1L 1M8, *in the United Kingdom* by The New English Library Limited, Barnard's Inn, Holborn, London EC1N 2JR, England.

First Printing, March, 1980

1 2 3 4 5 6 7 8 9

PRINTED IN THE UNITED STATES OF AMERICA

Preface

The Concise Jewish Encyclopedia comprises information on all aspects of Judaism, Jewish history and literature, and Jewish communities around the world as well as on outstanding Jews both within a Jewish framework and in a world context.

The book was planned by Professor Cecil Roth, and the main work was prepared before his death. It was completed and brought up to date by his friends and published with the agreement of his wife, Irene.

To keep the book to a reasonable size, various conventions have been adopted. The parenthetical material that follows many entry words should be clear enough without special explanation. Cross-references to other entries, which are indicated by CAPITALS AND SMALL CAPITALS, have been used to avoid excessive repetition of information. Two or more members of the same family have often been discussed under the single heading of the family name. When an entry word is repeated frequently within an article it is denoted by its initial, and a few other easily understood abbreviations, such as "cent." for "century," have been used throughout. Finally, while an unreadably telegraphic style has been avoided, every effort has been expended to provide the essential information on each subject without excessive wordiness.

A simplified transliteration scheme has been adopted (see below). Proper names from the Bible and biblical quotations have been taken from the Jewish Publication Society version of the Bible. Common biblical proper names are given in their familiar English form (except for contemporary Israeli names). An asterisk appearing immediately before an entry on a person indicates that the subject of the entry is a non-Jew.

Encyclopedias and other reference works are frequently used simply to determine a correct, or at least an acceptable, form of a word: whether it should be capitalized or not, whether it should be italicized, and so on. In this encyclopedia, capitals and italics are used according to conventions common in English-language publishing; even the transliterations of Hebrew follow English-style typographical conventions. It should be remembered, of course, that the Hebrew alphabet, like other non-roman alphabets, does not have these conventions, and consequently decisions of how to treat transliterated or adopted Hebrew words are somewhat arbitrary.

Abbreviations

abbr.	abbreviation
Arab.	Arabic
Aram.	Aramaic
b.	born
BCE	Before Common Era (= BC)
c.	circa (about)
CE	Common Era (= AD)
cent.	century
d.	died
Deut.	Deuteronomy
E	East
Ecc.	Ecclesiastes
Est.	Esther
Exod.	Exodus
Ezek.	Ezekiel
fl.	flourished
Fr.	French
Gen.	Genesis
Ger.	German
Gk.	Greek
Hab.	Habakkuk
Hag.	Haggai
Heb.	Hebrew
Hos.	Hosea
IK	Ihud ha-Kibbutzim
Is.	Isaiah
It.	Italian
Jer.	Jeremiah
Josh.	Joshua
Judg.	Judges
KA	Ha-Kibbutz ha-Artzi
KM	Ha-Kibbutz ha-Meuḥad
Lev.	Leviticus
Lam.	Lamentations
Lat.	Latin
m.	mile
Macc.	Maccabees
Mal.	Malachi
MH	Ha-Moetzah ha-Ḥaklait
Mic.	Micah
Mt.	Mount
N	North
Neh.	Nehemiah
Num.	Numbers
PAI	Poale Agudat Israel
PM	Ha-Pocl ha-Mizrahi
Pop.	Population
Prov.	Proverbs
Ps.	Psalms
R	Rabbi; River
S	South
Sam.	Samuel
Sp.	Spanish
TM	Tenuat ha-Moshavim
W	West
Y	Talmud Yerushalmi
Zech.	Zechariah
Zeph.	Zephaniah

* indicates a non-Jew.

System of Hebrew Transliteration

א is not transliterated	ו = v (where not a vowel)
בּ = b	ז = z
ב = v	ח = ḥ
ג,גּ = g	ט = t
דּ,ד = d	י = y
ה = h	כּ = k
	כ = kh

ָ = a	ֶ = e
ַ = a	ִ = i
ֹ, וֹ = o	ֻ = u
וּ = u	ֱ = e
short ָ = o	ֳ = o
ֵ = e	ֲ = a

ל = l	פ = ph
מ = m	צ = tz
נ = n	ק = k
ס = s	ר = r
ע is not transliterated	שׁ = sh
	שׂ = s
פּ = p	ת,תּ = t

vocal *sheva* = e
silent *sheva* is not transliterated

The
Concise
Jewish
Encyclopedia

Aaron: First high priest; great-grandson of LEVI; elder brother of MOSES and his spokesman before Pharaoh. When Moses was on Mt. Sinai, A. yielded to the Israelites' demands to make the GOLDEN CALF (Exod. 20). He and his descendants were selected to serve as PRIESTS. A. officiated for almost 40 years in the wilderness until his death and burial on Mt. Hor (on the Edomite border), age 123 (Num. 20:23 ff.). Rabbis saw him as the personification of peace.

Aaron ben Elijah (c. 1330–1369): KARAITE theologian. He lived in Nicomedia (Asia Minor), died in Constantinople. His major work was *Etz Ḥayyim*, modeled after MAIMONIDES' *Guide of the Perplexed*.

Aaron ben Jacob ha-Cohen (late 13th–early 14th cent.): Provençal rabbinic scholar. After the expulsion of the Jews from France in 1306, he lived in Spain, then in Majorca, where he compiled the code of ritual laws and customs called *Orḥot Ḥayyim*. This became popular later in an abbreviated version as *Kol Bo*.

Aaron (Abu Aharon) ben Samuel (9th cent.): Mystic. Born in Baghdad, he took Babylonian mystical traditions to Italy, where they were then transmitted to Germany. A. had a reputation as a wonder-worker.

Aaronson, Aaron (1876–1919): Agronomist in Eretz Israel and a founder of the underground NILI organization. Taken as boy from Rumania to Zikhron Yaakov in Eretz Israel, he trained as an agronomist, discovering Wild Emmer Wheat in Palestine in 1906, and founding the Athlit Agricultural Experimental Station in 1911. He was one of the main organizers of Nili, spying for the British against the Turks during World War I. A. attended the Paris Peace Conference in the Zionist delegation. He was lost in an airplane over the English Channel. His sister Sarah Aaronson (1890–1917), also active in Nili, was arrested by the Turks, but she shot herself to avoid disclosing secrets.

Abarbanel see **Abravanel**

abba (Aram., modern Heb. "father"): Title of honor with some early rabbis, it passed into Christian usage to denote ecclesiastical office (cf. "abbot").

Abba Mari ben Moses ha-Yarhi (late 13th–14th cent.): French talmudist. A bitter opponent of philosophical studies as pursued by followers of MAIMONIDES, he was influential in securing a decree forbidding anyone under 30 to study philosophy. His book *Minhat ha-Kenaot* contained correspondence on this dispute. Originally from Montpellier, he lived in Arles and Perpignan after the 1306 expulsion of the Jews from France.

Abbahu (c. 279–320):

Palestinian AMORA who headed the rabbis of Caesarea. He was highly regarded by the Roman authorities. A. has been credited with editing the legal sections of the Jerusalem Talmud.

Abbaye (278–338): Babylonian AMORA, often called Nahmani. From childhood he studied with his colleague RAVA, and their discussions over a period of many years are reported throughout the Babylonian Talmud. A. became head of the academy at PUMBEDITA, which closed after his death.

Abel: Second son of ADAM and EVE. A shepherd, he was killed out of jealousy by his elder brother CAIN, a farmer, when God accepted Abel's animal sacrifice but rejected Cain's offering (Gen. 4).

Abiathar: Priest of the family of ELI; son of Ahimelech; priest at the sanctuary of Nob. The sole survivor of Saul's massacre of the priests, A. was devoted to David throughout his reign, including the period of Absalom's revolt. However, because he supported Adonijah as David's successor, Solomon, after his accession, banished him from Jerusalem to Anatooth (I Sam. 22:19–23; I Kings 2).

Abigail: Wife of DAVID, who married her shortly after the death of Nabal, her first husband (I Sam. 25).

Abijah (Abijam): King of Judah and son of Rehoboam, A. reigned c. 914–912 BCE. Throughout his reign he was at war with JEROBOAM, king of Israel (I Kings 15).

Abimelech: (1) King of Gerar who maintained friendly relations with ABRAHAM (Gen. 20) and Isaac (Gen. 26). (2) Son of GIDEON by a concubine (c. 12th cent. BCE). He killed his 70 brothers (with one exception) and was king in Shechem for 3 years before being killed (Judges 9).

Abiram: Together with his brother DATHAN, head of the tribe of Reuben, the two leaders joined KORAH in his rebellion against Moses, and were punished by being swallowed up by the earth (Num. 16).

Abishag: Young Shunammite woman who was the companion of the aged David (I Kings 1). Adonijah's request to marry her after David's death was interpreted by Solomon as a bid for the throne, for which he was put to death.

Abishai: DAVID's general and probably his nephew; brother of JOAB. He served David faithfully and saved his life in battle (I Sam. 26; II Sam. 2; etc.).

ablution: Jewish law deals with both total and partial a. for ritual purposes. Complete immersion, in a specially constructed ritual bath (MIKVEH), was prescribed for the high priest on the Day of Atonement and for other priests participating in the Temple service. Today it is required for postmenstruant women (see NIDDAH) and PROSELYTES. Washing of the feet and hands was a requisite for the priests before taking part in the Temple service. Washing of the hands, according to the rabbis, is obligatory before partaking of bread, after leaving a privy, on waking up, before prayer, etc.

Abner: Son of Ner and cousin of SAUL, whose army he commanded. After Saul's death he first made Saul's son ISH-BOSHETH king but later changed his allegiance to David. However, he was killed by Joab, whose brother Asahel he had slain (II Sam. 3).

Abner of Burgos (c. 1270–1340): Spanish apostate who was baptized at the age of 50, taking the name Alfonso of Valladolid. His anti-Jewish works were the basis of subsequent anti-Jewish polemics by Christians.

Aboab: Family of Spanish origin. Its members included *Isaac A.* (14th cent.), a talmudic scholar and author of *Menorat ha-Maor*, a popular collection of ethical rabbinical teaching arranged according to subject matter. Another member, *Isaac de*

Fonesca A. (1605–1693), was the first rabbi in the Americas. Born a Marrano in Portugal, he was brought as a child to Amsterdam, where he became rabbi. In 1641 he went to Recife in Brazil, then under Dutch rule, where he officiated for 13 years until the Portuguese reconquest. He returned to Amsterdam, where he headed a rabbinical academy and was signatory of the ban of excommunication on SPINOZA in 1656.

Abraham: First patriarch and ancestor of the Hebrew people. He was born in Ur, the son of Terah. The family moved to Haran (Gen. 11) and then to the land of Canaan. There God made a covenant with A., the result of which was that the descendants of A. would be recognized as God's people. A. for his part undertook to worship the one God and is hence regarded as the father of monotheism. The sign of the covenant was CIRCUMCISION. A.'s wife was SARAH; they visited Egypt for a time and returned to live in Hebron. There, on one occasion, A. and his men went down into the Jordan Valley and defeated a group of armies who had captured his nephew LOT. As Sarah was childless, she gave A. her handmaid HAGAR, by whom he had a son, ISHMAEL. However, in their old age, Sarah gave birth to ISAAC. God tested A. by asking him to sacrifice Isaac (AKEDAH) on Mt. Moriah but at the last moment told him to substitute a ram. Shortly thereafter Sarah died and A. bought a family plot at MACHPELAH. He himself was buried there at the age of 175. In rabbinical literature he was regarded as the epitome of hospitality (see Gen. 18). The Arabs also regard themselves as descendants of A., through Ishmael.

Abraham bar Ḥayya (late 11th–early 12th cent.) : Spanish scholar who lived in Barcelona. His pioneer scientific writings in Hebrew covered astronomy, geometry, mathematics, geography, music, etc. He was active in the translation of Arabic scientific works into Latin. He also wrote ethical and philosophical works strongly influenced by Neoplatonism.

Abraham ben David of Posquières (c. 1125–1198): French talmudist, known as Ravad. The outstanding French rabbinical authority of his time, his decisions were accepted as authoritative by subsequent generations. His responsa were collected in *Temim Deim*, and he became famous for his *Hassagot*, which criticized Maimonides' *Mishneh Torah*.

Abraham ben Moses ben Maimon (1186–1237): Egyptian communal philosopher and physician, the son of Moses MAIMONIDES. He succeeded his father as leader (*nagid*) of Egyptian Jewry. Like his father he was also physician to the caliph. He wrote various works, notably *Kifayat al-Abidin* (in Arabic) on Judaism and Jewish ethics.

Abraham ibn Daud see **Ibn Daud**

Abraham ibn Ezra see **Ibn Ezra**

Abraham Joshua Heshel (c. 1745–1825): Polish Ḥasidic rabbi, "The Rabbi of Opatov (or Apt)." He taught the importance of "loving and fearing God." A believer in the transmigration of the soul, he claimed that his own soul had had ten previous existences.

Abrahams, Israel (1858–1925): English scholar, reader in rabbinics at Cambridge from 1902. His works include *Jewish Life in the Middle Ages*, a reconstruction of Jewish social life; *Studies in Pharisaism and the Gospels*; and *Hebrew Ethical Wills*. He was a leader of Liberal Judaism in England. He was joint editor (with Claude MONTEFIORE) of the first series of the scholarly periodical JEWISH QUARTERLY REVIEW (1888–1908).

Abramsky, Yehezkel (1886–1976): Talmudic scholar. In the 1920s he was active in promoting Jewish life and rabbinic studies in the USSR, for which he was arrested and sent to Siberia. On his release, he went to London, where he was appointed *dayyan* of the BET DIN and greatly influenced British orthodoxy. From 1951, he lived in Jerusalem. His best-known work is *Ḥazon Yeḥezkel* on the *Tosephta*.

Abravanel (Abarbanel): Sephardi family. *Isaac A.* (1437–1508) was a statesman, religious philosopher, and biblical commentator. He was treasurer to Alfonso V of Portugal, and then became an influential minister at the court of Ferdinand and Isabella of Spain. His efforts to prevent the expulsion of the Jews from Spain in 1492 were unsuccessful. He himself went to Italy, where he was first at the court of Naples and finally at Venice. His discursive commentary on the Bible, largely philosophical, covered all books except the Hagiographa; in Latin translation, it influenced subsequent Christian Bible commentaries. Isaac's son *Judah A.* (Leone Ebreo; c. 1460–1523) was a philosopher, poet, and physician, whose *Dialoghi d'Amore*, one of the first philosophical works written in Italian, was strongly linked to Neoplatonism. It had widespread influence, more in non-Jewish than Jewish circles.

Absalom: Third son of David. He killed his half brother Amnon, who had raped their sister Tamar. He fled to Aram but after 3 years returned and was reconciled with his father. Later he used his personal popularity to organize a revolt against David which enjoyed great initial success. David fled across the Jordan. Eventually when battle was joined, David's army was victorious and Absalom was killed by David's general, Joab, who found him caught by his long hair in a tree (II Sam. 13–19). His death occasioned a famous lament from David.

Abu Isa Alisfahani (8th cent.): Persian pseudo-messiah. He claimed to be the forerunner of the Messiah and announced his mission as the reestablishment of Jewish political independence. He led an army of followers against the Abbasid rulers in Persia. The revolt was suppressed and he was killed. His followers claimed that he had gone into hiding and would reemerge. Known as Isunians, they continued to exist until the 10th cent. They influenced ANAN, founder of Karaism.

Abudarham, David ben Joseph (14th cent.): Spanish liturgic commentator. His popular encyclopedic prayer-book *Sepher Abudarham* explained liturgical customs and practice and is an important source for medieval practices.

Abulafia: Sephardi family. *Abraham ben Samuel A.* (1241–after 1291) was a Spanish mystic who journeyed extensively. He visited Rome to try to convert Pope Nicholas III to Judaism. The Pope's death saved him from being burned at the stake. His prophecy of the imminent end of the world caused the hostility of the rabbis. He founded a new school of mysticism ("Prophetic Kabbalah") based on contemplation of the letters of the Hebrew alphabet. Another family member, *Samuel ben Meir Halevi A.* (1320–1361), a Spanish financier, was treasurer to Pedro the Cruel, king of Castile. He built several synagogues in Toledo, where one of them (Sinagoga del Transito), as well as his home, still stand. He was tortured to death and his wealth confiscated.

Abyssinia see **Ethiopia**

academy (*yeshivah;* Aram. *metivta*): Academies of rabbinical studies flourished in Palestine and Babylonia. They existed in Palestine as early as Second Temple times but their significance became crucial after the destruction of the Temple (70) when the academy at JABNEH founded by JOHANAN BEN ZAKKAI played a vital role in adapting Jewish practice to the new circumstances. Here the liturgy was established, biblical canon determined, and work begun on codifying the ORAL LAW. Subsequent Palestinian academies included those at Lydda (under ELIEZER BEN HYRCANUS), Pekiin (JOSHUA BEN HANANIAH), USHA, SHEPHARAM, BET SHEARIM, SEPPHORIS (where JUDAH HA-NASI compiled the Mishnah), CAESAREA (R. ABBAHU), and TIBERIAS (where the Jerusalem Talmud and the Masorah were compiled). The Palestinian academies began to decline in the 5th cent. The main academies in Babylonia in the period of the TANNAIM were in NISIBIS and NEHAR PEKOD. One of the most distinguished eras began in the 3rd cent., when SAMUEL headed the school at NEHARDEA and RAV established the SURA academy. The former was replaced by the academy at PUMBEDITA in 259. The academies of Sura and Pumbedita were the authoritative centers of learning and authority for many centuries; the Babylonian Talmud was edited in the former. The heyday of the Babylonian academies had passed by the 12th cent., but they continued to exist (in Baghdad and elsewhere) until the 13th cent.

Academy of Hebrew Language: Israeli institution recognized as the official authority on the Hebrew language. Established in 1953, it succeeded the Vaad ha-Lashon ha-Ivrit ("Hebrew Language Council"), which had been founded by Eliezer Ben-Yehuda and David Yellin in Jerusalem in 1890, then reorganized in 1904. The academy determines Hebrew language, usage, grammar, and pronunciation.

accents (*taamei hamikra; neginot*): Signs inserted in the Hebrew Bible, both for punctuation and as notes for cantillation. These signs were introduced in the 8th–9th cent. As for the vowel signs, there were originally three systems: Babylonian, Palestinian, and Tiberian. The a. indicate division of sentences as well as accent, because they are placed on the tone-syllable of the word. They are divided into disjunctive a. (*melakhim*) and conjunctive a. (*mesharetim*). The cantillation varies according to Jewish communities, and there are also differences among the books of the Bible (the Pentateuch, Prophets, and the Books of Psalms, Proverbs, and Job each have their own tunes). The a. are not marked in the Scroll of the Law. Tradition says that the a. were first given to Moses, then forgotten, and later revived by Ezra.

Acosta (da Costa), Uriel (Gabriel) (c. 1585–1640): Philosopher. Born in Portugal to a Marrano family; his study of the Bible led him to doubt Christianity, and he escaped with his family to Amsterdam, where he openly professed Judaism (1615). However the biblical Judaism he had studied in Portugal differed from rabbinic interpretation, and A. openly attacked rabbinical teaching, in particular denying immortality of the soul and resurrection. He was then excommunicated. After 15 years he recanted. But soon afterward he repeated his ideas. Again he was excommunicated, again he recanted, but this time he was sentenced to flogging and other public humiliations. He committed suicide.

Acre (Acco, Akko; under the Romans, Ptolemais; under the Crusaders, St. Jean d'Acre): Town on northern coast of Israel. Mentioned in the 19th cent. BCE, it became noted as a commercial and manufacturing (e.g. glass) center. After the Israelite conquest of Canaan, it remained outside the area they controlled and was not included in the traditional boundaries of the "Holy Land." Jews lived there at various periods. The town took on special importance at the time of the Crusaders, and for a century (from 1191) was their capital of Palestine. When Napoleon endeavored to move through the Middle East, his armies were stopped at A. as a result of British intervention (1799). Many years later, in 1947, Jewish underground fighters interned by the British in A.'s ancient jail staged a spectacular breakout. Most of its Arab population fled in 1948. Subsequently it was a mixed Jewish-Arab town, and in 1975 had 34,800 inhabitants, of whom nearly 9,000 were Arabs. Impressive Crusader remains have been excavated at A., and it is also the site of the el-Jazzar mosque. Its ancient port is still used by fishermen.

Adam ("Man"): The first man, created by God on the sixth day in the Divine image as the climax of the Creation process. He was made out of the earth and instructed to look after the Garden of Eden. Out of his rib a woman and "helpmeet," Eve, was created. Persuaded by the cunning serpent, A. and Eve disobeyed the Divine command not to eat of the fruit of the forbidden Tree of Knowledge. They were punished by expulsion from the Garden, and A. was destined to become a toiler. He lived for 930 years and had many children, of whom the eldest were CAIN and ABEL (Gen. 1–5).

Adar: Twelfth month of the Jewish religious year, 6th month of the civil year. Corresponds approximately to Feb.–Mar., with the zodiac sign of Pisces. Major dates: 7th, traditional date of birth and death of Moses; 13th, Fast of Esther; 14th, Purim; 15th, Shushan Purim. A. lasts 29 days in an ordinary year and 30 days in a leap year when there are two months of A. (Adar I and Adar II) and the festivals and other anniversaries are observed in Adar II. Because of its festive days, the rabbis said, "When A. come in, joy increases."

Additional Service see **Musaph**

Aden: City on south western Arabian coast. Jews lived there in medieval times, and its Jewish community had a long and prosperous history; it was the home also of many noted scholars. Jews from Yemen moved there after the British annexation in 1838. The Arabs attacked the Jewish quarter in 1947, and after 1948 most of its Jews left. The remaining Jewish community came to an abrupt end in 1967 when all Jews left the city after the Arab-Israeli war.

Adiabene: District in upper Tigris region in Mesopotamia. In the 1st cent. CE, when it was semi-indepen-dent, its queen HELENA con-verted to Judaism together with her sons King Monobaz II and Izates (c. 30 CE).

Adler: Family of rabbis in Britain. *Nathan Marcus* A. (1803–1890), born in Han-over, was appointed chief rabbi of the British Empire in 1845. He was largely re-sponsible for founding JEWS' COLLEGE and the UNITED SYNAGOGUE. He was the au-thor of *Netinah la-Ger*, a standard commentary on Tar-gum Onkelos. His son *Her-mann* A. (1839–1911) suc-ceeded his father as chief rabbi in 1891.

Adler: US family. *Samuel* A. (1809–1891) was a Re-form rabbi in Germany before going to the US in 1857 as rabbi of Temple Emanu-El in New York. His son *Felix* A. (1851–1933) left Judaism after studying for the rab-binate. He founded the New York Society for Ethical Cul-ture (1876) and was professor of ethics at Columbia Uni-versity, 1902–28.

Adler: US family of ac-tors. Its founder was *Jacob* A. (1855–1926), who first acted in Russia. When the Czarist government prohibited the Yiddish theater he went to London (1883). In 1888 he arrived in New York, where he subsequently became the outstanding actor-manager of the Yiddish theater in the US. His wife *Sarah* (c. 1858–

1953) played opposite him. Their children *Stella* A. (1902–) and *Luther* A. (1903–) both achieved renown on the English-speaking stage.

Adler, Alfred (1870–1937): Austrian psychologist. He broke with his teacher FREUD and developed his own theory of "Individual Psychology," emphasizing the problems caused by inferiority complexes. In 1934 he moved to the US.

Adler, Cyrus (1863-1940): US communal leader and scholar. From 1892 he was librarian of the Smithsonian Institution in Washington. He founded and headed many US Jewish cultural organizations, including the American Jewish Historical Society and the Jewish Publication Society of America. He also served as president of the Jewish Theological Seminary and of Dropsie College. A. was editor of the *Jewish Quarterly Review* and the *American Jewish Year Book*. His autobiography was titled *I Have Considered the Days*.

Adler, Jankel (1895–1949): Expressionist painter. Born in Lodz, he settled in France in 1935 and eventually moved to England. Many of his works, especially in his early and last periods, had Jewish themes.

Adloyada (Aram.):

Purim carnival (especially in Israel). The term comes from the statement that on Purim a man should drink until he does not know (*ad de-lo yeda*) the difference between "Blessed be Mordecai" and "Cursed be Haman."

Admor: Abbr. of *Adonenu, Morenu ve-Rabbenu*, "Our Lord, Our Master and Our Rabbi," a title given by the HASIDIM to their rabbi or TZADDIK.

Adon Olam ("Lord of the Universe"): Hymn of unknown authorship (sometimes attributed to Solomon ibn Gabirol), recited at the beginning of the Morning Service in the Ashkenazi rite, and in many other rites at the conclusion of the Additional Service. It is also recited before falling asleep and on a deathbed. It praises the unity and eternity of God and expresses confidence in Divine Providence.

Adonai ("My Lord"): Metonym substituted to avoid reading the Divine name YHWH. As early as the 2nd cent. BCE, it was used in all Bible reading.

Adoshem: Artificial word constructed from ADONAI and *ha-Shem* ("the [Divine] name") so as to avoid pronouncing *Adonai* when uttering the Divine name outside prayer.

Adorno, Theodor (1903–1969): German sociologist,

who later lived in the US (1938–56). Co-author of *The Authoritarian Personality*, which made an impact on both psychology and sociology. Adorno was an important influence in New Left circles for a time.

Adret, Solomon ben Abraham (1235–1310): Spanish rabbinical authority, known as Rashba, a rabbi in Barcelona for more than 40 years. He issued thousands of responsa which greatly influenced rabbinical thought and decisions in subsequent centuries. He also wrote novellae based on the Talmud. In 1305 he issued a ban on students under the age of 30 studying philosophy.

Adrianople (Edirne): Town in Turkey. Jews lived there from the Byzantine period. Its Jewish community became particularly noteworthy after it attracted many Spanish Jews following the Spanish expulsion of 1492. A. was a center of Jewish learning, and many Hebrew books were printed there. Close to 20,000 Jews were living there in the early 20th cent., but many left for other parts of Turkey and, from 1948, for Israel. By 1971 the Jewish population had diminished to 250.

Aelia Capitolina: Name given by the Romans to city built on site of Jerusalem after the Bar Kokhba war (135); formed from names of the emperor (Aelius Hadrianus) and the god Jupiter Capitolinus. Jews were allowed in the city only on the fast of Av 9.

Afghanistan: The medieval Jewish community ended with the Mongol invasion (1222). The modern community grew in the 19th cent. as a development of the Jews of Persia. In the 20th cent. their numbers dwindled and in recent years most have emigrated, many to Israel. In 1976 their numbers were estimated at 200 living in Kabul, Herat, and Balkh.

Africa, North: The early history of the Israelites is closely bound up with EGYPT, whose Jewish community dates back at least to the 6th cent. BCE. In the course of time they moved westward along the N. African coast (e.g., to CYRENE). In addition, there is evidence that many among the Berber tribes of MOROCCO adopted Judaism. After the Muslim invasion in the 7th cent., Jewish life and learning flourished there; for a time the N. African academies were outstanding in the Jewish world. The Jews were subject to severe persecutions from time to time. From the end of the 14th cent., and especially after 1492, many Spanish and Portuguese Jews found refuge in N. Africa, in many cases transforming the nature of the local communities to take on SEPHARDI overtones. Gradually their position became depressed, and they were often restricted to the MELLAH (Jewish quarter). The situation improved only with the arrival of the European powers, especially the French, from the mid-19th cent. The ALLIANCE ISRAÉLITE UNIVERSELLE opened a network of schools in N. African countries, while the Crémieux Decree of 1870 conferred French citizenship on the Jews of Algeria. This gradual improvement in conditions was halted before and during World War II in the countries falling under Fascist and Nazi control. Only with the advances of the Allies into some territories were former conditions gradually restored. However, rising Arab nationalism and the Palestinian conflict exacerbated relations between Jews and Moslems in the postwar period. From 1948, Jews left Africa, mostly for France, Israel, and other destinations such as Canada. The ancient Jewish communities of Egypt and Libya were virtually ended after the Six-Day War in 1967; almost all the Jews of Algeria left when that country attained independence in 1962. Of the estimated 750,000 Jews in N. Africa in 1948, less than 40,000 remained by 1977.

Africa, South: Jews first settled in S. Africa in number from the early 19th cent., with the first congregation formed in CAPE TOWN in 1841. Gradually the Jews moved inland, often as itinerant peddlers, with some settling in smaller towns as storekeepers and as farmers. Jewish immigration increased at the end of the 19th cent., especially with the discovery of gold. JOHANNESBURG and the Transvaal were now the main centers of attraction, and Jews played a large part in the development of the diamond industry in the Kimberley area. Another large wave of immigration came after World War I, mainly of Jews from Lithuania. From the 1930s onward, restrictions were imposed on immigration, and the number of Jews entering the country gradually diminished. After 1948, Israel attracted many S. African Jews, and several thousand went there to settle. The S. African Jewish community is centrally organized, with a Board of Deputies, a strong Zionist Federation, and active boards of Jewish education. Most of the Jews living in rural areas have moved into the towns. The main communities are in Johannesburg and Cape Town, with smaller groups in Durban, Port Elizabeth, and East London. There were 117,900 Jews in

S. Africa in 1976.

Afternoon Service see **Minḥah**

Afula: Town in Israel, in the Valley of Jezreel. Founded in 1925, it did not fulfill the early hopes of the settlers, growing slowly until 1948. After that, however, many immigrants settled there, and it had 18,700 inhabitants in 1974. The central hospital for the region is situated there.

Agam, Yaacov (1928–): Israeli painter, working mostly in Israel and Paris. He has made original contributions to optic and kinetic art. In many of his paintings, the picture is changed by the movement of either the picture or the viewer.

aggadah: Those sections of the TALMUD and MIDRASH devoted to ethical and moral teaching, legends, folklore, etc., as opposed to the legal sections (HALAKHAH). There is little a. in the Mishnah, but about a third of the Palestinian Talmud and a quarter of the Babylonian Talmud consist of a. The other major repository is MIDRASHIC LITERATURE, which is entirely based on a., emanating primarily from homiletic expositions of the Bible, applied directly or by implication to topical situations. No aggadic work is known before the 4th cent., but thereafter these are numerous, appearing until the 10th or 11 cent. The aggadic sections of the Talmud were collected by Jacob and Levi ibn Ḥaviv in *Ein Yaakov*; the outstanding English compilation is Louis Ginzberg's 7-volume *Legends of the Jews* (1909–28), which presents the major aggadot according to biblical chronology.

Agnon, Shemuel Yoseph (1888–1970): Hebrew novelist, winner of the 1966 Nobel Prize for Literature. Born in Buchach, Galicia, he settled in Palestine in 1909, lived again in Europe (mostly Germany) from 1912 to 1923, and then finally settled in Jerusalem. He is the outstanding writer of modern epic Hebrew literature. His tales are set either in his native Galicia (*Hakhnasat Kallah, Oreah Natah la-Lun*) or Israel (*Temol Shilshom, Shirah*). His Hebrew blends biblical and rabbinical styles.

Agrippa I (10 BCE–44 CE): Herod Agrippa I, king of Judea; son of ARISTOBULUS and grandson of HEROD. Due to his friendship with Caligula, he was appointed as king over some of the territories that had been ruled by his grandfather, including parts of Transjordan (37). Later his jurisdiction was extended, eventually covering Galilee, Samaria, and Judea. His religious observance earned him the affection of his Jewish subjects.

Agrippa II (28–92): Herod Agrippa II, last of the Herodian kings; son of AGRIPPA I. He received the title of king from Claudius, ruling initially over Chalcis and later receiving other territories. He never ruled Judea. He was disliked by the people, and his attempts to intervene at the outbreak of the Jewish revolt against Rome ended in ignominy. He joined Titus during the siege of Jerusalem, and Vespasian subsequently granted him additional dominions.

Agudat (Agudas) Israel ("Union of Israel"): Ultra-orthodox worldwide Jewish movement. Founded in Kattowitz in 1912, it strongly opposed political Zionism. In Europe, its main constituents were in Poland, Lithuania, Hungary, and Germany, and it was supported by the Hasidic *tzaddikim*. Many of its supporters perished in the Holocaust, and after World War II its main centers developed in Israel and the US. When the State of Israel was established, A.I. dropped its opposition to the State (although still refusing to become a part of the World Zionist Organization) and participated in Knesset elections; it joined the government coalition from 1948 to 1952. A.I., together with its workers party, POALEI AGUDAT ISRAEL, has had a steady representation of 5–6 seats in every Knesset.

Aguilar, Grace (1816–1847): English novelist and poet. Her best-known work, *Vale of Cedars*, is an idealized story of the Marranos in Spain.

Agunah: Woman separated from her husband who cannot remarry either because she cannot obtain a bill of divorce or because there is no evidence of his death. The potential hardships involved have been recognized by rabbis who from early times were often as lenient as they could be within the framework of the law (e.g., by accepting the evidence of a single witness regarding the husband's death). Nevertheless the problems that remain have led to attempts to amend the wedding contract so as to cover the possible contingencies.

Aha (Ahai) of Shabha (680–752): Babylonian rabbinical authority. A. taught for many years at Pumbedita, but when a rival was appointed GAON, he moved to Palestine. He is best known for *Sepher Sheeltot* ("Book of Queries"), one of the first rabbinic works to appear after the editing of the Babylonian Talmud. It contains homilies in Aramaic arranged according to the weekly Torah readings, and it deals with many problems raised subsequent to the closing of the Talmud.

Ahab: King of Israel, son of OMRI; he ruled c. 874–852 BCE. He married JEZEBEL, princess of Tyre who introduced the Baal cult into Israel. This led to conflict with the prophets, led by ELIJAH, culminating in the contest on Mt. Carmel (I Kings 18). Elijah rebuked A. severely for his conduct over NABOTH's vineyard (I Kings 21). A. joined forces with Ben-Hadad, king of Damascus, to check the advance of Shalmaneser II of Assyria. He was fatally wounded while fighting against Damascus. The ruins of his palace have been excavated at Samaria.

Ahad ha-Am ("One of the People"; 1856–1927): Pseudonym of Asher Ginzberg, Zionist thinker and essayist. Born in the Ukraine, he was an early supporter of the Zionist ideal; he founded the secret order of BENE MOSHE. Visits to Palestine in the 1890s led him to write critiques of the settlement program, and he also criticized Herzl's political Zionism. He expounded a "cultural Zionism," according to which Zionism must first face the spiritual problems of Judaism. Thus Palestine would be first and foremost a spiritual center for Jews everywhere, which would in turn influence all aspects of Jewish life.

From 1896 to 1903 he edited the journal *Ha-Shiloah,* which he founded. From 1908 to 1922 he lived in London, where he took part in some of the negotiations leading to the 1917 Balfour Declaration. From 1922 he lived in Tel-Aviv.

aharonim ("later ones"): The later rabbinical authorities, as contrasted with the *rishonim* ("the early ones"). The commencement of the period of the *a.* is sometime in the late Middle Ages.

Ahasuerus: King of Persia, in the story of the Book of ESTHER. Scholars differ as to his identification, but many take him to be Xerxes I (reigned 486–465 BCE). The name is also applied to the WANDERING JEW.

Ahavah Rabbah ("[with] Great Love"): Prayer recited before the *Shema* in the Morning Service in the Ashkenazi rite. In the Sephardi rite the prayer begins with the words *Ahavat Olam* ("Eternal Love"), which is the beginning of the version of the prayer in both rites in the Evening Service.

Ahaz: King of Judah who ruled 743–727 BCE. Under severe attack from various kingdoms, he turned to Assyria for aid despite the warnings of ISAIAH. As a result he became a vassal of Assyria (II Kings 16 ff.).

Ahaziah: Name of two

biblical kings. (1) A. of Israel ruled c. 853 BCE for a short period during which he was bitterly condemned by Elijah for his corrupt practices (II Kings 1). (2) A. of Judah also had a short reign, c. 842–841 BCE. He continued the evil ways of his parents, Jehoram and Athaliah, and was fatally wounded in battle with Jehu (II Kings 8–9).

Aḥdut Avodah ("Unity of Labor"): (1) Zionist socialist party founded in 1919, merging in 1930 with Ha-Poel ha-Tzair to form Mapai. (2) Israeli socialist party, which broke away from Mapam in 1954 and existed indepen dently until 1968, when it merged with Mapai and Rafi to form the Israel Labor Party (Maarakh). Its backbone was the KIBBUTZ ME'-UḤAD movement.

Ahijah: Prophet of Shiloh ("the Shilonite"), active in the reigns of Solomon and Jeroboam I. He prophesied the latter's accession and fall (I Kings 11:29–40).

Aḥikar: Hero of legend popular in ancient Near East. Translations exist in various languages, and it was already known in the 5th cent. BCE. It falls in the category of WISDOM LITERATURE since, after the first part telling the story of its hero, the second part is devoted to maxims and axioms. The folktale has a considerable Jewish basis, either original or derived in the course of its various versions.

Ahithophel: David's adviser. He supported Absalom when the latter rebelled against David, but sensing failure when Absalom refused to accept his counsel, he committed suicide (II Sam. 17).

Ai: Place near Bethel, north of Jerusalem. It was captured by Joshua following an attempt whose lack of success was attributed to Achan, who took for himself dedicated spoils (Josh. 7). The site has been excavated.

Aijalon: Plain between Jerusalem and the Mediterranean Sea, the site of Joshua's victory over the Gibeonites. It is here that the sun stood still at Joshua's command to enable him to complete his victory (Josh. 10:12 ff.).

Akdamut Millin (Aram. "Introduction"): Aramaic poem recited in Ashkenazi synagogues on the first day of the Feast of Weeks immediately preceding the Reading of the Torah (or inserted after the first verse of the Torah reading). Its author was the 11th-cent. rabbi Meir ben Isaac Nahorai of Worms.

Akedah ("binding"): The binding of ISAAC (Gen. 22). The story was taken as the epitome of selfless devotion to God, becoming the prototype of the Jewish ideal of complete submission to the Divine will and, when necessary, to martyrdom. The story and its implications appear frequently in Hebrew poetry and literature, and it may at one time have served as a contrast to the Christian story of the crucifixion.

Akiva ben Joseph (c. 50–c. 135): Palestinian TANNA. Little is known about his early life. Tradition relates that he did not begin his studies until the age of 40. He studied with R. Joshua and R. Eliezer, arranging the foundations for the Oral Law as eventually codified in the MISHNAH. According to his influential method of biblical exegesis, every word and letter in the Bible has its own importance and can be utilized for the exposition of the Scriptures. A. was acknowledged to be the outstanding scholar of his time, and his academy at Bene Berak attracted many students. He keenly supported the BAR KOKHBA revolt against Rome and is said to have hailed Bar Kokhba as "king-messiah." He resolutely refused to obey the Roman regulation forbidding the teaching of the Law, and for this he was arrested, imprisoned, and eventually executed at Caesarea. Both his life and death profoundly influenced Jewish history and legend.

akkum (abbr. for "worshipers of stars and planets"): Idol worshiper. When Christian critics of the Talmud implied that the use of the terms *nokhri* or *goy* (non-Jew) referred to Christians, the Jews in the Middle Ages substituted the term *a.* to show that the reference was to an idolator or heathen.

Al ha-Nissim ("[We thank Thee] for the Miracles"): Thanksgiving prayer inserted into the AMIDAH and the grace after meals on PURIM and ḤANUKKAH. It contains a résumé of the events of the respective deliverances commemorated on those two festivals.

Al Ḥet ("For the Sin"): Formula of confession recited in every prayer service on the Day of Atonement (except the Concluding Service) and on the previous afternoon. The congregation says the prayer silently and it is then repeated aloud by the cantor. The sins are listed in alphabetical order (one per letter in the Sephardi rite; two in the Ashkenazi). The confession is phrased in the first person plural as a corporate act.

Al Tikre ("do not read"): Term used in the Talmud and Midrash to denote slight changes introduced into the biblical reading for exegetical purposes, e.g., by altering the vowels of a word in order to extract a new meaning.

Alabama: US state. Jewish traders traveled there in the mid-18th cent., but the first community, at Mobile, dates from 1820s. Communities were subsequently founded at Montgomery (1849), Huntsville (1860), and Birmingham (1882). The Jewish population fell steadily in the first part of the 20th cent., but became stabilized after World War II. In 1976 there were 9,050 Jews in the state.

Alaska: US state. The number of Jews there has always been small. A cemetery was opened in Fairbanks in 1905. A small community emerged after World War II at Anchorage. The first state senator was Ernest GRUENING.

Alav ha-Shalom ("on him be peace"): Phrase said when mentioning a dead person (cf. R.I.P.).

Albania: Balkan country. Jewish refugees from Spain settled here, especially in the ports (e.g., Berat, Durazzo, Valona), in the early 16th cent. SHABBETAI TZEVI was imprisoned in A. and died in Dulcigno. A small Jewish community, including some refugees from Germany, lived in A. before World War II. In 1977, there were 300 Jews, mostly in Tirana.

Albany: Capital of State of New York. Its first congregation was Beth El (later Beth Emeth), founded in 1838. From 1846 to 1854 its rabbi was Isaac Mayer WISE, whose reforms in the service led to a split in the congregation. The city has a Jewish population of 13,500 (1976).

Alberta: Canadian province. Jews began to settle at the end of the 19th cent. Calgary and Edmonton have always been the largest communities; many of the smaller ones have now disappeared. In 1971 there were 7,320 Jews in A.

Albo, Joseph (c. 1380–c. 1435): Religious philosopher in Spain. He participated in the DISPUTATION of Tortosa in 1413–14. His *Sepher Ikkarim* ("Book of Principles") was the last major work of Jewish medieval philosophy, distinguishing between conventional, natural, and Divine law, with only the last offering salvation. He postulated three basic principles of religion: The Existence of God, Revelation, and Reward and Punishment. From these are derived secondary dogmas, and to deny any of these major principles constitutes heresy.

Alenu ("It is our duty [to praise]"): First word of hymn on the unity of God and His kingship over the universe; from the 12th cent. on, it was recited at the end of every service. Although possibly written earlier, it was placed by Rav (3rd cent.) in the New Year Additional Service. The A. prayer became the subject of a lengthy persecution by Christians, who misconstrued certain passages, and it was banned in various countries at different times. Sometimes it was deleted entirely, and the Sephardim still recite only the first paragraph.

Aleph (א): First letter of the Hebrew alphabet. Numerical value: 4. Pronounced

Aleppo: Town in Syria; called by Jews Aram-Zoba (see Psalms 60:2). The Jewish community there dates from ancient times and had a long tradition of Jewish scholarship. Some 5,000 Jews were living there in the 12th cent., and the community prospered under the Mamluks. In the 19th cent. there was a decline. After World War I, 6,000 Jews lived in A., but most of these subsequently emigrated, especially after riots in 1947, in which all the synagogues were destroyed. The 1,000 Jews still there in the 1970s suffered severely, together with the rest of Syrian Jewry. The famous 10th-cent. Aleppo codex of the Bible, corrected by BEN ASHER, reached Israel in the 1950s.

*Alexander the Great (356–323 BCE): Macedonian ruler. He marched through the land of Israel on his way to Egypt, and many legends grew up around this occasion (e.g., his visit to Jerusalem, his encounter with the high priest). Later, he hastened back from Egypt to put down a Samaritan revolt. He played an important role in Jewish legends and romances, and the name Alexander became accepted as a Jewish name.

Alexander Yannai (Jannaeus) (c. 126–76 BCE): Hasmonean king of Judea and high priest, who ruled 103–76 BCE; son of John HYRCANUS. He alienated many of his own subjects, breaking completely with the Pharisees. A civil war ensued when the latter sought the support of the Syrians. However when A. was defeated by the Syrians near Shechem, he evoked the sympathy of his opponents, many of whom returned to his ranks. He was then able to be victorious and take a cruel revenge on his internal enemies. In the course of his reign, he extended considerably the territories of his country, annexing the coastal region and the Greek cities of Palestine, and obtaining land in Transjordan.

Alexander, Moses (1853–1952): First Jewish governor of a US state. A., who was born in Germany, was a popular governor of Idaho, 1915–19, and the town of Alexander, Idaho, is named for him.

Alexander, Samuel (1859–1938): British philosopher. Born in Australia, he taught in Manchester from 1893. His writings, especially on relationships of time and space, were influential; he was a leading representative of the school of metaphysical realism.

Alexandra Salome see Salome Alexandra

Alexandria: Principal port of Egypt. In ancient times, Alexandria was the main Jewish center outside Palestine. Jews lived there from the 3rd cent. BCE, and much of the city was Jewish. A center of Jewish Hellenistic culture, the Bible was translated into Greek (SEPTUAGINT) there, and it was also the home of the philosopher PHILO. Frequent clashes occurred with the non-Jewish population, and A. became one of the earliest cradles of anti-Jewish feeling. At the time of the great Jewish revolt in 115–17 CE, the Jews of A. were attacked and suffered serious losses, including the destruction of their synagogue, the most magnificent and famous in antiquity. The Jewish community never again attained the same importance. Jews were expelled in 414 but returned within a couple of centuries. In the 19th cent. the community grew again, and many Italian Jews settled there. However, it declined steadily after World War II, particularly following the 1948, 1956, and 1967 wars with Israel, and by 1977 less than 100 remained.

Alfasi, Isaac (1013–1103): Talmudist and codifier, known as Rif. He was a major link in the transfer of the center of talmudic study from Babylonia in the East to North Africa and then to Spain in the West. Until he was 75 he taught at Fez. He was then compelled to flee to Spain, where he established an academy at Lucena, playing an important role in developing talmudic studies in Spain. His *Sepher ha-Halakhot* (also known as *Alfas*) is one of the basic works of codification of Jewish law, summing up both the talmudic legislation and the subsequent rulings of the *geonim* (see GAOU).

Algeria: N. African country. Jews were living there as early as Roman times. Certain local Berber tribes embraced Judaism in the early medieval period. Jewish life generally flourished, except for periods of reaction, such as under the Almohades (12th cent.) when the community of Tlemcen was destroyed. The nature of the community changed completely as a result of its absorption of Jews from Spain at the end of the 14th and in the 15th cent. Under the Turks, from the 16th cent., conditions were generally good, and some Jews played prominent roles in politics and economic life. The Jews welcomed French rule in 1830, benefiting from the CRÉMIEUX Decree (1870), by which they were granted French citizenship. This was canceled by the Vichy government during World War II but restored by De Gaulle. The Jews identified largely with French culture, and when the French settlers left in 1961–62, at the approach of Algerian independence, the Jews left with them, mostly to France, with a minority going to Israel. About 120,000 Jews lived in A. until the early 1960s, but by 1977 only 1,000 remained in Algiers and Constantine.

Alḥarizi, Judah (c. 1170–c. 1235): Hebrew author. His best-known work is *Taḥkemoni*, a series of narratives in rhyming prose. He translated works from Arabic into Hebrew, including Maimonides' *Guide of the Perplexed*. He was one of the first Hebrew authors to write in a light, humorous style.

Aliyah ("going up"): (1) The honor of being "called up" to the READING OF THE LAW in the synagogue service. (2) The immigration of Jews to Israel. Ever since the Diaspora began, Jews have aspired to return to Israel, and there were several early cases of group immigration, starting with the Return to Zion from the Babylonian Exile in the 6th cent. BCE. Modern organized *a.* began in the early 1880s with the arrival of the BILU. Zionist immigration waves are divided into the following. *First A.* (1882–1903), led by the Bilu and partly motivated by the Russian pogroms. About 25,000 immigrated—mostly from E. Europe—and several agricultural settlements were founded, although these generally had a difficult economic struggle. *Second A.* (1904–14), also derived chiefly from Russia. About 40,000 came in this *a.*, most of whom subsequently left. The pioneers of the Second A. played a major role in setting the patterns for the subsequent development of the country, and there was a drive at cooperation in many spheres, with emphasis on Hebrew culture, language, etc. *Third A.* (1919–23), when some 35,000 went to Palestine, mostly from Eastern Europe. *Fourth A.* (1924–28) brought almost 70,000, most of them in 1924–25, when there was widespread economic depression in Poland. A middle-class element entered with this a. *Fifth A.* The First Period (1929–35) saw the beginnings of Hitler's rule, and many newcomers came from Germany, including a high proportion of professional men. In the Second

Period (1936–40), when immigration was restricted by the British authorities, over 250,000 arrived in that decade. *Sixth A.* (1941–47) covered the worst war years and the struggle against the British in Palestine for the right of Jews to immigrate freely. During this period 85,000 Jews arrived. From 1948 onward there was unrestricted immigration for Jews to the State of Israel, and 1,540,000 immigrated between 1948 and 1975.

Alkabetz, Solomon ben Moses (c. 1505–1584): Hebrew poet and mystic. Born in Turkey, he settled in Safed, where he headed a group of kabbalists and was a colleague of Joseph Caro and teacher of Moses Cordvero. His most popular composition is the Sabbath hymn Lekhah Dodi, which entered all Jewish rites in Friday evening services.

Alkalai, Judah ben Solomon Hai (1798–1878): Rabbi and a forerunner of modern Zionism. He served as rabbi in Serbia and became acquainted with Balkan nationalism. His booklet *Shema Yisrael* (1834) proposed the return of the Jews to their homeland through natural colonization, which should precede supernatural redemption. His work was widely disseminated and influenced the formation of the religious Zionist movement.

Allen, Woody (1936–   ): US humorist. After writing filmscripts, plays, and articles, Allen made a name for himself on stage and especially in movies (*Play It Again, Sam, Bananas, The Front, Annie Hall, Interiors, Manhattan*).

Alliance Israélite Universelle: French organization, founded in 1860, to defend Jewish liberties wherever threatened and to provide Jewish education, especially in N. Africa, the Balkans, and Middle Eastern countries. It played a significant role—often in conjunction with similar organizations from other countries—in intervening on behalf of oppressed Jews up to World War II. It founded the first agricultural school in Palestine (at Mikveh Israel in 1870), and its network of schools in Moslem lands was crucial in improving Jewish education. Although the number of schools fell after World War II, the A.I.U. remains active in France, Israel, Morocco, Tunisia, Syria, Lebanon, and Iran and runs 64 schools.

Allon, Yigal (1918–   ): Israeli military and political leader. A founder of the Palmah, he was its commander from 1945 to 1948. He then commanded Israeli armies on various fronts in the 1948–49 War of Independence, including the Southern Front, where he directed the operation leading to the occupation of Elath on the Red Sea. Subsequently he was a leader of the Ahdut Avodah party, and when this merged, of the Israel Labor Party. A member of the Knesset from 1955, he held various government offices, including minister of labor (1961–68), minister of education (1969–74), and foreign minister (1974–77).

almemar (Arab. *al-minbar*, "pulpit"): Raised platform in the center of the synagogue from which the Scroll of the Law is read. The word is used among Ashkenazim (who also use *bimah*). Sephardim call it *tebah*.

alphabet: The Hebrew a. is in the family of North Semitic alphabets. It consists of 22 letters, all of them consonants. (The vowels, marked first by the insertion of *yud*, *vav*, and, less frequently, *aleph* as vowel-letters, and subsequently by PUNCTUATION of the consonants, were inserted only much later.) The Early Hebrew a., which belonged to the Canaanite family of alphabets, was used until the period of the Babylonian Exile. The same script was used by other peoples in the vicinity (e.g., the Moabites). After the Exile it was gradually replaced by the Square Script, derived from the Aramaic a., then commonly used throughout much of the Near East. For a time the former script was also in use, and it is found as late as some of the Dead Sea Scrolls and the coins of Bar Kokhba. The Square Script developed in the course of time into the modern printed Hebrew script. Five of the 22 letters in the Square Script have special forms when they are the final letters of the word. Various cursive scripts developed for writing Hebrew by hand, and these often took on local differences. One of the best known was the rabbinic Rashi script (so called because it was first used in a printed commentary by Rashi). All the letters have a numerical value, and the letters are also used for writing numbers.

Alroy, David (12th cent.): Pseudo-messiah; real name, Menahem ben Solomon. He succeeded his father as head of a messianic movement which developed among the Mountain Jews of the Caucasus before 1121. When this was defeated, A. shifted the revolt to Kurdistan. Many followed him, but the revolt collapsed with his sudden death (possibly by assassination). Even after his death some of his followers, called Menahemites after his real name, continued to believe in his messianic mission.

Alsace: Province of France. In the Middle Ages, Jews were settled throughout A. They were the victims of frequent attacks, including the ARMLEDER (1336–38) and BLACK DEATH (1348) massacres. There were various expulsions and readmissions, but when A. became French in the 17th cent., the Jews were permitted to remain and were among the first Jews in Europe to receive civil rights (1791). During the following century they constituted one of the outstanding elements of French Jewry and had a strong communal and cultural life. In 1940, the community was expelled by the Nazis, and many met their deaths. In 1975, 50,000 Jews lived in Alsace-Lorraine, especially at Strasbourg (12,000), one of the most vital Jewish communities in Europe.

altar: Place where sacrifices were offered to the deity. First mentioned after the Flood (Gen. 8:20), altars were built by all the patriarchs. When the Israelites entered Canaan there were initially numerous local altars ("high places"), but this was against the legislation of the Pentateuch, which commanded one central a. Eventually this command was fulfilled, first in the TABERNACLE and then in the Jerusalem TEMPLE. The a. had "horns" at its corners, which were seized by a person seeking asylum. Apart from the central sacrificial a., the Temple also had an a. for burning incense.

Alter of Gur: Hasidic dynasty, founded in the small town of Gur near Warsaw (the *Gerer rebbe*). It was established by Isaac Meir Alter (1799–1866). His greatnephew, Abraham Mordecai A. (1864–1948), urged his followers to move to Israel, where he himself settled after the Nazi period.

Alterman, Nathan (1910–1970): Hebrew author. Born in Poland, he settled in Tel Aviv in 1925. He was noted for his serious poetry, light verse (some of which was written for satirical theater performances), topical poems, and plays as well as for his translations of Shakespeare and Molière.

Altneuschul: Synagogue in Prague; probably the oldest existing synagogue in Europe. The present building dates from the 14th cent., though an earlier one on the site was built in the 11th cent.

Altona: German port, now suburb of Hamburg. The Jewish community, originally from Portugal, received a charter in 1641. Ashkenazim became numerous in the 17th cent. Jews played an important role in the development of the town's commerce and shipping industries. The three adjacent Ashkenazi communities of A., Hamburg, and Wandsbeck (known as AHW) were united during the years 1664 to 1811, and various famous rabbis served there. Some 5,000 Jews lived in A. when the Nazis came to power, but the community ended during World War II, after which only a small number of Jews returned.

Altschuler, Jehiel Hillel (18th cent.): Galician rabbi. He completed and arranged a commentary on the Bible started by his father *David A.* Its two volumes, *Metzudat David* (giving the literal meaning of every word) and *Metzudat Zion* (explaining the meaning of the text), became standard Bible commentaries, often reprinted.

am ha-aretz ("people of the land"): In the Bible, the general population. After the Babylonian Exile, the term was applied to the section of the rural population that had assimilated with the surrounding peoples. In the Mishnah, it was applied to the common people, who were lax in their ritual observances, especially regarding the laws of tithes and ritual cleanliness. Later the term was generally used to mean a person ignorant of religious matters.

Am Olam ("Everlasting People"): Russian Jewish society founded after the 1881 pogroms with the object of leaving Russia and establishing agricultural socialist communes. The US was their principal goal. The longest-surviving settlement was New Odessa near Portland, Oregon (1883–86). Two settlements in S. Dakota lasted from 1882 to 1885.

Amalek: Nomadic people living in the Sinai Peninsula in early biblical times. When the Children of Israel were crossing the wilderness, they were attacked by the Amalekites at Rephidim, but after a hard battle they succeeded in driving them off. The Amalekites were regarded as an inveterate foe who should be obliterated (Exod. 17:16, Deut. 25:19), and this obligation was annually recalled on Sabbath Zakhor, the Sabbath preceding Purim. The A. remained a threat to the Israelites until defeated by David (Saul's failure to observe the annihilation command led to the kingdom being removed from his family). They were finally wiped out in the reign of Hezekiah, although traditionally Haman and his ten sons were the last of their descendants.

Amarna, Tel el: Ancient town in Middle Egypt which was the capital of Pharaoh Akhnaton. Here Egyptian royal archives were discovered, including many documents relating to current conditions in Canaan (18th–14th cent. BCE). These letters, from vassal rulers, were written mostly in Akkadian. There are references to the invasion of the "Habiru," which may be the first mention of the Hebrews.

Amatus Lusitanus (1511–1568): Physician. Born a Marrano in Portugal, he studied medicine at Salamanca University. He moved to Antwerp (1533), then to Ferrara, where he taught at the university. He was ordered to Rome on several occasions to treat Pope Julius III. Later, at Ragusa, he openly embraced Judaism and finally settled in Salonica. He published seven volumes of *Centuriae curationum*, a major contribution to medieval medical science.

Amaziah: King of Judah, who ruled c. 798–c. 780 BCE. He succeeded his murdered father JOASH and executed his assassins. He conducted a successful campaign against the Edomites, capturing their capital, Sela. His unwise challenge to King Jehoash of Israel led to his defeat and virtual subjection to Israel. He was murdered at Lachish.

amen ("so be it"): Formula of confirmation in public response after prayer; in the Temple it was part of a longer formula (Ps. 72:18–19). In the synagogue it is uttered at the conclusion of every benediction. The term passed into Christian, and less frequently Islamic, usage.

America: The first European to set foot on American soil was Luis de Torres, a converted Jew, who was Columbus' interpreter. The discovery of A. coincided with the expulsion of the Jews from Spain, and before long Marranos found a haven in the Spanish and Portuguese colonies of the New World, although they soon encountered intolerance and the Inquisition. When the Dutch ruled BRAZIL (1631–54), the first open Jewish communities were established, but when the Portuguese reconquered the country, the Jews fled to other countries, including the WEST INDIES and New Amsterdam (New York, 1654). The early Jewish settlement in S. America came to an end, leaving only indirect traces. The UNITED STATES community grew, especially from the early 19th cent., with successive waves of European immigration, and Jews also came to CANADA. The early settlers in N. America were Sephardim, but they were soon outnumbered by Ashkenazi arrivals. The entire nature of American Jewry changed as a result of the mass immigration from Eastern Europe following the pogroms of the

1880s. Over 2,000,000 Jews arrived between 1881 and 1924 (when immigration restrictions were imposed). The US was the main goal of the immigrants, but communities were developed and founded throughout the Americas. In the late 19th cent. attempts were made to found Jewish agricultural colonies in AR-GENTINA and Brazil under the auspices of the JEWISH COLONIZATION ASSOCIATION. A further influx came as refugees from Nazi persecution during the 1930s, and numbers settled in Latin America, but the doors of American countries were increasingly closed; this was the last large-scale immigration. Throughout the years there was a much smaller influx of Jews from Mediterranean countries than from other parts of Europe. After World War II, there was a tendency for Jews to move from smaller to larger communities, and in Latin America, from the smaller to the larger countries. The early generations lived by peddling, opening small stores, and working in sweatshops. Successive generations, however, were able to achieve a general degree of affluence. The great majority of the younger generation are university students, and the Jewish communities are faced with problems of assimilation, mixed marriage, and inadequate Jewish education. In 1976 there were an estimated 6,800,000 Jews in A., of whom almost 6,000,000 were in the US, 305,000 in Canada, 300,000 in Argentina, and 165,000 in Brazil. Altogether 580,000 live in S. America; 9,500 in Central America and the West Indies; and 6,182,000 in N. America.

American Association for Jewish Education: Organization founded in 1939 to promote Jewish education in N. America. It provides service in educational research, curricula, etc. and publishes educational material and journals. It helped to found over 30 bureaus of Jewish education throughout the US.

American Council for Judaism: Anti-Zionist organization founded in 1942, asserting that Judaism is a religion of universal values and not a nationality. It sharply opposed "double loyalties" (to the US and Israel) and opposed the establishment of the State of Israel. Its main support came from Reform circles. Its membership was never high, dwindling sharply after the 1967 Six-Day War period.

American Jewish Committee: Organization founded in 1906 to protect Jewish rights being threatened anywhere in the world and to secure equality for Jews. It fought against anti-Semitism in Czarist Russia and Nazi Germany. After World War II it was active in the US in fighting discrimination and prejudice. It also worked to foster intergroup and ecumenical relations. Traditionally non-Zionist, it adopted a pro-Israel position after the establishment of the State. Its membership, obtained by voluntary subscriptions, was put at 60,000 in 1977. It publishes the prestigious monthly *Commentary* and the annual *American Jewish Year Book* (the latter in conjunction with the Jewish Publication Society). Its presidents have included Mayer Sulzberger, Louis Marshall, Cyrus Adler, and Joseph M. Proskauer. Outside the US, it maintains offices in Latin America, Paris, and Jerusalem.

American Jewish Congress: Organization established in 1917. Its objective was to work for Jewish rights in Europe and Palestine. Founded by Zionists, it has always been pro-Israel. It sent a delegation to the 1919 Peace Conference. Organized on a permanent basis in 1922, the AJC's subsequent activities have included fighting Nazism, the organization of the WORLD JEWISH CONGRESS, and the fight for civil rights in the US. It publishes *Congress Monthly* and *Juda-*

ism, the latter a monthly on Jewish religious subjects. Presidents of the AJC have included Rabbis Stephen S. Wise, Israel Goldstein, Joachim Prinz, Arthur J. Lelyveld, and Arthur Hertzberg.

American Jewish Historical Society: Society established in 1892 to pursue research into American Jewish history. Its headquarters, formerly in New York, are now on the campus of Brandeis University in Waltham, Mass. Its *Publications* appears quarterly.

American Jewish Joint Distribution Committee: Organization (known as the "Joint" or JDC) for relief to Jews in need in other countries. Founded in 1914 by a group of American relief organizations, it initially succored Jews hard hit by World War I in Europe and Palestine. After the war, attention was paid to emergency relief and reconstruction, with emphasis on helping Jews in Eastern Europe. A major challenge was posed by the advent of Nazism, especially during World War II. Until 1941 the JDC was able to work openly in various parts of Europe, and from 1941 to 1945 it financed rescue activities wherever possible. After the war, the JDC was the major organization working for the rehabilitation of the survivors of the Holocaust, their maintenance in the Displaced Persons camps of Europe, their emigration to Israel, etc. Over a longer period, it financed the reestablishment of Jewish life in Europe, relief and education for Jews in Moslem lands, and care of aged immigrants in Israel (through the Malben organization). The JDC now derives its funds through the United Jewish Appeal.

Amichai, Yehuda (1924–): Israeli author. Born in Germany, he went to Jerusalem in 1936. His poems, appearing from the mid-1950s, were very influential and pioneered in the poetic use of everyday terms. His novel *Not of This Time, Not of This Place* deals with the problem of the attitude of Israelis to Germans.

amidah ("standing"): Prayer recited at all synagogue services while standing. It is also known among Ashkenazim as *Shemoneh Esreh* ("18") because there were 18 blessings in its original form. The most frequent form now recited at regular weekday services consists of 19 blessings. These are (1) praising the God of the Patriarchs, (2) praising God's power, (3) praising God's holiness; petitionary benedictions for (4) knowledge, (5) penitence, (6) forgiveness, (7) redemption, (8) healing of the sick, (9) blessing of agricultural produce, (10) ingathering of the exiles, (11) righteous judgment, (12) punishment of heretics, (13) reward of the pious, (14) rebuilding of Jerusalem, (15) restoration of the Davidic dynasty, (16) acceptance of prayer, (17) restoration of the Temple service, and (18) thanksgiving; and (19) a prayer for peace. On festivals and holy days the number is reduced and special blessings are inserted in the middle, but nos. 1 to 3 and nos. 17 to 19 are recited on all occasions. The *a.* is recited first silently by the congregation and then repeated aloud by the reader, with additions such as the KEDUSHAH; at the evening service, however, there is no reader's repetition. The prayer is ancient; it was formulated largely at the time of the First Temple.

Ammon: Ancient country east of the Jordan. The people were known as Ammonites, and their capital was Rabbath-Ammon (modern Amman, capital of Jordan). Together with the people of MOAB they were looked on as sworn enemies of Israel (Deut. 23:4), and Israelite women were forbidden to marry Ammonites. The Ammonites were defeated by Jephthah, Saul, and David, but subsequently Ammon threw off Israelite rule. In the Second Temple period, they disappeared as an independent people.

Amnon see **Absalom**

Amnon of Mainz: Legendary martyred rabbi ascribed to the Crusader period. The story is told that he refused to accept the demand of the archbishop of Mainz that he convert to Christianity. In punishment, his limbs were cut off. The dying rabbi was then taken to the synagogue—it was on Rosh ha-Shanah—and uttered the *Netanneh Tokef* prayer, which thereafter was recited on the High Holidays in all Ashkenazi and some Sephardi rites. In fact, the prayer dates from an earlier period.

Amon: King of Judah, who reigned 642–640 BCE. Son and successor to MANASSEH, he was murdered by servants in his palace and succeeded by his son Josiah (II Kings 21:19–26).

amora (pl. *amoraim*; "speakers," "interpreters"): Name given to a rabbinic teacher in Palestine and Babylonia during the period between the completion of the Mishnah and the compilation of the Talmud (c. 3rd–6th cent.). The discussions of the *amoraim* based on the Mishnah are recorded in the *gemara* (the Mishnah together with the *gemara* constituting the Talmud). There was constant communication and influence between the

amoraim in Palestine and Babylonia. The former had the title *rabbi*, the latter *rav*. Over 2,000 *amoraim* can be identified.

Amorites: Early Semitic inhabitants of Palestine. The name is applied in two ways in the Bible, both generically to the pre-Israelite population of the country, and specifically to one of the peoples there. They are mentioned as early as the times of the Patriarchs. The A. lived on both sides of the Jordan, and Moses conquered two Amorite kingdoms—Heshbon and Og. The rabbis called all idolators A., and "the ways of the A." was a general term for superstition.

Amos (8th cent. BCE): Prophet. Born in Tekoa, he prophesied in the northern kingdom of Israel. A simple shepherd, he was moved to go to the shrine at Bethel and inveigh against the moral corruption of his contemporaries. He prophesied doom unless the people reformed, condemning the widespread social injustice of the times. He extended his message to all nations, preaching a universal ethical monotheism. But the Israelites, chosen for responsibility and not for privilege, were particularly called upon to lead a moral life. Although not opposing the sacrificial system, A. attacked the hypocrisy of sacrifices unaccompanied by sincere repentance and devotion to God. The Book of A., third of the twelve minor prophets, has 9 chapters.

Amram ben Sheshna (9th cent.): Head of the SURA academy. The first complete prayerbook (*Sedar Rav Amram*) was ascribed to him. It had a great influence on the development of Sephardi liturgy.

Amsterdam: Dutch city. The community was founded early in the 17th cent. by Marranos from the Iberian Peninsula. Later in that century, Jews arrived from Germany, and before long the Ashkenazim were in the majority. However, the Sephardi community retained a special distinction, and its synagogue (1675) remains a noted monument. It was in A. that Rembrandt painted his Jewish neighbors, that MANASSEH BEN ISRAEL established his printing press, and that SPINOZA and URIEL D'ACOSTA were excommunicated. A. Jewry remained one of the most distinguished communities in Western Europe. The town's diamond-polishing industry was almost entirely run by Jews. Some 80,000 Jews lived there at the outbreak of World War II, but most were deported by the Nazis to their deaths in extermination camps. In 1976, 20,000 Jews were living there, forming the largest community in the Netherlands.

amulet: Protection against evil spirits. In Jewish circles they were widely used in talmudic times and usually contained a verse from the Bible. They became even more widespread under the influence of the Kabbalah, now containing the Divine name represented by various letter combinations and kabbalistic formulae. Most amulets were worn, but some were hung on walls (e.g., directed against the demon LILITH in a room where a woman was giving birth) or put in places where danger or the evil eye was feared. Amulets are still used, especially among Oriental Jews.

Anan ben David (8th cent.): Founder of the KARAITE sect (traditionally, after he had been passed over to succeed his father as exilarch in Babylon). The sect, originally known as Ananites, venerates him as the "principal teacher." His *Sepher ha-Mitzvot*, of which only portions have survived, represents a strict interpretation of Pentateuchal law, which was modified by later Karaite tradition.

Anatoli, Jacob ben Abba Mari (c. 1190–1240): Philosopher and translator. Born in Provence, he settled in Naples. His collection of homilies, *Malmad ha-Tal-*

midim, was strongly influenced by Maimonides.

Anav (Anau): Leading Italian family (traditionally, among those taken to Rome by Titus). *Zedekiah ben Abraham* A. (13th cent.), who lived in Rome, wrote *Shibbolei ha-Leket*, which is an important halakhic compendium on the liturgy and ritual.

angel of death (*malakh ha-mavet*): Angel who destroys life. Originally a function of the Divine will, he gradually acquired a demonic individuality. He is connected (and at times identified) with SATAN or with Samael, the prince of the demons. Many Jewish folk customs are designed to ward him off.

angels: Supernatural, celestial beings. They appear in the Bible as messengers of God and even perform practical, sometimes punitive functions. Their place is in the heavens but in First Temple times they lacked individual names, although certain types (seraphim, cherubim, ophannim) were recognized as being particularly connected with the Divine throne. Under Babylonian and Persian influence, angelology developed in Second Temple times, when a. began to receive individual names (the Book of Daniel refers to Michael and Gabriel). Angelology is particularly prevalent in post-biblical apocalyptic literature, where the a. is God's medium of revelation and the instrument by which He controls the world. Each nation of the world has its own guardian a. The fallen a., the progenitors of the DEMONS, now became prominent. Magian and Zoroastrian influence led to further developments in angelology, but in Jewish tradition the a. and the evil spirits were all controlled by the One God. The Talmud and aggadah accepted the belief in a., as did the medieval philosophers (some of whom rationalized their existence by equating them with Aristotle's higher intelligences). The Kabbalah indulged in extreme speculation regarding a., and appeals were made to them through amulets, incantations, and references in the liturgy, some of which have been retained (cf. the KEDUSHAH prayer and the SHALOM ALEIKHEM Sabbath table hymn).

Anglo-Jewish Association (AJA): British organization founded in 1871 to assist Jews in distress. In cooperation with other international Jewish organizations, it intervened on behalf of oppressed Jews, particularly in the period leading up to World War I. At one time non-Zionist, the AJA later modified its attitude to Zionism.

Ani Maamin ("I Believe"): Statement of faith based on Maimonides' "Thirteen Articles of Faith." Since the 16th cent. it has been incorporated in most Ashkenazi prayer books. The article, expressing confidence in the advent of the Messiah, was sung by Nazi victims being taken to their death.

Anielewicz, Mordecai (1919–1943): Commander of the Warsaw ghetto uprising. A member of the Ha-Shomer ha-Tzair movement, he was commander of the Jewish Fighting Organization in the ghetto, leading the heroic and desperate revolt, during the course of which he was killed.

Anilai and Asinai (1st cent. CE): Two brothers from Nehardea in Babylonia who established a robber state on the Upper Euphrates, which they ruled for 15 years (20–35 CE), with Parthian support. Eventually they were defeated.

aninut: Status of mourner in period between death and burial of relative. During this time, he is absolved from observing commandments (e.g., prayer) and forbidden to eat meat or drink wine.

Annenberg, Walter Hubert (1908–   ): US publisher and diplomat. His many publishing holdings include the Philadelphia *Inquirer*. He was US ambassador to Britain from 1969 to 1974.

Anointing: In a religious context, consecration by the application of oil. In ancient times, a. was the method of consecrating kings and priests, while the altar and sacred vessels were also anointed (Lev. 7:10–12). David was anointed by Samuel, and the descendant of David who would eventually redeem Israel was called the "anointed one" (*Mashiah*, from which the English word "messiah").

An-Ski, S. (1863–1920): Pseudonym of Solomon Zainwil Rapaport, Yiddish writer in Russia. He collected Jewish folklore in Eastern Europe, writing the *Destruction of the Jews in Poland, Galicia and Bukovina* following his journeys in these areas during World War I. His poem *Die Shvue* was the hymn of the Bund. His best-known work was the play. *The Dibbuk*, which achieved international renown, especially through the Habimah Theater's production of the Hebrew translation by Bialik.

Anti - Defamation League: US organization, under the auspices of B'nai B'rith, established in 1913 to fight anti-Semitism and discrimination and to assure equal rights for Jews. In the course of time, it extended its activities to fight discrimination and to secure civil rights for all Americans.

Antigonus (Mattathias): Last king of the Hasmonean dynasty, who ruled 40–37 BCE; youngest son of Aristobulus II. Taken to Rome by Pompey in 63 BCE, he returned to Judea in 49 BCE. He captured Jerusalem in alliance with the Parthians and ruled for 3 years, during which time he was also high priest. HEROD recaptured Jerusalem with Roman help and had Antigonus executed.

*Antiochus Epiphanes: Syrian king, who ruled 175–164 BCE. An ardent Hellenizer, his desecration of the Temple and harsh suppression of the Jewish religion sparked off national resistance which he endeavored to suppress ruthlessly. His excesses led to the HASMONEAN revolt.

Antipas, Herod (20 BCE–c. 39 CE): Son of Herod. After the latter's death (4 BCE), Augustus confirmed Antipas as ruler of Galilee and part of Transjordan with the title of tetrarch. Antipas founded TIBERIAS, which was his capital city. He had John the Baptist executed when John rebuked him for marrying his sister-in-law in contradiction to Jewish law. During the reign of Caligula he was accused of preparing for war against Rome, and he was exiled to Gaul.

Antipater: (1) Governor of Idumea; father of HEROD (d. 43 BCE). He was an ally of Hyrcanus in his struggle with his brother Aristobulus and in alliance with the Nabateans defeated Aristobulus. He also gave practical support to Julius Caesar in his fight with Pompey, as a result of which Caesar made him regent of Judea (47). A. paved the way for Herod's eventual accession to the throne. He met his death by poisoning. (2) Herod's son (d. 5 BCE), destined to succeed his father. But Herod suspected A. of plotting against him and had A. executed 5 days before his own death.

anti-Semitism: Term coined (by Wilhelm Marr) in 1879 to denote the organized movement directed against Jews but used to mean hatred of Jews generally. It is also projected back into earlier periods of history, although the nature of a. was then different. The earlier periods of a. were largely based on religious hostility. In the classical world, the Jewish rejection of paganism, refusal to worship images, and observance of ritual laws which meant a frequent social distancing from pagans led to suspicion and hatred manifested both practically and in polemical and literary works. The necessity for Jews to live near one another for religious and social reasons also marked their "differentness" and led to suspicion. However, it was under Christian rule that a. assumed its most serious character. Christianity developed the doctrine that the Jews had been rejected by God and that the Jewish people had to bear responsibility for the crucifixion of Jesus. Over the centuries the situation of the Jews deteriorated as the Christians sought their conversion and enforced a series of decrees designed to humiliate the Jews, who were frequently subject to attack, expulsion, and massacre. Jews were charged with ritual murder, BLOOD LIBEL, and DESECRATION OF THE HOST, and were identified with the forces of the devil. In the Muslim world a. was less extreme, although there were periods when the Jews were physically persecuted. In any case, Jews were second-class citizens among most peoples and subject to frequent humiliations. From the late 18th cent. on, the emphasis of a. changed. In the Age of Enlightenment, religion was a less powerful factor and the emphasis changed to hatred of the Jews as a people or race. The latter was based on an unsound racial theory which boosted the "superior Aryan" over the "inferior Semitic" races. In the 20th cent., the *Protocols of the* "ELDERS OF ZION" forgery spread the widely believed myth of Jewish attempts at world domination. A. was adopted as official government policy in various countries, climaxing with the Nazi rulers in Germany who preached hatred of the Jews, identifying them on the one hand with the dreaded Bolsheviks and on the other with the feared capitalists. Fascist and Nazi parties carried these doctrines throughout the world, and when the Nazis controlled Europe and pushed their theories to the extreme of physical extermination of the Jewish people, they found many collaborators and sympathizers among other peoples. On the other hand, the murder of 6,000,000 Jews led to a feeling of revulsion in the postwar world. Many Christian leaders, realizing the role played by traditional Christian doctrines in the events leading to the Holocaust, demanded and obtained revisions in Christian attitudes to Jews. Political parties preaching outright anti-Semitism won scant support in postwar years, but menacing manifestations continued to appear, although not always as openly as before (e.g., in the USSR). The general prosperity of the postwar world also served to brake a., but its continuing existence— now often masked as anti-Zionism—has been repeatedly confirmed (e.g., among certain black circles in the US, in South America, and, fostered by Arab propaganda, in many other parts of the world) and frequently manifests itself in one guise or another.

Antokolski, Mark (1843–1902): Russian sculptor, originally a woodcarver. Inspired mainly by Russian and general history, some of his works were on Jewish subjects. He was greatly honored by the czarist court, but because of anti-Semitic attacks he left Russia and spent his last years in Paris, where he created little apart from his statue of Spinoza.

*Antoninus Pius (86–161): Roman emperor, 138–161 CE. He repealed the anti-Jewish decrees (including the ban on circumcision imposed by his predecessor, Hadrian). Many legends are told in the Talmud of a Roman emperor "Antoninus" who held friendly discussions with R. Judah ha-Nasi. The identity of this Antoninus is uncertain.

Antwerp: Belgian port. A few Jews lived there before the 15th cent., and Marranos from Portugal reached A. in the 16th cent. Later there was a community of Jews from Central Europe and, in the late 19th cent., from Eastern Europe. Jews played a major role in building up the city's diamond industry. The Jews of A. suffered severely under the Nazis; most of the community of 50,000 was exterminated. The post-World War II community of 13,000 (1977), which again plays a key role in the diamond trade, is the most Orthodox-oriented Jewish community on the continent of Europe, with a considerable Hasidic element.

aphikoman: Section of the middle of three pieces of unleavened bread on the SEDER table which is broken off by the celebrant at the beginning of the service and eaten at the end of the meal. The custom has developed of its being hidden by the children, who reveal its whereabouts only on promise of a gift.

apikoros (derived from Gk. "Epicurus"): Talmudical term for a heretic or skeptic. From the Middle Ages, the term was also applied to anyone who was lax in his religious observance.

apocalypse: Divine revelation of the future disclosed in a vision or trance; the body of literature containing such revelations (particularly dealing with the End of Days) in Jewish and Christian writings. Apocalyptic literature flourished mainly from the 2nd cent. BCE to the 2nd cent. CE. Early traces of a. are to be found in the Bible (e.g.,

Book of Daniel); others are in the Apocrypha and Pseudepigrapha (e.g., Enoch, Jubilees). The Dead Sea Scrolls have shown that apocalyptic works were written in sectarian circles; they also appeared in Christian writing (e.g., Revelation of John). As prophecy was believed to have ceased in biblical times, most of these books were attributed to personalities of Bible times. The seeds of later Jewish mysticism are to be found in these writings. The authors believed that the end of the world was imminent, and there is therefore great emphasis on ESCHATOLOGY. There are also revelations of superhuman mysteries such as the nature of the heavens, the secrets of the world, accounts of Judgment Day, the day of the Messiah, etc.

Apocrypha and Pseudepigrapha: Body of Jewish literature written in later Second Temple times and for some subsequent decades; although similar in content and style to the biblical books, they were not incorporated in the Jewish canon. However, the books known as the Apocrypha were canonized by the Church and incorporated in the Catholic Bible; the noncanonized works were known as the Pseudepigrapha. Most of the works originated in Palestine and were written originally in Hebrew or Aramaic, although with few exceptions they have been preserved only in translation. The Apocrypha resemble the books of the Hagiographa section of the Bible; the Pseudepigrapha are largely apocalyptic. The Apocrypha consist of I and II MACCABEES (in some instances III and IV Maccabees are also included); I and II ESDRAS; ECCLESIASTICUS (or Ben Sira); WISDOM OF SOLOMON; TOBIT; JUDITH; Prayer of MANASSEH; Additions to the Book of Esther; BEL AND THE DRAGON; Song of the Three Holy Children; SUSANNAH; and BARUCH. Better-known works among the Pseudepigrapha include Psalms of Solomon, Testament of the Twelve Patriarchs, Assumption of Moses, and Sibylline Oracles. It is now thought that the large body of apocalyptic writings emerged from the eschatological movement that was widespread in Palestine and prevalent among the Essenes and related groups (e.g., the Dead Sea sect), as well as among the early Christians. These early Christians would have been drawn to such literature, unlike the mainstream of Judaism, which found their stress on an early direct Divine intervention in human affairs a hindrance to their grappling with urgent religious problems and challenges which required immediate solution.

apostasy: Change of religion; the Hebrew words for one who leaves Judaism are *min, apikoros, meshummad,* or *mumar.* The first large-scale manifestation of a. among Jews was in the Hellenistic period, especially among the Jewish aristocracy who were attracted by Greek culture. Later a. was mainly to Christianity, with the apostate bitterly reviled in Jewish life and literature. In the Middle Ages, Jewish apostates took a prominent role in anti-Jewish disputations, polemics, denunciations, and anti-Talmud propaganda. A. to Islam was also common, but in these instances the Jewish apostates did not react to their former religion with the same virulence. Jews made a distinction between the voluntary apostate and the forced convert, or MARRANO. According to Jewish law, a Jew who abandons Judaism continues to be regarded as a Jew and requires no special ceremony in the event of his returning to Judaism.

Aquila (late 1st cent.–early 2nd cent. CE): Translator of the Bible into Greek. His translation of the Hebrew is most literal; it was meant to provide a translation more acceptable to the Jews than the SEPTUAGINT, which was being used by the Christians. The rabbis identified A. with ONKELOS and the two have been confused. Both were proselytes.

Arabah: Desert valley covering Jordan Valley and area south of Dead Sea.

Arabia: Country in southwestern Asia. The area figures prominently in the Bible (e.g., the queen of Sheba) and Jews were living there in Second Temple times. Their numbers increased, partly through immigration and partly through the conversion of Arabs to Judaism, including the 6th-cent. Himyarite king DHU NUWAS. Considerable Jewish communities developed in the Hejaz, especially near Medina. When Mohammed adopted a hostile attitude toward them, the Jews were annihilated or expelled. Thereafter Jewish settlement in the peninsula was mostly to be found in the YEMEN, HADRAMAUT, and ADEN, and the Jews were tolerated on payment of special taxes. In modern times there were no Jews in northern A., while nearly all the 50,000 Jews in Yemen and the south emigrated to Israel, especially after 1948. Only a few hundred remain.

Arabs: Semitic people who initially lived in the Arabian peninsula but after becoming Moslems conquered and brought their new religion (ISLAM) to vast areas of the then-known world. They trace their origin back to ISHMAEL, son of ABRAHAM. Many countries conquered by the A. had Jewish populations. In some areas the Jews assisted the A. in making their conquests. On the whole, the Jews were not persecuted, although they were subject to the disabilities imposed on nonbelievers; during certain periods of reaction (e.g., under the Almohades) the Jews suffered severely and were compelled to convert. Under Moslem rule in Spain, the golden age of that country's Jewish culture was achieved, while in N. Africa there emerged a Jewish cultural life and the Jews played a role in public life as well. In modern times the Jews of the Arab lands participated in the general lethargy of the countries in which they lived (especially in the last period of the Ottoman Empire). In the 20th cent., Jews, who had largely identified themselves with the European elements, suffered from the nationalist tendencies of the A., and relations took a turn for the worse with the impact of Zionism and later the establishment of the State of Israel. Jews emigrated from Arab lands, and in place of the 750,000 Jews who lived there in 1948, less than 50,000 remained by 1977.

Arad: Biblical city in the Negev captured by Joshua. Its remains, excavated by Y. Aharoni, have revealed a Canaanite temple and high place. The modern town, founded 6 miles from the historic site, had a population of 8,000 in 1974.

Aragon: Former kingdom in Spain. Jews lived there from the earliest years after the Christian reconquest. They were treated well until the end of the 13th cent., when they suffered greatly under hostile ecclesiastical pressures. Many were massacred in the 1391 outbreaks, and many others converted in the following decades. Those who remained, apart from the Marranos, left the country in the general expulsion from Spain in 1492.

Arakhin ("Valuations"): Fifth tractate in the MISHNAH order of *Kodashim*, with commentary in both the Jerusalem and Babylonian Talmuds. It discusses the valuation of persons, houses, or fields dedicated to the sanctuary (Lev. 25–27).

Aram: Group of western Semitic tribes, speaking ARAMAIC, who settled in the Fertile Crescent—particularly in the Syrian region—during the last part of the 2nd millennium BCE. They established a number of states, notably Aram-Dammesek (named after its capital, DAMASCUS). In the 10th–8th cent. BCE

Aram-Dammesek played an important role in the political situation of the area; it was often a danger to the neighboring kingdom of Israel, with which on occasion it was allied, and by which it was for a time annexed (in the reign of JEROBOAM II). Another known kingdom was Aram-Zobah, which lost its importance after the period of DAVID, by whom it was defeated on several occasions. In the latter part of the 8th cent., the Aramean states were subjugated by the Assyrians.

Arama, Isaac ben Moses (c. 1420–1494): Rabbi and preacher; in Spain until the expulsion of the Jews in 1492, when he went to Naples. His principal work is *Akedat Yitzḥak*, a homiletic commentary on the Pentateuch and Five Scrolls. He stated the basic Jewish tenets as belief in the Creation, in the Torah, and in Reward and Punishment.

Aramaic: Northwestern Semitic language (mistakenly known also as Chaldaic), closely related to Hebrew. Its written use is first known in 9th-cent. Syria, and shortly thereafter it appeared in Babylonia. It became the *lingua franca* of much of the Middle East, especially along the trade routes. It is found in the Bible, and parts of the Books of Daniel and Ezra are written in A. A. became the general language spoken in Palestine, and for this reason the Bible had to be translated in it; these translations are the TARGUMS. Both the Palestinian and Babylonian Talmuds are written in A.; it is also the language of certain prayers (e.g., the KADDISH, KOL NIDRE). It persisted as a literary tongue and was the language of the ZOHAR, from which it became the main language of Jewish mysticism. It is still spoken by a small number of Kurdish Jews.

arba kanphot see **tzitzit**

Archelaus (d. 16): Ethnarch of Judea from 4 BCE to 6 CE; son of Herod. Herod, before his death, designated him his successor as king, but in view of popular Jewish opposition, the Romans, while confirming A. as ruler of Judea, Samaria, and Idumea, gave him only the lesser title of ethnarch. His sometimes cruel rule provoked further opposition, and Emperor Augustus exiled him to Gaul, where he died.

archeology: Archeological discoveries — especially over the past century — have thrown fresh and important light on most aspects of ancient Jewish history. Moreover, the discoveries concerning ancient cultures throughout the Middle East have illuminated the world of the Bible and the early Jews and the cultural milieu which influenced their lives and thought. Discoveries in Mesopotamia (e.g., at Ur) have thrown light on the background of the early biblical narratives (e.g., the Flood), and the patriarchal period is further illuminated by the documents discovered at Mari in Mesopotamia and at Tel el Amarna in Egypt (the latter probably containing the first reference to Hebrews). Recent discoveries of a massive archive at Ebla in Syria promise to throw much light on the area in the pre-patriarchal period. Remarkably little has been unearthed to throw light on the events connected with the Exodus, which still poses many problems. Archeologists seeking evidence of Joshua's campaigns have dug at Jericho (the most ancient city in the world), Ai, Hazor, etc. The early Canaanite texts discovered at Ras Shamra (Ugarit) in Syria have brought a new understanding to both the historical and literary aspects of the early parts of the Bible. Various finds have shown the development of Hebrew epigraphy. These include the stela of Mesha, king of Moab; the inscription on the Siloam tunnel constructed by King Hezekiah in Jerusalem; ostraca found at Arad; and letters written at Lachish shortly before the destruction of the First Temple. Royal palaces were uncovered in Samaria. Other early sites extensively excavated have included Megiddo, Ashdod, and Dan. There is a dearth of material on the Persian period, but a wealth of discoveries date from the later Second Temple period, notably in Jerusalem (the area around the Temple, the Jewish quarter), Masada, the Tobiad palace in Transjordan, and Caesarea, and the Dead Sea Scrolls, as well as other discoveries in the Judean Desert. Among the main discoveries in the post-Temple period are the letters and other remains from the Bar Kokhba revolt; the synagogue and necropolis at Bet She'arim; synagogues in Bet Alpha, Capernaum, Biram, Nirim, etc.; and Nabatean remains in the Negev desert (Avdat, Subeita). Archeological discoveries made outside Israel have also proved important for Jewish history. These include the Elephantine papyri found at Yeb on the River Nile; synagogues from the early centuries CE at Ostia (Italy), Sardis (Asia Minor), Dura-Europos (Syria), etc.; and Jewish catacombs in Rome. In Israel today there is keen activity in all branches of a., which is conducted mostly under the auspices of the Israeli government's Department of Antiquities, the Israel Exploration Society, and the Hebrew and Tel Aviv Universities.

archisynagogos: Title of head of synagogue who was leader of the Jewish community in the classical period, especially in the Roman and Byzantine Empires.

archives: In ancient times, major documents were deposited in the Temple, and Jewish communities throughout the ages kept records, although few of these have survived from the Middle Ages or earlier. However, Jewish records have often been preserved in general a. From the 16th to 17th cent. many Jewish communities kept a record book (*pinkas*). After World War II, most of those that survived in Europe were transferred to the Central Jewish Historical Archives in Jerusalem. Other notable modern a. include the Central Zionist Archives (from 1933, in Jerusalem), the American Jewish Archives (Cincinnati), the Yivo Archives (from 1940, in New York), and archives on the Holocaust (e.g., in Yad vaShem, Jerusalem; Wiener Library, London; Centre de Documentation Contemporaine, Paris), as well as the Israeli State Archives.

Ardon (Bronstein), **Mordekhai** (1896–): Israeli painter. Born in Germany, he settled in Palestine in 1933. From 1940 to 1952 he directed the Bezalel Art School, Jerusalem. He painted in an expressionistic style. Some of his subjects were inspired by Jewish mysticism.

Arendt, Hannah (1906–1975): US political and social philosopher. Born in Germany, she lived in France from 1933 and in 1941 escaped to New York. Her learned and provocative works include *The Origins of Totalitarianism* and *On Revolution.* Her controversial *Eichmann in Jerusalem,* subtitled "The Banality of Evil," criticized the submissive conduct of European Jewry in World War II.

Argentina: Marranos settled in A. from the late 16th cent. but traces of them were lost. The modern Jewish settlement dates from the 19th cent., with the first community founded in 1862 in BUENOS AIRES (the synagogue in 1897). Major immigration began in the 1880s with the arrival of Eastern European Jews. From 1891, Baron de Hirsch promoted Jewish agricultural settlements in A. through the JEWISH COLONIZATION ASSOCIATION. A. also attracted many Sephardi immigrants from Mediterranean lands. In 1976, there were about 300,000 Jews in A. About 3,200 families remained connected with the land, but few of these were actual farmers. The main centers were Buenos Aires, Rosario, Cordoba, Santa Fe, and Bahia Blanca. The central communal body is the Daia (Delegacion de Associacones Israelitas Argentinas), the representative body of Argentine Jewry (founded in 1934) to which 100 organizations are affiliated. Much of its activity is directed to fighting anti-Semitism, which has occurred in A. under various auspices (e.g., the Tacuara movement), some of them inspired by Nazis who found refuge in A. after World War II and were financed from Arab sources.

Ari see **Luria, Isaac**

Aristeas, Letter of: Jewish-Alexandrian work purporting to be of non-Jewish origin. It gives the legendary account of the preparation of the SEPTUAGINT translation of the Bible into Greek (according to which 72 Jewish scholars, each working in isolation, produced identical versions). The work probably dates from the latter half of the 2nd cent. BCE.

Aristobulus I (Judah): King of Judea who ruled 104–103 BCE; eldest son of John Hyrcanus, who designated him high priest in his will. He murdered his mother, who was to have succeeded his father, and killed or imprisoned his brothers. He was the first Hasmonean to call himself king.

Aristobulus II (d. 49 BCE): Last independent Hasmonean king, who ruled 67–63 BCE; son of Alexander Yannai and Salome Alexandra. He prevented his elder brother HYRCANUS from acceding to the throne, seizing it for himself. To end the resultant civil war, Pompey intervened and established Roman control over the country, sending A. as a prisoner to Rome (63 BCE). Escaping in 56 BCE, A. returned to Judea and raised forces but was again defeated and sent back to Rome. Released by Julius Caesar (49 BCE), he planned to help Caesar to fight Pompey, but was poisoned by supporters of Pompey before leaving Rome.

Aristobulus III (Jonathan) (d. 35 BCE): Last Hasmonean high priest. He officiated during the reign of Herod, but his popularity aroused Herod's jealousy, and he had A. drowned in the baths in his Jericho palace.

Arizona: US state. Jewish merchants and businessmen arrived in the 1860s, many establishing themselves in the new mining towns. One of the first settlers was Michael Goldwater, grandfather of Senator Barry Goldwater. The first Jewish community was founded at Tombstone in 1881. In 1976 there were 22,665 Jews in

Arizona, mostly in Phoenix and Tucson.

ark: The place in the synagogue in which the Scrolls of the Law are kept. It is called *aron ha-kodesh* by the Ashkenazim, and *heikhal* by the Sephardim. In talmudic times, when it was portable, it was called *teivah* and was brought into the synagogue only for services. Eventually it was built into the wall facing Jerusalem (which for most Jews was the "eastern" wall) and became the major architectural aspect of the synagogue. In front of the a. is generally hung a curtain (*parokhet*). It became customary to place an abbreviated version of the Ten Commandments above the a. and to hang the perpetual light (NER TAMID) before it. The opening of the a., for the removal of the Scrolls and their return, is carried out with great solemnity, the entire congregation rising to its feet. The term "ark" is also applied to the vessel built by NOAH (Gen. 8).

Ark of the Covenant: Wooden chest which Moses was ordered by God to construct as a repository for the two Tablets of the Law. It was lined and overlaid with gold. Above it was a gold covering on which were the images of two cherubim, whose wings screened the ark cover. Throughout the wilderness wanderings of the Israelites, the ark was carried by the Levites; when stationary, it was placed in the Holy of Holies, where it was seen only once a year by the high priest. It was occasionally taken to the battlefield to inspire the Israelite fighters, and on one occasion fell temporarily into Philistine hands (I Sam. 4: 1–5). There is no record of its fate after First Temple times.

Arkansas: US state. The first Jews settled in 1830 in Hot Springs, but the major Jewish settlement dates from after the Civil War, when many congregations were founded. There were 3,490 Jews in 1976. The largest community is at Little Rock, with sizable ones at Hot Springs, Helena, and Fort Smith.

Arkin, Alan W. (1934–): US actor. He appeared in the Broadway play *Luv* and his movies include *The Russians Are Coming* and *Catch-22*.

Arlen, Harold (1905–): US composer. The son of a cantor, he sang in synagogue choirs in his youth. He wrote the Oscar-winning score for the movie *The Wizard of Oz* and many other films and musicals.

Arlosoroff, Chaim (1899–1933): Israeli labor leader. Raised in Germany, A. was active in Labor Zionist circles and settled in Palestine in 1924. He became a leader of the MAPAI movement, and from 1931 headed the Jewish Agency's Political Department. His murder on the Tel Aviv seafront led to accusations against members of the Revisionist movement, but they were acquitted after a trial which caused many bitter feelings.

Armenia: Region in western Asia, now partly in USSR, partly in Turkey. According to local traditions, Jews lived there in First Temple times; they are attested to from the Second Temple period. Later, many Jews settled there, and in the Talmudic period there was a rabbinical school at Nisibis. The numbers of Jews declined over the centuries, but small communities continued to exist. Armenian Jewry eventually disappeared as a separate entity, but a part was absorbed into the Jewry of KURDISTAN.

Armilus: In late eschatological literature, name of king who will make war on the Messiah. It was held that he would eventually be overcome by God or the Messiah (of the house of David) or Nehemiah and Elijah.

Armleder (Ger. "Armleather"): Anti-Jewish groups (probably so called from their leather armlets) who were responsible for murderous assaults on Jews in over 100 places in Alsace and Rhineland in 1336–39.

Arnon: River in Transjordan flowing for 50 miles and emptying into the Dead Sea. In biblical times it was the border between MOAB and the AMORITES.

aron kodesh see ark

Arrow, Kenneth (1921–): US economist; prof. of economics at Harvard from 1968. He was awarded the Nobel Prize for Economics in 1972.

art: Two opposing trends have marked the Jewish attitude toward a. One was negative, based on the interpretation of the Second Commandment forbidding the reproduction of human and other graven images. The other was positive, reflected in the artistic work embodied in the Tabernacle, Temples, and many archeological finds in Israel. The rabbinical interpretations of the prohibition varied from a strict ban on portrait painting to more liberal attitudes which only forbade the sculpting of the full human figure. There is, however, growing evidence of a strong and continuing Jewish artistic tradition. Coins, monuments, and buildings of late Second Temple times were followed by the synagogue decoration of the following centuries. Among the latter are mosaics (e.g., at BET ALPHA) and frescoes, of which the outstanding example is the remarkable series of depictions of scenes from the Bible on the walls of the DURA-EUROPOS synagogue, which even portrays the "hand of God." Under Muslim influence, figurative motifs gave way to geometric ornamentation, but in Christian countries Jews were strongly influenced by the prevalent artistic trends. Particular attention was paid to certain ritual objects on which Jews lavished their artistic talents. Manuscripts of the aggadah, prayer books, and the Bible were decorated with miniatures and illuminations. Loving attention was paid to spice boxes, Ḥanukkah candelabra, ornaments for the Scrolls of the Law, Sabbath lamps, and other objects used in religious context. The Scroll of Esther and the wedding document provided opportunities for painters. Walls of synagogues continued to be decorated with views of Jerusalem, the signs of the zodiac, etc., and the furnishings of the synagogue were objects for carved woodwork. From the period of emancipation, Jews played a significant role in the various general artistic movements and schools of painting, some of them achieving widespread recognition as painters (e.g., Pissarro, Lie-bermann, Modigliani, Chagall) and sculptors (Epstein). Israeli art dates from the foundation in 1906 by Boris Schatz of the Bezalel School of Arts. Since World War I, it has been strongly influenced by contemporary European styles. There is much artistic activity in the country and many art galleries.

Arukh see **Nathan ben Jehiel**

Arvit see **Maariv**

Asa: King of Judah, who reigned 908–867 BCE. His 40-year reign started with a decade of peace. Subsequently he had to counter invasion threats from Baasha of Israel and Zerah the Ethiopian. He is praised in the Bible as one of the few "good" kings; however, it is noted that although he removed heathen cults, the high places were not removed.

Asaph (6th cent.): Physician who gave his name to the first Hebrew book on medicine. It was written in the Middle East, not by A. but by his pupils. It contains important information on the medicine and medical ethics of the Jews as well as of other peoples, and also preserves excerpts from lost Greek medical works.

asceticism: Judaism does not encourage the practice of religious austerities, emphasizing rather the legitimacy of the pleasures of the world as long as they are enjoyed in moderation. In particular, celibacy was opposed as it negated the first precept to "be fruitful and multiply." The major ascetic practice among Jews was FASTING. From time to time, however, there have been groups or individuals who have adopted or advocated ascetic measures. These included certain sects in the Second Temple period, the Mourners for Zion (a KARAITE group), the medieval German Hasidim, and groups influenced by the Kabbalah.

Asch, Sholem (1880–1957): Yiddish writer. Born in Poland, he subsequently lived in other European countries and in the US; in 1954, he settled in Israel. His first stories were written in Hebrew but he soon devoted himself to writing in Yiddish. He wrote books about Jewish life in Eastern Europe (*Three Cities, Salvation*) and America (*East River*). Turning to the historical novel, he wrote a trilogy about early Christianity (*Mary, The Nazarene, The Apostle*) which aroused considerable controversy in Jewish circles. He also wrote novels about Moses (*Moses*) and Isaiah (*The Prophet*). He was one of the first Yiddish playwrights to achieve international fame, his plays including *Mottke the Thief* and *God of Vengeance*.

Ashamnu ("We have trespassed"): Formula of confession of sin, citing 24 sins in alphabetical order. Probably originally recited (in a somewhat different form) by the high priest in the temple, it became part of the liturgy on the Day of Atonement, when it is recited in all services.

Ashdod: Israeli port. In ancient times, it was one of the five cities of the Philistines where they built a temple to the god Dagon. The historical town—some distance from the modern town —has been excavated. Modern A. was founded in 1956, and many new immigrants settled there. An industrial complex was built, as was a deep-water harbor, which became the main Mediterranean port for southern Israel. The population in 1975 was 55,-000.

Asher: Eighth son of JACOB (2nd of his concubine Zilpah) and progenitor of the tribe of A. (Gen. 30:12). The tribe's territory was in the Plain of Acre and W. Galilee.

Asher ben Jehiel (c. 1250–1327): Talmudic scholar. Known as the Rosh, he was pupil of MEIR OF ROTHENBURG, and after his teacher's death was looked on as the outstanding halakhic authority of German Jewry. He left Germany in 1303, settling in Toledo, Spain. His responsa threw important light both on the development of HALAKHAH in his time and on contemporary events. His chief work, *Piskei ha-Rosh*, influenced subsequent halakhah, particularly through the *Tur* of his son, JACOB BEN ASHER.

Asherah: Canaanite fertility and mother goddess. Worship of A. became popular in Judah and Israel and was condemned by the prophets. The name was also given to a wooden pole representing the goddess and placed near her altars.

Ashi (c. 335–427): Babylonian AMORA, who was the chief editor of the Babylonian Talmud. He reopened the SURA Academy, which he headed for 52 years, and was regarded as the head of Babylonian Jewry. The editing of the Talmud, according to tradition, lasted 30 years, and was completed after his death.

Ashkelon: Port in Israel. One of the ancient towns in the country, it is mentioned from the 20th cent. BCE. A. was one of the five cities of the Philistines and remained independent during the period of the Israelite kingdom. It was also independent during the late Second Temple period, when it was a center of Greek culture. It was captured by the Crusaders but was destroyed in 1270 by the sultan Baybars. The town grew after 1948, when it incorporated the former neighboring Arab town of Migdal (Majdal). New immigrants were settled there, and it was developed as a resort and as the terminal of the oil pipeline from Elath. The population in 1974 was 46,700.

Ashkenazi: Term applied to Jews of Germany and their descendants (especially in contradistinction to the SEPHARDIM, the descendants of the Jews of Spain). The A. tradition developed in the Rhineland communities of Speyer, Worms, and Mainz, then spread through France under the influence of Rashi and his school, then eastward to Germany and Bohemia. In these areas of Central Europe, it established a unified custom and law. The ritual was closer to the old Palestinian rite than the Sephardi (which was influenced by Babylonia). The A. pronunciation of Hebrew differed from the Sephardi. The A. provided the main reservoir of Jews going to American countries in the 19th and 20th cent. The great majority of the Jewish people are A. In Israel, there was originally a considerable A. majority, but Sephardi immigration and their offspring are now 60% of the population. The country has both an A. and a Sephardi chief rabbi.

Ashkenazi, Bezalel (c. 1520–c. 1591): Talmudic authority. He was chief of the Egyptian rabbis and later chief rabbi of Jerusalem. He traveled extensively, collecting funds for Palestinian institutions and encouraging immigration to the Land of Israel. His *Shittah Mekubbetzet* collected comments on the Talmud from medieval Ashkenazi and Sephardi authorities.

Ashkenazi, Jacob (c. 1550–1626): Author of devocational works; born in Poland, he died in Prague. His Yiddish work *Tz'enah u-Re'enah*, a homiletical commentary on and exposition of the Pentateuch, became extremely popular among Jewish women, providing favorite reading, especially on Sabbath afternoons.

Ashkenazi, Solomon (c. 1520–1602): Physician and Turkish diplomat. Of Italian birth, he was physician to the king of Poland and settled in Turkey in 1564. There he entered the service of the sultan and was employed on various diplomatic missions. He wielded great influence, especially in Turkey's foreign policy.

Ashkenazi, Tzevi (1660–1718): Talmudic scholar, known as Ḥakham Tzevi. Born in Moravia, he became rabbi of Altona and then of Amsterdam, where he uncompromisingly opposed Shabbetaism. He eventually had to resign, and spent the rest of his life in Poland. He was widely respected during his lifetime as an outstanding rabbinic authority.

Ashre: First word of prayer recited in the morning and afternoon services. It begins with Ps. 84:5 ("Happy are they who dwell in Thy house"), Ps. 144:15, and continues with the alphabetic Ps. 145.

Ashtoreth: Pagan goddess, also called Astarte. Various A. plaques and figurines have been discovered in Israelite levels of occupation. A. was a Canaanite war and fertility goddess to whom temples were dedicated.

Asia: Until Temple times, Jewish history originated in western A., and the first main Diaspora was in Babylonia. For many centuries the Jewish communities of Babylonia and Persia were outstanding, and for almost 1,000 years Babylonia was the hub of Jewish learning, its academies guiding Jews in all parts of the world. Gradually Jews spread eastward, and already in the Middle Ages some reached China on trade missions. Other significant Jewish communities were in India, Yemen, and Arabia, as well as southern Russia (e.g., Georgia, Bokhara). Others lived in Syria and Lebanon, and in western A. the communities were augmented by Spanish and Portuguese refugees from the end of the 15th cent. The 20th cent. saw the return to Israel; the move of many Jews to Asian parts of Russia, especially during World War II; and after 1948, the evacuation of most Asian Jewish communities, mostly to Israel. Within a few years, few Jews were left in Iraq, Yemen, and China, and the Indian community and Afghanistan had dwindled considerably. Outside Israel the largest remaining community was in Iran, and smaller groups lived in other parts of A., including Japan, Singapore, and Hong Kong. In 1976, 100,000 Jews lived in A., apart from 3,000,-000 in Israel.

Asimov, Isaac (1920–): US writer and biochemist. From 1955 he was professor of biochemistry at Boston Univ. and wrote on many aspects of science. He has published over 100 books and is best known for his science fiction (*The Caves of Steel, The Gods Themselves, Asimov's Mysteries*).

Asmodeus: Evil spirit identified with Ashmedai, king of the demons. First mentioned in the Apocryphal Book of Tobit, he appears frequently in early aggadic literature but was developed in later aggadot into a joyful sprite whose evil associations were lost.

Assembly, Great see **Keneset Gedolah**

Assembly of Notables see **Sanhedrin, Grand**

assimilation: Process by which individual or group loses identity by merger with another group. It is applied to varying phenomena ranging from an inevitable acculturation process (the adoption of the dominant clothing or speech) to the complete abandonment of all Jewish ties and identity (short of a formal act of conversion). Already in ancient times, a. posed a problem, with the most striking challenge coming from the Hellenistic way of life, even in Palestine. But even in its severest forms, a. has become a major challenge only in modern times. A certain amount of cultural a. occurred at all times but did not threaten Jewish identity. As long as religion was a major force, Jews could not leave the Jewish fold without formally adopting Christianity or Islam, and this was regarded as the problem of apostasy rather than a. It is only in recent centuries, particularly under the impact of emancipation and secularization, that Jews have had the opportunity of forsaking their Jewish identity and replacing it with that of the majority culture. This frequently started with an estrangement from the religious aspects of Judaism, and was connected with a loosening of all Jewish ties and commitments. In many cases this led to intermarriage, following which subsequent generations had no Jewish commitment or allegiance whatsoever. This process was particularly noticeable in Western Europe (e.g., Germany, France, England) from the 19th cent., and the tendency has continued in all Diaspora communities, although it has been slowed by the emergence of Zionism and Israel and by manifestations of anti-Semitism, notably the Holocaust. In recent years, Jewish leaders have paid considerable attention to combating a., especially by improvements in the scope and standard of Jewish education. It is recognized that a certain degree of a. is inevitable in any open society, and Jews outside Israel face the prospect of rapid attrition through the assimilatory process.

Assyria: Ancient western Asian empire. Assyrian armies on various occasions reached the territory of Israel and Judah, where they were regarded with dread. Evidence of these contacts are to be found not only in the Bible but also in monuments discovered in A. which depict the Assyrian wars and also mention names of kings of Israel and Judah. The first Assyrian king mentioned in the Bible is Tiglath-pileser III (745–27 BCE), who took many from the Kingdom of Israel into captivity. Shalmaneser V (727–22 BCE) besieged Samaria for 3 years, and its capture was effected by his successor Sargon II (722–705 BCE), who was responsible for the mass exile of inhabitants from the northern kingdom of Israel and their replacement by Syrian and Babylonian prisoners. His son Sennacherib (705–681 BCE) invaded Judah in 701, conquered Lachish, and besieged Jerusalem, but was compelled to withdraw as a result of a plague in his army. In the next century the Assyrian empire gave way to that of BABYLONIA.

Astarte see **Ashtoreth**

astrology: The study of celestial phenomena for their supposed influence on human events. Although Jewish authorities could be found among both its supporters and detractors, the general trend in the ancient and medieval world was for Jews—like other peoples—to believe in it. This belief found its way into popular usages, superstitious beliefs and practices, and even everyday speech (e.g., the popular greeting *mazzaltov* means, literally, "a good constellation"). Talmudic rabbis who deny the efficacy of a. do so with respect to the Jewish people but do not deny its validity for others. In the Middle Ages, belief in a. was widespread among Jews, and the only authority to reject it was Maimonides, who classed it with witchcraft and sorcery. Nevertheless, belief in a. continued to flourish. Jews were among the noted astrologers of the Middle Ages, and some of their works on the subject have survived. A. also played an important role in kabbalistic literature, especially in "Practical Kabbalah."

astronomy: In ancient times, a. was studied for its religious implications but never as star worship—the stars themselves were created by God and they themselves worshiped Him. Much of the interest in celestial phenomena derived from ASTROLOGY. Another important motivation was the need to determine the CALENDAR, which caused many rabbis to become expert astronomers (R. SAMUEL claimed that he knew the paths of heaven as well as he knew the streets of his hometown). The expertise was particularly important in determining new moons and leap years. Talmudic a. accepted the views universally held at the time, according to which the earth is the center of the world. In the Middle Ages, Jews played a major role in astronomic study and in the transmission of Greek and Arab traditions to the Christian world. They acted as official astronomers, wrote and translated important works, and compiled astronomical tables. They were also responsible for inventions (e.g., concerning the astrolabe and quadrant).

asylum see **cities of refuge**

Athaliah (d. 836 BCE): Queen of Judah who ruled 842–836 BCE. Daughter of AHAB, king of Israel, and his Phoenician wife JEZEBEL, she was married to Jehoram, king of Judah. After the death of her husband and son Ahaziah a year later, she seized power and had the entire royal family killed, with only the young prince JOASH escaping. She introduced Baal worship into the kingdom. She was killed when JEHOIADA led a conspiracy to have Joash crowned king.

Athens: Capital of Greece. Jews are known to have lived there from the 1st cent. CE. The community remained small throughout the ages. After the Balkan wars, Jews from Salonica and elsewhere moved there, and in 1939 the community numbered 3,000, many of whom were sent to their death in Auschwitz. In 1977, 2,000 Jews lived there.

Athlit: Village in Israel. It was an important port in ancient times and was a major stronghold of the Crusaders when its name was Castrum Peregrinorum (evacuated in 1291). In 1911, Aaron AARONSOHN founded there an agricultural experimental station which was a NILI center during World War I. Under the British, a detention camp for "illegal" immigrants was constructed there. The moshavah, founded in 1903, has 2,467 inhabitants (1972). Prominent on the shore are the ruins of the Crusader castle.

Atlanta: Capital of Georgia, US. The first Jewish settler arrived in the early 1840s, the first congregation was founded in 1867, and the first synagogue was built in 1877. In 1976, A. had 21,000 Jews with 7 congregations. Sam Massell, a Jew, was mayor of the city from 1970 to 1973.

atonement: Overcoming of sin, effected through the performance of certain rituals (in Temple times, through sacrifice), through the payment of compensation for wrong committed or inflicted, through suffering, or through contrition and REPENTANCE, accompanied by a rectification of conduct. The popular belief in biblical times that sacrifice alone sufficed for a. was attacked by the prophets, who insisted on the element of contrition. Prayer and fasting were also advocated as methods of achieving a., as was the giving of charity. A. was particularly stressed during the Penitential Period during the month of Elul and particularly during the Ten Days of Penitence culminating in the Day of Atonement.

Atonement, Day of (Yom Kippur; Yom Ha-Kippurim): Annual fast; the most solemn occasion in the Jewish year when, according to Jewish tradition, God seals the fate of every person for the ensuing year. The rabbis connected it with the New Year ten days earlier and described the entire period as the Ten Days of Penitence during which sincere repentance can prevent an unfavorable decision on the D. of A. In ancient times, the day was the occasion of a solemn Temple ceremonial (based on Lev. 16). This was the one annual occasion when the high priest entered the Holy of Holies. Another feature of the ceremonial was the symbolic transference of the sins of the community to a goat (scapegoat), which was then taken to the wilderness to die there (see AZAZEL). After the destruction of the Temple, the solemnity was conveyed in the liturgy (including a detailed description of the Temple ritual). There are five prayer services during the 25-hour observance of the fast. The first is the initial Evening Service, generally known after its introductory prayer as KOL NIDRE. During the following day the Morning, Additional, Afternoon, and Concluding (NEILAH) prayers are recited. During the entire period it is forbidden to partake of food or drink, to have marital relations, to anoint with oil, or to wear leather shoes. A feature of the prayers is the confession prayers (AL ḤET and ASHAMNU), which are couched in the plural to convey the collective guilt responsibility of the community. The Law is read at both the Morning and Afternoon Service, and prayer shawls are worn at all services; the Orthodox also wear a white coat (*kittel*). In 1973, Egypt and Syria attacked Israel during the D. of A.

Auschwitz (Pol. Oswiecim): Town in Poland, site of the largest Nazi extermination camp, where over 1,000,-000 Jews perished during World War II. It consisted of three main sections: the main camp (where few Jews were housed), Birkenau, and outside groups. Prisoners were sent there from all parts of Europe, with altogether some 4,000,000 to 5,000,000 passing through. Most non-Jews were used for slave labor, but the overwhelming majority of Jews were sent immediately on arrival to their death in the gas chambers; their remains were burned in vast incinerators. Even those Jews at first selected for slave labor were eventually put to death. When the Russians reached the camp in January 1945, they found only 5,000 survivors. The most notorious commandant, Rudolf Hoess, was executed in A. in March 1947 as a war criminal.

Australia: Jews were living there in the second decade of the 19th cent., with the first communities established in SYDNEY in 1828 and in MELBOURNE in 1840. Many Jews arrived following the discovery of gold in the mid-19th cent., and a number of country communities were founded, some of which subsequently disappeared as the Jews moved to the larger towns. Jews immigrated from various places, including Europe and Britain. There was a considerable influx of refugees from Nazi Germany in the 1930s, and again of homeless Jews after World War II. Some 72,000 Jews were living there in 1976 (34,000 in Melbourne, 28,-000 in Sydney). The community has an active religious life (Orthodox communities recognize the authority of the British chief rabbinate), widespread educational networks, and strong Zionist affiliations.

The Executive Council of Australian Jewry is the representative body. Outstanding Australian Jews have included Sir John MONASH, who commanded the Australian Expeditionary Force in World War I, and Sir Isaac ISAACS and Sir Zelman COWAN, governors-general.

Austria: Its Jews originated mostly from S. Germany, Bohemia, Hungary, Galicia, and Rumania. Records go back to the 10th cent. In the 13th cent., the Jews received a charter of privileges. Subsequently there were frequent persecutions, of which the most serious was the *Wiener Gezerah* of 1420, when 270 Jews were burned, and the others expelled or forcibly converted to Christianity. There were Jews in A. during the following centuries, and they were also subject to harassment and expulsions (notably that ordered in 1669–70). A change for the better resulted from Joseph II's Edict of Toleration (1782), and full rights were granted in 1867. Jews played a large role in the cultural life of the country in the 19th and 20th cent. There were 180,000 Jews in A. at the time of the Nazi Anschluss in 1938. Severe persecutions ensued (some of the major Nazi leaders, including Hitler and Eichmann, were of Austrian origin). About 70,000 Austrian Jews were killed in the following years. The 1976 community numbered 13,000, mostly in Vienna. In 1970, Bruno Kreisky became the first Jew to be chancellor of A.

auto-da-fé: Ceremony of pronouncement of sentences of the INQUISITION. Often attended by large crowds, those who were condemned for heresy were handed over by the Church to the secular authorities, who were responsible for burning them. Between 1481 and 1826, some 2,000 rituals are known to have been held in Spain, Portugal, and their overseas dependencies, and over 30,000 people were put to death—mostly on accusations of Judaizing—while perhaps another 400,000 received other sentences.

autonomy: Even after the Jews lost their national independence under the Romans, they continued to enjoy some degree of self-government in almost all countries where they lived. In Babylonia, the exilarch had widespread powers and authority including the imposition of taxation. Jewish courts were in most places empowered to try all cases in which only Jews were involved, while the Jewish authorities were entrusted with taxing the community not only for its own needs but also to pay the general taxes levied on the community. In Spain, the Jewish courts could even impose capital punishment. Outstanding in Eastern Europe was the COUNCIL OF THE FOUR LANDS, which was responsible for the self-government of the Jewish communities. Fines and excommunication were among the means of punishment used by such bodies to ensure respect for their authority. Civic emancipation ended a. for Jews in Europe.

Av: Fifth month of the religious year, 11th of the civil; corresponding to July/ August, it has 30 days and its zodiac sign is Leo. Its first 9 days are a period of semi-mourning, culminating in the fast of Tisha be'Av (see Av, NINTH OF). In Temple times, Av 15 was a holiday to celebrate the bringing of wood offerings for the Temple altar. It was also a day when young men chose their brides.

Av, Ninth of (Tisha be'Av): Annual day of mourning to commemorate the destruction of the Temples, both of which were destroyed around this date. It was traditionally the date of other tragedies in Jewish history. It is the only fast, apart from the Day of Atonement, to be observed from nightfall to nightfall (the others are from dawn to dusk). The highlight of the synagogue service is the reading of the Book of Lamentations in the Evening and Morning Services and the recital of dirges (*kinot*). Customarily these are recited while sitting on the floor, and only in dim light. The prayer shawls and phylacteries are worn not at the Morning but at the Afternoon Service. If the date falls on the Sabbath, the fast is postponed until its conclusion. There is a traditional belief that it will be the day of birth of the Messiah. Throughout the centuries it became a custom, in the Land of Israel, to pray at the Western Wall on this day.

av bet din ("father of the lawcourt"): In Second Temple times, the vice-president of the Supreme Court of Justice. In modern times, the title is given to heads of Jewish local law courts.

Av ha-Rahamim ("Father of mercy"): Prayer recited on Sabbath (with certain exceptions) in the Ashkenazi rite. It is a dirge composed in the Middle Ages in memory of martyrs.

Avadim ("Slaves"): Minor tractate appended to the Talmud dealing with the purchase and manumission of slaves, etc.

Avdat: Ancient city in the central Negev, the southern part of Israel. Originally built in the 1st cent. CE by the Nabateans, it was later inhabited by Byzantines, and destroyed in the 7th cent. Extensive remains from both periods have been excavated and reconstructed.

Avele Zion ("Mourners of Zion"): Groups of Jews who after the destruction of the Second Temple adopted ascetic practices for the purpose of hastening redemption. They did not eat meat or wine. The name and customs of the A.Z. were again adopted in the 9th cent. by KARAITES who settled in Jerusalem, and groups existed in other countries. They are known to have been in existence until the end of the 11th cent.

averah: Trespass; transgression of religious commandment; the opposite of MITZVAH. The three most serious *averot* are the shedding of innocent blood, adultery, and idolatry; a person must give up his life rather than commit any of these three sins.

Avignon: Town in southern France where Jews were settled from the 4th cent. As the town fell under papal rule, its Jews were able to remain there, even when those in the rest of France were expelled in the 14th cent. Later they were enclosed in a ghetto called the Carrière des Juifs. In the Middle Ages, the Jews of A. and the entire Comtat Venaissin developed their own liturgical customs. The modern settlement, numbering 2,500, is largely composed of recent immigrants from N. Africa.

Avinu Malkenu ("Our Father, Our King"): Invocation of God recited during the Ten Days of Penitence (except on Sabbaths) and on fast days (except Av 9). Each of its 44 verses (29 in the Sephardi rite) begins with the words A.M.

Aviv (Abib): First month of the year in the Bible, corresponding to NISAN. The word in Hebrew also means "spring."

avodah ("service"): The sacrificial service in the Temple and the special ritual for the Day of Atonement performed by the high priest. The latter is graphically described in the prayers read in the Day of Atonement Additional Service. This was also the subject for medieval poems also called by the same name.

Avodah Zarah ("Idolatry"; "Strange Worship"): Tractate in the MISHNAH with commentary in both Talmuds. It deals with the prohibition of idolatry and steps to be taken concerning idols and idol worshipers.

Avot ("Fathers"): Also known as *Pirkei Avot*, "Chapters of the Fathers"; often called "Ethics of the Fathers." Treatise of the MISH-

NAH containing the ethical maxims of the early rabbis. It became very popular and was incorporated into the Ashkenazi synagogue service, being read on Sabbath afternoons between Passover and the New Year (the Sephardim read it in the home between Passover and Pentecost). It originally had five chapters, but a sixth, dating from amoraic times, was later added. The work was the subject of many commentaries, the best known being *Avot de-Rabbi Natan*, which was printed in Talmud editions after A. (which had no Talmud commentary).

avot see **patriarchs**

ayin (ע): Sixteenth letter of the Hebrew alphabet. Numerical value: 70. Among Ashkenazim it is not pronounced, but among Oriental Jews it is sounded in the back of the throat. European Sephardim pronounce it as *ng*.

Azazel: According to Lev. 16, the goat to which the sins of the people were symbolically transferred in Temple times was designated "to A." and sent to the wilderness to meet his death. The term A. has been variously interpreted as referring to the goat, to the wilderness, and to a wilderness demon. In later rabbinical literature, A. was seen as a fallen angel. In modern Hebrew, saying "Go to A." is a curse ("Go to hell").

Azharot ("warnings"): Liturgical poems based on the exposition of the 613 precepts (the numerical value of the word *a.* in Hebrew = 613). They are recited by Sephardim in the Shavuot service before the Afternoon Service.

Azulai, Hayyim Joseph David (1724–1806): Rabbinical scholar, known as Hida. Born in Jerusalem, he traveled extensively on behalf of the Hebron community, spending his last years in Leghorn. Wherever he went he consulted and copied Hebrew manuscripts. The best known of the hundred works he wrote were the bibliographical *Shem ha-Gedolim* and the diary *Maagal Tov*.

Baal: A chief god of the Canaanite pantheon. He was the god of fertility, of the heavens, and of thunder. The name was also given to various local gods (e.g., Baal Gad, god of good fortune, and Baal Peor, the god worshiped at Mt. Peor in Moab). The worship of B. influenced the Israelites in Canaan, who tended to adopt the rites of B. worship, for which they were denounced by the prophets. This conflict is a major theme of the Book of Kings, which includes the dramatic confrontation between Elijah and the prophets of B. supported by Jezebel (I Kings 18:19–40). Baalist practices and worship persisted until the Babylonian Exile. In Hebrew, B. means "owner," "husband."

Baal ha-bayit ("master of the house"; in Yiddish, *balebos*): Houseowner; landlord. In Yiddish, a man of substance.

baal kore (baal keriah): The reader of the Scroll of the Law in the synagogue (Ashkenazi usage).

baal shem ("master of the [Divine] name"): Person who used the Divine name to work miracles. The title became familiar in the Middle Ages, especially in mystical and, later, Hasidic circles. It was frequent in Eastern Europe for those who cured the sick (especially the mentally sick) by means of amulets, etc.

Baal Shem Tov, Israel ben Eliezer (c. 1700–1760): Founder of HASIDISM. Few facts are known of his life.

He lived in Podolia, was a teacher, charcoal burner, and sexton, and was called Baal Shem Tov (abbr.: Besht) by virtue of his reputation as a healer of the sick. His intensive study culminated in his "revealing" his teachings (c. 1740). At this time, he settled in Medzibozh and pupils gathered in great numbers to study his teachings. He himself did not write down his doctrines, but they were collected and recorded by his students. In addition, many legends were related about his personality and teaching. He was strongly influenced by the mystical teachings of the Kabbalah and Isaac LURIA, but nonetheless made his own original contributions. Man must seek a cleaving (*devekut*) to God, and this is attained primarily through prayer, which must be recited with devotion (*kavvanah*) and ecstasy (*hitlahavut*). His teachings appealed to the uneducated, and the movement he inaugurated soon won a mass following in Eastern Europe.

baal tekiyah: The person who blows the ram's horn (*shophar*) at the synagogue service in the penitential season during the month of Elul and on the High Holidays.

Baasha (d. 883 BCE): King of Israel who ruled 906–883 BCE. He conspired against and slew Jeroboam's son Nadab and succeeded him (I Kings 15:27 ff.). His contemporary, and enemy, in the Kingdom of Israel was ASA, who, in alliance with Ben-Hadad of Aram, defeated A. in battle and wrested territory from him.

Baazov, Herzl (1904–1945): Georgian playwright and poet. Much of his subject matter was drawn from Jewish life. He was arrested and exiled in 1937 and died in Siberia.

Babel, Isaac (1894–1939?): Russian short-story writer. In the Civil War, he served in the Soviet cavalry, the subject of some of his stories. Other stories by him center around life in his native Odessa, especially among the Jews (e.g., *Benia Krik*, about a gangster); he also wrote plays. He is regarded as one of the outstanding writers of modern Russian literature. Arrested in 1939 for unknown reasons, he was never seen again.

Babel, Tower of: According to the Bible (Gen. 11), a structure erected by the inhabitants of Shinar (Babel-Babylon) in an effort to reach heaven. Their plan was prevented by God, who confused their languages and scattered them over the earth. The story is designed to explain the multiplicity of languages. Scholars have connected the T. of B. with the

Babylonian tower-temple, or ziggurat.

Babi Yar: Ravine outside Kiev; scene of mass slaughter of Jews by the Germans in September 1941. In postwar Soviet Russia, the Jewish martyrdom in B.Y. was played down, a housing project built on the site, and no memorial erected to commemorate the massacre. This called forth a notable poem in protest from the Soviet poet Evgeni Yevtuchenko (1962), and inspired a novel by Anatoli Kuznetzov.

Babylon: Ancient city and country (the latter being more generally known as Babylonia). The Bible regards B. (which roughly corresponds to the modern Iraq) as the place of origin of the first patriarch, ABRAHAM (who came from Ur of the Chaldees). The two other major impacts of B. in biblical times resulted from (1) the continuing invasions of ASSYRIA (the predecessor of B.) and of B. toward the Mediterranean, which frequently brought Babylonian armies in and near the Land of Israel; (2) the conquest of Judah by Babylonia in the early 6th cent. BCE, as a result of which many inhabitants of Judah (including the prophet EZEKIEL) were exiled to B. This was the Babylonian EXILE, and although some exiles returned a few decades later, after B. was conquered by the Persians under Cyrus, many continued to live in B. The position of the Jews remained favorable, and they built up their own communities, although remaining in constant touch with the Jews in the Land of Israel. Eventually they achieved considerable autonomy under the EXILARCH. Their intellectual role became supreme in Jewish life, and for centuries B. was the great center of Jewish religious life, through the activities of its great academies, notably those of SURA and PUMBEDITA. There the Babylonian TALMUD—which became the main subject of study of Jews the world over —was compiled and the authority of their spiritual heads (GAON) was recognized by all Jewish communities. In 637 CE, B. was conquered by the Arabs; for subsequent history, see IRAQ.

Bacharach, Jair Ḥayyim (1638–1702): German talmudical authority. He is best known for his *Ḥavvat Yair*, responsa which show a wide knowledge of rabbinical literature and which reject casuistry.

Bacher, Wilhelm (1850–1913): Hungarian scholar and orientalist; one of the best-known, most prolific, and most versatile scholars writing in the WISSENSCHAFT period. His works on talmudic aggadah have remained standard authorities.

Bachrach, Burt (1928–): US composer. After working as accompanist and arranger for Marlene Dietrich, he composed popular music, with many hits, including the musical *Promises, Promises* and the Oscar-winning score for the movie *Butch Cassidy and the Sundance Kid*.

badge, Jewish: The distinguishing mark on clothing for Jews (and other nonbelievers) originated in a Muslim milieu. The fourth Lateran Council (1215) laid down that Jews and other infidels should wear distinguishing clothing, and this often took the form of a b. The b. was usually yellow, although there were variants in color and form. In some countries, the Jews were made to wear a special hat. This lasted for many centuries and fell into disuse only in the 18th cent. (it was finally abolished in the Napoleonic period). The concept was used by the Nazis, who during World War II made the Jews of Europe wear a distinguishing yellow b. in the form of a Shield of David, with the word "Jew" inside it.

badhan ("joker"): A Jewish jester in Eastern Europe. He was a familiar feature at weddings and other celebrations.

Baeck, Leo (1873–1956): German theologian and Liberal Jewish leader. He was a rabbi in Berlin from 1912, and from 1933 headed the German Jewish communal organization. From 1943 to 1945 he was imprisoned by the Nazis in THERESIENSTADT. After the war he settled in London and headed the World Union for Progressive Judaism. In his theological works (notably *The Essence of Judaism*) he depicted Judaism as the classical religion of the concrete in contrast to Christianity as the romantic religion of the abstract.

Baer, Max (1909–1959): US boxer. In 1933 he won the world's heavyweight boxing championship from Max Schmeling. Two years later he lost it to Jim Braddock.

Baer, Yitzhak (Fritz) (1888–): Historian. Born in Germany, he taught at the Hebrew University, Jerusalem, where he became a professor from 1928. He wrote *History of the Jews in Christian Spain* as well as works on the Second Temple period.

Baerwald, Paul (1871–1961): Banker and philanthropist. He went to the US from his native Germany in 1896. He was active in Jewish communal affairs, especially the American Joint Distribution Committee, of which he was chairman from 1932 to 1945.

Baeyer, Adolf von (1835–1917): German organic chemist; son of a Jewish mother. Professor in Berlin and Munich, he worked on organic dyes and hydroaromatic compounds, discovering synthetic indigo. He was awarded the Nobel Prize in Physics in 1905.

Baghdad: Capital of Iraq. Jews lived there from the time of its foundation (762 CE), and its Jewish community became the largest and most influential in the country. In the 9th cent. the academies of SURA and PUMBEDITA were established there. In the 12th cent. the number of Jews was put at 40,000. The community declined in the 15th cent. but was again important from the 17th. In the 19th and early 20th cent., many of its Jews became prominent in other Asian communities, including in the Far East. Hundreds were killed and wounded in the pogroms during the brief rule of the pro-Nazi Rashid Ali in 1941. 77,000 Jews lived in B. in 1947 and had many religious and educational institutions. Most Jews of B. immigrated to Israel together with the rest of Iraqi Jewry in Operation Ezra and Nehemiah, 1950–51. Less than 5,000 remained, and their numbers had dropped to around 500 by 1977. Nine B. Jews were publicly hanged in 1969 on charges of spying for Israel.

Bahia: Port in Brazil. Marranos settled there in the 16th cent., but from the late 16th cent. were persecuted by the Inquisition. About 200 returned to Judaism under the Dutch occupation (1624) but suffered after the Portuguese reconquest. The Jewish community was refounded in 1912, with the immigration stemming from Eastern Europe, mainly Bessarabia. It numbered 1,300 in 1974.

Bahir, Sepher ha-: Earliest work of Jewish mystical literature. Traditionally ascribed to the 1st-cent. R. Nehunya ben ha-Kanah, it first appeared in the 12th cent. in Provence but it incorporates ancient texts which had been transmitted to Europe from the East. Written in Hebrew and Aramaic, the style of this short book is obscure. Its teachings greatly influenced later KABBALAH.

Bahur, Elijah see **Levita, Elijah**

Bahya ben Asher ibn Hlava (13th cent.): Bible commentator and kabbalist who apparently lived in Spain. His best-known work is his commentary on the Pentateuch along the four lines of interpretation known as PARDES—literal, philosophical, homiletical, and mystical.

Bahya ben Joseph ibn Paquda (late 11th cent.): Moral philosopher and ethical writer who probably lived in Saragossa, Spain. His *Hovot ha-Levavot* ("Duties of the Heart"), written in Arabic and influenced by Muslim mystics, was the most influential of medieval Jewish ethical works. It teaches the "duties of the heart" which the Jew must observe to reach spiritual perfection.

bakkashah ("supplication"): Name given to a class of synagogue hymns resembling SELIHOT, recited by Sephardim on the High Holidays. B. is also the name given to a service of religious hymns printed at the beginning of Sephardi prayer books since the 17th cent., and recited while waiting for the Morning Service. Originally this was done daily, but later only on the Sabbath.

Balaam: Heathen soothsayer summoned by BALAK, king of Moab, to curse the Israelites who were advancing into the Jordan Valley. However, Divinely inspired, he blessed the Israelites instead of cursing them ("How goodly are thy tents, O Israel"). He subsequently instructed the Midianites to entice the Israelites into idol worship and was killed by the Israelites on the battlefield (Num. 22–24; 31:1–8, Josh. 13:22). Late Jewish commentators debated whether the story of his talking ass was to be taken literally or allegorically.

Balaban, Meir (1877–1942): Historian of Polish and Russian Jewry. He taught in Warsaw and died in the Warsaw ghetto.

Balfour Declaration: Document issued by the British government on November 2, 1917, expressing the British intention to establish a Jewish national home in Palestine, newly conquered from the Turks. It was the result of intensive activity by Zionist leaders (WEIZMANN, SOKOLOW, etc.) in various countries, notably England, the US, and France. It was also preceded by intensive discussions at government level in London initiated by Herbert SAMUEL. It was supported by Prime Minister David Lloyd George and Foreign Secretary Arthur J. Balfour. The final text was somewhat modified, however, as a result of pressure by anti-Zionist British Jews (Edwin MONTAGU). The final text, which was communicated to Lord Rothschild, announced that "His Majesty's Government views with favour the establishment of a national home in Palestine for the Jewish people and will use their best endeavours to facilitate the achievement of this object, it being clearly understood that nothing shall be done which may prejudice the civil and religious rights of existing non-Jewish communities in Palestine or the rights and political status enjoyed by Jews in any other country." The document was incorporated into the Palestine mandate issued to Britain on behalf of the League of Nations.

Baltimore: US city. Founded in 1729, few Jews settled there until the 19th cent., and the first congregation was established in 1830. The early settlers were mostly of German origin. The first Reform congregation was founded in 1842. About 10,000 Jews lived in B. by the 1880s. It expanded rapidly in the 20th cent., and by 1976 had 92,000 Jews.

Bamberger, Simon (1846–1926): Democratic Governor of Utah, 1916–20; the first non-Mormon to hold that position. B., who was of German birth, was a banker and railroad builder before entering politics.

ban see **excommunication**

Bank Leumi le-Israel: Israeli bank; until 1948 the bank of Palestinian Jewry, and from 1948 to 1951, the bank of the State of Israel. It was founded in 1903 as the Jewish Colonial Trust. From 1931 to 1951 it was called the Anglo-Palestine Bank.

Bank of Israel: Israel's national bank, set up in 1954. It is responsible for the conduct of the country's monetary policy in accordance with government directives.

banking: Jews rose to prominence in modern b. with the development of the international economy which favored the growth of merchant-bankers, and firms such as the Rothschilds grew rapidly. They played an important role in the growth of joint stock banks, among the pioneers of which were Ludwig Bamberger in Germany and Sir David Salomons, the Sterns, and the Seligmans in England. Private banks declined in the 20th cent., and Jews played only a minor role in the major banks thereafter. In the 19th cent., US Jews played a significant role in banking (Erlanger, Guggenheims, Schiff, Kuhn-Loeb, Warburg), but their role declined too in the 20th cent.

Banu Kainuka: Jewish tribe in Medina at the time of Mohammed, who forced them to surrender after a 2-week siege. Initially he wished to execute the males but spared them on condition that they leave the town. They migrated to elsewhere in Arabia.

Banu Kuraiza: Jewish tribe in Medina at the time

of Mohammed, who attacked them. On their surrender he executed the males and sold the women and children into captivity.

Banu-l-Nadir: Jewish tribe in Medina, besieged by Mohammed (c. 626). On their surrender they were allowed to move north and relocated in Khaibar and Syria.

baptism, forced: Forced conversions to Christianity as a result of mob violence occurred in the Roman Empire during the 4th to 6th cent. and became state policy in Visigothic Spain and elsewhere. The Catholic Church from the time of Pope Gregory I (590–604) condemned f.b. but *post facto* accepted it as valid. During the Crusades many in the Jewish community were given the alternative of baptism or death; with few exceptions, they chose the latter. In Spain, however, when faced with a similar alternative, a large number chose baptism, even though many continued to practice Jewish rites in secret (see MARRANOS). F.b. of children, although officially condemned by the Church, was recognized as valid once performed, and many zealous Catholics engineered the secret baptism of children who were henceforth regarded as Catholics, despite the efforts of their families. The most notorious such example, in the mid-19th cent., was the MORTARA case. Forced conversion also occurred under Moslem rule. In Jewish law, it was laid down that the descendants of forced converts returning to Judaism did not require the customary ceremony for proselytes.

Bar Giora, Simeon (d. 70): Zealot leader at the time of the revolt against Rome. Born in Jerash in Transjordan, he may have been the son of a convert. He led a group of zealots and declared equality for all and the liberation of slaves. He took over the fortress of Masada, and gained control of much of Judea. Invited to Jerusalem by the opponents of John of Giscala, he took the upper city. Civil war raged, but in face of the growing Roman strength in the year 70, the two rivals made peace with each other. Prominent in the last defense of the city, he was captured by the Romans and displayed in the triumphal procession of Vespasian and his sons, at the conclusion of which he was put to death.

Bar-Ilan (Berlin), Meir (1880–1949): MIZRACHI leader; son of Naphtali Tzevi Judah BERLIN. From an early age he was active in religious Zionist circles, and before World War I was secretary of the Mizrachi World Executive and editor of its weekly journal, which he continued to edit in New York after moving there in 1914. He was president of Mizrachi in the US. In 1926 he settled in Palestine and from then was president of World Mizrachi. He strongly opposed the 1937 Palestine partition scheme. In 1937 he founded the religious daily *Ha-Tzopheh*. He also initiated the ambitious *Talmudic Encyclopaedia* project (1947).

Bar-Ilan University: Israeli university under Orthodox religious auspices, situated near Ramat-Gan. It was founded in 1955 by the American MIZRACHI organization. In 1974 it had 7,000 students. Its president is R. Emanuel Rackman.

Bar Kokhba, Simeon (d. 135 CE): Leader of the Jewish revolt against Rome, 132–35 CE. As now known from recently discovered documents, his real name was Bar (or Ben) Kosiba (Bar Kokhba = "son of a star," an idealization). Sources of his career and personality are scant. During the revolt R. Akiva called him the Messiah, but this view was not universally accepted. Initially his forces took over the entire country, including Jerusalem, and B.K. was declared "Nasi of Israel" (coins being struck accordingly). However, the Roman emperor Hadrian concentrated his best forces, who

gradually recovered the areas taken over by the Jews. B.K.'s last stronghold was at Betar, near Jerusalem, where he held out for some time before this too was taken by the Romans and B.K. was killed. The net result of the revolt was tragic: the Jewish casualties were enormous, through the war and through disease; many Jews were sold into servitude; the land was laid waste; Jerusalem was barred to the Jews. In modern Hebrew literature and in Israel, the figure of B.K. has become a symbol of the Jewish militant struggle for independence. Evidence of the revolt was discovered in excavations (conducted 1952–61) in Judean Desert caves where warriors of B.K.'s army sought refuge.

Bar-Lev, Haim (1924–): Israeli military and political figure. Born in Austria, he went from Yugoslavia to Palestine in 1939. He served in the Haganah and the Palmah, and in various positions in the Israeli army; from 1968 to 1971 he was chief of staff. From 1972 to 1977 he was minister of commerce and industry.

bar mitzvah (literally "son of the commandment," i.e., one who is responsible to perform the commandment): An adult male Jew; hence, the ceremony marking the initiation of a 13-year-old boy into the adult Jewish religious community. He is now obliged to perform the commandments and is reckoned together with other adult males for purposes of prayer (e.g., in the ten-man *minyan* for communal prayer or the three-man *mezumman* in the grace after meals). The b.m. ceremony is comparatively modern, being known only from the 13th–14th cent.; previously a boy was regarded as reaching his religious majority on puberty, reckoned at 13 years and a day, but no special ceremony was held. The religious ceremony consists of calling up the boy to the altar to read from the Scroll of the Law on the Sabbath following his 13th birthday (he generally reads the MAFTIR and HAFTARAH). The father is also called to the Reading of the Law and recites a blessing (*Barukh shepetarani*) thanking God for being released from religious responsibility for the child. In observant circles, the boy now begins to lay his phylacteries daily, and in certain Oriental communities, this too is the occasion of a special (weekday) festivity. From the Middle Ages it became the custom for the b.m. boy to deliver a talmudic discourse. More recently he is addressed in the synagogue by the rabbi. The religious ceremony is followed by social festivities.

baraita (Aram. "external teaching"): Teachings of the *tannaim* not included in the MISHNAH. The largest collection is in the TOSEPHTA, and others are found in the halakhic Midrashim. Many *baraitot* are contained in the Jerusalem and Babylonian Talmuds.

Barak: Commander of the Israelite forces—together with DEBORAH—in their war against the Canaanites (12th cent. BCE). He gathered 10,000 men from the tribes of Zebulun and Naphtali on the slopes of Mt. Tabor and led the Israelites to a resounding victory.

Barash, Asher (1889–1952): Israeli writer. Born in Galicia, he settled in Palestine in 1914 and taught at high schools. He wrote extensively and was best known for his fiction. His chief themes were Jewish life in Galicia, the pioneering period in Palestine, and stories from Jewish history.

Barbados: Island of the WEST INDIES. Its first Jews settled there in 1655. For a time Jews controlled the sugar industry there. Economic decline in the 19th cent. led to the dwindling of the Jewish community, and by 1925 not one was left. However, a small group of Jews settled there from the mid-1930s, numbering 85 in 1976.

Barcelona: Mediterranean port with important Jewish community in Spain between the 9th and 14th cent., the home of a number of distinguished Jewish scholars. In 1263 it was the scene of a famous DISPUTATION. The Jews were attacked in 1348, community leaders were executed on a charge of host desecration in 1367, and the community was annihilated in the 1391 riots. A modern community was established in the 20th cent., which numbered 3,000 in 1972.

Barenboim, Daniel (1942–): Israeli pianist and conductor. Born in Argentina, he was taken to Israel in 1952. An infant prodigy at the piano, he later achieved an international reputation as a conductor as well as pianist.

Bari: Southern Italian port. In early medieval times it was an important center of Jewish learning. Subsequently the community declined and ended when the Jews were expelled from the Kingdom of Naples in 1541.

Barnato, Barnett Isaacs ("Barney") (1852–1897): S. African financier. Born in England, he went to S. Africa during the diamond rush in 1873. He became a diamond magnate and, together with Cecil Rhodes, founded De Beers Consolidated Mining Company. He was also prominent in gold mining in the Johannesburg area.

Baron, Salo Wittmayer (1895–): Historian. Born in Galicia, he went to the US in 1926 and from 1930 was professor of Jewish history at Columbia University, New York. One of the outstanding Jewish historians of the 20th cent., his major work is *Social and Religious History of the Jews* (16 vols. by 1978). Other books include the 3-volume *The Jewish Community*. He founded the periodical *Jewish Social Studies* and for many years headed the American Academy for Jewish Research.

Baron de Hirsch Fund: Incorporated in New York (1891), this trust was established by Baron Maurice de HIRSCH to help Jewish refugees arriving in the US. It assisted immigrants in different ways and also founded an agricultural school in Woodbine, New Jersey, supporting various efforts to settle Jews on the land.

Barsimson, Jacob (mid-17th cent.): Probably the first Jewish settler in New Amsterdam (New York). He arrived on July 8, 1654, from Holland. He fought for equal rights for Jews.

Baruch: Secretary and friend of JEREMIAH, who dictated to him his prophecies of doom. B. then took the scrolls to the Temple area and read them to the people (Jer. 36). After the fall of Jerusalem and the murder of Gedaliah, he was taken to

Egypt together with Jeremiah. He was highly regarded in Jewish tradition, and a number of later works were pseudepigraphically ascribed to him. One of these, the Book of Baruch, was incorporated in the APOCRYPHA; it was probably written in the late Hasmonean period in Hebrew, but it has survived in many translations. The Syriac, Greek, and Ethiopic Apocalypses of Baruch all apparently date from the 2nd cent. CE. All center around the personality of B., with some relating his ascension to heaven and what he found there.

Baruch, Bernard Mannes (1870–1965): US financier and public figure. He was a key figure in managing the US economy during and after World War I. Later, as one of the main confidants of President Franklin D. Roosevelt, he was a leading planner of the New Deal. After World War II, as US representative to the UN Atomic Energy Commission, he proposed a plan for the control of atomic weapons, which was vetoed by the USSR.

Barukh ha-ba ("Blessed be he who comes"): Hebrew equivalent of "Welcome"; a common greeting (cf. Ps. 118:26).

Barukh she-petarani ("Blessed be He who has relieved me [from religious responsibility for my son]"): Benediction recited by father at son's BAR MITZVAH.

Bashan: Region east of the Jordan. Its ancient inhabitants were the REPHAIM, who terrified the Israelites. They were succeeded by the AMORITES. During the Exodus period, its king was the semi-legendary OG. After conquest by the Israelites, B. was settled by half the tribe of MANASSEH. In 732 BCE it was conquered by Tiglath-pileser III of Assyria, who exiled many of its inhabitants. Later it came under Persian, Seleucid, and Roman rule, and was given by the emperor Augustus to Herod, who settled Idumeans there, as well as Jews from Babylonia.

Bashevis Singer see **Singer, Isaac Bashevis**

Baskin, Leonard (1922–): US artist. The son of a rabbi, B. studied in the US and Europe. From 1953, he taught printmaking and sculpture at Smith College. Many of his works are on Jewish subjects.

Basle: Swiss city. The Jewish community, founded in the 13th cent., ended with the Black Death massacres (1349). There was a further settlement in the 14th cent., lasting until 1397. The modern community dates from the late 18th cent. Basle was the scene of the First Zionist Congress in 1897 and several later congresses. The Jewish population in 1976 was 2,300.

*Basnage, Jacques Christian (1653–1725): French Protestant clergyman. He wrote a 5-volume work which was the first systematic account of post-biblical Jewish history.

Bass, Shabbetai (1641–1718): First Jewish bibliographer. Born in Poland, he lived later in Prague, Amsterdam, and Dyhernfurth, where he established a printing press in 1680. His great achievement was his *Siphte Yeshenim*, a Hebrew list of 2,200 works on Hebraica and Judaica and a listing of manuscripts.

bat kol ("daughter of a voice"): A divine voice revealing God's decisions to man. Unlike prophecy, in which the recipient had to be predisposed, it could be received by any person or group of persons. Instances are related in the Talmud of a b.k. resolving halakhic problems, but these decisions were not always taken as binding.

Bat-Miriam, Yokheved (1901–): Israeli poet. Born in White Russia, she settled in Israel in 1928. Her poetry, written in Hebrew, is profoundly influenced by the European Jewish tragedy of the 20th cent.

bat mitzvah: Girl aged 12 years and a day who is obligated to fulfill the religious commandments appli-

cable to adult women. In modern times, the occasion is often marked by a celebration, and in some congregations is marked in the synagogue.

Bat Yam: Israeli city on the Mediterranean just south of Tel Aviv; founded in 1926. The population as of 1971 was 90,700.

Bath-Sheba: Wife of DAVID and mother of SOLOMON. While she was the wife of URIAH the Hittite, David committed adultery with her and then arranged Uriah's death in battle in order to marry her. For this he was rebuked by Nathan the prophet, and the death of their firstborn son was regarded as punishment. She persuaded David to name Solomon as his successor.

batlan: A loafer or good-for-nothing.

Bauer, Otto (1881–1938): Austrian statesman. A leading figure in European socialism, he was the first foreign minister of the Austrian republic (1918–19). His views were Marxist and he favored Jewish assimilation.

bava (Aram. "gate"): Part of a book. The first tractate of the MISHNAH order of *Nezikin* was divided into three parts: (1) *Bava Kamma* ("First Gate") deals with the four principal categories of damage to property (cf. Exod. 21:33; 22:5 ff.); (2) *Bava*

Metzia ("Middle Gate") deals with laws of acquisition, of lost and found property, interest, labor relations, etc.; (3) *Bava Batra* ("Last Gate") discusses ownership of real estate, acquisition of property, inheritance, the preparation of legal documents, etc.

Beaconsfield, Benjamin Disraeli, Earl of (1804–1881): British statesman and novelist. When B. was 13, his father—the writer Isaac D'Israeli—had him baptized. A flamboyant figure, he was first elected to the British Parliament in 1837 as a Tory. He became leader of the party, served in various governments, and in 1868 and from 1874 to 1880 was prime minister. Among the highlights of his period of office were his acquisition for England of a dominant holding in the Suez Canal, his activities as British representative at the Congress of Berlin (1878), his proclamation of Queen Victoria as empress of India, and extensive social legislation. He wrote a series of brilliant novels, some of which reflect his abiding interest in the Jewish people and its history.

Beame, Abraham David (1906–   ): First Jewish mayor (Democratic) of New York City (1974–77); he previously served as comptroller of the city.

bedikah ("examination"): Inspection of an animal after ritual slaughter to ascertain that the animal is not diseased and that the slaughter is ritually correct.

bedikat hametz ("examination for leaven"): Search carried out in the home on the night before Passover to ensure that no leaven remains in the house. It is customary to hide some pieces of bread so that the search will not be in vain. These are burned the following morning (*Nisan* 14).

Beersheba: City of southern Israel, first settled in the Chalcolithic Period. Abraham and Isaac dug wells in its vicinity. It became the traditional southernmost limit of the country ("from Dan to Beersheba"). It was settled in Second Temple times but was deserted in the Middle Ages. Under the Turks it was a small town, but developed rapidly under the State of Israel as the key town of the Negev. The railroad reached there, industries were opened, a university was founded (Ben Gurion University of the Negev). By 1974 its population was 93,400.

be'ezrat ha-Shem ("with God's help"): Expression of pious hope, often written (generally in abbreviation) at the top of letters.

Begin, Menahem (1913–   ): Israeli political

leader. Born in Poland, he headed the BETAR movement there before going to Palestine, where he settled in 1942. The following year he became commander of the underground IRGUN TZEVAI LEUMMI, which he led in its struggle with the British until 1948. After the establishment of the State, he founded the ḤERUT party, which was one of the main opposition groups. After Ḥerut merged with the General Zionists to form GAḤAL in 1965, he was a leader of the new party, serving as minister without portfolio in the government of national unity, 1967–70. In 1977 he became prime minister in the first Israeli government not dominated by the Labor parties.

behemoth: Animal described in the Book of Job (40:15–24), perhaps the hippopotamus. In post-biblical literature, it became a legendary animal which in the messianic age will engage in a massive fight with another legendary animal, the LEVIATHAN. The flesh of the b. will be the reward for the righteous at the messianic banquet.

Beilis, Menahem Mendel (1874–1934): The accused in a blood libel which received worldwide attention in 1911–13. The body of a boy was discovered in Kiev and B. was imprisoned for two years while investigations were carried out. There were clear anti-Semitic motivations in this case, and they were accompanied by an anti-Jewish campaign inspired by Russian government circles. These in turn brought a liberal countercampaign. Despite the efforts of the prosecution, the jury acquitted B., who went to live in Palestine and later in the US.

Beisan see **Bet She'an**

Bekhorot ("Rights of Firstborn"): Fourth tractate of the MISHNAH order of *Kodashim* (with *gemara* in the Babylonian Talmud) dealing with laws concerning the FIRSTBORN of men and animals (Exod. 13:2 ff; Num. 18:15 ff.).

Belasco, David (1859–1931): US theatrical figure. He was an outstanding producer, noted for his extravagant effects. He opened his own theater, the Belasco, in New York. Two of his own plays—*Madame Butterfly* and *The Girl of the Golden West* —provided Puccini with opera libretti.

Belgium: The first Jewish settlements in the area were established in the 13th and 14th cent. but were destroyed in 1348 and 1370. From the 16th cent. MARRANOS began to settle, especially at ANTWERP. Ashkenazi Jews arrived in the 18th cent. Religious equality was a basic provision of the independent kingdom of B., established in 1830, and Belgian Jewry was organized under a consistory with its center in Brussels. Until World War II, the main community was at Antwerp, where Jews played a key role in developing the diamond industry. More than half of B.'s 100,000 Jews were deported to their deaths by the Germans. In postwar B., Jews have again played an important role in Antwerp (where there is a community of 13,000, most of them Orthodox), but the larger community is now in Brussels (24,500). Some 40,000 Jews were living in B. in 1976.

belief see **creed**

Belkin, Samuel (1911–1976): US Orthodox leader. Born in Poland, he settled in the US at the age of 18. From 1935 he taught in Yeshiva College (later Yeshiva University), of which he became president in 1943. Many of his studies deal with the Hellenistic period.

Bellow, Saul (1915–   ): US novelist, winner of the Nobel Prize for literature (1976). Born in Canada, he has taught at various universities in the US. Regarded as one of the outstanding post-World War II novelists, Bellow has written often on Jewish themes. His major successes include *Herzog, Mr. Sammler's Planet, The Ad-*

ventures of Augie March, and *Humboldt's Gift.*

Belz: Small town in Ukrainian SSR from which originated the Rokeah family of Hasidic rabbis. The dynasty was founded by Shalom of B. (1799–1856). It emphasized rabbinic learning and insisted on a specific Jewish garb and appearance. The dynasty was influential in the development of Galician Hasidism.

Belzec: Nazi extermination camp situated in a small Polish town, operating in 1942–43. More than 600,000 perished there.

Ben Asher, Aaron ben Moses (10th cent.): Palestinian Hebrew grammarian and scholar of the MASORAH. A representative of the Tiberias school of masoretes, his carefully edited biblical text, complete with vowel points and accents, became the basis for all Bible editions. Some scholars have suggested that he was a KARAITE.

Ben-Gurion,   David (1886–1973): Israeli statesman. Born in Plonsk, Poland, he settled in Palestine in 1906. By this time he was already one of the leaders of the Labor movement in the country. During World War I, he was expelled by the Turks. Together with his close friend Itzhak BEN-ZVI, he went to the US, where he helped to organize volunteering for the JEWISH LEGION, in which he himself served. After the war, he played a leading role in the development of the Labor movement, being among the founders of AHDUT AVODAH in 1919, of MAPAI in 1930, and secretary-general of the HISTADRUT from 1921 to 1935. He became one of the key figures of the entire Palestinian Jewish community; from 1935 to 1948 he served as chairman of the JEWISH AGENCY Executive. He took the lead in influencing the Zionist Movement to adopt a program aimed at establishing a Jewish state, and he led the Jews of the country through the difficult days up to the establishment of the State in 1948, which he himself declared as head of the provisional government. From then until 1963 he was prime minister (except for a brief period of semi-retirement in 1953–55), as well as minister of defense. His period of premiership saw the winning of the War of Independence, mass immigration programs, and the successful Sinai campaign. After his retirement he continued for a time in political activities, now in opposition to his successors, but eventually he returned to his Negev home at Sedeh Boker, where he concentrated on writing.

Ben-Haim, Paul (1897–): Israeli composer. Born in Germany, he settled in Tel Aviv in 1933. One of the country's most distinguished composers, he helped create the Eastern Mediterranean school of composition, combining Western techniques with Near Eastern music.

Ben Naphtali, Moses ben David (10th cent.): Palestinian masoretic scholar. Nothing is known of his life, and even his name is doubtful. He probably lived in Tiberias and, like his contemporary BEN ASHER, edited the punctuation and accentuation of the Hebrew Bible. Although the accepted MASORAH is largely that of Ben Asher, details have been incorporated from B.N.

Ben Sira, Simeon ben Jesus (2nd cent. BCE): Sage and scribe in Jerusalem. He collected his aphorisms and wise sayings in a book known as the *Wisdom of Ben Sira* (or *Ecclesiasticus*), which was translated into Greek by his grandson in 132 BCE and was included in the APOCRYPHA. The book contains many ethical maxims which influenced later works; it identified wisdom with the observance of the Torah. The Hebrew text was lost, but much of it was rediscovered at the end of the 19th cent. in the Cairo Genizah, while further sections were found among the Dead Sea Scrolls.

Ben-Yehuda (Perelman), Eliezer (1858–1922): Hebrew lexicographer, considered the father of modern Hebrew. Born in Lithuania, he studied in Europe but in 1881 moved to Jerusalem, where he engaged in teaching and Hebrew journalism. His insistence on speaking only Hebrew attracted other enthusiasts, and it was largely due to his inspiration that the new Jewish settlers adopted Hebrew as their language. He founded the Vaad ha-Lashon ha-Ivrit ("Hebrew Language Council") and devoted much time to preparing a Hebrew dictionary, which was completed after his death by his widow Hemdah and other Hebrew linguists.

Ben Zvi, Yizhak (1884–1963): Palestinian labor leader and second president of the State of Israel. Born in the Ukraine, he went to Palestine in 1907, where he was active in the Poalei Zion party and in the Jewish self-defense organization. During World War I, he was in the US with his friend David Ben-Gurion, and returned with him to Palestine as a soldier in the Jewish Legion. He played a leading part in Labor politics during the following years, and from 1931 to 1948 was president of Vaad Leummi ("National Council"). He was a Mapai member of the Knesset from 1949 until 1952, when he succeeded Weizmann as president of Israel. He was a popular president, especially in view of his deep scholarly interest in various Jewish communities, notably the Oriental ones, about which he wrote many research studies. He also published studies on the Samaritans and on the history of Jewish settlement in Palestine. He founded the Ben-Zvi Institute for research into Middle Eastern communities. His wife, Rachel Yannait Ben-Zvi (1886–), was also a labor leader, active in the Jewish self-defense movement, and prominent in the women's agricultural training movement.

Benaiah: A member of King David's bodyguard (II Sam. 23:20–23). He remained loyal to the king during the rebellions of Absalom and Adonijah, and he supported Solomon as David's successor. Solomon appointed him commander-in-chief of his army in succession to Joab, who was killed by B.

Bene Akiva ("Sons of Akiva"): Religious youth movement founded in 1929, affiliated with Ha-Poel ha-Mizrachi. In 1974 it had 18,000 members in Israel. It founded 3 kibbutzim in Israel, and was active as well in other countries. Its motto is *Torah va-Avodah* ("Religion and Labor").

Bene Berak: Town near Tel Aviv, founded in 1924 by religious settlers. It has maintained its Orthodox character, and several yeshivot are situated there. Its population in 1974 was 81,000. It is close to the ancient site of B.B., where R. Akiva established his academy.

Bene Israel: Jewish community of ancient but obscure origin in India. For many centuries the people here were isolated and out of touch with other Jews, and their religious customs differed in many details from the Jewish norm. From the 18th cent., Jews from other communities (especially Cochin and Iraq) instructed them in traditional Judaism. From the 19th cent., their main center was Bombay, and many Jews there achieved good positions under the British, in the professions and in white-collar occupations. Their numbers were 24,000 in 1947, but less than half remain in India. The majority have moved to Israel in recent years, with most of them living in the southern parts of the country.

Bene Mosheh ("Sons of Moses"): Small exclusive Zionist group founded by Aḥad ha-am in Odessa in 1889 within the Ḥoveve Zion movement to develop cultural and educational activities. It founded Hebrew schools and established the Aḥiasaph Pub-

lishing Co. It dissolved in 1897 on the foundation of the Zionist Organization.

benediction (*berakhah*): Expression of blessing, praise, or thanksgiving incorporated in the liturgy and also recited on many other occasions. The general formula begins *barukh attah adonai* ("Blessed art Thou, O Lord") and concludes with the specific reason for the blessing. The pattern is biblical (Ps. 119:12; II Chron. 29:10) but underwent modifications, although all the statutory forms had been fixed by the 3rd cent. CE. Benedictions form a basic component of the liturgy; the weekday Amidah, for example, is based on 19 blessings. Other short blessings regularly recited can be divided into: (1) Blessings of enjoyment, recited before eating, drinking, etc. The concluding phrase varies according to the type of food to be eaten. There are also b. before enjoying the smell of flowers, spices, etc. (2) Blessing before the performance of a commandment, e.g., putting on *tallit* or *tephillin*, sounding the *shophar*, taking the *lulav*. (3) Blessings of praise and thanksgiving, such as those recited on seeing thunder and lightning, a rainbow, a king, or a great scholar, and on hearing good or bad news. Special blessings are recited for new things or on the advent of a holiday (*she-heheyanu*), and on recovery from a serious illness or escape from death. Traditionally, a Jew should say a hundred blessings each day. The whole subject is discussed in the talmudic tractate BERAK-HOT.

Benjamin: Twelfth and last son of JACOB by his favorite wife, RACHEL. JOSEPH was his full brother. His mother died in childbirth, and B. was particularly beloved by Jacob. This link is a central feature in the story of Joseph and the move of Jacob and his sons to the land of Goshen (Gen. 42–44). After the conquest of Canaan, the tribe of B. received land between Ephraim and Judah, including Jerusalem. Israel's first king, SAUL, was a Benjaminite. After the division of the kingdom, Israel and Judah disputed the territory of B., which was eventually divided between the two kingdoms.

Benjamin, Judah Philip (1811–1884): US lawyer and politician. A Louisiana lawyer, he was elected to the state legislature in 1842 and to the US Senate as a Whig in 1852. A supporter of the Confederacy in 1861, he was its attorney-general; for a time he was acting secretary of war, and secretary of state from 1862. On the collapse of the Confederacy, he escaped to England, where he pursued a distinguished legal career, being appointed a queen's counsel.

Benjamin of Tudela (12th cent.): Traveler. He left Spain (about 1159 or 1167) and journeyed for between 5 and 14 years before returning. In the course of that time he visited hundreds of places in Europe and the Middle East. His notes record information on the Jewish communities and on the hundreds of places he visited, as well as information he collected on many places he did not actually visit. These notes are of major importance, especially for Jewish history of that period.

Benny, Jack (1894–1977): US entertainer. Born in Waukegan, Mich., he became one of the best-known comedians of vaudeville, radio, and movies, portraying a character noted for stinginess. His films included *To Be or Not to Be*.

bensh (old Fr.; probably from Lat. *benedicere*): To pronounce a benediction. Used particularly for grace after meals, blessing children, and the recitation of the *Ha-Gomel* blessing.

Bentwich: English Zionist family. *Herbert B.* (1856–1932), a lawyer, was a leader of the English Hovevei Zion. Many of his children settled or were active in Eretz Israel. These included *Norman B.*

(1883–1971), who was attorney-general of the Mandatory government from 1920 to 1931, and professor of international relations at the Hebrew University from 1932 to 1951. He was active in many humanitarian causes, especially on behalf of refugees during the Hitler period, and was the author of a wide variety of books on Jewish subjects.

Berab, Jacob (1474–1546): Halakhic authority. Born in Spain, he was rabbi of Fez in Morocco at the age of 18, later moving to Egypt and eventually to Safed. B. initiated the attempt to revive the traditional rabbinical ORDINATION (*semikhah*), which had lapsed in the amoraic period. His object was eventually to reestablish the SANHEDRIN. His attempt was opposed by Levi Ibn Haviv, and B. had to take refuge in Damascus after a violent controversy. His scheme eventually failed.

berakhah see **benedictions**

Berakhot ("Benedictions"): First tractate of the MISHNAH order of *Zeraim*. It deals with the components of the SHEMA, recital of prayers and BENEDICTIONS. There is *gemara* to it in both the Palestinian and Babylonian Talmuds.

Berdichev: City in Volhynia, now Ukrainian SSR. Jews lived there from the 18th cent., and by the end of the 19th cent. 80% of the town's population were Jews. It became a center of Hasidism when LEVI ISAAC settled there. It was also a Haskalah center. Some 40,000 Jews lived in B. before World War II, and there were large massacres under the Nazis. In 1970 the estimated Jewish population was 15,000.

Berdyczewski, Micha Joseph (Bin Gorion) (1865–1921): Hebrew writer. Born in Podolia, he studied in Berlin where, under the influence of Nietzsche, he called for a change of values in Jewish thinking. He advocated that Hebrew literature should draw its inspiration from life and nature. Subsequently he was influenced by Hasidism, and his works became more influenced by the Jewish past. He also wrote in German and Yiddish.

Berechiah ben Natronai ha-Nakdan (12th–13th cent.): Writer of fables. His Hebrew book of fox fables, *Mishle Shualim*, mostly originating from non-Jewish sources, was widely read by Jews. He lived in southern France but has been identified with Benedict le Pointur, who lived in Oxford.

Berek Joselovicz (c. 1763–1809): Polish patriot and soldier. Born in Lithuania, he lived in Warsaw and commanded a cavalry battalion composed of Jewish volunteers. Most of these were killed during the Kosciuszko uprising in 1794. He himself was killed fighting the Austrians.

Berenice (28 CE–after 79): Judean princess. Daughter of AGRIPPA I, she was married for a while to her uncle Herod of Chalcis. She fled with her brother Agrippa II to the Romans after the outbreak of the Jewish war with Rome in 66. She accompanied the Roman general Titus during the siege of Jerusalem, and he installed her in a palace in Rome but eventually had to sever the connection under pressure from Roman authorities.

Bereshit see **Genesis**

Bergelson, David (1884–1952): Russian Yiddish author. He went to Berlin in 1920, returning to Moscow in 1934. B. wrote several novels, plays, and stories in a strong Communist spirit. Nevertheless, he was put to death with other leading Yiddish writers.

Bergen-Belsen: Nazi concentration camp in Germany. Between 1943 and 1945, 30,000 Jews died there. It was a center to which prisoners from camps more to the east were transferred, especially in the course of the German retreat. 20,000 (including Anne FRANK) died there in March 1945. When the British freed the camp in 1945, they found 55,000 prisoners, but within the next days, a further 14,000 died.

Bergman, Samuel Hugo (1883–1975): Philosopher. In his young days he was a leading figure of the Czech Zionist movement. He settled in Palestine in 1920 and directed the National and University Library until 1935. He taught philosophy at the Hebrew University, where he was rector from 1936 to 1938.

Bergson, Henri Louis (1859–1941): French philosopher. In 1927 he was awarded the Nobel Prize for Literature. His best-known works include *Creative Evolution* and *Laughter*. Although not connected with Jewish activities, he identified himself with the Jews under Nazi rule despite an opportunity to be excluded, actively protesting the Vichy government's anti-Jewish legislation.

Berihah ("Flight"): Underground operation organized in the aftermath of World War II to move Jews out of Eastern Europe. Their immediate destination was central and southern Europe, but the ultimate objective for most of them was Palestine. The B. was largely organized by Zionist youth movements, and about 250,000 Jews were saved under its auspices.

Berit Ivrit Olamit

("World Hebrew Union"): Organization, with its center in Jerusalem, for the dissemination and promotion of Hebrew as a spoken language and of Hebrew culture. It was founded in 1931.

Berit Shalom ("Covenant of Peace"): Society founded in Jerusalem in 1925 by Jews hoping to promote a rapprochement with the Arabs. It advocated an Arab-Jewish binational state in Palestine. It was headed by Judah L. MAGNES. In the early 1940s it was replaced by a similar group called Ihud. Membership of both organizations was never large, and after 1948, that of Ihud became tiny.

Berkowitz, Yitzhak Dov (1885–1967): Hebrew writer. Born in Belorussia, he lived in the US from 1914 to 1928, and from then on in Tel Aviv. His short stories and plays deal with Jewish life in Eastern Europe, in the US, and in Palestine; he also wrote several volumes of memoirs. He translated the works of his father-in-law, SHOLEM ALEICHEM, from Yiddish into Hebrew.

Berle, Milton (1908–): US entertainer. As "Uncle Milt," he was a popular performer in vaudeville, movies and on Broadway. He was one of the first comedians to have a regular TV show.

Berlin: German city. Jews first appeared there in 1295, and there were expulsions in 1349, 1446, 1510, and 1573. Settlement was renewed in 1671, and the first synagogue was opened in 1714. The brilliance of Moses MENDELSSOHN (who became a protected Jew in 1763) was the spark for the EMANCIPATION era, and by the late 18th cent. Jewish salons were playing a prominent role. In 1808 Jews were recognized as town citizens. In the 19th and 20th cent. many central German-Jewish organizations were situated or had their headquarters in B., including the Hochschule (Lehranstalt) für die Wissenschaft des Judentums, the Orthodox Berlin Rabbinical Seminary, and ADAS ISRAEL. Over 160,000 Jews were living in B. in 1933; the community was completely destroyed by the Nazis. A few Jews returned to B. after the war, and in 1976 there were 5,300 Jews with synagogues and a communal life in West B., and 700 in East B. with one synagogue.

Berlin, Irving (1888–): US songwriter. Born in Russia, he was taken to the US in 1893. Many of his songs have become classics ("*God Bless America*," "*Alexander's Ragtime Band*," among others). He wrote music for many Broadway musical comedies (*Annie Get Your Gun, Call Me Madam*) and movies.

Berlin, Sir Isaiah (1909–): English political scientist. During World War II he served at the British embassies in Washington and Moscow. In 1957 he was appointed professor of sociology and political theory at Oxford; in 1966, the first president of Oxford's Wolfson College; and in 1974, president of the British Academy. His works deal with modern political thought and philosophy.

Berlin, Meir see **Bar-Ilan, Meir**

Berlin, Naphtali Tzevi Judah (1817–1893): Talmudist known as Ha-Netziv; from 1854 he was head of VOLOZHIN yeshivah, where he fought Haskalah, opposed *pilpul*, and stood for logical approaches. He was a Hovevei Zion leader.

Bernhardt, Sarah (1844–1923): French actress. The illegitimate child of a Jewish mother, she was raised as a Catholic. The outstanding French actress of her time, she was known as the "divine Sarah." She continued acting even after the amputation of a leg in 1914.

Bernstein, Leonard (1918–): US composer and conductor. He was the first American-born musical director of the New York Philharmonic Orchestra, which he conducted from 1957 to 1969. His compositions include symphonic works (such as the *Jeremiah* and *Kaddish* symphonies) and Broadway musical shows (e.g., *Wonderful Town, Candide, West Side Story*). He has appeared frequently in Israel and toured various countries with the Israel Philharmonic Orchestra.

Beruryah (2nd cent. CE): Talmudic sage and wife of the *tanna* R. MEIR. She is often quoted in the Talmud; in one instance her opinion was accepted as authoritative. She bore stoically a series of family tragedies.

besamim: Spices, especially those used in the HAVDALAH service.

Besht see **Baal Shem Tov**

Bessarabia: Region of southeastern Europe; now in the Ukrainian SSR. About 20,000 Jews were living there in 1812 when it was annexed to Russia, many of them were in commerce and the liquor trade. B. was frequently the scene of anti-Semitism, including the period it was under Rumanian rule (1918–40). In World War II, about half of the Jews were driven into Transnistria, and many of the others were murdered by Germans and Rumanians.

Bet (ב): Second letter of the Hebrew alphabet. Numerical value: 2. Pronounced *b* (with *dagesh*) and *v* (without).

Bet Alpha: Israeli kibbutz in the Valley of Jezreel (affiliated to HA-KIBBUTZ HA-ARTZI) with 837 members in 1972. It is the site of a mosaic floor of a 6th-cent. synagogue which depicts the wheel of the zodiac among other things; it is one of the outstanding examples of early Jewish synagogue art.

bet din ("house of judgment"): Jewish law court. There were various kinds of such courts in Second Temple times. The 71-member SANHEDRIN was the highest court; there was a lower court with criminal jurisdiction of 23 judges and local courts for civil suits with at least 3 judges. After the decline of Palestinian Jewry, Jewish communities everywhere established their own b.d. with rabbinical judges who adjudicated civil, criminal, and religious matters according to the Halakhah, and also ruled on the internal affairs of the community. In the framework of Jewish AUTONOMY, the authority of these courts in criminal jurisdiction was recognized in various countries. With the advent of EMANCIPATION, the authority of Jewish courts was confined to ritual matters. In the Ottoman Empire, Jewish courts, parallel to those of other faiths, had authority in matters of personal status, and this has been carried down today to the State of Israel, where the rabbinical b.d. has full authority over Jews in such matters.

bet ha-Kneset see synagogue

Bet Hillel and Bet Shammai ("House of HILLEL and House of SHAMMAI"): Two schools flourishing in the 1st-early 2nd cent. CE. The Talmud records 300 differences between them in interpreting the Oral Law. In most cases (but not exclusively), the view of the Shammaites was the more severe. It has been suggested that the differences reflected political, economic, and social differences. The synod at Jabneh (c. 90 CE) decided that the final decision would be according to the School of Hillel. Traditionally, this followed a proclamation by a Divine voice (BAT KOL).

bet midrash ("house of study"): School for advanced study of rabbinic texts. In mishnaic times the b.m. was independent of the synagogue, but later was closely associated with it, often situated in the same building; frequently prayer services would be held in the b.m. In Germany it was known as the klaus; in Eastern Europe, the kloiz or shtibel; in Muslim lands, as the midrash. It was a place for senior study as well as for popular classes. It also contained a library.

Bet She'an (Beisan): Israeli town. In the second millennium BCE, it was a center of the Egyptians, who were then occupying Palestine. The Israelites conquered it only during the period of the monarchy. In the Hellenistic period it was called Scythopolis and was a member of the DECAPOLIS. Jews lived there until the Middle Ages, and again in the 20th cent. until the 1936 riots. The Arabs left in 1948, and the town was resettled by new immigrants. After the Six-Day War in 1967, it came under fire a number of times from beyond the Jordan. There have been extensive excavations of the ancient site as well as of the old Roman theater. The population in 1974 was 12,000.

Bet She'arim: Ancient Jewish city in the western Jezreel Valley. In the late 2nd cent., JUDAH HA-NASI established his academy there, and made it the seat of the Sanhedrin. It was the outstanding burial place for Jews both inside and outside Palestine; Judah ha-Nasi and his family were interred there. Since 1936, extensive excavations have revealed catacombs and tombs, as well as an ancient synagogue.

Betar: Ancient town near Jerusalem, which was the scene of the last stand of BAR KOKHBA in his revolt against the Romans (134–35).

Betar: Abbreviation for Berit Trumpeldor, the "Trumpeldor League," Zionist Youth movement. It was founded in 1923 and associated with the REVISIONIST movement, being particularly strong in pre-World War II Eastern Europe. Its principles are a militaristic, nonsocialist, and activist Zionism. Its center is now in Israel. It was led until 1940 by Vladimir JABOTINSKY and later by Menahem BEGIN.

Bethel: Town frequently mentioned in the Bible. Situated north of Jerusalem, its original name was Luz. ABRAHAM built an altar there (Gen. 12:8), and it was the site of JACOB's dream (Gen. 28:17), as a result of which it received the name B. ("House of God"). Jeroboam I, ruler of the Kingdom of Israel, built a shrine at B: to rival the Jerusalem Temple; its central feature was the idol of a calf. Despite the denunciations of the prophets, the B. shrine remained standing until defiled by Josiah in 621 BCE (II Kings 23:15). The town was destroyed by the Babylonian army (II Kings 23:15), but Ezra and Nehemiah refer to subsequent settlement on the site. Remains from various periods have been uncovered in excavations at B.

Bethlehem: Town 5 miles south of Jerusalem, particularly revered by Jews as the traditional birthplace of David and by Christians as that of Jesus. From the 4th cent. CE, when the first Church of the Nativity was built, it became a prime object of Christian pilgrimage. Jerome lived there when translating the Bible into Latin, and the grotto associated with him is still visited. In 1967, when the town passed into Israeli hands as a result of the Six-Day War, it had 27,000 inhabitants, of whom just over half were Christian. It is the site of many Christian institutions. The traditional Tomb of Rachel is situated at the entrance to B.

Bettelheim, Bruno (1903–): US psychologist. Born in Austria, he used his own experience as an inmate of Nazi concentration camps to describe human behavior in extreme situations. Much of this work has dealt with the treatment of autistic and disturbed children.

Betzah ("Egg"): Tractate of the MISHNAH order *Mo'ed*, containing 5 chapters with *gemara* in the Palestinian and Babylonian Talmuds, and dealing with the laws of festivals. Its original title was *Yom Tov* ("Festival").

Beur see **Mendelssohn, Moses**

Bezalel: (1) Son of Uri of the tribe of Judah. He was the architect of the tabernacle and designer of the sacred vessels in the wilderness (Exod. 35:30). (2) Academy of arts and design founded in Jerusalem in 1906 by Boris SCHATZ. It pioneered in the development of the arts in the renewed Jewish settlement in Eretz Israel. The Bezalel Museum, founded in association with the school in 1906, became independent in 1925. Its art collection, specializing in works by Jewish artists and works of Jewish religious art, was incorporated with the Israel Museum in 1965.

Bialik, Ḥayyim Naḥman (1873–1934): The outstanding modern Hebrew poet. Born in Zhitomir, he studied at Volozhin yeshivah and went to Odessa in 1891. His first poem, "To a Bird," appeared that year. From then on he published a flow of lyric, national, love, and nature poetry. He spent periods as a timber merchant and as a teacher, and also founded the Moriah publishing house. His great works include *Ha-Matmid*, dealing with yeshivah life and his revolt against the traditional environment; *Mete Midbar; Ir ha-Haregah*, inspired by the 1903 Kishinev pogrom and calling for a self-defense movement; and *Me-*

gillat ha-Esh, reflecting the struggle between faith and despair. Together with Y. H. Ravnitsky, he edited the popular aggadic anthology *Sepher Aggadah.* He also wrote children's poems, published the works of the medieval poets Solomon Ibn Gabirol and Moses Ibn Ezra, and translated world classics into Hebrew (Shakespeare, Cervantes, etc.). In 1921 he went to Berlin, and in 1924 settled in Tel Aviv. He headed the Vaad ha-Lashon ("Hebrew Language Council"), while his Saturday-afternoon *Oneg Shabbat* became a major cultural activity of the Jewish community. B. was the leading poet of the modern Hebrew renascence and of the Jewish national movement.

Bialystok: Polish city. The community became autonomous in the 18th cent. The development of its textile industry was largely due to Jewish initiative. In 1939, over 40,000 Jews lived there. In 1941 they were herded into a ghetto and eventually transferred to various death camps. Few Jews lived there after the war.

Bible (*mikra, kitve-kodesh; Tanakh*): The Hebrew B., which constitutes the basis of the Jewish religion, consists of 24 books divided into 3 sections: (1) The Pentateuch (Torah) containing the Five Books of Moses, GENESIS, EXODUS, LEVITICUS, NUMBERS, and DEUTERONOMY. These relate the story of the Creation, the early patriarchs, the formation of the Israelite nation, the sojourn in Egypt, the Exodus, the giving of the Law at Sinai and its contents, and the wanderings in the wilderness under Moses. (2) The Prophets (Neviim) is subdivided into: (a) The Former Prophets, continuing the narrative and relating the conquest of Canaan under Joshua, the settlement of the country, the establishment of the kingdom under the initial kings (Saul, David, and Solomon), the division of the kingdom into two, and the history and fate of the northern kingdom until its destruction by the Assyrians and of the southern kingdom until its destruction by the Babylonians. The books of this section are JOSHUA, JUDGES, SAMUEL (divided into 2 parts), and KINGS (divided into 2 parts). (b) The Latter Prophets, containing the writings of the outstanding prophets (the 3 Major Prophets, ISAIAH, JEREMIAH, and EZEKIEL) and the 12 Minor Prophets (which can be reckoned as one book but also as 12, relating the prophecies of HOSEA, JOEL, AMOS, OBADIAH, JONAH, MICAH, NAHUM, HABAKKUK, ZEPHANIAH, HAGGAI,

ZECHARIA, and MALACHI).
(3) The writings of Hagiographa (Ketuvim), containing the 3 major literary books of PSALMS, PROVERBS, and JOB, the 5 smaller scrolls (RUTH, SONG OF SONGS, LAMENTATIONS, ECCLESIASTES, and ESTHER), the Book of DANIEL, and the historical works of EZRA and NEHEMIAH (originally one work) and CHRONICLES (now divided into 2). The Christians call all of the above the Old Testament, adding the APOCRYPHA (in certain churches) and the Christian writings comprised in the New Testament to form the Christian B.

The Jewish B. was written in Hebrew with some small exceptions in Aramaic (notably certain chapters of the Books of Daniel and Ezra). The biblical canon evolved gradually. According to traditional belief, the Pentateuch was concluded by Moses under Divine guidance; critical scholarship suggests that its final form was determined much later, possibly about the 5th cent. BCE. According to tradition, the final editing of the whole B. was carried out in the Persian period by the men of the GREAT ASSEMBLY. Modern scholars suggest that the collection of the Prophets was accomplished about the 2nd cent. CE, and that the final

composition of the Hagiographa was decided at the synod of Jabneh (90 CE). The tripartite division was certainly known in the 2nd cent. CE, at which time the Pentateuch was already being read in the synagogue.

The books were originally written on parchment scrolls. The ancient script was Phoenician, and the transition to the familiar square alphabet was gradual, accomplished by Second Temple times. The text was consonantal, with only a few vowel letters used for vocalization. An extensive tradition (MASORAH) was handed down concerning its punctuation and reading. This was only committed to writing in the 6th to 10th cent. CE, when vowel signs were added to the manuscripts (but not to the Scrolls of the Pentateuch read in synagogue). In the 13th cent., numbered chapters and verses were introduced.

The first translation was the Aramaic TARGUM, which developed in the Palestinian synagogues. The Greek SEPTUAGINT (3rd cent. BCE) was of great influence and was followed by a number of other Greek translations. Other early translations were into Syriac (the Peshitta) in the 2nd cent. CE, and the Latin (VULGATE) made by Jerome in the 4th cent. CE.

The version of the Pentateuch preserved by the Samaritans is also of special interest. SAADIAH translated the B. into Arabic in the 9th cent., and Moses Arragel into Spanish in the 15th cent., from which period Yiddish translations also began to appear. The Reformation gave an impetus to translations into European languages, with Luther's German translation and the English Authorized Version among the outstanding examples. Later English translations include the Revised Version and the New English Bible, while that produced by the Jewish Publication Society of America is the outstanding English translation under Jewish auspices.

Bible Commentators: Two basic trends in Jewish biblical interpretation were early apparent in *peshat* (the literal interpretation) and *derash* (the homiletical exposition). The former can be already discovered in the Bible translations (TARGUM, SEPTUAGINT), the latter in the MIDRASH and the TALMUDS. The *tannaim* developed hermeneutic principles for the interpretation of the Bible. Further trends that developed were the allegorical interpretation, of which the outstanding exponent was PHILO, and the esoteric, later fully developed in the KAB-

BALAH. An impetus to biblical studies was provided by the challenge posed by the KARAITES in the Middle Ages. This inspired the commentaries of SAADYAH, who also applied philological and grammatical criteria. These were developed in Spain, where the outstanding medieval Bible commentators, Abraham IBN EZRA and David KIMHI, lived. The former combined literal interpretations with philosophical interpretations; the latter excelled in plain exegesis. Another great commentator in Spain was NAHMANIDES, whose exegesis was rational but introduced midrashic and kabbalistic elements. The outstanding commentator of the Middle Ages was RASHI, who lived in France, and whose simple, straightforward explanations have been an essential adjunct to Jewish Bible study to this day. The last of the outstanding medieval commentators was Isaac ABRAVANEL, whose works were erudite and discursive. The modern period of Jewish Bible commentary was ushered in by the *Biur* of Moses MENDELSSOHN and his school, and now Christian standards of criticism began to influence Jewish commentary. A few traditional commentators made their appearance, such as MALBIM, but the emphasis was on a modern approach, often directed at refuting the more extreme attitudes of the Bible critics. Outstanding names in 20th-cent. Jewish Bible scholarship have included U. CASSUTO, M. Z. SEGAL, and Y. KAUFMANN.

Bible study: The critical approach to the Bible text is divided into Literary or Higher Criticism, dealing with literary and historical questions, and Textual or Lower Criticism, dealing with textual problems. Although certain earlier scholars had raised problems of a critical nature, SPINOZA is regarded as the pioneer of modern B.s. Its modern form was developed in the late 19th cent. especially by Graf and Wellhausen, who propounded the theory that the Pentateuch is a composite text based on various sources or "documents." Similar methods of analysis were used for the later books of the Bible. More recently there has been a reaction against some of the more extreme theories advanced by the Higher Critics, based on further research and a deeper understanding of the ancient Middle East. The textual study has been based largely on a comparison of the Hebrew text with that of early translations, versions, and documents (notably from the Dead Sea Scrolls). It has also relied on the possibilities of scribal errors, as well as an examination of Semitic languages and of the nature of literary composition in biblical times (notably, poetic parallelism). It has been increasingly recognized that many difficulties can be attributed not to faulty copying but to the existence of divergent textual traditions.

bibliography: The first systematic b. of Hebrew books was Bartolocci's *Bibliotheca Magna Rabbinica* (1675–93). Shabbetai Bass's *Siphte Yeshenim* (1680) lists 2,200 titles of Hebrew books. Other important works were compiled by Johann Christian Wolf, Giovanni Bernardo de Rossi, and Ḥayyim Joseph David Azulai. The outstanding figure in modern Jewish b. is Moritz STEINSCHNEIDER, whose vast works include an important catalogue of the Bodleian Library, Oxford (1852–60). H. D. Friedberg's *Bet Eked Sepharim* (1928–31) lists all works in Hebrew type. S. Shunami published a comprehensive *Bibliography of Jewish Bibliographies* (1965; Supplement, 1975). The standard bibliographical journal is *Kiryat Sepher*, published since 1926 by the National and University Library, Jerusalem.

bikkur holim see **sick, visiting of.**

Bikkurim ("First Fruits"): Last tractate of the MISHNAH order of *Zeraim* dealing with the laws related to the FIRST FRUIT offering. It has *gemara* in the Palestinian Talmud only.

Bilhah: Maidservant of Rachel who was given by her to become Jacob's concubine. She was the mother of Dan and Naphtali (Gen. 30:18; 35:25–26).

Biltmore Program: Zionist declaration of policy calling for the establishment of Palestine as a Jewish commonwealth. It was adopted at a conference held at the Biltmore Hotel, New York, in 1942 and marked the beginning of the open struggle by the Zionist Movement for a Jewish state.

BILU (acronym of *Bet Yaakov lekhu ve-nelkhah,* "House of Jacob come ye and let us go"; cf. Is. 2:5): First group of Russian pioneers to go to Palestine. The ideology emerged among young Jewish intellectuals and students in Russia in reaction to the 1881 pogroms. It had about 5,000 members, but only several dozen went to settle in Palestine (the beginning of the First ALIYAH). They were motivated by socialist and cooperative principles, and some of them settled the village of Gederah (1884). Others settled in various other villages, with some going to Jerusalem to form a handicraft cooperative.

binding of Isaac see **akedah**

Bin-Gorion see **Berdichevsky, Micah Joseph**

Birnbaum, Nathan (1864–1937): Early Zionist, philosopher, and writer, using the pseudonym Mathias Acher. From his student days he was active in Zionist movements; he was credited with coining the word "Zionism" (in 1890). Joining Herzl, he was the first general secretary of the World Zionist Organization. However, he subsequently moved away from Zionism, becoming an ardent Yiddishist. Eventually he became general secretary of AGUDAT ISRAEL, the ultrareligious movement which at that time was strongly anti-Zionist.

Birobidjan: Autonomous region in southeastern Siberia which the Soviet government in 1928 designated for autonomous Jewish settlement. Tens of thousands of Jews went there, but most left after a short period, owing to inauspicious conditions. The ambivalent attitudes of the Soviet authorities also prevented its development. Some 30,000 Jews were living there in 1948 (about a quarter of its population), but by the mid-1970s the number had dropped to about 11,000. Russian, not Yiddish, was the spoken language (a small Yiddish newspaper continued to appear 3 times weekly), but there was little specific Jewish activity, and the project to develop B. as an autonomous Jewish region has been dropped.

birth: The pains of childbirth are associated with Eve's sin (Gen. 3:16). According to the Bible, a mother was considered ritually impure for a period of 33 days after giving b. to a boy, 66 days after giving b. to a girl (Lev. 12:1–8). Many superstitious practices developed (e.g., the use of AMULETS) around childbirth, and these often brought on rabbinic censure. It became customary for a mother to visit a synagogue after recovery, and a special prayer has been prescribed for her to recite. Barrenness was regarded as the greatest of misfortunes for a woman, and a husband could (and even should) divorce a wife who was still barren after ten years of marriage, according to talmudic law (Yev. 64a).

biur ḥametz ("destruction of leaven"): The destruction, generally by fire, of leaven, on the morning before Passover (see BEDIKAT ḤAMETZ). After the burning, an Aramaic formula is recited, renouncing ownership of any leaven which may have been undetected.

Black Death: Plague which swept Europe in 1348–49. It led to extensive massacres of Jewish communities, who were accused of originating the epidemic by poisoning wells. Despite condemnation of the libel by the Pope, the masses all over Europe—especially in Germany—attacked the Jews, and many communities were totally exterminated; others were expelled or fled.

Black Hundreds: Popular name for an organization founded in Russia after 1905 directed against the liberal movement. It was virulently anti-Semitic and played a significant role in organizing pogroms.

Black Jews (in the US): Individuals have converted to Judaism since the 19th cent. but most Black Jews belong to urban sects who have declared themselves Jewish, without going through the traditional conversion procedure. A few dozen such groups with a membership of several thousand exist in large cities, the best known being the Commandment Keeper Congregation of the Living God in Harlem. Some Black Jews from Chicago have settled in Israel in Dimona.

blasphemy: Abuse of God is punishable, in biblical law, by death by stoning (Lev. 24:15–16). The rabbis prescribed corporal punishment for the blasphemer. Later Jewish courts usually punished the offense with excommunication. A special procedure was laid down for hearing such cases.

blessing see **benediction**

blessing of the new moon see **new moon**

Bloch, Ernest (1880–1959): Composer. Of Swiss birth, he lived in the US from 1917. He was deeply influenced by Jewish musical tradition. His compositions include *Avodat Hakodesh* (a setting of the Sabbath Morning Service), the rhapsody for cello and orchestra *Shelomo*, the operas *Macbeth* and *Jezebel*, and numerous chamber works.

Bloch, Ernst (1885–1977): German philosopher. He lived in the US from 1938 to 1949 and then returned to East Germany, moving to West Germany in 1960. His philosophy is characterized by a Marxist humanism.

Block, Herbert Lawrence (1909–): US cartoonist known as Herblock. After working on various papers, he joined the Washington *Post* and achieved national recognition for his pointed satire. He was twice awarded the Pulitzer Prize.

blood: The Bible regarded the b. as the bearer of life (Deut. 12:23). The absolute prohibition on eating it is a basic law, already proclaimed to Noah (Gen. 9:4);

it is repeated several times, being regarded as equivalent to eating a living animal. Even the b. of a slaughtered animal is forbidden. The draining of the b. after slaughter is essential for ritually permitted meat. The abhorrence of b. extended also to the menstrual discharge, which was regarded as especially unclean. B. was sprinkled on the Temple altar as the climax to the atonement rites (Lev. 17:11, 14).

blood libel: The accusation that Jews use the blood of Christians for their religious rites, particularly in the preparation of the unleavened bread for Passover. It had its roots in ancient times but became widespread from the Middle Ages, when the first recorded accusation was made at Norwich, England (1144). It became widespread, and torture was often used to obtain "confessions" with grim consequences for Jewish communities. Despite condemnation by the Popes, the libel persisted down through the ages. There were many instances in the 19th and early 20th cent., the most famous being the DAMASCUS AFFAIR (1840), the Tisza-Eszlar accusation in 1882, and the notorious BEILIS case in Russia, which roused the world's conscience shortly before World War I. The libel was revived and widely propagated by the Nazis, most obscenely in their publication *Die Stürmer*.

Bloomgarden, Solomon see **Yehoash**

Blum, Léon (1872–1950): French socialist statesman. He headed the French Socialist Party from 1920. The first Jew to be premier of France, he served in that position in 1936–37, and for short periods in 1938 and 1946–47. During World War II, he was imprisoned by the Vichy regime and put on trial, where his courageous demeanor made a profound impression. The Germans imprisoned him in the Buchenwald concentration camp, from which he was freed in 1945.

B'nai B'rith ("Sons of the Covenant"): International Jewish Organization, originally founded in New York in 1843 as a fraternal society. The first lodge in Germany was established in 1882 and was a strong movement, until it was closed down by the Nazis in 1937. In the mid-1970s B.B. had over 500,000 members in 40 countries, the great majority, 210,000 men and 135,000 women, in the US. It was also active in Latin America, Europe and Britain, Australia, South Africa, and Israel. Its youth organization had 50,-000 members. Its branches include the B'nai B'rith Youth Organization (including Aleph Zadik Aleph and B.B. Girls), the ANTI-DEFAMATION LEAGUE, and HILLEL HOUSES for Jewish students on many college campuses. Headquarters of the B.B. are in Washington.

B'nai Zion see **fraternal societies**

Board of Deputies of British Jews: Official body representing British Jewry. Founded in 1760, its members are elected by synagogues and other Jewish institutions in the British Commonwealth. It has c. 400 members. From 1881, it dealt with foreign affairs together with the ANGLO-JEWISH ASSOCIATION, but from the mid-1940s, the board acted on its own in such matters.

Boas, Franz (1858–1942): US anthropologist. He taught at Berlin and participated in expeditions to the Arctic and elsewhere before settling in New York in 1887. From 1899 he taught at Columbia Univ. He established the cultural-relativist school of anthropology in the English-speaking world.

Boaz: Wealthy landowner in Bethlehem who married Ruth and was the ancestor of David (Ruth 2–4).

Boethusians: Religious and political sect which flourished in the late Second Temple period. They were closely associated with the high priesthood and were close to, but not identical with, the Sadducees.

Bohemia see **Czechoslovakia**

Bohr, Niels (1885–1962): Danish physicist; son of a Jewish mother. His researches revolutionized the study of the structure of the atom, for which he was awarded the 1922 Nobel Prize for Physics.

Bolivia: Marranos lived in the region in the 16th cent. Jews lived there from the early 20th cent., but only in any numbers in the 1920s. Immigration was mainly from Europe. Some 10,000 were living there in 1939, but many left after the war; by 1976 the Jewish community numbered 2,000, of whom over 1,000 were in La Paz and 400 in Cochabamba.

Bombay: City in India. Permanent Jewish settlement was established in the latter 18th cent. by the BENE ISRAEL. From the 19th cent., Iraqi Jews (especially from Baghdad) had their own community there. In 1971, 11,000 Jews were living in B., but their numbers dropped to 3,600 in 1975 as most left for other countries, especially Israel.

*****Bomberg, Daniel** (d. 1549): One of the first and best-known printers of Hebrew books. From 1516 to 1548, the press he established in Venice printed nearly 200 books. These included editions of the Pentateuch and Hebrew Bible, and of the Palestinian and of the Babylonian Talmuds, for which his pagination became standard.

books: Jews have traditionally had a deep love and reverence for b. going back to the Book of the Law (Sepher Torah) and other biblical and early books which were regarded as conveying the word of God. These and other sacred b. were kept with particular care (if one fell on the floor, it was immediately picked up and kissed). Ethical literature stressed the need for special care of b. The possession of b. and the lending of them to scholars was particularly meritorious, especially in the pre-printing era. Religious b. that were no longer usable were never destroyed but were put away in a storeroom (GENIZAH). Heretical b. were occasionally burned. The mass destruction of Jewish b. by the non-Jewish authorities was regarded with horror. Notable instances of this were the burning of 24 cartloads of copies of the Talmud in Paris in 1242, the burning of Jewish b. in Rome in 1332 and 1553, and the burning by the Nazis of b. by Jewish authors in 1933.

Book of Life: According

to Jewish belief, a volume in which the fate of human beings is recorded by God. The concept dates from the Bible (cf. Exod. 32:32; Mal. 3:16; Ps. 69:28) and was subsequently linked with the belief in an annual Day of Judgment (Rosh ha-Shanah), when God determines who will live throughout the subsequent year. This concept plays an important role in the liturgy for Rosh ha-Shanah and for the Day of Atonement (when the decision is traditionally "sealed").

Boorstin, Daniel J. (1914–   ): US historian. He taught at the Univ. of Chicago from 1944. From 1969 he directed the National Museum of History and Technology at the Smithsonian Institute in Washington. From 1975, he was head of the Library of Congress. He has written extensively on US history.

Born, Max (1882–1970): German physicist; lived in England 1933–53. An authority on the quantum theory, he was awarded the Nobel Prize for Physics in 1954.

Borochov, Dov Ber (1881–1917): Socialist Zionist. Born in Russia, he was one of the founders of POALEI ZION in 1906 and one of its leaders for the rest of his life. He lived in Europe from 1907, in the US from

1914. A major ideologist of the socialist Zionist movement, the conclusion of his Marxist analysis of the abnormal economic and social structure of the Jewish people was the necessity to achieve economic normalization by resettlement in Palestine.

Boston: US city. A number of Jews lived there from the latter half of the 17th cent., but the first congregation was not founded until 1842. The Jewish community grew rapidly with the Eastern European immigration of the 1880s, and in 1976 numbered 180,000, with 75 congregations in the Greater B area. B. is the site of the Hebrew Teachers' College and of BRANDEIS UNIVERSITY.

Brandeis, Louis Dembitz (1856–1941): US jurist and Zionist. Born in Louisville, Kentucky, he practiced law in Boston until 1916, when he was appointed to the Supreme Court, serving until 1939. He was noted for his judicious liberalism. His involvement in Jewish affairs began in 1911, and he soon led the American Zionist movement. He helped to influence official US views on Zionism during World War I, and was made honorary president of the Zionist Organization of America (1918–21) and of the World Zionist Organization (1920–21). However, a clash with WEIZMANN on economic policies to be pursued in Palestine led to his resignation from official positions in the Zionist Movement in 1921.

Brandeis University: Nonsectarian university in Waltham, Massachusetts, under Jewish sponsorship, named for Louis Dembitz BRANDEIS. It was opened in 1948 as a coeducational liberal-arts college. Its first president (later chancellor) was Abraham Sachar.

Bratislava (Ger. Pressburg): Capital of Slovakia. Its first Jews may have come with the Romans. Jews lived there from the 13th cent.; its first synagogue dates from 1335. Its Jews were expelled with the rest of Hungarian Jewry in 1526. A synagogue was again built in 1695, and a ghetto was enforced from 1712 to 1840. Many noted rabbis lived there, and it was the site of a distinguished yeshivah founded by Moses SOPHER in the 19th cent. Under the Nazis, the Jewish community was destroyed. It was refounded after World War II, but diminished considerably during the 1960s, and in 1970 was estimated at only 1,500.

Brazil: Marranos lived there in the 16th cent., and during the period of Dutch rule in the 17th cent. many returned to Judaism while Jewish immigrants came in numbers from Holland. However, the Portuguese reconquest (and the reestablishment of the Inquisition) caused most of the Jews to flee. Some went back to Holland, and others, including the founders of the New York community, went elsewhere in the Western Hemisphere. The modern community dates from the 19th cent. It grew in the 20th cent., with the major influx from Eastern and Central Europe. Jewish agricultural settlements were established in the early 20th cent. but were liquidated by 1952. In 1976, 165,000 Jews lived there. The main communities were SAO PAULO (65,000), RIO DE JANEIRO (50,000), and Porto Alegre (12,000).

bread: Bread prepared from one of the five species of grain (wheat, barley, rye, oats, spelt) was traditionally considered the main element of a meal. The blessing over b. (". . . who brings forth b. from the earth") is therefore considered adequate for the entire meal, and so when b. is consumed no further blessing is required. The full GRACE AFTER MEALS is recited only when b. has been eaten. A portion of the dough (HALLAH) was formerly given to the priest, and the Sabbath b. is known as *hallah.*

breastplate (*hoshen mishpat*): Priestly vestment

in which were set the URIM AND THUMMIM. It was worn by the high priest and consulted for oracular purposes. The term b. is also used for the metal shield hung over the Scroll of the Law.

Brenner, Joseph Ḥayyim (1881–1921): Hebrew writer. His early writings depicted the sorry state of the Jews in the Pale of Settlement. Drafted into the Russian army, he deserted and fled to London, where he published the Hebrew monthly *Ha-Meorer*. After a period in Lvov he moved to Palestine and settled in Jaffa in 1909. He was one of the outstanding writers and journalists of the latter Second Aliyah period, and was a leader of the workers' movement. He edited newspapers, published essays, and translated world classics into Hebrew. He was killed by Arabs in the 1921 riots.

Breslau (Wrocław): Polish city, formerly in Germany. Jews are known to have lived there from the 13th cent. The community was destroyed in 1453 after an accusation of host desecration (when 41 were burned at the stake and the rest expelled). The modern community dates from the 18th cent. Its rabbinical seminary (founded 1854) was the first in Germany, and remained one of the most distinguished. 10,-000 Jews lived there in 1939, but Jewish life ended under the Nazis. The community was refounded after World War II, with 5,000 Jews living there in 1968, but most subsequently left for Israel.

Brest-Litovsk (Brisk): Town in Belorussia, USSR. From the 14th to the 17th cent., it was the main community of Lithuanian Jewry. There was a massacre during the Chmielnicki pogroms of 1648–49, from which the community recovered very slowly. B. was a center of MITNAGGEDIM and of rabbinic learning. From the early 20th cent. a majority of its inhabitants were Jews. In 1941 about 30,000 Jews lived there, but the community was ended by the Nazis. About 2,000 Jews lived there in 1970.

Breuer: German Orthodox family. Its members included *Solomon B.* (1850–1926), who succeeded his father-in-law Samson Raphael HIRSCH as rabbi of the Orthodox community in Frankfort-on-Main and cofounded AGUDAT ISRAEL; and his son *Isaac* (1883–1946), also an Agudat Israel leader, who lived in Frankfort until settling in Palestine in 1936.

Brice, Fanny (1891–1951): US actress and singer. One of the leading comediennes of Broadway, she appeared in the *Ziegfeld Fol-*

lies. Her career formed the basis for the musical and movie *Funny Girl*, and for the movie *Funny Lady*.

Bridegroom of Genesis (*Ḥatan Bereshit*): Person called on SIMḤAT TORAH to the reading of the Law of the section beginning the new cycle; the opening verses of Genesis.

Bridegroom of the Law (*Ḥatan Torah*): Person called on SIMḤAT TORAH to the reading of the Law of the section concluding the old cycle; the concluding verses of Deuteronomy.

bris: Ashkenazi form of *berit*, "covenant."

British Columbia: Canadian province. Jews came in the wake of the gold discoveries of the mid-1850s, and a community developed in Victoria from 1859. The VANCOUVER community dates from the beginning of the 20th cent. In 1971, there were 12,175 Jews, nearly all in Vancouver.

Brod, Max (1884–1968): Writer. He lived in Prague and wrote novels, plays, etc., in German. He was one of the first to recognize the qualities of his friend Franz Kafka. In 1939, he moved to Tel Aviv, where he continued to write, and compose music.

Broderzon, Moshe (1890–1956): Yiddish poet. Before World War II, he was an outstanding figure in the younger group of Yiddish writers in Lodz. During the war he escaped to the USSR, where he continued to write. He was imprisoned during the period of the anti-Yiddish terror of the last years of Stalin and was released only in 1956; he died shortly thereafter.

Brodetsky, Selig (1888–1954): British Zionist and mathematician. He was professor at Leeds Univ. from 1920 to 1949, during which time he was prominent in Zionist political activities, serving on the Jewish Agency Executive from 1928. He was president of the British BOARD OF DEPUTIES from 1940 to 1949, when he went to Jerusalem as president of the Hebrew University, an office he held until 1952.

Brodie, Sir Israel (1895–): British rabbi. He was minister in Melbourne, Australia (1922–37); senior chaplain to the British Forces during World War II; and chief rabbi of the British Commonwealth (1948–65).

Bronfman, Samuel (1891–1971): Canadian industrialist, who headed the Seagram's liquor concern. He was active in many Jewish organizations, including the CANADIAN JEWISH CONGRESS, of which he was president from 1940. He also supported various organizations working for Israel.

Brown, Harold (1927–): Physicist. From 1959, he headed California's Livermore Radiation Laboratories. He was secretary of the air force in the President Johnson administration, and President Carter appointed him secretary of defense in 1977.

Bruce, Lenny (1926–1966): US comedian. His scatological night-club commentary on current affairs became a cult among some and angered others. He was convicted of obscenity and died from an overdose of drugs. His career formed the basis for the musical *Lenny*.

Buber, Martin (1878–1965): Philosopher. Born in Vienna, he was active early in the Zionist movement, editing its journal *Die Welt* from 1901. He was prominent in the intellectual life of Germany, and cooperated with Franz ROSENZWEIG on a German translation of the Bible. In 1938 he went to Jerusalem, where he was professor of social philosophy at the Hebrew University. B.'s religious thought encompassed mysticism and Jewish existentialism. He was noted as a philosopher (*I and Thou, Between Man and Man*), biblical theologian (*Moses*), and interpreter of Hasidism (*Tales of the Hasidim*). His conception of religious faith as a dialogue between man and God ("I and Thou") has had a considerable impact on modern Christian theology.

Bucharest: Capital of RUMANIA. Jews settled there first in the 16th cent., and were massacred in 1593. An Ashkenazi community was founded in the 17th cent. The position of the Jews remained difficult until after World War I; later 100,000 Jews suffered greatly during World War II. In the 1970s it had 14 synagogues, a Talmud Torah, and maintained the last Yiddish theater in Europe. Its Jewish population in 1976 was 40,000.

Buchenwald: German concentration camp opened in 1937. During the following years many prisoners were sent there, including a large proportion of Jews. Over 56,000 prisoners died there of hunger, disease, and maltreatment, or else they were executed.

Buchler, Adolf (1867–1939): Scholar. Born in Hungary, he went to London in 1906 and headed JEWS' COLLEGE. Much of his scholarship dealt with the history of the Second Temple period.

Buchwald, Art (1925–): US journalist. He first wrote for the Paris edition of the *New York Herald Tribune*, and from 1952 his popular column, in which he treated topical events and personalities with humor and irreverence, appeared in the

US. Collections of his articles have been published in book form.

Budapest: Capital of HUNGARY. Jews lived in Buda in the late 11th cent., and were expelled in 1348 and 1360. Jews lived in Pest from 1786, and a rabbinical seminary was opened in 1877. B. became a leading Jewish community, and c. 200,000 Jews lived there at the outbreak of World War II. Many were deported to their death by the Nazis. About 90,000 Jews were living there in 1956, the time of the uprising against the Soviet Union, but 20-30,000 fled in the latter part of the year. In 1976 an estimated 65,000 Jews were living in B.

Buenos Aires: Capital of ARGENTINA. Organized Jewish life there dates from the 1860s. Jews arrived in numbers only from the 1880s (mainly from Eastern Europe, but also Sephardim). Many German Jews arrived after 1933. The Ashkenazi Burial Society, founded in 1894, initiated a number of charitable organizations. The Ashkenazi community of B.A. (Asociacón Mutual Israelita Argentina, known as Amia) was founded in 1939. B.A. now has the largest Jewish community in Latin America, numbering over 250,000 (of whom c. 50,000 are Sephardim). There is a broad educational network and an extensive cultural and social life.

Bukhara: City and region in Uzbek SSR. Jews are first known there in the 13th cent. In the 17th and 18th cent. it was a center for poets and translators working in the Tajiki-Jewish dialect. It subsequently declined but was revived in the 19th cent. From the 1890s there was considerable immigration to Palestine. In 1970, 8,000 Jews lived in B., but from the early 1970s many left for Israel.

Bukovina: Region in Eastern Europe; southern part now in Rumania and northern part in the USSR. Jewish communities first sprang up there in the 14th cent. In the 18th cent., the number of Jews was severely limited, but the following century many newcomers came from Galicia. An estimated 90,000 Jews lived there in 1890. B. was a center of Hasidism. After World War I, when B. was part of RUMANIA, the position of its Jews deteriorated. Most of its Jews were deported in World War II to the death camps in Transnistria.

Bulgaria: Jews were living there as early as Roman times; from the 8th cent., B. was a country of refuge for Jews from the Byzantine Empire, and in the 14th cent., for Jews from Hungary. Sephardi communities were established as a result of the influx of refugees from Spain after 1494. The Sephardim soon became the dominant element in the Jewish community. Religious equality resulted from the Berlin Congress of 1878. Although allied to Nazi Germany in World War II, the Jews of B. escaped virtually unharmed and were not subjected to the horrors experienced by other European Jews, as the local population opposed the German deportation policy. After the war the great majority of Bulgarian Jews (44,000 of 48,000) emigrated to Israel. About 7,000 were living there in 1976, with a communal life.

Bund (Algemeyner Yidisher Arbeterbund in Lite, Poilen un Russland, "General Jewish Workers' Union in Lithuania, Poland, and Russia"): Jewish socialist party founded in 1897 which became widespread and influential among Eastern European Jews until World War I. From 1898 it was part of the international socialist movement. Its membership was mainly in Russia, where it served as both a trade union and a political party. Banned in Russia, it grew strongly in the 1904–05 period, but declined after the failure of the 1905 revolution. Other branches were established elsewhere, including England

and the US. Inside Soviet Russia, the B. groups joined the Communist Party, and only the Polish B. was of significance between the two wars. The B. felt that Jews were strongly bound to the countries of residence; hence they opposed Zionism. World War II ended the last major manifestations of the B.; small groups continued to exist in other lands, but were no longer of influence.

burial: Burial of the dead was the general Jewish custom already in biblical times. According to traditional practice, b. is in the earth or in sepulchers (see CATACOMBS). In ancient times, the body was often buried first in the ground, with the bones being subsequently gathered and reburied in an ossuary. Cremation and embalming were not allowed, although the former is now sometimes practiced by Reform Jews. Wherever possible b. was on the day of death. The body is ritually washed and wrapped in a simple shroud. The use of a coffin is according to local custom; it is usual in Western countries but not among Oriental Jews or in Israel. The body is carried to the grave on a bier and interred after a short ceremony. The males present assist in filling the grave, after which the mourners recite the KADDISH. It became a widespread practice in the Diaspora to place some soil from the Holy Land in the coffin. Responsibility for b. was given to the heads of a communal organization — the ḤEVRA KADDISHA — membership in which was regarded as particularly meritorious.

Burla, Yehuda (1886–1969): Hebrew writer. Born in Jerusalem, he was one of the first modern authors to write about the Oriental and Sephardi communities in Israel. He also wrote a number of novels based on personalities in Jewish history.

burning bush: The thorn bush in the wilderness from which God spoke to Moses (Exod. 3:1–10), calling him to his mission. Although the bush was aflame, it was not consumed.

Burns, George (1896–): US stage, radio, and film comedian. He had a long career in partnership with his wife Gracie Allen. After her death, he continued on his own and won an Oscar for his performance in *The Sunshine Kids*.

Byzantine Empire: Jews were living there from its foundation in the 4th cent. They were discriminated against in its juridical codes, notably that issued by Justinian, who also intervened in issues concerning synagogue service and forbidding the study of the Oral Law. Later some Byzantine emperors forbade the practice of Judaism, although Jewish religious life soon reestablished itself. Jewish communities were to be found throughout the Byzantine Empire, including in southern Italy. They had their own prayer rite (*minhag*), which was contained in a special prayer book (*Maḥzor Romania*).

Caesarea: Ancient Palestinian coastal city. It was originally called Straton's Tower. Herod was responsible for its major expansion into a large harbor city; he renamed it C. in honor of Augustus, from whom he had received it. Under the Romans, C. was the capital of Judea; both Jews and gentiles lived there, and disputes frequently broke out. It was also one of the main early centers of Christianity. The Crusaders fortified it, making it one of their main harbors. In modern times, many of its ancient sites have been excavated, including the Roman theater and the Crusader city. Israel's only golf course is also situated there.

Cahan, Abraham (1860–1951): US Yiddish writer and journalist. He had to leave Russia because of his revolutionary activities and went to the US in 1882. He became an outstanding workers' leader, founding the first Jewish tailors' union. He established several Yiddish periodicals, and was best known as editor-in-chief of the *Jewish Forward*. His novel *The Rise of David Levinsky* (written in English) is one of the outstanding American-Jewish books of the pre-World War I era.

Cain: Firstborn son of ADAM and EVE; brother of ABEL. When God preferred the offering of the shepherd Abel to that of the farmer C., C. killed Abel. In punishment, C. was condemned to be a wanderer.

Cairo: Capital of EGYPT.

Jews lived in the Old City (Fostat) from the time of the Arab invasion in the 7th cent., and in the New City since its foundation in the 10th cent. It was the center of Egyptian Jewry and the seat of its leaders, the exilarchs and *negidim*. Many refugees from Spain came at the end of the 15th cent. It was in an ancient C. synagogue that the famous GENIZAH was discovered. The community grew in the 19th and 20th cent., numbering 40,000 Jews in 1948 (including 2,000 KARAITES). The situation of the community deteriorated after 1948, and there were riots and expulsions. The Jews of C. left for elsewhere, and by 1977 only about 100 remained.

Caleb: A leader of the tribe of Judah. One of 12 selected to spy out the land, only he and JOSHUA brought back favorable reports (Num. 13–14). As a reward they were the sole survivors of the Jews who left Egypt to enter Canaan. Joshua assigned Hebron and its neighborhood to C., and his descendants, the Calebites, remained an important element in the tribe of Judah.

calendar: The Jewish c. is lunisolar ("bound lunar") and is of such accuracy that, unlike the Gregorian calendar, it has never had to be adjusted. It consists of 12 months, but in order to adjust to the solar year, a full month (Adar II) is added in the 3rd, 6th, 8th, 11th, 14th, 17th, and 19th year of each 19-year cycle (5730 began such a cycle); these are called leap years. The months are counted from Nisan in the spring and the names as known are of Babylonian origin: Nisan (30 days), Iyyar (29), Sivan (30), Tammuz (29), Av (30), Elul (29), Tishri (30), Marheshvan or Heshvan (29 or 30), Kislev (29 or 30), Tevet (29), Shevat (30), and Adar (29; 30 in leap years). Non-leap years have 353–55 days and leap years 383–85 days. Adjustments are made so that certain festivals do not fall on inconvenient days of the week (e.g., Hoshana Rabbah does not fall on a Saturday nor the Day of Atonement on a Friday or Sunday). This constant c. was introduced by the patriarch Hillel II (330–65). Previously the fixing of the NEW MOON was determined by observation and the evidence of witnesses. The practice of adding a second day to festivals outside Palestine was introduced because of the doubts which arose in these communities as to when the new moon had been officially recognized in Palestine. Some sectarians advocated a purely solar c., and it is probable that there was tension between the Dead Sea Sect (see DEAD SEA SCROLLS) and the rest of the Jewish population owing to their observing a different c. The Jewish era is reckoned from the Creation of the World. On biblical data this was reckoned to have occurred in 3760 BCE. The year is reckoned from the first of the month of Tishri (Rosh ha-Shanah). Thus Rosh ha-Shanah in 1979 CE is, in Jewish tradition, Tishri 1, 5740.

California: US state. The 1849 gold rush first brought Jews to the West Coast, and a decade later there were many communities throughout C. Jews became prominent in trade and commerce in the northern part of the state, centered on SAN FRANCISCO, which had a Jewish newspaper, the *Weekly Gleaner*, from 1857. In the 20th cent. LOS ANGELES attracted many Jews who played an important role in the growth of its entertainment industry. After World War II, the Jewish population of C. rose rapidly and in 1976 numbered 662,610.

Calvin, Melvin (1912–): US biochemist. He taught at the University of California at Berkeley. He was awarded the 1961 Nobel Prize for Chemistry for his work using carbon-14 isotopes as radioactive tracers to study photosynthesis.

camps, Nazi: In 1933 the Nazis had already begun to establish a network of concentration camps to which their political opponents were sent. Individual Jews were consigned to camps during the early years, but a mass transfer of Jews did not occur until after KRISTALLNACHT in November 1938; the great majority of those who were imprisoned at this time were soon released. During World War II, however, deportation to camps took on a more lethal aspect, with the establishment of camps for mass extermination. In the early part of the war, Jews were herded into ghettos, and from 1941 on were sent to such camps. From 1942, Jews from all over Europe were transported directly to the death camps, in which gas chambers had been installed. It has been estimated that some 4,000,000 Jews were killed in these camps, of which the most notorious were AUSCHWITZ (over 1,000,000 Jewish victims), TREBLINKA (750,-000), BELZEC (600,000), CHELMNO (152,000), SOBIBOR (230,000), and MAIDANEK (125,000). Many died in camps in the Reich area, including MAUTHAUSEN (110,-000), BUCHENWALD (51,500), BERGEN-BELSEN (30,000), and DACHAU (36,000). Some 34,-000 Jews died in THERESIENSTADT, but most of its inmates were transported to their death in other camps.

Canaan, Canaanites: In ancient times, the Land of Canaan denoted the area between the Jordan and the Mediterranean from Egypt into Syria; it was also applied to the low-lying coast of Palestine. Its inhabitants were regarded as descended from Canaan, son of Ham. When the Israelites conquered the land, they were repeatedly warned against Canaanite worship (mostly fertility cults) and customs (e.g., Exod. 23:23–4) and intermarriage with the Canaanites. Although certain Canaanite influences did occur, the Israelites generally were not affected by the Canaanite culture. The conquest of the Land of Canaan was accomplished gradually, but eventually the Canaanites were defeated entirely or assimilated by the Israelites, Philistines, and Arameans.

Canada: Under the French, Jews were excluded, and Jewish settlement commenced only after the British conquest. A Sephardi congregation was established in MONTREAL in 1768. Ashkenazi congregations were founded in Montreal in 1846, in TORONTO in 1856, and in Victoria in 1863. The Quebec assembly granted Jews full civic rights in 1832. Jews arrived on the west coast during the 1858 gold rush. The major influx came from Eastern Europe, starting in the early 1880s (in 1881, there were 2,442 Jews in Canada; 16,493 in 1901; over 100,000 in 1919; and 300,000 in 1975). Canada was one of the few countries, apart from Israel, in which there was sizable Jewish immigration after World War II. New arrivals, in addition to those coming from Europe, included emigrants from Israel and Jews from North Africa. The Canadian Jewish community has developed in the 20th cent. into one of the most active and best organized in the world. Its representative body is the CANADIAN JEWISH CONGRESS; it has an outstanding Zionist organization and education network. There are over 200 Jewish congregations in the country. The vast majority are Orthodox, but these are mainly smaller groups; there are large Conservative and Reform congregations affiliated to the respective bodies in the US. Two-thirds of Canadian Jewry are concentrated in the cities of Montreal and Toronto. In recent years, Jews in Quebec have been concerned about aspects of Quebec nationalism, and some have left Montreal for Toronto and elsewhere.

Canadian Jewish Congress: Representative organization of Canadian Jewry. It was founded in 1919, originally to assist East European Jewry, and is affiliated with the WORLD JEWISH CONGRESS. Its activities include group relations, the combating of anti-Semitism, education and culture, overseas relief and rehabilitation, and public relations.

candelabrum see **menorah**

Canticles see **Song of Songs**

cantillation see **accents; cantor and cantoral music**

cantonists: Forced recruits in the Czarist army, 1805–56. Jews became subject to military duty in 1827, and during the following three decades a large number of children were forced into the army at a very young age; while they were in service, every effort was made to convert them to Christianity. The Jewish communities had to supply the recruits (aged between 12—or even 8—and 25), and service lasted for at least 25 years. Sometimes professional kidnappers were employed. The Jewish recruits were generally stationed in distant areas, such as Siberia. Many converted and others died as a result of the difficult conditions and cruel treatment.

cantor and cantoral music: The term *hazzan* now used in Hebrew for the cantor originally referred to a community official. Lay members of the congregation led the prayers; they were known as the *sheliah tzibbur*, i.e., the emissaries of the congregation. The professional cantor only emerged in the gaonic period, (6th–11th cent.) as a result of both the lack of knowledge of Hebrew among the laity and the introduction of PIYYUTIM (many of which were composed by the *hazzanim*). The cantors were increasingly influenced by the secular music of their environment. Big differences developed between the Sephardi tradition (often influenced by an Arab environment) and the Ashkenazi cantoral music (*hazzanut*), which tended to the florid. Over the last century the importance of the choir increased, and in Reform tradition the service is sometimes conducted by rabbi and choir. Musically, the cantor was always allowed a great amount of latitude within a certain framework. A wide variety of influences made themselves felt, ranging from church music in the late Middle Ages to, more recently, opera. The last two centuries have seen systematic musical study by cantors. In the early 19th cent., Solomon SULZER brought form to cantoral chant and synagogue music. In recent decades, schools for the training of cantors have been opened.

Many cantors have achieved fame and popularity beyond their own communities, often by personal tours and especially with the advent of recordings.

Cantor, Eddie (1892–1964): US comedian. Famous as a vaudeville performer and as star of the Ziegfeld Follies, he achieved even more widespread popularity through films and broadcasting. C. was very active in philanthropic activities, both general and Jewish.

Cape Town: City in S. Africa. The first Jewish congregation in S. Africa was established there in 1841 and the first synagogue in 1849. For some time C.T. was the center of Jewish life in the country, but with the discovery of rich minerals elsewhere, many Jews moved northward from the latter part of the 19th cent. The main synagogue, which also houses a Jewish museum, was dedicated in 1904. In 1976 C.T. had 25,650 Jews, with 1 Reform and 12 Orthodox synagogues.

Capernaum: Site on the banks of the Sea of Galilee which in ancient times was a port of the lake. It is mentioned on a number of occasions in the New Testament as Jesus' main center in Galilee. Jews lived there until the 6th cent. The remains of the 3rd-cent. synagogue were excavated and restored by Franciscan monks, who acquired the site in the late 19th cent.

capital punishment: Biblical law prescribes c.p. for certain major offenses, notably murder; adultery, incest, and certain other sexual sins; blasphemy; idolatry; Sabbath desecration; witchcraft; kidnapping; and striking or dishonoring parents. However, this form of punishment was seldom carried out in practice. Rabbinic interpretation laid down that there had to be two witnesses to the crime and that the offender had to be given a specific warning as to the consequences prior to his committing the crime. Some rabbis regarded a court which imposed a death sentence once in 70 years as "bloodthirsty." Capital cases had to be tried by a court of 23 judges. The Bible mentions three forms of c.p.— stoning, burning, and killing with a sword. The rabbis added strangulation. Hanging was not permitted. Exceptional cases of c.p. imposed by Jewish courts are mentioned in the Middle Ages. The death penalty has been abolished in the State of Israel, except in cases of genocide and wartime treason. The sole instance of an execution resulting from an Israeli court decision was in the case of Adolf EICHMANN.

captives: The Bible legislates on the subject of c. only in the case of the marriage of an Israelite and a captive woman (Deut. 21: 10–14). Later sources paid much attention to the problem of Jews in captivity, and the duty of their ransom was regarded as the most sacred obligation that could be observed. Money collected for another purpose could be used in order to ransom captives. A woman taken into captivity by foreign soldiers was barred from marrying a priest out of presumption that her chastity may have been defiled. Many communities established Societies for the Redemption of Captives.

Cardozo, Benjamin Nathan (1870–1938): US jurist. He was on the New York Court of Appeals from 1914 (chief judge, 1927) and in 1932 succeeded Oliver Wendell Holmes on the Supreme Court. He was a staunch defender of New Deal legislation.

Carmel: Mountain range on Israel's northern coastal plain. The city of HAIFA extends up its western slopes, and there are two Druze villages in its coastal area. In biblical times, it was within the boundaries of the tribe of Asher, and it was here that Elijah triumphed over the prophets of Baal (I Kings 18–19). From the 12th cent., the Christian Society of Carmelites have had a monastery there. At the foot of the hill is a cave traditionally associated with Elijah, and revered by Jews, Christians, and Muslims. Most parts of Mt. Carmel are being developed as a nature reserve.

Caro, Joseph (1488–1575): Codifier, talmudist, and mystic. On the expulsion of the Jews from Spain (1492) he left with his family, and eventually settled in Constantinople (1498). He was rabbi in Adrianople and Nicopolis before going to Palestine in 1536 and settling in Safed, where he founded a yeshivah. There he joined Jacob BERAV's attempt to renew ORDINATION and was himself ordained by him in 1538. He was one of the outstanding codifiers of Jewish law. His major work is *Bet Yoseph*, a commentary on JACOB BEN ASHER's *Arbaah Turim*. On this he based his shorter code, the SHULHAN ARUKH, which became the standard guide to Jewish law and practice, particularly with the addition of Moses Isserles' *Mappah*, which appended Ashkenazi tradition to C.'s primarily Sephardi work. C. was a student of the KABBALAH, and in his diary, *Maggid Meisharim*, he describes his own mystical experiences, communicated by a *maggid* (heavenly agent).

Carpentras: French town in the former COMTAT VE-NAISSON whose ancient Jewish community was in existence from the 10th to the 19th cent. It flourished especially from the 13th to 18th cent., although from about 1477 the Jews were confined to a ghetto. It had its own prayer rites, and its 14th-cent. synagogue (rebuilt 18th cent.) is a national monument. A community, largely of N. African origin, was established in the late 1950s, and numbered 150 in 1971.

Casablanca: City in Morocco. Jews have lived there since the Middle Ages. The community came to an end when the town was destroyed by the Portuguese in 1468 and was reestablished only in the 19th cent. After the French occupation it grew rapidly, exceeding 70,-000 by 1948, when it was the largest Jewish community in N. Africa. The Jewish population subsequently diminished as a result of emigration; it was estimated at about 30,000 in 1973. The Jews lived in a crowded quarter (MELLAH) but were assisted by outside Jewish organizations such as the ALLI-ANCE ISRAÉLITE UNIVER-SELLE, which ran various schools there.

Caspi, Joseph ben Abba Mari (1297–1340): Biblical exegete and philosopher who lived in southern France. He wrote Bible commentaries and a commentary on Maimonides' *Guide of the Perplexed,* which were regarded by some rabbis as heretical because of his naturalistic explanations of biblical miracles.

Cassel, David (1818–1893): German scholar and educator. From 1872, he taught at the Hochschüle fur die Wissenschaft des Judentums in Berlin. He wrote many studies on Jewish literature and published critical editions of Hebrew classics.

Cassin, René (1887–1976): French jurist and Nobel Peace Prize laureate (1968). He taught at the Sorbonne, and from 1924 was French delegate to the League of Nations. During World War II he joined De Gaulle and the Free French Forces, serving as commissioner of justice and education. He was a French delegate to the UN General Assembly, 1946–51, and from 1944 was vice-president of the Conseil d'Etat. Active in Jewish affairs, he was president of the ALLIANCE ISRAÉL-ITE UNIVERSELLE.

Cassuto, Umberto (Moses David) (1883–1951): Bible and Semitic scholar and historian. He was chief rabbi of his native Florence from 1922, heading the rabbinical seminary there.

From 1933 he taught at Rome, but after the introduction of Fascist anti-Semitic legislation, he moved to Jerusalem, where he was professor of Bible at the Hebrew University from 1939. His Bible commentaries and studies, which were widely influential, were based on modern research yet preserved a conservative attitude to tradition. He was editor-in-chief of the *Entziklopedia Mikrait* ("Biblical Encyclopedia"). C. was also a noted historical scholar, particularly of the Italian Jewish community.

Castile: Former kingdom in central and northern SPAIN. Jews lived there from the 11th cent., and with the conquest of Toledo, C. became the major center of Spanish Jewry. At first the Jews were well treated, but in the course of time their situation deteriorated. The 14th and 15th cent. saw a gradual decline until their general expulsion from Spain in 1492.

catacombs: Underground tunnels used as burial galleries. The c. of BET SHE'-ARIM in Israel were a central burial place for Jews from many countries. Six Jewish c. have been excavated in Rome; in them were discovered many Jewish inscriptions and adornments. In Rome this method of burial ceased in the 5th cent. Other Jewish c. have been found in Sardinia, Venosa (southern Italy), Malta, etc.

Catalonia: Region in northeastern Spain, with its capital in BARCELONA. Jews lived there when it was under Arab rule, and in the Middle Ages it had a large Jewish population. It was an important focus of cultural activities. It suffered severely in the 1391 massacres, and the Jewish community ended with the 1492 expulsion from Spain.

Catholicism see **Christianity; Church Councils; Popes**

Caucasus: Mountainous region in the USSR. It includes an ancient Jewish community living in Georgia; the Mountain Jews, living mainly in Azerbaijan and Daghestan (of Persian origin, they have lived there since the 6th cent.); and the Ashkenazi community, which has lived in the C. since the mid-19th cent. The first two groups speak largely their own dialect (Judeo-Georgian, Judeo-Tat). Their total numbers were estimated at about 125,-000 in 1959, but subsequently there was considerable emigration to Israel. The main centers were Baku and Tbilsi (Tiflis).

Cellar, Emanuel (1888–): US politician. Congressman from New York from 1923 to 1972, he was chairman of the House of Representatives Judiciary Committee from 1948 to 1952. He strongly supported the New Deal and political Zionism.

cemetery (*bet kevarot* or *bet olam*, "everlasting house"; *bet ḥayyim*, "house of life"): Since dead bodies, in Jewish law, are a source of ritual impurity, Jewish cemeteries have generally been situated beyond town limits. Buildings connected with burial rites were usually attached. Priests (*kohanim*) are forbidden to enter the c. so as not to become ritually defiled. Suicides (unless regarded as of unsound mind), as well as apostates and people of evil repute, are buried outside the line of graves, near the c. wall. Graves are generally visited on the anniversary of death and on certain days of the year, but the rabbis warned against visiting cemeteries too frequently. Some cemeteries (e.g., Prague, Venice, Curaçao) became famous for their artistic monuments.

censorship: Hebrew books, at various periods, have been subject to either internal or external c. The rabbis prohibited the reading of immoral or heretical books, and the custom developed of prefixing an approbation (HASKAMAH) by eminent authorities to printed books. External c. began with the campaign undertaken by the Christian Church in the Middle Ages and continued until the end of the Czarist regime in Russia. In the 13th cent., Jews were ordered to delete references to Jesus in Maimonides' *Code*. The most extreme c. consisted in destroying complete works (including the Talmud). More generally it consisted of orders to replace passages or words judged as offensive. From 1554, extensive c. was undertaken in Italy, often with apostates acting as the censors. As a precaution, Jews in some places themselves censored their own publications.

Central British Fund for Jewish Relief and Rehabilitation (CBF): British refugee-relief agency founded in 1933 initially to help German refugees. After World War II, it assisted Jewish refugees from other areas.

Central Conference of American Rabbis (CCAR): Organization of Reform rabbis in the US and Canada. Founded by I. M. WISE in 1889, it had reached a membership of over 1,000 rabbis by the late 1970s. It publishes a unified prayer book for Reform congregations (the *Union Prayer Book*) and other liturgical handbooks and directives. In the early 20th cent. it was strongly anti-Zionist, but its position changed from the 1930s and it subsequently became strongly pro-Zionist.

Central Yiddish Culture Organization (CYCO): Society founded in New York in 1935. It has published the monthly *Zukunft*, Yiddish scholarly works, and works by leading Yiddish authors.

Chagall, Marc (1887–): Artist. Born in Vitebsk, he left Russia in 1922 and settled in Paris; during World War II he lived in New York. One of his main inspirations was Eastern European Jewish folklore. He designed murals, tapestries, frescoes, and stained-glass windows for many public buildings, including the UN, the Vatican, the Metropolitan and Paris opera houses, the Israeli Knesset, and Hadassah Hospital in Jerusalem.

Chain, Sir Ernst Boris (1906–): Biochemist. Born in Berlin, he taught in England (Oxford, London University) from 1933, except for the period 1949–60 when he was in Rome. In 1945 he was awarded the Nobel Prize for Medicine for his role in the discovery of penicillin.

Chajes, Hirsch (Tzevi) Peretz (1876–1927): Scholar; grandson of Tzevi Hirsch Chajes (1805–1855), scholar and pioneer in the scientific study of Jewish subjects in Galicia. C. taught at the rabbinical seminary of Florence, was chief rabbi of Trieste, and (from 1918) chief rabbi of Vienna. He had a reputation as a noted scholar and a gifted orator.

Chaldeans: Semitic tribe who penetrated S. Babylonia and, assisted by the Medes, conquered Assur in 614 BCE, giving their name to the area. The C. were noted as astrologists. ARAMAIC was wrongly called Chaldaic (or Chaldee).

charity: Provision for the needy has always been regarded as a sacred duty in the Jewish tradition. Special provisions are made in biblical law, although these are largely geared to an agricultural society. These provisions were extensively developed by the rabbis, who stated that a man should give 10% to 20% of his income to assisting the needy. They also stressed the spirit in which c. should be given, with emphasis on consideration of the feelings of the recipient. Organized c. was an early, continuing, and characteristic feature of Jewish communal life throughout the ages. It included provision for the poor, the dowering of indigent brides, the ransom of captives, and provision for education, hospital services, old-age homes, and free burials. The past century has seen the development of professional c. workers, playing key roles in the increasingly complex and varied operations of Jewish charitable organizations. In recent years, the directions of Jewish c. have been affected considerably by the growth of welfare activities by the State of Israel.

Charleston: City of SOUTH CAROLINA, US. It was the home of one of the earliest Jewish communities in N. America. Jews lived there from shortly after its foundation in 1670, and the first congregation was founded in 1749. The first Jewish Reform community in America was formed in C. in 1824. The C. community declined, especially after the Civil War when many Jews went north. It had 3,000 Jews in 1976.

Chayefsky, Paddy (1925–): US scriptwriter. He has written for TV, films, and stage and excels in his naturalistic depiction of simple people. His best-known works include *Marty*, *The Tenth Man* (based on the legend of the Dybbuk), *The Passion of Joseph D.* (on the 1917 Russian Revolution), and the Oscar-winning film *Network*.

Chelm: Polish town. Jewish settlement may date from the 12th cent. C. is best known among Jews for the tradition of the supposed simplemindedness of its inhabitants, which inspired many humorous folk stories. The community of 15,000 was de-stroyed by the Nazis in World War II.

Chelmno: Nazi concentration camp in Poland where 152,000 Jews (out of a total of 170,000 victims) were put to death during World War II.

Chemosh: Chief god of the Moabites, whose worship resembled that of MOLECH. Solomon, under the influence of his foreign wives, built an altar to C. in Jerusalem (I Kings 11:7) which stood for three centuries until the reformation of Josiah (II Kings 23:13).

Cherniakov, Adam (1881–1942): Chairman of the council (Judenrat) of the Warsaw ghetto. An engineer by profession, he was appointed head of the council by the Germans. When their demands to supply them with Jews for deportation to death camps grew insupportable, he committed suicide.

Chernovtsy (Cernauti; Ger. Czernowitz): City in Ukrainian SSR; formerly in Austria and, between the world wars, in Rumania. Jews are mentioned there from the 15th cent. In the 19th cent. it was a center for various cultural trends ranging from Hasidism to Haskalah. C. was the site of a conference in 1908 which proclaimed Yiddish as the Jewish national tongue. Over 50,000 Jews lived there in 1939, most of whom were deported to their death during World War II. After the war, Jews went to C. from other parts of the USSR, and in 1970, 70,000 Jews lived there.

cherubim: Winged creatures with both animal and human characteristics. Mentioned in the Bible, they were derived from Near Eastern mythology, and the motif was common in various countries. C. guarded the entrance to the Garden of Eden after the expulsion of Adam and Eve. Gold likenesses of c. extended above the Ark of the Covenant in the Tabernacle, and they were used subsequently in decorating Solomon's Temple. In Ezekiel's vision (Ezek. 1), the four-faced cherubim (one human face and the others an ox, a lion, and an eagle) carry the Divine throne. Later literature identifies c. with angels.

chess: Jews were early devotees of the game of c., which they learned from the Arabs. Games of c. were sometimes described in medieval Jewish literature. A number of world champions and a high percentage of international masters have been Jews. The best known include Wilhelm Steinitz, Emanuel Lasker, Mikhael Botvinnik, Mikhail Tal, Samuel Reshevsky, Boris Spassky, and Bobby Fischer.

Chicago: US city in ILLINOIS. Jews lived there from the 1830s, and the first congregation was organized in 1846. The first Reform group dates from 1861. In the late 19th cent. the community grew rapidly, developing a wide network of institutions (e.g., the Michael Reese Hospital, the United Hebrew Relief Association). The Jewish Federation was established in 1900, and the Welfare Fund in 1936. In 1976, 253,000 Jews lived in the metropolitan area of C. Centers of Jewish learning included the College of Jewish Studies and the Hebrew Theological College. As in other large cities, there has been a great movement of Jews to the suburbs and to satellite towns in recent years (e.g., West Rogers, Skokie).

Chile: Marranos settled there in the 16th cent. but the Inquisition, established in 1570 in Lima, had jurisdiction over this area. Jews began to arrive in the 19th cent. but a formal community was organized only after World War I. In 1976 there were about 27,000 Jews in C. (90% Ashkenazim), of whom about 15,000 had arrived between 1934 and 1946 (3,000 of them after World War II). The largest settlements are in Santiago (25,000) and Valparaiso (1,200).

China: The first evidence of Jews in C. dates

from the 8th cent. Their community at KAI FENG FU in Honan Province lasted for 800 years from the 10th cent. before becoming assimilated. Jews, mainly from Iraq, established communities in Shanghai and Hong Kong in the mid-19th cent. Russian Jews arrived from the late 19th cent. and founded various communities, including that of Harbin. During World War II many refugees from Nazi Germany were stranded in C., especially in Shanghai. Some 25-30,000 Jews were then living in the country, including Manchuria. They were subject to restrictions by the Japanese but survived the war, and once this was over they began to leave. Their exodus was hastened under the Communist regime, and by the 1960s no Jews were left in C. About 200 Jews live in Hong Kong, of whom a third are Sephardim.

*Chmielnicki, Bogdan (1595–1657): Leader of Cossack uprising in 1648–49. One of the targets of the rebellion was the Jews, and hundreds of communities were exterminated. Tens of thousands of Jews were murdered, and only those accepting baptism were spared.

choir: A c. of Levites sang in the Temple. In the Second Temple this consisted of at least 12 adult voices. After the Temple was destroyed, music was prohibited. The earliest account of a synagogal c. outside Israel was in 10th-cent. Baghdad. In the Renaissance, the c. began to be reintroduced, although opposition was expressed in some quarters. However, it was not until the 19th cent. that choral singing was developed on a widespread scale in Western synagogues. Reform synagogues introduced mixed (male and female) choirs, but Orthodox services limited the choirs to men and boys.

cholent: Sabbath food among Ashkenazim consisting of a stew. It is prepared on the Friday and kept warm in an oven, to be eaten on the Sabbath lunch. A similar dish among the Sephardim is called hamin.

Chomsky, Noam Avram (1928–): US linguist. Son of William C., a noted Hebrew scholar (1896–1977). C. revolutionized linguistic theory. From 1957 a professor at MIT, he is a noted advocate of radical views and policies.

chosen people: A designation expressing the belief that the Jews have a special relationship with God. The concept is based on the covenant with Abraham and the other patriarchs and renewed at Sinai. The Bible (Deut. 14:2) states, "The Lord hath chosen you to be a treasured people." The prophets stressed that chosenness was conditional on social righteousness. Various blessings regularly recited refer to the Jews as a c.p. Interpretations of the concept vary from a narrow idea of superiority to universalist explanations. Christianity claimed that the Jews had lost their chosenness through their rejection of Jesus and that it was believers in the latter who were now chosen. Generally the talmudic rabbis stressed the role of Israel in bringing God's message to other nations. Medieval philosophers (except JUDAH HA-LEVI) paid little attention to the notion of chosenness, but it assumed an important role in mystical doctrine. With EMANCIPATION, the concept became problematical, and certain Reform as well as Reconstructionist prayer books have removed all references to the doctrine of the c.p. The traditional attitude has never been exclusivist, and any person accepting Jewish law (viz., the convert) became included as part of the c.p.

Christ see **Jesus**

Christianity: Christianity began as a Jewish sect. JESUS, the apostles, and PAUL were all Jews. Many scholars have found in the DEAD SEA SCROLLS added evidence for the Jewish influence on early Christian teaching. C.

adopted the Hebrew Bible and many of its traditional interpretations, and after the crucifixion of Jesus, his followers saw themselves as Jews who believed in Jesus as Messiah. It was Paul who developed C. so as to lead it toward a complete break with Judaism. He taught that the Law had been superseded and that the Christians had displayed the Jews as the elect of God through their belief in Jesus. The breach between the two communities became complete, although C. maintained a special attitude to Judaism, acknowledging that its own roots were to be found in Judaism. At the same time the Jews were regarded by Christians as rejected and even cursed. When C. became the official religion of the Roman Empire, the Jews were deprived of many rights, and hostile legislation was enacted. However, Jews were tolerated in the belief that they should be allowed to live but in severe deprivation, as a living witness to their not having accepted Jesus. The long history of Jewish persecution in Christian countries was the result of religious intolerance and hatred, of which outstanding manifestations included the BLOOD LIBEL and the charge of the DESECRATION OF THE HOST, the CRUSADES, the INQUISITION, the

GHETTO system, forced conversions, and religious DISPUTATIONS. Nonetheless, there was also a certain amount of friendly contact between Jews and Christians. Many Jews adopted C., often under pressure (see APOSTATES), and a smaller number of Christians became Jews (PROSELYTES). There are also many instances of mutual influences in various spheres, both political and theoretical. During the Renaissance many Christians studied Hebrew and other Jewish subjects, but the attitudes of the early Reformation leaders (e.g., LUTHER) were as intolerant as those of the Catholics. It is only in recent years, and especially since World War II, that a considerable number of Christians have actively worked to alter the traditional stance. This was most clearly expressed in the Catholic Church by the declaration on Jews adopted at the Vatican Council in 1965. In many Western countries this new relationship has been expressed by interfaith activities and "dialogue." This latter development has been opposed by certain factions in Orthodox Jewry, who feel that the ultimate attitude of Christians toward Jews is postulated on the hope and belief in their eventual conversion.

Chronicles, Book(s) of
(*Divrei ha-Yamin*): Last book in the Hebrew Bible. Originally a unit, it became customary to divide it into two books, known as I Chronicles and II Chronicles. They describe the history of the Jews, starting from Adam and down to the Babylonian Exile. The main stress is on the centrality of the Temple and its cult, and of the role of the House of David. Scholars differ as to the date of composition, but many hold that C. was written in the Persian period c. 4th cent. BCE.

chronology: In biblical times, certain major events were taken as determinant (e.g., x years after the flood, or y years after the earthquake, or regnal years). The accepted method of dating years among Jews is from the Creation, which, according to this tradition, occurred in 3760 BCE. This system became widespread in the 10th cent. Previously, years had been dated from the Seleucid era (i.e., from 312 BCE); this era was used by Eastern Jews until the 16th cent., and by Yemenite Jews until the present day. Occasionally Jewish dates were calculated from the destruction of the Second Temple (which was previously held to have occurred in 68, and not in 70 CE). Jews in English-speaking countries use BCE (Before the Common Era) and

CE (Common Era) so as not to use BC and AD, which are based on Christianity.

Chuetas: Derogatory name (of disputed origin) given to the crypto-Jews of Majorca. Severely persecuted by the Inquisition, especially in the 17th cent., they no longer maintained their secret Judaism but nonetheless were outcasts and had to live in the former Jewish quarter.

church councils: Councils of clergy vary from those called by a single bishop to general (ecumenical) councils. The decisions of the general councils had a great impact on the life of the Jewish communities. Thus the Council of Nicaea (325) forbade the celebration of the Christian Sabbath on Sunday and endeavored to prevent Easter from falling on Passover. The 7th-cent. Council of Toledo supported the Visigothic persecutions. Major decisions were made at the Fourth Lateran Council (1215), which legislated to separate the Jews completely from Christian society; it enacted, for example, the legislation forcing Jews to wear a distinguishing badge. The Ecumenical Council of Basle in 1434 adopted a policy of compelling Jews to attend conversionist sermons. A completely new atmosphere prevailed at the Second Vatican Council (1962–65), in which a declaration was passed deploring anti-Semitism and stating that the Jewish people as a whole cannot be blamed for the death of Jesus.

Chwolson, Daniel (1819–1911): Russian Orientalist. He received a yeshivah education. After baptism in 1855, he was appointed professor of Oriental languages at St. Petersburg. He wrote on many aspects of ancient Oriental life and religion, and on Semitic epigraphy. He fought anti-Semitism, defended the Jews against the BLOOD LIBEL, and frequently intervened with the Russian authorities on behalf of Jews.

Cincinnati: US city in Ohio. Its first Jews came from England, and in the 1830s Jews came from Germany. The first congregation was founded in 1824, and the first rabbi was Max Lilienthal. Rabbi Isaac Mayer WISE served in C., which became the center of Reform Judaism in the US, although orthodoxy continued to flourish there. It was the home of HEBREW UNION COLLEGE, and it was here that Wise founded the earliest US Anglo-Jewish weekly, the *American Israelite*, as well as the German-language *Deborah*. Its federation, the United Jewish Charities, founded in 1896, is the oldest of its kind in the US, and several Jews have served as mayor. The

Jewish population in 1976 was 30,000.

circumcision (*milah*; *berit* or *bris milah*, "covenant of circumcision"): Rite of symbolizing the entrance of a male child into the traditional Jewish covenant with God. It consists of removing the foreskin of the penis, performed on all Jewish male infants on the eighth day after birth (health permitting). Male converts to Judaism also undergo the ceremony. Originally commanded by God to Abraham for himself and his descendants (Gen. 17:10–12), c. is often called the "covenant of Abraham." In Hellenistic times, assimilated Jews sought to obliterate the sign of the covenant. It may have been in reaction to this that the rabbis added the obligation of *periah*—laying bare the glans. A third requirement was *metzitzah*, sucking off the blood, originally performed by the *mohel* (circumciser) with his lips but now generally by a glass tube. The ceremony is performed even on a Sabbath or the Day of Atonement if that is the eighth day. The occasion is festive, and the chief participants, apart from the child and the *mohel*, are the father and *sandak* (godfather who holds the child on his lap during the ceremony). The chair on which the child is placed prior to c. is called the Chair of Elijah.

cities of refuge: Six places of asylum—three east and three west of the Jordan —allotted by Moses and Joshua as a refuge for the accidental killer to be safe from the blood avenger. The killer had to remain there until the death of the reigning high priest (Exod. 21:13; Num. 35:9–25; Deut. 19:1–7). The deliberate murderer was not allowed to find refuge in the cities.

citron see **etrog**

Cleveland: US city in Ohio. Its first Jews arrived in 1839. Many Eastern European Jews settled there in the late 19th and early 20th cent. Outstanding rabbis included Abba Hillel Silver and Barnett Brickner. The Tels yeshivah was reestablished there after World War II. The Jewish population in 1976 was 80,000.

Coblenz: German city. Jews first settled there in the 12th cent. They played an important role in the economic affairs of the region. They frequently were attacked, and the community was destroyed in 1349. Jews returned in 1356 but were expelled by the archbishop in 1418. During succeeding centuries there were a number of other expulsions. About 700 Jews lived there in 1933, but the community was destroyed by the Nazis. A couple of dozen Jews were living there in the 1970s.

Cochin: Town and former state in southern India. Two copper plates, still preserved, constitute the earliest evidence of settlement of Jews on the Malabar Coast; their most likely date is c. 1000 CE. The three main elements are the "Black Jews," living there from at least the 16th cent.; the White Jews, who arrived subsequently from Syria, Turkey, etc.; and the Freedmen, descended from converted native slaves. They maintained an active religious and intellectual life. After 1955, about 2,200 Jews emigrated to Israel, only a few hundred remaining in 1977.

cohen (kohan) see **priests and priesthood**

Cohen, Hermann (1842–1918): German philosopher. He was the founder of the Marburg School of Neo-Kantian philosophy. Only from 1880 did he interest himself in Judaism, replying to anti-Jewish attacks of the historian Treitschke. In his later years he devoted himself to writing about Judaism, strongly affirming the values of Jewish tradition.

coins and currency: The earliest coin regarded as Jewish is a half-shekel, dating from the Persian period. Some 4th cent. c. bear the word "Yahud," and the Hasmoneans issued many c. with traditional Jewish symbols. After the time of Herod, Palestinian c. bore the likenesses of Roman emperors. The rebels against Rome in 66–70 issued silver shekels reproducing Jewish emblems with archaic Hebrew lettering. BAR KOKHBA issued c. dated according to the year of his revolt. Subsequently these were defaced by the Romans, who also issued c. depicting defeated Judea. In Palestine at the time of the Mandate, the British issued coinage in English, Arabic, and Hebrew. C. issued in the State of Israel have gone back to the ancient Jewish coinage for many of their motifs.

College of Jewish Studies: Chicago educational institution founded in 1924 to teach Jewish subjects and to train teachers.

Collegio Rabbinico Italiano: Italian rabbinical college founded in 1829 in Padua. The school was transferred to Rome in 1887, to Florence in 1899, and back to Rome in 1934. Closed during the later Fascist period, it was reopened in 1955.

Cologne: W. German city. A Jewish community was known there in Roman times. Nothing is then known of Jews in C. until the 11th cent. The community suffered severely from rioters in

1096, when a thousand Jews were killed, and it was destroyed during the Black Death outbreaks in 1349. A few Jews lived there again 1372–1424. Jews returned to Cologne only in 1798. Almost 20,000 Jews lived there in 1933, but they were annihilated by the Nazis, who deported them to extermination camps. A new community was founded after 1945, numbering 1,350 in 1971.

Colombia: Marranos settled there in the 16th cent., but life was difficult in the wake of the Inquisition. Some Jews arrived from the late 18th cent., but settlement in numbers began only after World War I, with many Sephardim arriving in the 1920s. There has been no Jewish immigration since 1950. 10-12,000 Jews lived there in the 1970s, divided equally between Sephardim and Ashkenazim. About 6,000 live in Bogota and over 1,000 each in Barranquilla and Medellin. There are 9 synagogues and an active communal life.

Colorado: US state. Jews were to be found in mining camps with the 1859 gold rush, and there were many congregations throughout the state. However, they later were largely concentrated in DENVER, where 30,-000 of the state's 31,500 Jews live.

Columbus: US city in Ohio. Jews were there from 1838. The first Reform congregation was organized in 1846, the first Orthodox congregation in 1883, and a Conservative congregation, started by Hungarian Jews, in 1901. Around 14,000 Jews were living there in 1976.

Columbus, Christopher (1451–1506): Italian explorer, discoverer of America. A number of scholars have suggested that he was of Jewish or Marrano origin and have cited various cryptic pieces of evidence. It is impossible to confirm or deny the hypothesis. His interpreter, Luis de Torres, was the only member of his crew of Jewish origin.

Comité des Délégations Juives: Body founded in 1919 representing Jewish organizations in Europe and America to protect Jewish interests at the Paris Peace Conference and put forward demands for Jewish national rights, especially in the new states of Eastern Europe. It was headed by Leo Motzkin and succeeded in having some of its demands accepted. After the Peace Conference, it was not disbanded; and after the death of Motzkin, it evolved into the WORLD JEWISH CONGRESS.

commandments, 613 (*taryag mitzvot*): According to rabbinic tradition, Moses was given 613 commandments which are to be found in the Pentateuch. They consist of 249 affirmative precepts (corresponding to the traditional count of the bones of the body) and 365 negative (muscles). As no count of the Pentateuchal laws gives this number exactly, various enumerations were made by rabbinical scholars—some in prose, others in verse (in poems called *azharot*). The most accepted listing is that of Maimonides in his *Sepher ha-Mitzvot*.

Commandments, Ten see **Decalogue**

Communism: Revolutionary movement based on the teachings of Karl MARX. In prerevolutionary Russia, most Jewish socialist parties (including the BUND) opposed C., but there was considerable enthusiasm for the Revolution in certain Jewish quarters which welcomed the break with the hostile Czarist regime and the outlawing of anti-Semitism. Both the February and October Revolution of 1917 had a number of Jewish leaders, for example, Trotsky, Zinoviev, Kamenev, Radek, and Litvinov. In other countries, too, a number of Jews adhered to Communist groups (e.g., Bela Kun, Rosa Luxemburg), especially in the 1930s when the Communists took a strong anti-Nazi stand. A series of disillusionments caused by Soviet Russia's attitude to its Jews and to Zionism and Israel contributed to a dwindling of support among Jews for C. In Israel the Communist Party remained legal but small, drawing its main strength from the Arab sector.

community: Communal autonomy has been a feature of Jewish life throughout history. Patterns initially developed in Babylonia served as foundations of communal structure in other countries. From the 2nd cent. BCE the Jews of ALEXANDRIA had a council (*gerousia*) to regulate affairs according to Jewish law, and this example was followed elsewhere in the Hellenistic world. The EXILARCHS, whose home was in Babylonia, exercised authority over a wide area, as did the *negidim* of Egypt and Kairouan. In Christian countries, communities developed new forms of organization. Authority rested with the communal assembly, which delegated responsibility to elected officials and executives. Generally the government would make the community collectively responsible for many obligations, including tax collecting. Considerable discretion was left to the community, including, on occasion, the right to impose the death penalty. An outstanding central communal body was the

COUNCIL OF FOUR LANDS, representing the Jews of Poland and Lithuania. In the Ottoman Empire, Jewish communal life was carefully organized under the *ḥakham bashi* in Constantinople. With EMANCIPATION, the Jews entered the general life of the country, and the community's concern was largely restricted to religious affairs. However, in more recent times the community has undertaken wider responsibilities. In the US, central communal councils regulate varying activities, including fundraising, defense, education, etc. These have also carried on the basic democratic traditions of the Jewish c.

Comtat Venaissin: District in Provence, southern FRANCE. Since C.V. was under papal rule, Jews continued to live in its four communities of Avignon, Carpentras, Cavaillon, and L'Isle after they were expelled from the rest of France. They developed individual liturgical rites.

concentration camps see **camps**

Conference of Presidents of Major American Jewish Organizations: National coordinating body representing 24 US Jewish organizations. Founded in 1954, it speaks on behalf of the community, particularly concerning external affairs and US relations with Israel.

Conference on Jewish Material Claims Against Germany: Roof organization established in 1951 by 23 Jewish organizations to obtain funds from Germany as restitution for physical losses suffered by Nazi victims. More than \$110,000,000 was received over a 12-year period and allotted mostly to relief, rehabilitation, and resettlement, and also to cultural and educational reconstruction. The conference thereafter wound up but before dissolving established in 1965 the Memorial Foundation for Jewish Culture as an ongoing project to fund Jewish cultural projects.

confession of sin (*viddui*): In Jewish tradition, c. is said before seeking atonement. It is made directly to God and may be said individually, in private prayers, or collectively in public congregational c., as on the Day of Atonement. Although originally there was no fixed wording, formulas emerged and were incorporated into the liturgy. These are worded in the plural, to emphasize the collective responsibility of the community for the sins of its members. In the Temple, verbal c. accompanied sin offerings. Private c. is made in some customs by bride and groom before the wedding, and a special formula evolved for deathbed c.

Connecticut: US state. Some Jews were living there in the 18th cent. but little is known about communities until the mid-19th cent. The earliest congregations were in Hartford and New Haven. The Jewish population grew considerably from the late 19th cent. and developed an active communal life. In 1976 there were 97,945 Jews in C.

Conservative Judaism: Ideological trend which developed in American Judaism in the 20th cent. It was influenced by the 19th cent. Historical School of Judaism in Europe, notably by Zacharias FRANKEL, who maintained that Judaism had always reacted to the contemporary exigencies of the Jewish people, but opposed the Reform movement in its belief that the Halakhah should be adapted in terms of its own spirit. The founders of the movement (especially Solomon SCHECHTER) stressed the concept of Jewish nationhood, and this brought them to a strong emphasis on Zionism, especially the cultural Zionism of AḤAD HA-AM. The platform of C.J. has always allowed for considerable latitude of interpretation, even in its basic concepts of Catholic (= the community of) Israel, Zionism, halakhah, etc. It opposes extreme changes in observance but permits modifications in liturgy and practice (e.g., the seating of men and women together during worship). The American experience has made a strong mark on the movement. The spiritual and educational center of the movement is the JEWISH THEOLOGICAL SEMINARY OF AMERICA. Its rabbis are organized in the RABBINICAL ASSEMBLY, and its synagogues and lay membership in the UNITED SYNAGOGUE. In recent years it has extended its activities outside North America. Numerically, it is the largest trend in the U.S.

consistory (Fr. *consistoire*): Governing body of the Jewish congregations of a communal district. The first c. was convened by Napoleon in Paris in 1808, and the system has remained in France and Belgium. The local c. in France represents the Jews of the area and sends representatives to Paris to the central c. The Belgian c. meets in Brussels.

Constantinople (Istanbul): Turkish city. Probably the first Jews lived there under Constantine in the 4th cent. Under Byzantine rule, they suffered frequent persecution in C., but its commercial importance attracted more Jews. In 1165 there were 2,000 Jews and 500 KARAITES in C. The Turkish conquest (1453) led to a great improvement in the situation of the Jews, and their numbers increased through transfer from Ottoman provinces and through the arrival of refugees from Spain and Portugal (from the end of the 15th cent.). In the mid-16th cent. the Jews numbered nearly 50,000. They had 44 congregations, according to places of origin, the Sephardim being predominant. The supreme religious authority was the ḥakham bashi (chief rabbi). C. was an important center for scholarship and the printing of Jewish books. From the 17th cent. the Jewish community began to decline, economically and culturally, but in the 20th cent. it increased numerically (to 90,000 after World War I). Many left for Israel after 1948, and in 1976, 30,000 Jews were living there.

converts: From Judaism, see APOSTASY; to Judaism, see PROSELYTES.

cookery see **food**

cooperatives: In 1914 there were already over 400,-000 members of 678 Jewish c. in Russia. These were nearly all credit c., with members mostly from the middle classes. The movement was liquidated in Soviet Russia but continued strongly in other Eastern European countries such as Poland and Rumania, until World War II. Little headway was made in the US toward a c. movement among Jews. but much successful initiative took place among the Jews of Argentina, both in agricultural settlements and in the urban population. The c. movement in Israel began with the new settlement at the end of the 19th cent. The movement developed rapidly during the period of the Second Aliyah before World War I, which saw the foundation of the first agricultural cooperatives (KEVUTZAH, MOSHAV OVDIM), while immediately after the war the foundation of the HISTADRUT led to the systematic development of c. Agricultural forms now included the KIBBUTZ and MOSHAV. C. later expanded to cover many aspects of economic life (e.g., transport and marketing). In the 1960s the c. sector employed 15% of the total employed in the country.

Copenhagen see **Denmark**

Copland, Aaron (1900–): US composer. He has written many forms of concert music (symphonies, suites, piano concertos, chamber music), ballets (*Billy the Kid, Rodeo, Appalachian Spring*), and film scores (*Louisiana Story*). Well known are his symphonic compositions, *El Salon Mexico* and *A Lincoln Portrait*.

Cordoba (**Cordova**):

City in Andulasia, southern Spain. Under Muslim rule it was one of the major cities of the peninsula, and it was a Jewish cultural center. HASDAI IBN SHAPRUT lived there, and MOSES BEN ENOCH established there the first yeshivah in Spain. The Jewish community retained its importance until after the end of the Caliphate (1002) but came to an end in the Almohade persecutions of 1148. It was in existence again under Christian rule (from 1236), but suffered severely during the 1391 massacres; it was completely expelled in 1483. MAIMONIDES was born in C., and a square in the modern town has been named for him.

Cordoba: Province and town in Argentina. Jews have lived there since the beginning of the 20th cent. The early settlers came from the Middle East and from agricultural colonies elsewhere in Argentina. Over 9,000 were living in the province in the 1960s with considerable Jewish communal activity, much of it organized within separate Sephardi and Ashkenazi frameworks.

Cordovero, Moses ben Jacob (1522–1570): The outstanding kabbalist in Safed before Isaac LURIA. He attempted to synthesize varying kabbalistic trends. His works include *Pardes Rimmonim*

and the more popular *Tomer Devorah*. These cover many subjects and teach that all creation is a unity, with the human soul containing the image of all the upper worlds.

Corfu: Greek island. The Jewish community developed in the 13th cent., through immigration from the Greek mainland. This community followed the Byzantine prayer rite (*Minhag Corfu*), and other groups were formed by Spanish refugees (after 1492) and by fugitives from Apulia (16th cent.). The Venetian rule was not oppressive, and Jews participated in the defense of the island against Turkish attacks. Full rights for Jews were finally obtained when C. was united to the Kingdom of Greece in 1864. There were several RITUAL MURDER libels in the 19th cent., and many Jews left. About 1,750 were living there in 1939, but only 175 survived the German rule. In 1977 there were 50 Jews, with one synagogue.

corporal punishment: Such punishment is provided for in the Bible (Deut. 25:1–3). A maximum of 40 lashes (interpreted by the rabbis as 39) is prescribed—a third on the chest and the remainder on the back. The number could be reduced in multiples of three in certain cases. Flogging was the usual punishment for infringing a negative commandment where death was not the punishment. MAIMONIDES listed 207 offenses punishable by c.p.

Costa Rica: Sephardi Jews arrived there late in the 19th cent., and after World War I, Ashkenazim (now constituting a majority) came from Poland and, later, Germany. In 1976, 1,500 Jews lived there, most of them in San José.

costume: The only relevant biblical commandments on c. are the prohibition on wearing cloth woven of wool and linen (Lev. 19:19); the obligation to place fringes on the four corners of one's garment (Num. 15:37–41); and the instruction not to wear the clothes of the opposite sex (Deut. 22:5). From talmudic times, it became customary for Jews to wear distinctive garb. However, the enforcement by the Church of the wearing of a special badge for the Jews indicates that in Europe Jews must have been generally indistinguishable from non-Jews in their clothes. A pointed hat was at one time considered specifically Jewish, and Jews also wore a special coat on festivals. In more modern times, Eastern European Jews retained some of the older general clothing fashions and even venerated them, so that the fur-trimmed hat (*streimel*) and long ungirdled coat became the standard dress of the Orthodox Jew (still retained notably in some parts of Israel and in some sectors in New York). Otherwise Jews in the Western world adopted the prevailing c. Under Muslim rule in N. Africa, Jews were forbidden to wear bright colors, and this led to the development of the characteristic black skullcap and robe. Ostentatious c. among Jews was controlled by the Jewish communities themselves in sumptuary laws.

Council of Jewish Federations and Welfare Funds: Association of community organizations in the US and Canada. It was established in 1932, and by the 1970s represented 220 federations, welfare funds, and community councils, serving 800 communities.

Council of the Lands: Central institution of Jewish self-government in Poland and Lithuania. The original Council of "Four Lands" covered Great Poland, Lesser Poland, Red Russia (Lvov area and Volhynia), and Lithuania. However, the area differed at various periods, and the council was at times "of Five Lands" or "of Three Lands." The first records date from the 16th cent. In 1623 the Jews of Lithuania broke away and formed their own Council of Lithuania. The council met twice a year at the fairs of Lublin and Yaroslav (less regularly in the 18th cent.). Representatives came from the provinces and principal communities. The council made tax allotments for the Jewish population. It also dealt with internal disputes, religious life, education, charity, and economic problems. In 1764 the Polish parliament instituted a new system of allocating Jewish taxation. A central assessment was therefore unnecessary, and the council dissolved.

Council of Lithuania see **Council of the Lands**

Counting of the Omer see **Omer**

court Jews (Ger. *Hofjuden*): Jews who were commercial and financial agents in European courts from the late 16th cent. The court Jews were affluent and enjoyed personal privileges and were often able to intercede for fellow Jews and to obtain rights for the Jewish community. They helped develop international credit facilities.

covenant (*berit*): The agreement between God and Israel was termed a c. As with covenants between men, it was symbolized by some kind of ritual. The c. made with Abraham (and subsequently confirmed with the other patriarchs) was made "between the pieces" (Gen. 15:9–17). It was renewed with the entire people at Sinai. Outward signs of the c. on the part of Israel are the act of circumcision and the observance of the Sabbath. More specific covenants were with the house of Aaron to receive the priesthood (Num. 25:12–13) and with the house of David for the monarchy (II Sam. 23:5; Ps. 132).

covering the head: The Orthodox custom of always having one's head covered is based in custom rather than law. The rabbis prescribed head covering for married women, but among men it was initially only a sign of special dignity. Gradually it became usual, partly under Islamic influence, to cover the head during prayer. The custom was later explained as being adopted to differentiate from Christian practice. Orthodox Jews cover their head at all waking hours. Reform Jews do not cover the head even during prayer.

Cowen, Sir Zelman (1919–): Australian jurist. He was vice-chancellor of the Univ. of New England, New South Wales, 1967–70, and of the Univ. of Brisbane, 1970–77. In 1977, he was appointed governor-general of Australia.

Cracow: Polish city. Jews lived there from the 14th cent. During the 15th cent. there were struggles with the non-Jews, and Jews were often attacked. In 1495, they were expelled to the adjacent town of Kazimierz (now part of C.), to which they were confined for the following centuries. Many distinguished Jewish scholars (Jacob Pollack, Moses Isserles, Meir Lublin) lived there. It was only when the city was under Austrian rule and Jews were granted emancipation in 1867 that they moved out from Kazimierz and again settled in C. It was a leading center of Polish Jewish life and in 1939 had a Jewish pop. of 60,000. The Nazis established a ghetto there, and its inmates were deported to their death in 1943. Some Jews returned after World War II, but most of them left after a short period; only about 700 were left by the early 1970s.

Creation: Jewish tradition starts from the belief that God created the world (Gen. 1). Most Jewish thinkers, including the rabbis and the philosophers, held that the C. was from nothing (*ex nihilo*), but there were some who held that a belief in C. from preexistent matter was consonant with the biblical story. It was also generally thought that one day our world would end, although some held it to be eternal. The biblical belief in C. by the One God was unique, but many elements in the biblical narrative have striking parallels in the C.

mythology of other ancient Near Eastern peoples. The systematic study of the C. was a recognized discipline (MAA-SEH BERESHIT), which was restricted to the initiated because it was felt the inadequately trained would be susceptible to heresy (dualism, gnosticism). Medieval Jewish philosophers were influenced in their attitudes to the subject by the teachings of Neoplatonism and Aristotelianism. The former also influenced the kabbalists.

creed: Judaism in its biblical and talmudic periods did not lay down a group of doctrines as a test of faith. Its basis was the commandments, i.e., how to act rather than what to think. In postbiblical times, thinkers endeavored to formulate a Jewish c. The most widely accepted was MAIMONIDES' Thirteen Principles of Faith, although this was never regarded as formally binding. Hasdai CRESCAS produced an 8-point formulation based on a division into fundamental beliefs, true beliefs, and opinions. Joseph ALBO formulated three fundamental dogmas— the existence of God, revelation, and retribution. From the 19th cent. the REFORM movement issued declarations or platforms which were creedal in nature (although not necessarily dogmatic).

Crémieux, Isaac-Adolphe

(1796–1880): French lawyer and statesman. From 1842 he sat in the Chamber of Deputies; in 1848 he was minister of justice in the provisional government. In 1843–45 he was president of the Central Consistory of French Jewry. During the Second Empire, he was a leader of the opposition movement of the Freemasons. On several occasions he intervened with the French government on behalf of persecuted Jews. In 1870 he was again minister of justice, this time in the Government of National Defense. He signed the decree granting French nationality and political emancipation to the Jews of Algeria, which became known as the Crémieux Decree. In 1875 he was elected life senator. C. was a founder of the ALLIANCE ISRAÉLITE UNIVERSELLE (president, 1863–80).

Crescas, Hasdai (c. 1340–c. 1412): Religious philosopher, rabbi and statesman. From 1387, he acted at Saragossa as crown rabbi of the Jews of Aragon. After the 1391 massacres (in which his son was murdered) he played an important part in rebuilding the destroyed Spanish Jewish community. His main work, *Or Adonai* ("Light of the Lord"), is a criticism of Aristotle and Aristotelian thought in Judaism as represented by Maimonides. He also wrote a critique of Christianity designed to win back Jewish apostates.

Crete: Greek island, apparently identified with the biblical Caphtor (Amos 9:7). Jews were living there in the 2nd cent. BCE. Under Venetian rule, there were 500–1,000 Jews, closely organized under a "constable." Many refugees from Spain arrived in the late 15th cent., swamping local Byzantine traditions. After the Turkish conquest in 1669, the Jews shared the fate of their co-religionists in the rest of the Ottoman Empire. Their numbers dropped. In 1939 there were 400 Jews, but almost all lost their lives when the Germans deliberately sank the ship on which they were being deported to the mainland. No Jews now live there.

CRIF: Conseil représentatif des Juifs de France, the representative organization of French Jews, founded in 1943. It is composed of delegates nominated by major Jewish bodies.

Crimea: Peninsula in southern Russia. Jews lived there by the end of the 1st cent. CE. C. was one of the main strongholds of the KHAZARS. From the 12th cent. it was a major KARAITE center. The Jewish community continued to flourish under various rulers, although they suffered disabilities until 1917 (the Karaites until

1863). In 1924 the Soviet government experimented in settling Jews there on the land, but only a few thousand families went into agriculture. In 1939 there were 60,000 Jews, of whom 20,000 were on the land. Under German occupation, the settlement was annihilated (except for the Karaites). Jews returned after the war, and over 26,000 were living there in 1970 (main centers: Simferopol with 15,000 Jews, Yevpatoria, Sevastopol).

Croatia see **Yugoslavia**

*Cromwell, Oliver (1599–1658): Protector of England, 1653–58. His Puritan views led him to sympathize with the Jews, whom he also regarded as a potentially useful economic element. He therefore favored their readmission to England, from which they had been expelled in 1290. With this object, he summoned the Whitehall Conference (1655). When this proved indecisive, he connived at the return of the Jews, and by the time of his death a considerable number had already settled in England.

Crusades: Holy wars launched by European Christians between the 11th and 14th cent. to recover Palestine, particularly Jerusalem, from the Muslims. European Jewry suffered severely, since there were those Christians who urged that the "enemies of Christ" encountered en route should be attacked. Thus the first Crusade (1096–99) was the signal for attacks on the Jews of northern France and massacres in many Rhineland cities. When Jerusalem was captured in 1099, its Jewish and Karaite communities were driven into a synagogue in which they were burned to death. Further anti-Jewish outbreaks in France and the Rhineland occurred during the Second Crusade (1147–49), although the number martyred was smaller than previously. The Third Crusade (1189–92) saw attacks on Jews in England, but fewer than previously on Jews elsewhere. The Jews were less affected by subsequent Crusades, except for financial damage. The Jews in northern Spain and southern France were attacked in the "Shepherds' Crusade" (1320). Apart from the physical toll resulting in the death of tens of thousands of Jews and the destruction of many Jewish communities, the C. had unfavorable economic repercussions.

crypto-Jews: Nominal converts to Christianity or Islam who continue to retain Jewish beliefs in secret and, sometimes, practices. These included the MARRANOS in Spain and Portugal, the CHUETAS of Majorca, the

JEDID AL-ISLAM in Persia, the followers of Shabbetai Tzevi, the DÖNMEH in Turkey, the Daggatun of the Sahara, and the Tschola of Bokhara.

Cuba: Some Marranos lived there in the 16th cent. The modern community dates from the beginning of the 20th cent. Many of the Jews who settled there before World War I came from the Near East; after the war Jews arrived from Eastern Europe and after 1933, from Germany. The Central Committee was organized in 1939. Prior to the establishment of the Castro government in 1959, there were 10–12,000 Jews, most of them in Havana. Of these 4,000 were Sephardim. Most Jews left after 1959, since they belonged to the classes that suffered from the new regime. Castro's attitude to the Jewish community and the Zionist movement (the latter until 1967) was friendly. Even though the community dropped to 1,500, all five synagogues remained open. Many Cuban Jews moved to the US and settled in and around Miami.

Curaçao: Its Jewish community dates from the 1650s and has enjoyed great prosperity and influence. Jews have been landowners and shipowners, and have held a central position in the economic life of the island. Even after the country began to decline, the Jewish community continued to be of great importance. The Sephardi synagogue, built in 1732, is still in use. A Reform congregation was founded in 1863, and the two merged in 1964, accepting the Reconstructionist aegis. Most of C.'s 700 Jews live in Willemstad. About half are Sephardim. There is also an Ashkenazi synagogue, opened in 1955.

Curtis, Tony (1925–): US movie actor, born Bernard Schwartz. His successes include *Some Like It Hot* and *The Boston Strangler*.

custom (*minhag*): A religious practice dating from post-biblical times that has become accepted not by virtue of authority or biblical origin but as a result of long folk usage. It became a major factor in the development of Jewish law and religious observance. Not all customs were accepted, and some were abolished. Some were accepted only in limited areas, and customs could therefore differ between one area and another (for example between Ashkenazi and Sephardi Jewry or between Ḥasidim and Mitnaggedim). Customs are less binding than formal enactments, but in some instances they can take precedence over law. Examples of generally accepted customs are the observance of second days of festivals in the Diaspora, and the COVERING OF THE HEAD.

Cyprus: Jewish settlement developed from the 3rd cent. BCE and was flourishing by the time of John Hyrcanus. In 117 CE they participated in the great rebellion against Trajan and killed 240,000 people and destroyed the city of Salamis. The revolt was put down, and Jews banned from the island, although not for long. In the Middle Ages there were Rabbanite and Karaite communities. In the late 19th cent. some attempts were made to establish Jews on the land, but without success. From 1946 to 1948 the British deported boatloads of over 50,000 would-be immigrants to Palestine to internment camps on C. They went to Israel after the establishment of the State. Only 30 Jews were living there in 1976.

Cyrenaica: Province of LIBYA. Jews lived there from ancient times as soldiers and farmers. The Jewish revolt in 115–17 CE devastated the country and was bloodily suppressed, leading to the end of the Jewish community. Jews were again there in the 4th cent. and continued to develop. New communities, including that of Benghazi, were founded in the 15th cent. Jews began to leave,

mostly for Israel, from 1945, and none remained after the 1967 Six-Day War.

*Cyrus (d. 529 BCE): King of Persia, who reigned 559–529. In 539 he defeated the Babylonian army and shortly thereafter permitted the Jews exiled in Babylonia to return to Judah. They were permitted to take with them the Temple vessels and to rebuild the Temple. C. was greatly admired in Jewish tradition.

Czechoslovakia: Jews settled in Bohemia from its earliest period and were in PRAGUE from Roman times. They suffered severe attacks in the 11th, 12th, and 15th centuries. Later they underwent a number of expulsions, notably in the 16th cent. The community was refounded, and flourished economically and culturally. From 1781 to 1919 the country was ruled by Austria, and increased opportunities led to cultural assimilation. After World War I, the Jews played a full role in all aspects of Czech life. 357,000 Jews lived there in 1930. Under German rule, the Jews suffered severely. Some managed to leave before September 1939; 75,000 were sent to their death. Only 42,000 remained at the end of World War II. About 24,000 of these emigrated to Israel by 1953. Initially many Jews took leading parts in the Communist regime, but anti-Jewish elements soon predominated, culminating in the 1952 SLANSKY trial. More Jews left after 1968, and in 1976 the Jewish population of C. was put at 12,000.

Dachau: German concentration camp in Bavaria. One of the first camps established by the Nazis, it was in existence almost the entire period of their rule (1933–45). At least 40,000 died there, of whom 80 to 90% were Jews.

dagesh: A dot placed in a Hebrew consonant. There are two categories. D. *kal* gives the letter a hard sound (*v* becomes *b*; gh becomes *g*; *dh* becomes *d*; *kh* becomes *k*; *ph* becomes *p*; and *th* becomes *t*). The other category is the *d. ḥazak*, which "doubles" the pronunciation of the letter.

Dagon: Syrian god worshiped by the Syrians and Canaanites. D. also occupied an important place in the Ugaritic pantheon. D. was a god of vegetation.

Dahia al Kahinah (d. 702): Queen of Berber tribe converted to Judaism in Algeria. Initially victorious in wars against Arab invaders, she was eventually defeated and killed in combat. The stories about her contain much legend.

DAIA: Acronym of Delegacion de Asociaciones Israelitas Argentinas, the representative body of Argentine Jewry. Founded in 1933 to combat anti-Semitism, it had over 100 affiliates in 1974. It deals with political matters of common interest and maintains ties with Jewish bodies in other countries.

Dalet (ד): Fourth letter of the Hebrew alphabet. Numerical value: 4. Pronounced *d*.

Dallas: US city in Texas. The Jewish community dates

from the 1870s, the first Reform Temple from 1874, and an Orthodox congregation (which became Conservative) from 1884. In 1976 there were 20,000 Jews in D.

Damascus: Capital of SYRIA. David made D. a tributary, and from the reign of Solomon it was the capital of Aram-Dammesek. In the time of Herod, many Jews lived there in their own quarter. The community continued to exist through the following centuries and was unaffected by the Arab conquest (635). Many Karaites lived there in the 9th and 10th cent., and for a time there was a Samaritan community. After 1492, Spanish refugees settled in D. The community was noted for its scholarship and prosperity. After the DAMASCUS AFFAIR (1840) the community started to decline, and after World War I, Jews left D. in numbers. About 10,000 were living there in 1940. After 1948 they suffered severely, and by 1973 only about 1,500 were left, subject to severe discrimination.

Damascus Affair: Ritual-murder charge leveled against Damascus Jews in 1840. The charge was the result of the disappearance of a Franciscan friar and his servant. The leading Jews of D. were imprisoned and tortured, and a "confession" was extracted. Tried by the French consul, they were sentenced to death. The incident aroused a great outcry in the West, and Sir Moses MONTEFIORE and Adolphe CRÉMIEUX went to Alexandria to make representations to Mehemet Ali, ruler of Syria. The charges were canceled and the surviving accused released, while the sultan issued a denunciation of the ritual-murder libel.

Damrosch: Family of US musicians. *Leopold D.* (1832–1885) founded the Breslau Philharmonic Society and in 1873 the New York Oratorio Society. His son *Walter D.* (1862–1950) conducted the New York Symphony Society Orchestra. Another son, *Frank D.* (1859–1937), was chorusmaster at the Metropolitan Opera.

Dan: Fifth son of Jacob, his mother was Bilhah, Rachel's maid (Gen. 30:1–6). The tribe of D., after the conquest of Canaan, was allocated land south of Jaffa but failed to conquer the coastal region. The majority of the Danites then sought territory farther north, where the tribe obtained control of the city of Laish (which it renamed D.) and its surroundings. A temple was built there; Jeroboam made it one of his centers of calf worship. D. was the northernmost limit of Israelite settlement (cf. "from

Dan to Beersheba"). The ancient city has been extensively excavated and remains of the ancient temple have been uncovered. Nearby is the modern kibbutz of D.

dance: Dancing has expressed joy and religious ecstasy in Judaism from ancient times. Examples are the d. of Miriam and the women of Israel after the crossing of the Red Sea, the d. of the Israelites around the Golden Calf, and David's d. before the Ark. In talmudic times, the rabbis used to dance at weddings, but the men and women danced separately. One of the earliest treatises on dancing was written by the 15th-cent. Jewish-Italian dancing master Guglielmo da Pesaro. The *Tanzhall*, where wedding dances were held, was a familiar feature of German Jewish communities. In more recent times, the Ḥasidim have been enthusiastic exponents of dancing on festive occasions. In the synagogue it has become customary to dance with the Scrolls of the Law on Simḥat Torah. Many folk dances have developed in Israel, based on the traditions of the communities (Ḥasidic, Eastern European, Oriental), while a number of dance companies have won international reputations (Inbal, Batsheva, Bat Dor). Many Jews have become famous as dancers and choreographers; these include Ida Rubinstein, Marie Rambert, Alicia Markova, David Lichine, Nora Kaye, Miya Plisetskaya, and Jerome Robbins.

Daniel: Central figure in biblical book named after him. The first part of the book (which is largely in Aramaic) tells about D. and the miraculous events that befell him and his colleagues at the Babylonian court. The second half is apocalyptic, and the visions, although ostensibly referring to ancient times, are apparently to be taken as alluding to the kingdoms of Babylonia, Persia, Media, and Greece. Scholars have dated the composition at least of the second part to the early Maccabean period, although traditionally the entire work was ascribed to the men of the GREAT SYNAGOGUE.

Danzig (Gdansk): Polish port, formerly in Germany; between the world wars it was a free port. There was a *Judengasse* in the 15th cent., but the community was subjected to persecution until 1773, when they benefited by a charter to Jews from the Prussian monarch. During the mass emigration from Eastern Europe, it was an important embarkation port for the West. About 10,000 Jews lived there in 1933, and those who did not manage to leave were exterminated by the

Nazis. A few Jews settled there after the war, but nearly all of these had left by the 1970s.

darshan ("expounder"): Teacher or preacher in the synagogue or school of study. The *d.* originally expounded both halakhah and aggadah. According to tradition EZRA was the first *d.* From talmudic times, the *d.* generally preached and taught in the synagogues on Sabbath and festivals. Later the *d.* concentrated on aggadah.

Dathan and Abiram: Reubenites who joined the rebellion of Korah against Moses and shared his fate in being swallowed up by the earth (Num. 16).

Daugavpils (Dvinsk): Latvian city. Jews lived there from the 18th cent.; for many years most of the population was Jewish. Over 56,000 Jews lived there before World War I, but thereafter their numbers declined; by the outbreak of World War II the Jewish population had dropped to 11,000. These were herded into a ghetto and eventually murdered. A new community was refounded after the war; in 1970 it numbered 2,000, with one synagogue.

daven (Yiddish): To pray.

David: Second king of Israel; he reigned c. 1010–970 BCE. Born at Bethlehem, the youngest son of Jesse, he was first a shepherd of his father's flock. He was secretly anointed by SAMUEL as Saul's successor. Brought to court, D. cured the king's melancholia with his musical talents and became SAUL's armor bearer, intimate friend of his son JONATHAN, and—after showing his military prowess —husband of Saul's daughter Michal. His victory over Goliath made him a popular hero. This aroused Saul's jealousy, and thereafter D. and his followers had to seek refuge with the king of Gath. After Saul's death, D. settled in Hebron and was crowned king of Israel (II Sam. 2). At first his succession was disputed by Saul's son Eshbaal, but after the latter's murder, D. remained sole king. In the eight years of his reign, he conquered Jerusalem from the Jebusites and made it his capital. During his reign the tribes were consolidated into one people and the threat of Philistine power broken. Victories over the Edomites, Ammonites, Moabites, and Arameans led to a considerable extension of territory, extending as far as the Euphrates. D. brought the ark up to Jerusalem, and the cultic unification was accomplished by the building of the Temple in the reign of his son and successor, SOLOMON. In his old age, his son ABSALOM led a rebellion against him, but D. proved victorious. The Bible portrays both his virtues and his faults, but in the course of time he became the great Jewish ideal, and the kingdom—as well as the eventual Messiahship—was promised to his descendants. He was traditionally ascribed with the authorship of the Book of Psalms and the organization of Temple Music. Christianity and Islam both derived from Judaism an admiration for D., the former regarding him as an ancestor of Jesus. A site in Jerusalem has been venerated as his tomb since the Middle Ages, but modern scholars regard the most probable site as farther to the east.

David ben Samuel ha-Levi (c. 1586–1667): Polish halakhic commentator. His chief work is a commentary on *Shulḥan Arukh,* called *Ture Zahav,* and he is widely known after the initials of this work as Taz.

Davis, Sammy, Jr. (1925–): US black entertainer who converted to Judaism. A versatile actor, impersonator, singer, and dancer, he is a star of stage and screen. His autobiography is *Yes I Can.*

Day of Atonement see **Atonement, Day of**

Dayan, Moshe (1915–): Israeli soldier and public figure. He served in the Haganah and Palmaḥ, losing an eye in World War II while serving with the British in Lebanese territory. For part of the Israeli War of Independence, he was commander of the Jerusalem region. From 1953 to 1958 he was chief of staff of the Israeli army, and was responsible for conducting the victorious Sinai Campaign. In 1959 he was elected to the Knesset on behalf of MAPAI and was minister of agriculture from 1959 to 1964. He was appointed minister of defense in the National Unity Government formed on the eve of the Six-Day War. In this position, he had an important part in postwar policies, including those in the areas occupied during the war which remained under military government. After the Yom Kippur War, he was the subject of public criticism because of army unpreparedness at the outbreak of the war, and he resigned from the Cabinet (1974), but joined Menaḥem Begin's Cabinet in 1977 as foreign minister.

dayyan ("judge"): Judge in rabbinic court.

Dayyenu ("It would have satisfied us"): Refrain of a thanksgiving litany in the Passover Seder service, listing the accumulation of Divine favors for Israel. It dates possibly from the 6th or 7th cent. CE.

Dead Sea: Large lake in

Israel. Its length is 47–49 miles and its width 11 miles (less than its original size, according to geologists). It lies between the mountains of Moab and the hills of Judea. Since 1948, it has been partly in Israel and partly in Jordanian territory. It is the lowest point on earth, its surface lying 1,300 ft. below sea level. Its name derives from its high salinity, which does not allow living things to flourish in its waters. The salts (potash and bromine compounds) are extracted by the Dead Sea Works at Sedom at its southern end. Its waters also have therapeutic effects.

Dead Sea Scrolls: Ancient manuscripts written in Hebrew, Aramaic, and Greek, the first of which was discovered in the vicinity of the Dead Sea in 1947. Because of the dry climate, many of the scrolls were well preserved. The initial finds were made in caves at Qumran, near Jericho; subsequent excavations in the vicinity revealed extensive remains of a monastic-type settlement, as well as a cemetery with over 1,000 graves. Evidence of occupation dated from the 1st cent. BCE and the 1st cent. CE. The scrolls were presumably the possession of this settlement and may have been written there. The settlement ended at the time of the Roman subjugation of the Jewish revolt (c. 68 CE). Scholars have propounded various theories about the identity of the Dead Sea sect, the most widely accepted theory identifying them with the Essenes (or a section of them). Some of the scrolls (e.g., the *Manual of Discipline*) describe the rules of the community. Others include manuscripts from many parts of the Bible, constituting the oldest Bible manuscripts known and of great importance for Bible research. There are commentaries on various books of the Bible incorporating the sect's own interpretation of the biblical text as it applies to their own history and circumstances; fragments of apocryphal and apocalyptic works; and special works connected with the community, including their psalms and their own eschatology (describing the final war between the "Sons of Light" and the "Sons of Darkness"), as well as a copper scroll indicating the location of hidden treasure. The D.S.S. are also of interest to students of Christianity, as they portray a milieu which probably had influence on Jesus. As a result many of his doctrines, previously thought to derive from Hellenistic sources, are now seen to derive from Jewish sectarian circles. Most of the scrolls are housed in the

Shrine of the Book in the Israel Museum, Jerusalem. The thousands of fragments are mostly in Jerusalem's Rockefeller Museum.

death: In rabbinic thought, d. is the end of man's striving upon earth, after which he will be punished or rewarded for his actions in this world. D. came to the world through sin, and there is a widespread tendency to explain premature death as the consequence of sin. D. itself acts as a kind of atonement. The time of d. is determined by God, and man is forbidden to take matters into his own hands (by murder or suicide). It is also forbidden to hasten d., and thus euthanasia is forbidden. A person should not be allowed to die alone, and on his d. his eyes are closed; those present say the TZIDDUK HA-DIN and rend their garments. It became customary to spill out water near the dead person in the belief that the angel of d. cleans his knife in water. Another custom is to cover all mirrors. The dead corpse renders ritually unclean everything under the same roof. See also IMMORTALITY.

Deborah: Israelite judge fl. c. 115 BCE. Together with Barak, she led the Israelites against Jabin, the Canaanite king of Hazor, and his commander Sisera. The story of their victory is given in Judg. 4, and the next chapter consists of the "Song of D.," one of the oldest examples of Hebrew poetry.

Decapolis: League of ten Hellenistic cities in Palestine in the Roman and Byzantine periods. The D. probably dates from 63 BCE. Its members enjoyed a certain amount of internal autonomy. The D. controlled the trade route from Arabia to Syria. Its composition was not identical throughout its existence but it included Philadelphia (Rabbath-Ammon), Scythopolis (Bet She'an), and Gerasa (Jerash).

Deganyah: First Israeli communal settlement, was founded in 1908 and established on its permanent site the following year. It was known as the "mother of the kevutzot" and was the home of A. D. GORDON. A second settlement was founded in 1920, and the first was then called Deganyah Aleph and the second Deganyah Bet.

Delaware: US state. Jews arrived in the late 19th cent. and were never very numerous. In 1976 they numbered 9,200, nearly all living in greater Wilmington.

Delilah: Philistine woman who was SAMSON's paramour. She persuaded him to reveal to her that the secret of his strength was in his unshorn locks. She then had his hair shaved and betrayed him to the Philistines (Judg. 16).

Delmedigo: Cretan family. *Elijah D.* (c. 1460–1497), philosopher and talmudist, taught philosophy in Italy, where his pupils included Pico della MIRANDOLA. His main work, *Behinat ha-Dat*, is on the relation between faith and philosophy. He died in Crete. *Joseph Solomon D.* (known as Yashar; 1591–1655), astronomer, mathematician, physician, and philosopher, was born in Crete, traveled extensively throughout Europe and the Middle East, and died in Prague. He wrote on Jewish and secular topics.

Demai ("Produce on Which Tithes May Not Have Been Taken"): Third tractate in the MISHNAH order of *Zeraim*, with *gemara* only in the Palestinian Talmud. It deals with agricultural produce about which there is doubt whether it has been properly tithed.

Democratic Fraction: Zionist group, 1901–04, led by Leo Motzkin and Chaim Weizmann. It advocated greater democracy and more cultural activity. It existed for only a short time, but its impact was considerable.

demons: In official Judaism d. were relatively unimportant, but they played a considerable role in popular practice. The existence of harmful supernatural beings was acknowledged in the Bible and rabbinical thought, but with the proviso that they were subject to the will of God. An important source of d. was the fallen ANGELS. SATAN, originally a servant of God, was metamorphosed into the king of the d. Persian influence developed the belief in d.; Christianity enlarged on the role of the Devil; and the medieval mystics fancifully embroidered on the activities of the d. who controlled a cosmic sphere parallel to the Divine. In rabbinic teaching, d. belong mainly to folklore and legend and rarely influenced halakhah, although a number of customs were the outcome of these beliefs. D. mentioned in early literature include AZAZEL and LILITH. Later major d. included Asmodeus (or Samael) and Agrat bat Mahlat. Although generally malevolent, d. could also be friendly and useful. Protection against d. was afforded by observance of the commandments and by the use of amulets. D. have played a role in Jewish folk belief up to modern times.

Denmark: Jews first settled there in 1622. The first Jews were Sephardim, later joined by Germans. Citizenship was received in 1814 and the last restrictions were abolished in 1849, with Jews becoming prominent in the public and cultural life of the country. More Jews arrived from Eastern Europe in the 20th cent. The friendly attitude of the non-Jewish population received its outstanding expression during World War II in the movement which rescued Danish Jews from the Nazis by conveying them to neutral Sweden. From 1920, about 6,000 Jews lived in Denmark, nearly all of them in COPENHAGEN. There was an influx of some 2,000 from Poland in 1968–69. The Jewish population in 1976 was 7,000.

Denver: US city in Colorado. Jews lived there from the 1860s, and the first (Reform) congregation was founded by German Jews in 1872. In 1899, the National Jewish Hospital for Consumptives was established there, and D. became a leading Jewish health center. In 1976 it had 30,000 Jews.

derashah see **homiletics**

derekh eretz ("way of the land"): Proper behavior toward one's fellow man.

Derekh Eretz: Minor tractate appended to the Babylonian Talmud. The first part, *D. E. Rabbah*, contains laws of forbidden marriages and ethical instructions. The second part, *D. E. Zuta*, contains ethical sayings.

desecration of the host: Charge leveled at Jews concerning defilement of the sacred wafer used in the Christian communion service. After the doctrine of transubstantiation was accepted in 1215, Jews were accused of endeavoring to pierce the host in order to reenact the passion of Jesus. Proof often rested on red spots found on the host, later believed to have been caused by a tiny scarlet fungus, *Micrococcus prodigiosus*. The accusations were often the starting point for attacks and massacres. The first recorded instance was at Belitz, near Berlin, where many Jews were burned following the charge. The allegation recurred repeatedly during the late Middle Ages.

Detroit: US city in Michigan. Individual Jews lived there in the 18th cent. The first Jewish settlers, who arrived from the 1840s, came from Germany; the first congregation was founded in 1850. The Jewish population grew rapidly in the late 19th and early 20th cent. The Community Council, founded in 1937, represents over 260 organizations. In 1976, D. had 80,000 Jews.

Deuteronomy: Last book of the Pentateuch. In Hebrew it is called *Devarim*, after an initial word. It is also known as *Mishneh Torah* ("Repetition of the Torah"). Its 34 chapters cover the events of the last month of the Israelites' journey through the desert, incorporating Moses' survey of developments that had occurred after the Israelites had left Sinai, ethical exhortations (including a repetition of the Ten Commandments), a summary of legislation, Moses' final speeches, his last poem and blessing, and an account of his death. Jewish tradition holds that the book was written by Moses, but critics have suggested that it comes from a source different from most of the rest of the Pentateuch; they refer to the "Deuteronomic Source" (called "D"). The tendency is to regard its composition as early, identifying D. with the Book of Law found by Josiah (II Kings 22–23).

Deuteronomy Rabbah: Aggadic Midrash on the book of Deuteronomy, incorporated into MIDRASH RABBAH. The date of its compilation has been put at the 9th cent. CE.

Deutscher, Isaac (1907–1967): Historian. He escaped from his native Poland in 1939 and settled in England. His main works were on Soviet Russia and included a biography of Stalin and a trilogy on the life of Trotsky.

Devarim see **Deuteronomy**

devekut ("cleaving"): Communion with God. The concept was important in the Kabbalah and it played a central role in Hasidic thought, which developed the concept of meditative as well as ecstatic d. Through d. man sheds all barriers between himself and God in order to establish complete spiritual communion.

Dhu Nuwas (d. 525): Ruler of the independent kingdom of Himyar in southern Arabia. He ruled 517–18 and converted to Judaism before his accession, taking the name Yusuf. He was defeated and killed and his kingdom was destroyed in a war against the Ethiopian monarch.

dialects, Jewish: In the Diaspora, Jews often adopted the language of the environment but gave the words a Jewish color, often writing them in Hebrew letters. Such cases include Judeo-Arabic, Judeo-Persian, Judeo-Italian, and Judeo-Provençal. The particular Jewish aspect results also from the preservation of old forms of speech and the varying Hebrew content. Jews also brought languages from one region to another. Two such outstanding instances are YIDDISH, based on Judeo-German, and LADINO, which is Judeo-Spanish. These latter display regional variations according to where they were used.

Diaspora (Gk. "dispersion"): Jewish settlement outside the Land of Israel. From the 6th cent. BCE there were considerable Jewish settlements in Babylonia and Egypt. In the classical period they spread to many other centers, and by the Roman period, Jews lived throughout the Roman orbit, including Western Europe. In the centuries after the destruction of the Second Temple, the Jewish settlement in Palestine decreased, and eventually almost all Jews were living in other parts of the world. The special conditions prevailing in each different country influenced Jewish religious customs, and external factors made their impact on all aspects of Jewish life and many spheres of creativity. Until modern times, Jews almost unanimously regarded their exile as an evil. But with the period of emancipation and the effects of assimilation, many Jews also held that D. was a natural condition of the Jews and that at best only a part of the Jewish people would return to their Jewish homeland.

dibbuk ("attachment"; same root as DEVEKUT): Soul of disembodied sinner which finds no peace after death and enters the body of a living person. The concept evolved in late mystical circles, and appropriate exorcism was practiced, especially by wonder-workers and Ḥasidic *tzaddikim*. A play on the theme by AN-SKI was the first great success of the HABIMAH theater.

dietary laws: The Jew is forbidden to eat certain foods. These consist of: (1) meat from animals and birds listed as "unclean" in the Bible; (2) animals or birds not ritually slaughtered, or found, after slaughter, to be defective in a vital organ; (3) certain parts of "clean" animals, including the abdominal fat of cattle and the sinews of the hip; (4) fish with no fins and scales. Meat and milk foods may not be eaten together, and if meat has been eaten, a period of time must elapse before partaking of a milk product. The blood of beasts and birds is forbidden. Flesh may not be taken from a living animal. Animals and birds (but not fish) require ritual slaughter (SHEḤITAH). A flaw in the slaughter renders the food unfit for consumption by a Jew. The by-products of unclean animals is forbidden (e.g., ass's milk). Blood specks in an egg render it forbidden. Wine touched by an idolator is forbidden. The Reform movement does not regard the d.l. as binding. The Conservative movement recognizes their halakhic importance but stresses their educational value more than the actual letter of the law.

Dimonah: Town in Negev, Israel. It was first established in 1955 and later became a center for industries and the site of an atomic reactor. The population in 1974 was 26,900.

Dimshits, Benjamin (1910–): Soviet economist. He held various leading economic posts and was minister for the construction of metal and chemical industries, 1955–57. He became a deputy premier and head of the economic council of the USSR in 1962, when he was the only Jew in a top position in Russia.

din: A legal decision; a religious law; a lawsuit. Theologically, it denotes the Divine attribute of judgment, which is balanced by the attribute of mercy.

Dinur (Dinaburg), Ben Zion (1884–1973): Israeli historian and educator. Born in the Ukraine, he settled in Jerusalem in 1921. He directed a teachers' seminary and later became professor of Jewish history at the Hebrew University. He sat in the Knesset on behalf of the NAPAI party, 1949–51, and was minister of education and culture from 1951 to 1955. His historical researches viewed Jewish history from a Zionist perspective.

***Dio Cassius** (c. 150–235): Roman historian. His accounts of the Jewish revolt against Rome, 66–70, and of the Jewish uprisings in the time of Trajan and Hadrian are important sources for Jewish history of the period.

Displaced Persons (DPs): People uprooted from their homes by the Nazis in World War II. The Jewish DPs who survived the war did not, for the most part, wish to resettle in their old homes but preferred to remain in camps and await resettlement elsewhere, in most cases preferably in Palestine. About 230,000 Jews were in DP camps in 1947, and their plight had an important influence on the developments leading to the establishment of a Jewish state, to which two-thirds went in 1948–50. About 80,000 went to the US.

disputations: Organized discussions between participants of different faiths. D. between Jews and pagans are recorded from classical and talmudic times. From medieval times, Jews were compelled to engage in d. with Christians. The Church spokesman was often an apostate Jew. Famous medieval d. include that at Paris in 1240 in which the Jews defended the Talmud from charges of blasphemy but were not able to prevent its condemnation and burning; the 1263 d. at Barcelona, in which the chief Jewish representative, Nahmanides, won a moral victory but as a result was forced to flee Spain; and the lengthy d. at Tortosa in Spain starting in 1413 in the presence of the entire papal curia. Two d. were held under Church auspices in Poland in 1757–59, between Jews and FRANKISTS.

Disraeli, Benjamin see **Beaconsfield, Benjamin Disraeli, Earl of**

divorce: In Jewish law a marriage is dissolved by a bill of divorcement (*get*) given by the husband to the wife in the presence of a rabbinical court. Strictly, a husband can give a d. arbitrarily, but from early times safeguards were set up to prevent him from acting capriciously. Mutual consent is sufficient ground for d., although a rabbinical court will make every effort at reconciliation. Specific grounds for d. include refusal to cohabit, apostasy, misbehavior, ill treatment, adultery by the wife, impotency of the husband, and ten years of childlessness. From the 11th cent. Ashkenazi Jews have accepted the regulation forbidding a husband to divorce his wife against her will (unless he has recognized grounds). A divorcée may not marry until 91 days after the d. The marriage of an adulterous wife and her paramour is forbidden after her d. A wife cannot be divorced on grounds of insanity, but if the illness is incurable, the husband may receive permission, on the basis of the signature of 100 rabbis, to marry a second time. At the time of d., the rabbinical court determines monetary settlements and custody of children (alimony is unknown in Jewish law). Civil d. is not recognized unless it is accompanied by religious d. Judaism regarded d. as a calamity and looked on it as contrary to the Divine will.

Divre ha-Yamim see **Chronicles**

Dizengoff, Meir (1861–1936): First mayor of Tel Aviv. Born in Bessarabia, he settled in Palestine in 1905. He laid the cornerstone for the future city in 1909, and from 1921 until his death, except for the years 1925–28, was its mayor.

Djerba see **Jerba**

Dominican Republic: From the mid-19th cent. Jews settled there. At first there were West Indian Sephardim, with later arrivals from Europe. During the Nazi period, the D.R. expressed its readiness to receive 100,000 Jewish refugees. The project as a whole did not work out, but several hundred Jews arrived and a farming colony was set up at Sosua. After the war, most of the Jews left. In 1975 there were 110 Jews.

Dönmeh: Turkish sect of adherents of SHABBETAI TZEVI. In 1666 they followed his example and adopted Islam but continued to observe in secret many Jewish customs as well as Sabbetaian prayers and rituals. The sect later split into two or more groups, their main center being in Salonica. Some of them were prominent in the Young Turk movement. In recent decades, they have been disintegrating.

Donnolo, Shabbetai (913–c. 982): Medical authority in southern Italy. Physician to Church dignitaries and to the Byzantine governor of Calabria, he was the first medical writer in Hebrew in medieval Europe. He also wrote a commentary on the SEPHER YETZIRAH.

Dori (Dostrovski), Yaakov (1899–1973): First chief of staff of the Israeli Defense Forces. He was chief of staff of the Haganah from 1938, continuing in this office with the army of the new State throughout the War of Independence. From 1951 to 1965 he was president of the Haifa Technion.

Dov Ber of Mezhirich (c. 1710–1772): Hasidic leader, called the Maggid of Mezhirich. The leading disciple of the founder of Hasidism, Israel BAAL SHEM TOV, he succeeded to the leadership of the movement, and his residence in Mezhirich became its focus. He sent advocates of the move-

ment to many parts of Eastern Europe. His main talent was as a teacher, and although he wrote no books, his teachings were collected and published. He developed the concept of the central role played by the TZADDIK.

dowry (*nedunyah*): In biblical times it was the groom who paid a sum of money to the bride's father. The bridal d. became an institution only in talmudic times. A bride received a d. from her father, according to his means; a poor bride received her d. from charity funds. The marriage contract stipulated that the d. went back to the wife in the event of a divorce or the death of the husband, and the law states that a husband may not dispose of his wife's immovable property without her agreement.

dream: The ancient Hebrews saw great significance in dreams, which were regarded as a channel of Divine communication. The Talmud contains a lengthy section dealing with d. interpretation (Ber. 55a–57b) but it also says that "dreams neither help nor harm." The practice of fasting after a bad d. (*taanit halom*) was observed even on the Sabbath. A special prayer was also composed for recitation after a bad d.

dreidel (*trendel*): Top spun in a traditional Hanukkah game. The four sides bear the initials of the Hebrew phrase "A great miracle happened there [in Israel: here]."

dress see **costume**

Dreyfus, Alfred (1850–1935): French army officer who was the central figure in a historic case that rocked the French Republic. D. was a captain on the French general staff who was falsely accused (1894) of selling military secrets to Germany. He was convicted of treason by a military court, publicly degraded, and sentenced to life imprisonment on Devil's Island (off French Guiana). The charge, which had partly anti-Semitic motivations, was supported by army, royalist, and Church circles. D.'s friends conducted a campaign to prove his innocence, but when the real traitor, Esterhazy, was tried, he was acquitted (1898). D.'s cause was taken up by liberal circles, of which the most famous expression was Emile Zola's *J'accuse*. The case aroused deep passions in France. It transpired that the evidence against D. had been forged by a French officer, Colonel Henry, who committed suicide. D. was retried in 1899 and again found guilty, but this time exonerating circumstances were admitted. He was pardoned by the president of France but legally acquitted only in 1906. He resumed his army career, reaching the rank of lieutenant colonel. The Dreyfus Affair contributed greatly to the separation of Church and state in France.

drink offering (*nesekh*): Wine offering which formed part of sacrifice in the Temple.

Dropsie University: Institution in Philadelphia for advanced Jewish and Semitic studies, until 1969 known as Dropsie College for Hebrew and Cognate Learning. Founded with the bequest of a Philadelphia lawyer, Moses Aaron Dropsie (d. 1905), the college opened in 1909. Its presidents have been Cyrus Adler (1919–40), Abraham A. Neuman (1941–1967), and Abraham Katsh (1967–1976). It publishes the scholarly periodical Jewish Quarterly Review.

Dubinsky, David (1892–): Outstanding personality in the US labor movement. He emigrated from Poland to the US in 1911. D. became president of the International Ladies' Garment Workers' Union in 1932 and was vice-president of the American Federation of Labor. He was also active in New York politics.

Dublin: Capital of Ireland. A small Jewish community lived there in the Middle Ages. In the mid-17th cent., some former Marranos settled there, and a community developed which was dissolved in 1791. Reestablished in 1822, it was greatly augmented by Jews from Eastern Europe in the late 19th cent. In 1976 it had 3,600 Jews, a chief rabbinate, and a representative council.

Dubnow, Simon (1860–1941): Historian. Born in Belorussia, he worked in St. Petersburg and Odessa until 1922, when he left Russia, settling first in Berlin and later in Riga. He was murdered by the Nazis in the Riga ghetto. D. was one of the outstanding modern Jewish historians. His 10-volume history of the Jewish people pioneered in its emphasis on sociological factors, and he wrote extensively on Eastern European Jewry. D. was the leading exponent of Autonomism, which sought to solve the Jewish question in the Diaspora by creating a cultural autonomy for the Jewish minorities.

dukhan ("platform"): To recite the priestly benedictions.

Dunash ben Labrat (10th cent.): Linguist and poet. Born in Baghdad, he settled in Cordova, where he engaged in the study of philosophy, supported by Ḥasdai IBN SHAPRUT. He was the first to introduce Arabic meter into Hebrew poetry. His criticisms of MENAHEM BEN SARUK's grammar led to bitter disputes.

Dura-Europos: Ancient city on the Euphrates where the ruins of a synagogue were discovered and excavated in 1932–35. The well-preserved remains contained several walls with frescoes depicting biblical scenes and figures. The discovery threw much light on the development of Jewish art in the early centuries of the Christian Era.

Duran: Family of scholars of Provençal origin. *Profiat D.* (14th–15th cent.), who lived in Barcelona, was a philosopher, grammarian, and polemicist. He was forced to adopt Christianity and lived in Perpignan as a Christian for 12 years. Nevertheless he wrote an anti-Christian satire and a criticism of Christianity. His other works include a Hebrew grammar. *Simeon ben Tzemaḥ D.* (Rashbatz; 1361–1444), codifier and philosopher, was born in Majorca and emigrated to Algiers as a result of the 1391 persecutions. He practiced medicine and in 1408 became rabbi of the community. He wrote works on many branches of Jewish studies, including responsa and the philosophical *Magen Avot.* His son *Solomon* (Rashbash; c. 1400–1467) succeeded him as rabbi and wrote a defense of the Talmud.

Durkheim, David Emile

(1858–1917): French sociologist, professor of sociology at Bordeaux (1887) and Paris (1902). He founded a school of sociology that stressed the importance of precision and scientific methods in all social investigations.

Dylan, Bob (Robert Zimmerman; 1941–): US folk singer and composer. He was one of the leading personalities in the 1960s folk-music revival and protest-song movement. He later turned to concerts and ballad music.

E

ban (Even), Abba (1915–): Israeli diplomat; raised in England. He was a member of the Jewish Agency delegation to the UN in 1947–48, and represented Israel at the UN until 1959 and was also ambassador to the US (1950–59). Elected to the Knesset in 1959 to represent MAPAI (later the Israel Labor Party), he held various Cabinet positions, including minister of education and culture, 1960–63, and minister for foreign affairs, 1966–74.

Ebionites: Judeo-Christian movement in the early Church, probably encompassing several groups. Its followers observed Mosaic law (e.g., Sabbath, circumcision) but did not sacrifice; some believed Jesus to have been divine but did not ascribe to him any kind of transcendental nature (other E. rejected his divinity but maintained his messiahship). Most E. lived in Transjordan and eastern Syria. As Christianity moved away from Judaism, some of them returned to the latter. The group disappeared in the 5th cent.

Ebla: Ancient city in Syria. Its massive archives, dating from c. 2000 BCE, were discovered in excavations in the 1970s. Preliminary work indicated that they revolutionize knowledge of the Middle East and of the background to the early period of the Patriarchs.

Ecclesiastes (*Kohelet*): Book of the Bible in the Hagiographa section. It is read in the synagogue during the Feast of Tabernacles. It contains 12 chapters of pessimistic meditations, summed up in the opening phrase, "Vanity of vanities—all is vanity." It ends on a more optimistic note, and modern scholars have suggested that this ending is a later addition. Some of the early rabbis wished to exclude the book from the canon, but the traditional ascription of its authorship to King Solomon ensured its inclusion. Modern scholars maintain that it was written c. 3rd cent. BCE.

Ecclesiasticus see **Ben Sira**

Ecole Rabbinique de France see **Séminaire Israélite**

Ecuador: Few Jews lived there before 1933. Some went as a result of Nazi persecution, but many who settled at that time subsequently left. In 1976 there were 1,000 Jews, most of them in Quito.

Edelman, Gerald (1929–): US immunologist who discovered chemical structure of antibodies. He was awarded the Nobel Prize for Medicine in 1972.

Edels, Samuel Eliezer (1555–1631): Polish talmudist, known as Maharsha. His main work was *Ḥiddushei Halakhot*, appended to almost all subsequent editions of the Talmud; it expands the talmudic text and adds explanations to the comments of Rashi and TOSAPHOT.

Eden, Garden of: First home of man. It was created by God as the dwelling place for Adam and Eve. However, on eating of the fruit of the forbidden tree of knowledge, they were expelled. In later literature it became identified with paradise.

Edom: Mountainous country in southern Transjordan. Its inhabitants were related to the Hebrews and according to the Bible were descended from Esau. They took the country from its previous (Horite) inhabitants but were conquered by David, who made E. into an Israelite province. They subsequently regained their independence. The Hasmoneans conquered their kingdom, and John Hyrcanus forcibly converted them to Judaism. From then on they were part of the Jewish people (Herod was of Edomite descent). They supported the extremist elements in the war against Rome (66–70), but are not heard of thereafter. In the Talmud the name of E. was applied to Christian Rome, and then used for Christianity in general.

education: A strong educational tradition has characterized the Jewish people from its earliest days. The Bible often stresses the duty of instructing the people in the Divine commandments. Originally this was the obligation of the parents, but by late First Temple times there is evidence of instruction by Levites. Ezra instituted regular public readings of the Torah, and this led to the extension of organized e. In Second Temple times, Simeon ben Shetah established local schools for boys of 15 to 17, and elementary schools were instituted by the high priest Joshua ben Gamla (c. 65 CE). The talmudic period saw the organization of extensive e., from the elementary *heder*, Talmud Torah, or *bet sepher* to the advanced *bet midrash*. Adult e. was conveyed through public discourse. This system long remained the basis of subsequent Jewish e. Generally, e. was restricted to boys, but some girls did receive a good e. In the Middle Ages e. among the Jews was universal and generally financed by the community. Higher e. was in the yeshivah. Secular e. was often minimal. With the advent of emancipation and enlightenment, Jewish children began to attend general schools. Their Jewish e. then became supplementary —sometimes daily, sometimes once a week—and eventually there were many who received no Jewish e. (apart from a brief pre-BAR MITZVAH course). Since World War II, there has been a big increase in Jewish day schools, in which the pupils study both secular and Jewish subjects. Efforts have been made by national and local Jewish bodies to promote e. Nevertheless half the Jewish children in Western lands receive no Jewish e. In the USSR, the last Jewish school was closed in the late 1940s. In Israel, e. is compulsory up to the age of 15, but most children attend high school. After that there are various universities and institutes of higher learning.

Eduyyot ("Testimonies"): Tractate in the MISHNAH order of *Nezikin* with no *gemara* in either Talmud. It collects testimonies given by the scholars at Yavneh concerning doubtful cases.

Efros, Israel (1890–): Hebrew poet. Born in the Ukraine, he lived in the US from 1905, serving at first as rabbi and then teaching in various colleges. He has written Hebrew poetry, translated classics into Hebrew, and co-authored a Hebrew dictionary. In 1955 he settled in Israel, where he was rector of Tel Aviv University until 1959.

Eger, Akiva (1761–1837): German rabbi and codifier. He founded a yeshivah at Posen. One of the outstanding rabbinical authorities of his time, he strenuously opposed Reform Judaism and secular education. His published writings include novellae, responsa, and glosses.

eglah eruphah: A heifer whose neck was broken in the event of an untraceable murder (cf. Deut. 21:1–9). The court of the city nearest to the murder had to recite a formula over its body proclaiming their innocence. The ceremony ceased in mishnaic times "when murders increased in number" (Sota 9:9).

Egypt (*Mitzrayim*): E. frequently had a close relationship with the Land of Israel. ABRAHAM visited E., and JACOB spent his last years there, joining his son JOSEPH, who had become one of the country's chief officials (it has been conjectured that this occurred during the period when the country was dominated by the HYKSOS.) Jacob's descendants, the Israelites, were later harassed by the Egyptians and, under MOSES, left E. (the EXODUS) via SINAI to return to Israel. The Tel el AMARNA tablets give a broad picture of Egyptian suzerainty over Canaan in a somewhat earlier period. There were constant relations between E. and the Jewish monarchy. Solomon married an Egyptian princess, and subsequently E. invaded both Judah and Israel. The history of the latter years of the monarchy was profoundly influenced by the rivalry between E. and Assyria-Babylonia. E. was with Babylonia, the scene of the first DIASPORA, and the prophet JEREMIAH fled there after the murder of Gedaliah. A Jewish military colony existed at Yeb (ELEPHANTINE) in the River Nile; its temple was destroyed in the 5th cent. BCE. After the conquests of Alexander the Great, many Jews settled in E., and ALEXANDRIA became the outstanding Jewish settlement outside Israel, with a strong Jewish communal and cultural life. It has been estimated that a million Jews lived in E. in the 1st cent. CE. Their position deteriorated as a result of anti-Jewish feelings, riots, and the Christianization of the Roman Empire. An uprising by the Jews in 115 was put down with cruelty. For several centuries the community was unimportant, but it revived in the later Middle Ages. There was a flourishing KARAITE community there down to modern times. MAIMONIDES settled in Fostat-CAIRO, and he and his descendants served as the leaders (NAGID) of Egyptian Jewry. Under the Ottoman Empire, the history of Egyptian Jewry was undistinguished until Western influences penetrated in the 19th cent. The Jews were mainly to be found in Cairo and

Alexandria, and about 90,000 lived there in 1947. The Jews suffered greatly as a result of the tensions that followed the establishment of the State of Israel. Subject to imprisonment and other discrimination, their numbers rapidly dwindled, particularly in the aftermaths of the 1948, 1956, and 1967 wars. In 1976, only 400 Jews remained.

Ehad Mi Yodea ("Who Knows One?"): Hymn of medieval origin sung in Ashkenazi rites at the end of the Seder services. Its authorship is unknown.

Ehrenburg, Ilya (1891–1967): USSR author. At first he was anti-Bolshevik, and lived in Western Europe, but he returned to the USSR and became a publicist for the Stalin regime. His treatment of Judaism and Zionism reflected the official line. He received the Stalin Prize for his novels *The Fall of Paris* and *The Storm*. The title of his novel *The Thaw* was widely adopted to characterize the post-Stalin era. He wrote several volumes of memoirs.

Ehrlich, Paul (1854–1915): German biochemist and Nobel Prize winner. He taught at Frankfort-on-Main. He discovered salvarsan, a cure for syphilis, and a cure for sleeping sickness.

Ehud: One of the Judges. He killed Eglon, king of Moab, and judged Israel (Judg. 3:15–4:1).

Eibeschütz, Jonathan (c. 1695–1764): Talmudist and kabbalist. An outstanding preacher and rabbinic authority, he founded and headed the Prague yeshivah; he was rabbi in Metz, and from 1750 was rabbi of the three communities of Altona, Hamburg, and Wandsbeck. While in the last position he was accused of being a secret Sabbetaian on the evidence of kabbalistic amulets he had given to the sick and women in childbirth. The opposition to him was led by Jacob EMDEN, and the quarrel spread throughout Europe. The argument has never been solved, although modern scholars tend to find substance in Emden's charges.

Eichmann Trial: Trial conducted in Jerusalem in 1961–62 of Adolph Eichmann (1906–1962), senior Nazi official who was charged with being one of the main instigators and implementers of the policy of Jewish extermination. As the head of the Jewish section of the Gestapo, he was directly responsible for all Jewish deportations and exterminations. At the end of World War II he went into hiding and escaped to Argentina, where he lived under an assumed name. Discovered by the Israeli security service, he was kidnapped and taken to

Israel to stand trial, charged with crimes against humanity. The four-month trial unrolled the entire story of the fate of European Jewry under the Nazis and received worldwide attention, as did Eichmann's detailed defense. Eichmann was found guilty and sentenced to death, the first such sentence in an Israeli law court. After the Supreme Court confirmed the verdict, the execution was carried out by hanging. His body was cremated and the ashes scattered over the Mediterranean Sea.

eighteen benedictions see **amidah**

Einhorn, David (1809–1879): Reform rabbi and theologian. Born in Bavaria, he officiated in Germany and Hungary and, from 1855, in the US. He was the spokesman of the radical Reform element, denying the continued authority of the Talmud and introducing such changes as Sunday services. He was an active abolitionist. He compiled the prayer book *Olat Tamid.* ·

Einstein, Albert (1879–1955): Physicist and mathematician. Born in Germany, he taught in Switzerland; from 1913 he directed the Kaiser Wilhelm Institute of Physics, Berlin. He was deprived of his post by the Nazis in 1933 and became a member of the Princeton In-

stitute for Advanced Study. In 1902–09 he published his Theory of Relativity, which revolutionized physics. He was awarded the Nobel Prize in 1921. E. was an active Zionist. After the death of Chaim Weizmann in 1952, BEN-GURION invited E. to stand for president of Israel, but he declined the invitation.

Eisendrath, Maurice Nathan (1902–1973): US Reform rabbi. After serving in Charleston and Toronto, he became in 1943 president of the Union of American Hebrew Congregations.

***Eisenmenger, Johann Andreas** (1654–1704): Anti-Jewish German writer. After a long study of Jewish sources, he published his *Entdecktes Judentum,* attacking the Jews and collecting rabbinical sources which could be used against Jews. The book remained a chief source for anti-Semitic calumnies.

Eisner, Kurt (1867–1919): German socialist politician. A leader of the Social Democrats before World War I, he was imprisoned for his pacifism during the war. After the fall of the monarchy, he became leader of the revolutionary movement in Bavaria, and was later elected president of the Bavarian republic. He was assassinated within three months and his government was overthrown.

Ekhah see **Lamentations**

Ekhah Rabbati see **Midrash Rabbah**

Ekron: One of the five cities of the PHILISTINES. Its god was Baal Zebub. The site is identified with a mound 10 miles east of Ashdod.

El see **God, names of**

El Al ("Skyward"): Israeli airline, founded in 1948. It runs extensive passenger and freight services, to Europe, America, and South Africa.

el-Arish, Wadi: Known in the Bible as "the Brook of Egypt," river just inside Sinai which was the traditional boundary of Palestine; site of the town of El-Arish. A proposal in 1902 that the area should be used for Jewish settlement was rejected by the authorities in Egypt. The area was captured by Israel after the Sinai Campaign in 1956 and again after the Six-Day War of 1967.

El Elyon ("the most high God"): Name of God first mentioned in the story of Abraham, which describes Melchizedek of Salem as his priest.

El male raḥamim ("God, full of compassion"): Prayer recited for the peace of the departed. It originated in Europe in the Middle Ages. It is recited in some Ashkenazi rites in memorial prayers.

El Salvador see **Salvador**

El Shaddai see **God, names of**

Elah: King of Israel, the son of Baasha. He reigned two years (c. 883–82 BCE) and was killed, while drunk, by his successor, Zimri, in his capital, Tirzah (I Kings 16: 6–14).

Elam: Ancient land near Iranian plateau; its capital was Susa (Shushan). Its king Chedorlaomer participated in an alliance that was defeated by Abraham (Gen. 14). Ashurbanipal transferred Elamites to Samaria (Ezra 4:9–10), where they continued an identifiable existence until the gaonic period.

Elath: Port in southern Israel on Red Sea. Mentioned in the Bible, it was in the vicinity of EZION-GEBER. The site was captured by Israelis in March 1949, and the town was developed. Its growth at first was slow, but when the Gulf of E., leading to Asia and East Africa, was opened to Israeli shipping as a result of the 1956 Sinai Campaign, it developed more rapidly. A port was built there, as was an oil pipeline terminal. E. also became one of the country's leading tourist resorts. Its 1976 population was 14,-900.

Elbogen, Ismar (1874–1943): Scholar. He taught in Florence and then in Berlin until 1938, when he went to the US. His major work was a history of Jewish liturgy, and he also wrote works on other aspects of Jewish history.

Eldad ha-Dani (9th cent.): Traveler. His origin remains a subject of controversy. According to his own account he belonged to the tribe of Dan originating from the Red Sea region. He visited Egypt, Mesopotamia, North Africa, and Spain, arousing great excitement by his vivid accounts of the Lost Ten Tribes who, he maintained, were living in independence in the Ethiopia area, surrounded by the legendary SAMBATYON river. He reported that their rabbinical observances differed from rabbinic Judaism. His stories enjoyed great credence at the time.

elder (*zaken*): In ancient Israel, a member of the consulting body ruling a city or the nation. Moses appointed such a body, and subsequently it is mentioned as a representative—but not legislative—body. The elders shaped the form of government down to early Second Temple times. The e. was selected for his learning, and was often not necessarily advanced in age.

"Elders of Zion," Protocols of: Anti-Semitic forgery which gained widespread credence in the earlier part of the 20th cent. About 1902 there was published in Russia an alleged plan by a secret world Jewish "government" purporting to overthrow Christian society. Its preposterous nature prevented it from immediately achieving acceptance, but after World War I it became widely circulated, being introduced by Russian émigrés to Western Europe. It was translated into various languages and was taken seriously by politicians. However, in 1921 an exposé in the London *Times* showed it up as a forgery, adapted from a satire written in 1865 against Napoleon III. Although this destroyed the credibility of the Protocols, and, although they were condemned in legal actions, they have continued to be reprinted and circulated by anti-Semites. They played a great part in Nazi propaganda and more recently have been disseminated under Arab auspices.

Eleazar: Third son of AARON and his successor in the priestly office (Num. 20: 28). He was the ancestor of the high priests of the house of Zadok.

Eleazar (d. 163 BCE): Hasmonean warrior, fourth son of MATTATHIAS. He was killed fighting the Syrians in the battle of Bet Zechariah.

Eleazar ben Jair (d. 73 CE): Leader of the Sicarii who took his forces in 66 from Jerusalem to Masada, where he held out against the Romans for 7 years. When the situation became untenable he led the defenders in committing suicide rather than falling prisoner.

Eleazar ben Judah of Worms (c. 1165–c. 1230): German kabbalist, talmudist, and religious poet, called Rokeah. His wife and children were killed in front of him by Crusaders at Erfurt. From 1201 he was rabbi at Worms. His writings developed the mystical system of his teacher JUDAH BEN SAMUEL HE-ḤASID, and his best-known work is the halakhic *Sepher ha-Rokeah*, describing the doctrines of the German Ḥasidim.

Elephantine (Yeb): Island in the Nile River in southern Egypt, opposite Aswan. Jewish mercenaries were stationed there from the early 6th cent. BCE and throughout the Persian era, and a Jewish Temple was built there. It was destroyed by Egyptian priests in 411, but apparently rebuilt following a petition from the Jews of E. to Bagoas, satrap of Judah. Considerable light was thrown on this episode and on the history of the way of life of the E. Jews by the discovery of Aramaic papyri on the site early in the 20th cent.

Eli (11th cent. BCE): Chief priest at Shiloh; one of the last of the Judges. He trained SAMUEL, who was his successor. He served for 40 years and died on learning of the defeat of the Israelites by the Philistines, the capture of the ark, and the death of his two sons (I Sam. 4).

Eli Zion ("Wail O Zion"): Dirge recited on the fast of Av 9, an alphabetic hymn of unknown authorship dating from the Middle Ages.

Eliezer of Damascus: Steward of Abraham (Gen. 15:2). He was identified with the messenger sent by Abraham to find a wife for his son Isaac, but this is not explicitly stated in the Bible.

Eliezer ben Hyrcanus (1st–2nd cent.): TANNA, disciple of Johanan ben Zakkai and teacher of AKIVA. After the destruction of the Temple he followed his teacher to Jabneh; eventually he established and headed his own academy at Lydda. In 95–96 he accompanied the patriarch R. GAMALIEL on a mission to Rome. He was excommunicated by his colleagues for refusing to accept the majority decision on a point of law.

Elijah (9th cent. BCE): Prophet in the Kingdom of Israel during the reigns of AHAB and AHAZIAH. He challenged Ahab's wife, JEZEBEL, who sought to introduce BAAL worship into the kingdom. In a dramatic confrontation on Mt. Carmel, E. was victorious over the prophets of Baal, who were slain by E. and his supporters (I Kings 18). E. also took a courageous stand against the king in the matter of NABOTH's vineyard (I Kings 21). He was forced on various occasions to live in hiding to escape the royal wrath. The biblical account also relates to a number of miracles performed by him. It also states that he did not die, but in the presence of his disciple ELISHA ascended to heaven in a fiery chariot. E. is a leading figure in Jewish folklore, which says traditionally that E. will return to earth as the harbinger of the Messiah. Many stories were told of him wandering in disguise, appearing at moments of danger, and acting as a Divine messenger. In the Passover Seder service, a cup of wine is poured in his honor, and he is associated with the *havdalah* and circumcision ceremonies. He is also a prominent figure in Christian and Muslim folklore.

Elijah, Chair of: Chair placed at the circumcision ceremony, on which it is believed that ELIJAH is invisibly present. Chairs were often made especially for this purpose.

Elijah Bahur see **Levita, Elijah**

Elijah ben Solomon Zalman (1720–1797): Rabbinical authority, called the Vilna Gaon. He founded his own yeshivah in Vilna but refused the position of rabbi, although he was recognized as the outstanding talmudist of his times. He lived in seclusion and devoted himself to his studies, which also covered relevant secular subjects. His approach to the Talmud was characterized by keen logic and a critical approach aimed at establishing an accurate text. He maintained the validity of every detail in the Torah. He led the opposition to the Hasidic movement, ordering its excommunication and the destruction of its literature; his rigorous measures checked the spread of Hasidism in Lithuania. At about age 60, he set out alone for Palestine, but for reasons never explained he returned to Vilna without reaching his destination. His works in many spheres were published posthumously, and continued to be very influential for a long time.

Elimelech of Lizensk (1717–1787): Hasidic rabbi. After the death of his teacher DOV BER OF MEZHIRICH in 1755, he was the recognized leader of the Hasidim in Galicia and Poland. His main work, *Noam Elimelekh*, develops the concept of the role of the TZADDIK.

*Eliot, George (1818–1880): English novelist, born

Mary Anne Evans. Her novel *Daniel Deronda* (1876) shows her sympathy for the Jewish people and has a strong Zionist motif.

Elisha (9th cent. BCE): Prophet in the Kingdom of Israel; a disciple of ELIJAH. He continued the latter's policies and, through his support of JEHU, brought about the downfall of the House of Omri. Many miracles are attributed to him.

Elisha ben Avuyah (2nd cent. CE): TANNA. At first a colleague of R. Akiva and a noted authority, he later adopted heretical opinions. Thereafter the rabbis only referred to him as Aḥer ("the other one"). Affected by the failure of the BAR KOKHBA revolt and influenced by mysticism, he rejected rabbinic Judaism, doubting the Unity of God, Reward and Punishment, and the Resurrection of the Dead.

Elkan, Benno (1877–1960): Sculptor. He worked in Germany until 1933, when he moved to London. Many of his works are of Jewish interest, including the historical candelabrum at the Knesset in Jerusalem.

Elman, Mischa (1891–1967): Violinist. Of Russian birth, he lived in the US but traveled widely.

Elohim see **God, names of**

Elul: Sixth month in the religious calendar, last in the civil. It has 29 days and its zodiacal sign is Virgo. In anticipation of the High Holiday season, it is a month of penitence when SELIḤOT are recited and the SHOPHAR sounded.

emancipation: Removal of the disabilities placed upon Jews. Throughout the Middle Ages, both in Christian and Muslim countries, Jews were subject to far-reaching restrictions affecting all aspects of their life. The climax of this was the GHETTO system, aimed at the total exclusion of Jews from Christian life. Formal e. was first achieved in the US where the Declaration of Independence forbade religious tests for public office (although in individual states full e. was not immediately implemented). In Europe, the first formal step was the French Declaration of the Rights of Man in 1789, although the process in France was not completed until 1831. The armies of the French Revolution introduced Jewish e. to the countries they conquered. The reaction after the defeat of Napoleon led to these innovations being canceled or diluted, but the seeds of e. had been sown; throughout the 19th cent. European countries continued to remove disabilities from the Jews. In England it was removed in stages in the mid-

19th cent., while in South Africa and Australia there was never discrimination. In Russia, full legal e. was obtained only as a result of the 1917 Revolution. Thereafter legal disabilities remained only in Muslim lands, with the exception of the Nazi period when the Germans reimposed the most extreme disabilities on all Jews in lands under their influence. The effect of e. was to bring the Jew out of the ghetto and permit him to live and be educated on terms of equality with his fellow-citizens. A resultant trend was that of ASSIMILATION.

Emden, Jacob Israel (1697–1776): Rabbinical authority. Noted scholar, called Yavetz; son of Tzvi Hirsch ASHKENAZI. After serving as rabbi in Emden he returned to his native Altona, where he established a printing press. Here he produced many books attacking Jonathan EIBESCHÜTZ, accusing him of being a secret Sabbetaian. The resultant conflict affected communities throughout Europe. He wrote many works on halakhic subjects, polemics, and responsa.

emek (valley; plain): The "Emek" now generally refers to Emek Yizreel (the valley of Jezreel). The term is also used in combination for other regions in Israel, for example in Emek Bet She'an (Bet She'an Valley), Emek Hepher (Hepher Plain), Emek Zevulun (Zebulun Plain).

Emet ve-Emunah ("True and Trustworthy"): First words of blessing in Evening Service recited after the reading of the three paragraphs of the *Shema*. The corresponding blessing in the Morning Service begins *Emet ve-Yatziv* ("True and Firm").

En Gedi: Oasis on the western shore of the Dead Sea; now the site of a communal settlement. David found refuge there from Saul (I Sam. 24:1–2). It was a significant town at the time of the war with Rome, and much light has been thrown on the situation there in the BAR KOKHBA period by documents discovered in the 1960s in nearby caves where its leaders hid as the revolt was collapsing. It was a Jewish village in later Roman times, noted for its dates. Recent excavations under B. Mazar have revealed much of the ancient history of the site. A synagogue was discovered with a beautiful mosaic floor.

En Harod: Two kibbutzim in the Valley of Jezreel. The original E.H. was founded in 1921 near Harod spring (see Judg. 7:4–6). In 1929, the settlement was transferred to a permanent site on a nearby hill. It became one of the best-known settlements in the country, with a museum, art gallery, and printing press. As a result of the split in the Kibbutz Meuḥad movement, the settlement divided into two in 1956.

En ke-Elohenu ("There is None Like our God"): Popular hymn recited in Ashkenazi rites at the end of the Additional Service on Sabbaths and festivals, and among Sephardim at the end of the daily Morning Service.

En Soph ("Infinite"): Kabbalistic term used as a name of God.

En Yaakov see **Ibn Ḥabib**

Engel, Yoel (1868–1927): Composer. In 1908 he founded in Moscow the Society for Jewish Folk Music. He composed the incidental music to AN-SKI's play *The Dybbuk*. He settled in 1924 in Tel Aviv and was a significant influence in the early development of Israeli music.

England: Jews settled in E. following the Norman conquest (1066). The main center then was LONDON, but the Jews also lived elsewhere and were traders and financiers. The first BLOOD LIBEL on record occurred at Norwich in 1144. There were anti-Jewish riots throughout the country, especially in London and York, at the time of the Third Crusade (1189–90). During the next century Jews were subject to cruel extortion by the king, and were expelled from the country in 1290. Their return was negotiated at the time of Oliver CROMWELL, when in 1655 MANASSEH BEN ISRAEL was invited from Amsterdam to discuss readmission. Although the return was not immediately recognized, it was in fact connived at, and before long a Jewish community was functioning in London. The original Sephardi settlers were soon joined by Ashkenazi settlers from Germany and Central Europe. Although they did not officially receive civil rights until the 19th cent., the Jews enjoyed broad toleration; their numbers increased, and they prospered. From the 19th cent., English Jewry began to play an important role in world Jewry, especially through such outstanding figures as Sir Moses MONTEFIORE and members of the ROTHSCHILD family. The mass emigration from Eastern Europe (beginning 1881) brought large numbers of Jews to E., completely transforming the nature of the community. Many settled in the East End of London; others went to provincial cities such as MANCHESTER, LEEDS, and GLASGOW. Large-scale immigration ended with World War I, and the only other major influx was of refugees from Nazi Europe in

1933–39. English Jewry is highly centralized, with the main bodies being the Chief Rabbinate and the Board of Deputies. As a result of the 1917 BALFOUR DECLARATION E. also became a center of Zionist activity; this period ended in Jewish-British tension in the immediate postwar years, but this disappeared with the establishment of the State of Israel. The Jewish population in 1976 was put at 410,000.

Enlightenment see **Haskalah**

Enoch: Father of METHUSALEH (Gen. 5:18 ff.). According to the Bible, "Enoch walked with God and he was not; for God took him." This was understood to mean that he did not die a natural death but was taken to heaven in his lifetime. Several apocalyptic books (e.g., the Abyssinian Version and the Slavonic Version of the Book of Enoch) were written around his ascension to heaven.

ephod: Upper garment worn by the high priest (Exod. 28:6–8). To it was fastened the breastplate containing the URIM AND THUMMIM. The e. is not mentioned after the time of David.

Ephraim: Younger son of Joseph and his Egyptian wife Asenath (Gen. 41:50–52). It was also the name of the twelve tribes which re-ceived hill country in central Canaan with its capital at SHECHEM. The tribe of E. led the secession after the death of Solomon, and was the dominant tribe in the Northern Israelite kingdom.

Epstein, Isidore (1894–1962): English rabbinical scholar. He taught in Jews' College, London (principal, 1945). He edited the English translation of the Talmud (Soncino edition) and wrote books on Judaism.

Epstein, Sir Jacob (1880–1959): Sculptor. Born in New York, he lived in England from 1904. He was one of the most influential of 20th-cent. sculptors. His works include public monuments (Coventry Cathedral, British Medical Association), symbolic figures ("Genesis," "Adam"), and busts of famous personalities (Shaw, Einstein, Weizmann). His great works were sculpted in stone or marble.

Epstein, Jacob Nahum (1878–1952): Talmudic scholar. He taught in Berlin and, from 1925, at the Hebrew University in Jerusalem. An outstanding authority, he inaugurated new approaches to the study of the Talmud, notably on the original text of the Mishnah.

Eretz Yisrael: Land of Israel.

Erter, Isaac (1791–1851): Hebrew satirist. He

lived in Brody, Galicia, and worked as a physician. He wrote five satires in biblical Hebrew, largely directed against Hasidism for blocking HASKALAH.

erusin: Betrothal; first stage in marriage.

eruv ("mixture"): Term for halakhic devices to remove difficulties as related to Sabbath restrictions. *Eruv Tehumim* ("Union of Sabbath Limits") enables a person to walk farther than the permitted Sabbath day's journey of 2,000 cubits beyond an inhabited area by previously placing food for a meal at the journey's limit. *Eruv Hatzerot* ("Union of Courtyards") makes it possible to carry on a Sabbath within specified limits. *Eruv Tavshilin* ("Mixture of Dishes") makes it possible to cook on a festival for the following day if this is a Sabbath.

Eruvin ("Mixtures"): Tractate in MISHNAH order of *Moed* with commentary in both Talmuds. It deals with the law of ERUV.

eschatology: Branch of theology dealing with the final destiny of man and the universe (*aharit ha-yamim*, "end of days"). Such thought is to be found in many religions. In Jewish tradition, central aspects of eschatological thinking are the ingathering of the dispersed Jewish exiles to the Holy Land, the last battle between the forces of righteousness and of evil (the wars of GOG and Magog), the day of Judgment, the advent of the MESSIAH, the RESURRECTION of the Dead, and the reestablishment of paradise on earth. While Jewish thought may have from the earliest been influenced from external sources, it was invested by the prophets with original, moral content which became its characteristic. On the final day, God would reform the world and reign in perfect justice. Faced with national tragedies, the eschatological, apocalyptic predictions and expectations became more intense. The multiplicity of views on the subject is vividly illustrated by the ample speculation that has survived from Second Temple times, including that of early Christianity and the Dead Sea sect. After the destruction of the Second Temple, many eschatological elements were incorporated into normative rabbinic beliefs, finding expression in Maimonides' formulation of the principles of faith. Reform and other modern interpretations see the messianic era as the attainment of complete justice on earth as a result of human efforts.

Esdras, Book of: Two apocryphal works ascribed to the Biblical EZRA (Esdras).

In the SEPTUAGINT, the Book of Ezra is I Esdras, and the Book of Nehemiah is II Esdras. The two apocryphal works are known as III Esdras and IV Esdras. The former contains a history of Israel from the period of Josiah to that of Ezra. It was written in the first cent. BCE or earlier. The latter is a major Jewish apocalyptic work, originally written in Aramaic, probably shortly after the destruction of the Temple in the 1st cent. CE. It seeks to find an explanation for the tragedy that had befallen the Jewish people.

Eshkol (Shkolnik), Levi (1895–1969): Third prime minister of Israel. Born in the Ukraine, he settled in Palestine in 1914 and was active in the agricultural settlement movement before entering public service, where he was particularly engaged in the direction of settlement activities. From 1951 he was a member of BEN-GURION's government, in which he was minister of finance from 1952. When Ben-Gurion retired in 1963 he was succeeded by E., who was noted for his talents as a conciliator. The outstanding event of his period of office was the successful direction of the SIX-DAY WAR in 1967.

Essenes: Jewish religious sect of an ascetic nature which flourished in Palestine from the Hasmonean period until the destruction of the Second Temple. Information on them is contained in the writings of Josephus and Pliny, which has led many scholars to identify them with the sect which produced the DEAD SEA SCROLLS. Although close to the Pharisees, they were more strict, particularly with reference to dietary and purity laws. They lived an ascetic communal life; celibacy was common, but some married. Novices underwent a 3-year initiation period and were sworn to secrecy. In Philo's time, they numbered 4,000 and were scattered throughout Judea; some are reported to have participated in the fighting against the Romans. Pliny mentions that they were located near the shores of the Dead Sea. Their main occupation was farming, and their earnings were given to the community. Nothing is known of them after the end of the Roman War (70 CE).

Esther: Central character in the biblical book of that name. She was married to the Persian king Ahasuerus, and it was at her intervention that the Jews of the kingdom were saved from the destruction plotted against them by their enemy, the vizier Haman. The Book of Esther (*Megillat Ester*, "Scroll of Esther") is incorporated in the Hagiographa section of the Bible. It is read at the Evening and Morning Services on PURIM. Scholars dispute its origins; it is thought to have been written not later than 330 BCE. The Scroll of E. was frequently illustrated and illuminated by Jewish artists.

Esther, Fast of (Taanit Ester): Fast observed on Adar 13 (the day before PURIM). If this date falls on a Saturday, the fast is observed on the preceding Thursday. The fast is first mentioned in sources dating from the 8th cent. CE but may be older. It is not connected with the fasting mentioned in the Book of ESTHER. The fast is especially observed by Persian Jews.

Esther Rabbah see **Midrash Rabbah**

Estonia: Soviet Baltic republic. Jews were living in E. from the mid-19th cent. onward. When it became a republic after World War I, they received civil and political rights. Before World War II, the Jews numbered 3,500, of whom 2,000 were in Tallinn and 1,300 in Dorpat. The Jews suffered during World War II. In 1970 they numbered 5,300.

Estori ha-Parhi (1280–1355): First Palestinian topographer. Born in Provence, he went to Palestine c. 1313 and settled in Beisan (Bet

She'an). His *Sepher Kaphtor va-Pherah* is a pioneering work on the historical geography of the Holy Land.

Ethics of the Fathers see **Avot**

Ethiopia (Abyssinia): Traditionally identified with the biblical Cush (e.g., Is. 20:3). Its former royal house claimed descent from the union of Solomon with the Queen of Sheba. Its native Jewish population consists of the FALASHAS. About 300 other Jews live in the country.

ethnarch: Title used for heads of Jewish state or community in the classical period. It was conferred on Simon the Hasmonean, Hyrcanus II and his heirs, and Archelaus. An e. was in no sense an independent ruler. The title was also used by community heads, e.g. in Alexandria.

etrog: The citron fruit, one of the four species used in the synagogue service on the Feast of Tabernacles. In ancient times it was also a popular Jewish symbol.

Etzel see **Irgun Tzevai Leumi**

Europe: Jews probably first reached E. via the Greek islands. Alexander the Great's conquest of Palestine brought them into a European orbit, and by the 2nd cent. BCE Jews were living in GREECE and ROME. By the 2nd cent. CE they were in SPAIN and

Gaul, and by the 4th cent. had reached the Rhineland. With the Christianization of the Roman Empire they became a despised religion, and their status and conditions deteriorated. An improvement resulted from the initial triumph of Islam in southern Europe (especially Spain) and the accession of the Carolingians. European trade moved largely into the hands of Jews and settlements grew up in FRANCE, GERMANY, and BRITAIN. By the year 1000, E. was the main Jewish center. From the period of the Crusades, they were subject to large-scale attacks and frequent expulsions. Charges of RITUAL MURDER and DESECRATION OF THE HOST became common. They were excluded from many occupations and tended to be restricted to moneylending. They were expelled from England (1290), France (14th cent.), Spain (1492), PORTUGAL (1497), and many smaller states and cities. They suffered widespread attacks and expulsions during the period of the BLACK DEATH (1348–51). By the late 15th cent. they were virtually excluded from Western E. and were mainly concentrated in Eastern E., notably in POLAND and TURKEY. The Jewish position in Poland deteriorated as a result of the CHMIELNICKI massacres (1648–49). From

about the same time, there was a revival in the West, partly fostered by fugitive Marranos. EMANCIPATION ushered in by the French Revolution spread eastward during the 19th cent., although not reaching the major concentration in RUSSIA, which, as a result of the partition of Poland, had the largest Jewish population in the world. Before the 1880s, 85% of the Jews of the world lived in Eastern Europe. However, as a result of the Russian pogroms (beginning 1881), there was large-scale emigration, primarily to America but also to Western Europe. The Jews of Russia received emancipation with the 1917 Revolution, but the Bolshevik system suppressed their national and cultural life. The extreme anti-Jewish policy advocated by the Nazis was implemented on their accession to power in Germany in 1933 and subsequently in the other countries they occupied. The HOLOCAUST of European Jewry was effected by the cold-blooded murder of 6,-000,000 Jews during World War II. This deliberate extermination policy resulted in the end of the period of hegemony of European Jewry. About 11,000,000 Jews had been living in E. in 1939; after the war there were 2,000,000 to 2,500,000 in Russia, and less than 1,500,-

000 elsewhere, including over 500,000 in France (many of them immigrants from North Africa during the 1950s and early 1960s) and 410,000 in Britain.

Eve: The first woman; wife of ADAM. Under the influence of the cunning serpent, she tempted Adam to sin in the Garden of Eden, as a consequence of which they were expelled from the Garden. The particular punishment meted out to E. and her descendants was the pangs of childbirth. She was the mother of CAIN, ABEL, and Seth.

Evel Rabbati: Minor tractate appended to the talmudic order *Nezikin*, dealing with the laws of death, funerals, and mourning. The original was written in Palestine in the mishnaic period; there are later additions. The work is also euphemistically known as *Semaḥot* ("Joys").

Even, Abba see **Eban, Abba**

Even Shetiyyah ("Foundation Stone"): A rock in the Holy of Holies of the Temple in Jerusalem. According to legend, it was here that the world was founded; it was also the site where Isaac was bound for sacrifice. In the First Temple, the ark was placed on it. The traditional site is to be seen in the Mosque of Omar ("The Dome of the Rock").

Evening Service see **Maariv**

evil see **good and evil**

evil eye (*Ayin ha-Ra*): Superstition that individuals can malignantly affect others by their glance. The belief was common in the Talmud and Kabbalah and still persists among certain circles. Formulas were prepared to ward off the e.e., and amulets were used extensively, especially among Oriental Jews.

excommunication (ḥerem): Exclusion from the community and from its religious privileges. Commonly imposed from Talmudic times, it was either a punishment for transgressions or a method of securing obedience to communal enactments. The culprit was completely ostracized until he repented. It was used extensively in the Middle Ages but lost its significance from the 18th cent., partly due to the consequences of emancipation.

exilarch (*Resh galuta*): Lay head of the Babylonian Jewish community. Although rabbinic traditions claim that the office existed in biblical times, clear evidence dates only from the mid-2nd cent. CE. The office was hereditary, and the exilarchs were legendarily descended from David. The e. was officially recognized by the authorities, held an important position at court, and was responsible for the internal government of the community (collecting taxes, appointing judges, and acting as a final appeal). Frequently there was friction between the e. and the GAON. The exilarchate flourished during the first two centuries after the Arab conquest (642) but thereafter declined. The last outstanding holder of the office, Hezekiah, died in 1040, but the office continued in existence at least until the 13th cent. From the 11th cent., a similar office existed in Egypt.

Exile see **Diaspora**

Exile, Assyrian: After the Assyrians completed their conquest of the Kingdom of Israel, they deported many of its inhabitants to Assyria. They were settled mainly in the upper Mesopotamian provinces. There is no certain information about their fate, despite the many legends about the Lost Ten Tribes. It appears that some of the exiles achieved a high economic and social status and most were eventually absorbed into their environment. Some, however, preserved their distinctive character and later merged with the Judean exiles.

Exile, Babylonian: Exiles from Judah deported to Babylonia in the 6th cent. BCE. Not all Jews were exiled to Babylonia; a nucleus remained in Judah during all

that period. Nor did all return, since a permanent Diaspora remained in Babylonia. The outstanding spiritual figure in Babylonia during this period was the prophet EZEKIEL. It was apparently during the B.E. that the institution of the SYNAGOGUE was developed, and this period also saw the beginnings of the prayer book. After CYRUS of Persia conquered Babylonia, he permitted the Jewish (and other) exiles to return to their homes.

Exodus: The departure of the Israelites under Moses from Egypt, as related in the Book of Exodus (but unknown from any other source). Various theories have been propounded as to the date of this event, between the 15th and 13th cent. BCE. The route of E. is also the subject of controversy.

Exodus, Book of: Second book of the Bible and of the Pentateuch. The Hebrew name is *Shemot*. It relates the oppression of the Israelites by the Egyptians, the call to Moses, his negotiations with Pharaoh and the TEN PLAGUES, the Exodus, and the Revelation at Sinai. As part of the Pentateuch, its authorship is traditionally assigned to Moses, but modern scholarship regards it as a compilation from several sources.

Exodus 1947: Ship carrying over 4,500 survivors of Nazi Europe to Palestine in 1947. The British, who at that time opposed Jewish emigration to Palestine, seized the ship, and in the ensuing fight, three of the refugees were killed. The rest were sent back to Germany. The British action was received unfavorably in world public opinion.

Exodus Rabbah see **Midrash Rabbah**

expulsions: Although e. of Jews occurred in antiquity, the phenomenon took on major dimensions only under Christianity. Jews were often given the alternative of baptism or expulsion. The large-scale e. were from England (1290), France (three times in the 14th cent.), much of Germany after the Black Death massacres (1348–50), Spain (1492), and Portugal (1497). There were other frequent e. from similar states and cities. Sometimes Jews were excluded only for a short time, sometimes for centuries.

Ezekiel (6th cent. BCE): Prophet who prophesied in the Babylonian Exile. In the first part of the Book of E., he foretells the imminent fall of Jerusalem; in the second part, he foretells its restoration and the return of the exiles. He described in detail this vision of the rebuilt Temple. His vision of the Divine throne (chap. 1)

became the basis for an entire section of Jewish mysticism (*Maaseh Merkavah*). According to the rabbis, the book was edited by the Men of the GREAT ASSEMBLY; critics are divided on a dating for the book.

Ezion Geber: Place on the Gulf of Akaba which served as port and shipyard during the reign of Solomon. It continued to be used in the period of the Kingdom of Judah. Its remains were identified by Nelson Glueck with those he discovered to the east of Elath, but other locations have been proposed.

Ezra: Priest and scribe who led settlers from the Babylonian exile to Palestine; he was responsible for introducing major reforms into Jewish life. He was a scribe of the Persian administration in Babylonia, and when Jews began to return to Palestine, he led a group, after receiving permission from the Persian king to impose the law of the Torah on the community. He brought back with him the sacred vessels of the Temple. He persuaded the people to observe the Torah and reject intermarriage. The Talmud attributes to him the establishment of the GREAT ASSEMBLY, the final determination of the text of the Pentateuch, and the introduction of the square Hebrew script. The Book of E., (partly in

Aramaic) was originally a unit with the Book of NEHEMIAH. It relates events in the 6th–5th cent. BCE. The relationship between E. and Nehemiah and their respective chronology remain a matter of controversy.

F

able (*mashal*): Short moral story, in which the characters are beasts. The two main biblical examples are found in Judg. 9:8–15 and II Kings 14:9. The Talmud and Midrash are rich sources, and fables are frequent in medieval Hebrew literature in Europe. Modern Hebrew literature also provides many examples.

Factor, Max (1877–1938): US cosmetician. Born in Poland, he lived in the US from 1904. He founded the cosmetics firm that bears his name in 1909.

Faïtlovitch, Jacques (1881–1955): Orientalist, whose special interest was the FALASHAS. Born in Lodz, he lived successively in France, Switzerland, the US, and Palestine. He visited Ethiopia regularly from 1904 and obtained help for the Falashas throughout the Jewish world. He also organized educational activities among the Falashas.

Fajans, Kasimir (1887–): Physical chemist. Born in Warsaw, he taught in Munich and from 1936 in Michigan. He discovered the chemical element 91 (uranium X2 or brevium) and formulated the radioactive displacement law.

Falaquera, Shemtov ben Joseph (c. 1225–1295): Philosopher, poet, and translator living in Spain or southern France. He endeavored to show the harmony of Judaism and Aristotelian philosophy. He wrote a defense of MAIMONIDES' *Guide* against attacks by French rabbis.

Falashas: Ethiopian Jews

living in the Gondar region surrounding and to the north of Lake Tana. Their origin is disputed, but probably they are descended from Ethiopians who converted to Judaism many centuries ago. They live in a number of villages and their economy is mainly based on agriculture; some work in handicrafts, and an increasing number work in the towns. At one time they were apparently powerful, but they were defeated in battle and lost many of their numbers to Christian missionary activity. Their present numbers have been estimated at 25–30,000. Their religion is based on the Bible, which they read in their language of Ge'ez. Their religious leaders are priests, claiming descent from Aaron. Although their existence was known much earlier, the first authentic information on their existence reached the West at the end of the 18th cent. In the 20th cent., great efforts on their behalf were made by Jacques FAITLOVITCH. Some young F. have been educated in Israel under the auspices of the Jewish Agency; they then returned to Ethiopia to be teachers.

Familianten Law: Law limiting the number of Jewish marriages in Bohemia, Moravia, and Silesia. In order to restrict the number of Jews, severe restrictions were imposed and younger sons had to emigrate or remain single. Many Jews had to marry in secret and their children were not recognized as legitimate. The number was determined in 1726, and the law finally abolished in 1859.

fast: The only f. in Mosaic legislation is the Day of Atonement (the instruction "Ye shall afflict your souls" in Lev. 23:27 being interpreted as a call to f.). Other statutory fasts mourn historical events—Tammuz 17 (Shivah Asar be-Tammuz), Av 9, Tishri 3 (F. of Gedaliah), and Tevet 10. Only the Day of Atonement and Av 9 are observed from sunset to sunset; the others are from sunrise to sunset. Fasts instituted later include the F. of Esther and the F. of the Firstborn. Other f. days included that of the bride and groom on their wedding day, fasts on Yahrzeit, and fasts undertaken after a bad dream; some extremely pious Jews f. every Monday and Thursday. F. days falling on Saturdays are postponed (or occasionally held earlier), with the exception of the Day of Atonement. Fasting among Jews involves complete abstention from food and drink. The talmudic tractate *Taanit* is devoted to the subject. *Megillat Taanit* lists dates on which fasting is forbidden because they constitute the anniversary of miraculous or joyous events.

Fast, Howard (1914–): US author. At one time an active Communist, he related his break with Communism in *The Naked God*. His historical novels include *Citizen Tom Paine*, *My Glorious Brothers* (based on the story of the Maccabees), and *The Immigrants*. He also wrote a history of the Jews.

Fefer, Itzik (1900–1952): USSR Yiddish poet. Most of his poems praise the Soviet regime. Together with S. MIKHOELS he visited Western Jewish communities during World War II on behalf of the Jewish Anti-Fascist Committee. He was murdered, along with other leading Russian Yiddish writers, during the last days of Stalin.

Feierberg see **Feuerberg**

Feinberg, Avshalom (1889–1917): NILI leader in Palestine during World War I. He was killed by Bedouin in Sinai while en route to Egypt. His remains were discovered after the 1967 Six-Day War.

Feiwel, Berthold (1875–1937): Zionist leader. He worked closely with HERZL in organizing the first Zionist Congress. In 1901 he was a key figure in the DEMOCRATIC FRACTION. After World War I he moved from the Continent to London, where he directed Keren Hayesod (1920–26). From 1933, he lived in Palestine.

Felsenthal, Bernard (1822–1908): US Reform rabbi, serving in Chicago from 1861. He belonged to the moderate Reform circles and supported Zionism.

Ferber, Edna (1887–1968): US writer. Her novels include *So Big, Giant, Show Boat,* and *Cimarron,* several of which were dramatized. Her popular plays include *Dinner at Eight* and *Stage Door*.

Ferrara: Northern Italian city. Jews lived there from the late 13th cent. It became an outstanding community and an important cultural center. A Hebrew printing press was in operation there from 1477. Many Spanish and Portuguese refugees settled there in the late 15th cent. and Jews from Central Europe from 1532. When F. came under papal rule at the end of the 16th cent., a ghetto was introduced, and the Talmud was burned there in 1553. Full emancipation came with annexation to the kingdom of Italy in 1859–60. The community suffered severely during World War II; 150 Jews lived there in 1970.

*Ferrer Vicente (c. 1350–1419): Spanish Dominican friar. His preaching to Jews who were compelled to listen to him in synagogues led to many conversions.

festivals: Five are mentioned in the Bible—the three Pilgrim F. (Passover, Weeks, and Tabernacles), "the day of blowing the *shophar*" (cf. Rosh ha-Shanah), and the Day of Atonement. The first three were harvest and historical f., the last two purely religious occasions. Shemini Atzeret, at the end of Tabernacles, is, in some views, a separate festival. Originally new moons had a semi-festive character. Rosh ha-Shanah is observed for two days and the Day of Atonement for one. On other occasions (the beginning and end of Passover and Tabernacles, and the Feast of Weeks) one holy day is observed in Israel, two elsewhere. On all these occasions work is forbidden and prohibitions similar to those of the Sabbath (but in some cases somewhat less stringent) are enforced. Outside Israel the ninth day of Tabernacles is observed as the Rejoicing of the Law (Simhat Torah), but in Israel this coincides with Shemini Atzeret. The observance of the second days of f. has been abolished by Reform Jews and is not insisted upon by the Conservatives. F. are marked by liturgical changes, including the recitation of Hallel and Musaph. These are also recited during the Intermediate Days of Passover and Tabernacles (Hol ha-Moed),

when, however, work is permitted. Post-biblical f. (notably Hanukkah and Purim) involve certain liturgical additions and home observances, but they are regular working days.

*Fettmilch, Vincent (d. 1616): German anti-Semitic agitator. In 1614 he incited the population which seized control of Frankfort-on-Main and expelled its Jews. Eventually he was arrested and executed.

Feuchtwanger, Lion (1884–1958): Historical novelist and playwright. He had to leave his native Germany in 1933, moving first to France and in 1940 escaping to the US. His historical novels include a trilogy about Josephus, *Jew Süss,* and *The Ugly Duchess.*

Feuerberg, Mordecai Zeev (1874–1899): Russian Hebrew author. His outstanding novel, *Le'an,* depicting the problem of Diaspora youth in modern times, had a great impact.

Feyman, Richard Phillips (1918–): US physicist; from 1950, professor at the California Institute of Technology. In 1965 he won the Nobel Prize for Physics for work in quantum electrodynamics.

Fez: Town in Morocco. Jews lived there from the 9th cent. For some time F. was one of the leading intellectual centers of the Jewish world, with many outstanding scholars, including Isaac ALFASI. From the 11th to the 16th cent. there were periods of persecution. Refugees from Spain settled in F. in the late 14th and 15th cent. The position of the Jews improved under French rule in the 20th cent., but most of the community left F. in the 1950s and 1960s. Some 22,000 Jews lived there in 1947; only about 1,000 remained in 1970.

Fichman, Yaakov (1881–1958): Poet and essayist. Of Bessarabian origin, his early career was largely spent in Warsaw and Odessa. He lived in Palestine from 1919. He edited a literary journal, wrote critical works (on Bialik and others), and edited textbooks, anthologies, and other works.

Fiedler, Leslie Aaron (1917–): US literary critic. He has taught English at various American universities and writes novels and poems as well as sharp critical works, applying Freudian and Jungian concepts to American literature.

Filene: Boston family of merchants. *Edward Albert F.* (1860–1937) was a pioneer of the US consumer-cooperative movement. Together with his brother, A. *Lincoln F.* (1865–1927), he founded one of Boston's best-known department stores.

final solution: Nazi term for the extermination of the Jews. The order for the complete extermination of European Jewry was given by Hitler in March 1941, and the term f.s. was first used two months later. The details were worked out at a conference in Wannsee, Berlin, and implementation was centralized in the hands of Adolf Eichmann.

Fine, Reuben (1914–): US chess master and psychoanalyst. He was US chess champion in 1934 and wrote several books on the subject. He is professor of psychology at City College, New York.

Finkelstein, Louis (1895–): US scholar and educator. He taught Talmud and theology at the JEWISH THEOLOGICAL SEMINARY in New York, of which he became president (1940) and chancellor (1951). He played a role in the development of CONSERVATIVE JUDAISM. His scholarly work has dealt largely with Jewish history, especially in the mishnaic period, with emphasis on social and economic factors.

Finland: Jews have lived there since the first part of the 19th cent. Although under German influence during part of World War II, no anti-Jewish measures were taken. In 1976, 1,320 Jews lived there, most of them in Helsinki.

Firkovich, Abraham (1786–1874): KARAITE leader and scholar in Russia. He traveled widely in search of ancient manuscripts, many of which he acquired. In order to demonstrate the antiquity of Karaite settlement in Russia, he forged or falsified dates. This threw doubt on his scholarly writings, many of which were of considerable importance. His manuscript collections are housed in the Leningrad Public Library.

firstborn: In biblical times, the f. son inherited a double portion from his father's estate (Deut. 21:17). The f. also received the responsibility of caring for the other children. A father cannot by testation deprive his f. of his privilege, although he may circumvent this by dividing his property in his lifetime. The f. may renounce his right. The privilege is not enjoyed by a posthumous child or one born by Caesarean section. In modern Israel, the law recognizes no special privileges for the f.

firstborn, redemption of (*pidyon ha-ben*): According to the Bible, every f. male— of man or beast—belongs to God (Exod. 13:11–16). In the case of humans, the father redeems his f. by paying a priest a ransom of five shekels or its equivalent in goods. The redemption is effected at a ceremony on the 30th day after birth. Since the basis of redemption is exemption from Temple service, the children of priests and LEVITES (or wives of priestly or levitical descent) are exempted. Also exempt are those born as the result of a Caesarean operation or subsequent to a miscarriage. The f. of clean animals had in Temple times to be sacrificed as peace offerings. After the destruction of the Temple, the Orthodox Jews left the f. of such animals to pasture and derived no benefit from them.

first fruits (*bikkurim*): According to the Bible, the f.f. of fields and trees had to be taken to the Temple, and on that occasion Deut. 26:5–10 was recited. The obligation applied only in Temple times and applied solely to produce of the land of Israel. The f.f. were brought between the Feast of Weeks and Ḥanukkah. They had to be of the seven species for which Israel was renowned—wheat, barley, figs, vines, pomegranates, olives, and honey. The legislation is contained in the talmudic tractate *Bikkurim*.

Fischer, Robert (Bobby) (1943–   ): US chess master. He won the world chess championship in 1972 by defeating Boris Spassky but forfeited the title in 1975 when he refused to defend it. F. joined a Christian Sabbatarian sect.

fiscus Judaicus: Tax levied on Jews in the Roman Empire after the destruction of the Second Temple. The proceeds were devoted to the Temple of Jupiter Capitolinus in Rome.

flag: Herzl proposed for the Jewish State a f. with 7 stars representing his proposed 7-hour working day. However, the Zionist Movement took as its f. a Shield of David on a blue and white background, said to have been inspired by the TALLIT. This became the f. of the State of Israel, where a number of other flags have been adopted by the various municipalities as well as the armed forces.

flagellation: Physical punishment administered by flogging. The punishment was administered for transgressing various biblical precepts. The Bible prescribes a maximum of 40 lashes (interpreted by the rabbis as a maximum of 39) for any one offense— one-third on the chest and the others on the back. The number of lashes administered could be reduced by the court passing sentence. Mystics introduced f. as a voluntary penance. The punishment was used by the British in Palestine in the period

of the Mandate but was abolished by the State of Israel.

Flavius Josephus see **Josephus**

Fleg, Edmond (1874– 1963): French author. His work, which includes many plays and poems, was largely based on Jewish themes.

Flexner: US family. *Abraham F.* (1866–1959), educator and scholar, was the first head of the Institute for Advanced Study at Princeton (1930–39). He published studies of American universities, especially concerning medical education. His brother *Bernard F.* (1865– 1945), a lawyer and economist, was active in Zionist work. He was the first president of the Palestine Economic Corporation. A third brother, *Simon F.* (1863– 1946), a medical scientist, isolated the dysentery bacillus and discovered the virus which caused polio. He directed the Rockefeller Institute for Medical Research from 1903 to 1935.

flood: In the time of NOAH God caused the destruction of mankind because of its sinfulness (Gen. 6–9). Only Noah, his family, and specimens of all animals were saved in the ark. After 150 days of flood, the waters subsided and the ark came to rest on Mt. Ararat. God promised never to repeat this punishment, and the RAIN-

BOW was to be a sign of His covenant. The biblical story has striking parallels in the Babylonian Gilgamesh epic, but is unique in presenting its monotheistic concept of history as a moral issue.

Florence: Italian city. The community was established in 1437 when Jews were invited to settle there to open loan banks. The community generally prospered under the Medici. However, under Cosimo I (1537–54), the papal policy of repression was strictly applied. The Jewish BADGE was introduced in 1567 and the ghetto from 1571; the latter was abolished by the French revolutionary armies at the end of the 18th cent. Jewish emancipation was completed in 1860. F. was the seat of the Italian Rabbinical College (1899–1930). During World War II, 230 Jews were deported to their deaths, and the beautiful synagogue was badly damaged. In 1973, 1,400 Jews lived there.

Florida: US state. Jews played a prominent role in public life in Florida already before the Civil War. Jews settled in Jacksonville in the early 1850s, and its first congregation was opened in 1867. Numbers remained small until after World War I, but it was especially after World War II that F. became a major Jewish center with the Miami area in particular attracting many Jews both as permanent residents and as winter visitors. The other large communities are in Jacksonville, Tampa, St. Petersburg, Orlando, Palm Beach, Fort Lauderdale, and Hollywood. 393,815 Jews were living there in 1976.

Folkspartei: Jewish political party in Poland, advocating Jewish national and cultural autonomy. Founded in 1916, it was most active in the 1920s.

food: Jews throughout the world have adopted the dishes of their environment, and many examples of what is called "Jewish f." are not Jewish in origin. However the DIETARY LAWS have often compelled an originality and ingenuity in adapting dishes to Jewish requirements. The two main trends of Jewish cooking are generally referred to as the Ashkenazi and Sephardi. The former originated especially in Eastern Europe and makes considerable use of fats and sugar. The Sephardi cooking is largely influenced by Mediterranean environment and its characteristics include many spices, olive oil, and rice. Special foods are traditionally connected with most of the festivals, and an outstanding feature is the Sabbath loaf (ḥallah).

*Ford, Henry (1863–

1947): US automobile manufacturer, who was responsible for widespread anti-Semitic activities in the 1920s. His dissemination of the Protocols of the "ELDERS OF ZION" libel ceased following a lawsuit. In his later years he retracted his anti-Semitism.

Fortas, Abraham (1910–): US lawyer. He was undersecretary of the interior from 1942 to 1946. In 1965 he was appointed to the Supreme Court, of which he was nominated chief justice in 1968, but the nomination was dropped under Republican pressure. The following year he resigned from the Court under threat of impeachment.

Forverts ("Jewish Daily Forward"): New York City's daily newspaper in Yiddish. The last large-scale Yiddish paper in the US, it has appeared since 1897. It presented the views of the Jewish labor movement, and its best-known editor was Abraham CAHAN.

four species (*arbaah minim*): Four plants taken during the Festival of Tabernacles—the palm (*lulav*), myrtle, willow, and the ETROG. After a special benediction recited during *Hallel* on each day of the festival, the f.s. are waved in each direction and their owners carry them as they make a circuit around the synagogue.

France: Individual Jews lived in F. from the 1st cent. In the third cent., they were to be found in Marseilles and other trading centers. They spread considerably, and were well integrated into the economy, including agriculture. They flourished initially, but in the course of time their position deteriorated under the influence of the Church. From the time of Charlemagne they were to be found throughout F., many of them as merchants, concentrating much of the trade in their hands both internally and internationally (RADANITES). By the 11th cent. F. was a major Jewish intellectual center, reaching its zenith with RASHI and the TOSAFISTS, and with scholars in Provence. When the Jews were excluded from trade, they were driven into moneylending. There were persecutions in the 11th cent. and in the First Crusade (1096). Jews were attacked in Rouen and Lorraine, and 31 Jews were burned at the stake in Blois following a blood libel (1171). The Talmud was burned after the DISPUTATION of Paris (1240). The 14th cent. saw a series of expulsions, the first in 1306 and the final one in 1394. Jews remained only in Provence (where royal authority was weak) and the papal dominions in Comtat Venaisson. In the 16th cent., Marranos escaping from the Iberian Peninsula settled in western F., and when Alsace-Lorraine passed under French rule Jews were living there. The French Revolution brought emancipation. The Jewish communities were organized by NAPOLEON into consistories after he had convened an ASSEMBLY OF NOTABLES in 1806 and a SANHEDRIN the following year. In the 19th cent. French Jewry was prominent in activities on behalf of Jews elsewhere (ALLIANCE ISRAÉLITE UNIVERSELLE). The end of the cent. saw the DREYFUS AFFAIR and its manifestations of anti-Semitism among various factions in the country. The Jews suffered severely during World War II, and 83,000 were deported to their deaths by the Germans, often with the assistance of the Vichy government. The French Jewish population received two main infusions in the 20th cent.—from Eastern Europe (1880 onward) and from North Africa (in the 1950s and early 1960s). By 1976 there were 550,000 Jews in F. Close French-Israeli cooperation, inaugurated prior to the 1956 Sinai Campaign, was terminated by De Gaulle shortly before the 1967 Six-Day War.

Franck, James (1882–1964): Physicist; born in Germany, he lived in the US from 1935. He shared the 1925 Nobel Physics Prize for his discovery of laws governing the effect of the impact of electrons on the atom.

Frank, Anne (1929–1945): German-born girl whose posthumously discovered diary of her teenage experiences while in hiding from the Nazis in Amsterdam achieved worldwide renown. The group in hiding was eventually discovered and deported. A.F. died in the Bergen-Belsen concentration camp. The house where she hid was turned into a museum after the war.

Frank, Jacob (1726–1791): Pseudo-messiah and founder of the Frankist sect, which emerged in Podolia, and was the last stage in the development of Sabbetaism. He taught antinomian doctrines and advocated a rapprochement with the Catholic Church (similar to that with Islam adopted by SHABBETAI TZEVI); his mystical festivities were alleged to have been marked by sexual orgies. He repudiated the Talmud and accepted the Trinity. After various disputation with the rabbis, he had himself baptized in Warsaw Cathedral (with Emperor Augustus III as his godfather). As his followers still regarded him as the Messiah, the church authorities isolated him in the seclusion of a monastery for 13 years. He lived his latter years in Offenbach (Germany), which became the center of the sect. After his death, his place was taken by his daughter Eve (the "high priestess" of the group). Eventually the Frankists were absorbed into Polish society, many being prominent in the nobility.

Frankel, Zacharias (1801–1875): Rabbinical scholar and theologian. After serving as chief rabbi of Dresden, he became head of the Breslau Rabbinical Seminary in 1854. He combined traditional Judaism with European scholarship, and while he opposed religious reforms, he advocated liturgical changes and modernized Jewish education. He was a leader of the movement for "Historical Positive Judaism," out of which CONSERVATIVE JUDAISM developed. His best-known work was *Darkhe ha-Mishnah*, on the Mishnah.

Frankfort, Henri (1897–1954): Historian and archeologist. He taught in his native Amsterdam until 1938, when he went to the Oriental Institute of the Univ. of Chicago. He participated in excavations in Egypt and Mesopotamia and wrote cultural histories of the Ancient Near East.

Frankfort-on-Main: German city. Jews were living there in the latter 11th cent. In 1462 they were confined to one street (the Judengasse). Inside the town the Jews were restricted to hawking and peddling. The FETTMILCH Riots in 1614 led to a short-lived expulsion. The Jewish quarter was destroyed by a fire in 1711. Emancipation was attained during the 19th cent. The success of the Reform movement led to the formation of a separate Orthodox community under Samson Raphael HIRSCH. F. Jews—notably the ROTHSCHILDS—were prominent in the city's economic life. It was the home of many distinguished rabbis and scholars and was also a center of Hebrew printing. 26,000 Jews were living there in 1933, but few were left by 1942. A new community was organized there after World War II and numbered 4,950 in 1973.

Frankfort-on-Oder: E. German city. Jews lived there from the late 13th cent. There were expulsions in 1510 and 1573. F. was a center of Hebrew printing. Some 800 Jews lived there before the Nazi period. A community was refounded there after World War II but declined in the 1960s.

Frankfurter, Felix (1882–1965): US lawyer. Born in Vienna, he was taken to the US at age 12. He was professor of administrative law at Harvard (1914–39) and was then appointed associate justice of the Supreme Court (1939–62), in which he became the leading representative of the liberal tradition, upholding civil liberties in particular. Until 1921 he worked with BRANDEIS in the leadership of the Zionist Organization, and in 1919 was legal adviser to the Zionist delegation at the Paris Peace Conference. In 1965 he was awarded the Presidential Medal of Freedom.

fraternal societies: Organizations for mutual aid. The modern type of f.s. was known among Jews in England in the late 18th cent. but developed most strongly in the US in the 19th and 20th cent. Initially they mostly brought together immigrants from the same places of origin (*Landsmannschaften*) and provided insurance and burial benefits. The oldest and largest is B'NAI B'RITH (founded 1843). Others in the US include Free Sons of Israel (1849), B'rith Abraham (1887), Workmen's Circle (1900), B'nai Zion (1910), and Fārband (1913).

free will offering (*nadavah*): Sacrifice offered voluntarily. It could be a burnt offering or a peace offering (Lev. 22:18, 21).

Freiman: Canadian family of Zionist leaders including *Archibald Jacob F.* (1880–1944), national president of the Zionist Organization of Canada, 1920–44, and his wife *Lillian F.* (1885–1940), president of Canadian Hadassah, 1919–40.

Freimann: Family of scholars. *Abraham Ḥayyim (Alfred) F.* (1889–1948), jurist, was born in Moravia, taught at the Hebrew University, Jerusalem, and was killed by Arabs in the Mount Scopus convoy. *Aron F.* (1871–1948), historian and bibliographer, was librarian in Frankfort until 1933, when he moved to New York, where he was consultant to the New York Public Library.

Freud, Sigmund (1856–1939): Austrian originator of psychoanalysis. He treated hysteria by methods of hypnosis, subsequently replacing this with free association and other psychoanalytic techniques. He spent most of his life in Vienna but lived in London after the 1938 Anschluss. F. saw some of the opposition which he encountered as motivated by anti-Semitism. He was identified with various Jewish activities, and almost all his disciples were Jewish. His *Moses and Monotheism* presented a psychoanalytical approach to the Bible story and concluded that Moses was an Egyptian. His daughter *Anna F.* (1895–) is a noted child psychologist in London.

Fried, Alfred Hermann

(1864–1921): Austrian pacifist. A bookseller and publisher by profession, he founded the German and Austrian peace societies. In 1911 he was awarded the Nobel Peace Prize. Accused of treason, he had to spend World War I in Switzerland.

Friedan, Betty Naomi (1921–   ): US feminist. Her book *The Feminine Mystique* attacked the concept that women could find fulfillment only in the roles of wives and mothers. She founded the National Organization for Women in 1970.

Friedberg, Abraham Shalom (1838–1902): Hebrew writer. He worked for the Warsaw Hebrew paper *Ha-Tzephirah* and on other literary projects. He wrote and translated many books, his best-known composition being *Zikhronot le-Vet David*, a popular series of Jewish historical stories.

Friedenwald: Baltimore family of physicians and public workers. *Aaron F.* (1836–1902), ophthalmologist, was among the founders of the Jewish Theological Seminary and other institutions. His sons included *Harry F.* (1864–1950), also an ophthalmologist, Zionist, and author of studies on the history of Jewish medicine.

Friedlaender, Israel (1876–1920): US historian and orientalist. Born and educated in Europe, he was professor of biblical literature at the Jewish Theological Seminary in New York. He wrote on Islamic sects, Judeo-Arabic literature, and many other subjects. In 1920 he was sent to the Ukraine, with Rabbi Bernard Cantor, on a relief mission on behalf of the Joint Distribution Committee, and both were murdered by brigands.

Friedlander, David (1750–1834): German communal leader who was prominent in the fight for equal rights for Prussian Jewry. After the death of his close friend Moses MENDELSSOHN, F. was the outstanding figure in the German Jewish Enlightenment Movement. He was a founder of the Jewish Free School in Berlin, and in 1809 became the first Jew to be elected to the Berlin City Council. He fought for political assimilation, made proposals for radical reform, and even expressed his readiness to join the Protestant Church if not required to accept all the dogmas of Christianity.

Friedman, Milton (1912–   ): US economist; professor at the University of Chicago from 1947. He criticized the theories of Keynes and advocated a simplified taxation system. In 1976 he was awarded the Nobel Prize.

Frischmann, David (1859–1922): Hebrew writer.

He edited various Hebrew periodicals in St. Petersburg and Warsaw and wrote a wide variety of works, including short stories, satires, essays, poems, and literary criticism. He also translated classics (including Nietzsche and Tagore) into Hebrew. One of his best-known works was *Ba-Midbar*, a series of biblical stories. F. also wrote in Yiddish.

Frohman: Two brothers —*Charles F.* (1860–1915) and *Daniel F.* (1851–1940) —who were noted New York theatrical managers. Charles, who dominated the New York stage, was drowned on the *Lusitania*.

Fromm, Erich (1900–): Psychoanalyst and phi-losopher. Born in Germany, he went to the US in 1934. His works (*The Art of Loving, Be Ye Like Gods*) apply psychoanalysis to the problems of contemporary society.

Frug, Simon Samuel (1860–1916): Russian poet. He began by writing Russian poems and was a contributor to leading Russian periodicals. Later he wrote in Yiddish, including satires, stories, and *feuilletons*.

Funk, Casimir (1884– 1967): Chemist who worked in Berlin, London, and New York. He discovered vitamins (and originated the word) and also pioneered in the use of sex hormones in the treatment of certain illnesses.

Gabbai: Treasurer or warden of a synagogue. The term originally meant a "collector" and "tax gatherer," with unfavorable associations. However, the *gabbaei tzedakah* ("charity collectors") were highly regarded.

Gabo, Naum (originally Pevsner; 1890–1977): Sculptor. Born in Russia, he lived in Berlin (1922–32), Paris (1932–36), and England (1936–46), and in the US from 1946. He was a pioneer of Constructivist sculpture and made the earliest example of kinetic art.

Gabor, Dennis (1900–): British physicist. He was a pioneer in the development of the laser beam and was awarded the Nobel Prize in 1971.

Gabriel: Archangel. He and MICHAEL are the only angels named in the Bible (Dan. 8–10). In later literature he is depicted as a leader of the host of heaven.

Gad: (1) Semitic deity of fortune. (2) Israelite tribe descended from G., son of Jacob and Zilpah (Gen. 30: 10–11). The tribe settled in Gilead. When the kingdom divided, it became part of the Northern Kingdom. (3) Prophet at David's court (II Sam. 24) to whom is ascribed a lost book (I Chron. 29:29).

Gadara (Geder): Ancient city in Gilead near the confluence of the Yarmuk and Jordan rivers. Pompey included it in the cities forming the DECAPOLIS. It was noted for its hot springs and was a center of Hellenistic culture.

Gadna (abbr. of *gedude noar*, "youth corps"): Israeli youth movement under government auspices for training 13-to-18-year-olds in defense and national service. Founded in 1939 by the Haganah, it functions in schools and youth clubs.

Gahal (abbr. for "Herut-Liberal bloc"): Israeli party composed of LIBERAL and HERUT parties formed in 1965, receiving 26 seats in the Sixth and Seventh Knesset. It joined with some smaller parties to form the LIKKUD, which obtained 39 mandates in the 1973 elections and 43 in 1977. It participated in the government of national unity (1967–1970); the rest of the time it was the largest opposition party, until 1977, when it was the largest party and its leader Menahem BEGIN became prime minister.

Galicia: Eastern European region, north of Carpathian mountains. Jews lived there from 11th cent. (see POLAND). When G. became part of the Hapsburg Empire in 1772, about 200,000 Jews were living there. The Austrian government tried to "civilize" the Jews, but the reforms did little good and were soon dropped. G. saw many quarrels between HASIDIM and MITNAGGEDIM. It was also a HASKALAH center, leading to further conflicts with the Ḥasidim. In 1860 Jews of G. received the franchise; complete political freedom was obtained with the Austrian constitution of 1867. ḤIBBAT ZION and the Zionist movement attracted many supporters there. For economic reasons many Jews emigrated to the West, especially to the US, before World War I. In 1919, G. was annexed to Poland. After World War II part was in Poland, part in the Ukrainian SSR.

Galilee: Region in northern Israel between the Mediterranean Sea and the Jordan River. In biblical times it was divided among the tribes of Naphtali, Asher, Zebulun, and Issachar. In 732 BCE it became an Assyrian province, but many Jews continued to live there, and it was incorporated into the Hasmonean kingdom in 104 BCE. G. joined the war against Rome in 66 and was one of the first areas taken by Vespasian. After the failure of the BAR KOKHBA revolt (135), G. was the focus of Jewish settlement in Palestine, the seat of the patriarchate and of the talmudic academies (e.g., Tiberias, Sepphoris). Jews remained on the land in G. throughout subsequent history but sometimes in small numbers. From the 16th cent., Safed became an important kabbalistic center. Modern settlement started there in 1882 with the foundation of Rosh Pinnah. In 1948 G. became part of the State of Israel. (See also SEA OF GALILEE.)

Galili, Israel (1911–): Israeli soldier and politician. He was head of the Haganah's land forces and a founder of the Palmah. He was a founder of MAPAM and later a leader of Ahdut Avodah and of the Israel Labor Party. From 1966 to 1977 he was minister without portfolio in the Israeli government.

Galut ("Exile"): The Jewish people outside Israel; the DIASPORA.

Galveston Plan: Project to divert Jewish immigrants to the US away from the East Coast to the interior, with Galveston, Texas, as the port of entry. The plan, initiated by Jacob Schiff and Israel Zangwill, settled 10,-000 Jewish immigrants between 1907 and 1914.

Gamaliel: Name of six Palestinian sages, descendants of Hillel. The best known were *Gamaliel I ben Simeon* (1st cent. CE), a member of the Sanhedrin at the time of Caligula. He introduced important judicial reforms. G. receives favorable mention in the New Testament. *Gamaliel II of Yavneh* (1st-2nd cent. CE) was patriarch (with the title NASI) after the death of Johanan ben Zakkai. He was responsible for many important halakhic decisions based on the need for religious readjustment after the destruction of the Temple. He was also active in combating the early Christian movement. Because of his autocratic methods, he was temporarily deposed from his office. *Gamaliel III* (3rd cent.) succeeded his father Judah ha-Nasi as *nasi*. During his time the Mishnah received its final form.

Gans, David (1541–1613): Astronomer, mathematician, and historian. He lived in Prague from 1564 and was acquainted with Kepler and Tycho Brahe. His *Tzemah David* is a chronicle of Jewish and general history.

gaon (pl. *geonim*): Title for heads of the SURA and PUMBEDITA academies between the 6th and 13th cent.; it was an abbreviation of the description of their position as *resh yeshivat geon Yaakov* ("head of the academy which is the pride of Jacob"). Although the EXILARCHS held temporal power, the role of the g. was considerable. The *geonim* fostered and developed talmudic law, and their influence extended over the entire Jewish world. The best-known g. at Sura was SAADYAH, under whom the academy reached its peak. Toward the end of the 9th cent., both academies moved to Baghdad, although retaining their original names. The Pumbedita academy increased its importance from the mid-9th cent. when its g. Paltoi made contact with the North African community (previously connected only with Sura). The outstanding *geonim* of Pumbedita were SHERIRA and his son HAI. It was long thought that the gaonate ended in the 11th cent., but it is now known that this was not so; the academies were united and headed by a g. until the 13th cent., although in the last cent. their influence was primarily local. A competing gaonate also developed in Palestine toward the end of the 9th cent., and this lasted until the early 12th cent. Many important religious decisions were taken by the *geonim*. Their main activities were the determination of the law in places where the Talmud did not give a clear decision, replying to queries from Jewish communities, and training talmudic experts. The term g. remained in Hebrew usage for an outstanding scholar or genius.

Gaon, Solomon (1912–): Rabbi. Of Yugoslav birth, he was educated in England and was *ḥaham* of the Sephardi community in London 1949–77.

Garden of Eden see **Eden, Garden of**

Gaster, Moses (1856–1939): Rabbi, scholar, and Zionist. He taught Rumanian language and literature at the university of his native Bucharest (1881–85). Expelled from the country for his protests on the treatment of Jews, he went to England, and in 1887 was appointed *ḥaham* of the Sephardi community, serving until 1918. An early Zionist, he helped in the negotiations leading to the Balfour Declaration. His scholarly works covered many fields, from general folklore to studies of Samaritan history and literature.

Gath: One of the five Philistine cities. It was captured by David and its fortunes thereafter fluctuated. Its site is disputed.

Gaza: Chief and most southerly of the five Philistine cities. In the 15th-13th cent. BCE it was a base for Egyptian operations in Canaan. In the 12th cent. it was occupied by the Philistines. From the 8th cent. BCE G. came under various rulers (Assyrians, Persians, Greeks, Syrians) and was rebuilt by the Romans in 57 BCE. Jews lived there throughout the Middle Ages, and its 6th-cent. synagogue has been excavated. In the 17th cent. it was a center of Sabbetaism and home of SHABBETAI TZEVI's "prophet," Nathan of Gaza. The last Jews left following Arab attacks in 1929. In 1948 it became the center of the GAZA STRIP, and its population of 30,000 was considerably swollen by Arab refugees. It came under Israeli control with the Six-Day War of 1967, when its population was 119,000 (including 30,000 in the refugee camp).

Gaza Strip: Strip of land, including the town of GAZA, which remained occupied by the Egyptians after the 1948 war, although inside the traditional boundaries of Palestine. It extended along the southwestern coast of the country for 22 miles, with an average width of 8 miles; its 1967 population was 352,000, of whom 172,000 were Arab refugees. It was frequently the focus of tension. The area came under Israeli control with the Six-Day War.

Gedaliah: Jewish governor of Judah appointed by Nebuchadnezzar after the destruction of Jerusalem in 586 BCE (II Kings 25:22). Shortly thereafter he was assassinated by Ishmael of the royal house, who was apparently part of a plot to overthrow Babylonian rule. G.'s followers fled to Egypt, taking with them the prophet Jeremiah. The anniversary of the murder—Tishri 3—is observed as an annual fast in the Jewish calendar.

Gederah: Israeli MOSHAVAH with municipal-council status in the southern central plain. Founded in 1884 by BILU pioneers from Russia, its economy was originally based on grapes and grain; later, citrus, cotton, and other crops were added. The population in 1971 was 5,200.

Gedud ha-Avodah ("Labor Legion"): National organization of Jewish laborers in Palestine which became a large collective undertaking work, such as roadbuilding. Its members began to settle the eastern part of the Jezreel Valley, and others worked in building in Jerusalem. Founded in 1920, it split into groups and disintegrated. Over 2,000 pioneers belonged to its ranks.

Gehinnom: Valley south of Jerusalem. During the period of the Monarchy, children were sacrificed there to the god Moloch at a place called Topheth, and consequently G. became the name for hell.

Geiger, Abraham (1810–1874): German theologian and religious reformer. In 1837 he convened the first meeting of Reform rabbis. He was rabbi in Wiesbaden, Breslau, Frankfort, and finally in Berlin, where he helped to establish the Hochschule für die Wissenschaft des Judentums, which he directed until his death. He regarded Orthodoxy as petrified and stressed the "mission" element in Judaism, seeking to eliminate national aspects. His researches ranged over almost every sphere of Jewish studies.

Gell-Mann, Murray (1929–): US physicist. For his discoveries concerning the classification of elementary particles, he was awarded the 1969 Nobel Physics Prize.

gematria: Hermeneutic method of discovering hidden meaning of Hebrew texts by calculating the numerical value of each word (where every letter has such a value) and determining other words or phrases of equal value. This was first used by the *tannaim* in the 2nd cent. and is frequently found in *midrashim* and kabbalistic writings.

gemilut ḥesed ("bestowal of kindness"): Any act of kindness or benevolence. Personal kindness is among the most praiseworthy of human qualities and is also considered an attribute of God. The term came to be applied to the act of lending money to a needy person free of interest, and *g.ḥ.* societies were established with this object.

General Zionists: Zionist party. It emerged early in the 20th cent. in contrast to the socialist and religious trends. It incorporated two groups—one aimed at an overall approach above parties, the other at the formation of a center party. There were a number of splits in the G.Z. groups in both the Diaspora and Israel. Inside Israel, the two main groups were called the G.Z. or Liberals (which united with the Ḥerut Party to form Gaḥal and later the Likkud) and the Progressive and Independent Liberal Party. The World Confederation of G.Z. divided in two in 1963.

Genesis (*Bereshit*): First book of the Pentateuch. It contains an account of Creation and the beginning of mankind, the story of Noah and the Flood, and the lives of the three patriarchs (Abraham, Isaac, Jacob) and of Joseph. Although parallels have been found between its early chapters and the sacred literature of the Mesopotamian peoples, the monotheistic approach is unique, as is the ethical teaching. God, the sole Deity, has laid down a moral code and man is judged according to his adherence to that code. God has also made a covenant with Abraham and his descendants to be their God, and they will be His people;

He also promises them the Land of Canaan as their home. Critics regard this book, as the rest of the Pentateuch, as being of composite authorship, but they are divided as to the likely date of redaction. Traditionally its author was Moses.

Genesis Rabbah see **Midrash Rabbah**

genizah ("storing"): Storage place for worn-out and heretical Hebrew books. In the Middle Ages, most synagogues designated a room as a g. for old and imperfect books. The famous g. is that discovered at the end of the 19th cent. in the external storeroom of the synagogue at Fostat, Cairo. Its value was fully recognized by Solomon SCHECHTER, who took some 100,000 pages of medieval documents and manuscripts to the library at Cambridge; others reached elsewhere in the world. This g. has proved a most fruitful source of material for scholars in many fields of medieval Jewish studies. Finds include part of the lost version of Ecclesiasticus, extracts from Aquila's Greek translation of the Bible, the "Zadokite Documents" (related to the subsequently discovered Dead Sea Scrolls), commercial documents throwing light on Jewish economic life, and medieval poems and liturgies.

genocide: The liquidation of a people. It was defined in the UN as a coordinated set of acts intended to destroy a nation, ethnic, racial, or religious group. Influenced primarily by horror at the fate of the Jews in Nazi Germany, the UN in 1948 adopted a convention declaring g. a crime against modern international law.

gentile (*nokhri* or *goy*): A non-Jew. The child of a Jewish mother or a person converted to Judaism is Jewish; all others are gentiles. A marriage between a Jew and a g. is not valid under Jewish law. The g. is obliged to observe the seven commandments given to Noah, and "the pious of all nations have a share in the world to come." In the late Second Temple times, when relations between Jew and non-Jew were very strained, the rabbis enacted several decrees to minimize contact between Jew and non-Jew. To avoid the trend toward assimilation, rabbis often set up barriers to limit social contacts with non-Jews. Modern developments have led to a closer contact with non-Jews. This has led both to greater assimilation and to the development of greater understanding and interfaith activities.

Georgia: Soviet Socialist Republic in the Caucasus. Jews lived there from an early date and are mentioned in the Talmud. In the 12th cent. they were noted for their devotion to Rabbanite Judaism. From the 15th cent. onward, they underwent persecution. They received equal rights in 1918. About 30,000 Jews were living there before World War II but their numbers reached 80,000 by the 1960s, largely as a result of the influx of newcomers during World War II. The native Georgian Jews maintained their religious observances and were prominent among those who left Russia for Israel in the 1970s.

Georgia: US state. Jews first settled in Savannah in the year of its foundation, 1733. The number of Jews grew after the 1750s and by the 1850s there were congregations in Augusta, Columbus, and Macon. Many Jews were prominent in public office, and the first Jewish governor of any US state was David Emmanuel, who was governor of G. in 1801. There are 12 Jewish communities in G., the largest ones in Atlanta (21,000), Savannah (3,000), Augusta (1,500), and Columbus. In 1976 there were 30,695 Jews in Georgia.

Gerizim: Mountain (height 2,600 ft.) facing Mt. Ebal (2,800 ft.); in between stands the town of SHECHEM (Nablus). G. is the Holy Mountain of the SAMARITANS, on which they built their temple in antiquity. It remains their religious center and the site of their annual paschal sacrifice.

Germany: Jews were living in Cologne in the 4th cent. CE. The main settlement developed in the Rhineland, which also became an intellectual center. The massacres perpetrated by the Crusaders in 1096 was a turning point, and thereafter the Jews in G. frequently came under attack and persecution. They were also often subject to expulsion, but the fact that G. was fragmented meant that when they were expelled from one state, they could find refuge in another. Major persecutions were the Rindfleisch massacres (1298), the Armleder massacres (1336–37), and the widespread attacks and expulsions at the time of the BLACK DEATH (1348–50) in which 300 communities were wiped out. Despite the many vicissitudes, G. remained a center of Jewish scholarship and thought. After a couple of centuries during which the number of Jews dwindled, the position of Jews improved in the 17th cent., when many Jews were in positions of influence (e.g., COURT JEWS). Moses MENDELSSOHN inaugurated the period of EMANCIPATION, and Jews were now to be found in most aspects of secular life in G. The HEP! HEP! riots of 1819 had no permanent effect on the increasing momentum to grant Jews full civil rights. Jews entered German society with enthusiasm, frequently being completely assimilated and converted. Religious modernization trends led to the foundation of the REFORM movement. The application of general scholastic disciplines to Jewish studies brought about the WISSENSCHAFT DES JUDENTUMS. Jews became prominent in many spheres. At the same time, ANTI-SEMITISM in its modern form—hatred of the Jews as a "race"—had its focus in G. This intensified after the German defeat in World War I and the accusation that the Jews had "stabbed G. in the back." The resulting anti-Jewish feeling did much to sweep Adolf HITLER and his Nazi Party to power in 1933. He immediately inaugurated a vicious anti-Jewish policy, which by degrees reached the extreme horror of the HOLOCAUST of World War II. Many German Jews escaped to other countries in the 1933–39 period, but over 200,000 were still there at the outbreak of war. 160–180,000 of them were killed during the war years. After the war the number of survivors was augmented by Eastern European Jews who settled in Germany. In 1976, 32,000 Jews lived in West G., 1,500 in East G. Despite the impact of the Holocaust, relations between West G. and Israel improved following the granting of reparations and restitution in 1952. Eventually (in 1965), diplomatic relations were established between the two countries. East G., however, continued to maintain a hostile attitude.

Gerondi: Name of various scholars whose families came from Gerona in Spain. They included *Jonah ben Abraham G.* (1180–1263), who headed the rabbinic academy in Toledo. His novellae on talmudic tractates were widely used. *Nissim ben Reuben G.* (Ran; d.c. 1380), rabbinical authority and author of commentaries on talmudic tractates and responsa, was prominent in the Barcelona community. *Zerahiah ben Isaac G.* (12th cent.), who lived in Lunel, was a noted talmudist and liturgical poet.

Gershom ben Judah (c. 960–1028): Talmudic scholar, known as Meor ha-Golah, "Light of the Diaspora." He headed a rabbinical academy at Mainz, where he laid the foundation of Ashkenazi scholarship. He determined correct readings of the *Masorah* and of the Talmud. Only segments of his Talmud commentary have been preserved. His son was forcibly baptized. He was the author of legal regulations, accepted as binding by Ashkenazim, and many such *takkanot* were issued by or ascribed to him, the best known being a ban on polygamy.

Gershwin, George (1898–1937): US composer. He wrote musical comedies and film scores as well as symphonic jazz (*Rhapsody in Blue*), orchestra music (Piano Concerto in F), and the opera *Porgy and Bess*. Many of his songs have retained their popularity and are regarded as classics of their kind.

Gersonides see **Levi ben Gershom**

Gerusia: Council of 71 elders which assisted the high priest; probably the forerunner of the SANHEDRIN.

*****Gesenius, Wilhelm** (1786–1842): German theologian and Hebraist. His Hebrew grammar and lexicon became standard works.

Gestapo: Nazi secret police. They were involved in the persecution of Jews from the outset of the Nazi regime. They headed the *Einsatzgruppen*, which carried out the physical killing of the Jews in Eastern Europe in the first years of the war, and played a central role in the dispatch of Jews to the gas chambers.

get see **divorce**

Gezer: Ancient Palestinian city. Joshua defeated the king of G., but the town was held by the Israelites only for short periods in biblical times. It has been extensively excavated on various occasions in the 20th cent., and a Hasmonean palace was discovered there. The best-known find is a Hebrew inscription from the 10th cent. BCE, giving a list of agricultural seasons (the "Gezer Calendar").

ghetto: Section of a town designated as compulsory living area for Jews. The name may derive from the foundry or *ghetto* in Venice, where Jews were segregated in 1516. Jewish quarters had, in fact, been in existence already for some centuries (e.g., the *juderia* in Spain, the *Judengasse* in Germany). In 1555, the Jews in the Papal States were ordered into separate quarters. On the one hand, the g. enabled the complete observance of Jewish religious life and moral codes, and it preserved Jewish culture and communal life. On the other, it was overcrowded and made the Jews ready targets for attack. In North Africa, the widespread ghettos were called *mellah* and existed until the dissolution of these Jewish communities. European ghettos came to an end by the 19th cent. (in the sense of compulsory isolation and not a voluntary Jewish neighborhood). During World War II, the Nazis reintroduced the concept of the g. when they concentrated Jews in restricted sections of specific towns. The Jews were then subject to terrible privations, many dying of disease and hunger. From the ghettos they were removed to be shot or sent to the death camps. In some ghettos (notably the biggest one, in Warsaw) desperate revolts were organized.

Gibeon: Ancient levitical city north of Jerusalem. It was the scene of David's victory over the Philistines (II Sam. 2:12 ff). In the time of Solomon it was the site of a high place. Its pool, the scene of a fight between the followers of David and of Ishbosheth (II Sam. 8), has been excavated.

Gibraltar: Jews came there from Morocco after 1729 and increased in number after the siege of 1779–83. The Jews have played an important role in commerce there; at one time they numbered 2,000 and controlled most of the retail trade, but by 1976 this was down to 625. The first incumbent of the office of chief minister (1964–69, 1972–   ) was a Jew, Sir Joshua HASSAN.

Gideon (Jerubaal) (12th cent. BCE): Judge who delivered Israel from the Midianites (Judg. 6–8). He refused an offer to become king of Israel, maintaining that only God was Israel's king.

Gihon: (1) One of the four rivers of the Garden of Eden (Gen. 2:10–13). (2) Spring in the Kidron Valley which was the main source of water for ancient Jerusalem. Hezekiah made a tunnel to connect the waters of G. with the pool of SILOAM.

Gilboa: Mountain ridge bordering the Valley of Jezreel. Its highest point is 1,709 feet above sea level, and it is 10½ miles long. The best-known biblical event associated with G. was the victory of the Philistines over the Israelites, when SAUL and three of his sons, including Jonathan, were killed.

Gilead: Central region east of the Jordan, south of the river Yarmuk, and north of the river Arnon. It was settled in the south by the tribes of Reuben and Gad, and in the north by half the tribe of Manasseh. When the kingdom split, G. belonged to the northern kingdom of Israel, and its inhabitants were sent into exile when the Assyrians conquered the area in 733 BCE.

Gilels, Emil Grigoryevich (1916–   ): Russian pianist. He won the Stalin and Lenin Prizes and acquired an international reputation.

Gimbel: US merchant family. *Adam G.* (1817–1896) went to the US from Germany in 1835. He founded a dry-goods store in Vincennes, Indiana, and his descendants developed this into a chain, including one of the biggest and best-known department stores in New York.

gimmel (ג): Third letter of the Hebrew alphabet. Numerical value: 3. It is pronounced like a hard *g*. When written without a *dagesh*, some communities pronounce it like the French *r*.

Ginsberg, Allen (1926–   ): US poet. One of the best-known figures of the "beat" generation of the 1950s. His poems include *Howl* and *Kaddish*.

Ginsberg, Asher see **Ahad ha-Am**

Ginsburg, Christian David (1831–1914): Biblical scholar. Born in Warsaw, he converted to Christianity in 1846. Later he settled in England, where he pursued research in the masoretic text and published two standard editions of the Hebrew Bible based on manuscript texts. He also wrote on the Kabbalah, the Karaites, and the Essenes.

Ginzberg, Louis (1873–1953): Rabbinic scholar. Born in Lithuania, he settled in New York in 1899. Many of his contributions to the *Jewish Encyclopedia* remain standard statements. From 1902 he taught Talmud at the Jewish Theological Seminary. His writings cover a vast range of subjects and his erudition was remarkable. Among his outstanding studies were *The Legends of the Jews* (7 vols.) and his work on the Palestinian Talmud and on the gaonic period. His son *Eli G.* (1911–   ), economist and social planner, was appointed professor at Columbia University in 1955.

Gittin: ("Divorces"): Fifth tractate in the MISHNAH order of *Nashim*, with *gemara* in both Talmuds. It deals with the laws of divorce.

Givat Brenner: Communal settlement (affiliated with Ha-Kibbutz ha-Meuhad) in central Israel. Founded in 1928, it became the country's largest kibbutz, with a population of 1,572 (1972).

Givatayim: Township in central Israel with a population of 41,900 in 1974.

Glanz, Leib (1898–1964): Cantor. Born in Russia, he emigrated to the US in 1926 and in 1954 settled in Tel Aviv. He pursued research into cantoral music and also composed.

Glaser, Donald A. (1926–): US physicist; professor at the University of California, Berkeley. He won the 1960 Nobel Prize for work on the development of the bubble chamber to photograph the atom.

Glasgow: City in Scotland. The first Jewish community dates from 1830 and the oldest synagogue from 1858, but the Jewish community remained small until the 1880s, when many Jews arrived from Russia. The 1976 Jewish population was 13,-400, with 10 synagogues.

Glatstein, Jacob (1896–1971): Yiddish writer. Born in Lublin, he lived in the US from 1914. He was among the founders of the *Insikh* introspectivist tendency in Yiddish poetry in the US. He was also a critic and columnist for the Yiddish newspaper *The Day–Morning Journal*.

Glicenstein, Enrico (1870–1942): Sculptor, painter, and printmaker. Born in Poland, he lived in Italy (twice winning the Prix de Rome) and from 1928 in the US. He was a keen Zionist, and a museum in Safed was named for him posthumously.

Glückel of Hamelin (1645–1724): Yiddish memoir writer. Living in Hamburg, she wrote her memoirs in Yiddish after her husband's death in 1689. They are an important source of information about 17th-cent. Jewish life, and have been translated into various languages.

Gluckman, Henry (1893–): South African public official. A physician by profession, he was elected to Parliament in 1938, and served as minister of health in the Smuts government, 1945–48, the only Jew to serve in a South African cabinet.

Glueck, Nelson (1900–1971): US archeologist. He directed the American School of Oriental Research at Jerusalem (1932–33, 1936–40, 1942–47) and at Baghdad (1933–34). He carried out a survey of archeological sites in Transjordan and in the Negev. From 1947 he was president of Hebrew Union College in Cincinnati (from 1950 of the merged H.U.C.–Jewish Institute of Religion), of which he himself was a graduate rabbi. He wrote studies of Transjordan, the Negev, and the Nabateans, among others.

Gnesin, Michael Fabianovich (1883–1957): USSR

composer. In 1913 he was a founder of the Society of Jewish Folk Music and devoted considerable attention to Jewish folklore. In 1935 he was appointed professor at Leningrad Conservatory.

Gnessin, Uri Nisan (1881–1913): Hebrew author. He was born in Russia but led a wandering life. He was one of the first Hebrew writers whose subject matter was rootlessness and alienation.

God: The existence of G. is presupposed in the Bible from its outset, and no proof is attempted. Similarly the uniqueness of G. is taken as axiomatic (MONOTHEISM). Moreover, unlike other early civilizations, the concept of G. has no mythological quality. G. is incorporeal and completely spiritual. All depends on Him and He on nothing. He is the Creator of the Universe, the Judge and ruler of history. He has a special relationship with Israel, which has accepted the challenge of being G.'s people. To Israel, G. has revealed His Torah. However, G. rules over all nations, and His message is universal. After the Bible, philosophical concepts influenced the Jewish concept of G. The rabbis often used anthropomorphic descriptions to bring G. close to the people—they depicted His weeping, rejoicing, and praying—but these were never meant to be taken literally. They were meant to encourage the "imitation of God." Medieval philosophers in some cases sought proofs for the existence of G.; they were concerned with His attributes. MAIMONIDES stressed Divine transcendence, while JUDAH HALEVI emphasized the role of G. in history. Whereas medieval philosophy sought to reconcile revelation and reason, more recent thought has often queried revelation. SPINOZA propounded a doctrine of pantheism. Later influences on Jewish concepts of G. included Kant and existentialism. With few exceptions, the "death of God" school had little impact on Jewish thinkers. Generally speaking, the Jews have been a "God-intoxicated" people, keenly conscious of the traditional special relationship. The essence of Judaism, and the last expression of the dying and of Jewish martyrs throughout the ages, was the SHEMA—the key phrase of the Jewish religion—"The Lord Our God Is One."

God, names of: Biblical names include *El* (occurs in all Semitic languages); *Eloah*, and, more usually, *Elohim*; *YHVH* (the Tetragrammaton, whose original pronunciation was unknown, but scholars have suggested

Yahweh—to avoid pronouncing it, *Adonai* was substituted, and later *Ha-Shem* or *Adoshem* were used); *Yah*, probably an abbreviation for *YHVH; Shaddai* ("Almighty"); and more poetical names. Bible criticism discerns two different biblical traditions in the Pentateuch —one using YHVH, the other *Elohim*. The rabbis said that *YHVH* was used when referring to the Divine attribute of mercy and *Elohim* of justice. Rabbinical names for God included *Ha-Makom* ("The Place"), *Ribono shel Olam* ("Lord of thc Universe"), *Ha-Kadosh Barukh Hu* ("The Holy One blessed be He"), and the *Shekhinah* ("Divine Presence"). Kabbalists added other terms (e.g., *Ein Soph*, "The Infinite"), and medieval poets also coined many terms and epithets.

Gog and Magog: Ruler and country who will fight Israel (Ezek. 38:2). The concept was developed into that of the anti-Messiah, who at the end of days would head the forces of evil spirits against the forces of good in the final battle. G. and M. will be defeated by God himself or by the Messiah. The idea figures also in Christian legend.

Golah: Exile. See GA-LUT.

Golan: Western region of BASHAN, named after its chief town of the same name. In Greek, it was called Gaulanitis. Upper G. extended from Mt. Hermon to the Sea of Galilee. The G. Heights (Ramat ha-Golan) are the hills that were held by the Syrians overlooking Upper Galilee and used for bombarding Israeli kibbutzim below. They were captured by the Israelis in the 1967 war, and a number of Jewish settlements were established. Excavations uncovered many ancient synagogues on the G. Heights.

Gold, Ze'ev (Wolf) (1889-1956): Religious Zionist leader. Born in Poland, he went to the US in 1906. He was a founder of the Mizrahi movement in the US and its president from 1931. He settled in Palestine in 1935 and was a member of the Jewish Agency executive from 1946.

Goldberg, Arthur Joseph (1906–): US legal and public figure. Born in Chicago, he was a noted arbiter in labor disputes and was largely responsible for the A.F.L.–C.I.O. merger in 1955. Under Kennedy he was secretary of labor (1960–62) and was then appointed to the Supreme Court, resigning in 1965 to become senior US delegate to the UN, a post he held until 1968.

Goldberg, Lea (1911–

1970): Hebrew poet and critic. Born in Königsberg, she settled in Palestine in 1935. Her poems were influenced by the European Jewish tragedy and were marked by melancholy. She taught comparative literature at the Hebrew University, Jerusalem (professor, 1963).

Goldberg, Rube (Reuben Lucius) (1883–1970): US cartoonist, noted for his drawings of exaggeratedly complicated inventions.

Golden, Harry Lewis (1902–): US author and publisher. He was brought up in New York, but settled in North Carolina, where he published *Carolina Israelite* from 1942 to 1969. He took a strong stand favoring black integration. He published excerpts from his newspaper writings in *Only in America* and other volumes.

Goldfaden, Abraham (1840–1908): Yiddish author and producer, known as the father of the Yiddish theater. Born in the Ukraine, he published Yiddish poems and songs. Then, going to Rumania, he founded in 1876 the first professional Yiddish theater, which achieved great success throughout Eastern Europe. However, in 1883, the Russian government banned performances in Yiddish, and G. spent the rest of his life in Western Europe and the US. He wrote 60 plays which achieved great popularity, including *Shulamis* and *Bar Kokhba*, the former including the famous cradle song "*Rozhinkes mit Mandlen.*"

Golding, Louis (1895–1938): English novelist. Many of his works deal with Jewish life in his native city of Manchester, the best known being *Magnolia Street*. He also wrote travel books (*In the Steps of Moses*), essays, and literary studies.

Goldman, Edwin Franko (1878–1950): US bandmaster. The Goldman Band, which he formed in 1911, toured widely and influenced band music in the US.

Goldman, Emma (1868–1940: US anarchist. She left Eastern Europe for the US in 1885 and achieved notoriety before World War I for her advocacy of birth control. During the war, her opposition to conscription led to her imprisonment. In 1919 she was deported to the USSR, but was disillusioned there and left after 2 years. She lived in Europe.

Goldman, Solomon (1893–1953): U.S. Conservative rabbi and Zionist leader. From 1929 he served at Congregation Anshe Emet in Chicago. He was president of the Zionist Organization of America and co-chairman of the United Jewish Appeal. His writings include a series on the Bible.

Goldmann, Nahum (1895–): Jewish and Zionist leader. Born in Lithuania, he lived in Germany from the age of 5, and in the 1920s was a founder of the Eshkol Publishing house, which published the German-language *Encyclopaedia Judaica*. In 1933 he became chairman of the COMITÉ DES DÉLÉGATIONS JUIVES and from 1935 to 1939 he represented the Jewish Agency at the League of Nations. He helped to organize the WORLD JEWISH CONGRESS, of which he was president from 1953 to 1977. From 1955 to 1968 he was also president of the WORLD ZIONIST ORGANIZATION. He played a leading role in many developments in postwar Jewish history, including the REPARATIONS agreement with Germany. He lived in the US from 1940 and subsequently in Israel and Switzerland.

Goldmark, Karl (1830–1915): Austrian composer. He wrote operas (of which the most successful was *The Queen of Sheba*) and orchestral and chamber music. His nephew *Rubin Goldmark* (1872–1936) was a well-known composer and music teacher in the US, heading the Julliard School Department of Composition from 1924.

Goldschmidt, Lazarus (1871–1950): Scholar and bibliophile. He first specialized in Ethiopian language and literature but his best scholarly work was his translation of the Babylonian Talmud into German. He was also a collector of rare books and published a number of bibliographical studies.

Goldstein, Herbert S. (1890–1970): US Orthodox rabbi. He officiated in New York synagogues, taught at Yeshiva University, and was president of major Orthodox organizations in the US.

Goldstein, Israel (1896–): US Conservative rabbi and communal worker. He was rabbi of B'nai Jeshurun congregation, New York, from 1918 to 1961, when he moved to Jerusalem to become head of the Keren Hayesod. G. was president of many Jewish and Zionist organizations in the US, including the Zionist Organization of America and the Jewish National Fund.

Goldwyn, Samuel (1882–1974): US movie producer. Born in Warsaw, he went to the US in 1895 and was in the motion picture industry from 1913. He founded Goldwyn Pictures, which later merged to become Metro-Goldwyn-Mayer.

Goldziher, Ignaz (1850–

1921): Hungarian scholar of Islam. He was secretary of the Budapest Reform Jewish community and taught at the University of Budapest and at the Budapest Rabbinical Seminary. He published extensively on the history and religion of Islam, on which he was an outstanding authority, as well as Jewish studies.

golem: A creature usually in human shape, magically formed, especially through the use of divine names. The idea developed from mystical interpretations of the early medieval SEPHER YETZIRAH. The concept of creating a g. developed among the ḤASIDEI ASHKENAZ in the 12th cent. Legends that such creatures had been created spread from the 15th cent., and the best-known story was associated with Rabbi JUDAH LOEW of Prague.

Goliath: Philistine warrior. Despite his massive arms, the giant G., who was the Philistine champion, was killed by a stone slung by the young, inexperienced David (I Sam. 17).

Gollancz: English family. *Sir Hermann* G. (1852–1930) was a Hebrew scholar, teaching at University College, London, and the first rabbi to be knighted. His brother *Sir Israel* G. (1864–1930) was a noted literary scholar, specializing in the works of Shakespeare. He was secretary of the British Academy. Their nephew *Sir Victor* G. (1893–1967) was a publisher whose Left Book Club was influential in the 1930s. He was involved in humanitarian causes, on which he wrote extensively.

Golomb, Eliyahu (1893–1945): Leader of the Jewish Self-Defense, Palestine. After World War I, he was one of the main organizers of the HAGANAH and from 1931, the chief figure on its national command. During the Arab riots of 1936–39, he established its field units but was a chief advocate of the policy of self-restraint during this period. During World War II he supported the enlistment of Palestinian Jewish volunteers into the British army. He was a founder of the PALMAḤ.

gomel, blessing of: A benediction of thanksgiving recited after recovery from serious illness or escape from danger. It is usually recited by the person delivered, after being called to the Reading of the Law in the synagogue.

**Gompers,	Samuel** (1850–1924): US trade unionist. He was born in London and settled on New York's Lower East Side in 1863 and became a leader of the cigar makers' union while in his twenties. In

1886, he helped to establish the American Federation of Labor, of which he was president and editor of its journal. He played a major role in the development of the American labor movement and was prominent in mobilizing the support of trade unions for the American war effort in World War I.

Goodhart, Arthur Lehman (1891–): Legal scholar. Born in New York, he taught law at Cambridge, England, from 1918 and edited the *Cambridge Law Journal*. He was professor of law at Oxford from 1931 and in 1951 was appointed master of University College, Oxford, the first Jew to head an Oxford College.

Goodman, Arnold Abraham, Lord (1913–): British lawyer. Legal adviser to many British leaders, he arbitrated many industrial disputes and was sent by the British premier, Harold Wilson, to attempt to negotiate the Rhodesian situation. He was chairman of the Arts Council, 1965–72, and president of University College, Oxford.

Goodman, Benny (1909–): US musician. An outstanding exponent of clarinet playing, he was known as the "King of Swing," leading a large jazz orchestra and also smaller groups. He also appeared with symphony orchestras and chamber ensembles.

Goodman, Paul (1911–1972): US educator. He taught at several universities and wrote on a variety of subjects ranging from social problems to Gestalt therapy. His critique of the American social scene brought him widespread popularity among the New Left in the late 1960s. His brother *Percival G.* (1904–) was professor of architecture at Columbia University and designed many synagogues in the US.

Gordimer, Nadine (1923–): South African writer. She has published novels and short stories and is among the small number of novelists who have created a distinctive South African literary tradition.

Gordin, Jacob (1853–1909): Yiddish playwright and journalist. Born in the Ukraine, he was influenced in his early days by Tolstoy and Christian Evangelism and established the "Spiritual Biblical Brotherhood" in the Ukraine. Its attempts to found a commune failed and G. fled to the US in 1891. Here he turned to drama and wrote over 100 plays, some of which achieved great popular success, such as *The Yiddish King Lear* and *Mirele Efros*.

Gordon, Aharon David (1856–1922): Zionist labor

philosopher. Born in Russia, he worked as an official until the age of 48. He then went to Palestine, where he was an agricultural laborer in various villages, spending his last years in Deganyah. His teachings, known as the "Religion of Labor," were a great influence in socialist Zionism and the Israeli labor movement. He taught that the return to nature through physical labor would bring man to religion and to a sense of holiness.

Gordon, Cyrus Herzl (1908–): US Semitic scholar. He has taught at various universities and from 1956 at Brandeis Univ. He wrote pioneering studies on Ugaritic grammar and literature and published on many aspects of the ancient Near East. He claimed that there were close relationships between the ancient Greek and Semitic cultures.

Gordon, Lord George (1751–1793): English proselyte. The son of the duke of Gordon, he headed the United Protestant League in England and led violent riots against popery in London. In 1787, he became Jewish, taking the name Israel ben Abraham. He was imprisoned from 1788 for libeling the British government and lived his last years as an Orthodox Jew in jail.

Gordon, Judah Leib

(1830–1892): Hebrew poet, known by his acronym Yalag. He lived in Vilna, where he was one of the leading advocates of the HASKALAH. Later, he moved to St. Petersburg, where he was for a time secretary of the Jewish community. A prolific author, he wrote novels, essays, and criticisms as well as editing in Hebrew and Russian journals. His chief importance was as a poet; he wrote historical poems and poems satirizing aspects of Jewish life in Eastern Europe.

Goren, Charles Henry (1901–): US bridge expert. He was American bridge champion over 30 times, and his bridge methods, expounded in a number of books, were followed all over the world.

Goren, Shlomo (1917–): Israeli rabbi. He was chief chaplain of the Israeli Defense Forces from their establishment in 1948. In 1968 he was elected Ashkenazi chief rabbi of Tel Aviv, and in 1972 Ashkenazi chief rabbi of Israel.

Gottheil, Gustav (1827–1903): Reform rabbi. After officiating in Germany and England, he went to Temple Emanu-El in New York in 1873. He was the outstanding American Reform rabbi to support Herzl when he started the Zionist movement and was a founder of the Federation of American Zionists. His son *Richard James Horatio G.* (1862–1936) taught Semitic languages at Columbia University and directed the Oriental Department of the New York Public Library. He too was an active Zionist and was president of the American Federation of Zionists (1898–1904).

Gottlieb, Maurycy (1856–1879): Polish painter. Although his career lasted only a few years, he succeeded in producing some of the best-known paintings depicting Eastern European Jewish life. His brother *Leopold* (1883–1934), born four years after Maurycy's death, also became a famous painter.

Gottlober, Abraham Baer (1810–1899): Hebrew and Yiddish writer, known by his pseudonym, Mahalalel. He lived in Eastern Europe as a teacher and Talmud instructor. He published Hebrew poems and works of scholarship and was one of the early advocates of Jewish nationalism and the Hebrew revival. His memoirs and short stories are important sources of information on Eastern European Jewish life of his time.

Gould, Morton (1913–): US musician. He is a popular conductor, pianist and composer. His light and classical compositions often use American folk and popular sources, incorporating jazz elements.

grace after meals (*birkat ha-mazon*): The obligation to recite g. is on adult males after a meal which included bread. It contains three benedictions—for food, for the land of Israel, and for the rebuilding of Jerusalem—to which later prayers have been added. On Sabbaths and festivals, additions are prescribed. If three or more males have eaten together, there is a special introductory formula (*mezumman*). Sometimes a shorter form is recited. Before meals, a single blessing is recited, varying according to the type of food about to be consumed.

Grade, Chaim (1910–): Yiddish poet and novelist. In his youth, he was a key figure in the Yiddish movement in his native Vilna. In World War II he escaped to the USSR and from 1948 lived in the US, where he published poems, novels, and short stories and contributed to the Yiddish press. Many of his works deal with Polish Jewish life before World War II.

Grade, Lew, Lord (1906–): British television producer. Born in Russia, he grew up in England and headed the Associated Television Company, producing spectacular series on the lives of Moses, Jesus, etc.

Graetz, Heinrich (1817–1891): German Jewish historian. From 1853 he taught at the Breslau Rabbinical Seminary and from 1869 also at Breslau Univ. His outstanding work is his *History of the Jews*, which became one of the most popular and influential Jewish histories in its original German and in many translations, especially in its abridged form. G. was also a Bible scholar and editor of the scholarly journal *Monatschriften für die Geschichte und Wissenschaft des Judentums*.

Granada: City and province in Spain. Jews lived there from the 4th cent. and under the Muslims it was one of the outstanding Jewish communities in Spain. Samuel ha-Nagid was vizier to the king, and other Jews occupied high office. The community declined from the late 11th cent. and came to an end with the Christian conquest and expulsion of 1492.

Gratz: US family in Philadelphia. Founded in the 18th cent. by two brothers who came from London, its members in the 19th cent. included *Hyman* G. (1776–1857), whose bequest enabled the establishment of the Jewish teachers training seminary, Gratz College,

opened in 1897; and *Rebecca* G. (1781–1869), pioneer of Jewish social welfare and the Sunday-school movement and reputedly the prototype of Rebecca in Scott's *Ivanhoe*.

Great Assembly (*Keneset ha-Gedolah*): Institution of the Second Temple period, listed as the link between the time of the prophets and the time of Simeon the Just (200 BCE) as responsible for transmitting the oral tradition. It made important contributions in liturgy, the canonization of the Bible, and the Oral Law.

Great Britain see **England; Scotland; Wales**

Greece (*Yavan*): Jews were living on the Greek mainland from the 3rd cent. BCE. The influence of Greek culture was long dominant over the Jewish countries in the Middle East (Hellenism). In the Hasmonean period Jewish communities were established in all the main Greek cities. Under Christian rule, they shared the fate of Jews throughout the Byzantine Empire. Many refugees from Spain arrived at the end of the 15th cent., changing the nature of the community. The main Jewish settlement now was in Salonica. In the early 20th cent. there were 10,000 Jews in G. but after the upheaval of the Balkan wars and the period after World War I, the numbers grew to 100,000. Under German rule during World War II, the Jews of G. suffered the same fate as the Jews of the rest of Europe—65,000 out of 77,000 being deported to their deaths. The historic Salonica community now lost its importance. Over 2,000 Greek Jews emigrated to Israel after 1948, and in 1976, there were 6,000 Jews in G. (2,800 in Athens, 1,300 in Salonica).

Greenberg, Hank (Henry) (1911–): US baseball player. He was a star of the Detroit Tigers and was elected to the Baseball Hall of Fame.

Greenberg, Hayyim (1889–1953): Zionist essayist and editor. Of Bessarabian birth, he edited in Berlin the weekly of the World Zionist Organization, *Ha-Olam*, 1921–24; and from 1924 in the US, he edited *Der Yidischer Kemfer* and the *Jewish Frontier*. A leading theoretician of the Labor Zionist movement, he was a member of the Jewish Agency Executive from 1946.

Greenberg, Uri Zevi (1894–): Hebrew poet. He was born in Galicia. His earliest poems were in Hebrew and Yiddish. From 1924, he lived in Tel Aviv, where he wrote exclusively in Hebrew. Some of his verse is on topi-

cal issues, influenced by G.'s support of the Revisionist and Herut movement (he represented the latter in the KNESSET, 1949–51). Since World War II much of his work has been devoted to the Holocaust.

Grock (Charles Adrien Wettach) (1880–1959): Swiss clown; son of a Jewish father. He appeared in England 1911–24 and then throughout Europe. His act as a musical clown was the most famous of its kind.

Grodno: City in Belorussian SSR. It was one of the oldest Jewish communities in the duchy of Lithuania and received a charter in 1389. G. was a seat of Jewish learning, and the first Hebrew book printed in Lithuania was printed there. From the late 19th cent. it was a center of the Jewish socialist and Zionist movements. There were pogroms under Polish rule in 1935 and 1939. Over 20,000 Jews were living there at the outbreak of World War II; they were sent to extermination camps by the Nazis.

Gropper, William (1897–1977): US artist. He was well known as a cartoonist and in the 1930s executed murals for the WPA. His work was marked by its social realism.

Gross, Chaim (1904–): US sculptor. Born in

Galicia, he lived in the US from 1921. He worked in various media; his wood sculpture is outstanding.

Grossinger, Jenny (1892–1972): US hotelier. In 1914 she opened a boarding house in the Catskill Mountains near Liberty, New York, which eventually grew to a resort covering over 1,000 acres. She wrote *The Art of Jewish Cooking*.

Grossman, Meir (1888–1969): Zionist leader and journalist. He worked on newspapers in Eastern Europe, leaving Russia after the Bolshevik Revolution. He helped to establish the Jewish Telegraphic Agency and in 1925 founded an English daily in Jerusalem. He was active in the Revisionist Party but split away in 1933, when he established the Jewish State Party. Later he became a General Zionist and was a member of the Jewish Agency Executive (1948–61).

Gruenberg, Louis (1894–1964): US composer. His works include the opera *Emperor Jones*, based on O'Neill's play, and *Jack and the Beanstalk*. He utilized Negro spirituals and jazz in his compositions.

Gruening, Ernest (1887–1974): US politician and journalist. He edited *The Nation* (1920–23) and *The Portland Evening News*. He was territorial governor of Alaska (1939–53), and when Alaska was admitted to the Union, G. was its first senator (1958–68).

Grünbaum,   Yitzhak (1879–1970): Zionist leader in Poland and Israel. Born in Warsaw, he worked on Jewish newspapers and after World War I was elected to the Polish parliament, where he headed the "club" of Jewish members. In 1933, he was elected to the Jewish Agency Executive and settled in Palestine. He was the minister of the interior in Israel's provisional government (1948–49). For most of his life he was active in the General Zionist Party, but in his later years became a supporter of Mapam. He wrote and edited on Zionist subjects and Eastern European Jewry.

Grusenberg,   Oscar (1866–1940): Russian advocate and communal leader. He defended many political prisoners and conducted the brilliant defense in the BEILIS case. Under the Kerensky regime (1917) he was appointed senator but left the country after the Bolshevik Revolution and lived in Berlin and Riga.

Guatemala: Marranos lived in G. in the colonial period. Jews reached there from the mid-19th cent. Some refugees arrived in the

1930s and many more after World War II. In 1976 there were 1,900 Jews, nearly all of them in Guatemala City, with three synagogues.

Güdemann, Moritz (1835–1918): Rabbi at Magdeburg; from 1891, chief rabbi of Vienna. He wrote on Jewish cultural history and on apologetics. He opposed political Zionism.

Guggenheim: US family of philanthropists, originating from Baden and Switzerland. *Meyer G.* (1828–1905) established a smelting and refining business in which he was joined by his seven sons. These included *Isaac G.* (1854–1922), known as the "Copper King"; *Daniel G.* (1856–1930), who established foundations to promote the "well-being of mankind" and to promote aeronautics; *Solomon Robert G.* (1861–1949), arts patron for whom the Guggenheim Museum in New York is named; and *Simon G.* (1867–1941), who was US senator from Colorado, 1907–13. Daniel's son *Harry Frank G.* (1890–1971) was US ambassador to Cuba, 1929–33. *Benjamin G.* (1865–1912) drowned on the *Titanic*. His daughter *Peggy G.* (1898–) was a noted art patron, living in Venice.

Günzburg: Russian family of philanthropists and communal leaders. *Baron Joseph Yozel G.* (1812–1878) founded the G. Bank in St. Petersburg, which became a leading Russian financial institution. He participated in the financing of railroads and gold mines in Asiatic Russia. He fought for Jewish rights and was responsible for receiving permission to build the first synagogue in St. Petersburg. G. supported the settlement of Jews on the land in southern Russia and was a founder of the Society for the Promotion of Culture among the Jews of Russia. He was ennobled in 1874. His son *Baron Horace G.* (1833–1909) directed his father's bank and was an alderman in the St. Petersburg municipality. He was a generous patron of Jewish scholars and artists. He headed the Jewish community in St. Petersburg and actively intervened with the government in attempts to combat their anti-Semitic activities. His son *Baron David G.* (1857–1901) was a distinguished Jewish scholar who published works on Semitic languages, medieval Arabic poetry, and manuscripts of medieval Jewish authors. His major collection of Judaica is now housed in the Lenin State Library in Moscow. He also headed the St. Petersburg Jewish community, created an Institute of Jewish Studies, and was an editor of the Russian Jewish encyclopedia.

Gutt, Camille (1884–1971): Belgian statesman. He was minister of finance (1934–35, 1939–40) and during World War II was a minister in the Belgian government in exile. From 1946 to 1951, he was chairman of the board of directors of the International Monetary Fund.

Guttmacher, Elijah (1795–1874): Rabbi and early Zionist, one of the best-known rabbis in Eastern Europe. His interest in mysticism and in contemporary problems led him to the conviction that Jews should cndcavor to resettle in Eretz Israel without waiting for the arrival of the Messiah. He supported Tzevi Hirsch KALISHER in his efforts to organize practical settlement in Eretz Israel.

Guyana (formerly British Guiana): Jews arrived in the 17th cent. and Jews from Italy founded the settlement of Nieuw-Middleburgh in 1648. The Jews, however, eventually emigrated or assimilated. Only a few individuals lived there before World War II; 130 found temporary refuge during the war. A British plan to settle Jewish refugees there, announced in May 1939, proved impractical.

Haapalah: Movement to take Jews into Palestine against the regulations of the British Mandatory authorities. Transports began in 1934, and by 1938 these "illegal" immigrants were arriving in considerable numbers. Largest proportions were reached during the 1945-48 period. Those "illegal" immigrants caught by the British in 1946–48 were sent to detention camps in Cyprus.

Ha-Aretz ("The Land"): Newspaper founded in Jerusalem in 1919 but from 1922 published in Tel Aviv. Among its editors have been Moshe Glickson and Gershom Schocken. It has an independent liberal orientation.

Haas, Jacob de (1872–1937): Zionist writer. Born in London, he lived in the US from 1902. Prominent in US Zionism, he occupied various positions in Palestine development organizations. He was author of a life of Herzl and editor of *The Encyclopedia of Jewish Knowledge.*

Habad: Trend in Hasidism founded by SHNEOUR ZALMAN OF LYADY. The name is taken from the initials of *Hokhmah Binah Daat* ("Wisdom, Understanding, Knowledge"). It emphasized an intellectual approach in contrast to the more emotional approach adopted by other Hasidic trends. Stress was placed on the study of the Torah, while the role of the *tzaddik* was more spiritual. The movement was led by the Shneersohn family of

Liubavich. Its headquarters are now in New York, and its followers have been active in many countries, including Israel, the Soviet Union, North Africa, and Australia.

Habakkuk: Prophet of the 7th cent. BCE, author of book of the Minor Prophets. Nothing is known about him or his life. He foretold the rise of the Chaldeans and includes a protest at their success and an assurance of the ultimate doom of the wicked. "The just shall live by his faith," the prophet is assured (Hab. 2:4). A Hebrew PESHER on the work was discovered among the DEAD SEA SCROLLS.

Habe, Hans (1911–1977): Novelist. Born in Budapest of parents who had been converted, he was in the US army during World War II and after the war founded the American-supported newspaper *Neue Zeitung* in Munich. His writings are strongly anti-Nazi. They include the novels *The Mission* (about the EVIAN conference) and *The Wounded Land* (about the murder of President Kennedy).

Haber, Fritz (1868–1934): German physical chemist. He directed the Kaiser Wilhelm Institute at Dahlem, Berlin. His discovery of the synthesis of ammonia from its elements, was invaluable to the German military efforts in World War I. In 1918 he was awarded the Nobel Prize for Chemistry. H., who was baptized, refused to dismiss the Jews on his staff as demanded by the Nazis in 1933. He resigned and went into exile in Switzerland.

Habimah ("The Stage"): Hebrew repertory theater, founded in Moscow in 1917. Its early productions, staged by Stanislavsky's associate Vachtangov, created a profound impression, notably the performance of An-Ski's *The Dybbuk*. In 1926 the company left Russia and in 1928 made its headquarters in Tel Aviv. It played a major cultural role in Palestine and later in Israel, being officially recognized as the Israeli National Theater in 1958. Its repertoire includes both foreign and Israeli plays.

Habiru: A group of people mentioned in the Tel el-AMARNA tablets (2nd millennium BCE). The H. are reported as threatening certain Canaanite cities, and some scholars have connected the term with the word for Hebrews (*Ivrim*).

Habonim ("The Builders"): Zionist youth movement. Founded in Great Britain in 1929, it spread to other countries, especially in the British Commonwealth. It founded several settlements in Israel and established its headquarters in Tel Aviv. The movement is now called H. Tenuah Meuḥedet, following its merger with the movement of the latter name.

Ḥad Gadya (Aram. "An Only Kid"): Poem in Aramaic recited by Ashkenazim in the Passover SEDER service since the late Middle Ages. Its theme is retribution. The structure is of a nursery rhyme, and it may have been introduced to interest the children at the late hour when it is usually sung or recited.

Hadassah: Women's Zionist Organization of America. It was founded in 1912 by Henrietta SZOLD. Its major activity has been raising funds for medical and public-health programs in Israel. Its other activities in Israel include support for YOUTH ALIYAH and vocational education projects. The Hadassah Hospital in Jerusalem on Mt. Scopus was inaccessible in the period 1948–67, and a new hospital was built at Ein Kerem which incorporated a medical school, run with the Hebrew University. After 1967 the Mt. Scopus hospital was restored and reopened in 1976. In the US, H. is responsible for widespread educational and social programs among its 325,000 members (1973) in 1,440 chapters and groups (including publication of Hadassah Magazine). Jun-

ior H. has members between the ages of 17 to 25.

Ḥaderah: Town in central Israel, founded in 1891 by immigrants who had first to drain malaria-infested swamps. Its economy is based on industry, commerce, and intensive agriculture in the vicinity. The population in 1971 was 34,500.

Ha-Doar ("The Mail"): US Hebrew paper, founded in 1922 as a daily. Since 1923 it has appeared as a weekly, stressing literary topics. Its editor from 1923–53 was Menahem Ribalow.

Hadramaut: Region in SAUDI ARABIA. Its ancient Jewish community in its entirety moved to Israel after 1948.

*Hadrian (76–138): Roman emperor, 111–38. At first Jews hoped his policy would lead to an improvement in their position, but his prohibition of castration, which included circumcision, aroused fierce opposition. When he attempted an intensified Hellenization policy in Palestine, the Jews rebelled under BAR KOKHBA, and it took four years (132–35) for him to suppress the revolt. After it was over, a statue of H. was erected on the Holy of Holies, and Jerusalem was renamed Aelia Capitalina in his honor (his name being P. Aelus Hadrianus).

Haffkine, Waldemar

Mordecai Wolfe (1860–1930): Bacteriologist. Born in Odessa, he worked in Paris, where he developed a vaccine against cholera and the bubonic plague. From 1893 he was very active fighting plagues in India. H. was an Orthodox Jew who left a large bequest to yeshivot.

Haganah ("Defense"): Underground Jewish paramilitary organization in Palestine during the British Mandate. It took the place of Ha-Shomer in 1920 and developed rapidly. During the 1936–39 disturbances, Special Field Squads (commanded by Yitzhak Sadeh) and Special Night Squads (commanded by Orde Wingate) were set up. The H. sponsored "illegal" immigration and carried out instant settlement operations. It worked under the instructions of the Jewish Agency. During World War II, 30,000 members of the H. volunteered for service with the British army. From 1941 it had a commando unit (Palmah). The H. engaged in a bitter struggle with the British after the war, assisting immigration and resisting British measures in the country. Conflict often arose with the other underground groups. From late 1947, the H. concentrated on opposing attacks from Arabs, and in 1948 its members were transferred to Tzeva Haganah le-Israel.

Hagar: Egyptian maidservant of Sarah, who gave her to Abraham as his concubine. By him she was the mother of Ishmael. At Sarah's insistence, H. and her young son were banished to the desert but were saved from death by Divine intervention.

Haggadah, Passover: The prescribed service and narrative, relating the Exodus from Egypt, and recited in the Jewish home on the first night (or first two nights, outside Israel) of Passover. The obligation to relate the story of the Exodus and the name H. ("narration") are based on Exod. 13:8. After the sacrifice of the paschal lamb ceased, the rabbis ordained the festival meal accompanied by a fixed ritual with a prescribed order (seder). The H. is a series of excerpts from the Bible, Mishnah, and Midrash, which assumed its present structure by the end of the talmudic period, and appears in the 8th-cent. prayer book of Amram Gaon. After the preliminaries (including *kiddush*), the youngest present asks four questions, meant to evoke an explanation of the reasons for the Passover celebration. The reply, which is the H. proper, is in set form which includes the *Midrash on the Four Sons*, a detailed commentary on Deut. 26:5–8, an account and midrashic exposition of the Ten Plagues, and the thanksgiving hymn DAYYENU. This is followed by HALLEL—interrupted by partaking of the unleavened bread (*matzah*), the bitter herb (*maror*), the meal, and the recitation of grace. At the end of the service, a number of songs of folk origin (originating in the late Middle Ages) are sung in the Ashkenazi rite. Other features of the service include the drinking of four cups of wine and the placing of a special glass of wine for ELIJAH, who, it is believed, will reappear on the Passover. The H. text became one of the most popular of Jewish books and the subject of artistic decoration and illumination. In modern times, modified *Haggadot* have been produced by various groups, including Israeli kibbutzim and Jewish radical youth circles in the US.

Haggai (c. 520 BCE): Hebrew prophet of the era after the Babylonian Exile; contemporary of ZECHARIAH. His prophecies are contained in the Book of H., the tenth book of the Minor Prophets. It deals with the reconstruction of the Temple and the future glory of ZERUBBABEL.

Hagigah ("Festival Offering"): Last tractate in the MISHNAH order *Moed* dealing with the peace offerings brought by worshipers to the Temple on the Pilgrim Festivals. It has *gemara* in both the Babylonian and Palestinian Talmuds. It also contains important information on early rabbinic mysticism.

Hagiographa (*Ketuvim*, "Writings"): Last of the three divisions of the Bible. Its 11 books are: Psalms, Proverbs, Job, Song of Songs, Ruth, Lamentations, Ecclesiastes, Esther, Daniel, Ezra, Nehemiah, and Chronicles.

haham: Chief rabbi of the Sephardi community in England; a variant of *hakham*.

Hai (939–1038): Last *gaon* of the PUMBEDITA academy, which under his direction reached the zenith of its fame. A son of SHERIRA Gaon, he became chief of the *bet din* in 986 and *gaon* in 998. He issued thousands of responsa and continued to teach until the age of 99. He wrote Hebrew and Arabic commentaries on the Bible and Talmud, halakhic works, liturgical compositions, and other works.

Haidamaks: Paramilitary Ukrainian bands, active from early 18th cent. but especially from 1734. Their major anti-Jewish outbreaks were in 1734, 1750, and 1768 (the last witnessing the massacre of the Jews of Uman). Their deleterious effect on everyday life led to their eradication by Russian and Polish troops.

Haifa: Third-largest city in Israel with a population of 225,000 in 1974. In ancient times it was a small settlement. Its modern importance dates from the latter 19th cent., with the development of its port, and from 1905 it was linked with the Hejaz railroad. The Jewish community grew from the 1880s and the Technion was founded there in 1912. Under the British Mandate, its importance increased with the completion of a deep-water harbor and the pipeline connection between its oil refineries and the Iraqi oilfields. The entire region became an industrial center, which was further developed under the State of Israel. A university was opened there in the 1960s. H. is the world center of the Bahai movement.

hakham ("sage"): Term used by Sephardim for a fully ordained rabbi. In Mishnaic times, it was the title of a high official of the Sanhedrin.

hakham bashi ("chief sage"): Chief rabbi, under Ottoman rule. The office was recognized by the government as the representative of the Jewish community. It applied to chief rabbis both in the capital and in provincial towns.

hakhnasat kallah ("bringing in the bride"): A rabbinic commandment providing a poor girl with a dowry. This was ranked as a major *mitzvah*, and the Talmud stresses that it should be performed anonymously. From the Middle Ages, Jewish communities have had *h.k.* societies.

hakhnasat orehim ("welcoming guests"): Hospitality. One of the highest virtues in Jewish tradition, its prototype was seen in the action of Abraham in welcoming his visitors (Gen. 18:1–8). The relevant laws are expounded in rabbinical literature, and *h.o.* societies were established to extend hospitality to travelers.

hakhsharah ("preparation"): Training for settlement in Israel. Pioneering youth movements, set up special *h.* centers in various countries, especially for agricultural training.

Ha-Kibbutz ha-Artzi ha-Tzair: Union of kibbutzim of the Ha-Shomer ha-Tzair movement. Founded in 1927, it had 77 affiliated kibbutzim with 31,945 members in 1973. Its headquarters are at Merhavyah.

Ha-Kibbutz ha-Dati: Kibbutz federation of the Ha-Poel ha-Mizrahi religious settlements. In 1973, it had 15 affiliated kibbutzim, with 5,200 members. It is connected with the youth movements Torah va-Avodah and Bene Akiva.

Ha-Kibbutz ha-Meuḥad: Kibbutz movement, formerly associated with the AHDUT AVODAH party. Founded in 1927, it had 60 kibbutzim with over 25,000 members in 1973. Its headquarters are in En Harod.

hakkaphot ("circuits"): Processional circuits made on several occasions including: around the synagogue *almemar* during Tabernacles (by worshipers carrying *lulav* and *etrog*), on Hoshana Rabbah (Seven circuits are made), and Simḥat Torah (by worshipers carrying Scrolls of the Law); at the cemetery circuits are made at the consecration of the cemetery and by Sephardim around the grave prior to burial; in a number of communities, it is customary for the bride to walk 3 or 7 times around the bridegroom under the wedding canopy.

halakhah ("law"): Legal side of Judaism (as contrasted with AGGADAH, the nonlegal material). Originally h. was a legal formula laid down in the Oral Law. The best-known early systematic collection of halakhot was that of R. AKIVA. This served as the basis for the MISHNAH, the compilation of JUDAH HA-NASI.

Halévy: French family. *Élie H.* (1760–1826), writer in Hebrew, was an official of the Paris community. He wrote a poem in honor of Napoleon. His son *Jacques François Fromental H.* (1799–1862), composer, wrote operas, including *La Juive*, and taught music at the Paris Conservatoire. His brother *Léon H.* (1802–1883), novelist and playwright, was a follower of Saint-Simon. Leon's son *Ludovic H.* (1834–1908) wrote the libretti for several operettas for Offenbach, including *Orpheus in the Underworld* and Bizet's *Carmen*. His son *Elie H.* (1870–1937), philosopher, and historian, was raised as a Protestant.

halitzah ("taking off"): Ceremony performed when a man refuses to marry his brother's childless widow (cf. Deut. 25:9–10). Prior to this ceremony the widow is not allowed to remarry. At the ceremony she takes off her brother-in-law's shoe and declares, "So shall be done to the man who will not build his brother's house." See also LEVIRATE MARRIAGE.

Halkin, Shimon H. (1898–): Hebrew writer and educator. He was born in Belorussia, lived in the US from 1914, and became professor of modern Hebrew at the Hebrew University in 1949. He has written poetry, novels, literary criticism, and many translations. His brother *Abraham Solomon H.* (1903–) taught Hebrew at New York universities and at the

Jewish Theological Seminary. He settled in Israel in 1970. He wrote on medieval Jewish literature. Their cousin *Shmuel H.* (1897–1960), Russian Yiddish poet, was arrested with other leading Yiddish writers in 1948 but was one of the few who survived; he was released in 1955.

ḥallah: Type of bread, especially the Sabbath loaves; originally part of the dough separated as a gift for the priest (Num. 15:7–21). If not taken from the dough, it must be removed from the bread. Originally applicable only in Israel, the rabbis ruled that it must be observed in the Diaspora. Since most baking was done by women, the command was especially enjoined on them. It is also the name of a mishnaic tractate on the subject.

Hallel ("Praise"): Name applied to a group of Psalms (113–8, 136) recited in the synagogue on special occasions, viz. after the Morning Service on Passover, Shavuot, Sukkot, and Ḥanukkah as well as on new moons and at the Passover Seder service. An abbreviated version (half H.) is recited on the latter days of Passover and on new moons. In Israel it has become the custom to recite H. on Independence Day.

hallelujah ("praise the Lord"): Liturgical expression appearing as the opening or closing word of certain psalms. It is also frequently used in Christian liturgy.

Halprin, Rose Luria (1896–1978): US Zionist leader; national president of HADASSAH 1932–34 and 1947–52). From 1946 to 1968 she was a member of the Jewish Agency Executive, for a time heading its New York Executive.

ḥalukkah ("division"): System of relief for the poor in Palestine from contributions made in other countries. From ancient times, money was collected for the upkeep of the Jewish community in Palestine, but the collection was organized systematically from c. 1600. Emissaries (known as *sheliḥim, meshullaḥim,* or *shadarim*) were sent to Jews throughout the world to collect funds. The Jews living in Palestine who subsisted from these collections were known as "ḥ. Jews."

ḥalutz ("pioneer"): A pioneer in modern Israel, especially one working on the land.

*Haman: Vizier of the Persian emperor Ahasuerus. According to the Book of Esther (the only source for the entire episode), he planned to kill all Jews in the Persian Empire, but his plan was foiled by ESTHER and her uncle MORDECAI. H. and his sons were hanged in punishment. The story is the basis of the festival of Purim. H. became regarded as the archenemy of the Jews.

Ha-Mavdil ("Who Distinguishes"): Hymn sung in the home after the HAVDALAH ceremony at the close of the Sabbath.

Hamburg: City in West Germany. In the late 16th cent., ex-Marranos from Spain and Portugal were living there. They played an important role in commerce, and by 1611 there were three congregations. Ashkenazi Jews settled in the neighboring town of ALTONA, and in 1671 the two communities, together with that of Wandsbeck, were united. Among the outstanding rabbis of the community were Tzevi ASHKENAZI and Jonathan EIBESCHÜTZ. The foundation of a Reform temple in 1818 led to bitter strife within the community. Full equality of rights were obtained in 1850. There were 20,000 Jews in H. in 1933, but the community ended under the Nazis. After World War II, a new community was founded, numbering 1,485 in 1973.

Ha-Measseph ("The Gatherer"): The first secular Hebrew periodical. It appeared from 1784 to 1829. See ME'ASSEPHIM.

hametz see **leaven**

Hammerstein, Oscar H. (1847–1919) US theatrical manager. After making a fortune from his invention of a cigar-making machine, he turned to the theater and built and managed several New York theaters. His grandson *Oscar H. (II)* (1895–1960) wrote librettos and lyrics for many successful musicals (*Show Boat, Oklahoma, The King and I, South Pacific, Sound of Music*).

*Hammurabi: King of Babylon who ruled 1792–1750 BCE. His legal code, discovered early in the 20th cent., contains interesting parallels with biblical legislation, probably deriving from similar origins.

Ha-Motzi ("Who Brings Forth"): Key word and name of blessing over bread. As bread is held to characterize a meal, the *H.* blessing became a grace before meals.

Hananiah ben Teradyon (2nd cent.): TANNA. For defying the Roman prohibition on teaching Torah, he was sentenced to death, and burned at the stake wrapped in a Torah scroll. He was the father of BERURIAH.

Handlin, Oscar (1915–): US historian. Professor of history at Harvard, his studies include a series on American immigrants, combining historical and sociological insights, that was awarded the Pulitzer Prize.

Hannah: Wife of El-kanah, mother of SAMUEL. Long childless, she vowed that if she were vouchsafed a son, he would be dedicated to the service of God. As a consequence, she took Samuel to Eli, who raised him (I Sam. 1).

Hannah and her seven sons: Family killed by Antiochus Epiphanes for refusing to commit idolatry. Among Christians, they were called the Maccabees, and venerated as saints.

Ha-Noar ha-Tziyyoni ("Zionist Youth"): Pioneering Zionist youth movement, founded in Eastern Europe. Its world organization was set up in the early 1930s and established the settlements of the HA-OVED HA-TZIYYONI movement. Its 2,000 members in Israel have 6 kibbutzim.

Ha-noten teshuah ("He who gives salvation"): Beginning of prayer for the welfare of the government. It has been said in the synagogue on Sabbaths and festivals in many countries since the 14th cent. In Israel it is replaced by a prayer for the State.

Hanukkah ("Dedication"): Festival celebrated for eight days starting from Kislev 25 to commemorate the successful struggle of the HASMONEANS, under JUDAH THE MACCABEE, and the miracle in the Temple when the undefiled oil sufficient for only one day lasted for eight. Lights are kindled in the Jewish home on each evening (one on the 1st, two on the 2nd, etc.), and the MAOZ TZUR hymn is sung. HALLEL is recited in the liturgy and the story of the miracle is related in the AL HA-NISSIM addition to the *amidah* and the grace after meals. The 8-branched H. lamp (*hanukkiah*) has often been the object of artistic design. Among the special games which developed around the festival is the spinning of the H top (*dreidel* or *trendl*).

Ha-Oved ha-Tziyyoni ("The Zionist Worker"): Israel labor movement, part of the Independent Labor Party. It has 18 moshavim with 5,400 members.

Haphetz Hayyim (1835–1933): Rabbinical scholar and Orthodox leader in Lithuania, born Israel Meir Kahan. His works include *Haphetz Hayyim*, on the laws of talebearing and slander, and *Mishnah Berurah*, summarizing the views of commentators on Karo's *Shulhan Arukh*.

haphtarah ("conclusion"): Reading from the prophetical books of the Bible following the Reading of the Law in the Morning Service in the synagogue on Sabbaths and festivals. On fast days, a h. is read in the Afternoon Service. The person called to read the h. is called the *maphtir* and is first called to a reading from the Pentateuch (generally repetition of the last few verses). A special benediction is recited before and four benedictions after the prophetical reading. The prophetical portions have been chosen because of a connection with the pentateuchal section or the relation to the festival or special Sabbath. The reading of the *h.* goes back to Second Temple times. The selection varies somewhat between communities. In modern times, it has become a custom for a boy on his BAR MITZVAH to read the *h.*

Ha-Poel ("The Worker"): Israeli workers' sports organization affiliated with the HISTADRUT. The first branch was established in 1924 and by 1974 it had 90,000 members. Its international sports conventions are known as the Poeliad.

Ha-Poel ha-Mizrahi ("The Mizrahi Workers"): Religious pioneering and labor movement. From its foundation in 1921, it was part of the Zionist organization. It has joined almost all coalition governments in Israel. In 1955 it merged with MIZRAHI to form the NATIONAL RELIGIOUS PARTY. Its youth movement is Bene Akiva and its kibbutz organization HA-KIBBUTZ HA-DATI.

Ha-Poel ha-Tzair ("The Young Worker"): Labor party in Eretz Israel from 1905 until 1930, when it merged with Aḥdut Avodah to form MAPAI. Its members set up the first kevutzah (at Deganyah) and the first *moshav ovedim* (at Nahalal).

Harkavy, Albert H. (1835–1919): Russian orientalist and scholar of Jewish history. In 1877 he became librarian of the Hebrew department in the Imperial Public Library in St. Petersburg. He wrote on the history of Russian Jewry, the Karaites, and many other aspects of Judaica. *Alexander H.* (1863–1939), Yiddish lexicographer, was born in Russia and settled in the US in 1886. He was a Yiddish journalist and published standard dictionaries of Yiddish.

Harman, Avraham (1914–): Israeli public figure. Born in London, he settled in Palestine in 1938. He was a member of the Jewish Agency Executive (1955–59) and Israeli ambassador to the US (1959–68). From 1968 he was president of the Hebrew University. His wife ZENA H. (1914–) was elected chairman of UNICEF in 1964.

ḥaroset: Paste made of ground apples, walnuts, almonds, cinnamon, and other spices with wine, eaten in the course of the Passover Seder service. It was held to symbolize the mortar of which the Israelites had been deprived in Egypt.

Harris, Julie (1925–): US actress. She made her name in the play and movie version of *Member of the Wedding* and *I Am a Camera* (creating the role of Sally Bowles). Among her stage successes was a solo performance about Emily Dickinson.

Hart: Canadian family of early settlers. Its members included *Aaron H.* (1724–1800), who settled in Trois Rivières, Quebec, and became one of the wealthiest men in the British Colonies; and his son *Ezekiel H.* (1770–1843), who was elected to represent Trois Rivières in the Canadian Assembly in 1807 and 1809 but was not allowed to take his seat, as authorities thought he could not be faithful to the Christian oath, being a Jew. Descendants of the family held prominent positions in public life in Canada.

Hart, Aaron (1670–1756): First English chief rabbi. Born in Breslau, from 1704 he served as rabbi of the London Ashkenazi community, officiating in the Great Synagogue.

Hart, Lorenz Milton (1895–1943): US lyricist. He collaborated with Richard Rodgers in a series of popular musicals. He was noted for his witty and literate lyrics.

Hart, Moss (1904–1961): US playwright. He wrote many successful comedies, some of them in collaboration, such as *You Can't Take It with You* and *The Man Who Came to Dinner*, written with George S. KAUFMAN. He wrote an autobiography, *Act I*.

harvest, harvest festivals: In the biblical period, harvesting was the occasion for merrymaking. All three PILGRIM FESTIVALS are specifically mentioned as h.f. PASSOVER was the occasion for bringing the barley-flour offering to the Temple; the Feast of WEEKS was the first-fruit harvest festival; and Tabernacles designated the end of the entire harvest. In modern Israel, their agricultural significance has been revived.

Ḥasdai Crescas see **Crescas**

Ḥasdai ibn Shaprut see **ibn Shaprut**

Ha-Shiloaḥ: Hebrew literary monthly, founded in 1896 and edited in Odessa until 1920. Its editors included Aḥad ha-Am, Bialik, and J. Klausner. From 1920 until 1926 it appeared in Jerusalem. It was regarded as a model of Hebrew writing, both in form and content.

Ha-Shomer ("The Watchman"): Jewish self-defense organization in Palestine. It was set up in 1909 and commanded by Israel Shochat. Its functions were later assumed by the Haganah.

Ha-Shomer ha-Tzair ("The Young Guard"): Zionist-socialist youth movement. The formation of its first groups, in Galicia in 1913, coincided with the postwar period of national and social awakening. Many immigrated to Palestine and founded the settlement organization Ha-Kibbutz ha-Artzi. Its ideology was influenced by Marxism. Until World War II, the main membership was in Eastern and Central Europe. In 1946, it became a political party in Palestine, advocating a bi-national state. In 1948, it fused with Aḥdut ha-Avodah–Left Poalei Zion to form Mapam.

Ḥaside Ashkenaz ("Pious Men of Germany"): Name given to German school of pietists and mystics in the 13th cent. Its main figures were Judah ben Samuel He-Ḥasid and Eleazar ben Judah of Worms. The most important collection of its teachings is in the *Sepher Ḥasidim*.

Ḥasideans: Obscure Jewish pietist sect which flourished during the Second Temple period. They prayed frequently, meditating for one hour before and after prayer, and were zealous in fulfilling the commandments. They chose martyrdom rather than accept the decrees of Antiochus Epiphanus and ceased to support the Hasmoneans when the latter became overconcerned with political affairs. It has been surmised that they were the forerunners of the Pharisees.

ḥasidei ummot ha-olam ("pious of the nations of the world"): Righteous non-Jews who, according to the Talmud (*Sanh.* 13:2), "have a share in the world to come." In recent times, the term has been applied to non-Jews who risked their lives to save Jews under the Nazis.

Ḥasidism: Religious movement founded by Israel Baal Shem Tov in Volhynia and Podolia in the 18th cent. His teachings appealed especially to the uneducated, by rabbinic standards. He taught that zeal, prayer with emotional feeling, and humility were superior to study. He was succeeded by Dov Ber of Mezhirich, who organized the growing movement and attracted many followers from Lithuania. His opponents (of whom the Vilna Gaon was outstanding) regarded the teachings as heretical. The opposition became even stronger when the movement was led by Shneour Zalman of Lyady, who introduced Ḥabad Ḥ. founded on a more rationalist approach than that of his predecessors. The opponents (MITNAGGEDIM) issued repeated bans on Ḥ. and its practices. Inside Ḥ. the *tzaddik* was elevated to the role of intermediary between God and man. This special status was taken by different *tzaddikim* in various ways, but the overall consequence was a decline in the movement, rent between the various dynasties of *tzaddikim* and often the bearer of superstitious practices. In the course of time, the situation stabilized and the Ḥasidim even found common ground with the Mitnaggedim in their struggle against HASKALAH. Under the Nazis, the European Ḥasidic centers were destroyed. Only a few *tzaddikim* escaped and reestablished their "courts," in Israel and the US. Ḥ's teachings were mostly concerned with morality and religion. Central were the doctrines of joy, enthusiasm, and communion with God (DEVEKUT). Another principle was inner devotion (KAVVANAH) at prayer. The *tzaddik* (or *admor* or *rebbe*) is linked to God and could be asked to mediate with God. He was ascribed with holiness, and his every action given a holy aura. The main teachings of Ḥ. have a mystical basis. In the 20th cent. they received a new currency (neo-Ḥasidism) and were popularized by such writers as Martin Buber,

Abraham Joshua Heschel, and Elie Wiesel.

Haskalah ("Enlightenment"): Movement for the dissemination of modern European culture among Jews. In the mid-18th cent. certain Jews in central Europe desired to conform with the non-Jewish population and break away from the exclusiveness of Jewish life. Its cradles were in Holland and Italy, but the movement really began in Germany, and its pioneer was Moses MENDELSSOHN. Important influences were the German translation of the Bible, together with the commentary issued by Mendelssohn and his friends, and the journal HA-MEASSEPH. The movement spread eastward and met considerable opposition in Galicia at the hands of the Orthodox, including the Ḥasidim. H. also penetrated southern Russian Jewry. The center of H. in Eastern Europe was Lithuania, especially Vilna. An extensive literature in Hebrew and Yiddish appeared throughout the 19th cent. The Russian government intermittently encouraged H., and this was seen by the Orthodox as an assimilationist tendency to be fiercely resisted. H. developed Hebrew as a modern literary language and neglected Yiddish. Outstanding figures included the scholars N.

KROCHMAL and S. J. RAPOPORT, the satirists J. PERL and I. ERTER, and writers I. B. LEVINSON, M. J. LEBENSOHN, and A. MAPU. The H. movement came to an end toward the end of the century under the impact of assimilation on the one hand and nationalism on the other. The adherents of the H. were known as *maskilim*.

haskamah ("approbation"): Official authorization added at the beginning of a book. After the introduction of printing, it became customary to incorporate an approbation from the rabbinic authorities, a measure taken to avoid unnecessary friction with the Church censorship. Later Jewish writers sought the h. as an official recommendation of their scholarship (and often of their orthodoxy). Among Sephardi communities, a communal regulation is called h. (or often *ascama*).

Hasmoneans: Family name of priestly dynasty starting with MATTATHIAS. The origin of the name is uncertain. In 166 BCE Mattathias and his five sons, JUDAH THE MACCABEE, JONATHAN, SIMON, JOHN, and ELEAZAR, revolted against the Syrian ruler Antiochus Epiphanes, who was imposing a policy of extreme Hellenism on his subjects. In the course of time they succeeded in obtaining victories over the Syrians and reestablishing Jewish rule in the country. This proved a major factor in the development of Judaism, encouraging the rise of pietists and WISDOM teachers. Jonathan secured the high priesthood, which was combined with civil power also by his successors. Simon's son JOHN HYRCANUS (135–105 BCE) considerably extended the area of the State, and his rule marked the transition of the H. to a semi-Hellenized secular military dynasty. He broke with the PHARISEES and allied himself with the SADDUCEES. The reign of ALEXANDER YANNAI (104–76 BCE) was marked by frequent warfare. His opposition to the Pharisees led to a civil war, and the situation improved only under the rule of his widow, SALOME ALEXANDRA (76–67 BCE), under whom the Pharisees resumed a position of leadership. After her death, her sons contested the succession and the country was plunged into civil war. From 63 CE the country was a Roman province, with the Romans holding the real power. The last of the H. were put to death by HEROD (including his wife MARIAMNE and her sons).

Hassan, Sir Joshua Abraham (1915–): Gibraltar statesman. He was mayor of Gibraltar from 1945 to 1950 and again from 1953. He was chief member of Gibraltar's Legislative Council from 1950 to 1964 and became its first chief minister, holding office until 1969 and again from 1972.

Ḥatam Sopher see **Sopher, Moses**

Ha-Tenuah ha-Meuḥedet ("The United Movement"): Israeli pioneer youth organization, founded in 1944 by MAPAI supporters. In 1951 it joined the World HA-BONIM Organization.

Ha-Tikvah ("The Hope"): National anthem of Israel; originally the hymn of the Zionist movement. The words were written by Naphtah Herz IMBER and first published in 1886.

Ha-Tzephirah ("The Dawn"): Hebrew paper founded as a weekly by Ḥayyim Selig Slonimsky in Warsaw in 1862. In 1886 it became a daily. There were several intervals in its publication. From 1904 its editor was Nahum SOKOLOW. Originally devoted to science and technology, it became increasingly a literary paper and journal.

havdalah ("differentiation"): Ceremony designating the termination of Sabbaths and festivals. It consists of blessings over wine, spices, fire, and on the "differentiation" between the sacred and the everyday. It is recited both in the synagogue and in the home. A briefer form is incorporated in the Saturday-evening *Maariv amidah*. Connected with the ceremony are folk songs, often associated with ELIJAH, who, it is believed, will return as forerunner of the Messiah on a Saturday evening, as well as folk art (especially in the design of the spice box).

haver ("member"): In the Second Temple period, term used for one belonging to a group which was punctilious in its ritual observances. Later it was a title given to a scholar. In modern times, the term means "comrade."

havlagah ("self-restraint"): Policy adopted by the *yishuv* in Palestine during the Arab revolt of 1936–39, based on self-defense without retaliation.

Hawaii, US state. Jewish traders visited there in the mid-19th cent. The first Jewish institution was the Hebrew Benevolent Society, founded in 1901, and the community was established in 1938. Most of the present population of H. have arrived since World War II. 1,500 Jews were living there in 1976.

Ha-Yom ("The Day"): First Hebrew daily newspaper. It appeared in St. Petersburg in 1886–88 and was edited by Judah Leib Kantor.

Hayon, Nehemiah (c. 1655–c. 1730): Kabbalist and Sabbetaian. Born in Palestine, he became a rabbi and wandered throughout Europe. He joined the believers in SHABBETAI TZEVI and published kabbalistic works, for which he was excommunicated by many rabbis. He died in North Africa.

Hays, Arthur Garfield (1881–1954): US advocate. He fought for civil rights, and was defense attorney in the Scopes trial and the Sacco-Vanzetti case. He was general counsel of the American Civil Liberties Union.

Hayyim ben Isaac of Volozhin (1749–1821): Rabbi and educator; founder of the Volozhin yeshivah. He was a disciple of the Vilna Gaon, whom he succeeded as the accepted leader of Lithuanian Jewry.

Hayyuj, Judah ben David (c. 945–c. 1000): Hebrew grammarian. He was born in North Africa but lived most of his life in Spain. H. wrote in Arabic, producing two main grammatical works dealing with "weak" verbs.

hazak ("be strong") or **hakaz ve-ematz** ("be strong and of good courage," cf. Josh. 1:19): a congratulatory phrase said upon completion of a piece of work. On concluding the reading of a book of the Pentateuch in the synagogue, all present say *hazak hazak ve-nithazzak*. Sephardim congratulate a person who has performed a *mitzvah* with *hazak u-varukh*.

hazakah ("taking possession"): Talmudic term for the act of acquiring ownership of property. It is also used for the presumptive right resulting from undisturbed possession (for land, over 3 years).

Hazaz, Hayyim (1897–1973): Hebrew author. Born in the Ukraine, he lived in Jerusalem from 1931. His novels are set among Jewish communities in various parts of the world (Ukraine, Yemen, Israel) and at different historical periods.

Hazon ish see **Karelitz, Avraham Yeshayahu**

Hazor: Ancient city in Galilee. One of the largest cities in early Palestine, it is known from the 19th cent. BCE. Later it was destroyed by Joshua. Its king led the alliance defeated by Barak and Deborah (Judg. 4–5). H. was rebuilt by Solomon. Extensive excavations have been conducted there, first by J. Garstang (1928) and then by Y. Yadin (1955–58 and 1968–69). The town of H. (population in 1974 5,400) is in Lower Galilee. The kibbutz of H. is in the southern coastal plain.

ḥazzan: Originally a communal official; now, a cantor. In talmudic times, his functions included the preservation of order, the security of the town, and the administering of certain punishments. He was also responsible for arrangements in the synagogue. The ḥ. was often the poet and stood beside the cantor; eventually the title was transferred to the cantor himself. As such he had not only to possess a good voice but also a good character. (See also CANTOR AND CANTORAL MUSIC.)

he (ה): Fifth letter of the Hebrew alphabet. Numerical value 5. Pronounced as h. At the end of words it is silent, unless there is a dot (mappik) inside it.

Heaven: The upper part of the universe, according to the traditional Jewish world view. It is regarded as the home of God and the "heavenly hosts." It was only in Second Temple times that there developed the concept of H. as the abode of souls after death. This was identified with paradise or the Garden of Eden. Vivid descriptions of the life of the righteous in H. are to be found in midrashic and mystical sources. Reform Jews and other modern thinkers tend to refer the concept of H. to a spiritual state rather than an actual place.

heave-offering (terumah): Temple offering to the sanctuary or to the priests. It is used especially for the tithe of produce, but also refers to the dough offering given to the priests; this may not be consumed by anyone but a priest.

Hebrew Immigration Aid Society see HIAS

Hebrew language: H. belongs to the Canaanite branch of Semitic languages and was spoken in Palestine before the Israelite conquest. It is the language of the Bible (with a few exceptions in the cognate language of ARAMAIC). It borrowed many words from surrounding languages. After the Babylonian Exile, its usage gradually diminished as Aramaic, the lingua franca of the Near East, became generally spoken. However, H. remained a literary language. After about 200 CE, even Palestinian Jews no longer used H.; they wrote in Aramaic and Greek. From the 6th cent., literary works were again written in H., at first in Palestine, then throughout the Diaspora. For a time the language, in various countries, was influenced by the predominant Arabic. In the 18th and 19th cent., H. was again used for general as well as religious literature (under the influence of HASKALAH). The writers of this period returned to the Bible for their inspiration. The modern era of H. began in the 1880s. It became again a living language with its everyday use by the new settlers in Palestine. In 1921 it was recognized under the British Mandate as an official language in Palestine. Its usage was officially directed by the Vaad ha-Lashon, which in 1953 became the ACADEMY OF THE HEBREW LANGUAGE.

Hebrew Teachers' College: College for training Jewish teachers, established in Boston in 1921. It offers graduate degrees in education and Hebrew literature.

Hebrew Theological College: Orthodox rabbinical school in Chicago, founded in 1922. In addition to ordination, it offers degrees in Hebrew literature.

Hebrew Union College–Jewish Institute of Religion: US Reform rabbinical seminary, consisting of the Hebrew Union College, Cincinnati (founded by I. M. WISE in 1875), and the Jewish Institute of Religion, New York (founded by S. S. WISE in 1922), which merged in 1950. The Cincinnati school houses the American Jewish Archives. It has graduated over 800 rabbis. It also has centers in Los Angeles and Jerusalem. Nelson GLUECK was president of HUC-JIR from the merger until his death in 1971, when he was succeeded by Alfred Gottschalk.

Hebrew University: University in Jerusalem. Proposals to found such a university were made from the early period of the Zionist movement. Land was purchased in 1914 on Mt. Scopus, and the cornerstone was laid by Chaim Weizmann in 1918. The H.U. was opened by Lord Balfour in 1925. It developed steadily, but as a result of the 1948 war, the Scopus campus was cut off from the rest of Jerusalem and the H.U. had to use other premises, eventually developing another campus at Givat Ram, Jerusalem. Its medical school was situated at Ein Karem, Jerusalem, in conjunction with the Hadassah Hospital, and its agricultural faculty in Rehovot. After the 1967 war, the Mt. Scopus campus was reopened and extended. The H.U. had 16,000 students in 1976, including 3,000 from abroad. It has seven faculties (humanities, social sciences, science, law, medicine, dental medicine, agriculture) and four schools (education, pharmacy, social work, library). The Jewish National and University Library is an outstanding part of the university. The budget comes from fees, contributions from "Friends of the H.U." in many parts of the world, and the Israeli government. Its first president was J. L. MAG-NES, who was succeeded by S. BRODETSKY, B. MAZAR, E. ELATH, and A. HARMAN.

Hebrews (*Ivrim*): In the Bible, the Jewish people. The term originates either from descendants of Eber (Gen. 10:24) or from those who came from the other side of (*ever*) the river Euphrates. It is first found in Gen. 14:13. It has been identified with HABIRU, but this is now questioned.

Hebron: City south of Jerusalem, with a population of 38,309 (1967). Abraham bought from the Hittites a plot of land there—the Cave of Machpelah—in which to bury his wife Sarah. The other Patriarchs and their wives were also traditionally buried there, and a mosque now stands on the reputed site, revered by Muslims and Jews. H. was David's capital before he moved it to Jerusalem. A Jewish community existed in the Byzantine period and under Arab rule. It was one of the four sacred cities of the Jews. The SLO-BODKA yeshivah was transferred there in 1925. Many Jews were massacred there by Arabs in 1929, and the others left. Between 1948 and 1967, H. was under Jordanian rule. After 1967, Jews again settled there, establishing an area

known by one of the town's biblical names, Kiriath-Arba.

Hecht, Ben (1893–1964): US novelist and playwright. He wrote novels, an autobiography (*A Child of the Century*), plays, and film scenarios (including scripts for the MARX BROTHERS). He was one of the leading US supporters of the IRGUN TZEVAI LEUMI in the 1940s.

ḥeder ("room"): Elementary religious school of the type prevalent in Eastern Europe. Frequently it consisted of a single room, sometimes in the house of the teacher. In the 19th cent. an attempt to moderate the institution led to the *ḥ. metukkan* ("improved ḥ.").

He-Ḥalutz ("The Pioneer"): Association of pioneering youth movements, aiming to prepare and train for settlement on the land in Israel. The first H. group in the US was founded in 1905. Groups were formed throughout Europe, especially after World War I. World War II saw the end of the Central and Eastern European branches of the movement. It operated within the framework of the Histadrut.

Heifetz, Jascha (1901–): Violinist. Born in Vilna, he settled in the US after the Russian Revolution. He first played in public at the age of four and eventually became recognized as one of the world's outstanding violinists.

Heine, Heinrich (1797–1856): German poet and essayist. He became a Protestant in order to advance his legal career. His *Reisebilder und Buch der Lieder* (1827) established his reputation. In 1831 he settled in Paris, where he remained for the rest of his life. From 1847 he suffered from a spinal disease and for the rest of his life was a helpless invalid, confined to what he called his "mattress grave." Some of his poems were set to music by Schubert, Brahms, and others. His prose style was also brilliant and his satire biting. His most popular poem was *Die Lorelei*. He became increasingly interested in Jewish history and culture in his late years and wrote *Hebräische Melodien* and the unfinished novel *Der Rabbi von Bacherach*.

Hekhalot, Books of: Mystical Midrashim of the talmudic and gaonic period. Many describe the perilous ascent to heaven to behold the divine glory and the heavenly palaces (*hekhalot*).

Helena (d. 56 CE): Queen of Adiabene; wife of Monobaz I. Her son Izates converted to Judaism (c. 30 CE). She lived her latter years in Jerusalem and made gifts to the Temple. Buried in the Tomb of the Kings in Jerusalem, her sarcophagus was discovered and is now in the Louvre.

hell see **Gehinnom**

Hellenism: Greek culture dominant in the Middle East from the 4th cent. BCE. Palestine and many Diaspora centers came within the orbit of H. Outside Palestine Greek became the language of these Jews, and by the 3rd cent. BCE the Bible had been translated into Greek (SEPTUAGINT). In Palestine tension between the Hellenists, supported by the Seleucid rulers, and the anti-Hellenists led to the Maccabean Revolt. The success of the Maccabees ensured the dominance of the anti-Hellenists, although the influence of H. continued to be felt in many ways within the Jewish cultural development, and especially among the non-Jewish population of the country. Material life was predominantly Hellenist, and many Greek words entered the vocabulary. Outside the country, a Jewish-Hellenist culture developed, notably in Alexandria, where the outstanding figure was PHILO. The pagan character of H., however, prevented the Jews from entering entirely into its civilization. The impact of H. declined from the 2nd cent.

Heller, Bunim (1908–   ): Yiddish writer. His first

writings reflect his early Communist sympathies but in the 1950s, he became disillusioned, and he left his native Poland for Tel Aviv in 1957. Some of his later poems are inspired by independent Jewish life in Israel.

Heller, Joseph (1923–): US novelist. His *Catch-22* was a powerful satire on modern warfare, juxtaposing realism with farce, which had a strong impact in the 1960s. He also wrote *Something Happened*.

Heller, Yomtov Lipmann (1579–1654): Rabbinic scholar and commentator on the MISHNAH. Born in Bavaria, by the time he was 18 he was a *dayyan* in Prague. Later he served in Vienna and other cities. His chief work, on the Mishnah, is *Tosephot Yom Tov*.

Hellman, Lillian Florence (1905–): US playwright. Her major plays include *The Children's Hour*, *The Little Foxes*, *The Autumn Garden*, and *Watch on the Rhine*. Her autobiographical writings in *Pentimento* and *An Unfinished Woman* achieved critical and popular success.

Helsingfors Program: Zionist policy program aimed at settlement in Palestine adopted at a conference of Russian Zionists, held in 1906.

Henriques: Anglo-Jewish family of Marrano origin. They included *Henry Straus Quixano H.* (1865–1925), lawyer and president of the Board of Deputies of British Jews, 1922–25; *Sir Basil Lucas Quixano H.* (1890–1961), social worker and authority on juvenile delinquency; and *Robert David Quixano H.* (1905–1967), soldier and author, who wrote novels and *A Hundred Hours to Suez*, on the 1956 Sinai Campaign.

Hep! Hep! Derogatory anti-Semitic cry; name given to riots in Germany in 1819. According to one theory it originated from the initials of the phrase *Hierosolyma est perdita* ("Jerusalem is lost").

hephker: Ownerless property and renunciation of ownership. In Jewish law, such property can be legally acquired by the person who first takes possession of it.

Herberg, Will (1906–1977): US sociologist. At first active in Communist circles, he later concentrated on general sociological studies. On Jewish topics, he wrote *Judaism and Modern Man* and *Protestant, Catholic, Jew*.

Herem: Originally, property separated for sacred purposes. Later an excommunication or ban.

hermeneutics, talmudic: Rules evolved by the rabbis for interpreting biblical texts. Their origin is unknown but they were first classified by HILLEL, who formulated seven basic principles, viz.: (1) *Kal va-Homer, a fortiori,* deduction from a minor to a major case; (2) *Gezervah Shanah,* inference by the analogy of words; (3) *Binyan Av mi-Katuv Ehad,* principles derived from a single verse, applied generally; (4) *Binyan Av mi-Shnei Ketuvim,* which is the same as (3) but based on two verses; (5) *Kelal u-Pherat u-Pherat u-Kelal,* limitation of a general principle derived from a particular (and vice versa); (6) *Ka-Yotze Bo be-Makom Aher,* exposition by reference to a similar passage; (7) *Devar ha-Lamed me-Inyano,* deduction from context. These principles were expanded to 13 by R. ISHMAEL and to 32 by R. Eluezer b. Yose ha-Galili. Other principles of interpretation included apparently superfluous words and letters, GEMATRIA and NOTARIKON.

Hermon: Mountain range in Lebanon and Syria; from 1967, partly under Israeli rule. Its highest peak is 9,232 feet above sea level and is always covered with snow.

Herod I (c. 73–4 BCE): King of Judea, Samaria, Galilee, and Idumea. He was appointed by his father ANTIPATER to be governor of Galilee (47). His high-handed actions led to his being brought before the Sanhedrin, but he was saved by his Roman protectors. After Antipater's death, the Parthians made ANTIGONUS king, but H. escaped to Rome and with Roman help seized Jerusalem and was appointed king (37 BCE). He was an energetic ruler and greatly enhanced the wealth of the country, engaging in ambitious projects (such as rebuilding the Temple), and extending the territory of the state (defeating the Nabateans and being granted extensive areas). He was, however, unpopular with his subjects, who remained attached to the Hasmoneans and who resented his heavy taxation. His private life was tragic, and he put to death his wife, the Hasmonean Mariamne, their two sons, and his firstborn son Antipater. He also executed leading Sadducees. In the New Testament he is associated with the "Massacre of the Innocents," unknown from any other source.

Herod Agrippa I see **Agrippa I**

Herod Agrippa II see **Agrippa II**

Herod Archelaus see **Archelaus**

Hertz, Joseph Herman (1872–1946): British chief rabbi. Of Slovakian birth, he was taken as a child to New York and was the first gradu-

ate of the JEWISH THEOLOGI-
CAL SEMINARY. He held office
in Johannesburg but was expelled for his pro-British
views during the Boer War.
In 1913 he was elected chief
rabbi of the British Empire.
His strong support of Zionism played a part in the negotiations leading to the
Balfour Declaration. His
works include *The Book of
Jewish Thoughts*, and a
prayer book and Pentateuch,
both with English commen-
taries.

Herut ("Freedom"):
Israeli political movement,
founded in 1948 by members
of IRGUN TZEVAI LEUMI. It
was led by Menahem BEGIN.
Its program included the territorial integrity of the land
of Israel and liberal economic
policies. It was one of the
largest opposition parties. In
1965 it aligned with the
LIBERAL party to form
GAḤAL.

Herz, Henriette (1764–
1847): Society leader in Berlin. Daughter of a Hamburg
Sephardi physician, at the
age of 15 she married *Marcus H.* (1747–1803), physician and philosopher. He
was a noted doctor and received the title of professor
of medicine. His correspondence with Kant is of importance for understanding the
development of the latter's
thought. His wife's charm,
beauty, and education made
her salon outstanding. She
was baptized in 1817.

Herzl, Theodor (1860–
1904): Founder of the
World Zionist Organization,
journalist, and author. Born
in Budapest, he lived in Vienna from 1878 and achieved
a reputation as social dramatist and feuilletonist in the
Neue Freie Presse. He was
sent by his paper as its
representative in Paris. His
interest in the Jewish problem was intensified by the
Dreyfus Trial, and in 1896
he published *Der Judenstaat*
("The Jewish State"), advocating the establishment of
an independent Jewish state
endorsed by the big powers.
This stimulated various elements throughout the Jew-
ish world, including the HIB-
BAT ZION. Thereafter H.'s
main preoccupation was with
Zionism, and in 1897 he convened the first ZIONIST CON-
GRESS at Basle. Here he
founded the World Zionist
Organization, which he
headed until his death, jour-
neying extensively to seek
support for Zionism. He had
meetings with the Sultan of
Turkey in Constantinople,
with the German Emperor
Wilhelm II in Palestine in
1898, and the czar's minister,
Von Plehve, in Russia. He
also worked at establishing a
financial basis for Zionist activities (the JEWISH COLONIAL
TRUST, 1899). He was en-

thusiastically received everywhere by the Jewish masses. Persistent contacts in Britain led to the British colonial minister, Joseph Chamberlain, proposing a region of UGANDA for Jewish settlement. H. at first tended to accept the proposal, but the firm opposition of the Russian Zionists at the Sixth Zionist Congress in 1904 led him to modify his views. In his last years he had interviews with the Pope and the King of Italy. His health gave way under the strain of his activities, and he died at the age of 44. In 1949 his remains and those of his family were reburied on the highest hill west of Jerusalem, which was renamed Mt. Herzl. His novel *Altneuland* gave a utopian picture of a Palestine settled by Jews.

Herzliyyah: Israeli town in southern Sharon, founded in 1924. One section (H. Pittuah) is a leading holiday resort. The population in 1972 was 40,100.

Herzog, Yitzhak ha-Levi (1888–1959): Rabbi. Born in Lomza, Poland, he was appointed rabbi of Belfast in 1915 and of Dublin in 1919 (chief rabbi of the Irish Free State in 1925). In 1936 he was elected Ashkenazi chief rabbi of Palestine. He wrote *The Main Institutions of Jewish Law*.

Heschel, Abraham Joshua (1907–1972): Philosopher and scholar. Born in Poland, he settled in the US in 1940 and from 1945 taught at the Jewish Theological Seminary, New York. His religious philosophy was influenced both by modern existentialism and by Hasidic tradition. He was active in various humanitarian causes, including the civil-rights movement and the struggle for Soviet Jewry.

Heshvan see Marheshvan

hesped: A eulogy in honor of a dead person.

Hess, Moses (1812–1875): German socialist and father of Zionist Socialism. His philosophical works were largely about Spinoza and Hegel, whom he interpreted in a socialist direction. At first he worked closely with Marx and Engels, but broke with them, especially after the publication of the *Communist Manifesto*. He eventually settled in Paris, and took an increasing interest in Jewish history. His *Rome and Jerusalem* (1862) presented a Zionist ideology and a program for its realization.

Hess, Dame Myra (1890–1965): British pianist. She appeared with symphony orchestras as soloist and in chamber ensembles. During World War II, she inaugurated and ran daily lunch-hour concerts at London's National Gallery.

het (ח): Eighth letter of the Hebrew alphabet. Numerical value: 8. Pronounced like *ch* in "loch."

hevrah kaddisha ("holy brotherhood"): Society devoted to burying the dead. Although mentioned earlier, it became a recognized institution in the 17th cent. Its members worked on a voluntary basis. They often visited the sick and comforted mourners.

Heym, Stefan (1913–): German writer; in the US 1935–52, where he was active in the Communist Party. In 1952 he returned to East Germany. His writings include political works, biographies, and novels (*The King David Report*).

Hezekiah: King of Judah who reigned c. 727–698 BCE. He is regarded in the Bible and Talmud as one of the most commendable kings. He eliminated foreign religious practices from the worship, and rid Jerusalem of pagan altars and idols. His reign was also one of material prosperity. He was influenced by the prophets, notably ISAIAH. He fortified Jerusalem and constructed the SILOAM tunnel to ensure its water supply. H. led an alliance which challenged Assyrian suzerainity. This led to the siege of Jerusalem by the Assyrians under Sennacherib. For some reason the city did not fall, and the Assyrians returned home.

HIAS: Acronym of Hebrew Sheltering and Immigrant Aid Society, formed in New York in 1906 in order to assist Jewish immigration to America. After World War I, it established offices in Eastern Europe to help Jews preparing to leave. It has also been active in Israel. From 1954, it became part of the American Joint Distribution Committee. In the 1970s it was active in Vienna assisting Russian Jewish immigrants bound for the US.

Hibbat Zion ("Love of Zion"): Zionist organization founded in Russia in 1882. Societies were organized especially in Eastern Europe but also Western Europe and the US. The first group of young settlers went to Palestine in 1882 (BILU). A federation of the societies was formed as a result of the Kattowitz Conference in 1884. The leader of the movement was Leon PINSKER. The practical trend in the movement, headed by LILIENBLUM, concentrated on promoting settlement activities; the intellectual current headed by AHAD HA-AM stressed cultural activity. A third trend was represented by the religious Zionists. In 1897 nearly all the H.Z. societies joined the newly founded World Zionist Organization. The movement continued an independent existence until 1920, and for most of its latter years was headed by USSISHKIN.

HICEM: Organization established in 1927 to assist Jewish migration. Its name came from the initials of the three sponsoring bodies (HIAS, ICA, and *Emig-Direkt*). Its work extended during the Nazi period. In 1945 its activities were transferred to Hias.

hiddushim see **novellae**

high commissioner of Palestine: Chief executive official appointed by the British during the period of the MANDATE. The first h.c. was Sir Herbert SAMUEL (1920–25), the only Jewish h.c., during whose period of office the foundation of the Jewish National Home was firmly laid, although some of his actions disappointed the Jewish community. He was followed by Lord Plumer (1925–28), whose administration was energetic. He was followed by Sir John Chancellor (1928–31) and Sir Arthur Wauchope (1931–37), the latter in particular being sympathetic to Jewish aspirations. Sir Harold MacMichael (1938–44) was unpopular with the Jews, notably as a result of his refusal to be flexible on the admittance of refugees from Nazi Germany. The last h.c. was Sir

Alan Cunningham (1945–48).

high place (*bamah*): Place for worship, usually made of stones. It was frequently built on a hill, but sometimes in a valley. The Canaanite h.p. consisted of an altar, a pillar, and a sacred tree. Although worship at high places was banned after the conquest of Canaan, it remained widespread until the establishment of the Temple at Jerusalem. Although they were sometimes used for the God of Israel, they tended to be associated with pagan cults. They were finally removed by Hezekiah and Josiah. Remains have been found in modern excavations.

high priest: Chief ecclesiastical authority in the TEMPLE. The office was held by AARON and his descendants. The h.p. was in charge of the Temple administration and entitled to officiate at all sacrificial services. He was the only ministrant on the Day of Atonement, when he wore white robes and entered the Holy of Holies (the only person permitted so to do, and only on this occasion). He could only marry a virgin and was forbidden to become defiled by proximity to a corpse. In the time of Herod, the h.p. was nominated by the Jewish or Roman ruler. During the Roman War

(66–70), it was filled by lot.

Hildesheimer, Azriel (Israel) (1820–1899): German Orthodox rabbi and scholar. He founded the Berlin Rabbinical Seminary in 1873 and headed it until his death. His scholarly works include an edition of the 8th-cent. talmudic codification *Halakhot Gedolot*.

Hilfsverein der Deutschen Juden (Ger. "Relief Organization of German Jews"): German Jewish charitable society founded in 1901 to assist Jews in Eastern Europe. It supported schools in the Balkans and Palestine from 1903 to 1918 and took the initiative in founding the Haifa TECHNION. It also assisted Jewish emigration from Eastern Europe. After 1933, the H. helped Jews to leave Germany. It ceased to exist in 1941.

hillazon: Marine animal mentioned in the Talmud as the source of the dye used for the blue fringes of the TALLIT. It was very scarce and supposed to appear only once in 70 years. To obtain the right color, it had to be captured alive. In view of the problems involved, the rabbis permitted its use to be dispensed with.

Hillel (1st cent. BCE): Rabbinic authority and Pharisaic leader. Born in Babylonia, he settled in Palestine and studied with Shemaiah and Avtalyon. Eventually he became president of the Sanhedrin. He and his colleague SHAMMAI were the last of the ZUGOT; they differed on many basic issues, and the two schools of the followers continued the disputes long after their deaths; the legal decision generally followed the view of H. H. was noted for his leniency and humility. Very few of his decisions are known, but one of the most important was the institution of the PROSBUL. He also determined the basic rules of HERMENEUTICS. Asked to define the essence of Jewish law, he replied, "What is hateful to yourself, do not do to your neighbor" (Shab. 31a). He exerted a major influence on the development of Judaism.

Hillel II (2nd half of 4th cent.): *Nasi* of Palestinian Jewry. He abolished the proclamation of the new month by observation of the New Moon and substituted a permanent calendar, which meant that the Diaspora was no longer dependent on Palestine for the determination of dates. It has remained the standard Jewish calendar.

Hillel Foundation: Nationwide institution offering services to Jewish students in colleges and universities in many parts of the world, especially in North America. Founded in 1923, it is supported by B'NAI B'RITH. On many campuses it has permanent residences and facilities (Hillel Houses).

Hillman, Sidney (1887–1946): US labor leader. Born in Lithuania, he lived in the US from 1907. He was president of the Amalgamated Clothing Workers Union, 1915–46. H. was moderate in his views and was closely associated with President Franklin D. Roosevelt.

Hillquit, Morris (1869–1933): US socialist and lawyer. Born in Riga, he went to the US in 1886. He was a founder of the Socialist Party of America.

ḥillul ha-shem ("profanation of the [Divine] name"): A disreputable act by a Jew, especially toward a non-Jew. In some instances, the offense was punished by excommunication.

***Himmler, Heinrich** (1900–1945): German Nazi leader, a key figure in the massacre of European Jewry. He headed the SS from 1929 and the German police system from 1936. On his instructions, the FINAL SOLUTION was implemented and millions of Jews were sent to their deaths. He committed suicide shortly after his arrest by the British forces.

Hinnom, Valley of see **Gehinnom**

***Hiram**: King of Tyre during the reign of David and Solomon. He sent gold, wood, and craftsmen for the construction of the Temple, as well as sailors for Solomon's Red Sea fleet. In return he received, among other things, twenty towns in Galilee.

Hirsch, Baron Maurice de (1831–1896): German financier and philanthropist. Born in Munich, he lived in Brussels, and later in Paris. He made his fortune from financing railroads in Turkey, Russia, and Austria. H. made large donations to the ALLIANCE ISRAÉLITE UNIVERSELLE. After the Russian government refused his offer of a large sum to found crafts and agricultural schools in Russia, he turned to the possibility of settling Jews on the land in Argentina, and for this purpose founded the JEWISH COLONIZATION ASSOCIATION (ICA). He also created the Hirsch School Fund in Galicia and the Baron de Hirsch Fund in New York for the technical training of immigrants.

Hirsch, Samson Raphael (1808–1888): Leading exponent of Jewish Orthodoxy in Germany. He was rabbi in various congregations and, from 1851 in Frankfort. He built up its Orthodox community and turned it into the center of German orthodoxy. His writings were widely influential and he is regarded as the founder of Neo-Orthodoxy. His best-known works were *Nineteen Letters of Ben Uzziel* and *Horeb*. He also published a translation of and commentary on the Pentateuch and an annotated prayer book.

Hirsch, Samuel (1815–1889): Rabbi and philosopher. He served in Luxemburg and in 1866 went to Congregation Keneseth Israel in Philadelphia, where he was active in the Reform movement. His son, *Emil Gustav H.* (1851–1923), was also a Reform rabbi, serving in Chicago from 1880. He advocated extreme Reform and was the author of scholarly publications.

Hirschbein, Peretz (1880–1948): Yiddish dramatist, poet, and novelist. Born in Eastern Poland, he lived in the US from 1911. At first he wrote in Hebrew but in 1906 turned to Yiddish. His best-known plays include *The Idle Inn* and *Green Fields*.

Histadrut: Ha-Histadrut ha-Kelalit shel ha-Ovedim be-Eretz Yisrael ("The General Federation of Labor in Israel") is an Israeli federation of trade unions, founded in 1920. In 1973 the H. had 1,259,200 members, including 89,000 Arabs and Druze, covering manual and white-collar workers, urban and rural workers, wage workers, and the self-employed. Its Solel Boneh is the largest contractor and industrialist in the country. The H. runs a sick fund (Kupat Holim), Noar Oved for working youth, and Ha-Poel sports organization. Its press includes *Davar* and the easy-Hebrew *Omer.*

Histadrut ha-Ovedim ha-Leummit ("National Labor Federation"): Israeli non-socialist labor organization affiliated with the Herut movement. It had 81,000 members in 1973. It runs the Kupat Holim Leummi sick fund.

Histadrut Ivrit of America: Organization for the promotion of Hebrew in the US. It was founded in 1917 and since 1923 has published the weekly *Hadoar.*

*Hitler, Adolf (1889–1945): German Nazi leader. Born in Austria, he led the German National Socialist Party from the early 1920s, giving it its vicious anti-Semitic direction. In 1933 he became German chancellor, and eventually dictator, enforcing his policy against the Jews (see HOLOCAUST). As a result 6,000,000 Jews were sent to their deaths. He committed suicide after Russian troops entered Berlin.

Hittites: Ancient people

in Anatolia. From the 14th cent. BCE they pushed to the south, including Syria. The Bible mentions the H. as one of the seven nations living in Palestine prior to the Israelite conquest (Gen. 15:20). Abraham purchased the Cave of Machpelah from a Hittite, and there are other references to the H., but the term seems to have been used vaguely, not always with reference to the great Hittite Empire.

Hochschule (Lehranstalt) für die Wissenschaft des Judentums: Institute for Jewish studies and Reform rabbinical seminary, founded in Berlin in 1872. It remained in existence until 1942, its last head being Leo BAECK.

Hoffman, Dustin (1937–): US movie actor. He made his name in the title role of his first film, *The Graduate*. His other successes have included *Midnight Cowboy* and *All the President's Men*.

Hoffmann, David Tzevi (1843–1921): Bible and Talmud scholar. Born in Slovakia, he taught at the Berlin Rabbinical Seminary, which he directed from 1899. He was a vigorous proponent of Orthodoxy. He wrote on early rabbinic texts, publishing a commentary on Leviticus and Deuteronomy which strongly attacked the critical approach of Wellhausen and others.

Hofjude see **Court Jews**

Hofmannsthal, Hugo von (1874–1929): Austrian dramatist and poet. Several of his works, including *Elektra* and *Der Rosenkavalier*, were made into operas by Richard Strauss. His adaptation of *Everyman* (*Jedermann*) was also well-known.

Hofstadter, Robert (1915–): US physicist; professor at Stanford University. He won the 1961 Nobel Physics Prize for his investigation of the structure of atomic nuclei.

hol ha-moed ("the weekday of the festival"): The intermediate days of the festivals of PASSOVER (3rd-6th day in the Diaspora, 2nd-6th in Israel) and TABERNACLES (3rd-7th in Diaspora, 2nd-7th in Israel). Only essential work should be done on these days. Marriages are not performed and mourning is restricted. HALLEL is recited (half-*Hallel* on Passover), as is the Additional Service and other liturgical additions.

Holdheim, Samuel (1806–1860): German exponent of Reform Judaism. Rabbi in Berlin, he introduced radical innovations, including services on Sundays, prayers in German, and family pews. He strove for the complete integration of Jews into the German people.

holiness (*kedushah*): In an ethical context, h. implies the attainment of moral purity and perfection through right conduct and through imitating the Divine attributes. In ceremonial practice, it is repeatedly stressed in connection with dietary laws and family purity. Originally it meant "separation," and Israel, in accepting a state of h., separated itself as a holy people. It is the obligation not of the few but of the entire people. The rabbinical regulations were aimed at the sanctification of all of human life and behavior. In Judaism, h. is attained not by fleeing the world but by investing all one's deeds and thoughts with appropriate sanctification.

Holland: The history of Dutch Jewry dates from the 15th cent. and the following century, when MARRANOS from the Iberian peninsula began to settle there. AMSTERDAM was their main settlement, and from the early 17th cent. they were granted freedom of worship there. Communities were established in other cities, and Ashkenazim came into the country as well as Sephardim. The Jews were important in Dutch commercial life and also began to make an impact on intellectual life. Dutch Jewry were prominent in establishing communities in London, the US, and elsewhere. Jews were early admitted to the parliament (1797) and to high public office. In the 19th cent., the community's relative importance began to decline, although Amsterdam in particular continued to be a major Jewish center. In 1939, there were 140,000 Jews in H. (apart from refugees from Germany). The Germans introduced their annihilation policy during the war years and, despite protests from the general population, the great majority of Dutch Jewry perished in the extermination camps. In 1976 there were 30,000 Jews in H., of whom 14,000 lived in Amsterdam.

Holocaust: The persecution of European Jewry by the Nazis, 1933 to 1945, culminating in the murder of approximately 6,000,000 Jews. The National Socialist Party (Nazis) came to power in GERMANY in January 1933 and shortly thereafter defined as "non-Aryan" any person having a non-Aryan—particularly Jewish—parent or grandparent. Discrimination was applied to Jews in all walks of life. Anti-Jewish legislation was organized in the Nuremberg Laws, promulgated in September 1935. Jews were rapidly forced out of all aspects of German life. The anti-Jewish legislation was applied in AUSTRIA after the Anschluss of March 1938. The murder of a German diplomat in Paris in November 1938 was taken as a pretext for mass attacks on Jews, the destruction of dozens of synagogues, the looting of Jewish stores, the imposition of a crippling fine, and the transfer of many Jews to concentration camps. During this period the Jews of Germany (and Austria) were still able to escape, and many fled as refugees to other lands. Before World War II, 225,000 left Germany, 100,-000 left Austria, and 35,000 left Czechoslovakia (which had come under Nazi domination in 1938–39). The outbreak of World War II was the signal for mass killing of Jews. This began in the parts of Poland that were overrun by the Germans. Jews in many places were herded together, taken outside the towns, and shot *en masse*. Under the direction of Hitler, it was decided to implement the "final solution," viz., the extermination of the Jews. At first this was carried out by the concentration of European Jews in ghettos, where they lived in inhuman conditions, many dying of hunger and disease. In the course of time extermination camps were set up to which Jews were transported and gassed to death, their bodies being then burned in vast crematoria. This policy was decided on at the Wannsee Conference in January 1942. The conference was called by Heydrich, and one of the key figures charged with its implementation was Adolf Eichmann. Transports were organized from all parts of Europe to the death camps. For example, 300,000 Jews were deported in boxcars from the Warsaw ghetto to their death in Treblinka. At first healthy Jews were selected for labor battalions, where they were put to work under slave conditions; later they too were sent to their death. Around 1943, a number of revolts broke out among Jews in the ghettos and camps, but they were desperate and hopeless attempts at resistance. Other Jews escaped and joined partisan movements, many being killed fighting the Germans. In many instances in Eastern Europe the Germans were assisted by members of the local population in murdering the Jews, although in other cases (e.g., in Denmark) the local population endeavored to rescue the community or individual Jews. The H. was the most barbarous episode not only in Jewish history but in all world history. Many of those responsible were punished after the war by death or imprisonment.

holy days see festivals
Holy Land see Israel
Holy of Holies see Temple

holy places: Shrines in the Holy Land held sacred by adherents to Judaism, Christianity, or Islam because of their association with events described in the scriptures of the three faiths. There are also later sites associated with the pious men and saints. The term applies especially to specific places of pilgrimage including for Jews the Temple area and the WESTERN WALL; for Christians sites in Bethlehem, Nazareth, Galilee, and Jerusalem; and for Muslims the Mosque of Omar. Some of the shrines were the object of dispute between different religions or sects. Their guardianship has been governed by the "Status Quo," a decree issued by the Turkish government in 1757 and accepted by all subsequent governments in the Holy Land. Jews have throughout the ages made pilgrimages to their holy sites in and near Jerusalem, and from the Middle Ages to traditional tombs of rabbis in Galilee. Among Oriental Jews, even outside Israel, various sites have been sanctified as the result of reputed connections with biblical and later figures.

homiletics: In talmudic times, there were two types of preachers—those who lectured on halakhah and those who lectured on aggadah. As shown by the MIDRASH the method was to begin with a biblical verse which was illustrated by another verse. After appropriate exegesis and legend, the preacher would return to the original verse. Preaching in synagogue was common on Sabbaths and festivals. Many Midrashim are based on sermons, and many medieval ethical works originated in sermons. In several European countries preaching was in the vernacular. But there were regions where sermons were rare, often delivered only twice a year, on the Sabbaths before Passover and the Day of Atonement. From the 17th cent., a type of Yiddish preacher called the MAGGID emerged in Eastern Europe and Germany. The Reform movement introduced the vernacular sermon into 19th-cent. Germany and elsewhere. More recently there has been a tendency to build the sermon around topical events.

Hong Kong: British crown colony in southern China. Jews arrived there after the British conquest in 1842, including several noted families of Iraqi origin such as the Sassoons and the Kadoories. The Jewish population in 1976 was 200.

Honi ha-Meaggel ("Honi the Circle-Drawer"): Sage in the 1st cent. CE, considered a miracle worker. His name is said to have derived from an episode when, during a drought, he drew a circle and refused to budge from inside it until rain had fallen. He is also the hero of a legend of the Rip Van Winkle type. Josephus states that he was put to death by soldiers of Hyrcanus when he refused to curse his enemy Aristobulus.

Horayot ("Rulings"): Short tractate in the MISHNAH order of *Nezikin*, with *gemara* in both Talmuds. It deals with the procedure to be followed in the event of erroneous decisions by the Sanhedrin or high priest (cf. Lev. 4:1–21).

Hore-Belisha, Leslie Isaac, Lord (1898–1957): British statesman. A Liberal (later, National Liberal) member of Parliament from 1923, he was minister of transport (1934–37), minister of war (1937–40), and, briefly, minister of national insurance in 1945.

Horeb: Mountain near which Moses saw the burning bush (Exod. 3). In Deuteronomy and later tradition, it was identified with Sinai. Elijah fled to H. from Beersheba (I Kings 19).

Horovitz, Vladimir (1904–): Pianist. Of Russian birth, he toured Europe from 1925 and later settled in the US. In later years, his public appearances were rare but he remained widely popular through his recordings.

Horowitz, Isaiah (c. 1565–1630): Moralist and kabbalist, known as Shelah after the initials of his main work. He was rabbi in various Eastern European communities, then in Frankfort-on-Main, Prague, and from 1621 in Jerusalem. He later moved to Safed and died in Tiberias, where his grave, next to that of Maimonides, is still revered. His main work is *Shene Luhot ha-Berit*, an encyclopedic compendium of theology, mysticism, ethics, and law.

Hosea (8th cent. BCE): Prophet whose book of prophecies is contained among the Minor Prophets. He lived in the kingdom of Israel and was active during the reign of Jeroboam II. He chides Israel for its unfaithfulness to God, comparing it with his own unfaithful wife (it is not known whether this is based on fact or metaphor). The work ends with promises of consolation and salvation, resulting from Divine mercy.

Hoshana Rabba: The 7th day of the Feast of TABERNACLES. In Temple days it was the occasion for worshipers to make seven circuits around the altar, waving the Four Species and crying *Hoshana* ("O Deliver"). On this day the willow branches were beaten (to indicate dependence on rain), a custom still retained. From the Middle Ages, a serious element was introduced when H.R. was identified as the culmination of the repentance season—when God finally passes decisions on man's fate sealed on the Day of Atonement, 11 days earlier. Solemn melodies are recited and white robes worn to mark the solemnity of the occasion. The synagogue service combines the liturgy for the Intermediate Days of festivals with a sevenfold circuit of the *al-memar* carrying the Four Species and singing *hoshana* prayers. The calendar is adjusted so that H.R. never falls on a Sabbath.

Hoshea: Last king of Israel, who ruled 732–724 BCE. He succeeded Pekah, whom he assassinated, and was a vassal of Assyria, to whom he paid heavy tribute. However, he rebelled unsuccessfully against Assyria, and was imprisoned by Shalmaneser of Assyria. His ultimate fate is unknown.

hospitality see **hakhnasat orehim.**

Host, desecration of: Charge that Jews desecrated the sacred wafer used in the communion to reenact the agonies of Jesus' passion. The accusation became current in Europe from the early 13th cent., and was frequently the pretext for persecution and massacre of the Jews. The first recorded case was at Belitz near Berlin in 1243. It has been suggested that the accusation that the wafer shed drops of blood was the result of the appearance on the wafer of a small scarlet organism (*Micrococcus prodigiosus*) which sometimes forms on stale food kept in a dry place.

Houdini, Harry (1874–1926): US escape artist, born Ehrich Weiss. The son of a rabbi, he specialized in magic, acrobatics, and spectacular escape feats.

Houston: US city in Texas. Jews lived there from the late 1830s. The first congregation was founded in 1860. By 1976 H. had a Jewish population of 24,000.

Hovevei Zion see **Hibbat Zion**

Howe, Irving (1920–): US critic. He has taught English literature at Brandeis Univ. and Hunter College, New York. His works include studies of English and American literature, anthologies of Yiddish literature, and *The World of Our Fathers*, on Jewish life in New York during the period of mass immigration.

Huberman, Bronislaw

(1882–1947): Violinist. Born in Poland, he was a child prodigy and a pupil of Joachim and became recognized as one of the great violinists of his time. In 1936 he founded the Palestine Symphony Orchestra (later the ISRAEL PHILHARMONIC ORCHESTRA).

Ḥuleh: Former lake in Upper Galilee (known also as Lake Semechonitis and the Waters of Merom). The surrounding area, known as the Ḥuleh Region, was acquired by the Jewish National Fund in 1934 and subsequently settled. In the 1950s, the lake itself was drained off (apart from small areas retained as a nature reserve) and the rich land developed.

Ḥullin ("Profane Things"): Tractate in the MISHNAH order of *Kodashim*, with *gemara* in the Babylonian Talmud. It deals with the law of ritual slaughtering and is a main source for the dietary laws.

Ḥummash (from *ḥamesh*, "five"): Pentateuch (the five books of Moses), frequently printed as a separate volume.

Hungary: Jews lived there as early as Roman times, and there were communities recorded in the 11th cent. In the 13th cent. many Jews settled in H. They were first expelled after the Black Death in 1349. They returned, were expelled again in 1360, and returned in 1364. During the 15th cent. there were persecutions, ritual-murder libels, and burnings at the stake. The Jews enjoyed comparative liberty in the areas under Ottoman rule in the following centuries but continued to suffer in the Christian part of H. The number of Jews increased following the expulsion from Vienna in 1670 and the restrictions in Moravia early in the following century. Jews from Poland established important Talmud study centers. Maria Theresa endeavored to make life difficult for the Jews and imposed heavy taxes. Joseph II (1780–90) introduced many alleviations for Jews, but these were canceled with his death, following which there was a long struggle for civil rights. Jews supported the Hungarian independence movement in 1848 and in 1867 received full civil rights. The 19th cent. saw a sharp cleavage in the Jewish community between the Orthodox and the Reform. Anti-Semitism grew from the early 1880s (cf. TISZA-ESLAR). Many Jews figured prominently in the short-lived Bela KUN government after World War I. Anti-Semitic laws were passed in the 1930s and during World War II. The worst horrors hit Hungarian

Jewry after the Germans took control of the country in 1944; their massacre of Hungarian Jewry was the last major action in the HOLOCAUST. Of the 825,000 persons registered as Jews in 1941, 565,000 perished. After the war communal life continued under the Communist regime (although its institutions were nationalized). About 20,000 Jews left after the 1956 uprising was suppressed by the Soviets; 80,000 remained there with a communal and religious life.

huppah: The bridal canopy; the term is also applied to the wedding ceremony. The canopy takes various forms, ranging from richly embroidered baldaquins to a simple *tallit* held over the couple.

Hurok, Sol (1890– 1974): US impressario. Born in Russia, he went to the US in 1906. The artists he presented included Chaliapin, Isadora Duncan, Arthur Rubinstein, and Anna Pavlova. He also brought the USSR's Bolshoi Ballet to the US.

Hurst, Fannie (1889– 1968): US author. She was active in various social causes (including women's rights), and some of her novels were inspired by these themes. Her books included *Back Street* and *Lummox*.

Hurwitz, Henry (1886– 1961): US editor. He founded the Intercollegiate Menorah Association and edited the *Menorah Journal*, US Jewry's first literary periodical in English, throughout its entire appearance.

Husserl, Edmund (1859– 1938): German philosopher. His influential system of phenomenology was based on the relationship of the conscious mind and objects. H., who was baptized, taught at Halle, Gottingen, and Freiburg.

Hyksos: Asiatic dynasty which overran Egypt c. 1655–1570 BCE. It was probably at this time that the Children of Israel entered Egypt and were well received, while the period of slavery was after the H. had been expelled from Egypt. Little is known of them, but remnants of their culture have been discovered in Israel.

Hyrcanus, John: Ethnarch of Judea and high priest from 135 to 104 BCE. He threw off the oppressive Syrian sovereignty over Judah and entered into a relationship with Rome, in order to protect his independence. He attacked the Samaritans and destroyed their temple. Subsequently he defeated the Idumeans and imposed Judaism on them. He broke with the Pharisees and in his last years came closer to the Sadducees.

Hyrcanus II (c. 103–30 BCE): Hasmonean. He was regarded as heir to the throne, but on the death of his mother, SALOME ALEXANDRA, in 67 BCE, his brother Aristobulus seized power. This led to civil war. H. obtained the support of the Roman general Pompey, who made him high priest. In 40 he was deprived of power and mutilated so as to disqualify him for the high priesthood. Herod accused H. of treason and had him executed.

Ibn Balam, Judah ben Samuel (10th–11th cent.): Spanish Hebrew grammarian. He wrote works analyzing the biblical text and comparing Hebrew and Arabic grammar.

Ibn Daud, Abraham (c. 1110–c. 1180): Spanish historian and philosopher. *Emunah Ramah* (written in Arabic) reflects Aristotelian philosophy. He tried to show that science (Aristotelianism) and religion (Judaism) were not at variance. His historical work *Sepher ha-Kabbalah* related the chain of rabbinic tradition from Moses to the author's own time and contains much information about Spanish Jewry.

Ibn Ezra, Abraham (1089–1164): Spanish poet and exegete. After 1140, he traveled extensively, visiting Italy, France, England, and, in his old age, Palestine. His known writings (in Hebrew) date from this period. They include poetry, Bible commentary, philosophy, grammar, and astrology. His commentary on the Bible (on which fifty supercommentaries were subsequently written) interprets the text in a grammatical, literal sense, occasionally containing remarks that at the time were original and even daring. His philosophy was Neoplatonic.

Ibn Ezra, Moses (c. 1055–c. 1135): Spanish philosopher and Hebrew poet. In 1190, he had to leave his native Granada, and his subsequent life was one of hardship. He wrote religious and secular poetry, and many of his 200 sacred compositions have been incorporated in the High Holiday prayers in the Sephardi rite. He wrote a Neoplatonic philosophical work.

Ibn Gabirol, Solomon (c. 1021–c. 1058): Spanish philosopher and Hebrew poet. He lived mostly in Saragossa. One of the outstanding medieval Hebrew poets, he wrote both secular and religious poetry. The former concerns wine, friends, life, love, and loneliness. His best-known religious poem is his *Keter Malkhut,* in part a philosophical meditation, in part a prayer. His known philosophical works are the ethical code *Tikkun Middot ha-Nephesh* and *Mekor Hayyim.* The latter work was translated into Latin and as *Fons Vitae* was extremely influential among non-Jewish philosophers, who were not aware of the identity of its author. Only when excerpts of the Hebrew translation of the Arabic original were discovered in the 19th cent. did the scholar Solomon Munk identify Ibn Gabirol as its author. This is the outstanding work of Neoplatonic philosophy in medieval Jewish thought.

Ibn Habib: *Jacob I.H.* (1445–1516), rabbinic scholar, was born in Spain but fled to Portugal when the Jews were expelled from Spain. In 1501 he escaped to Salonika. His *En Yaakov* as-

sembled the aggadic sections of both Talmuds. Jacob completed only the first section, and the work was finished by his son *Levi I.H.* (c. 1480–1545), the chief rabbi of Jerusalem and a leading opponent of BERAB's scheme to reintroduce ORDINATION.

Ibn Janah, Jonah (c. 990–c. 1050): Spanish Hebrew grammarian. He practiced medicine in Saragossa. His *Sepher ha-Dikduk* (written in Arabic) was a basic work in Hebrew grammatical studies and included alphabetical lists of Hebrew roots. His influence on Hebrew philology was unparalleled.

Ibn Pakuda, Bahya see **Bahya**

Ibn Shaprut, Hasdai (c. 915–c. 970): Spanish statesman and scholar. He was physician to the caliphs Abdel-Rahman and Al-Hakim II at Cordova. His linguistic versatility made him a useful negotiator. He munificently supported Jewish scholarship and himself collaborated with a Greek monk in translating Discorides' work on botany into Arabic. When he heard of the existence of the KHAZAR kingdom on the Volga, he entered into correspondence with its king, and their exchange of letters is a main source of information on the Khazars.

Ibn Tibbon: Family of

Jewish scholars, originating in Spain and then living in southern France, who were among the most important translators into Hebrew during the Middle Ages. Its members included *Jacob ben Makhir I.T.* (c. 1236–1304), who translated works of Euclid and Averroes into Hebrew. His own astronomical tables were translated into Latin. *Judah ben Saul I.T.* (c. 1120–after 1190) translated into Hebrew several of the major Jewish philosophical works, which had originally been written in Arabic. *Moses ben Samuel I.T.* (d. c. 1280) translated works by Maimonides, Euclid, Averroes, and others. *Samuel ben Judah I.T.* (c. 1150–c. 1230) translated Maimonides' *Guide of the Perplexed*.

Ibn Tzaddik, Joseph ben Jacob (c. 1075–c. 1149): Spanish philosopher; *dayyan* at Cordova. His best-known work is *Olam Katan*, a largely Neoplatonic work, which sees man's soul as a microcosm of the world.

Ibn Verga, Solomon (15th–16th cent.): Historian. He left Spain, went to Portugal, became a Marrano, went to Italy in 1506, and reverted to Judaism. His *Shevet Yehudah* is a chronicle of Jewish persecutions and disputations, of both historical and literary value.

Ibn Yaish (Abenaes),
Solomon (d. 1603): Statesman. Born into a Portuguese Marrano family, he escaped to Turkey and openly embraced Judaism. A diplomat at the Turkish court, he arranged the Anglo-Turkish league against Spain; subsequently he was made duke of Mytilene.

ICA see **Jewish Colonization Association**

Idaho: US state. The Jewish population has always been small and in 1976 was only 630 for the state. There are communities in Boise and Pocatello. The former was first organized in 1895 by Moses ALEXANDER, who was to become governor of the state.

Idelsohn, Abraham Zvi (1882–1938): Musicologist and composer. Born in Lithuania, he settled in Jerusalem in 1906. From 1924 he taught in the US at the Hebrew Union College, Cincinnati. He collected the melodies of Oriental and Occidental Jews, which he published in *Jewish Music*, and many other works.

idolatry: Although Judaism opposed i., it had to contend with widespread idol worship. Biblical literature contains many bans on i., as well as indications that there was a tendency among the Israelites to revert to idolatrous cults. This was especially problematic in the northern kingdom, where Jeroboam erected golden calves as the center of worship. The most frequently mentioned idols in the Bible are BAAL and ASTARTE. I. appears to have finally disappeared among the Jews during the Babylonian Exile. The talmudic tractate AVODAH ZARAH ("Idol Worship") is devoted to regulating relations between Jews and heathens. Thus Jews were forbidden to eat the food or drink the wine of idolators.

Idumea see **Edom**

Ihud Habonim see **Habonim**

Ihud ha-Kevutzot Veha-Kibbutzim ("Federation of Kevutzot and Kibbutzim"): Organization of collective settlements in Israel, founded in 1951. In 1973 it had 80 villages with a population of 30,000.

"illegal" immigration see **haapalah**

Illinois: US state. In the mid-19th cent. Jewish communities were established in CHICAGO, Peoria, and Springfield. By the 1970s there were over 30 communities and several thousand Jews in other towns, but 253,000 of the state's 269,300 Jews lived in the greater Chicago area.

Immanuel of Rome (1261–c. 1328): Italian poet and exegete. He lived in various places in Italy, writing works of biblical exegesis and poetry in both Hebrew and Italian. I. introduced the sonnet form into Hebrew literature. His verse ranges from the devotional to the erotic. His poems, including an imitation of Dante's *Divine Comedy*, appeared in *Mahberot Immanuel*.

immortality of the soul: The Bible does not state a doctrine of the immortality of the soul, nor does this clearly emerge in early rabbinical literature. Opinions differed as to whether the concept of the World to Come implied immortality of the soul, while there was also confusion with regard to the relation to the Resurrection of the Dead. Maimonides came under criticism for minimizing the significance of resurrection and stressing the doctrine of the immortality of the soul. Eventually the belief that some part of the human personality is eternal and indestructible became part of the rabbinical creed and was almost universally accepted in later Judaism. It was also accepted by medieval and later Jewish philosophers. The kabbalists believed in the immortality of the soul, although they connected it with the doctrine of metempsychosis. The traditional belief that evolved was in a hereafter where departed souls are rewarded and the wicked punished for their deeds in this world, until the time of Resurrection and Last Judgment, which will inaugurate a completely new era. Reform Judaism generally denies belief in Resurrection but accepts immortality of the soul.

impurity see **purity, ritual**

incense: The burning of i. was an essential element of the sacrificial system in the Tabernacle and in the Temple (only the sin offering of the poor and the meat offering of the leper were not accompanied by i.). The Bible and Talmud prescribe which ingredient may be used. A special i. altar stood in the Temple in front of the Holy of Holies. The burning of i. played no part in Jewish ritual after the destruction of the Temple.

incunabula: Books printed before 1500. 175 Hebrew i. are known, most of them from Italy. 22 Hebrew presses are known to have printed i.

Independence Day, Israel (Yom Atzma'ut): Anniversary of Israel's declaration of independence, observed annually on Iyyar 5.

India: The COCHIN Jews are known to have been established in Cranganore by the 10th cent. Settlement in the Malabar Coast is known

from the 12th cent. The BENE ISRAEL Jews centered around Bombay, but their origin is not known. In the 19th cent. Jews arrived from Iraq, settling in Calcutta, Bombay, and other cities. Many members became distinguished in Jewish affairs throughout Asia (Sassoon, Gubbay, Ezra). Later settlers from Europe arrived after World War I, including German refugees in the 1930s. Before World War II, there were 25,000 Jews in I. but most of them have emigrated, the majority to Israel and several thousand to London. By 1976, 10,000 remained.

Indiana: US state. Jews lived in the state in the early 19th cent. and the first communities were in Fort Wayne (1838), Lafayette (1849), and Indianapolis (1856). In 1976, 26,215 Jews lived in I., the largest communities being in Indianapolis (11,000), Gary-Hammond (6,500), and South Bend (2,800). The weekly *National Jewish Post and Opinion* is published in Indianapolis.

Indonesia: Jews have lived in the Dutch East Indies from the mid-19th cent. After World War I there were 2,000 Jews in Java, including some from Holland. Others came from Eastern Europe and from Asia. After Indonesian independence most left; in 1976 there were only 100 mostly of Iraqi origin.

Industrial Removal: US movement, which functioned from 1901 to 1917, directing Jewish immigrants throughout the US rather than encouraging them to settle along the East Coast.

informer: In talmudic and medieval times, informing was regarded as the most heinous of crimes. Every punishment was permitted in order to safeguard the community, and in medieval Spain the civil authorities permitted the Jews to impose the death sentence under these circumstances.

inheritance: The Bible accepts the principle of primogeniture, but following the rule of Moses in the case of daughters of Zelophehad (Num. 27:8–11), daughters inherit where there are no sons. The basic rules of i. in Jewish law are: (1) it always passes in the direct line of immediate descent (or ascent); (2) a daughter inherits only in the event of the absence of a direct male descendant; (3) a person born out of wedlock or through illegal wedlock is entitled to inherit; (4) the right to inherit can be conveyed via a deceased person to his heirs. The order of i. is (1) sons and their descendants (with the firstborn receiving a double portion); (2) daughters and their descendants; (3) fathers; (4) brothers and their descendants; (5) sisters and their descendants; (6) father's father; (7) father's brothers and their descendants; (8) father's sisters and their descendants. A son born of a slave or a non-Jewess was excluded from i., but provision could be made by making him a gift. A husband inherits his wife's property, but not vice-versa. Support of a widow is the first charge on the husband's estate as long as she does not remarry.

Inquisition: Catholic ecclesiastical tribunal dealing with the detection and punishment of heresy. At first it dealt only incidentally with Jews, but from 1478, it was established in SPAIN to deal with MARRANOS. *Autos-da-fé* were held in Spain, Portugal, and in Latin America (until the 19th cent.). The I. was introduced in Portugal in 1536, in Peru in 1570, in Mexico in 1571, and so on. It had no jurisdiction over Jews but only those Jews who had embraced Christianity and were suspected of observing Judaism in secret. It also concerned itself with issuing certificates of purity of blood, which were a prerequisite before taking up certain positions. At least 2,000 *autos-da-fé* were held, in almost all of which persons of Jewish descent were featured. Over 350 years, some 400,000 persons were tried by the I. in Spain and Portugal on charges of being secret Jews or influencing others to keep Jewish observances, and some 30,000 were put to death.

intermarriage: Marriage between a Jew and a non-Jew. This became frequent from the 19th cent. in Central and Western Europe and in North America. Since World War II, the rate of i. has continued to rise, especially as the host societies in which Jews live have become increasingly open. Reliable statistics are available only in a few areas, but although the rate differs considerably, the increase is constant throughout the Diaspora. Although i. is contrary to Jewish law (unless the non-Jewish partner has first converted), there are a number of Reform rabbis in the US willing to officiate at such marriages. In Jewish law the status of the child follows that of its mother. Since i. is invalid, no divorce is required to dissolve it in Jewish law.

International Council of Jewish Women: Organization representing Jewish women from 25 countries with a membership of 700,000. It was founded in 1912 and is accredited to the UN.

Iowa: US state. Jewish peddlers visited the state from the 1830s. The first community was established at Keokok in 1855. In 1976, 6,555 Jews lived in I., of whom 3,000 were in Des Moines and 1,100 in Sioux City.

Iran see Persia

Iraq (formerly called Mesopotamia): For its early history see BABYLONIA. The large and flourishing Jewish community welcomed the Arab conquerors in 634. Its EXILARCH, GAON, and ACADEMIES were recognized authorities throughout the Diaspora. The position of the Jews was weakened through internal strife and the interference of the caliph, and with the end of the gaonate and the closing of the academies, I. was no longer the focus of the Jewish world (from c. 12th cent.). The position of the Jews improved after the Turkish conquest (1534). Under the British (1917–1932), the condition of the Jews there was satisfactory. Many Jews were in commerce and the professions. Hundreds of Jews were killed in the 1941 Baghdad pogrom. Nearly all Iraqi Jewry—numbering over 120,-000—left for Israel in a special airlift (known as Operation Ezra and Nehemiah) in 1950–51. Those who remained were subject to severe restrictions, especially after the Six-Day War, when 3,000 Jews were still in the country. By 1976, their numbers were reduced to a few hundred.

Ireland: A few Jews lived in I. in the Middle Ages, but a small Sephardi community was first in existence in the late 17th cent., when DUBLIN was the second community in the British Isles after London. They were later outnumbered by Ashkenazim, but by the early 19th cent. the community had disappeared. The Dublin community was reformed in 1822, and 450 Jews were living in I. in the early 1880s, when their number grew considerably with immigration from Eastern Europe, especially Lithuania. Communities were now founded also in Cork, Belfast, Waterford, and Limerick (the last-named experiencing anti-Semitic manifestations in 1904). In the course of the 20th cent. the provincial communities disintegrated, and by 1976, the only sizable communities were in Dublin (3,600) and Belfast (1,200).

Irgun Tzevai Leummi ("National Military Organization"): Jewish underground organization in Palestine, known from its initials as Etzel. Founded in 1931 by a number of ex-HAGANAH commanders, it linked with the REVISIONISTS. It carried out retaliation for Arab attacks, but after the 1939 White Paper, attacked the British. At the outbreak of World War II it declared a truce, and its head, David Raziel, fell in Iraq working with the British. Under Menaḥem BEGIN, it declared war on the British in 1944. The British arrested and exiled many of its members. Relations with the Haganah varied from extreme tension to close cooperation. After November 1947, it came out of hiding and joined in repulsing Arab attacks. When the State of Israel was proclaimed, it announced its entry into the Haganah. After a showdown with BEN-GURION, it was disbanded.

Isaac: Biblical patriarch; son of ABRAHAM and SARAH. To test Abraham's faith, God commanded Abraham to sacrifice I. on Mt. Moriah. However, at the last minute, on being convinced of Abraham's willingness, He forbade the sacrifice (AKEDAH). I. married REBEKAH, his cousin from Mesopotamia, and they had twin sons ESAU and JACOB. Jacob took advantage of his father's poor eyesight to obtain the blessing intended for the firstborn, Esau. I. died near Hebron and was buried in the Cave of Machpelah (Gen. 17–35).

Isaac ben Moses of Vienna (13th cent.): Rabbinic authority, known as Isaac Or Zarua. Born in Bohemia, he lived in various European towns and died in Vienna. His main work is the methodically organized code

Or Zarua, which deals with religious but not criminal and civil law. Its sources included the Jerusalem Talmud. It contains important information on the history of medieval European Jewry.

Isaac ben Sheshet Perfet (1326–1408): Spanish talmudic authority, known as Ribash, who lived his latter years in Algeria. His responsa influenced later halakhah. His grave near Algiers remained a center for pilgrimage.

Isaac, Jules (1877–1963): French historian. Before World War II, he was an education inspector. Losing his family during the war, he devoted himself to the study of Christian anti-Semitism, about which he wrote several works. He influenced the decision of Pope John XXIII to introduce the statement concerning Jews at the Second Vatican Council.

Isaacs, Rufus see Reading

Isaacs, Sir Isaac Alfred (1855–1948): Australian public figure. He was Australian attorney-general, a justice of the high court, and chief justice. In addition he helped to frame the Australian Constitution. In 1931 he was appointed as the first Australian-born governor-general of Australia, serving until 1935.

Isaiah: Prophet living in the 8th cent. BCE. He prophesied in Jerusalem from the period of Uzziah until the middle of Hezekiah's reign (c. 701 BCE). He belonged to a socially prominent family and was close to the court and the rulers, in particular to Hezekiah. The prophet condemned moral backsliding among the people. He saw all nations as in the hands of God, and therefore warned against putting trust in foreign alliances, saying that Israel must trust only in God. He foresaw the punishment of Israel for its sins but not its destruction; a remnant would revive the connection between God and His people in the Land of Israel. Modern scholars feel the book is not a unit. They ascribe Chaps. 1–39 to the historical I., and Chaps. 40–66 to another author (called by them Deutero-I.), who wrote in the Babylonian Exile. Many discern a third author (Trito-I., to whom they ascribe Chaps. 56–66).

Isaiah, Ascension of: Apocryphal work of composite origin. It is extant only in the Ethiopic version, but fragments have been found in Greek, Latin, and Slavonic. It is by a Christian writer but may be based on a Jewish apocryphal legend. It tells of the martyrdom of ISAIAH and his transportation to Heaven. It dates from c. 2nd–3rd cent. CE.

Ish-Bosheth: Son of

SAUL. On his father's death, he tried to rule all the tribes (II Sam. 2:10), but Judah refused allegiance. He attempted to rule initially with the support of his general ABNER. The latter, however, deserted him, and I. was murdered by two of his generals. They took his head to his rival DAVID, expecting a reward, but instead were killed by David for regicide.

Ishmael: Son of ABRAHAM and his Egyptian concubine HAGAR. He was circumcised at the age of 13. Jealousy between SARAH and Hagar led to the expulsion of the latter with her son into the desert, where they were miraculously rescued from death (Gen. 21:15ff.). Subsequently I. lived in Paran but joined his half-brother ISAAC in burying their father. His daughter married ESAU. He is the traditional ancestor of the Arab peoples. The Bible refers to 12 tribes in North Arabia who were regarded as the Ishmaelites (Gen. 25:12ff.).

Ishmael ben Elisha (1st–2nd cent. CE): TANNA. Of priestly descent, he was ransomed from the Romans, who had taken him as a captive to Rome after the fall of Jerusalem in 70 CE. He formulated the 13 rules for the HERMENEUTICS of the Talmud. Many of the halakhic Midrashim emanated from his school.

Islam: Monotheistic religion founded by MOHAMMED. Jewish elements are to be found in the KORAN as well as in many of the beliefs and institutions of I. Mohammed's first formulation was very close to Judaism, but when Jews failed to follow him, he added legislation which widened the gap. However, Jews were still regarded as superior to pagans and, together with Christians, as "the people of the book." Jews were placed in an inferior position but were not looked on as infidels against whom a Holy War was to be fought. I., for its part, influenced Judaism, e.g., in medieval thought and literature and ascetic piety. For Muslims, Jerusalem is the third holy city. Under I., Jews knew periods of persecution, periods of toleration, and periods of cultural creativity. Although life in Islamic lands was often not easy, it was far less difficult in most cases than in Christian countries.

Israel, Land of: *Geography.* The Bible gives various definitions of its borders but the common biblical description is: the Mediterranean Sea to the West; the Syrian Desert to the East; on the "Brook of Egypt" (Wadi el-Arish) in the South; and in the North, Mt. Hermon. This represents 17,500 square miles, of which 45% lies east of the Jordan. The actual area under Jewish control has varied at different times in history. The 1949 armistice agreements left Israel with 8,000 square miles; after the 1967 Six-Day War she was in control of 34,500 square miles including Sinai, Judea, and Samaria, and part of the Golan Heights. After the Yom Kippur War she withdrew from parts of Sinai. Historical I. consists of four longitudinal belts—the coastal plain, the western highlands, the Jordan rift, and the eastern highlands. The highest point is Mt. Meron (3,682 feet) and the lowest, the Dead Sea, is 1,300 feet below sea level, the lowest point in the world. Transjordan is a high plateau with three natural regions—Bashan, Gilead and Moab, and the Mount of Edom. In northern Israel, precipitation favors agriculture and the growth of forest trees. The southern part (the Negev) is desert, although its northern region has been cultivated since 1948. The main river is the Jordan, whose tributaries include the Arnon, the Jabbok, and the Yarmuk. The two main lakes are the Sea of Galilee and the Dead Sea; the former Huleh lake has been drained in recent years. The country has a Mediterranean climate, but regions along the Jordan Valley have a tropical temperature. Rains fall between November and April. There are considerable regional variations in temperature; the coast has mild winters and hot, humid summers; the hills have a moderate summer, but in winter temperatures occasionally dip to the freezing point.

History. Prehistoric remains have been discovered, and Jericho is one of the oldest known cities in the world. In historic times, the first known inhabitants were the Canaanites. The country was divided into small states, and the whole region was a bone of contention between Egypt and Assyria. The Israelite settlement eventually brought a unity. David (c. 1000 BCE) ruled over a large area, conquered the key city of Jerusalem, and made it his capital. His son Solomon built the magnificent Temple which made Jerusalem the undisputed center of the nation. After Solomon's death, his kingdom split into two separate states—the Kingdom of Israel in Samaria and the smaller Kingdom of Judah in the south. The former fell to the Assyrians in 721 BCE, and many of its inhabitants (the Ten Tribes) were deported. The Kingdom of Judah was conquered by Babylonia, and the Temple was destroyed in 586 BCE.

The elite were deported, but in c. 539 BCE they were permitted to return and begin rebuilding the Temple. Judea was now a Persian vassal. The area became a frequent battleground after the invasion of Alexander the Great. When the Syrian Seleucids gained control and endeavored to proscribe practice of Judaism, the people rose in revolt under the Hasmoneans and reestablished their independence. Victorious wars extended the boundaries. However, the brief independence ended in 63 BCE when the Roman general Pompey conquered Jerusalem. The unsuccessful revolt against Rome (66–70 CE) led to the destruction of the Second Temple. After the failure of a second revolt under Bar Kokhba (132–35 CE), the Jews were expelled from Jerusalem, spiritual life was persecuted, and the last vestiges of independence were destroyed. Leadership now rested in the intellectuals and the heads of the Sanhedrin, while the main center of population was in Galilee. The following centuries saw continuing cultural activity and the completion of the Mishnah and Palestinian Talmud. The Jewish position in the country became more difficult after the triumph of Christianity. Under the Muslims, who conquered the country in 634, they at first prospered, but later their position deteriorated. They suffered considerably during the period of the Crusaders. During the Mamluk Period (1291–1561), they recovered and consolidated their position. Jews from Spain settled in the main cities. Ashkenazim from Eastern Europe began to arrive from the late 18th cent., and during the following 100 years, the number of Jews increased rapidly, especially in Jerusalem. The new era began with agricultural colonization from the last two decades of the 19th cent., and Jews began to come in ever-increasing numbers after 1882, within the framework of the Zionist Movement. During World War I, the British under Allenby conquered the country from the Turks, and the British government issued the Balfour Declaration (1917), undertaking to support a Jewish national home in Palestine. This aroused the opposition of Arabs, both in Palestine and in neighboring countries, and increasing friction built up between Jews and Arabs. The Jews were alarmed by the British policy of reducing immigration in view of Arab threats, especially during the Nazi period when Palestine seemed a potential refuge for the doomed Jews of Europe. The situation deteriorated rapidly in the immediate post-war period when the British refused to admit the remnants of European Jewry. Eventually the question was referred to the United Nations which decided on November 29, 1947, to partition the country into Jewish and Arab states. Despite Arab armed opposition to this decision, the Jews proclaimed the State of Israel on May 14, 1948.

Israel, Kingdom of: The northerly of the two kingdoms into which Solomon's kingdom was split after the success of the revolt led by Jeroboam against Solomon's son and successor Rehoboam (933 BCE). It is also known as the Kingdom of Samaria after the city which became its capital. I. was the larger of the two kingdoms, having three times the area and twice the population of the southern kingdom (JUDAH). The leading tribe of the ten tribes which formed this kingdom was Ephraim. Politically, it was the more important kingdom but was frequently subject to internal dissension and revolution. The rulers of I. set up shrines to rival those of Jerusalem (Dan, Bethel, Samaria). Relations between the two kingdoms were sometimes friendly, sometimes hostile. Frequent warfare, especially with Damascus, weakened the kingdom, and in 721 BCE it finally fell to the Assyrians under Sargon, who exiled many of its inhabitants, settling alien peoples in their place. Of the biblical prophets, Elijah and Elisha were the most prominent who were active in I., and of the literary prophets, Amos and Hosea.

Israel, State of: After the proclamation of the S. of I. on May 14, 1948, the first major problem faced was the attack on the State by the armies of the surrounding Arab nations. Despite the UN decision in 1947 to partition the Land of Israel, I. received no outside assistance in her fight, but with her newly created army succeeded in beating back the attacks and in signing a series of armistice agreements in 1949. At the same time, I. received a mass immigration—the Jews who had been lingering in European Displaced Persons camps, Jews from the detention camps in Cyprus, communities from Eastern Europe, and the entire Jewries of Yemen and Iraq. Jews from many other lands also flocked to I., which adopted a law conferring citizenship on every Jew immediately upon landing on I.'s soil. Severe economic difficulties accompanied the early years, and an austerity regime was instituted. Immense sums were spent on settlement and whole new regions developed.

The Arabs did not reconcile themselves to the situation and demonstrated unremitting hostility in various directions, endeavoring to impose an economic blockade on the one hand, and infiltrating saboteurs on the other. Tension built up to the 1956 SINAI CAMPAIGN, which removed the immediate threat to shipping in the Gulf of Elath and of terrorist acts emanating from the Gaza Strip. But these suddenly became a renewed challenge in 1967, when Egypt's President Nasser proclaimed a blockade of the Gulf of Elath and moved his forces back into the Sinai Desert. The resultant SIX-DAY WAR (fought also against Egypt's allies, Jordan and Syria) brought I. to the Suez Canal and brought under its control the Gaza Strip, Eastern Palestine, and the Golan Heights. In 1973, Egypt and Syria attacked Israel in the YOM KIPPUR WAR but were beaten back. I.'s Jewish population increased from 650,000 in 1948 to over 3,059,000 in 1977. In addition there were over 550,000 Arabs and Druze, making a total of 3,628,000. This excludes a further 1,000,000 Arabs in the areas controlled by I. as a result of the Six-Day War. Israel is a republic at the head of which stands a president, whose functions are largely representative. Effective power is in the hands of the prime minister and government, chosen by a parliament (KNESSET) democratically elected every four years. The judges are appointed by the president on the recommendation of an independent nominations committee. The residence of the president and the Knesset are in Jerusalem, capital of the country. There are 31 municipalities (2 Arab), 115 local councils (46 Arab and Druze), and 49 regional councils (one Arab) representing 850 villages. The main types of village are the MOSHAVAH (of which there are 56), KIBBUTZ (235), MOSHAV (349), and MOSHAV SHITTUPHI (28). There are 600 synagogues for Jews, 90 mosques for the Muslims, and 300 churches and chapels for the Christian community (the last being divided into 30 denominations). There are also Karaites, Samaritans, Druze, and Bahai. Israel maintains diplomatic and consular relations with over 70 countries; the number was higher but a number of countries (especially in Africa) broke off official ties after the Yom Kippur War; the Soviet bloc (with the exception of Rumania) had already severed ties in 1967. Israel became a member of the UN on May 11, 1949; it participates in many aspects of the work of the world organization, but on political issues relations have often been strained, particularly since the development of an automatic anti-Israel majority in any vote in the General Assembly. The Israeli armed forces conscript all young men and women at the age of 18 and after regular service they remain liable for reserve duty (for men, until the age of 55). The economy has been characterized by a virtually unprecedented rate of growth —10% per annum. There has been a steady rise in productivity and export. However, there has been a consistent rise in the adverse balance of payments, partly due to expenses involved in absorbing a large immigrant population and the soaring cost of armaments. Inflation has always been high, and in the mid-'70s was standing at an annual rate of 25–30%. The deficit has been covered by grants, loans, contributions, and investments. Education is compulsory up to the age of 15, and there is an extensive scholarship program for high school levels. The percentage of academically educated persons in the work force is the highest in the world. Hebrew is the first official language of the country; Arabic is the second. The development of Hebrew is guided by the Hebrew Language Academy.

Israel Labor Party: Political party formed in 1968 by a merger of the former MAPAI, AḤDUT AVODAH, and RAFI parties. In 1969 it formed an alignment with MAPAM. Until 1977 it was the dominant party in the Israeli government, holding 60 seats out of 120 in the Knesset in 1969 and 54 in 1973, but in 1977 it dropped over 20 seats and went into opposition.

Israel Museum: Jerusalem museum, opened in 1965, comprising the BEZALEL Museum, the Billy Rose modern-sculpture garden, a biblical and archeology section, and the Shrine of the Book containing the Dead Sea Scrolls.

Israel Philharmonic Orchestra: Formerly the Palestine Symphony Orchestra. It was founded in Tel Aviv in 1936 by the violinist Bronislaw HUBERMAN; initially it was composed of refugees from Nazi Germany. Its first concerts were conducted by Toscanini. The orchestra soon gained a worldwide reputation, and has been on frequent international tours.

Israeli, Isaac ben Solomon (c. 855–c. 950): Physician and philosopher. Born in Egypt, from c. 905 he lived in Kairouan, North Africa. He was the author of a number of treatises on medicine in Arabic, which were translated into various languages. His philosophical works were influenced by Neoplatonism.

Israëls, Jozef (1824–1911): Dutch painter; the best-known master of Dutch impressionism. He painted portraits, historical themes, and peasant life. Many of his pictures depict Jewish subjects.

Isru Hag ("Bind Festive Sacrifice"): The day following the termination of each of the three PILGRIM FESTIVALS (cf. Ps. 118:27). It is considered a minor festival for liturgical purposes.

Issachar: Fifth son of Jacob and Leah (Gen. 30:18). The tribe of I. settled land between Mt. Tabor, the Kishon river, and the Jordan.

Isserlein, Israel ben Pethahiah (1390–1460): Austrian rabbinical authority; rabbi at Marburg and Wiener-Neustadt. His book of responsa *Terumat ha-Deshen* is important both as a halakhic source and for its historical information concerning the Austro-German Jewish community in the 15th cent.

Isserles, Moses (Rema) (c. 1525–1572): Polish rabbi and codifier. He founded and supported a yeshivah in his home town of Cracow and also built a synagogue in memory of his wife which still stands (Rema Synagogue). His works *Darkhe Moshe* and *Nappah* complement the code of Joseph CARO by adding Ashkenazi practice and tradition to the Sephardi authorities on which Caro based his work. Through the addition of the *Mappah*, Caro's *Shulḥan Arukh* became accepted in the Ashkenazi as well as the Sephardi world.

Istanbul see **Constantinople**

Italy: Jewish settlement has been uninterrupted since before the Christian Era. Jews were living there in the Maccabean period—initially in Rome, then later in the southern ports. The considerable Roman community was augmented by Palestinian prisoners of war, and by the end of the classical period, Jews were living throughout the country. When the empire became Christian the condition of the Jews became one of subjection. The Popes, while not favoring them, protected them from violence. In the early Middle Ages, southern I. was an important center of Jewish learning. From the 13th cent., Jewish loan bankers spread out, and communities were established in central and northern I. Spanish authorities expelled Jews from Sicily and Sardinia in 1492 and from Naples in

1541. The Counter Reformation led to discriminatory edicts, and a bull issued by Pope Paul IV in 1555 confined the Jews to a ghetto; the wearing of the Jewish badge was now enforced, together with economic restrictions. This policy of degradation lasted until the late 18th cent. The Renaissance witnessed considerable cultural activity among Italian Jewry, and they continued to produce notable works in various branches of the arts and sciences. Emancipation was brought briefly by the Napoleonic armies, but was thereafter canceled. It was finally reintroduced with the establishment of a united Italy in the mid-19th cent. In the first years of the Fascist regime, the Jews were not affected, but under the Nazi pressure anti-Semitic legislation was introduced (1938). The German occupation during World War II led to thousands of Italian Jews being sent to their deaths. After the war, Jewish communal life was reconstituted, the main communities being in Rome and Milan. In 1976, 35,000 Jews lived in I.

Iyyar: Second month of the religious year, 8th of the civil. It has 29 days. Zodiac sign: Taurus. Israel's Independence Day falls on the 5th, Lag ba-Omer on the 18th.

Izmir (Smyrna): Harbor in Anatolia. Jews lived there in the early Christian Era. Their numbers diminished in the Middle Ages but grew again with the arrival of Spanish exiles in the 16th cent. Jews then played an important part in the flourishing economic life of the city, which was a center of Jewish learning. The community declined from the 19th cent., and its numbers fell from 40,000 in 1868 to 15,000 in 1948. 10,000 of these went to Israel. About 2,000 were living there in 1976.

Jabbok: Tributary of the Jordan river. By a ford of the J. Jacob struggled with an angel (Gen. 32).

Jabneh (Jamnia): Ancient Palestinian city, south of Jaffa (mentioned in the Bible as Jabneel). After the destruction of Jerusalem and the Temple in 70 CE, Johanan ben Zakkai received permission to open an academy there. He assembled a group of scholars and reconstituted the Sanhedrin—an act that proved a turning point in the history of Judaism. A modern Jewish town was founded there in 1948, and numbered 10,200 inhabitants in 1976.

Jabotinsky, Vladimir (Ze'ev) (1880–1940): Writer and founder of REVISIONIST Zionism. A journalist in Odessa, he became a leading force in Russian Zionism before World War I. During the war, he was instrumental in the formation of the ZION MULE CORPS (1915) and the JEWISH LEGION (1917), in which he served. In 1920 he organized Jewish self-defense in Jerusalem against Arab attacks, for which he was jailed by the British. From 1921 he was a member of the Zionist Executive, but he had a falling out with Weizmann and, in 1925, founded the Revisionist movement. In 1935 he and his supporters seceded from the World Zionist Organization to form the New Zionist Organization. From an early stage, he advocated the creation of a majority state in Palestine. In the late

1930s he was the nominal supreme commander of Irgun Tzevai Leumi. He was a brilliant orator in various languages and also a gifted writer in Russian and Hebrew, his works including novels, poems, and translations.

Jacob: Patriarch of the Children of Israel; son of Isaac and Rebekah and younger twin of Esau. He obtained his brother's birthright in return for a dish of lentils ("mess of pottage") and then, using a ruse, received the blessing Isaac intended for his firstborn. To escape his brother's revenge he fled to Mesopotamia. On the way, he had a vision ("Jacob's dream") in which God assured him that He would renew with him the covenant made with his father (Gen. 28). In Paddan-Aram he served his uncle Laban and married his two daughters, Leah and Rachel. From them and two concubines, he was father of twelve sons and a daughter. When Laban's attitude became unfriendly, J. took his family and fled to Canaan, where he was reconciled with Esau. On the way, an angel appeared to him by the Ford of Jabbok and, after they had wrestled, changed his name from Jacob to Israel. In his old age, the presumed death of his son Joseph left him inconsolable, but when Joseph was found in Egypt, J. went with his entire family to spend his last years there. After his death, his body was embalmed and returned to Canaan for burial in the Cave of Machpelah.

Jacob ben Asher (c. 1270–1340): Halakhist, the son of Asher ben Jeḥiel. Born in Germany, he fled with his father in 1303 to Barcelona, and later lived in Toledo. His code *Arbaah Turim* (from which he is commonly known as Baal ha-Turim) collected all halakhot and customs, and formed the basis of later authoritative works, notably the Shulḥan Arukh.

Jacob ben Meir Tam (c. 1100–1171): French rabbinic authority, called Rabbenu Tam; he was the grandson of Rashi and brother of Samuel ben Meir (Rashbam). In 1147 he was attacked by Crusaders and nearly killed. He was an originator and the chief exponent of the tosaphist method of Talmud exposition (see tosaphot). He also wrote on grammar and the Bible and composed religious poems.

Jacob ben Moses Mölln (c. 1360–1427): German rabbi and teacher, known as Maharil. He was rabbi in Mainz and Worms. One of the leading rabbis of his time, his responsa are a useful source of social history of the period.

Jacob ben Wolf Kranz (d.c. 1740–1804): Preacher and scholar, known as the Maggid of Dubno. The outstanding preacher of his time, he was noted for his use of parables and epigrams.

Jacob Joseph of Polonnoye (c. 1782): Hasidic rabbi, the first to formulate the principles of Hasidism in a book. His *Toledot Yaakov Yoseph* expounds the doctrines of his teacher, the BAAL SHEM TOV.

Jacobs, Joseph (1854–1916): Historian and folklorist. Born in Sydney, Australia, he settled in England as a young man. He wrote on medieval English Jewish history, Celtic folklore, and literary criticism. In 1900 he went to the US as revising editor of the *Jewish Encyclopedia*, and he also edited *The American Hebrew*.

Jacobs, Louis (1920–): British rabbi and theologian. His unorthodox views concerning the origin of the Pentateuch led to a dispute with the British chief rabbi, who disqualified him from holding a pulpit under his jurisdiction. J. founded his own congregation in London. His writings included *We Have Reason to Believe, Principles of the Jewish Faith,* and *A Jewish Theology*.

Jacobson, Dan (1929–): Novelist. He was born in South Africa, which is the scene of his early works (*The Beginners, The Price of Diamonds, Dance in the Sun*). Later he moved to London, where he wrote a biblical novel (*Rape of Tamar*).

Jacobson, Israel (1768–1828): Religious and educational reformer. In 1801 he established a school for Jewish and Christian children at Seesen, Brunswick, which existed until Nazi times. He also founded a Reform temple at Seesen (1810). Later he lived in Berlin, where he conducted Reform services.

Jael (12th cent. BCE): Wife of Heber the Kenite. When the defeated commander of the army of Hazor, Sisera, took refuge in her tent after being defeated by the Israelites, she killed him by driving a tent peg through his head while he was sleeping (Judg. 4–5).

Jaffa (**Joppa**): Former port in Israel; now merged with TEL AVIV. One of the oldest cities in the country, the oldest remains date from the 16th cent. BCE. It was an important port in biblical times; it was from here that Jonah sailed. The Greek legend of Andromeda was also located in J. In Hellenistic times, it was an independent city with a non-Jewish population, but it was conquered by the Hasmoneans. It managed to retain its importance under the Romans and the Crusaders. In modern times, Jews lived there from 1839, but many were killed in Arab attacks in 1921 and 1936. In 1948 it had nearly 100,000 inhabitants, of whom 30,000 were Jewish. In the 1948 War, the Arabs left and the city was subsequently united with Tel Aviv (which had been founded in 1909 as a suburb of J.). Its port, which had been of value for the citrus-growing belt in the vicinity, declined in importance with the development of Haifa (and latterly of Ashdod), and was closed in 1965. The old port area was developed as an artists' colony and tourist center.

Jaffee, Leib (1876–1948): Zionist leader. Born in Lithuania, he took part in the first Zionist Congress and was active in Zionist politics. In 1920 he settled in Palestine, becoming a director of the Keren Hayesod. He was killed in an Arab bomb attack on the Jewish Agency compound in Jerusalem.

Jaffee, Mordecai ben Abraham (c. 1535–1612): Talmudist and codifier. Born in Prague, he officiated in various Eastern European communities. His main work is *Levush Malkhut* (generally known just as *Levush*), a commentary on Jacob ben Asher's code.

Jaffe, Sir Otto (1846–1929): Irish industrialist. Born in Germany, he lived in Belfast, where he was prominent in developing the linen industry. He was lord mayor in 1899–1900 and in 1904–05.

jahrzeit see **yahrzeit**

Jakobovits, Immanuel (1921–): British rabbi. After officiating as chief rabbi of Ireland and rabbi of the Fifth Avenue Synagogue, New York, he was appointed in 1966 chief rabbi of the British Commonwealth. He has written on Jewish medical ethics.

Jakobson, Roman (1896–): Philologist. He was born in Moscow and lived in Prague until 1939. He reached the US in 1941 and was professor at Columbia, Harvard, and MIT. He has basically influenced the contemporary study of linguistics and in particular Slavic studies.

Jamaica: When the British conquered the island in 1655, Portuguese Marranos were already living there, and thereafter an open Jewish settlement, with Sephardi and Ashkenazi members, developed and flourished. Jews were granted the franchise in 1831 and played a leading role in many walks of life. The community declined for economic reasons from the end of the 19th cent. 500 Jews now live there, mostly in Kingston.

Japan: Traditions are to be found linking the Japanese with the Lost Ten Tribes. Jews lived there only from the 1860s, and communities were founded at Yokohama, Nagasaki, Kobe, and Tokyo. After a decline during the World War II period, the community revived with the US military occupation. In 1976 there were 500 Jews in J., mostly in Tokyo.

Japheth ben Ali ha-Levi (10th cent.): KARAITE scholar, living in Jerusalem. He translated the Bible into Arabic and wrote a commentary, widely used by Karaites.

Jassy: Town in Rumania, historic capital of Moldavia. The oldest community in Moldavia, Jews lived there from the 15th cent. The community increased, especially from the 17th cent. In 1832, J. came under Russian rule and Jews were henceforth treated as foreigners; if penniless, they were expelled. The situation improved with the Austrian occupation in 1853. J. at this time was the center of anti-Semitism in Rumania, and pogroms occurred. The community numbered 35,000 in 1930 but suffered severely in World War II, when 12,000 of its members were slaughtered. There were 18,000 Jews there in 1959, but many emigrated to Israel; in 1969 2,000 families remained.

Jastrow: *Marcus Mordecai J.* (1829–1903) was a rabbi in Warsaw, but he was expelled from Russia for his support of the Polish independence movement. He then went to the US, where he was a rabbi in Philadelphia. His dictionary to the Targums, Talmud, and midrashic literature has remained a standard work. Of his sons, *Joseph J.* (1863–1944) taught at the University of Wisconsin, and was president of the American Psychological Association in 1900, and *Morris J.* (1861–1921) was professor of Semitic languages at the University of Pennsylvania, writing on biblical and Assyriological subjects.

Javits, Jacob Koppel (1904–): US politician. He was a Republican member of Congress from 1946 to 1954, and of the Senate from 1956. He received wide support from liberal and Jewish voters.

Jawitz, Ze'ev (Wolf) (1847–1924): Historian. He lived in Eastern Europe, Palestine (1888–98), Berlin, Antwerp, and, from 1914, in London. He was a founder of the Mizraḥi movement. His 13-volume Jewish history is written from a theological point of view.

Jebusites: Canaanite people of obscure origin living in and around Jerusalem at the period of the Israelite conquest. They retained control of Jerusalem (then named Jebus) until this was captured by David (II Sam. 5: 6–7).

Jeconiah see **Jehoiachin**

Jedaiah ha-Penini (Bedersi) (c. 1270–1340): Physician, poet, and philosopher from Béziers in southern France; later he lived in Perpignan and Barcelona. Author of the ethical work *Behinat Olam* as well as poetical works, including *Eleph Alaphim*, which consists of 1,000 words, each beginning with the letter *aleph*.

Jedid al-Islam (Arab. "New Moslems"): Secret Jews of Meshed (Persia) who were forced outwardly to observe Islam (1839) but who continued with their Jewish observances in secret until they were able to leave Persia and return to open Judaism.

Jehiel ben Joseph of Paris (13th cent.): French tosaphist. He headed a talmudic academy in Paris, wrote TOSAPHOT, and was a recognized authority on Jewish law. In 1240, he was the chief Jewish spokesman in the DISPUTATION of Paris. He spent his last years in Palestine.

Jehoahaz (Joahaz): King of Israel, the son of Jehu, who ruled 814–800 BCE. During his reign, Israel became a vassal of Aram (II Kings 13:1–9).

Jehoahaz (Shallum): King of Judah for 3 months in 609 BCE; he was the son of Josiah. Deposed by Pharoah Necoh and exiled to Egypt, where he died (II Kings 23: 29–34).

Jehoash see **Joash; Bloomgarden**

Jehoiachin (Coniah, Jeconiah): King of Judah, the son and successor of Jehoiakim. He reigned in 597 BCE for 3 months, before being deposed by Nebuchadnezzar, and deported with his family to Babylon. He was in detention until 561 BCE, but was then released (II Kings 24–5; II Chron. 36:8–10). Babylonian food ration lists have been discovered throwing light on his captivity.

Jehoiada (9th cent.): Chief priest in the reigns of Ahaziah, Athaliah, and Joash. He rescued Joash, the one-year-old heir to the throne, from the murderous intentions of Athaliah. When Joash was 7, J. organized a *coup d'état* which made Joash king and himself regent. He had the Baal shrines destroyed, organized the Levites, and had the Temple repaired.

Jehoiakim (**Eliakim**): King of Judah, the son of Josiah; he reigned from 609 to 598 BCE. He was placed on the throne by Pharaoh Necoh in place of his exiled brother Jehoahaz. Within 7 years, he fell under Babylonian control. However, against the advice of Jeremiah, he rebelled against Nebuchadnezzar. This led to the siege of Jerusalem by the Babylonians in 598 BCE, during which he died.

Jehoram (**Joram**): (1) King of Israel, the son of Ahab; he reigned in 853–842 BCE. Jehoshaphat of Judah joined in the war against Mesha of Moab, leading to Moab's throwing off Israelite rule. He was wounded while fighting the Syrians and shortly thereafter was killed by Jehu, who seized the throne. (2) King of Judah, the son of Jehoshaphat; he reigned from 851 to 843 BCE. He married Athaliah, under whose influence Baal worship was encouraged in the kingdom. During his reign, there was a close alliance between Judah and Israel. The Edomites rebelled and regained their independence and Judah was invaded by Philistines (II Kings 8).

Jehoshaphat: King of Judah, the son of Asa; he reigned in 870–846 BCE. He formed an alliance with Israel, marrying his son Jehoram to Athaliah, daughter of Israel's king Ahab. His reign was prosperous, although some of his military expeditions, undertaken jointly with Israel, were unsuccessful (I Kings 22).

Jehovah: English transliteration of the Divine name, based on a misunderstanding of the Hebrew text, which should probably be read *Yahweh*.

Jehu: King of Israel, who reigned in 842–814 BCE. After being anointed by Elijah, he killed King Jehoram of Israel, King Ahaziah of Judah, the queen mother Jezebel, and the prophets of Baal. He lost part of his land to Syria and paid tribute to the king of Assyria.

Jellinek, Adolf (1821–1893): Rabbi, preacher, and scholar; he officiated first in Leipzig and, from 1856, in Vienna. He was the most celebrated Jewish preacher of his day; his sermons attracted large audiences. He wrote scholarly studies in many spheres of Judaica, including Midrash, Kabbalah, and medieval Jewish philosophy.

Jephthah (12th cent. BCE): Judge of Israel. He defeated the Ammonites, who threatened Gilead, where he lived. Before fighting the Ammonites, he vowed that should he return home safely, he would sacrifice whatever came out of his house. This proved to be his only child, a young daughter, whom he duly sacrificed (Judg. 11). He served as judge for six years.

Jerba (Djerba): Island off the coast of Tunisia. Jews lived there from at least the 10th cent. (although local tradition claims origins in Temple times). The Jews were almost all priests with few Levites. Many Hebrew books were printed there and the yeshivot were famous. Almost 5,000 Jews were living there in 1946, but most left for Israel; about 1,000 remained by the mid-1970s.

Jeremiah (7th-6th cent.): Prophet. A priest from Anathoth, he began to prophesy in 626 BCE, and his ministry lasted 41 years. He warned the people to keep the covenant, with dire consequences if they refused. His predictions made him unpopular in many circles, but he was backed in priestly and other circles. When Nebuchadnezzar became king of Babylon in 605, J. foretold his victory over Judah. King Jehoiakim ordered his arrest, and J. was in danger until the country submitted to Nebuchadnezzar. The new king, Zedekiah, admired J., and his intervention saved the prophet from death. J.

opposed Zedekiah's pro-Egyptian policy, and after the Babylonians conquered Jerusalem in 686 BCE, they afforded him protection. However, after the murder of Gedaliah, the survivors took the unwilling J. with them as they fled to Egypt, where he is last heard of, condemning the Jews in Egypt for idolatry. His prophecies were recorded at his dictation by his scribe BARUCH. The Book of J., one of the three Major Prophets, contains 52 chapters. He was torn between love of his people and the realization that they had set themselves on the road to doom. J. is traditionally credited with the authorship of the Book of LAMENTATIONS.

Jericho: Town in oasis in the southern Jordan valley, a few miles north of the Dead Sea and 820 feet below sea level. Excavations (by Garstang, Kenyon, and others) have revealed it as one of the oldest cities in the world, first settled in the 8th millennium BCE. According to the Bible it was destroyed by Joshua, rebuilt by Ahab, subsequently destroyed again, and further rebuilt under the Hasmoneans. Herod built himself a winter residence there (recently excavated). J. was destroyed by the Romans in 68 CE but rebuilt in the 4th cent. The remains of the palace built by the 8th-cent. Arab caliph Hisham still stands. In modern times, it has become an Arab town, whose 1946 population of 3,000 was swollen by refugees in the 1948–67 period. It was taken by Israel during the Six-Day War. Its 1968 population was 9,000.

Jeroboam I: King of Israel, who reigned 928–907 BCE. Originally a foreman of Solomon's conscripted labor, he planned a revolt against Solomon; upon being discovered, he fled to Egypt. After Solomon's death, he led a delegation on behalf of the northern tribes which presented demands to REHOBOAM; when these were turned down, the Kingdom of Israel was established with J. as its king and its capital at Shechem (later at Tirzah). To counteract the attraction of the Jerusalem Temple, he built calf shrines at Dan and Bethel.

Jeroboam II: King of Israel, who reigned 789–748 BCE. His reign was long, prosperous, and comparatively peaceful. He recovered territories that had been annexed by Aram and also conquered Aramean towns and made Israel a significant factor in the region. The internal religious and moral situation was condemned by the prophets Hosea and Amos.

Jerubaal see **Gideon**

Jerusalem: Capital of Israel, situated on the spur of the central range of the Judean hills, 2,500 to 2,800 feet above sea level. Ancient J. (today's Old City) is surrounded by the Kidron and the Hinnom valleys. The steepness of the approach to the city (except on its northern side) made it difficult to attack. The only source of water in J. is the Gihon spring; water supplies have had to be supplemented by cisterns and by aqueducts and pipelines. In the latter 19th cent., Jewish settlement developed outside the Old City, especially in the west and northwest (the New City). In Jewish tradition J. is also known as Zion and various other poetic names; before David captured it, it was Jebus and, originally, Salem. The Romans called it AELIA CAPITOLINA and the Muslims, El-Kuds (Arab. "The Holy"). The earliest settlement on the site was founded c. 2500 BCE. It is mentioned in the Ebla documents (c. 21st cent. BCE). David captured it from the Jebusites and made it the capital of his kingdom. His son Solomon built the Temple there, ensuring its place as the religious center of the people. After the division of the kingdom, J. was the capital of the southern kingdom of Judah. It was often in danger from the kings of Israel and Aram, was plundered by Shishak of Egypt, and was besieged by Sennacherib of Assyria. In the 8th cent. BCE, Hezekiah cut a tunnel to bring water to the city from the Gihon pool. The city fell to Nebuchadnezzar of Babylonia in 597 and 586 BCE; on the latter occasion the Temple was destroyed, and the elite of the population were exiled to Babylonia. However after 50 years, some of the exiles received permission to return from Cyrus of Persia (who had conquered Babylonia), and work was commenced on rebuilding the city and the Temple. The outstanding figures at this time were Ezra and Nehemiah. In Hellenistic times, the city was considerably Hellenized; this was a factor leading to the Maccabean revolt and the conquest of the city by Judah the Maccabee. The Temple service was restored, and J. became the center of the Hasmonean kingdom. In 63 BCE it was taken by the Roman general Pompey, and thereafter its rulers were Roman vassals. King Herod inaugurated a magnificent building program, which included the rebuilding of the Temple in the first cent. BCE. In the war against Rome (66–70 CE), J. was again declared the capital by the Jews who were besieged in its walls and at the same time were engaged in internecine strife. Finally the city fell to Titus and the Temple was destroyed again. It was again under Jewish control for a time during the Bar Kokhba revolt (132–35 CE). Thereafter it was a Roman city, and Jews were forbidden entry. From the 4th cent. J. became a holy city for the Christians, and Jews were living there again. From the 7th cent. it was regarded by Muslims as their third-holiest city. From 1099–1187 it was under Crusader rule (the Jewish population being massacred by the Crusaders); then it was in Muslim hands. It declined under Ottoman rule, but Jews now began to return there in ever-increasing numbers, constituting a majority by the 19th cent. New suburbs were built outside the Old City walls from 1855. During the British Mandate, J. was the capital of the British administration. The 1947 UN Partition Plan advocated the internationalization of J., but in 1948 the Arabs attacked the Jewish inhabitants, who suffered a severe siege. In the armistice agreements, J. was divided in two—one part under Israel control, the other under the Jordanians. This situation remained for almost 20 years. As a result of the Six-Day War in 1967, J. was reunited under the control of Israel, of which it had always been the capital. In 1975, J. had 355,500 inhabitants, of whom 259,400 were Jews. It was the site of places holy to the three faiths as well as the headquarters of Israel's parliament and government, the Hebrew University, the Israel Museum, and the Jewish Agency.

Jerusalem Post: English-language daily newspaper founded (as the *Palestine Post*) in 1932 by Gershon Agron. From 1955 to 1974 it was edited by Ted R. Lurie. Its weekly edition has a large circulation outside Israel.

Jerusalem Talmud see **Talmud**

Jesus (d. 30 CE): Founder of Christianity. Sources of information regarding his life are to be found in the NEW TESTAMENT, which, however, reflects the beliefs and opinions of the early Church rather than those of J.'s own times. The New Testament account therefore has to be used with caution. The mention in Josephus appears to be a later interpolation, while the references in the Talmud and TOLEDOT YESHU are po-

lemical. J. was a Jew from Galilee, greatly affected by the teaching of John the Baptist, who baptized him in his youth. John may have been in turn influenced by the Essenes and by the Dead Sea sect or a similar group. J. became a wandering teacher who preached in synagogues, exhorting repentance in view of the imminence of the Kingdom of God. The extent of his clashes with the Pharisees and his attacks on the Jews are hard to gauge, as they appear to have been exaggerated before being recorded. However, there was doubtless some clash with the Pharisees, although many of his sayings resemble contemporary rabbinic—especially Pharisaic—teachings. He apparently believed himself called to a messianic role. When he went to Jerusalem for Passover in 29 CE, he was seen by the Romans as a potentially dangerous dissident; for this he was arrested and crucified by order of the Roman procurator, Pontius Pilate. His followers (the Apostles) believed that after three days he arose from the dead. Although Jews may well have been involved in the events leading to his death, these were subsequently exaggerated in the New Testament account, which reflects the anti-Jewish feeling of the early Christians, as well as the desire to avoid laying blame on the then-dominant Romans. Jewish tradition maintained a hostile attitude to J. until modern times, when Jewish scholars have considered his life and teachings with more objectivity, sympathy, and understanding of the Jewish background.

Jethro: Midianite priest; father of Zipporah and wife of Moses. After Moses fled from Egypt, Jethro made him shepherd of his flock (Exod. 2–3). Subsequently J. visited Moses in the desert and advised him on the organization of a judicial system (Exod. 18). J. is revered as a prophet by the Druze, who honor him as Nebi Shueib, with his traditional tomb near Lake Tiberias.

Jew (*Yehudi*): Adherent of the Jewish religion; member of the Jewish people. Originally a tribal definition, it referred to members of the tribe of Judah.

Jewish Agency for Israel: International body centered in Jerusalem which is the executive of the WORLD ZIONIST ORGANIZATION. Its aims are to assist and encourage Jews throughout the world to help in the development and settlement of Israel. Before the establishment of the State of Is-

rael, its authority and functions derived from the MANDATE, during which period it was the spokesman of the Jewish population in Palestine. In 1948, this aspect of its work was taken over by the Israeli government. The J.A. Executive maintains headquarters in Jerusalem and New York. Its departments of Immigration, Youth Aliyah, and Agricultural Settlement (and, until the 1960s, Absorption) have assisted in the settlement of over 2,000,-000 Jews in Israel since 1948. The Departments of Education and Culture in the Diaspora and of Torah Education and Culture in the Diaspora have played an important role in developing Jewish, and especially Hebrew, education throughout the world. The Economic Department encourages investment in Israel. The Youth and Pioneer Department services Zionist youth movements and conducts work-study programs in Israel. In 1929, the J. A. Executive was enlarged when non-Zionist leaders joined it. After 1948, the J.A. was enlarged in various other ways, notably by encouraging the affiliation of major Jewish organizations throughout the world.

Jewish Brigade: British army unit in World War II, established in September

1944. It was the only independent Jewish military formation permitted in World War II. For political reasons, the British repeatedly turned down requests from the outset of the war from the Jewish Agency to form a Jewish unit and allowed only a Palestinian regiment, with separate Jewish and Arab units. The J.B. was commanded by Brigadier E. F. Benjamin. After the war it made contact with the Jewish survivors in Europe, and facilitated their move southward to Italy en route to Palestine. The J.B. disbanded in February 1946.

Jewish Chautauqua Society: US educational body established in 1893 by Henry Berkowitz. Since 1939 it has been sponsored by the National Federation of Temple Brotherhoods.

Jewish Chronicle: Oldest existing Jewish newspaper. It first appeared in London in 1841. A weekly, it is one of the most influential publications in the Jewish world. Its editors have included Abraham Benish, Asher Myers, L. J. GREENBERG (under whom it became strongly Zionist), William Frankel, and Geoffrey Paul.

Jewish Colonial Trust: The first Zionist bank, incorporated in London in 1899 following a decision of the First Zionist Congress. It commenced operations in 1902, financing development in Palestine. In 1934 it handed over its Palestine business to the Anglo-Palestine bank. First registered in Britain, it became an Israel company in 1955.

Jewish Colonization Association (ICA): Organization to settle Jews in productive employment, founded by Baron Maurice de HIRSCH in 1891. His prime object was to settle Jews from Russia and Rumania on agricultural colonies in North and South America. The main settlement was in Argentina, where over 20 settlements were founded by the end of the 19th cent., with about 7,000 inhabitants. Later, a few settlements were established in Brazil. In North America, ICA worked with other Jewish bodies in founding farms and factories to settle Jews away from the main concentrations of Jewish population. Some colonies were also founded in Canada. After World War I, it supported Jewish agricultural colonies in Eastern Europe. Of all these projects, only those in Argentina have remained in existence, and in 1966, 8,000 Jews were living in ICA colonies (although by now largely in managerial capacity). In Palestine, the settlements founded by Baron Edmond de ROTHSCHILD were transferred to ICA in 1899, and were later transferred to a new company called PICA. Since World War II, ICA has assisted a variety of Jewish institutions.

Jewish Legion: Jewish units in Allied armies in World War I. The concept emerged among Zionists, its leading proponents including JABOTINSKY and TRUMPELDOR. At first the British only allowed the establishment of the ZION MULE CORPS, which fought in Gallipoli. It was only in 1917 that the British agreed to recruit a Jewish fighting unit. The first Jewish battalion (38th Royal Fusiliers), commanded by Col. J. H. Patterson, went into action in Palestine in 1918, where it was reinforced by the 39th battalion (which had enrolled in the US and Canada) commanded by Col. E. Margolin, and the 40th battalion commanded by Col. F. D. Samuel. Numbering altogether some 5,000 men, they participated in the final attacks on the Turks. The J.L. was demobilized 1919–21, largely at the instance of anti-Zionist elements in the British administration.

Jewish National Fund (Keren Kayemet le-Israel): Land purchase and development institution of the World Zionist Organization. It was founded in 1901, following the suggestion of Hermann Schapira, in order to acquire land in Palestine which would remain the inalienable possession of the Jewish people. The land is leased to Jewish settlers on a hereditary tenure. Care is taken to avoid speculation in such land. The J.N.F. began to acquire land in 1905, and until 1920, was the only Zionist colonizing fund. Among its large acquisitions were the Jezreel Valley in 1921; tracts in the Plain of Zebulun in 1925; and the Hepher Plain in 1929. By 1947, it possessed more than half the Jewish landholdings in Palestine. After 1948, it became very much involved in land improvement and development. In 1960, the J.N.F. and the Israeli government established a Lands Authority. The J.N.F. has engaged in draining swamps, and land reclamation and afforestation, collecting funds in 52 countries to subsidize its activities. Its headquarters are in Jerusalem. By the early 1970s it had planted 130 million trees.

Jewish Publication Society of America: Society to publish Jewish works in English. It has published over 500 titles since its foundation in 1888. In 1917 it issued an English translation of the Bible prepared by Jewish scholars, and in 1963 began the publication of a new translation. It also copublishes the *American Jewish Year Book.*

Jewish Quarterly Review: Scholarly journal. Founded in England in 1888 by Israel Abrahams and Claude G. Montefiore, a "New Series" was commenced in 1910 under the auspices of Dropsie College (now University), Philadelphia, which has continued to sponsor it.

Jewish Science: Movement founded in the US by Rabbi Morris LICHTENSTEIN to promote a religious revival among the Jews and to combat the appeal of Christian Science. It maintains a group in New York led by Tehilla Lichtenstein, widow of the founder.

Jewish Telegraphic Agency (JTA): News agency gathering and disseminating news of Jewish interest. It was founded in the Hague in 1914; its headquarters were transferred to London, and later to New York.

Jewish Theological Seminary of America: Educational center of CONSERVATIVE Judaism. It opened in New York in 1887; its first president was Sabato MORAIS. In 1902, Solomon SCHECHTER became president and the seminary was reorganized. Many distinguished scholars joined its faculty and its library, which became one of the most important in the Jewish world, was established. Subsequently, it was headed by Cyrus ADLER (1915–1940), Louis FINKELSTEIN (1940–1974), and Gerson D. Cohen (1974–   ). Apart from a rabbinic school, the J.T.S. incorporates various other institutions and educational activities, including a Teachers' Institute and Cantors' Institute. Its Los Angeles branch is called the University of Judaism, and in Jerusalem, it is responsible for the Schocken Institute for Jewish Research and the American Student Center.

Jewish War Veterans of the United States of America: Veterans' organization established in 1896 by veterans of the American Civil War, with headquarters in New York City. Since 1954, the headquarters have been in Washington. It maintains services in the large American cities and cares for Jewish veterans and their families, particularly the wounded and disabled.

Jews' College: Rabbinical seminary in London, founded in 1856 by Nathan Marcus ADLER. It grants rabbinical and ministerial diplomas and has a department for training cantors. Its library contains 60,000 books and 700 manuscripts.

Jezebel (c. 891–841): Wife of Ahab. As daughter of the king of Sidon, she championed Baal worship and introduced it into the kingdom of Israel. This led to acute conflict with the prophets of God, led by Elijah. A noted example of her evil ways is in the story of Naboth's vineyard. As prophesied by Elijah, she came to a gory end in the uprising of Jehu.

Jezreel, Valley of (Plain of Esdraelon): Plain extending from the Mediterranean at Haifa to the Jordan Valley at Beth Shean. Its total area is 96 square miles. Throughout history it has been a vital communications route and the scene of many battles and events of strategic importance. Following its purchase by the Jewish National Fund in 1921, swamps in the vicinity were drained and the area became a center of Jewish settlement.

Joab (10th cent. BCE): Commander of David's army. He was David's nephew, first mentioned with reference to the capture of Jerusalem (II Sam. 5:8). He was a successful commander, with two of his outstanding victories being over the Ammonites and over the rebel forces supporting Absalom. J. was also a cruel man. He supported Adonijah's claim to succeed David and was killed by Solomon according to David's dying advice.

Joachim, Joseph (1831–1907): Violinist. His first public appearance was made at Budapest before he was eight. He was the leading violinist of his time and directed the Musical Academy in Berlin. J. was baptized.

Joash (Jehoash): (1) King of Israel, who reigned c. 800–786 BCE. He ended the long war with Aram. He defeated Amaziah of Judah and carried back Temple treasures to his capital at Samaria. (2) King of Judah, who reigned 835–798 BCE. As a young child he was the only member of his family to be saved from the murderous designs of his grandmother ATHALIAH. He was rescued by JEHOIADA, the high priest, who had him crowned when he was seven and reigned as regent until J. grew up. J. at first continued in the line of Jehoiada but subsequently deviated from moral reform. He was killed by conspirators.

Job: Central figure in biblical book that is called by his name. This tells the story of the righteous J., who lived in the land of Uz. In Heaven, Satan attributes J.'s piety to his good fortune, and God permits Satan to put J. through any trial in order to test him. He then suffers a series of calamities but refuses to "curse God." He is then visited by four friends (Eliphaz, Bildad, Zophar, and Elihu) who mostly maintain the view that suffering must be the consequence of sin, which J. refuses to accept. Eventually God speaks, emphasizing Divine omnipotence and the limitations of human understanding. Finally he restores J. to his former fortunes. Scholars are divided as to the date of the book—it has been put between the 7th and 4th cent. —but it is placed in the WISDOM LITERATURE. Its author is not known, and there have been suggestions that it contains Edomite elements. Rabbinical views were mixed as to whether J. was a real or fictitious character. In Temple times it was read by the high priest on the eve of the Day of Atonement; it is read by Sephardim on Av. 9.

Joel: Second book of the Minor Prophets. Nothing is known of J. or his life or period. Its 4 chapters tell of a locust plague, describing the "Day of the Lord" which the prophet saw as approaching.

Johanan ben Zakkai (1st cent. CE): Palestinian *tanna*, entitled Rabban. He was a pupil of HILLEL, who called him "a father of wisdom." He was the acknowledged head of the Pharisees, and his teachings reflect a noble, ethical outlook. During the siege of Jerusalem (66–70 CE), he was among the peace party; he had himself smuggled out of the city by his pupils while hidden in a coffin. According to tradition, he was taken to the Roman general Vespasian. He was allowed to found an academy at JABNEH, and with the fall and destruction of Jerusalem, this became the supreme authority of the Jewish people, enabling them to withstand the crisis of the destruction of the Temple cult by giving Judaism a character not bound to any particular place. J. taught that the continuation of Judaism depended firstly on loyalty to tradition.

Johannesburg: City in Transvaal, South Africa. The city was founded in 1886, and Jews played a prominent role there from its earliest days. The first synagogue opened in 1888 and was followed by many Jewish organizations. Jews were active in developing the gold mines and all aspects of the city life. The national Jewish institutions have their headquarters in J. Jews form a high proportion of the white population, and several Jews have served as mayor. The Jewish population in 1973 was 63,000.

John Hyrcanus see **Hyrcanus**

John of Giscala (Gush Halav) (1st cent. CE): Military leader. He quarreled with JOSEPHUS, who commanded the defense of Galilee against the Romans (66). J. suspected Josephus' loyalty, but was unsuccessful in having him removed. After the conquest of Galilee by the Romans, J. fled with his small army to Jerusalem. Here he fought other zealot factions for control of the city. Only in the final Roman onslaught did the rivals put aside their differences, but despite their bravery, in which J. was outstanding, Jerusalem fell. J. was taken prisoner to Rome, paraded in Titus' victory parade, and died in a Roman prison.

John the Baptist (1st cent. CE): Preacher and ascetic. Little is known of his life. Convinced of the imminence of Judgment Day, he preached repentance and advocated an austere way of life. One of his cardinal doctrines was that of baptism (ritual bathing) for spiritual purification. It has been surmised that he was close to the Essenes and perhaps to the Dead Sea sect (he was active in the Dead Sea area). JESUS was among those whom he baptized. He was put to death by Herod Antipas, but the sources disagree as to the reason for his execution.

Joiada see **Jehoiada**

Joiakim see **Jehoiakim**

Joint Distribution Committee see **American Jewish Joint Distribution Committee**

Jolson, Al (1886–1950): US singer. A star of vaudeville and screen, he played the lead in the early sound films *The Jazz Singer* and *The Singing Fool*.

Jonah: Fifth of the Minor Prophets. Unlike the other prophetic books, the Book of J. contains a historical narrative telling the story of J., who was unwilling to fulfill the Divine mission imposed on him of traveling to Nineveh and warning its citizens of their imminent destruction as a result of their wickedness. His attempt to journey elsewhere led to the famous incident with the fish. Eventually he reached Nineveh and delivered the message. The citizens' repentance led to the revocation of the decree for their destruction, to Jonah's disappointment. It is one of the most universalistic books of the Old Testament. Various dates have been suggested for its composition, from the 8th to the 3rd cent. BCE.

Jonathan (11th cent. BCE): Eldest son of Saul. He was a brave commander against the Philistines, a noble character and true friend of DAVID. He was killed together with his father when fighting the Philistines on Mt. Gilboa, and David composed a famous lament for him (II Sam. 1:1–27):

Jonathan (Appus): Head of the Jewish state, 160–143 BCE. The 5th of the Maccabee brothers, he succeeded Judah the Maccabee in the leadership of the revolt against the Syrians. He was very successful, being the real founder of the Hasmonean state, extending its territory, and being recognized both as high priest and as governor of Judah by the Syrian monarch. He was treacherously murdered at Acre by the pretender Tryphon.

Joram see **Jehoram**

Jordan: Chief river of the land of Israel and the boundary between East and West Palestine, running from the Anti-Lebanon mountains in the north down to the Dead Sea (186 miles following the course of the river). The river enters Lake Tiberias and then continues southward to the Dead Sea, dropping altogether over 3,000 feet. Its tributaries include the Yarmuk, Jabbok, and Heshbon. It is not navigable. The J. figured in Christian tradition as the scene of Jesus' baptism.

Jordan, Kingdom of: Kingdom in Transjordan. Originally established as an emirate in 1921, it was ruled by Abdullah of the Hashemite dynasty. His grandson Hussein became king in 1952. Eastern Palestine had been annexed in 1948, and from then on there was frequent tension between the Palestinians and the Transjordanians (where the Bedouin were the mainstay of the Hashemite regime). The kingdom was frequently at odds with other Arab kingdoms. After the 1967 Six-Day War, the former areas of Palestine came under Israeli control, leaving J. with its original area of Transjordan. It was a main base for terrorists until 1970, when they were driven out of the country.

Jordan Valley see **Emek ha-Yarden**

Joselman (Josel) of Rosheim (c. 1478–1554): German communal leader (SHTADLAN). He had the title "Chief of the Jews in German Lands" and repeatedly interceded for fellow Jews in danger and frequently appeared at imperial diets. He defended the Jews against attacks by Luther. J. was the author of several ethical works.

Joselowicz, Berek see **Berek Joselowicz**

Joseph: Son of JACOB and RACHEL. His dreams incurred his brothers' jealousy, and they plotted to kill him, but they were dissuaded and instead sold him to merchants traveling to Egypt. There he served in the household of Potiphar, captain of Pharaoh's guard, but, on a false charge by Potiphar's wife, was imprisoned. After several years in prison, he won a reputation as a dream interpreter. Pharaoh summoned him to interpret his dreams and was so impressed with the correctness of his interpretations that he made J. viceroy. He ruled with foresight, his policy of grain storage tiding the country over a lengthy famine. Eventually he resumed contact with his family and brought them down from Canaan, settling them in Goshen. He died at the age of 110; his embalmed body was ultimately taken to Canaan and buried near Shechem.

*Joseph II (1741–1790): Holy Roman Emperor. In 1782 his *Toleranzpatent* (Ger. "Edict of Toleration") relieved the Jews in the Austrian lands of various disabilities, granting them educational facilities. However, its effect was negligible.

Joseph ben Mattathias see **Josephus**

Joseph, Sir Keith (1918–): British statesman; son of *Sir Samuel J.* (1888–1944), Lord Mayor of London, 1933–34. J. held cabi-

net rank in Conservative governments, being minister for board of trade in 1961–62, minister of housing and Welsh affairs in 1962–64, and minister of health and social services in 1970–74.

Josephson, Brian (1940–): British physicist, who received the 1973 Nobel Prize for his work on electronic development.

Josephus Flavius (c. 38–after 100 CE): Historian. Of a priestly family, he was sent to Rome on a mission in 64 CE. Returning to Judea, he found the country on the brink of revolt. He was made commander of the Jewish army in Galilee, where he faced the army of Vespasian in 67. He directed the resistance against the Romans but was eventually besieged in Jotapata. Here he saved his life by going over to the Romans; he was on the staff of Titus during the siege of Jerusalem. Afterward he went to Rome, where he ingratiated himself with the emperors. His writings, therefore, on the one hand contain an apologia for his own actions and praise for those of the Romans, and on the other hand are the major source for knowledge of the events in the period up to the destruction of the Temple. Although their accuracy was questioned in the past, his veracity has been confirmed over many points as a result of recent archeological discoveries. His works are *The Antiquities of the Jews*, a general Jewish history down to the outbreak of the War with Rome; *The Jewish War*, giving a detailed account of the events leading up to the fight against Rome and the development of the war; an autobiography; and *Against Apion*, defending the Jews against the attacks of the Alexandrian anti-Semite Apion.

Joshua (Hosea): Successor of MOSES and commander of the Israelites during the conquest of Canaan. Shortly after the Exodus he led the Israelites in their war with the Amalekites (Exod. 17:14–16). Later, he was one of the twelve spies sent by Moses to spy out the land of Canaan, only he and CALEB opposing the negative views of the other ten, and for this were rewarded by being the only two participants in the Exodus permitted to enter the Promised Land. J. was appointed by Moses as his successor. He led the Children of Israel over the Jordan to capture most of the country, following which he divided the land among the Twelve Tribes. He died at the age of 110. The book called by his name is the first in the Former Prophets section of the Bible. Scholars regard it as ancient. According to Jewish tradition it was written by J.

Joshua ben Hananiah (1st–2nd cent. CE): Palestinian TANNA in the period following the destruction of the Temple. He had served in the Temple as a Levite. A pupil of Johanan ben Zakkai, he was favorably regarded by the Romans and traveled to Rome on national missions. After the death of GAMALIEL (110 CE) he headed the Bet Din. For a time his school was in Pekiin.

Josiah: King of Judah who reigned 640–609 BCE. He ascended the throne at the age of 8 following the murder of his father, Amon. When he grew up, he instituted a program of reformation in which all traces of idolatry were expunged. He discovered the Book of Law (apparently, DEUTERONOMY) hidden away in the Temple. At a Passover service in 621 BCE the king and his people entered into a renewed covenant with God (II Kings 22ff.). J. was killed while opposing the army of Pharaoh Neco of Egypt at Megiddo.

Josippon: Historical narrative, written in Hebrew, dealing with the Second Temple period, especially the last two centuries. It is in fact largely taken from Josephus, probably through the Latin version, and may have been compiled in southern Italy in the 10th cent. The author identified Josephus with Joseph Ben Gorion, a military leader in the revolt against Rome. It was frequently quoted in the Middle Ages.

Jost, Isaac Marcus (1793–1860): German educator and historian. A teacher in Frankfort, he wrote textbooks, a German translation of the Mishnah, a 9-volume history of the Jews, and a 3-volume history of Judaism. Although superseded by the more scientific writings of Graetz, the works have retained significance.

Jotham: King of Judah, who reigned 751–735 BCE. He began to reign in the lifetime of his ailing father Uzziah. He subjugated the Ammonites. His reign was prosperous and favorably regarded by the rabbis.

Jubilee, Book of: Pseudepigraphic work, also called Little Genesis. It is a Midrash on Genesis and part of Exodus written as a secret revelation by an angel to Moses. It divides Jewish history into "jubilee' periods of 49 years. It probably dates from the mid-Second Temple period and may stem from an Essene milieu—a Hebrew fragment has been discovered at Qumran. However, otherwise the original Hebrew is not known; the book has been preserved in Ethiopic and later translations from the Greek.

Judah: Son of JACOB and Leah. Due to his influence, Joseph was not left to die in a pit but was sold to passing merchants traveling to Egypt (Gen. 43–44). Although only the fourth son, he received a preferential blessing from his father. The tribe of J., one of the Twelve Tribes, received a large area in central Canaan. It became of major importance with the rise to power of David, who belonged to the tribe of J.; because of this it received a special place in Jewish tradition. After the division of the kingdom, the tribe adhered to the southern kingdom, which was known as the Kingdom of Judah. The word "Jew" derived from J.

Judah, Kingdom of: The southern kingdom of the divided monarchy following the death of Solomon. It was the smaller of the two, consisting of only the tribe of Judah, most of Benjamin, and probably of Simeon. It was landlocked and comparatively poor and insignificant. It was frequently at war with its northern neighbor, the Kingdom of Israel, but sometimes they worked in alliance.

It was, however, its comparative unimportance that spared the kingdom of J. extensive international involvements. However, it was the site of Jerusalem and the Temple and the main focus of the prophetic movement. As it was ruled by the Davidic dynasty, it was far less susceptible to palace revolutions and upheavals. The country was attacked by the Assyrians in 701 BCE and by the Babylonians in 597 BCE, and its independence finally fell to the Babylonians under Nebuchadnezzar in 586 BCE.

Judah ben Samuel he-Hasid of Regensburg (d. 1217): German mystic and ethical writer. He was the main author of *Sepher Hasidim,* the outstanding ethical work of the HASIDE ASHKENAZ.

Judah ha-Levi (c. 1075–1141): Poet and philosopher. He practiced as a physician in Cordova and other Spanish towns. In his old age, he was filled with the determination to settle in Palestine, and reached Egypt, but died there. (The story that he was struck down by an Arab horseman in sight of Jerusalem is a legend that has been disproved.) He began writing his poems in Hebrew at an early age and became one of the best-known Hebrew poets of all time. Many of his devotional poems have been incorporated in the liturgy. His *Zionides* consist of poems inspired by a love of Zion. His philosophical and religious views are also expressed in his book *Kuzari* ("The Khazar," so-called because written in dialogue form as a disputation conducted before the Khazar king). This was written in Arabic. It maintains that Judaism needs no logical proof, being based on revelation. Unlike other medieval Jewish philosophers, he does not feel the need to reconcile religion and reason. The Jewish people, he holds, are the heart of all nations.

Judah ha-Nasi (c. 135–c. 220): TANNA and redactor of the MISHNAH. He succeeded his father R. Simeon ben Gamaliel II as NASI. His *bet din* was first at Tiberias, then at Beth Shearim, and finally at Sepphoris. He is usually referred to just as "Rabbi." He used his great wealth to assist scholars and was highly regarded by the Roman authorities. His compilation of the Oral Law (based on the work of R. Akiva's pupils) was taken as authoritative, and his decisions were regarded as final. After the Bible, the Mishnah was accepted as the basic work of Jewish law. J.'s probable tomb has been discovered at Bet She'arim.

Judah Ḥasid ha-Levi (c. 1660–1700): Mystic. Born in Podolia, he was closely associated with the Sabbetaian movement in Poland. Together with several hundred followers he set out in 1699 for Palestine. J. died a few days after their arrival in Jerusalem.

Judah Löw ben Bezalel (c. 1525–1609): Prague rabbi and kabbalist, known as Der Hohe Rabbi Low or Maharal. He wrote ethical and homiletic works, often with mystical content, and was highly regarded by European Jewry. His philosophical works are still of influence. He was associated with the legend of the GOLEM, according to which he created a robot to serve him and, in case of need, to save the Jewish community.

Judah the Galilean (d. c. 6 CE): ZEALOT leader. He was one of the founders of the Zealots and was killed in resisting the Romans for taking a census. Two of his sons were crucified by the Romans, and a third, Menahem, was killed in the civil strife in Jerusalem in 66 CE.

Judah the Maccabee (**Judas Maccabeus**) (d. 160 BCE): Third and best-known son of Mattathias the Hasmonean, from whom he took over as leader of the uprising against the Syrians. He won a series of victories (Beth Horon, Emmaus) and in 164 CE entered Jerusalem, reestablishing Jewish worship in the Temple. He then led armies across the Jordan and into Samaria and Galilee. He fell in battle at Elasa.

Judaism: The Jewish religion; in a wider sense, the entire Jewish tradition and way of life. The term itself is comparatively late (first found in a Midrash). It is used to denote the entire corpus of Jewish thought based on MONOTHEISM, with its ethical imperatives. These fundamental concepts are bound up with two historical events which molded the Jewish people—the Exodus from Egypt and the Giving of the Law on Mt. Sinai. The basic Jewish experience is recorded in various sacred books, of which the BIBLE (and especially the Pentateuch) is focal. The subsequent traditions were first passed down by word of mouth (Oral Law) and then committed to writing (MISHNAH, TALMUD). There is a tradition that the number of commandments actually amounts to 613. There is no recognized CREED; the need for such only became felt in the Middle Ages, when MAIMONIDES' formulation

(*Thirteen Principles of the Faith*) was the most accepted version. Worship was originally centered around the TEMPLE, but in the course of time the SYNAGOGUE was developed as well as a LITURGY which could, if necessary, be recited on one's own. There was a strong mystic stream in J., which received its major expression in the ZOHAR. J., however, always emphasized the practical aspects of religion: ritual and ethical observance. Right action was always the central theme. Early Judaism has little to say about the World to Come; this concept developed in Second Temple times, largely under external impetuses. However the rabbis developed a theology which, while stressing this worldly righteousness, believed in REWARD AND PUNISHMENT in the afterlife, as well as a messianic era which would see the triumph of righteousness and a general RESURRECTION. Modern schools, e.g., REFORM Judaism, interpret this in terms of the ultimate perfection of man rather than the supernatural advent of the MESSIAH. In any case, J. is essentially an optimistic religion and rejects such concepts as original sin. The people of Israel were regarded as having a special mission, having been chosen by GOD to bring His word to mankind. Until the period of emancipation, ORTHODOXY was the sole form of J., but since the 19th cent., there have been modifications, notably Reform and CONSERVATIVE Judaism.

Judas Maccabeus see **Judah the Maccabee**

Judea: Latin form of JUDAH; the name given by the Romans to the southern province of Palestine, which they ruled from 63 BCE. The term is also used for the south-central part of the country, in which are found the Judean Desert and the Judean Hills.

Judges, Book of (*Sepher Shophetim*): Second book of the Former Prophets section of the Bible, telling the history of the Israelites in Canaan from the death of Joshua to the rise of Samuel. This was a period of stability and lack of unity among the tribes, but it is marked by the emergence of a succession of leaders (judges) who banded the entire people or large sections of it together, often in the face of external dangers. There were 6 major judges—Othniel, Ehud, Deborah, Gideon, Jephthah, and Samson—whose stories are told at length in the book; and 6 minor ones—Shamgar, Tola,

Jair, Ibzan, Elon, Abdon—who are mentioned briefly. Traditionally, the book was ascribed to Samuel, but scholars have put it later, although it contains some very early material (e.g., "Song of Deborah").

Judith: Heroine of apocryphal book. The beautiful J. used cunning to behead the Assyrian general Holofernes and raise the siege of her town, Bethulia. Many scholars have held that the work is a fictitious composition from the Hasmonean period or earlier, but there are indications of a historical basis in the Persian period (4th cent. BCE). The work was apparently originally written in Hebrew but has survived only in Greek translation.

*Julian (the Apostate) (c. 331–363): Roman emperor who ruled in 361–63. He left Christianity and revived paganism in the Roman Empire. He permitted the rebuilding of the Temple in Jerusalem. Work was commenced but was soon halted, and on J.'s death soon after, the project came to an end.

*Julius Caesar (c. 100–44 BCE): Roman statesman and military commander. Hyrcanus sent troops to assist him in the siege of Alexandria (48 BCE), and Caesar subsequently made administrative and territorial changes to Hyrcanus' advantage. His attitude toward the Jews in the Diaspora was tolerant and his death was mourned by the Jewish masses.

Jung, Leo (1892–　): Orthodox rabbi. From 1922, rabbi in New York; he taught ethics at Yeshiva University and wrote and edited many works.

justice: Quality regarded in Jewish tradition both as a Divine attribute and as a basis for human life. It is synonymous with righteousness (*tzedakah*). The rabbis spoke of the conflict between God's attribute of j. and His attribute of mercy. A corollary of Divine j. is the doctrine of Reward and Punishment. On the human level j. is the keynote of biblical legislation and the entire Jewish emphasis on social ethics.

*Justinian (483–565): Byzantine emperor, 527–65 CE. He adopted a rigid anti-Jewish policy as a result of his intolerance toward all religious minorities. His legal code forced Jews into an inferior status which was to last for many centuries. It included a ban on rabbinical expositions and, in Africa, on synagogues.

Justus of Tiberias (1st cent. CE): Historian. During the war with Rome he came into conflict with JOSEPHUS, who had him imprisoned. J. escaped and subsequently became secretary of Agrippa II in Beirut. Here he wrote an account of the Jewish War which is sharply critical of Josephus' role. The work has survived only in the form of citations in other sources.

Kabak, Aharon Avraham (1880–1944): Hebrew author. Born in Belorussia, he settled in Jerusalem in 1921. He wrote a trilogy about Solomon Molcho, a novel about Jesus, short stories, etc.

Kabbalah ("Tradition"): The mystical tradition in Judaism. There is evidence of mystic thought in biblical times, while apocalyptic literature is filled with mystic visions. K. was cultivated in small circles, including sectarian groups. Some of the *tannaim* indulged in mysticism, which was divided by the rabbis into two main categories—*maaseh bereshit* (study of cosmogony) and *maaseh merkavah* (study of the Divine chariot, celestial secrets, and the Divine nature). Mystic visions are only indirectly described in the Talmud, but more information is contained in the HEKHALOT literature composed in Babylonia in the 6th to 8th cent. These describe the experiences of those who have ascended to higher spheres. These made their impact on the Jewish liturgy (cf. the KEDUSHAH). Two important texts of the post-Talmudic period were the SEPHER YETZIRAH and the Book of BAHIR. The Jewish mystic tradition was taken in the 9th cent. to southern Italy by Aaron ben Samuel of Baghdad, from there penetrating Germany, where it reached its best-known expression in the 12th–13th-cent. school of ḤASIDEI ASHKENAZ (especially in the *Sepher Ḥasidim*). This school emphasized asceticism and devotion (*kavvanah*). Another strong mystic tradition developed in Provence and from there was incorporated into Spain, where classical K. developed. Its major accomplishment was the ZOHAR, which—according to the research of G. SCHOLEM—was composed by Moses de LEON, although it was traditionally ascribed to R. Simeon ben Yohai. This teaches the revelation of God through a series of emanations (*sephirot*). The human mind can grasp the *sephirot* but not the transcendental God (EN-SOPH). The Zohar traces all mysticism to the Pentateuch, on which it is a word commentary. Its teachings spread in Europe and, with the expulsion from Spain, the Jewish mind became messianically inclined; hence the study of K. was widespread. Various centers now developed, of which the outstanding was at SAFED. Here the key figure was Isaac LURIA, who added new motifs of a gnostic character (recorded by his pupil Hayyim VITAL). These included *tzimtzum* (God retracted Himself, thereby creating a vacuum in which Creation could take place) and *shevirat ha-kelim* (the Divine light broke the containing vessels and were scattered into the sphere of the demonic from which they must be rescued [*tikkun*]). The messianic character of Lurianic mysticism contributed greatly to the intellectual atmosphere that culminated in the SHABBETAI TZEVI phenomenon, including the most extreme manifestations among Sabbetaians and FRANKISTS. The teachings of Luria were also absorbed into HASIDISM, the last great mystical movement in Judaism. In the 20th cent. Rabbi A. Y. KOOK developed a mystic theology with a nationalist core.

Kabbalat Shabbat ("Receiving the SABBATH"): Service preceding *Maariv* on Friday evenings in most synagogues. It consists of Ps. 95–99; Ps. 29, LEKHAH DODI; and Ps. 92–93. The last two psalms were recited in olden times, but the rest of the service was introduced in the 16th cent.

kaddish (Aram. "holy"): Doxology recited at the conclusion of the main section of each synagogue service from the 13th cent. and used as a mourners' prayer (although unconnected with mourning). It was known during Second Temple times and probably was put in its present form in the 8th and 9th cent. Its language is Aramaic. There are five forms of *k*.: (1) short or half *k*., recited by the reader during the service; (2) full *k*., recited at the conclusion of the main part of the service; (3) mourners' k.; (4) rabbinical k., said after studying rabbinical literature or after a sermon; and (5) k. "of renewal," at funerals. The k. can only be recited when a *minyan* is present. In Conservative and Reform congregations, it has become customary for female as well as male relations to recite the mourners' k.

Kadesh Barnea: Important oasis in the wilderness of Zin, generally identified with a site in central Sinai. The children of Israel dwelled there for much of the period they were in the desert.

Kadushin, Max (1895–): Conservative rabbi and thinker. His books expound talmudic thought and rabbinic thinking. They include *The Rabbinic Mind* and *Worship and Ethics*.

Kafka, Franz (1883–1924): Czech-born German novelist. His works (including *The Trial, The Castle,* and *Amerika*) combine a seeming realism with a dream world and extensive symbolism, portraying the search of modern man for meaning in life and for personal salvation. After his death, he was recognized as a major figure in European literature and has been very influential. His work was preserved and published by his friend Max Brod, who also edited K.'s diaries, which show his Jewish consciousness.

Kaganovich, Lazar Moiseyevich (1893–): Soviet politician. In 1917 he was elected to the central executive of the USSR. He was active in directing economic activities in the Soviet Union. He became commissar of transportation, commissar of heavy industry, deputy minister of trade, and deputy prime minister. In 1957 he was expelled from the Central Committee and dismissed from high position.

kahal: A Jewish congregation, generally *kahal kadosh*. In Eastern Europe, the organized Jewish community was called k.

Kahan, Israel Meir see **Haphetz Ḥayyim**

Kahanovitz, Pinkhes (1884–1950): Russian Yiddish writer, known as Der Nister; one of the most outstanding modern Yiddish authors. He was a victim of the Stalinist campaign against Yiddish writers.

Kahn, Louis I. (1901–1974): US architect. He was noted for his work on housing projects and university buildings. He also designed many synagogues such as Congregation Mikveh Israel in Philadelphia. One of his best-known works was the Richards Medical Research Laboratories at the University of Pennsylvania, where he was a professor.

Kai-Feng-Fu: Chinese town which had a Jewish community from the 12th cent. Its synagogue was destroyed by floods and rebuilt in the 17th cent. Thereafter the community dwindled and disappeared in the 19th cent.

Kainuka see **Banu Kainuka**

Kairouan: Town in Tunisia. For a period, especially in the 11th cent., its scholars and academy composed the leading Jewish intellectual center in the West. The community decayed after the 12th cent.

Kalischer, Tzevi Hirsch (1795–1874): Rabbi and forerunner of Zionism; he lived in Thorn, Prussia. In 1832, he stated that the salvation of the Jews would result from a natural process of events, and he advocated the return of Jews to Palestine by their own efforts and not by awaiting Divine intervention. He showed from rabbinic sources the need to colonize the Holy Land, proposing the foundation of a colonization society to buy land in Palestine for Jewish settlement.

Kalisz: Polish town. Jews lived there from 1264, and it soon became one of the most important Jewish communities in Poland, economically and spiritually. The community was destroyed in 1656 but was renewed shortly thereafter. About 12,000 Jews were living there in 1939, but they were killed by the Germans.

Kallah ("Bride"): Tractate dealing with betrothal, marriage, etc. which is included in Talmud editions, although of post-talmudic origin.

kallah months: Term for the months of Adar and Ellul in Babylonia, when intensive study courses were conducted in a talmudic tractate at the academies of Sura and Pumbedita for students from all parts of the country. The custom began in the amoraic period. It has been revived in certain yeshivot in modern Israel.

Kallen, Horace Meyer (1882–1974): US philosopher and educator; professor at New York's New School for Social Research, 1919–52. K. propounded "cultural pluralism" as characterizing US society.

Kallir (Ben Kallir), Eleazar: Medieval liturgical poet. Details of his life are unknown, but he probably lived in Tiberias in Palestine about the 7th cent. He is the author of many *piyyutim*, some of which became standard liturgy.

Kalonymos ben Kalonymos (1286–after 1328): Hebrew philosopher and translator. He lived in various places in France and in

Rome. He translated Arabic mathematical and philosophical works into Hebrew and Latin. He wrote the ethical work *Even Bohan* and *Masekhet Purim*, a Purim parody of the Talmud.

kamatz: Hebrew vowel sign (ָ) pronounced short or long *a*.

Kamenev, Lev (1883–1936): Russian Bolshevik leader. He was arrested for revolutionary activities in 1902 and from 1908 lived in Switzerland, returning to Russia in 1914. He was a leading Bolshevik theoretician, and after the death of Lenin, was, together with Stalin and Zinoviev, one of a triumvirate who ruled the country. He was imprisoned in 1934, and executed.

Kaminski: Polish family of Yiddish actors. *Esther Rachel Kaminska* (1870–1925) appeared with her husband, the actor *Abraham Isaac K.* (1867–1918), in the Yiddish theater they had founded. Their daughter *Ida Kaminska* (1899–   ) was the leading Yiddish actress in Poland, until leaving the country during the anti-Semitic campaign in 1968, when she moved first to the US and then to Israel. She appeared in the Academy Award-winning film *The Shop on Main Street*. Her brother *Joseph K.* (1903–1972) was a composer and violinist in Israel; from 1937

he played in the Israel Philharmonic Orchestra.

Kanah, Book of: Kabbalistic work on the commandments, probably written in Spain in the 14th cent. by the author of *The Book of Peliah*. They draw on earlier mystical writings and influenced SHABBETAI TZEVI.

Kansas: US state. Jews were living there shortly after the establishment of Kansas Territory in the mid-19th cent. The first congregation was founded in Leavenworth in 1857 and the second at Wichita in 1885. The Jewish population has declined since World War II and in 1976 numbered 11,095, almost all in Wichita and Topeka.

Kansas City: US city in Missouri. The first Jewish organization was established in 1864 and the first congregation (Reform) dates from 1870. The first settlers were from Central Europe, and Jews from Eastern Europe came in the latter 19th cent. Jews played an important role in the city's economic development. In 1976 there were 22,000 Jews with 7 congregations.

kaph (כ): Eleventh letter of the Hebrew alphabet. Numerical value: 20. When it has a *dagesh* (כּ), it is pronounced *k*; without a *dagesh*, like *ch* in *loch*.

Kaplan, Jacob (1895–   ): French rabbi and author. He became chief rabbi of Paris in 1950 and of France in 1955. He was an ardent supporter of Israel, even during conflicts between Israeli and French policy.

Kaplan, Mordecai Menahem (1881–): US rabbi and founder of the RECON-STRUCTIONIST Movement. His books include *Judaism as a Civilization, The Future of the American Jew*, and prayer books. From 1909, K. taught at the Jewish Theological Seminary and was dean of its Teachers' Institute; K. was a key figure in the KEHILLA movement and created the idea of a Jewish Center. In 1971 he settled in Jerusalem. His influence was extensive and spread far beyond the members of the Reconstructionist Movement. His naturalistic theology, which rejects the traditional view of revelation and a transcendent God, assumes religion to be a human creation, expressive of a people's culture. Central to his thought is the stress on the historical Jewish peoplehood.

kapparah ("expiation"): Custom in which a person's sins are symbolically transferred to a fowl. It is performed on the morning before the Day of Atonement, and consists of swinging the fowl over one's head while reciting Psalm 107:17–20 and Job 33:23–24. A male takes a cock, a female a hen. The fowl is then given to charity. (Money is sometimes substituted for the fowl.) The custom arose in gaonic times; some authorities opposed it but others—especially those in kabbalistic circles—supported it.

Karaites: Jewish sect denying talmudic rabbinical edicts. Originally called Ananites. The sect was founded during the 8th cent. by ANAN BEN DAVID. He interpreted the Bible literally, and held it to be the sole source of law, basing on it a code of life without reference to the Oral Law and rabbinic authorities. The movement spread rapidly among communities in the Middle East, and after the 12th cent., into the Crimea and Eastern Europe. They were, however, hampered by internal schism and a shortage of scholars supporting their viewpoint. However, they constituted a threat to normative Judaism (the Rabbanites) until checked by a vigorous attack from SAADYAH GAON. His attacks, however, had the effect of eliminating internal differences and producing a number of scholars and writers of stature. Their "Golden Age" is generally put at the 11th to 12th cent., when their literature—in Hebrew and Arabic—included liturgical works, polemics, Bible commentaries, and codes. Their leading scholars include BENJAMIN BEN MOSES NAHAWENDI and Abu Yusuf Yakub KARKASANI. Thereafter the position of the K. weakened. There was a minor revival in Russia in the 19th cent., but after World War II only a few thousand survived in the USSR and the State of Israel. The name derives from *kara* ("a reader in Scripture"). Its main difference from rabbinism is the absence of certain customs (such as *tephillin* and *mezuzah*) and festivals (e.g., Hanukkah), as well as the rigid interpretation given to the observance and ritual cleanness. The liturgy is based largely on readings from the Bible.

Karelitz, Avraham Yeshayahu (1878–1953): Rabbinic authority who wrote under the pseudonym Hazon Ish, by which name he was generally known. He lived in Vilna until 1935, when he settled in Benei Berak in Palestine. The many volumes of his published works constitute halakhic commentary on the Talmud.

Karkasani, Abu Yusuf Yakub (10th cent.): Karaite exegete. He came from Karkasan near Baghdad. His major work described Karaite beliefs and customs. He also wrote biblical commentaries and theological works.

Kasher, Menahem (1895–): Talmudic scholar and yeshivah head. He went from Warsaw to Jerusalem in 1925, and to the US in 1939. He has produced the many-volumed *Torah Shelemah,* an encyclopedia of rabbinic interpretations of each verse of the Pentateuch.

kashrut: Regulations governing the DIETARY LAWS.

Kastein, Joseph (1890–1946): German writer and biographer. Born in Germany, he practiced law in Switzerland, and from 1933 lived in Tel Aviv. He wrote plays, novels (some about famous figures in Jewish history), and a history of the Jews.

Katsh, Abraham (1908–): US educator and scholar. Born in Poland, he lived in the US from 1925. He was professor of education at New York University and from 1967 to 1976 president of Dropsie University. He wrote *Judaism in Islam* and works on medieval Hebrew literature.

Kattowitz Conference: Convention of the HIBBAT ZION movement, convened by Leon PINSKER in 1884. The organization of the movement was restructured, Odessa was selected as its headquarters, and Pinsker was named as its president.

Katz, Sir Bernard (1911–): British physiologist. Born in Germany, he settled in London, where he finished his education and where he taught at University College. In 1970, he was awarded the Nobel Prize for Medicine. His main research was connected with the nerve impulse and nerve-muscle connections.

Katz, Mané (1894–1962): Painter. Born in the Ukraine, he settled in Paris in 1921. Many of his subjects were based on Jewish themes, ranging from the Bible to the ghetto. A gallery of his paintings was opened in Haifa.

Katzir, Ephraim (1916–): Scientist and fourth president of Israel, 1973–78. He headed the biophysics department at the Weizmann Institute of Science and was chief scientist of Israel's Defense Ministry, 1966–68.

Katznelson, Berl (1887–1944): Labor leader and ideologist in Palestine. Born in Belorussia, he went to Palestine in 1909 and became one of the leading personalities and influences in the labor movement. He was a founder of the Aḥdut Avodah party and later of Mapai, as well as of the Histadrut. An active journalist, he edited the labor daily newspaper *Davar*.

Katznelson, Isaac (1886–1944): Hebrew poet and dramatist. He lived in Lodz, Poland. His poems and plays were marked for their joy of life. In World War II, he continued to write, depicting the tragedy of the Holocaust. He was killed in Auschwitz.

Kaufman, George Simon (1899–1961): US playwright, stage director and wit. He collaborated on many successful plays, including *Of Thee I Sing* (with Morris Ryskind), *You Can't Take It With You* and *The Man Who Came to Dinner* (with Moss Hart), and *Stage Door* (with Edna Ferber).

Kaufmann, Yehezkel (1889–1963): Israeli Bible scholar. Born in the Ukraine, he settled in Palestine in 1920; he was professor at the Hebrew University from 1949. His two major works have had a great influence on modern Jewish thought. They are an 8-volume history of Israelite religion in Bible times, which took issue with many of the theories of the Bible critics and insisted on monotheism as an original Jewish concept; and *Golah ve-Nekhar*, a sociological study of the Jewish people.

Kaunas see **Kovno**

Kavvanah: Spiritual concentration, in particular applied to prayer or the fulfillment of a commandment. Medieval mystics developed the concept of devotion and stressed meditation before and during prayer. This method was of special importance in the teachings of Isaac Luria and later in Ḥasidism.

Kaye, Danny (1913–): US entertainer, a versatile comedian, actor, singer on stage and screen, and TV. His films include *Up in Arms, Hans Christian Anderson, Knock on Wood,* and *Me and the Colonel.*

Kazin, Alfred (1915–): US critic and educator. He has taught literature at Harvard and written books of criticism and studies of American literary figures.

kedushah: Prayers proclaiming the holiness of God. The name was given to the third of the blessings of the AMIDAH and later—popularly —to the insert in that blessing (recited by the reader with responses from the congregation) during the reading of the *amidah* by the reader. It is based on Is. 6:2, Ezek. 3:12, and Ps. 146:10, and is recited while standing. There are variations in the formulation between the Ashkenazi and Sephardi rites.

kehillah: A Jewish community or congregation.

Kehillah Movement: Attempt made to establish a central organized communal body for New York Jewry, made in 1908. Directed by J. L. MAGNES, it remained in existence for about ten years, but the size of the community made the operation impossible and the experiment was discontinued.

Kelim ("Vessels"): First tractate in the MISHNAH order of *Tohorot*; there is no *gemara* in either Talmud. It deals with the laws of ritual purity affecting utensils.

Keneset Gedolah see **Great Assembly**

Kenites: Nomadic clan in the Negev and Sinai desert in biblical times engaged in metalworking. Moses' father-in-law Jethro (Reuel) was a Kenite, and Israel maintained a treaty relation with the K. from the time of Moses.

Kentucky: US state. Jews were already in K. in the late 18th cent. but communal life dates only from the 1830s. In 1976 there were 11,525 Jews, the largest communities being in Louisville (9,200) and Lexington (1,200).

Kenya: East African country. The Nairobi community was founded at the turn of the 20th cent. and its first synagogue was built in 1913. Smaller groups lived elsewhere, including Eldoret-Kitale, the site of the UGANDA SCHEME. When K. gained independence in 1963, there were 650 Jews living there, but the number had dropped to 400 in 1976.

Kephar Ezion: Kibbutz in Hebron hills, one of four villages ("the Ezion bloc") destroyed by Arabs in 1948 and refounded in 1967. The other three settlements were

Massuot Yitzḥak, En Tzurim, and Revadim. It is affiliated with Ha-Poel ha-Mizraḥi.

Kephar Giladi: Israeli kibbutz situated in the northernmost part of the country in Upper Galilee; it was founded in 1916 and affiliated with the Iḥud ha-Kevutzot ve-ha-Kibbutzim movement. In 1920 it, together with neighboring Tel-Hai, was attacked by Arabs; among those who fell in their defense was Joseph TRUMPELDOR. The population in 1971 was 635.

kerei u-khetiv ("read and written"). Biblical text variants noted by the masoretes and registered in the margin of Bibles not used in the synagogue. There are over 1,300 such changes.

Keren Hayesod ("Foundation Fund"): Financial arm of the World Zionist Organization. Established in 1920, it was meant to attract all Jews, and not only Zionists, to participate in the building up of the Jewish National Home. Until 1948, it financed all the JEWISH AGENCY's activities in Palestine. With the establishment of the State, many of these functions were transferred to the government of Israel, and the K.H. has financed immigration, absorption, and developing settlements. The K.H. has its headquarters in Jerusalem, and it is active (with the additional title of United Jewish Appeal) in over 70 countries.

Keritot ("Excisions"): Seventh tractate in the MISHNAH order of *Kodashim*, with *gemara* in the Babylonian but not the Palestinian Talmud. It deals with the sins for which the Torah gives the punishment of *karet* ("cutting-off," cf. Gen. 17:14, Exod. 12:15).

Kern, Jerome David (1885–1945): US composer. He wrote the music for many successful musical comedies, including *Sunny, Showboat,* and *Roberta.* His songs include *Ol' Man River* and *Smoke Gets in Your Eyes.*

kerovah: Type of *piyyut* inserted mainly in the repetition of the *amidah.*

Kessel, Joseph (1898–): French writer. He was born in Argentina and lived in France from 1913. In 1964 he was elected to the French Academy. His books include *The Lion* and *The Road Back.*

ketubbah: A marriage contract. It is a document in Aramaic containing a statement of the husband's obligations to his wife, and is a prerequisite of marriage. It must be signed by two witnesses and is given to the bride to keep. It is read either just before or during the marriage ceremony. Conservative Jews have introduced certain modifications; Reform Jews have abolished the k. The ornamentation of the k. was a favorite form of Jewish art.

Ketubbot ("Marriage Contracts"): Second tractate in the MISHNAH order of *Nashim*, with *gemara* in both Talmuds. It deals mainly with the marriage contract and the amount of money to be allotted to a wife in the event of divorce or widowhood.

Ketuvim see **Hagiographa**

kevutzah see **kibbutz**

Khazars: A national group of Turkish origin who lived along the lower Volga in the region of the Crimea. During the 8th cent. their king Bulan and some 4,000 of their nobles adopted Judaism. The state religion was Judaism, although the Jewish element of the population always constituted a minority. News of the K. reached IBN SHAPRUT, who corresponded with their king. Judah HA-LEVI's philosophical work *Kuzari* (i.e., "The Khazars") used the story of the conversion of the K. as its framework. The K., who had been a powerful tribe, were defeated by the Russians in 1083. Thereafter they declined rapidly, and after the Tartar invasion of 1237 they disappeared, leaving few traces.

Ki Lo Naeh ("For to Him It is Fitting"): Alphabetical hymn in praise of God, recited in the last part of the Passover Seder service among Ashkenazim. It is first found in Western Europe in the Middle Ages, but its author is unknown.

kibbutz (kevutzah): Israeli collective community. The first kevutzah was founded in 1909 in DEGANYAH. The main k. movements are IHUD HA-KIBBUTZIM VEHA-KEVUTZOT, HA-KIBBUTZ HA-MEUHAD, HA-KIBBUTZ HA-ARTIZI HA-SHOMER HA-TZAIR, and HA-KIBBUTZ HA-DATI. The Israeli k. has attracted worldwide interest, but attempts to reproduce it in other countries have not been successful.

kiddush ("sanctification"): Prayer recited at the outset of Sabbaths and Holy Days, over a cup of wine (or, in its absence, over bread) before the meal. It also became customary from ancient times to recite it at the end of the evening prayer on these days in the synagogue service for the benefit of travelers and the poor, who often ate in the synagogue. It contains two benedictions —one for the wine or bread, and one for the festival. On Friday evenings it is generally preceded by a reading of

Gen. 2:1–3. On festivals the SHE-HEḤEYANU blessing is added. K. is also recited before the meal after synagogue on Sabbath morning.

kiddush ha-shem ("sanctification of the name"): Concept originally denoting martyrdom but later used of positive ethical actions which raise the prestige of Jews in non-Jewish eyes and hence "sanctify God." Its opposite is ḤILLUL HA-SHEM.

kiddush levanah see moon, blessing of the

Kiddushin ("Betrothals"): Last tractate in the MISHNAH order of Nashim, with gemara in Palestinian and Babylonian Talmuds. It deals with bethrothals, weddings, and marital status.

Kidron: Valley north and east of Jerusalem between the city and the Mount of Olives. It was the burial place of ancient Jerusalem, and here are ancient monuments such as "Absalom's Tomb." It continues eastward through the Wilderness of Judah.

Kielce: Town in Poland. Jews lived there from the 19th cent. Before World War II their community numbered 19,000, but most of them were killed during the war. In 1946, K. was the scene of a pogrom when 42 survivors of the Holocaust were murdered. This event led to a mass exodus of Jewish survivors from Poland.

Kiev: USSR city; capital of the Ukraine. KHAZARS lived there in the 8th cent. and later arrivals came from the Caucasus, the Crimea, and Persia. Despite persecutions from 1113, the Jewish population grew, but in 1240 the community was ravaged by Tartars, to return only at the end of the 14th cent. There were further expulsions in 1495 and 1619. In the late 19th cent. it became one of the largest Russian communities. It was the scene of pogroms in 1881 and the early 20th cent. Some 175,000 Jews were living there in 1939; many were killed by the Germans, including those murdered in the notorious massacre at BABI YAR. About 152,000 Jews were living there in 1970.

Kilayim ("Mixed Kinds"): Fourth tractate in the MISHNAH order of Zeraim, with gemara in the Palestinian Talmud only. It deals with the prohibition of mixed species of seeds, trees, clothes, and animals.

Kimḥi: Family of scholars in Spain and southern France. They include Joseph K. (c. 1105–1170), grammarian, poet, Bible commentator, translator, and polemicist; and his two sons. The better known was David K. (Redak; c. 1160–c. 1235), whose grammar and biblical lexicon (*Mikhlol*) and clearly written Bible commentary became very popular among both Jews and non-Jews. *Moses K.* (12th–13th cent.) also wrote a Hebrew grammar, as well as commentaries on books of the Bible.

kinah ("lament"): Form of elegy recited in ancient times. There are examples in the Bible and talmudic times. *Kinot* were composed by medieval religious poets, and the name was applied specifically to *piyyutim* for Av 9. Many dirges were written to commemorate the historical tragedies that occurred in Jewish communities, and some of them found a place in the liturgy.

Kings, Book of (*Sepher Melakhim*): Biblical book, concluding the Former Prophets section and covering the history of the kingdoms of Judah and Israel from the end of the reign of David to the destruction of the northern kingdom and to shortly after the fall of the southern kingdom. Following the SEPTUAGINT, the book is divided into two roughly equal sections—I Kings and II Kings. (In the Septuagint these appear as III and IV Kings, while I and II Samuel appear as I and II Kings.)

Kinneret: Kibbutz and village on the shores of the Lake of Galilee. A training farm was founded there in 1908, and the village the following year. K. is the second-oldest kibbutz in the country.

Kinneret, Lake of see **Sea of Galilee**

Kinnim ("Birds in a Nest"): Last tractate in the MISHNAH order of *Kodashim*, with no *gemara* in either Talmud. It deals with pigeons brought as sacrifices.

Kiryat Gat: Israeli town founded in 1955 in the southern coastal plain to serve as the urban center of the Lachish region. Industrial plants were set up there. The population in 1974 was 21,000.

Kiryat Shemonah: Israeli town in the Ḥuleh Valley. It was settled in 1949 and became a center for the rural villages of the area. Especially after 1967, it frequently came under fire from the nearby Lebanese hills. The population in 1974 was 15,500.

Kisch: Czech family, whose members included *Bruno K.* (1890–1966), medical authority and Jewish scholar who made discoveries in cardiology and biochemistry; *Egon Erwin K.* (1885–1948), German author and left-wing journalist; and *Guido K.* (1889–), Jewish historian who taught in the US from 1937, and in Basle from 1962, edited the journal *Historia Judaica*, and wrote on Central European Jewish history.

Kisch: English family, whose members included *Sir Cecil K.* (1884–1961), civil servant; *Hermann Michael K.* (1850–1942), Indian civil servant; and *Frederick Hermann K.* (1888–1943), soldier and Zionist, who fought in both World Wars and was killed while inspecting a minefield in North Africa. Between the wars he lived in Palestine, and in the 1920s was a leading member of the Zionist Executive.

Kishinev: Capital of Soviet Moldavia, formerly in Rumania. Jews lived there from the 18th cent. In a pogrom in 1903, 49 Jews were killed and 500 injured and the Jewish quarter was destroyed. This was an important factor in encouraging the Jewish self-defense movement in Russia, and worldwide horror was evoked. 19 Jews were killed when another pogrom occurred in 1905. In 1941, 65,000 of the town's inhabitants were Jews, 53,000 of those perished during World War II. The Jewish population in 1971 was 50,000.

Kishon: River crossing the Valley of Jezreel and entering the Mediterranean just north of Haifa; its length is 25 miles. It is mentioned in the Bible, notably in connection with the victory of Sisera (Judg. 4:13; 5:21). In recent years it has been transformed into an auxiliary harbor.

Kishon, Ephraim (1924–): Israeli satirist. Born in Hungary, he emigrated to Israel in 1949. He has written extensively, including books, plays, films, and regular columns in the Israeli press.

Kislev: Ninth month of the Jewish religious year, 3rd of the civil year. It has 29 or 30 days and its zodiac sign is Sagittarius. The festival of Hanukkah begins on the 25th of K.

Kisling, Moïse (1891– 1953): French painter. Born in Cracow, he lived in Paris from 1910. He painted portraits of women and children as well as flower still lifes and landscapes.

Kissinger, Henry (1923–): US political scientist and statesman. Born in Germany, he went to the US in 1938. In 1962 he was appointed professor at Harvard. An adviser to President Kennedy in 1961–62, K. achieved international prominence during the presidency of Richard Nixon, to whom he was chief adviser on foreign policy. He accompanied and advised Nixon on his 1972 visits to China and Russia, conducting much of the diplomacy related to efforts to end the Vietnam war. In 1973 he was awarded the Nobel Peace

Prize. Secretary of state from 1973 to 1976, he devoted much time to negotiations between Israel and the Arab States.

kitel: White gown worn at solemn services (e.g., New Year, Day of Atonement), at Seder services, and by bridegrooms. The *k.* is also the shroud—the only covering of the dead.

Klatzkin, Jacob (1882–1948): Philosopher and author. Of Polish birth, he lived in Germany and co-founded the Eshkol Publishing House, which produced the (unfinished) German-language *Encyclopaedia Judaica* under his editorship. After the Nazis came to power, he moved to Switzerland. His Zionism was founded on a complete denial of the Diaspora. Among his books is a thesaurus of Hebrew philosophical terminology.

Klaus (Ger. "enclosure"): A kind of *bet midrash,* where the Talmud was studied continually, usually serving also as synagogue. The term appears in Central and Southern Europe from the 17th cent. The Hasidim called their synagogue a *Kloiz.*

Klausner, Joseph Gedaliah (1874–1958): Israeli literary critic and historian. Born in Lithuania, he lived in Odessa from childhood until going to Palestine in 1919. He was appointed professor of modern Hebrew literature (1926) and of Second Temple history (1945) at the Hebrew University. He published hundreds of scholarly books and studies and was influential as editor of HA-SHILOAH (1903–27). His major writings include a history of modern Hebrew literature, a history of the Second Temple period, a history of the development of the messianic idea among Jews, and studies of Jesus and Paul. From 1950 he was editor-in-chief of the *Encyclopaedia Hebraica.* A supporter of the Ḥerut party, he unsuccessfully ran against Weizmann for the presidency of Israel in 1949.

Klein, Abraham Moses (1909–1972): Canadian poet and author. He published volumes of poetry deeply infused with his immersion in Jewish culture and topics. His semipoetic novel *The Second Scroll* was based on the theme of the Holocaust and the rebirth of Israel.

Klemperer, Otto (1885–1973): Conductor. He conducted in Berlin until the advent of the Nazis, when he went to the US and became conductor of the Los Angeles Symphony Orchestra. After World War II, he settled in Switzerland but continued to conduct in many parts of the world.

Klutznick, Philip Morris

(1907–): US community planner, diplomat, and communal leader. He was international president of B'nai B'rith in 1953–59 and was active in national and international Jewish bodies. He was federal housing commissioner in 1944–46 and a member of the US delegation to the UN in 1961–62. In 1977 he became president of the World Jewish Congress.

Knesset: Parliament of Israel. The first K. met in 1949. It is a single chamber with 120 members elected by proportional representation, based on the national vote. All Israelis—Jew and Arab both—above the age of 18 have suffrage. After a few months in Tel Aviv, the K. moved to temporary quarters in Jerusalem at the end of 1949, and in 1966 entered its permanent home. The language of the K. is Hebrew, but a simultaneous translation is provided in Arabic. Its standing committees—which discuss relevant bills after their first reading—are the House Committee, Constitution Legislation and Law Committee, Finance Committee, Foreign Affairs and Security Committee, Labor Committee, Economic Committee, Education and Culture Committee, Home Affairs Committee, and Public Service Committee. Bills are passed on second reading.

Distribution of seats after eight elections is shown on p. 314.

Knopf, Alfred A. (1892–): US book publisher. He started own firm in 1915, and it became one of the leading publishers in the US. In 1960, the firm merged with Random House.

Koch, Edward (1925–): US politician. After representing New York in Congress, he was elected mayor of New York in 1977 on the Democratic ticket.

Kodashim ("Sacred Things"): Fifth order of the MISHNAH, containing 11 tractates, of which 9 have *gemara* in the Babylonian, but none in the Palestinian, Talmud. They deal with the laws of sacrifice and meal offerings, ritual slaughter, and Temple procedure.

Koestler, Arthur (1905–): Hungarian-born author; he lived in England from 1941. His prewar books were based on visits to many countries, and include an account of his imprisonment in Spain during the Civil War; *Thieves in the Night* is about Palestine. He described his disillusionment with Communism in *The God That Failed* and the novel *Darkness at Noon*. His later works deal with political, scientific, philosophical, and autobiographical subjects. He also wrote *Promise and Fulfill-*

	1949	1951	1955	1959	1961	1965	1969	1973	1977
MAPAI (Israel Labor Party)	46	45	40	47	42	45	56	51	52
AHDUT AVODAH—POALE ZION			9	9	9	8			
MAPAM (United Workers' Party)	19	15	10	7	8				
RAFI (Israel Workers' List)						10			
HERUT	14	8	15	17	17 }				
GENERAL ZIONISTS (Liberals)	7	20	13	8	17 }	26	26	39	45
INDEPENDENT LIBERALS (Progressives)	5	4	5	6		5	4	4	1
Religious Parties: (MIZRAHI, HA-POEL HA-MIZRAHI, AGUDAT ISRAEL, POALE AGUDAT ISRAEL)	16	15	17	18	18	17	18	15	17
Communists (MAKI, RAKAH)	4	5	6	3	5	4	4	5	5
Arab Parties (Affiliated to MAPAI)	2	5	5	5	4	4	4	3	1
DEMOCRATIC PARTY FOR CHANGE									15
Others	7	3	0	0	0	1	8	3	4

ment on Zionism and *The Thirteenth Tribe* on the Khazars.

Kohelet see **Ecclesiastes**

Kohler, Kaufmann (1843–1926): US Reform rabbi and leader. He was raised in Germany and lived in the US from 1869. After officiating in Chicago and New York, he became president of Hebrew Union College in 1903. He saw the mission of the Jews in the teaching of ethical monotheism and had no place for Zionism. He was extremely influential in the Reform movement. K. wrote *Jewish Theology*.

Kohut, Alexander K. (1842–1894): Rabbi and talmudist. After officiating in Hungarian communities, he went to New York in 1885. He opposed the Reform movement and helped to found the Jewish Theological Seminary. He edited Nathan ben Jehiel's talmudic dictionary *Arukh* (9 volumes). His son *George Alexander K.* (1874–1933) was an educator, scholar, and bibliographer. Alexander's second wife, *Rebecca K.* (1864–1951), was a social worker who organized the Federated Employment Bureau for Jewish Girls.

Kol Bo ("Everything within"): Medieval Jewish legal work surveying all aspects of Jewish law, arranged according to subject matter. The name is also given to a comprehensive festival prayer book.

Kol Nidre ("All Vows"): Opening words of declaration which opens the service on the eve of the Day of Atonement, and the name is therefore also applied to the entire eve. The statement, made with extreme solemnity and repeated three times, annuls all vows rashly made. Originally this referred to the past year, but in the 12th cent. the formula was changed in the Ashkenazi rite so that the reference is to the forthcoming year. Nevertheless the prayer has been frequently cited by anti-Semites, who have quoted it with the claim that a Jew's word cannot be trusted. The rabbis have repeatedly emphasized that the annulment refers to vows made by a man to God and not by a man to another man. The recitation of the K.N. is one of the highlights of the entire liturgy, and its ancient traditional melody has made a deep impact.

Kollek, Theodore (Teddy) (1911–): Israeli public figure. Born in Vienna, he was active in European Zionist movements until he went to Palestine in 1934 and became a member of kibbutz Ein Gev. He held various public offices and was closely associated with Ben-Gurion. In 1965 he was elected mayor of Jerusalem and played a dynamic role in the city, founding the Israel Museum and making special efforts to foster Jewish-Arab cooperation and normalization of life following the reunification of Jerusalem in 1967.

Kook, Avraham Yitzhak (1865–1935): Rabbi and philosopher. He was born in Russia, officiating in Lithuania before going to Palestine in 1904 to become chief rabbi of Jaffa. In 1921 he was elected Ashkenazi chief rabbi of Palestine. He established the yeshivah known as Merkaz ha-Rav. K. was one of the outstanding modern religious thinkers, whose breadth of understanding won him the respect of the nonreligious as well as the religious. He wrote halakhic responsa, meditations, poetry, and a commentary on the prayer book. He stressed the centrality of Jewish nationalism and of the Land of Israel in Judaism. His thinking is in the mainstream of Jewish mysticism.

koph (ק): Nineteenth letter of the Hebrew alphabet. Numerical value: 100. Pronounced *k*.

Korah: A Levite who led a revolt against Moses' leadership in the desert (Num. 16–17). The rebels were swallowed by the earth. A guild of Temple musicians was known as the "sons of K.," and some of the Psalms were ascribed to them.

Korczak, Janusz (Henryk Goldszmidt) (1878–1942): Polish author and educator. His educational approach was influential in prewar Poland, where K. was noted as a broadcaster and author of children's books. In the Warsaw ghetto, he established an orphanage, which he directed until he and his wards were sent to their death in an extermination camp.

Kornberg, Arthur (1918–): US biochemist. He shared the 1959 Nobel Prize for Medicine for his study of enzymes involved in the natural synthesis and breakdown of nucleic acids. He is professor at Stanford University.

kosher see **kashrut**

Kostelanetz, André (1901–): US conductor. He went from Russia to the US in 1922. From 1929 he conducted his own orchestra, which was noted for its rich orchestration of light classical and popular music.

Koufax, Sandy (1935–): US baseball player and sportscaster. He played with the Brooklyn Dodgers (1955––57) and the Los Angeles Dodgers (1958–64), leading them twice to victory in the World Series. He established many major-league records and was one of the most successful pitchers in the history of the game.

Koussevitzky, Serge (1874–1951): Conductor. He began his career as a double-bass player. From 1910 to 1918 he directed orchestras in his native Russia and conducted the Boston Symphony Orchestra from 1924 to 1949. In 1935 he founded the Berkshire Summer Festivals at Tanglewood.

Kovner, Abba (1918–): Hebrew writer. During World War II, he led the Jewish partisans who escaped from the Vilna ghetto. In 1945 he settled in Palestine, where he became one of the country's best-known poets.

Kovno (Kaunas): Lithuanian city. Jews were living there in the 15th cent., but were expelled in 1472. However, it was soon refounded and continued to expand, despite periodic persecutions. By early 20th cent. 40% of the inhabitants were Jewish. K. was one of the most distinguished centers of Jewish learning; Isaac Elhanan SPECTOR and Israel SALANTER lived there. The SLOBODKA yeshiva was in a suburb of K. Before World War II, 38,000 Jews lived there (30% of the total population). They were confined to a ghetto by the Nazis, and all were killed by 1944, except

for a very few who escaped to join the partisans. The Jewish population in 1959 was 4,792.

Krauss, Samuel (1866–1948): Hungarian historian, philologist, and talmudic scholar. He taught at the Budapest and Vienna rabbinical seminaries. In 1938 he fled to England, where he lived in Cambridge. He wrote hundreds of books and studies ranging over many aspects of Judaica. His best-known works include *Greek and Latin Loan-Words in the Talmud, Midrash, and Targum* and *The Archeology of the Talmud*.

Krebs, Sir Hans Adolf (1900–): Biochemist. Born in Germany, he went to England in 1933 and taught at Sheffield and Oxford. He was a recipient of the 1953 Nobel Prize for Medicine for metabolism studies.

Kreisky, Bruno (1911–): Austrian statesman and the first Jew to become chancellor of Austria. During the war years he escaped to Sweden. In 1956 he was elected a Socialist member of parliament, becoming foreign minister in 1959 and chancellor in 1970.

Krimchaks: Group of Jews living in the Crimea from ancient times, who were distinguished in various ways from the more recent Ashkenazi settlers in Crimea and from the KARAITES. They spoke Judeo-Tartar, and many of their customs and dress were Turkic. They numbered c. 7,000 before World War I and were concentrated in a few towns. Under Soviet rule they declined rapidly, and they were exterminated during the German occupation in World War II.

Kristallnacht ("The Night of the Broken Glass"): The night of November 9–10, 1938, when the Nazis smashed Jewish stores, burned Jewish synagogues, and sent many Jews to concentration camps. Ostensibly this was in retribution for the murder of a German diplomat, Vom Rath, in Paris, by a Jewish refugee, Herschel Grynspan.

Krochmal, Nachman (1785–1840): Galician philosopher and historian, called Ranak. A merchant in Zolkiev, he devoted himself to his studies and was a founder of the SCIENCE OF JUDAISM. He wrote little, and his main work, *Moreh Nevukhe ha-Zeman* ("Guide to the Perplexed of the Time"), was published posthumously. This offers a philosophical interpretation of Jewish history, emphasizing spirituality as the basis of the Jewish mission.

kubbutz: Hebrew vowel - . Pronounced as short or long *u*.

Kun, Bela (1886–1939): Hungarian Communist leader. He was the virtual dictator of Hungary for over four months in 1919. On the fall of his government, he returned to Russia, and conducted propaganda from there. In the late 1930s, K. was disgraced and executed.

Kurdistan: Hilly region in Southwest Asia today divided among Turkey, Iraq, and Iran. Jews lived there from very early times, and there are Kurdish Jews up to the present who speak ARAMAIC. It was in K. that David ALROY appeared in the 12th cent. Most of the Jews lived in the Iraqi region. Before and after the establishment of the State, the great majority emigrated to Israel, but communities are still living in K.

Kusevitsky, Moshe (1899–1966): Cantor. He was chief cantor of the main synagogue in Warsaw, later officiating in England and the US. He toured widely and his records were also very popular. His brothers were also well-known cantors.

Kuznets, Simon (1901–): US economist. He taught at the University of Pennsylvania and from 1960 at Harvard. In 1971, he was awarded the Nobel Prize in Economics. He specialized in the understanding of modern economic growth.

Kwartin, Zavel (1874–1953): Cantor and composer. He officiated in Vienna and Budapest before going to New York in 1919. He spent the years 1919–27 in Palestine, and then returned to the US.

Laban: Brother of RE-BEKAH. JACOB served him for 14 years in Haran in Aram Naharaim, and in return received the hands of L.'s two daughters, LEAH and RACHEL.

Lachish: Ancient town in Palestine. Joshua captured it from the Canaanites and it was assigned to the tribe of Judah. The town was captured by Sennacherib of Assyria (701 BCE); the siege is depicted on reliefs discovered at Nineveh and now in the British Museum. Modern excavations uncovered 21 inscribed ostraca ("the L. Letters") written in 589 BCE, when L. was under a Babylonian siege. In modern Israel, the name has been given to a development region in the northern Negev.

Ladino: Judeo-Spanish dialect spoken by Jews of Spanish origin (SEPHARDIM) in the eastern Mediterranean areas. Its basis is medieval Castilian, but there is an admixture of other languages, including Hebrew, Greek, and Turkish. It is written in Hebrew letters. Literature in L. was written from the Middle Ages and contains much folk poetry, as well as works on religious and ethical subjects. From the 18th cent. newspapers and novels were also written. It was widely spoken in Balkan countries but was on the decline before World War II. This decline was hastened by the killings of World War II and the emigration of most Balkan survivors to Israel, where L.

is still spoken and read but its usage confined increasingly to the older generation.

Lag ba-Omer: Minor festival observed on the 33rd day of the OMER season corresponding to Iyyar 18. The semi-mourning of this period is lifted on this day, and weddings and other celebrations are permitted. The reason for this occasion is obscure. There is a legend that a plague among the pupils of R. Akiva was stayed on this date; the reference may be to some event connected with the BAR KOKHBA war. A later tradition said that this was the date of the death of R. Simeon ben Yohai, putative author of the *Zohar*; an annual pilgrimage to his traditional tomb at MERON is made on this date. Various customs grew up for this festival, especially for children. It was called the "scholars' holiday," and included the lighting of bonfires and games connected with bows and arrows.

La Guardia, Fiorello Henry (1882–1947): US public figure; son of an Italian father and a Jewish mother. As a Republican congressman, he sponsored resolutions condemning anti-Semitism in Eastern Europe. He was a flamboyant mayor of New York from 1933 to 1945 and in 1946 as director-general of UN relief operations in Europe gave considerable help to Jewish Displaced Persons.

Lamdan, Yitzhak (1899–1954): Hebrew poet and editor. Born in the Ukraine, he settled in Palestine in 1920. His best-known poem, *Nassadah*, reflected the spirit of the pioneers of the 1920s.

lamed (ל): Twelfth letter of the Hebrew alphabet. Numerical value: 30. Pronounced *l*.

Lamed Vav (=36): The 36 righteous men who, according to rabbinic tradition, live in every generation and are anonymous saints, for whom the world exists. According to legend, they reveal themselves at times of danger.

Lamentations: One of the 5 scrolls in the Hagiographa section of the Bible, known by its initial word *Ekhah*. Its 5 chapters of elegies lament the destruction of Jerusalem in 586 BCE. The first 4 chapters are alphabetical acrostics. The traditional author of the book is Jeremiah, although modern scholarship suggests a composite authorship. The book is read in the synagogue on the fast of the 9th of Av.

Lampronti, Isaac ben Samuel (1679–1756): Italian scholar, physician, and rabbi in Ferrara. His *Paḥad Yitz-ḥak* is an encyclopedic work, covering the whole range of talmudic studies.

Land, Edwin J. (1909–): US physicist and inventor. He invented Polaroid, a cheap means of polarizing light, and the Polaroid camera, which revolutionized photography. In 1937, he established the Polaroid Corporation to manufacture scientific instruments based on his inventions.

Landau, Ezekiel ben Judah (1713–1793): Talmudic authority, known as Noda bi-Yehudah after his main work, a book of responsa. He was rabbi of Prague and Bohemia from 1754.

Landau, Judah Leo (1866–1942): South African rabbi, scholar, and writer. He grew up in Galicia, and after a brief period in England went to Johannesburg in 1904 as rabbi (from 1915 chief rabbi). His literary output was in Hebrew, German, and English, and included poems, plays, and essays.

Landau, Lev Davidovich (1908–1968): Russian physicist. He won the 1962 Nobel Prize in Physics for studies of gases, and especially for his work in low-temperature physics. Seriously injured in a car accident in 1962, he spent his last years as an invalid.

Landowska, Wanda (1877–1959): Harpischordist and pianist. Born in Poland, she lived for many years in Paris and founded there a school for the study of ancient music. She settled in the US in 1941.

Landrabbiner: Title often given by German and Austrian rulers from the 17th cent. to government-recognized rabbis. In the 19th cent. their chief task was often to Germanize the Jews.

landsmannschaften: Organizations whose members all originate from the same city or zone L. played an important role in the new Jewish communities that were established in the West from the 1880s. Through mutual self-help, they solved many social and economic problems of the newcomers. Since 1948, such groups have been established in Israel to assist immigrants from other countries.

Landsteiner, Karl (1868–1943): Bacteriologist and pathologist. He taught in Vienna, the Hague, and, from 1922, at the Rockefeller Institute for Medical Research in New York. He was awarded the 1930 Nobel Prize for Medicine for his discovery of basic human blood groups and the Rh factor. L. was baptized.

Lasker: German-US family whose members included *Eduard L.* (1829–1884), German liberal politician, who led the German Liberal Party, was a member of the Reichstag, a strong opponent of Bismarck, and a champion of Jewish rights; and *Albert Davis L.* (1880–1952), an advertising pioneer in the US, chairman of Lord and Thomas (in Chicago), and founder of the Lasker Foundation for medical research.

Lasker, Emanuel (1868–1941): Chess master. Born in Berlin, he went to the US after the Nazis came to power. In 1894 he became world champion, defeating Steinitz, and held the title until 1921, when he was beaten by Capablanca.

Laski: English family. *Nathan L.* (1863–1941) was a communal leader in Manchester. His son *Harold L.* (1893–1950) was a brilliant political economist who had an international reputation as writer, teacher, and lecturer. From 1926 he taught at the London School of Economics. L. was a leader of the Fabian Society and chairman of the Labour Party Executive, 1945–46. His brother *Neville Jonas L.* (1890–1969) was a lawyer and judge. From 1933 to 1940, he was president of the Board of Deputies of British Jews. Neville's daughter *Margha-nita* (1915–   ) is a popular novelist.

Laskin, Bora (1912–   ): Canadian jurist. The first Jew to be appointed to the Canadian Supreme Court (1970), he became chief justice in 1973. He is noted for his liberal legal interpretations.

Lasky, Jesse L. (1880–1958): US film producer. One of the pioneers of the film industry, he worked with Adolf Zukor from 1916, introducing many famous stars and producing notable motion pictures.

Lassalle, Ferdinand (1825–1864): German socialist leader. An outstanding lawyer, he was a major influence on German politics, helping to establish the first German workers' political party in 1863. His writings took ideas from Marx but stressed the role of state socialism in which the workers constitute the most important class. He advocated that the worker should be his own producer and develop workers' cooperatives. L. was killed in a duel, the outcome of a love affair.

Latrun: Site on the Jerusalem-Jaffa road identified with the ancient Emmaus. Its Crusader castle was destroyed by Saladin in 1191. In modern times it is the site of a Trappist monastery. After heavy fighting, it remained under Jordanian control in the 1948 War but was captured by Israel in the 1967 Six-Day War.

Latvia: Soviet republic, formerly a Baltic republic. Jews lived in Courland from the 16th cent. On the establishment of the Latvian republic in 1919, Jews were granted minority status. About 85,000 were living there at the outbreak of World War II, about half of them in Riga. The Germans established ghettos in the main towns and proceeded to annihilate all the Latvian Jews. Some escaped to the partisans or to the Russian army. In 1970, 37,000 Jews were living in L.

Law, codification of: Once the Talmud had received its final form, it was accepted as the authoritative guide to Jewish law. It lacked schematic arrangement, however, and in many cases the final decisions were not clearly laid down. Legal codes based on the Talmud and arranged logically have subsequently appeared. The earliest were *Halakhot Gedolot* and *Halakhot Pesukot*, compiled in the 8th cent. and retaining the talmudic arrangement. The *Halakhot* of Alfasi was known as the "Small Talmud." Particularly influential was the *Mishneh Torah* of Maimonides, which rearranged the material according to subject matter and laid down the final decisions. It was widely accepted but was criticized for failing to cite its sources. Alfasi's work inspired Asher ben Jehiel in 14th-cent. Spain, and the work of his son Jacob ben Asher—*Arbaah Turim*—became the recognized code for Sephardi Jews, especially in the shorter summary *Shulḥan Arukh* by Joseph Caro. Caro follows Alfasi, Maimonides, and Asher ben Jehiel, and in the event of a difference of opinion decides for the majority view. Moses Isserles in his *Mappah* added Ashkenazi practice and views to the work of Caro and enabled the *Shulḥan Arukh* to be accepted as authoritative by Ashkenazi as well as Sephardi Jews.

Law, Oral (*Torah shebe-al Peh*): According to Jewish tradition, the part of the Divine revelation given to Moses on Sinai that was not written down by him but was conveyed by word of mouth from generation to generation, until eventually codified in the Mishnah. The oral tradition in Second Temple times was developed by the Pharisees, and private scrolls of halakhot existed prior to the compilation of the Mishnah, which was largely based on these sources. Even after the Mishnah was written, differing oral traditions of its contents continued to circulate, and these varying views and discussions were in turn committed to writing in the *gemara* (the Mishnah together with the *gemara* constituting the Talmud, of which there were two versions, one in Palestine and one in Babylonia). The KARAITES rejected the entire O.L. and founded their beliefs on literal interpretations of the Bible.

Law, Reading of the (*Keriat ha-Torah*): Portion of synagogue service consisting of public reading from the Pentateuch. Such readings are made on Sabbaths, festivals, new moons, Hanukkah, Purim, fast days, and on all Mondays and Thursdays. It takes place at the end of the Morning Service; on Sabbaths and fast days also during the Afternoon Service. The readings are made from a parchment Scroll of the Law. The person called to the reading recites a special blessing before and after; originally he read the section himself, but eventually just said the blessings and the reader read the Law according to the traditional cantillation. On Sabbath morning at least 7 men are called to the Reading; on the Day of Atonement, 6, on festivals, 5 (in all these instances, apart from the *maphtir*: see HAPHTARAH); on New Moons and the Intermediate days of Festivals, 4; on all other occasions, 3. The R. of the L. was already part of the service in Temple times. The complete Pentateuch is read over the period of a year (in ancient Babylonia and in some modern Conservative congregations over 3 years), concluding on SIMHAT TORAH.

Law, Rejoicing of the sec **Simhat Torah**

Laws of Noah: Seven commandments derived from God's words to NOAH which, according to the Talmud, are obligatory on all human beings—and not only Jews—to observe. They are prohibitions of (1) eating flesh taken from living animals; (2) blasphemy; (3) robbery; (4) murder; (5) idolatry; (6) immorality; and (7) the establishment of courts of justice.

Lazarus, Emma (1849–1887): US poet. Her books include *Songs of a Semite* and *By the Waters of Babylon*. Her poem *The New Colossus* is carved around the pedestal of the Statue of Liberty (1886). She translated medieval Hebrew poetry into English.

Lazarus, Moritz (1824–1903): German philosopher and psychologist. He introduced a new branch of psychology called the "psychology of nations." He wrote on

Jewish ethics and opposed Jewish nationalism. His wife *Nahida Ruth L.* (1849–1928), a convert to Judaism, wrote various works on Judaism.

League of Nations: International organization operating between the two world wars. Through its Mandates Commission it exercised theoretical supervision over the Palestine Mandate which had been entrusted by the Allied Powers to the British administration. The league endeavored to safeguard minority rights in certain Eastern European countries according to the peace treaties that had been signed after World War I. After the rise of Hitler, it was concerned with the plight of Jewish refugees from Germany and appointed a high commissioner of refugees, but this—like many other of its activities—had no substantial results.

Leah: Wife of JACOB; elder daughter of LABAN. Jacob planned to marry her younger sister RACHEL, but Laban substituted L. at the wedding. L. was the mother of six sons—Reuben, Simeon, Levi, Judah, Issachar, and Zebulun—and a daughter, Dinah.

leaven (*ḥametz*): Fermented dough kneaded from flour and water. In commemoration of the Exodus, when the Israelites fleeing Egypt could not wait for their dough to leaven, the annual festival of PASSOVER is observed as a "feast of the unleavened bread," when it is forbidden to eat l.; strict regulations are laid down to maintain its observance. A special ceremony (Search for Leaven) is held the night before Passover, in which the last crumbs of l. are removed from the house and burned. L. was also prohibited as a meal offering in most Temple sacrifices.

Lebanon: In biblical times, its cedars were famous. Jewish communities lived in Tyre and Sidon from ancient times. In modern times, the main community was in Beirut. As an Arab republic, L. participated in the 1948 War of Independence. However, its relations were the least inimical to Israel of all the Arab countries until tension was heightened after the 1967 war by the presence of terrorist groups. Some 6,000 Jews were living there after World War II, and their numbers were augmented after 1948 by Jews leaving Syria. However, the numbers diminished after 1967 and by 1975 were down to 1,000, most of whom left during the Civil War in 1976–77.

Lebensohn, Abraham Dov (c. 1794–1878): Hebrew poet, living in Vilna, known as Adam Ha-Cohen. He was the leader of the HASKALAH in Lithuania. His 3-volume *Shire Sepher Kodesh* collected his poems, which made a deep impression. He also wrote a Hebrew grammar and Bible commentary.

Lebensohn, Micah Joseph (1828–1852): Hebrew poet, known as Michal; the son of Abraham Dov L. He was stricken with tuberculosis at the age of 17 and his work is filled with the realization that he had not long to live. He published various translations and two volumes of poems on Jewish subjects.

Lederberg, Joshua (1925–): US geneticist. He was professor at the University of Wisconsin in 1948–59, and from 1959 at Stanford. He was awarded a Nobel Prize for Medicine and Physiology for his work on the organization of genetic material in bacteria.

Leeds: English city. Jews settled there in the 19th cent., especially in the latter part, when they played an important role in the woolen trade. Its Jewish population of 18,000 represents the largest proportion of Jews to the general population (3%) in Britain.

Leghorn (Livorno): Italian port. Jews lived there from the late 16th cent., and by the mid-17th cent. the Jewish community there was influential. Many Marranos settled in L., where the ghetto was never established. It became a center of Jewish intellectual life. Its importance dwindled after the French occupation in 1796. In 1974 about 600 Jews lived there.

Le-ḥayyim ("To life"): The most popular Jewish toast.

Leḥi see **Lohame Ḥerut Israel**

Lehman, Herbert Henry (1878–1963): US banker and public figure. He served as Democratic lieutenant-governor (1928–32) and governor (1932–42) of New York State. From 1943–46, he headed the United Nations Relief and Rehabilitation Agency, working in Europe in the latter part and aftermath of World War II. He was senator from New York in 1949–57. A vigorous supporter of the New Deal, he worked closely with President Franklin D. Roosevelt. He was prominent in Jewish organizations.

Lehranstalt für Wissenschaft des Judentums see **Hochschule für die Wissenschaft des Judentums.**

Leibowitz, Samuel Simon (1893–): US lawyer and jurist. A noted criminal lawyer, he participated in the defense of the Scottsboro Boys (1934–37). From 1940 he was a judge. His biography *Courtroom* was written by Quentin Reynolds.

Leinsdorf, Erich (1912–): Conductor. He conducted in Europe until 1937, when he went to the Metropolitan Opera House, New York. Later he conducted at Cleveland and Rochester and, from 1962, the Boston Symphony Orchestra.

Leivick, H. (Leivick Halper) (1888–1962): Yiddish author and playwright. He lived in Eastern Europe and was exiled for a time to Siberia until 1913, when he settled in the US. Many of his plays were highly successful, notably *Der Golem*. He was also a noted poet.

Lekah Tov ("Good Doctrine"): Midrash on the Pentateuch and the Five Scrolls composed in 11th cent. Germany by Tobiah ben Eliezer. It is also known as *Pesikta Zutrata*.

Lekert, Hirsch (1879–1902): Lithuanian revolutionary. He was active in the Bund and shot the governor of Vilna province, who had ordered the flogging of Jewish demonstrators. L. was executed, and his courage during his last days made him a folk hero.

Lekhah Dodi ("Come My Friend"): Poem recited in all synagogues on the Sabbath eve, welcoming Sabbath the bride. It was written in the 16th cent. by the Safed kabbalist Solomon ALKABETZ, whose name is to be found in the initial acrostic of the poem.

lel shimmurim ("a night of watching"): Name given in Exod. 12:42 to the night of the Exodus, and now referring to the first night (two nights in the Diaspora) of Passover, thought to be under special Divine protection. It was customary not to lock the door or to say the night prayer.

Lemberg see **Lvov**

Leningrad: Russian city and port, formerly St. Petersburg, Petrograd. Individual Jews lived there during the 18th cent., toward the end of which a community was established. The first synagogue dates from 1830. The community was seriously organized from the mid-19th cent., due largely to the efforts of the banker Horace GÜNZBURG. Schools were built there, and an active cultural life developed, even though Jews were required to have permits to live in L. Some 210,000 Jews lived there in 1941; their number was estimated at 165,000 in 1970 with one synagogue.

Leo Baeck Institute: Organization promoting research into the history of German Jewry. It was founded in 1955, with main branches in New York, London, and Jerusalem.

Leon of Modena see **Modena**

Leon, Moses de (1250–1305): Spanish kabbalist; putative author of the ZOHAR. He lived in Guadalajara until 1290 and in Avila thereafter. He wrote 20 kabbalistic works, of which two are known. Traditionally the *Zohar* was ascribed to R. Simeon ben Yoḥai, but modern scholars, notably G. Scholem, have reached the conclusion that its author was L., although older material was incorporated.

Leone Ebreo see **Abravanel, Judah**

Lerner, Alan Jay (1918–): US lyricist. He collaborated with Frederick LOEWE in many hits including *Brigadoon, Paint Your Wagon, My Fair Lady,* and *Gigi.*

Lerner, Max (1902–): US author. He taught at various universities, from 1949, at Brandeis. His books on American society include *America as a Civilization.* He was a regular columnist in New York daily newspapers and edited *The Nation,* 1936–38.

Lesser, Isaac (1806–1868): US rabbi and writer; born in Germany. From 1829 he was with the Mikveh Israel Congregation in Philadelphia. He was a founder of the first congregational union, the first Hebrew day school, the first Jewish college, and the first Jewish publication society. He edited the influential monthly *The Occident,* translated the Bible into English, and wrote books of Jewish instruction. He was the first American rabbi to preach in English.

*Lessing, Gotthold Ephraim (1729–1781): German writer. His play *Nathan the Wise* was a noble plea for toleration. The hero is inspired by L.'s close friend Moses MENDELSSOHN.

Lestschinsky, Jacob (1876–1966): Sociologist and economist. He was born in the Ukraine, lived in Germany from 1921, the US from 1938, and Israel from 1959. He wrote on the sociology, demography, and economy of the Jews in modern times.

Letter of Aristeas see **Aristeas**

Letteris, Meir ha-Levi (c. 1800–1871): Hebrew poet, writer, and educator. He lived in Vilna, Prague, and Vienna. His Hebrew translations include Goethe's *Faust* and Racine's biblical dramas. He edited the Hebrew Bible for the British and Foreign Bible Society.

Levi: Third son of Jacob and Leah. He and his brother SIMEON revenged the rape of his sister DINAH by killing the men of Shechem and plundering the city (Gen. 34). This aroused Jacob's displeasure, and he ordained that L.'s descendants (the LEVITES) should be scattered among the other tribes.

Levi ben Gershom (Gersonides) (1288–1344): Philosopher, exegete, mathematician, astronomer, Bible scholar, and talmudist, known as Ralbag. He lived for a while in Avignon, but little biographical information is known. His book *Milḥamot Adonai* is a work of religious philosophy, written in the spirit of Aristotelianism. L. also wrote supercommentaries on works of Averroes, commentaries on the Bible, and works on most of the sciences. He developed the use of the *camera obscura* and invented an instrument for measuring angles.

Levi of Berdichev (c. 1740–1810): Ḥasidic rabbi. He studied under Dov Ber of Mezhirich. He was known for his "love of Israel" and stressed the concept of "joy" in Ḥasidism. His prayers and Yiddish poems and songs were very popular. Many legends were related about him. Because of the veneration in which he was held, no successor was selected to replace him after his death.

Levi, Edward H. (1911–): US educator and legal scholar. A scion of a distinguished Reform rabbinical family, he was president of the University of Chicago from 1967 to 1975, when he was appointed US Attorney-General, serving until 1976.

Lévi-Strauss, Claude (1908–): French anthropologist. He conducted research and joined expeditions to South America and Asian countries. From 1959, he was professor of social anthropology at the Collège de France. He pioneered the structural school of anthropology, and sought to establish a science of myth.

leviathan: Sea animal, actual and mythological, mentioned in the Bible. It figures in ancient Middle East mythologies as a force of chaos and evil, and traces of the myth are preserved in the Bible. In rabbinic legend, the righteous will eat of the flesh of the l. in the world to come. In modern Hebrew, l. means "whale."

Levin, Meyer (1905–): Novelist. He wrote of his early life in Chicago; later he settled in Israel. His novels, many on Jewish themes, include *Compulsion, Eva, The Settlers,* and *Harvest.*

Levin, Shemaryahu (1867–1935): Writer and Zionist. Born in White Russia, he was crown rabbi in Grodno, Yekaterinoslav, and Vilna. He represented Vilna in the Duma. L. was a member of Zionist Executive (1911–18). He directed Zionist information in the US during World War I. He settled in Palestine in 1924. L. was a witty speaker and noted orator. He wrote in Hebrew and Yiddish for the press and published his memoirs.

Levin, Yitzhak Meir (1894–1971): AGUDAT ISRAEL leader. Born in Poland, he settled in Palestine in 1940. He represented the Agudat Israel in the Knesset from 1949, and was a member of the Israeli government 1949–52.

Levine, Jack (1915–): US expressionistic painter. His paintings depict satirically various aspects of US life.

Levinsohn, Isaac Ber (1788–1860): Russian Hebrew writer and educator. A founder of Haskalah in Russia, he was called "the Russian Mendelssohn." He advocated the modernization of Russian Jewry, proposing that secular and vocational subjects be taught along with traditional studies. He published anti-Hasidic satires.

The government supported his proposals and projects.

levirate marriage (*yibbum*): Marriage with the widow of one's brother who has died childless (Deut. 25: 5–10). If the brother had had children, the surviving brother may not marry her; but if there are no children he is obligated. Release from this obligation is possible only through the ceremony of ḤALITZAH. Although l.m. became customary in Sephardi communities, *halitzah* became general among Ashkenazim. The relevant regulations are discussed in the talmudic tractate *Yevamot*. In Israel, *halitzah* is the obligatory procedure. Reform Judaism has dispensed with the entire concept.

Levita (Bahur), Elijah (c. 1468–1549): Scholar. Born in Germany, he lived in Italy, where he taught Hebrew to Christian clerics and humanists. He wrote works —most of which were translated into Latin—on Hebrew grammar, biblical language, and *Masorah*. He also wrote a talmudic lexicon and an Aramaic dictionary. A pioneer Yiddish scholar, he produced the first Hebrew-Yiddish dictionary and translated Psalms and the Book of Job into Yiddish; his BAVA BUCH was a Yiddish adaptation of an Italian romance.

Levites: Descendants of
LEVI. This tribe was sanctified by Moses to be devoted
to the Divine service in the
Tabernacle, later the Temple. Each family was assigned
certain tasks in the wilderness, while that of AARON
was chosen for priestly functions within the Tabernacle.
After Palestine was con-
quered, the L., unlike the
other tribes, received no
tract of territory, but 48
cities were made over for
them to inhabit. They were
also allotted a tithe of all
agricultural produce. After
the destruction of the Temple, the special privileges of
the L. were restricted to
being called up second (after
the priest) to the Reading
of the Law in the synagogue
and to the honor of washing
the hands of the priest before he uttered the priestly
benediction.

Leviticus   (*Vayikra*):
Third book of the Penta-
teuch, formerly called *Torat
ha-Kohanim*. It continues the
Mosaic legislation that had
been begun in the preceding
Book of Exodus, and deals
largely with ritual and legal
subjects, including the laws
of sacrifice, regulations concerning the priests, the rules
of ritual impurity, and the
"Holiness Code" (a collection of ethical as well as ritual injunctions). Bible critics
suggest a separate authorship

to the Holiness Code. Early
critical scholarship assigned
the Book of L. a post-Exilic
date, but later views are that
it is much earlier. Traditionally it was written by Moses
as part of the Pentateuch.

Leviticus Rabbah: Midrashic commentary on the
Book of Leviticus, contained
in MIDRASH RABBAH. It dates
from the 5th cent. CE, and
was probably written in Palestine.

Levy,   Uriah   Phillips
(1792–1862): US naval of-
ficer. He fought in the War
of 1912 and became commo-
dore of the US fleet. He was
responsible for prohibiting
corporal punishment in the
navy.

Lévy-Bruhl,   Lucien
(1857–1939): French phi-
losopher, sociologist, and eth-
nologist. His achievement
rests primarily on his research into the primitive
mentality. He taught at the
Sorbonne.

Lewandowski,   Louis
(1821–1894): Choral director and composer of syna-
gogue music. At the age of
20, he was appointed choir-
master of the Old Synagogue
in Berlin. He composed and
arranged traditional music in
contemporary styles.

Lewin,   Judah   Leib
(1844–1925): Hebrew poet
and writer in Russia, known
as Yehalel. An early sociologist, he was one of the first

to discuss social and economic problems in Hebrew literature. Later he was an ardent Zionist.

Lewin, Kurt (1890–1947): Social psychologist and writer. He taught in Berlin until 1932, when he went to the US. He founded the Research Center for Group Dynamics at MIT. He introduced the system of topological psychology and studied minority group problems.

Lewis, Jerry (1926–): US comedian, born Joseph Levitch. He teamed with Dean Martin to make a comedy team that was successful on stage and in films. After they separated, L. starred in many movies (such as *The Nutty Professor*).

Lewisohn, Ludwig (1882–1955): US novelist, critic, and translator. He was professor at Ohio State University (from 1911) and at Brandeis University (from 1948). He wrote novels (some on Jewish subjects), criticism, autobiography, and books on aspects of Zionism.

Liberal Judaism see **Reform**

Liberal Party: Israeli political party, formed in 1961 when the GENERAL ZIONISTS joined the PROGRESSIVES. It obtained 17 mandates in the election held that year. Subsequently it broke up, the former General Zionists becoming part of GAHAL and the former Progressives forming the Independent Liberal Party.

Liberman, Yevsey Grigoryevich (1897–): Soviet economist; from 1959, professor at Kharkov University. He stressed profitability and rationality to increase plant efficiency, and brought about changes in Russian economic policy after 1956.

Libya: Jews lived there from pre-Roman times. For their subsequent history see CYRENAICA and TRIPOLI. Anti-Jewish riots broke out after World War II, and many Jews were killed in 1945. Some 30,000 Jews left for Israel after 1948. There were further anti-Jewish riots at the time of the 1967 Six-Day War, following which the 6,000 Jews who had remained left.

Licht, Frank (1916–): US jurist and governor. In 1956 he became justice of the Supreme Court of Rhode Island; in 1948 he was a state senator, and from 1969–72 was governor of Rhode Island.

Lichtenstein, Morris (1889–1938): Rabbi. In 1907 he went from Europe to the US, where he established the JEWISH SCIENCE movement in 1921. After his death it was continued by his wife, Tehilla.

Lieberman, Saul (1898–

): Talmudist. Born in White Russia, he taught in Jerusalem from 1931 until 1940, when he was appointed professor at the Jewish Theological Seminary of America. From 1967 he was also president of the American Academy of Jewish Research. One of the leading talmudists of the century, Lieberman published editions of the Palestinian Talmud and of the Tosephta; he has also written on Greek influence in Palestine during the talmudic period.

Liebermann, Aaron Samuel (1845–1880): Socialist writer. He had to flee Russia because of his socialist activities, going to London in 1875. The following year, he published the first Hebrew socialist manifesto and founded the first Jewish socialist journal, *Ha-Emet*. He committed suicide in the US after an unhappy romance.

Liebermann, Max (1847–1935): Painter, a founder and leader of German impressionism. He was president of the Berlin Academy of Fine Arts. His subjects included portraits and self-portraits. His grandnephew *Rolf L.* (1910–), composer, writes operas and has directed the Hamburg and Paris Operas.

Liebman, Joshua Loth (1907–1948): US rabbi. He officiated at Boston from 1939 and was widely known as a radio preacher and published the popular *Peace of Mind*, on the relations between psychology and religion.

Liebmann, Jost (d. c. 1702): Court Jew and mint-master to rulers of Brandenburg. He exercised a dominating influence on the affairs of the Berlin community.

Likkud (Union): Political alignment of non-socialist parties led by GAHAL with various smaller groups, established in 1973. It obtained 39 seats in the Knesset in 1973, and in 1977 became the largest party, with 45 seats. Its leader Menahem BEGIN was thereupon charged with forming a coalition government, in which L. was dominant.

Lilien, Ephraim Moses (1874–1925): Illustrator and printmaker. Born in Galicia, he lived in Germany from 1895. His pen-and-ink style is distinctive. His drawings were largely on Jewish themes, many being inspired by his strong Zionist interests.

Lilienblum, Moses Lieb (1843–1910): Hebrew writer, critic, and Zionist. After a talmudic education, he was drawn to Haskalah, and attacked the Orthodox. From 1869 he lived in Odessa.

After the 1881 pogroms he enthusiastically supported the Hibbat Zion movement, in which he was a leading figure.

Lilienthal, David Eli (1899–): US attorney and public official. In 1933 he was appointed director of the Tennessee Valley Authority; he was its chairman, 1941–46. From 1946–50 he chaired the US Atomic Energy Commission, playing an important role in civilian control of atomic-energy programs in the US. In 1955 he embarked on a private venture to execute development plans in backward countries.

Lilienthal, Max (1815–1882): Educator and rabbi. Principal of a Jewish school in Riga, he was selected by the Russian government to influence Jews to accept secular education. When he realized the anti-Semitic motivation behind the scheme, he left for the US (1845), where he was a noted Reform rabbi in New York and Cincinnati.

Lilith: Female demon. Mentioned in the Bible and Talmud, she became Queen of the Demons in mystical literature, regarded as seducer of men and strangler of children. It therefore became customary for women in labor to have amulets protecting them against her.

Linowitz, Sol M. (1913–): US businessman, lawyer, and ambassador. In 1959, he became head of the Xerox Corporation. He was US ambassador to the Organization of American States (1966–69). In 1977 he was co-negotiator of the US-Panama agreement over the Panama Canal.

Lipchitz, Jacques (1891–1973): Sculptor. He was born in Lithuania, settled in Paris in 1909, and lived in the US from 1941. An outstanding artist, his first "transparent" sculpture was completed in 1927. He also sculpted works on Jewish themes.

Lipkin, Israel see **Salanter, Israel**

Lipmann, Fritz Albert (1899–): Biochemist. Born in Germany, he went to the US in 1939 and was professor at Harvard (1949–57) and at the Rockefeller Institute for Medical Research in New York. He shared the 1953 Nobel Prize for Medicine and Physiology for his discovery of coenzyme A and its importance for intermediary metabolism.

Lippmann, Gabriel (1845–1921): French physicist. He was awarded the 1908 Nobel Prize for Physics for discovering a method of photographic reproduction through utilization of the interference process.

Lippmann, Walter (1889–1974): US writer. He edited *New Republic* and the New York *World* and from 1931 wrote a political column in the New York *Herald Tribune* and other journals. L. was the author of several books on international affairs and social philosophy.

Lipsky, Louis (1876–1963): US Zionist and journalist. He founded *The Maccabean*, the first English-language Zionist journal in the US, and later founded and edited *The New Palestine*. He was president of the Zionist Organization of America, 1922–30, playing a prominent role in Jewish communal life.

Lisbon: Capital of Portugal. Jews were living there from the 12th cent. Their quarter was sacked in 1373, and they suffered from attacks at various times in the 15th cent. L. was the principal center of the forced conversion of Portuguese Jews in 1497. Subsequently it was a Marrano center and a main seat of the Inquisition. In the 18th cent., Jews from Gibraltar settled there, and a community was founded in 1813. The Jewish population in 1973 was 565.

Lithuania: Jews are known to have lived there from the 14th cent., and in 1388 they received a charter modeled on that granted to Polish Jewry. From 1398 there was a community, mostly of KARAITES, at Troki, and by the late 15th cent. Jews were living in VILNA, GRODNO, and KOVNO. There was an expulsion in 1495, but the Jews returned in 1503. In 1566 a decree was enacted controlling Jewish dress and occupations. Originally represented in the COUNCIL OF FOUR LANDS, a separate Council of L. was formed in 1623. Their position declined during the 17th cent. and was hard hit at the time of the CHMIELNICKI uprising. L. was part of Russia from 1795 to 1918, during which time it became of major Jewish cultural importance. Here were to be found outstanding rabbis and yeshivot and the home of the MUSAR movement, and here also was a center of Haskalah. The Jews were severely affected during World War I. In independent L. (between the two world wars), Jews received national autonomy, and a Ministry for Jewish Affairs existed in 1918–24, but thereafter the powers of the Jewish community were curtailed. Lithuanian Jewry remained a cultural and educational center until World War II. 157,000 Jews were living there in 1937, but the great majority perished in the Holocaust. Some Jews escaped to Russia and subsequently returned. In 1970, 23,500 Jews were living in L.

Littauer, Lucius Nathan (1859–1944): US industrialist, congressman, and philanthropist. He made his money in glove manufacture, and became a member of Congress (1897–1907). He made many gifts to assist medicine and education and set up the Littauer Foundation.

liturgy see **prayer**

Litvinov, Maxim (1876–1951): Soviet diplomat. As a revolutionary he fled Czarist Russia and lived until 1917 abroad, mainly in London. From 1930 he was Soviet foreign minister, and from 1934 to 1938 he was the Russian representative at the League of Nations. At the time of Stalin's rapprochement with Hitler, L. was dismissed from his post, but he returned to public life after the German attack on Russia in 1941, when he was appointed ambassador to the US, where he served until 1943.

Liubavich: Russian village near Mohilev, formerly the center of Ḥabad Ḥasidism. It was a main center of the Shneersohn dynasty of Hasidic rabbis, whose leader was known as the Liubavicher.

Liuzzi, Giorgio (1896–): Italian soldier. His military career began in World War I, but he was dis-charged by Mussolini. He was reinstated in 1944 and was chief of staff of the Italian army, 1956–58.

Liverpool: English port. Its Jewish community dates from the 1750s, becoming the most important provincial community by the 19th cent. Later, however, it was overtaken by other communities. It now has 6,500 Jews with 9 synagogues.

Lod see **Lydda**

Lodz: Polish town, the center of a textile industry in which Jews have played a prominent part. The Jewish community was organized in the early 19th cent. Its 233,000 Jews (1939) had an active cultural and educational program. The Nazis concentrated the Jews into a ghetto, which was finally liquidated in 1944. After the war, some Jews returned to L, but by 1970, only 2,000 remained.

Loeb: US family. *Soloman L.* (1828–1903) was an original partner in the banking firm of Kuhn, Loeb & Co. His sons-in-law included Jacob H. Schiff and Paul M. Warburg. His son *James L.* (1867–1933) was a patron of the arts and established the Loeb Classical Library. Another son, *Morris L.* (1863–1912), professor of chemistry at New York University, was active in Jewish public and philanthropic affairs.

Loesser, Frank (1910–1969): US composer. Born in New York, he settled in Hollywood, where he wrote for films and musicals. His successes included *Guys and Dolls* and *How to Succeed in Business Without Really Trying.*

Loewe: English family. *Louis L.* (1809–1888) was an orientalist and traveler. Born in Germany, he went to England in 1833 and accompanied Moses MONTE-FIORE as his secretary on many of his journeys. He was principal of Montefiore College in Ramsgate and also of Jews' College, and he wrote works on Oriental languages. His grandson, *Herbert Martin James L.* (1882–1940), also an orientalist, taught at Oxford and Cambridge, publishing works on various aspects of Jewish literature and history.

Loewe, Frederick (1904–): US composer. Born in Vienna, he went to the US in 1924. He wrote music for *Brigadoon, Gigi,* and the popular *My Fair Lady* (the latter two in collaboration with Alan Jay LERNER).

Loewi, Otto (1873–1961): Physiologist and biochemist. He taught in Austria until 1938, when he went to England. In 1940 he went to the US, where he was re-search professor at the New York College of Medicine. He shared the 1936 Nobel Prize for Physiology and Medicine for his study of the chemical transmission of nerve impulses.

Lohame Herut Yisrael ("Fighters for Israeli Freedom": abbr. Lehi): Underground revolutionary organization fighting the British in Palestine from 1940 to 1948. It was known after its first leader, Avraham STERN, as the Stern Group. Lehi split originally from the IRGUN TZEVAI LEUMI, declaring a continuation of the war against Britain notwithstanding World War II. Its membership was some 300, and the deeds attributed to it included the murders of Lord Moyne in 1944 and of Count Bernadotte in 1948.

London: Capital of England. Jews lived there in the 12th and 13th cent. Many were massacred when disorders broke out during the coronation of Richard I in 1189. There were further massacres in 1263, and the Jews were expelled together with the rest of English Jewry in 1290. A secret Marrano community existed in the 16th cent. and again under the Commonwealth, forming a Sephardi community in 1663. An Ashkenazi community was established before the end of the cent.

The L. community retained its supremacy, and the rabbi of its Great Synagogue was recognized as chief rabbi of Britain. It was the center of all national British Jewish institutions. Restrictions on Jews were removed in the 19th cent., and in 1855 Sir David SALOMONS became lord mayor of L. From 1870 the Ashkenazi synagogues were federated in the United Synagogue, while the Federation of Synagogues (formed by newcomers from Eastern Europe) was established in 1887. The nature of the community was transformed from the 1880s with the mass migration from Eastern Europe; the majority of the new arrivals were concentrated in the East End. L. now became a flourishing Jewish center with 150,000 Jews. Immigration was virtually stopped in 1905, but there was another influx during the 1930s, this time from Central Europe. World War II and its aftermath, together with the growing affluence of the country, took the Jews away from the East End and into more suburban areas. In 1976 it was estimated that 280,000 Jews lived in greater L.

Lookstein, Joseph Hyman (1902–1979): US rabbi and educator. He officiated in New York and since 1923 had been professor of homiletics at Yeshiva University. He founded the Ramaz School in New York and became president of BAR-ILAN UNIVERSITY in 1958.

Lopez, Aaron (1731–1782): US merchant shipper in NEWPORT, Rhode Island. He helped to develop the whaling industry in Newport. In 1763 he laid the foundation stone of the Newport synagogue.

Lopez, Roderigo (1525–1594): Marrano physician. Born in Portugal, he completed his education in Spain and settled in London in 1559. There he became physician to the earl of Leicester and to Queen Elizabeth. His involvement in court intrigue made him enemies, including the powerful earl of Essex. He was accused of attempting to poison the queen and was executed.

Los Angeles: US city, whose 455,000 Jews constitute the world's second largest Jewish community (after New York). Jews lived there from the mid-19th cent., and the first congregation was founded in 1862. The main growth in the community began after World War I. The powerful Jewish Community Council was founded in 1934. After World War II, the growth was rapid. The Jewish Theological Seminary and Hebrew Union

College established L.A. branches. Jews have been very prominent in the city's entertainment industry.

Lost Ten Tribes see **Tribes, Lost Ten**

Lot: Nephew of Abraham (Gen. 11:27), with whom he traveled from Ur to Canaan. The two parted when L. went to settle in the Dead Sea area. Later he was rescued by Abraham when he was carried off by a hostile coalition (14:1–16). Subsequently, two Divine messengers rescued him and his family from the destruction of Sodom, but the refusal of his wife to heed their instructions led to her being turned into a pillar of salt. According to the Bible, he was the ancestor of the Moabites and Ammonites (Gen. 19:36–38).

Lots see **Purim**

Louisiana: US state. Until the territory became part of the US, the Black Code prohibited the practice of any religion other than Catholicism. There were Jews living in New Orleans in the early 19th cent., and the first congregation was founded in 1827. Several hundred Jews from L. fought in the Confederate army. Many communities were founded in the 19th cent. However, the tendency in the 20th cent. was for Jews to consolidate in larger communities, and the general number declined. In 1976 there were 15,630 Jews, including 10,500 in NEW ORLEANS, 1,500 in Shreveport, and 1,300 in Baton Rouge.

Low: Hungarian family. Leopold L. (1811–1875), rabbi and author, pioneered religious reform in Hungary and was the first rabbi to preach in Hungarian. He played an important part in the fight for Jewish Emancipation. He published a journal of Jewish studies and wrote on the history of Hungarian Jewry. His son *Immanuel L.* (1854–1944) succeeded his father as rabbi of Szeged. He sat in the Hungarian Upper Chamber from 1927 to 1940. He wrote on Hebrew and Aramaic philology, while his best-known work is *The Flora of the Jews.*

Lublin: Polish city. The Jewish community began in the 15th cent. but for a long time Jews were permitted to live only near the palace hill. L. was one of the meeting places of the COUNCIL OF THE FOUR LANDS. It was also a center of Jewish scholarship, and many noted rabbis officiated and taught there. Most Jews left as the result of persecutions in the latter 18th cent., but some returned after 1862, now settling in the Old City. About 37,000 Jews were living there at the outbreak of

World War II. The Germans established a ghetto and killed all its inhabitants. Some Jews resettled there after the war, but by 1968 all had left.

Ludomir, Maid of (c. 1805–1892): Ḥasidic leader. Noted for her extreme piety, she was revered by Ḥasidim, who flocked to her as to a *tzaddik*. A synagogue was built for her and she observed the religious duties of males. After her marriage, she ceased to occupy the same special position. She spent her last years in Palestine.

Ludwig (Cohn), Emil (1881–1948): German author. Born in Germany, he spent many years in Switzerland and died in the US. He was noted for his popular biographies of Napoleon, Marie Antoinette, Goethe, Bismarck, Beethoven, and others.

*Lueger, Karl (1844–1910): Anti-Semitic mayor of Vienna. He ousted Jewish officials and introduced segregation into municipal schools.

lulav ("shoot"): The palm branch, taken on the Feast of Tabernacles, together with the myrtle, willow, and citron as the FOUR SPECIES. The citron (*etrog*) is taken in the left hand, the other species in the right, and appropriate benedictions are recited. They are also carried around the synagogue during the recital of HOSHANOT. In ancient times, the *l.* was con-

sidered a Jewish symbol and was often represented artistically.

Luncz, Abraham Moses (1854–1918): Author and publisher. Born in Lithuania, he moved to Jerusalem in 1869. He went blind ten years later, but he continued with his research and published guides to Palestine, early sources on Palestinography, and other works.

Luria, Isaac (1534–1572): Kabbalist, known as Ari. Founder of a school of mysticism which profoundly affected the Jewish world and Jewish thought. Born in Jerusalem, he lived for a time in Cairo, and in Safed from 1569. He lived ascetically and never wrote down his teachings but taught them to a small group of disciples. After his death they were committed to writing by Ḥayyim VITAL. The Lurianic Kabbalah was based on three foundations: *tzimtzum* (the contraction of God, thus enabling existence outside the Divine, including that of evil); *shevirat ha-kelim* (see BREAKING OF THE VESSELS); and *tikkun* (the healing of the breach of the Divine order by a process of restoration). The last is associated with a doctrine of transmigration.

*Luther, Martin (1483–1546): German leader of Protestant Reformation. In the early stages of his reform movement, he looked hopefully to the Jews for support, but when they rejected him, he became bitterly anti-Jewish, encouraging the persecution and humiliation of the Jews. His German translation of the Bible is outstanding.

Luxemburg: Jews lived there in the 13th cent., and a community existed until 1391. Jews also lived there in the 15th cent. A community was reestablished after the French Revolution. It suffered under the Nazis but was strengthened again after World War II. In 1973 it numbered 1,000 (compared to 4,000 in 1939), with its largest settlements in Luxemburg (800) and Esch (100).

Luxemburg, Rosa (1871–1919): Revolutionary socialist. Born in Poland, she moved to Germany. She was imprisoned during World War I for her pacifism. L. worked with Karl Liebknecht in the German Communist Party. After an unsuccessful uprising in 1919, the two of them were murdered by soldiers. Her ideas continued to be influential in extreme leftist works; they appeared in *The Accumulation of Capital*, which expanded on Marxist thoughts.

Luzzato, Samuel David (1880–1865): Italian scholar, philosopher, and translator, called Shadal. He taught at the Padua Rabbinical College and published research on many aspects of Jewish history, literature, and philosophy. He edited the poems of JUDAH HA-LEVI. L. translated portions of the Bible into Italian, adding a Hebrew commentary. He is regarded as among the fathers of the WISSENSCHAFT DES JUDENTUMS.

Luzzatti, Luigi (1841–1927): Italian premier. He taught economy at Milan and Padua universities in Italy. He was minister of the treasury a number of times, minister of agriculture in 1909, and prime minister in 1910–11.

Luzzatto, Moses Ḥayyim (1707–1747): Italian mystic and poet, known as Ramḥal. Brought up in Padua, he was the center of a kabbalistic circle and apparently had certain messianic claims. He was persuaded to drop these on the insistence of the Italian rabbinate. L. went to Frankfort and then to Amsterdam, where he worked as a diamond polisher. In 1743 he went to Palestine, where he and his family died of the plague in Acre. He is regarded as a seminal figure in modern Hebrew literature. His poetical works include allegorical plays and psalms in the biblical style. His best-known work is the ethical tractate *Mesillat Yesharim*.

Lvov (Lemberg): Town in USSR, formerly in Poland

(Galicia). Jews began living there from the 13th cent., and in 1364 received privileges from Casimir the Great. There was a Jewish community outside the wall, which was destroyed during the CHMIELNICKI raids, and also a Jewish community inside the walls. The Jews frequently clashed with the Poles. Many famous rabbis and scholars lived in L., which was also a Haskalah and Zionist center. The Jews suffered during World War I and in pogroms in 1918. In 1939, 150,000 Jews were living there. During World War II, they were confined to a ghetto and eventually all were put to death. Jews returned after the war, and in 1970 there were 21,700 Jews.

Lydda (Lod): Israeli town. It is mentioned in biblical and Second Temple times. After the destruction of Jerusalem, it became an important rabbinic center, home of an academy where R. Eliezer ben Hyrcanus, R. Akiva, and others taught. From the 3rd cent. it was called Diospolis, and most of the inhabitants were Christians. L. was considered the home of St. George, and was called Georgiopolis for him. After the Arab conquest, L. was for a time the capital of Palestine (until this was moved to nearby Ramleh). In modern times, L. became a communications center, especially as the result of the establishment of the international airport nearby. Most of its Arab inhabitants left in 1948, and new immigrants settled there. The population in 1974 was 33,900, including 3,500 Arabs.

Maariv (Arevit): Evening Service, recited daily after nightfal. One of the three regular daily prayers, its institution is traditionally ascribed to the patriarch Jacob. Unlike the other daily prayers, M. did not originate as a substitute for sacrifice, and therefore there is a discussion in the Talmud as to whether its recitation is obligatory or optional. The accepted ruling is that it is optional, although it eventually became regarded as obligatory. It includes the recitation of the SHEMA and its benedictions and the AMIDAH (which is, however, not repeated by the reader). Some Ashkenazi communities incorporate *maaravot*—liturgical poems composed for M.

Maariv: Israeli afternoon newspaper, founded in 1948 by Azriel Carlebach. It has the largest circulation of any Israeli newspaper.

maaseh bereshit ("work of creation") and **maaseh merkavah** ("work of [the] chariot"): Topics of kabbalistic speculation—M. B. dealing with Creation (based on Gen. I), and M. M. with the composition of the Divine world (through the exposition of Ezekiel's vision of the throne-chariot). The Mishnah limits the exposition of these mysteries "from master to pupil." Only segments of these early esoteric topics have been preserved, for example in the HEKHALOT literature.

Maaseh Book: Yiddish anthology of ethical tales, often of a miraculous nature.

The main sources are the Talmud and folklore. It was first published in 1602.

Maaser Sheni ("Second Tithe"): Eighth tractate in the MISHNAH order *Zeraim* with *gemara* in the Palestinian Talmud only. It deals with second TITHE eaten in Jerusalem (Lev. 27:30–31 and Deut. 14:22–26) and when it may be exchanged for money.

Maaserot (Tithes"): Seventh tractate in the MISHNAH order of *Zeraim*, with *gemara* in the Palestinian Talmud only. It deals with the TITHE given to the Levite (see Num. 18:20–24).

Maccabee: Additional name (of uncertain derivation) given to Judas son of Mattathias and applied to the whole HASMONEAN dynasty and in Christian tradition to the seven martyred sons of Hannah.

Maccabees, Book of the: Four separate books of the APOCRYPHA. I Maccabees contains a reliable historical account of the Hasmonean revolt from 175 to 135 BCE. It was written in Hebrew during the latter part of the 2nd cent. BCE by·an admirer of the Maccabees. It has been preserved only in a Greek translation. II Maccabees is an abridgment of Jason of Cyrene's history of the revolt, but its aim is religious rather than historical, and it is less reliable. It was probably written in Greek in the 2nd cent. BCE (perhaps in Egypt). III Maccabees, which in fact is not connected with the Maccabees, describes the deliverance of the Temple from the hands of Ptolemy Philopater of Egypt. It belongs to the 1st cent. BCE and was written in Greek. IV Maccabees is a philosophical work influenced by Pharisaism and Stoicism. It was written in Greek by a Jewish author, probably in the 1st cent. CE.

Maccabi World Union: Jewish sports organization, founded in 1895. The German branch received official Zionist support and its headquarters were in Berlin from 1921; later it moved to London, and eventually to Tel Aviv. Under its auspices the Maccabiah, the international Jewish sports festival, is held generally once every four years; since 1932 it has been held in Tel Aviv.

Machpelah: Cave in Hebron. Bought by Abraham from Ephron the Hittite to serve as a burial place for Sarah, it was subsequently the burial place for all the patriarchs and their wives (except Rachel). The traditional site was hallowed from an early date; at different times, a church, a synagogue, and a mosque were erected there. From the 12th cent. it has been a mosque, with entry prohibited to non-Muslims, but since the 1967 Six-Day War, it has become a center for Jewish pilgrimage.

Mack, Julian William (1866–1943): U.S. judge and Zionist. He was professor of law at the Univ. of Chicago and Northwestern Univ. Active in Jewish and Zionist circles, he was president of the Zionist Organization of America, first president of the American Jewish Congress, and first chairman of the Comité des Délégations Juives at Versailles.

Magen David ("Shield of David"): Hexagram formed by two triangles which was an ancient mystical symbol and from about the 17th cent. became a specifically Jewish symbol. It was adopted as a Zionist symbol, and in 1948 was incorporated in the flag of Israel.

Magen David Adom ("Red Shield of David"): Israeli first-aid society, founded in Tel Aviv in 1930 as the medical wing of the Haganah. Gift ambulances are contributed by Friends of the M.D.A. in other countries.

maggid: (1) Popular preacher, especially in Eastern Europe. The itinerant *m.* went to the people and proved an important influence. The best known *m.* was Jacob ben Wolf Krantz (d. 1804), the M. of Dubno. These preachers played a key role in the dissemination of Ḥasidism. (2) In mystical literature, a heavenly agent communicating supernatural knowledge. Joseph Caro claimed to have been inspired by such a *m.*

Magnes, Judah Leib (1877–1948): US Reform rabbi, communal leader, and educator. After serving as rabbi in Temple Emanu-el, New York, M. was the moving spirit in the Kehillah movement in New York. During World War I, his pacifism aroused hostility. In 1921 he settled in Jerusalem, and when the Hebrew University was opened in 1925, he was its first chancellor; from 1935 he served as its first president. He strongly favored Arab-Jewish cooperation and was a founder of the Berit Shalom and Iḥud movements favoring a binational state.

Mah tovu ("How goodly"): Opening of blessing uttered by Balaam (Num. 24:5), which is used as the initial word of the prayer recited in the Ashkenazi rite on entering a synagogue.

Maharal see **Judah Löw ben Bezalel**

Mahler, Gustav (1860–1911): Austrian composer and conductor. M., after becoming a Catholic, conducted the Vienna Court Opera (1897–1907). He conducted the Metropolitan Opera and the New York Philharmonic

(1908–11). His compositions include nine symphonies, various song cycles, and art songs.

Mahoza: Babylonian town with Jewish community. The PUMBEDITA academy was moved in 338 to M., where it gained prominence under the direction of RAVA.

Mahzor: Festival prayer book; originally the entire liturgy of the Jewish year arranged chronologically.

maibarah: Transitional camp or quarter established in Israel during the period of mass immigration starting in 1948, to house newcomers until they could be transferred to permanent dwellings.

Maidanek: Nazi concentration and extermination camp near Lublin; established in 1941. By 1944, when it was liberated, some 125,000 Jews had been killed there. These included many Polish Jews sent from the Warsaw ghetto.

Mailer, Norman (1923–): US writer. He made his name with his early novel of World War II *The Naked and the Dead.* His subsequent works included other novels— *The Deer Park, The American Dream*—and documentary-style reportage, such as *The Armies of the Night* and *The Prisoner of Sex.*

Maimon (**Fishman**), **Judah Leib** (1875–1962): Rabbi and religious Zionist leader. He became involved in the Zionist movement in his native Bessarabia. In 1902, he participated in the founding conference of Mizrahi and settled in Palestine in 1913. He was a member of the Jewish Agency Executive (1935–48), Israeli minister for religions (1948–51), and Mizrahi member of the Knesset. He founded and directed Mosad Ha-Rav Kook and wrote prolifically on talmudic and Zionist subjects.

Maimon, Solomon (c. 1753–1800): Philosopher. Born in Lithuania, he had a varied career vividly described in his autobiography. He went to Germany in 1779 and, after living as a vagabond, settled in Berlin. With the help of Moses MENDELSSOHN, he became a member of the intellectual circles. Kant regarded him as one of his most perceptive critics.

Maimonides (**Moses ben Maimon,** also known as **Rambam**) (1135 or 1138–1204): Codifier, philosopher, physician; the outstanding Jewish personality of the Middle Ages. Born in Cordova, Spain, he left for N. Africa when he was 13. After living there for a time, he went via Palestine and settled in Fostat (old Cairo). He soon became the spiritual head of the Egyptian community, and from 1170 was physician to the viceroy of Egypt. He wrote a number of medical works, some of which were translated into Latin and were studied at European universities until the 17th cent. Already at the age of 30, M. concluded his commentary on the Mishnah (in Arabic). Its object was to make the Mishnah more accessible to the general reader and to systematize the Halakhah. His preface to tractate Sanhedrin leads up to his formulation of the Thirteen Articles of the Faith—the first attempt to lay down a sort of dogma—and despite criticism, this remained the popular formulation of the Jewish creed. His *Sepher Mitzvot* contains an enumeration of the 613 PRECEPTS, which was also widely accepted. This was the preface to M.'s great work on Jewish law, *Mishneh Torah* (also known as *Yad ha-Ḥazakah* because *yad* = 14 and it has 14 parts), which was written in Hebrew. This was the first complete compendium of Jewish law. Its object was to organize talmudic and other early rabbinic sources in the most concise way possible, clearly defining the actual law. The work has remained a standard code, although it was criticized for failing to indicate sources. M. rejected superstition and also incorporated theological and philosophical ideas. However, M.'s philosophical work was *Moreh ha-Nevukhim* ("Guide of the Perplexed"), which presents an exposition of Jewish faith. M.'s approach was strongly rationalist and influenced by Aristotelianism. His *Guide* seeks to reconcile the Torah with Aristotelianism as far as possible; when the two prove irreconcilable, the Torah is seen as holding the truth. M.'s strong rationalism led to the rejection of many traditional attitudes, and his work was the subject of bitter controversy among Jews in Christian countries, which lasted for at least a century after M.'s death. In general, it was accepted as authoritative and also influenced leading scholastic thinkers, such as Thomas Aquinas. After M.'s death, his body was taken for burial to Tiberias, where his grave is still visited. His descendants held the title of leader (*nagid*) of Egyptian Jewry for several generations.

Maine, U.S. state. Although individual Jews were living there around the beginning of the 19th cent., the first congregation was founded in Bangor in the middle of the century and most of the Jews arrived toward its end. Their numbers were not large, and in 1976 there were 7,945 Jews in M., of whom 3,500 lived in Portland and 1,300 in Bangor.

Mainz (Mayence): City

in W. Germany where Jews lived from the 10th cent. It was soon the main community in northern Europe, and despite persecutions and bloodshed, was the home of many famous rabbinic scholars. Massacres occurred during the Crusades and at the time of the Black Death, and several expulsions were ordered in the 15th cent. The community was well organized and was closely tied to its sister communities in Speyer and Worms. There was a complete expulsion in 1483. The community was refounded a century later but was weak until 1784. Before World War II, c. 3,000 Jews lived there. The Jewish population in 1970 was 122.

Majorca: Balearic island. The Jewish community was important in the Middle Ages and was the seat of an important school of cartographers. Many Jews left during the 1391 persecutions. There was a RITUAL MURDER LIBEL in 1435, and the Jews of M. were forced to accept Christianity. They continued as crypto-Jews, known as CHUETAS, who were hounded by the Inquisition and suffered in *autos-da-fé*. Some of their descendants can still be identified.

Makhshirin ("Things Which Render Fit"): Eighth tractate in the MISHNAH order of *Toharot*, with no gem-ara in either Talmud. It deals with the laws of ritual impurity for foods that have been moistened by water (cf. Lev. 11:34, 38).

Makkot ("Flagellation"): Fifth tractate in the MISHNAH order of *Nezikin*, with *gemara* in both Talmuds. It deals with the rules of flogging, as well as with plotting witnesses and cities of refuge.

Malachi: Last book of the Bible in section called Minor Prophets, named after prophet Malachi. Nothing is known of him, including his dates, and it is even possible that M. (literally "my messenger") is not a proper name. He condemns ritual and social abuses. He proclaimed the universal rule of God (1:11) and foretold the eschatological Day of the Lord after the coming of the prophet Elijah.

Malamud, Bernard (1914–): US novelist. His works reflect his interest in Jewish tradition. They include *The Assistant* and a novel based on the Beilis trial, *The Fixer*. He has taught at Oregon State College.

Malbim, Meir Leibush (1809–1879): Rabbi, preacher, and scholar. He served in various communities, including Bucharest, Mohilev, and Koenigsberg. The modernists found him too Orthodox and the Orthodox opposed his sympathy with Haskalah. He is best known for his Bible commentary, opposing the views of the Reform.

Mammeloshen (*lashon*, "tongue," "language," Yidd. "mother"): Colloquial term for Yiddish.

mamzer: Commonly translated as "bastard," it refers to the offspring of a forbidden (i.e., adulterous or incestuous) union. Such a child "unto the tenth generation" is not allowed to marry in the Jewish community.

Manasseh: Elder son of JOSEPH, like his brother EPHRAIM he received an equal portion with the sons of Jacob in the partition of Canaan. Half the tribe of M. was settled in Transjordan and the other half in the neighborhood of the Valley of Jezreel. It shared the fate of the other Ten Tribes in 721 BCE.

Manasseh: Son of HEZE-KIAH, king of Judah. He ascended the throne when he was 12 and ruled in 698–643 BCE. He is described by the Bible as one of the most wicked of all the kings. He abrogated the reforms instituted by Hezekiah and brought back pagan customs, including the worship of Moloch and the rite of passing living children through fire. According to II Chron. 33, he was a captive in Bab-

ylonia for some time, and this is the origin of the Prayer of M., a short work incorporated in the Apocrypha.

Manasseh ben Israel (1604–1657): Dutch rabbi, author, and printer. Born in Madeira of Marrano parents, he went to Holland and became rabbi in Amsterdam. Here he set up a printing press in 1626. His writings include *Conciliador*, reconciling apparent contradictions in the Bible, and *Hope of Israel*, dealing with the reputed discovery of the Lost Ten Tribes. This brought him in touch with the move to readmit Jews to England, in which he played a prominent role. His petition to Oliver Cromwell was of great importance, although he died without realizing that his mission was to prove successful. He was acquainted with Rembrandt, who painted his portrait.

Manchester: City in northern England. Jews lived there from the late 18th cent., and the 19th cent. saw Reform and Sephardi congregations grow up apart from Ashkenazi Orthodox ones. In the late 19th cent. there was a greater influx of Jewish immigrants to M. than to any other provincial city in England. Chaim Weizmann lived there early in the 20th cent., and it became a center of

Zionism. It remains the largest Jewish provincial community, with a population of 35,000 (1976).

Mandate for Palestine: Britain was entrusted with the M. by the Supreme Council of the Principal Allied Powers at the San Remo Conference in 1920. This was approved by the League of Nations in 1922. It gave "recognition to the historical connection of the Jewish people with Palestine, and to the grounds for reconstituting their national home in that country." The interpretation by the British of the M. was to cause continued friction with the Jews of Palestine over the subsequent quarter-century. Eventually the situation became so tense that Britain returned the M. to the United Nations—the successor to the League of Nations. The UN in 1947 decided on the partition of Palestine and the establishment of independent Jewish and Arab states.

Mandel (Rothschild), Georges (1885–1944): French statesman. He was private secretary to Clemenceau at the Paris Peace Conference, a member of the French parliament from 1919, and minister in various governments in the 1930s. He refused to surrender after the fall of France and was taken to prison in France. He was assassinated by the Vichy militia.

Mandel, Marvin (1920–): US politician. Born in Baltimore, he sat in the Maryland Legislature from 1953 and was its speaker from 1963. In 1969 he became governor of Maryland but in 1977 was deprived of office after being jailed for fraud.

Mandelstam, Osip Emilievich (1891–c. 1938): Russian poet. He was a co-founder of the neo-classicist Acmeist school, which opposed symbolism and stressed classical simplicity. He has been recognized by the outside world as one of the outstanding poets of Soviet Russia. He was arrested in 1934 and exiled until 1937. Rearrested in 1938, he died shortly thereafter in a Siberian prison as a result of ill treatment. His widow Nadezhda M. published her reminiscences in *Hope against Hope* and *Hope Abandoned*

Mane Katz see **Katz, Mane**

Manger, Itzik (1901–1969): Yiddish poet and writer, born in Rumania. He lived in London during World War II and subsequently in the US and Israel. His *Khumesh-Lieder* and *Megilla-Lieder* are satires that have been successfully produced on the stage.

Manitoba: Canadian

province. Its first congregation was opened in Winnipeg in 1882. Jews began to arrive in number after the beginning of the 20th cent. The numbers of Jews in the province has not changed greatly since 1930, and in 1971 numbered 20,010, mostly in Winnipeg.

manna: Food miraculously provided for the Israelites in the desert. It was collected every morning except the Sabbath, for which provision had been made by the collection of a double portion the previous day. Its form resembled seeds, white in color, and it tasted like honey wafers.

Mantua: Italian city. In the late 14th cent., Jewish money lenders were invited to settle, and a community was founded. It became of importance in the 16th cent., when Jewish actors and musicians gave performances at the court. In the early 17th cent., there was a reaction, and a ghetto was established. The community was expelled in 1630 after the city was captured by Germans. Later, under Austrian rule, Jews lived there and had 6 synagogues. Full civil rights came in 1866, but the community thereafter declined in numbers, almost totally perishing during World War II. 150 Jews lived there in 1970.

maot hittim ("wheat money"): Collections made before Passover to supply the needy with flour for unleavened bread. This was regarded as one of the most binding of taxes in the Jewish community.

Maoz Tzur ("Fortress Rock"): Hymn sung on Hanukkah by Ashkenazi Jews after kindling the lights. It was probably written in the 13th cent.

MAPAI: Initials of Miphleget Poalei Eretz Yisrael ("Israel Workers' Party"), Israeli labor party, formed in 1930 as the result of a merger between HA-POEL HA-TZAIT and AHDUT HA-AVO-DAH. From 1935 it was the largest party in the Zionist organization. Under the leadership of David Ben-Gurion, it was the biggest party in all elections in the State of Israel and the dominant party in government coalitions. In 1968 it merged with Rafi and Ahdut Avodah to form the ISRAEL LABOR PARTY, which dominated the government until 1977. M. was also the largest group in the HIS-TADRUT and controlled the IHUD HA-KEVUTZOT VEHA-KIBBUTZIM.

MAPAM: Initials of Miphleget Poalim Meuhedet ("United Workers' Party"), Israeli Marxist socialist party established in 1948 by the merger of HA-SHOMER HA-TZAIR and AḤDUT AVODAH—Left Poale Zion. It stresses pioneering and advocates a closer understanding with the Arab minority. It favored close cooperation with the USSR, until the Soviet attack on Zionism which led M. to dissociate itself from that policy. M. had 19 representatives in the first KNESSET, but after Ahdut Avodah seceded in 1954, representation was split fairly evenly between the two parties. In 1969, it entered an alignment agreement with the ISRAEL LABOR PARTY and, with it, was in the opposition from 1977. Its kibbutz organization is HA-KIBBUTZ HA-MEUḤAD.

maphtir: Person who reads the HAPHTARAH; also popularly used for the *haphtarah*.

Mapu, Abraham (1808–1867): First modern Hebrew novelist. He was a teacher in Kovno. He wrote *Ahavat Tziyyon*, set in biblical times; *Ashmat Shomron*, in the period of Ahaz; and *Hozeh Hezyonot*, in the period of Shabbetai Tzevi. His realistic *Ayit Tzavua* satirized Lithuanian Jewry.

mar ("master"): Honorary title given to exilarchs in Babylonia and to other dignitaries. In modern Hebrew, "Mr."

Marceau, Marcel (1923–): French mime. His father was killed by the Nazis during World War II and he worked for the French underground. After appearing with Jean-Louis Barrault, he embarked on his career as a solo performer and was soon recognized as the greatest living mime. His most famous characterization is the clown Bip.

Marcus, David ("Mickey") (1902–1948): US soldier. A graduate of West Point, he became assistant US attorney in the southern district of New York. He served in World War II, and went to Palestine in 1948 to serve as military adviser to the Haganah. He was accidentally killed while commanding the Jerusalem front during the Israeli War of Independence.

Marcus, Jacob Rader (1896–): US Jewish historian and Reform rabbi. Professor of Jewish history at the Hebrew Union College, Cincinnati, he founded the American Jewish Archives there in 1947.

Marcuse, Herbert (1898–1979): Philosopher and social theorist. Born in Berlin, he left Germany in 1934 and went to the US, teaching at Brandeis University and at the University of California at San Diego. His "critical theory," influenced by Marxism, was a critical analysis of current social and political institutions. In the 1960s, he was considered a major authority by members of the New Left, who were attracted by his critique of capitalism.

Marḥeshvan (Ḥeshvan): Second month in the religious, 8th in the civil year; zodiac sign, the scorpion. In the Bible it is called Bul. It has 29–30 days corresponding to October–November.

Mariamne (d. 29 BCE): Wife of Herod and daughter of the Hasmonean Alexander, son of Aristobulus II. She was proud of her Hasmonean ancestry and regarded Herod's family as upstarts. Although Herod loved her, she had a tragic family life and was eventually executed on a false charge of infidelity.

Maritime Provinces: Canadian provinces. Jews reached there in the mid-19th cent., and their numbers grew steadily until the early 1920s, after which they declined. The largest community in 1976 was in Halifax, Nova Scotia, numbering 1,500.

Markish, Peretz (1895–1952): Yiddish writer. Born in Volhynia, he lived in the 1920s in Warsaw, where he expressed trends in modern Yiddish poetry. In 1928 he moved to the USSR, writing poetry, plays, and novels, which expressed his Soviet patriotism. He was executed with other Yiddish writers in the last years of Stalin.

Markova, Alicia, Dame (1910–): English ballerina, born Lilian Alicia Marks. She joined the Diaghilev Company in 1925 and the Vic-Wells Company in 1932, and in 1935 formed her own company together with the dancer Anton Dolin. She co-founded the Festival Ballet in 1952 and became professor of ballet at the Univ. of Cincinnati in 1970.

Marks, Simon, Lord (1888–1964): British industrialist, Zionist leader, and philanthropist. Together with his brother-in-law Israel SIEFF, he formed the Marks and Spencer chain. The two men were also active in Zionist work, initially under the influence of Chaim Weizmann.

maror: Bitter herb, eaten as part of the Passover SEDER service to symbolize the fact that the Egyptians "embittered" the lives of the Israelites. It is ceremoniously eaten twice—once with ḤAROSET, once with unleavened bread (*matzah*).

Marranos: Crypto-Jews in Spain and Portugal who outwardly adopted Christianity but secretly followed Jewish rites and customs. The word means "swine" in Spanish; the Hebrew *anusim*, meaning "forced ones." Elsewhere the M. are called New Christians, and in Majorca, CHUETAS. M. became a significant factor after the anti-Jewish massacres of 1391 in Spain, when many Jews adopted Christianity to escape death. In the knowledge that many of them continued secretly as Jews, the INQUISITION was introduced to ferret out such cases. It was directed against the M. in the Iberian Peninsula and later also against their descendants in Latin America; tens of thousands were burned at *auto-da-fé*. Where possible, M. escaped to non-Catholic countries and there professed their Judaism openly (e.g., in the Netherlands or Turkey). Descendants of M. have been discovered in Portugal and South America, still observing Jewish customs but without knowing the reasons. A parallel in the Muslim world is the JEDID EL-ISLAM in Iran.

marriage: To marry and procreate are prime obligations of the Jew. However, there are certain prohibited m. relationships: near relatives may not intermarry, and a *kohen* (priest) may not marry a divorcée. The m. is performed in two stages—*kiddushin* (betrothal), which creates the husband-wife relationship, and *nissuin*, which imposes the mutual obligations of married life. Originally, the former ceremony could be performed by three methods—giving the wife money, giving her a deed, or by cohabitation. The last was frowned upon by the rabbis, and the second fell into disuse. The first is the modern practice (and a simple gold ring is generally given rather than money). It is performed by the man, but the woman must give her consent. Seven special blessings are recited for the *nissuin*. Most frequently *kiddushin* and *nissuin* are performed at the same ceremony. The talmudic rabbis protected the rights of the wives by insisting on the husband handing the wife a m. document (*ketubbah*), and this is read as part of the ceremony. M. customs include the fasting by the couple on their wedding day until the ceremony; the bride walking seven times around the groom; and the groom breaking a wine glass under his feet. The ceremony is customarily followed by a feast and traditionally by a week of celebrations. Marriages are not celebrated on Sabbaths, holidays, and during certain periods of semi-mourning (the OMER period, the three weeks up to Av 9). Marriageable age is 13 for males and 12½ for females. The rabbis recommended early m. M. between a Jew and a non-Jew is not possible under Jewish law. Original Jewish law is not based on monogamy; a man could have more than one wife. But this practice was stopped among Ashkenazim in the Middle Ages, and polygamy, with few exceptions, is not permitted in the State of Israel.

Marseilles: French port. Jews were living there in the 6th cent. In the Middle Ages, they had considerable liberty and conducted commerce with the East. From the 13th cent. they had their own quarter (*carrière*). Many noted scholars lived there. M. came under French rule in 1481. In 1484–5 there was a massacre of the Jews, and in 1501 they were expelled. They returned in the 18th cent. The community grew in the 20th cent., especially during the 1950s and 1960s, when many North African Jews settled there. The Jewish population was estimated at 70,000 in 1974.

Marshak, Samuel Yakovlevich (1887–1964): Russian author. In his early days he was an enthusiastic Zionist. A distinguished writer of children's literature, he was awarded the Stalin Prize four times. His translations from the English included works by Shakespeare.

Marshall, David Saul (1908–   ): Singapore public figure. A lawyer by profession, he led the United Labor Front Party to victory in the 1955 elections and was Singapore's first chief minister (1955–56). He was president of Singapore's Jewish Welfare Board, 1946–53.

Marshall, Louis (1856–1929): US Jewish leader. A noted constitutional and corporate lawyer, he was an outstanding defender of civil liberties. M. was a founder and president (1912–29) of the American Jewish Committee, founder and president of the American Jewish Relief Committee, and first president of the Comité des Délégations Juives after World War I. He was chairman of the board of the Jewish Theological Seminary, and although not a Zionist, he was first chairman of the Council of the Jewish Agency.

Marx Brothers: US comedy team made up of three brothers—the wisecracking *Groucho (Julius) M.* (1895–1977), the silent clown *Harpo (Arthur) M.* (1893–1964), and the Italian-accented *Chico (Leonard) M.* (1891–1961). Their films (*Horse Feathers, Animal Crackers, Duck Soup, A*

Night at the Opera, and others) have maintained their popularity.

Marx, Alexander (1878–1953): Historian, bibliographer and librarian. Born in Germany, he taught at the Jewish Theological Seminary in New York from 1903, and was for many years its librarian. He published many studies and (with Max Margolis) the one-volume *History of the Jewish People.*

Marx, Karl (1818–1883): German philosopher, founder of modern socialism. At the age of six, his parents had him baptized. From 1849, he lived in London. In 1848, M.—together with his friend, patron, and collaborator Friedrich Engels—prepared the *Communist Manifesto,* which contains the seeds of his subsequent writings. His major work was *Das Kapital,* of which only the first volume appeared in his lifetime. He developed the system of dialectical materialism, which was to play a powerful role in left-wing thought. M.'s references to the Jews were generally hostile.

Maryland. US state. Jews began moving to M. after the Revolution, but they had to wait until 1826 before being allowed to hold public office. In the mid-19th cent. newcomers arrived from Central Europe and in the latter 19th cent. from Eastern Europe. In 1976 the great majority of the state's 223,805 Jews lived in Baltimore and the suburbs of Washington.

Masada: Isolated rock near the Dead Sea in the Judean Desert. It was originally fortified in the Hasmonean Period. Herod built a palace there and his family took refuge in M., which was unsuccessfully besieged by Antigonus Mattathias in 40 BCE. Eleazar ben Jair escaped to M. in 66 CE and became its "ruler." After the fall of Jerusalem, a Zealot group under Eleazar took refuge there and withstood the Roman siege until 73. Finally finding their position untenable, the 960 defenders committed suicide rather than surrender. The story, as related by Josephus, has become in modern times a source of inspiration, especially in Israel. The site—which also saw a Roman post, a Byzantine church, and a Crusader fortress—was excavated in the 1960s by Yigael YADIN, whose extensive discoveries included scroll fragments and the ancient synagogue.

mashiv ha-ruaḥ ("who causeth the wind to blow [and the rain to descend]"): Phrase introduced in all prayer rites before the second benediction of the AMIDAH between the last day of Tabernacles and the first day of Passover. During the rest of the year it is replaced in the Sephardi rite with *morid ha-tal* ("who causes the dew to fall").

Maskil: Adherent of HASLALAH.

Masorah: Body of textual notes concerning the text of the Hebrew Bible. To counter divergent readings of the Pentateuch, standard readings were determined as far back as the time of the scribes (see SCRIBE). The work of determining the Masoretic Text continued for centuries, and those who dealt with this were called Masoretes. Standard texts of the Scroll of the Law were kept in the Temple. However, there were divergent texts, as is shown by the Dead Sea Scrolls and the early Bible translations. The Masoretes therefore began to determine and eventually record the exact tradition concerning each word—the division, punctuation, and accentuation; notes on unusual forms; lists of words that were written one way but pronounced another; defective spellings; and other abnormalities. These were committed to writing, and the accents and vocalization were noted from the 7th and 8th cent. CE. Chapter divisions and verse numberings were taken over from the Latin Bible in the 16th cent.

Massachusetts: US state. The first community was established at Leicester in 1777. The BOSTON community dates from the 1830s and has been dominant in the state. Many communities have been founded and still flourish throughout M., where there are over 200 synagogues and 85 centers. In 1976, 270,835 Jews lived in the state, of whom 180,000 were in Boston, 18,800 in Lynn, 11,000 in Springfield, and 10,000 in Worcester.

Matalon, Eli (1926–): Jamaican politician. He was mayor of Kingston in 1971 and was the first Jew elected to the Jamaican Parliament. In 1973 he was appointed minister of education.

Mattathias (d. 167/6 BCE): Initiator of the HASMONEAN revolt. A priest from the village of Modiin, he started the revolt against the decrees of ANTIOCHUS EPIPHANES directed against the observance of the Jewish religion.

Matthau, Walter (1920–): US character actor, noted for movie roles of both dry comedy and heavy villainy. Several of his successes were in cooperation with Jack Lemmon, including *The*

Fortune Cookie and *The Odd Couple*.

matzah: unleavened bread. See PASSOVER.

Maurois, André (1885–1967): French biographer and novelist, born Emile Hertzog. He wrote the novel *The Silence of Colonel Bramble*, a series of biographies (Shelley, Disraeli, Chateaubriand, George Sand, etc., a history of France, and a history of England. In 1938 he was elected a member of the Académie Française. In 1940, he fled to the US, where he stayed until after World War II.

Mauthausen: Concentration camp in Austria. It was established in 1938, expanded, and had satellite camps. Jews sent there, including many from Holland and Hungary, were killed immediately. Altogether, 132,000 prisoners were put to death in M.

May Laws: Series of laws confirmed in May 1882 by the czarist government in Russia, forbidding Jews to live outside the PALE OF SETTLEMENT. In the course of time, they were applied with increasing severity, helping to spur the mass Jewish migration from Eastern Europe. The laws were revoked during World War I.

Mayence see **Mainz**

Mayer, Daniel (1909–): French Socialist politician. He was secretary-general of the French Socialist Party after World War II, and minister of labor in various governments. From 1968 he was president of the League for the Rights of Man.

Mayer, Louis Burt (1885–1957): US motion-picture pioneer. In Hollywood, he formed various film corporations and in 1924 joined Samuel Goldwyn to form Metro-Goldwyn-Mayer (MGM).

Mayer, René (1895–1972): French politician. He held various Cabinet posts after World War II and was prime minister of France from December 1952 to May 1953. A moderate radical socialist, his policies were based on friendship with Britain and participation in the European Community. He was chairman of the European Coal and Steel Community (1955–58).

Mazar (Maisler), Benjamin (1906–): Israeli archeologist and historian. Born in Poland, he went to Palestine in 1929. He taught at the Hebrew University, of which he was president (1953–61). He directed archeological excavations at Tel el Kasile, Bet She'arim, En Gedi, and, from 1968, at the southern and western walls of the Temple compound in Jerusalem. He has written a history of Palestine up to the period of the monarchy and is an editor of the *Biblical Encyclopedia* and the *World History of the Jewish People*.

mazzal: Luck; originally a constellation, the latter meaning being influenced by astrological usage. *Massal tov* ("Good luck") is a popular festive greeting.

meal offering (*minhah*): Offering prepared of flour. Such an offering always accompanied an animal sacrifice, but there were occasions when it was offered independently. When made as a thanksgiving offering it was mixed with oil and frankincense, but when a sin-offering, it was offered on its own.

Me'assephim ("Gatherers"): Contributors to the Hebrew literary monthly HA-MEASSEPH (1783–1811). Most of the writers were minor literary figures, disciples of Moses Mendelssohn.

medicine: Throughout their history, Jews have greatly influenced medical science. The Bible mentions doctors (Job 13:4; Jerem. 8:22) and the physician is highly praised in Eccles. 37. The rabbis who practiced m. are mentioned in the Talmud. In the Middle Ages, Jewish doctors were famed throughout Europe and, despite restrictions, many of them were court physicians and even physicians to the Pope. They also played an important role in the translation of the Greco-Arabic medical classics into Latin. Famous medieval Jewish physicians include ASAPH, Shabbetai DONNOLO, Isaac ISRAELI, and MAIMONIDES. From Renaissance times, Jewish physicians studied in universities and wrote in Latin. Jews have played an important part in modern m. and many Nobel Prize winners in the field have been Jewish (Paul EHRLICH, Otto MEYERHOFF, Boris CHAIN, and Selman WAKSMAN, among others).

Megiddo: Ancient Canaanite and Israelite city controlling the strategic pass of the Valley of Jezreel. Extensive excavations have revealed that it was inhabited from the 4th millennium to 500 BCE. A number of historic battles took place there, including Deborah's victory over the Canaanites and Josiah's defeat by the Egyptians. Its situation was so crucial that the New Testament sets the eschatological battle between the forces of good and evil at Har Megiddo (Armageddon; Rev. 16:16).

megillah: A scroll. One of the five biblical scrolls (Ruth, Song of Songs, Lamentations, Ecclesiastes, Esther).

Megillah: Tenth tractate in the MISHNAH order of *Moed,* with *gemara* in both Talmuds. It deals primarily with the reading of the Bible in the synagogue, especially the Scroll of Esther on Purim.

Megillah Taanit ("Scroll of Fasting"): Ancient chronicle compiled at the beginning of the Common Era, recording 35 days to be regarded as anniversaries of glorious events in Jewish history, on which fasting is therefore forbidden. The work is written in Aramaic.

mehitzah: A partition in the synagogue separating men from women during prayer.

me'il ("mantle"): Cover for the Scroll of the Law, often elaborately embroidered.

Me'ilah ("Sacrilege"): Eighth tractate in the MISHNAH order of *Kodashim,* with *gemara* in the Babylonian Talmud only. It discusses the use of objects dedicated to the Temple.

Meir (2nd cent.): TANNA; pupil of R. Akiva. After the persecution by Hadrian, he was a leading member of the Sanhedrin in Usha. His MISHNAH compilation formed the basis of the standard MISHNAH compiled by JUDAH HA-NASI. Any source in the latter work not specifically ascribed is assumed to have been taken from Meir. He was a noted preacher and scribe. His wife *Beruriah* was also a scholar. Their life was marked by tragedies.

Meir Baal ha-Nes ("Meir the Wonder Worker"): Name given to a Rabbi Meir, whose tomb is venerated in Tiberias. He is generally, but probably incorrectly, identified with the *tanna* R. MEIR. From the 19th cent., collections throughout the world for poor Jews in Palestine were made in boxes labeled "The Charity of R. Meir Baal ha-Nes."

Meir ben Baruch of Rothenburg (c. 1215–1293): German rabbinical authority. He was the leading arbiter of his time on religious matters and was one of the last and greatest of the tosaphists. His responsa, of which over a thousand are known, were of major influence on Jewish laws and life throughout Europe. He also wrote liturgical poems. In 1286 the emperor imprisoned him for attempting to emigrate to Palestine. He died in prison, not allowing himself to be ransomed so as not to create a precedent.

Meir (Meyerson), Golda (1898–1978): Israeli head of state and labor leader. She was born in Russia but spent her youth in the US in Milwaukee, where she became a schoolteacher. In 1921 she settled in Palestine, and became active in Labor Zionism. After the establishment of the State, she was the first diplomatic representative in Moscow, where her appearance aroused great enthusiasm among Russian Jews. Subsequently she was labor minister and foreign minister, and in 1969 succeeded Levi ESHKOL as prime minister. She was in office during the period of the YOM KIPPUR WAR and resigned in 1974.

Meitner, Lise (1878–1968): Physicist and mathematician. Born in Vienna, she taught in Berlin. After the rise of the Nazis, she went to Stockholm, and from 1960 lived in Cambridge, England. She studied the disintegration products of radium thoria and actinium and of the action of beta rays. Her work on the bombardment of the uranium nucleus helped to develop the atomic bomb. In 1917, she was co-discoverer of the element protactinium.

Mekhilta ("Measure"): Tannaitic Midrash on the latter part of Exodus, probably compiled not earlier than the late 4th cent. Another M. attributed to the school of R. Simeon ben Yohai (M. de-Rabbi Shimon ben Yohai) was edited not earlier than the 5th cent.

melavveh malkah ("es-corting the queen [Sabbath]"): Meal and accompanying festivities at the conclusion of Sabbath. Just as the Sabbath is greeted as a bride on Friday night, so it is festively "escorted" at its conclusion. Special *zemirot* were composed for the occasion, which became enhanced by kabbalistic and Hasidic practice and customs. The final meal is prolonged so as to retain the Sabbath atmosphere as long as possible.

Melbourne: Australian city. The first synagogue opened in 1847. The community grew from the end of the 19th cent., due to the influx of Jews from Eastern Europe. It is now the largest community in Australia and has a thriving Jewish life, including the Mt. Scopus Jewish day school. The Jewish population was 34,000 in 1976.

Melchett see **Mond**

mellah: The Jewish ghetto in North African cities. The term is first encountered in 15th-cent. Fez; its origin is uncertain.

mem (מ): Thirteenth letter of the Hebrew alphabet. Numerical value: 40. It is pronounced *m* and has a special form when at the end of words (ם).

Memmi, Albert (1920–): Novelist and sociologist. He was brought up in Tunisia and moved to France in the 1950s. He has written the autobiographical novel *La Statue de Sel* and other works on Jewish identity.

memorbuch: Books kept in Central European Jewish communities containing prayers and listing martyrs and distinguished persons. The names were read out on the appropriate anniversaries.

memorial service: Prayers in memory of the dead, recited usually on the last day of Passover, on Shavuot, the Day of Atonement, and Shemini Atzeret. See YIZKOR.

Menahem: King of Israel, who reigned c. 746–737 BCE. He killed the previous ruler, Shallum, and took over the government (II Kings 15:14). He put down opposition ruthlessly and cruelly, and then had a fairly peaceful reign, partly bought by paying a heavy tribute to Tiglath-Pileser III of Assyria.

Menahem ben Judah the Galilean (d. 66 CE): Head of SICARII at the outset of the war against Rome. He led his forces to victory over Romans in Jerusalem. He then acted as the ruler, which antagonized other forces in Jerusalem, who killed him.

Menahem ben Saruk (10th cent.): Hebrew lexicographer and grammarian in Spain. He was secretary to Hasdai IBN SHAPRUT. He wrote the Hebrew dictionary *Mahberet*, systematically summarizing knowledge of grammar in his day.

Menahem Mendel of Kotsk (1787–1859): Hasidic leader. He lived austerely and for his last twenty years locked himself in a room seen by no one except his immediate family. His teaching was austere and zealous, holding that worship of God required abandonment of self.

Menahot ("Meal Offerings"): Second tractate in the MISHNAH order of *Kodashim*, with *gemara* in the Babylonian Talmud only. It deals with the rules of the meal-offering in the Temple (Lev. 2:1–14; 5:11–13).

Mendele Mocher Seforim (1835–1917): Yiddish and Hebrew writer. Born Shalom Jacob Abramowitsch in Minsk, he lived in various places, including Kamenetsk-Podolsk, Berdichev, Zhitomir, and, from 1881, Odessa. He first won a reputation as a Hebrew author but then turned to Yiddish; he became known as the "grandfather of Yiddish literature." His works include novels, stories, plays, and memoirs, the best known including *Fishke the Lame*, *The Mare*, and *Travels of Benjamin III*.

Mendelsohn, Eric (1887–1953): Architect. He lived in Germany until 1933, and subsequently in England,

Palestine, and (from 1941) the US. His buildings are noteworthy for their original shape and monumental nature. His works include the Einstein Tower at Potsdam, business houses and dwellings in Germany, the Hadassah Hospital on Mt. Scopus, Jerusalem, and synagogues in the US.

Mendelssohn, Moses (1729–1786): German philosopher, pioneer of the Enlightenment, and translator of the Bible. He was born in Dessau, and, after receiving a traditional Jewish education, went to Berlin, where he studied a wide variety of subjects. At first a teacher to the children of a silk manufacturer, he eventually became the manufacturer's partner. He became a leading figure in Berlin intellectual society. He was a close friend of the playwright Lessing, who depicted him in his character *Nathan the Wise*. He won the Berlin Academy of Sciences prize for the best essay on a metaphysical subject (another competitor being Kant) and wrote his philosophical dialogue *Phädon* on the immortality of the soul, which earned him the reputation of being the "German Socrates." Turning his attention to Judaism and the Jewish people, he became the outstanding representative of the Jews. His German translation of part of the Pentateuch with commentary, the *Biur*, was extremely influential and helped to familiarize Jews with the German language. In *Jerusalem*, he wrote on such subjects as religious and political toleration, and the separation of church and state. Although firmly advocating emancipation and full civil rights, M. himself remained a strictly observant Jew. However, most of his children and all his grandchildren became Christians. He was largely responsible for ushering in the modern era of Jewish history and thought.

Mendelssohn-Bartholdy, Felix (1809–1847): Composer; grandson of Moses Mendelssohn. The son of the banker Abraham Mendelssohn, he was raised as a Christian. He became a talented composer and conductor at a young age. He appeared frequently in England and founded the Leipzig Conservatoire of Music. His works include 5 symphonies, concertos for violin and piano, oratorios (of which *Elijah* is the best known), chamber music, and songs.

Mendes, Gracia see **Nasi, Gracia**

Mendes-France, Pierre (1907–   ): French statesman. A Radical Socialist, he was first elected to parliament in 1932. During World

War II, he was De Gaulle's finance commissioner in Algeria. As premier of France from June 1954 to February 1955, he ended the fighting in Indochina and pursued a vigorous North African policy.

Mendoza, Daniel (1764–1836: English boxing champion. He was still boxing at the age of 57. He was regarded as father of scientific boxing.

Mene, Mene, Tekel, Upharsin: Inscription which appeared on a wall, written by a detached hand, at feast given by Belshazzar, king of Babylonia (Dan. 5:25). Its meaning is enigmatic and it was construed by Daniel as a prophecy of doom—predicting the victory of the Persians over Belshazzar.

menorah: Candelabrum. The original one in Jewish tradition was made by BEZALEL in the wilderness and placed in the Tabernacle; it had seven arms and was made of fine gold. There were ten such candelabra in the First Temple, and one in the Second, along with copies; one of the copies was taken to Rome by the victorious Romans and is depicted on the Arch of Titus. The m. was the most frequent and popular Jewish symbol, and many examples can be found on tombs, catacombs, monuments, etc. In more modern times the HANUKKAH lamp was constructed on a similar model (but with 8 or 9 arms) and is popularly called a m. The m. has been adopted as the emblem of the State of Israel.

menstruation see **Niddah**

Menuhin, Yehudi (1916–): US violinist. He was a child prodigy, and soon won an international reputation. He is considered one of the world's foremost violinists. He appeared frequently in England, where he initiated the Bath festival. His sister **Hephzibah M.** (1920–), pianist, appeared with him in chamber music recitals.

Mephibosheth (**Meribaal**) (c. 1000 BCE): Son of JONATHAN; grandson of SAUL. He was crippled in childhood in an accident after his father and grandfather had been killed in battle. After David's accession, he called M. to court. Although M. supported Absalom in his rebellion, David treated him compassionately.

Meron: Place in Galilee; traditionally site of the tomb of SIMEON B. YOHAI, the reputed author of the *Zohar*, and became the destination of an annual *Lag ba-Omer* celebration which still attracts tens of thousands. Remains of an ancient synagogue were discovered nearby.

Meshed: Town in Iran.

Muslim fanatics compelled its Jewish community to convert to Islam in 1839. They continued to observe Judaism secretly, until such time as they could return to it openly (by fleeing abroad or eventually under a more tolerant rule in M.). Those who lived as crypto-Jews were known as JEDID AL-ISLAM.

meshullah see shaliah

Mesopotamia see **Iraq**

Messiah (*Mashiah*, "the anointed one"): The savior who will rule Israel at the End of Days. The concept developed in the period after the Babylonian Exile, when the ideal monarch of future days would not be just another "anointed" ruler but the ruler who would destroy Israel's enemies and establish a perfect era of peace and perfection. This ruler, it was maintained, would be a descendant of the House of David. The intense longing for the M. reached a climax in the 1st cent. CE, when various "messiahs" appeared; this was the atmosphere during New Testament times and affected Jesus' theology. The expectation grew more acute and poignant after the destruction of the Second Temple. During all this period, an extensive literature grew up describing the messianic, eschatalogical era. During BAR KOKHBA's revolt against Rome, some of his followers (including R. Akiva) hailed him as M. Throughout the centuries of Jewish exile, many pseudo-messiahs appeared, often attracting a considerable following, but generally leading to a tragic denouement. In the 7th and 8th cent. various messianic pretenders appeared in the Persia-Mesopotamia area (ABU ISSA AL-ISFAHANI, YUDGHAN, etc.). Other well-known names include David ALROY in the 12th cent. and Solomon MOLCHO in the 16th cent. The most famous was SHABBETAI TZEVI in 17th-cent. Turkey, whose messianic claims were accepted by Jews in all parts of the world, many of whom sold their belongings in anticipation of their triumphal return to their Holy Land. His abject failure caused great despondency. In the 18th cent. Jacob FRANK headed an offshoot of this movement in Poland, but by this time messianism was largely discredited. The Reform movement relates to the concept not as achievable through supernatural intervention but by man's self-perfection.

Metatron: Name of an angel (not mentioned in the Bible) who played an important role in Jewish angelology. In aggadah and the Kabbalah he was seen as the highest-ranking angel, who stood next to God. He is identified with the Angel of the Presence, Enoch.

Metullah: Village at northern tip of Israel in Upper Galilee. Founded in 1896 at the initiative of Baron Edmond de ROTHS- CHILD. Its growth was slow until the 1950s owing to water shortage. Its population in 1971 was 360.

meturgeman ("translator"): Originally, the translator of biblical selections at public readings. Later, the spokesman for talmudic teachers, who spoke quietly; their words would be repeated by the m. aloud.

Mexico: Marranos arrived there early in the 16th cent., and some were burned at the stake at an *auto-da-fé* in 1528. The Marranos, many of whom achieved distinguished positions, were eventually absorbed by the local population. The modern settlement dates from the 19th cent., and numbers increased after World War I. Ashkenazi Jews came from Eastern Europe, and Sephardim from the Balkans. The community is well organized and has an intense Jewish identity, with the highest proportion of Jewish children receiving Jewish education of any country in the Diaspora. About 90% of the country's Jews (37,500) live in Mexico City; there are small communities in Monterey and Guadalajara. A group of Mexican Indian Jews, although claiming Marrano descent, are apparently proselytes from a Christianizing sect.

Meyer, Eugene (1875– 1959): US financier and newspaper publisher. From 1933 he was publisher of the Washington *Post*. In 1932 he organized the Reconstruction Finance Corporation and in 1946 was appointed first president of the International Bank for Reconstruction and Development.

Meyerbeer, Giacomo (1791–1864): German composer, born Jacob Liebmann Beer. Son of a prominent banker, Jacob Herzl Beer, he made his debut as a pianist at the age of 7, and when he was 13 was considered Berlin's leading pianist. He settled in Paris, where his spectacular operas (*Robert le Diable, Les Huguenots,* and others) were highly successful. In 1842–47 he was music director to the king of Prussia.

Meyerhof, Otto Fritz (1884–1951): Biochemist. He was director of the Kaiser Wilhelm Institute and professor at Heidelberg University. He was awarded the 1923 Nobel Prize for Medicine for his research into the chemistry of muscles. He went to the US in 1940 and taught at the University of Pennsylvania.

mezuzah ("doorpost"): Small parchment on which are written the first two paragraphs of the SHEMA, which is rolled into a case and affixed to the doorpost of each door in a Jewish home. It is nailed in a sloping position on the upper-righthand doorpost of the entry to the home and its living rooms. A special blessing is recited as it is put in place. Pious Jews kiss the m. on entering or leaving rooms.

Mi she-berakh ("May He who blessed"): Initial words of petition recited in the synagogue for the congregation or for a named person. It is usually recited after the Reading of the Law and said by the reader at the request of the person called to the Reading. The person offering it frequently couples it with a gift to the synagogue or to charity.

Miami: City in Florida. The first Jewish resident came in 1895, and its first congregation was founded in 1912. M. attracts a large number of North American Jewish visitors, especially during the winter season. Its permanent Jewish community has been growing rapidly, and many Jews retire to M.; 225,000 were living there permanently in 1976.

Micah: Sixth of the Minor Prophets. He prophesied in Judah and witnessed Sennacherib's siege of Jerusalem. Of peasant origin, he condemned the oppression of the rulers, foreseeing their destruction and exile. He preached a noble ethical and religious message.

Michael: Angel (Dan. 10:13). One of the four archangels, he is often mentioned in apocryphal and aggadic literature, where he is described as God's vice-regent and as the heavenly high priest. He is God's messenger and executes Divine judgments. He is also the defender of Israel and the chief enemy of Satan.

Michelson, Albert Abraham (1852–1931): US physicist. He was professor at Clark University, and then at the University of Chicago. He worked on measurement of the velocity of light, for which he won a Nobel Prize in 1907, making him the first American to receive a Nobel Prize for Science. Einstein's Theory of Relativity owed much to his work.

Michigan: US state. The first Jew, Ezekiel Solomon, went there in 1761, and the first community was established in the 1840s in Ann Arbor. The major center is Detroit, where Jews settled in 1850. Other early communities were in Jackson (1862), Benton Harbor

(1865), and Grand Rapids (1871). In 1976 the state had 93,350 Jews, of whom 80,000 were in Detroit, 1,500 in Grand Rapids, and 1,150 in Ann Arbor.

Middot ("Measurements"): Tenth tractate in the MISHNAH order of *Kodashim*, with no *gemara* in either Talmud. It gives measurements and details of the building of the Temple.

Midian: Semi-nomadic people who traveled to Egypt and up the Jordan Valley. After fleeing from Pharaoh to M., Moses stayed there with JETHRO, whose daughter he married. Later the Midianites joined the Moabites against Israel. They pressured the Israelites in the period of the Judges until defeated by Gideon.

Midrash: The discovery of meanings other than the literal one in the Bible. The word derives from *darash*, "to inquire." It goes back to early origins, but the rabbis laid down definite rules to deduce new meanings from the Bible. There are halakhic Midrashim dealing with the Pentateuchal Law and aggadah which expound the non-legal part of the Bible. Eventually many of these were committed to writing, and a rich midrashic literature developed, continuing till about the 13th cent. These can be divided into works connected with books of the Bible and those based on readings for specific festivals. Midrashic subject matter ranges widely, including ethical teaching, fables and anecdotes, homilies and allegories, etc.

Midrash Rabbah: A Midrash on the Pentateuch and the Five Scrolls. It originated in Palestine but came from different periods; the works differ greatly among themselves. They are *Genesis Rabbah* (written in Hebrew with parts in Aramaic), *Exodus Rabbah*, *Leviticus Rabbah* (which unlike the preceding two is not a collection of comments verse by verse but rather a collection of homilies), *Numbers Rabbah*, *Deuteronomy Rabbah* (also homilies, each introduced by a halakhah), *Song of Songs Rabbah*, *Lamentations Rabbati* (of which one section is attributed to R. Simeon ben Yoḥai), *Ecclesiastes Rabbah*, and *Esther Rabbah* (which collects Palestinian and Babylonian aggadot).

Mikhoels, Solomon (1890–1948): Russian Yiddish actor, born Solomon Vovsi. From 1928 he directed the State Jewish Theater in Moscow. During World War II, as chairman of the Jewish Anti-Fascist Committee, he visited the US. His death at the hand of Stalin's agents was one of the harbingers of the anti-Semitic persecutions of Stalin's last years.

Mikvaot ("Ritual Baths"): Sixth tractate in the MISHNAH order of *Toharot*, with no *gemara* in either Talmud. It discusses details of ritual baths and ritual immersion.

mikveh: A ritual bath; originally, a gathering of water. According to Jewish law, ritual immersion was incumbent on persons or utensils that were ritually impure. Although many of these regulations have not been applicable since Temple times, the m. is still obligatory for converts and for women after menstruation and childbirth. Pious ascetics also practice regular ritual immersion. The m. has to contain sufficient water to cover the average body, and its water has to be derived from a natural source (spring or river). Early examples of such baths have been discovered at Masada and Herodion. They were an essential feature of Jewish communal life throughout the ages, and the building of a m. took precedence over the construction of a synagogue.

milah see **Circumcision**

Milhaud, Darius (1892–1974): French composer. He belonged to the circle of French composers known as Les Six. In 1940 he fled to the US. After the war, he lived both in the US and in France. His compositions include operas (*Christophe Colombe; David*), ballets (*Le boeuf sur le toît*), concertos, symphonies, chamber music, and Jewish liturgical music (Sabbath Morning Service).

Miller, Arthur (1915–   ): US dramatist. His plays include *All My Sons, The Crucible* (about the Salem witch trials), *Death of a Salesman* (which won a Pulitzer Prize), *After the Fall* (based on his married life with Marilyn Monroe), and *The Price*.

Millin: *Philip* M. (1888–1952) was a S. African judge who sat in the Transvaal Division of the Supreme Court from 1937. His wife, *Sarah Gertrude* M. (1892–1968), one of South Africa's best-known writers, wrote novels, plays, and biographies of Rhodes and Smuts.

Milstein, Nathan (1904–   ): US violinist. He was a child prodigy in his native Russia; he left there in 1925 and in 1929 settled in the US. M is regarded as one of the outstanding violinists in the world.

Milwaukee: US city in Wisconsin. Jews first settled there in 1844, with the first congregation organized in 1850. The Eastern European migration from the late 19th cent. laid the foundations for its Orthodox community. In 1976 it had 23,900 Jews. Golda MEIR grew up and taught school in M.

min: Sectarian, heretic, gnostic. The term is found in the Talmud and Midrash and came to be applied especially to Judeo-Christians. A prayer against the m. was added to the AMIDAH by Samuel ha-Katan as part of the Jewish struggle against early Christianity.

Minc, Hilary (1905–): Polish Communist leader. During World War II, he organized the Free Polish forces in the USSR. After the war he returned to Poland and served in various governments, holding the office of vice-premier (1952–56).

minhag: (1) Religious custom. Traditional customs according to rabbinic law receive the same validity as law. (2) Prayer rites. Many regional differences developed in liturgical customs, each group having its own m. in this respect.

minhah: (1) Meal offering (Lev. 2), partly offered on the altar, partly consumed by the priests. (2) Afternoon prayer. It replaced the meal offering offered each afternoon in the Temple. It can be recited any time between midday and sunset. It consists of *Ashrei*, the *amidah*, and *Alenu*. A portion of the Pentateuch is also read on Sabbaths and fast days. On Av 9 and the Day of Atonement, the *tallit* is worn during m. Traditionally it was instituted by the patriarch Isaac.

Minneapolis and St. Paul: Twin cities in Minnesota, US. Jewish life was organized in St. Paul in the 1850s. East Europeans came after 1881. The Jewish community in M. was founded in 1878. Its Talmud Torah is a noted educational institution. In 1976 M. had 22,085 Jews and St. P. 9,500.

Minnesota: US state. Jews were living there before it became a state in 1858. The first synagogue was opened in St. Paul in 1856. By the beginning of the 20th cent., Jews were to be found in every small town, but later the trend was toward the large cities. In 1976, 34,265 Jews lived in M., the largest communities being in Minneapolis (22,085), St. Paul (9,500), and Duluth (1,000).

Minor Prophets: Twelve books of sayings of literary prophecies (Hosea, Joel, Obadiah, Jonah, Micah, Nahum, Habakkuk, Zephaniah, Haggai, Zechariah, Malachi), called M.P. in distinction to the three "Major" Prophets —Isaiah, Jeremiah, Ezekiel. They appear in the Hebrew Bible as the last section of the Prophets, and they are sometimes reckoned as a single work, known in Hebrew as *Terei Asar* (i.e., "Twelve").

minority rights: Rights accorded to national minorities in Eastern Europe after World War I, largely at the instigation of Jewish organizations. The Allied Powers included such guarantees in the Peace Treaty, and the League of Nations was supposed to safeguard their fulfillment. By the 1930s the provisions were largely disregarded, and they were not specifically revived after World War II.

Minsk: Town in White Russia. Jews are mentioned there in 1489, and received a charter in 1579. In the 17th cent. they were the victims of massacres and expulsions. However, it remained an important Jewish center. About 90,000 Jews died there in 1941. During World War II, Jews were concentrated in the town and sent to extermination camps. About 47,000 Jews were living there in 1970.

minyan: ("number"): A minimum of 10 male Jews gathered for communal prayer. Certain prayers (e.g. KADDISH, KEDUSHAH) can only be recited in the presence of a *m*.

Mir: Small town in Belorussia with a famous yeshivah, founded in 1815, which flourished until World War II. The students who escaped were in Shanghai during the war. Successor institutions were subsequently founded in Jerusalem and Brooklyn.

Mirandola see **Pico Della Mirandola**

Miriam: Sister of MOSES and AARON. It was she who watched her baby brother when he was placed in an ark in the Nile. After the crossing of the Red Sea, she led the women of Israel in a dance of rejoicing. Later she and Aaron rebelled against Moses' leadership; for this, she was smitten with leprosy, but, following Moses' intercession with God, was healed.

Mishnah: Codification of Jewish law compiled by JUDAH HA-NASI c. 200 CE. It contains the basis of the ORAL LAW traditionally given to Moses at Sinai and handed down by word of mouth, side by side with the written Law (i.e., the Pentateuch), from generation to generation. At first there was a reluctance to committing it to writing, but when the transmission of the tradition appeared endangered, a number of authorities (e.g., Akiva, Meir), made collections of traditions in writing, and these were organized and unified in the M. The teachers whose views are recorded in the M are called TANNAIM. The M. is divided into six parts (each of which is a *seder*), each being divided into tractates (*masekhet*), and each tractate into sections (*pepek*), which in turn contain paragraphs (also called a *mishnah*).

Mishneh Torah see **Moses ben Maimon**

Mississippi: US state. Jews were already living there at the end of the 17th cent., and by the early 19th cent. there were Jewish cemeteries in Biloxi and Natchez. A few hundred Jews from M. served in the Confederate armies in the Civil War. In the early 20th cent., Jews lived in many towns in the state. In 1976 there were 4,165 Jews in M., the largest community being in Greenville (700).

Missouri: US state. Jews entered the area after the Louisiana Purchase in 1803. The first congregation in St. Louis was founded in 1841. Congregations were established in St. Joseph in 1860 and Kansas City in 1870. In 1976, M. had 75,425 Jews, of whom 50,000 lived in St. Louis and 22,000 in Kansas City.

Mitnaggedim ("Opponents"): Opponents of the Hasidim. The powerful personality of Elijah the Vilna Gaon in 1772 gave rise to this movement. The claims of the *tzaddik* were resented and Hasidic prayer customs aroused opposition. The conflict reached a climax with the arrest of the Hasidic leader Shneour Zalman of Lyady, as a consequence of the ban issued by the M., but the acerbity of the controversy subsided in the course of the 19th cent.

mitzvah ("commandment"): A commandment or religious duty contained in the Pentateuch. Traditionally there are a total of 613 positive and negative commandments. Further *mitzvot* derive from rabbinic decision. The Talmud distinguishes between *mishpatim*, commandments which could have been deduced rationally, and *hukkim*, the rational basis for which is not apparent. The opposite of a *m*. is an *averah* ("transgression"). A boy becomes liable to perform commandments at the age of 13 (hence the ceremony of BAR MITZVAH) and a girl at 12 (see BAT MITZVAH). A woman is exempted from performing those commandments that must be observed at a fixed hour. In a general sense, the term *m*. is used for any good deed.

Mizrachi: Abbr. of *merkaz ruhani* ("spiritual center"), the Religious Zionist movement. It was established in 1902 and its first world conference was held in 1904 at Pressburg, where it adopted a platform within the framework of the Zionist Organization. It engaged in settlement work in Palestine, and from the establishment of the State of Israel participated in coalition governments. It amalgamated with HA-POEL HA-MIZRACHI (its Labor wing) in 1955 to form the NATIONAL RELIGIOUS PARTY. It maintains a variety of religious, cultural, and economic institutions. Its women's federation in Israel is called Omen.

mizrah ("east"): Ornamental plaque hung on a wall designating the eastern wall—i.e., in the direction of Jerusalem toward which Jews turn while praying. The *m.* side of the synagogue came to be regarded as especially honorable, and community members would vie for the privilege of sitting there.

Moab: Ancient country east of the Jordan. According to the Bible, the Moabites were descended from Lot (Gen. 19:37). Their language was similar to that spoken by the Hebrews. They opposed the entry of the Children of Israel into Canaan and fought them during the period of the Judges (under Eglon). David subdued M. (II Sam. 8:2), but M. recovered its independence under Mesha (II Kings 1:1). M. disappeared as a power shortly after the invasion of Nebuchadnezzar (whom they assisted). The Pentateuch prohibits marriage with a Moabite. However, David's grandmother was Ruth the Moabitess, and the Talmud sees the prohibition as referring to marriage with a male Moabite.

Moabite Stone (Mesha Stele): Moabite inscription of King Mesha, recording the battles with Israel and his victorious revolt against Joram. The events referred to are described in the Bible, in II Kings 3:4, but the Moabite account is written from a different perspective. The stone was discovered in 1868 in the Moabite capital, Dibon; it is now in the Louvre.

Moch, Jules Salvador (1893–): French statesman and socialist leader. He held office in Léon Blum's 1938 government. During World War II he worked with General De Gaulle and held ministerial posts in various postwar cabinets. On one occasion (in 1949) he was nominated as premier but failed to secure a majority.

Modena, Leone see **Leone Modena**

Modigliani, Amadeo (1884–1920): Italian painter. He studied in Florence but soon went to Paris. His work was influenced by Cubism and Negro art. M.'s style was highly individual, using distortion for effect. His fame was posthumous.

Modiin: Town in ancient Israel where Mattathias and his sons, the Hasmoneans, lived. Part of their impressive mausoleum survives.

Moed ("Festival"): Second order of the MISHNAH, discussing the laws of Sabbaths and festivals. It contains 12 tractates, which have *gemara* in both Talmuds except for *Shekalim*, which has no *gemara* in the Babylonian Talmud.

Moed Katan ("Minor Festival"): Eleventh tractate in the MISHNAH order of *Moed*. It deals with work permitted and forbidden on the intermediate days of Passover and Tabernacles (Hol ha-Moed) and discusses the rules of mourning on Sabbaths and holidays. It has *gemara* in both Talmuds.

Moetzet ha-Poalim ("Workers' Council"): The local labor authority, under HISTADRUT auspices, in Israel. It is a workers' council which supervises the enterprise and institutions. The Moetzet ha-Poalot ("Women Workers' Council") is the central body of the women's labor movement in Israel and conducts varied activities (welfare, training, culture, recreation, etc.).

*Mohammed (c. 571–632): Founder of ISLAM. He grew up in Mecca and was familiar with Jews, being influenced by their traditions as well as by those of Christians. He believed that there was no contradiction between Judaism and Islam, and he attempted to win over the large Jewish community, especially in Medina, even adapting the ritual of his community to theirs. When the Jews refused to recognize him as God's prophet, he was deeply embittered, and he cruelly attacked several Jewish tribes, who were either annihilated or expelled. However, he legislated that Jews, like other "Peoples of the Book," should not be compelled to embrace Islam but should be permitted to continue to observe Judaism, although subjected to certain ignominies.

mohel: Trained person performing ritual CIRCUMCISION.

Mohilever, Samuel (1824–1898): Russian rabbi and pioneer of modern religious Zionism. He served as rabbi in various Polish communities and in 1881 established the first Ḥibbat Zion society in Warsaw. In 1884 he was one of the organizers of the KATTOWITZ CONFERENCE.

Molcho, Solomon (c. 1500–1532): Kabbalist and pseudo-messiah. Born of a Marrano family in Portugal, he was enthused by David REUVENI, returned to Judaism, and went to Salonica, where he studied Kabbalah. From there he went to Italy, where he impressed Pope Clement VII and was invited into the Vatican. He became convinced that he was the Messiah. With David Reuveni, he went to see Emperor Charles V at Regensburg; the emperor had them both arrested and handed over to the Inquisition. M. was burned at the stake in Mantua.

Moldavia: Former Rumanian province; now largely in the USSR Moldavian republic. Jewish settlement dates from the 16th cent. There was an expulsion in 1579, but in 1612 the Jews were allowed to return. The 17th cent. saw massacres and BLOOD LIBELS. In the 18th and 19th cent., the *boyars* invited many Jews to settle there. From 1859, M. was part of RUMANIA and suffered from the anti-semitic policies of that country. Some 165,-000 Jews lived there before World War II. They suffered greatly during the war. Afterward, in 1970, the Jewish population was 98,072.

Molnar, Ferenc (1878–1952): Hungarian playwright and novelist. His successful plays included *Liliom* and *The Guardsman*. From 1940 he lived in the US.

Moloch (Molech, Milcom): Semitic deity worshiped by the Ammonites. The Canaanites and others sacrificed their children to M., a practice strongly condemned by the Bible but which nevertheless persisted, even in Jerusalem in the valley of Hinnom. A HIGH PLACE to M. was erected by Solomon in his latter years.

Monash, Sir John (1865–1931): Australian soldier and engineer. He commanded a brigade at Gallipoli and then in France, where he was eventually appointed to the supreme command of all Australian forces, becoming lieutenant-general. Later he was vice-chancellor of Melbourne University. After his death, an Australian university was named after him.

Monatschrift für Geschichte und Wissenschaft des Judentums (Ger. "Monthly for the History and Science of Judaism"): German learned periodical devoted to Jewish studies founded by Zacharias FRANKEL in 1851 and edited by H. GRAETZ 1869–87. One of the most important publications of its kind, it appeared until 1939.

Mond: English family of Chemists and industrialists. *Ludwig M.* (1839–1909) was born in Germany and went to England in 1862. He established what became the world's largest alkali factory. He made many scientific discoveries. His great art collection was bequeathed to the British nation. His son *Alfred Moritz M., 1st Lord Melchett* (1868–1930), entered his father's firm and developed it into the Imperial Chemical Industries, of which he was chairman. He entered Parliament in 1906 and became commissioner of works (1916–21) and minister of health (1921–22) in Lloyd George's administration. In his later life he became a keen Zionist and was joint chairman of the Jewish Agency. His son *Henry M., 2nd Lord Melchett* (1898–1949), was raised as a Christian but returned to Judaism during the period of the Nazi persecutions, becoming chairman of the Council of the Jewish Agency. His son *Julian Edward Alfred M., 3rd Lord Melchett* (1925–1973), was in 1967 appointed chairman of the British Steel Corporation.

moneylending: The Bible forbids collecting interest on a loan to a fellow citizen but permits it from a stranger (Deut. 23:20ff). However, the Talmud interpreted the law most strictly to forbid interest. In the Middle Ages, the Church forbade Christians to become involved in m., while at the same time excluding Jews from other occupations. This forced the Jews into m., which in Northern Europe was almost a Jewish monopoly. The rates of interest were government-regulated, and most of their profits were taken from them by taxation. In Italy the Jewish loan bankers were generally the pioneers for the establishment of a Jewish community. With the emancipation, m. has ceased to be a typically Jewish occupation, and fewer and fewer Jews are engaged in it.

monotheism: Belief in one God. M. was the decisive characteristic of Jewish worship and the Israelite conception of the Deity. The Bible immediately depicts God as unique, above nature, and omnipotent. There are no other divinities, and the key statement is "Hear O Israel the Lord our God the Lord is one" (Deut. 6:4). The rabbis ascribe the monotheistic inspirations to Abraham; critical scholars tend to give a later date, possibly to Moses. The concept was not easily accepted by the Israelites, and throughout the period of the Kingdom there are reports of "backsliding," for which they were rebuked by the prophets. After the Babylonian Exile, idolatry was no longer a problem, although the rabbis had to fight the dualistic tendency of the gnostics. M. was Judaism's chief legacy to Christianity and Islam. Its exact implications exercised the medieval philosophers.

Monsky, Henry (1890–1947): US communal leader. He headed B'nai B'rith from 1938 and was prominent in the wider American community. M. was chairman of the American Jewish Conference, founded in 1943 to coordinate certain aspects of communal endeavor.

Montagu: English family. *Samuel M., Lord Swaythling* (1832–1911), financier, founded the merchant-banking firm of Samuel Montagu and played an important part in developing London as a center of the international money market. He was a Liberal member of Parliament. Strictly Orthodox, he founded the Federation of Synagogues in 1887. His second son, *Edwin Samuel M.* (1870–1824), statesman, in 1914 became minister of munitions and was secretary of state for India, 1917–22. An opponent of Zionism, his opposition to the Balfour Declaration led to the modification of the original text of the document. *Lilian Helen M.* (1873–1962), daughter of Lord Swaythling, was a founder and leader of the Liberal Jewish Movement in England and was the first Jewish woman to preach in England. *Ewen Edward Samuel M.* (1901–   ), son of the 2nd Lord Swaythling, served in the navy in World War II, and his account of one of his exploits, *The Man Who Never Was,* was a popular book and film. In 1945 he was appointed judge advocate of the British fleet. He was president of the Anglo-Jewish Association and of the United Synagogue.

Montana: US state. The first Jews arrived in the 1862 gold rush and a Hebrew Benevolent Society was organized in 1865 in Helena, named for the wife of a Jewish pioneer. Jews played a leading role in the political life of the state, although their numbers were never large. In 1976 there were 545 Jews in Montana.

Montefiore: English family. *Sir Moses M.* (1784–1885), philanthropist and Jewish leader, acquired wealth as a broker, retiring at the age of 40 to devote himself to public work. In 1837–38, he was sheriff of the City of London, and he was the first English Jew to be knighted. (He also received a baronetcy in 1846). He interceded on behalf of oppressed Jews in many lands, notably at the time of the DAMASCUS AFFAIR, when together with A. CRÉMIEUX he obtained a statement from the sultan denouncing the RITUAL MURDER libel. M. visited Palestine seven times and assisted in many ways in improving the conditions of its Jews, supporting agricultural schemes, promoting industries, new building developments, etc. He was president of the Board of Deputies of British Jews (1835–74), and his opposition to Reform Judaism checked its growth in Britain. His last years were spent at his country home in Ramsgate, where he had built a synagogue in 1833 and established the Judith Montefiore College in memory of his wife. His great-nephew *Claude Joseph Goldsmid M.* (1858–1939) was a scholar and a founder of the Liberal Jewish movement in England. Active in Jewish public life, and an anti-Zionist, he was president of the Anglo-Jewish Association, 1895–1922. He edited (and financed) the JEWISH QUARTERLY REVIEW. Much of his scholarship dealt with the period of the New Testament, which he felt should be read and respected by Jews.

Monteux, Pierre (1875–1964): Conductor. Born in France, he lived in the US. From 1911 to 1914, he conducted Diaghilev's Ballets Russes, and later conducted several US symphony orchestras, including those of Boston (1919–24) and San Francisco (1936–52).

Montreal: Largest city in Canada. Its first Jews arrived in 1760. The first (Sephardi) congregation, Shearith Israel, was founded in 1768. Government recognition was received only in 1831. The second (Ashkenazi) congregation, Shaar Hashomayim, was not founded until 1858. There was considerable Jewish immigration during the late 19th cent., and the Jewish population rose from 811 in 1881 to 46,000 in 1921. From 1903, Jewish children received equal educational opportunity within the framework of the Protestant School Board. The community's educational and cultural achievements have been noteworthy. Jews arrived there from Morocco in the 1950s, and many ex-Israelis also settled there. The Jewish population in 1976 was 114,000.

moon, blessing of the (*kiddush levanah*): Blessing recited at night when the moon is visible between the 4th and 15th of the month, preferably at the close of the Sabbath in the open air outside the synagogue. It is recited by a *minyan* and was influenced by mystical custom, concluding with the recitation of Psalm 67 and the *kaddish*.

*Moore, George Foot (1851–1931): US scholar, professor of the history of religion at Harvard. His 3-volume *Judaism in the First Centuries of the Christian Era* is a standard work, one of the first works on Judaism by a Christian scholar written with a profound inner understanding.

Morais, Sabato (1823–1897): US rabbi and educator. He was born in Italy, officiated at the Spanish and Portuguese Congregation in London (1846–51), and then was a rabbi in Philadelphia, where he also taught at Maimonides College. In 1886 he established the JEWISH THEOLOGICAL SEMINARY OF AMERICA, of which he was the first president.

Moravia: Region of Czechoslovakia; formerly in Bohemia, Austria. Although Jews may have been there earlier, the first written evidence comes from 1249. They suffered severely at the time of the Black Death and were expelled from parts of M. at various times in the 15th cent. The exiles drifted back and the Jewish population was increased by Polish refugees at the time of the CHMIELNICKI persecutions. They suffered from high taxes and restrictions until the general emancipation of 1867. The Jewish population of 45,000 remained stable until World War II, but few survived. In 1970, less than 2,000 Jews lived in M.

Moravia (Pincherle), Alberto (1907–   ): Italian novelist. His novels are realistic and psychologically penetrating. They include *The Conformist, The Woman of Rome,* and *Conjugal Love.*

Mordecai: Hero of the Book of ESTHER. He saved Persian Jewry from the wicked plan of HAMAN when he got his adopted daughter, Esther, who was married to King Ahasuerus, to intervene with the king and prevent the scheme to kill the Jews. Haman and his sons were hanged instead and M. was appointed vizier in his place.

morenu ("our teacher"): Title given in the 14th cent. to outstanding Ashkenazi rabbis and, subsequently, to all rabbis.

Morgenstern, Julian (1881–1977): US biblical scholar and Reform rabbi. He taught at Hebrew Union College in Cincinnati (1907–49) and served as president of the college (1921–47). He wrote many studies on biblical subjects, making original contributions in various spheres.

Morgenthau: US. family. *Henry M.* (1856–1946), diplomat and financier, went from Germany to the US in 1865. A lawyer by training, he made several successful real estate and banking ventures in New York. During World War I, he was US ambassador to Turkey, in which capacity he was able to give assistance to the Jewish population of Palestine. In 1919 he headed a commission (the "M. Commission") to investigate the situation of Polish Jewry. His son Henry M., Jr. (1891–1967), was secretary of the treasury under President Franklin D. Roosevelt (1934–45). The finances for the New Deal and then for the American war effort owed much to his initiative. Active in Jewish affairs, he headed the United Jewish Appeal (1947–50) and Israel Bonds (1951–55).

Moriah: Mountain in Israel where Abraham was instructed to sacrifice Isaac. It was later popularly identified with the hill in Jerusalem on which the Temple was built.

Morning Journal: New York Yiddish daily newspaper, an advocate of Orthodoxy. Established in 1901, it merged in 1954 with Der Tog, which ceased to appear in 1972.

Morning Service see Shaharit

Morocco: Jews already lived in Mauretania—as M. was then called—in Second Temple times. They prospered under the Romans and the Vandals but their position worsened under the Christians. Some Berber tribes were converted to Judaism, and there are stories of a warrior Jewish queen DAHIA AL-KAHINA. Jews were among the strongest opponents of the invading Arabs. The communities grew and became centers of Jewish learning, religious and secular. In the mid-12th cent. the fanatical Almohades introduced a century of persecution and forced conversion to Islam. Many refugees from Spain in the late 14th and 15th cent. settled in M. The new arrivals settled along the coast and played a major role in the economic and cultural life. Some Jews rose to prominence as diplomats, agents of the sultan, merchants, etc. Eventually, however, the general picture became one of poverty, with Jews living in ghettos (the MELLAH). The situation of the Jews improved under the French. From 1948 the Jews of M. began to leave, many going to Israel and also France and Canada. Of the 265,000 Jews living in M. (French and Spanish) in 1948, only 31,000 remained in 1976.

Mortara case: Kidnapping in 1858 by papal police of a 7-year-old boy in Bologna from his parents' home. Five years earlier, a Christian domestic servant, believing that the boy was dying, had secretly baptized him. The episode led to a widespread outcry throughout Europe, and Jewish leaders tried unsuccessfully to intercede to secure the boy's release. The boy, Edgardo Mortara, eventually became a high dignitary in the Catholic Church and a professor of theology, dying in 1940.

Moscow: Capital of the USSR. Jews were not allowed to reside there until the end of the 18th cent., when many Jewish merchants settled there, and CANTONISTS also were found in M. with their families. In 1891, some 30,-000 Jewish artisans and craftsmen were expelled. The 1905 Revolution led to a better situation. The Jewish population increased greatly after the 1917 Revolution, and M. became a center of Jewish culture for a short time, but gradually, Jewish life and expression were curtailed. There are now 1 large and 2 suburban synagogues, with the Jewish population put at 285,000, although it is thought the actual number is much larger.

Moses: Leader and lawgiver. Born in Egypt, he was hidden while an infant on the banks of the Nile when his mother tried to avoid Pharaoh's edict that all male children be killed. He was discovered by Pharaoh's daughter and brought up in the palace, but he had to flee following his defense of an enslaved Israelite. He went to Midian, where he met the priest JETHRO, for whom he worked as shepherd and whose daughter Zipporah he married. He experienced a theophany by the Burning Bush, as a result of which he went back to Egypt to appear before Pharaoh with his brother AARON and demand the release of the Israelites. Pharaoh refused, and the Ten PLAGUES followed. When Pharaoh eventually agreed to the departure, Moses led the EXODUS across the Red Sea (where the pursuing Egyptians were drowned) and on to Mt. Sinai. Here he received the Divine Revelation and the Ten Commandments, and he bound the people in a solemn covenant with the Lord. He also built the sanctuary, the tabernacle, and consecrated his brother Aaron as first high priest. He taught the people an entire legal code (recorded in the Pentateuch as traditionally written by M. himself, while Jewish tradition also held that M. received the ORAL LAW on Mt. Sinai). His leadership was challenged on various occasions but never successfully. M. led the Israelites through the wilderness for 40 years, although no information is recorded on events between the 2nd and 39th years. The older generation died, and only when a new generation had grown up were they adjudged fit to enter the Promised Land. M.

himself did not live to see that day. After a lengthy valedictory address and a farewell blessing, he handed over the leadership to Joshua and died on Mt. Nebo at the age of 120. The Bible and Judaism regarded M. as the greatest of all prophets. By giving the Torah, he in fact created Judaism and was the father of monotheism. He is also venerated by other monotheistic faiths.

Moses ben Maimon see **Maimonides**

Moses ben Nahman see **Nahmanides**

Moses de Leon see **Leon**

moshav ovedim ("workers' settlement") or **moshav:** Israeli cooperative village whose inhabitants possess their own homes and small holdings; purchasing, marketing, etc, are done together, and central buildings and equipment are owned in common. After World War I dissatisfaction with the kevutzah brought on the foundation of the big m.o. (Nahalal, Kephar Yehezekel). The roof organization of the m.o. is the Tenuat ha-Moshavim (founded 1928). This form of settlement became the most popular form of village after 1948. In 1974, there were 349 moshavim of various types, with a total population of 123,600.

moshav shittuphi ("collective settlement"): Israeli cooperative settlement based on collective economy and ownership (as in the kibbutz), but in which each family has its own home, receiving a fixed budget related to the size of the family. It combines features of the kibbutz and the moshav. Like the kibbutz, it has tended to develop industry in addition to agriculture. The first two m.s. were Kephar Hittim and Moledet, established in 1936–37. In 1974 there were 28 such villages with a total population of 5,700.

moshav zekenim: An old-age home.

moshavah ("settlement"): Israeli agricultural village based on private land ownership and private enterprise. The m. was the earliest form of modern settlement during the First Aliyah, from the 1880s. Many moshavot have expanded into towns or become partly urbanized. In 1973 there were 56 such villages.

Mostel, Zero (1915–1977): US stage and film actor. He was blacklisted in the McCarthy period for his left-wing views. He played the role of Leopold Bloom in *Ulysses in Nighttown*, and his greatest success was in *Fiddler on the Roof*.

Motzkin, Leo (1867–1933): Jewish leader and

Zionist. He was born near Kiev and became an ardent follower of Herzl. He was a founder of the DEMOCRATIC FRACTION. During World War I he headed the Copenhagen office of the Zionist Organization. After the war he served as secretary and later president of the COMITÉ DES DELEGATIONS JUIVES. He headed the Organization of European National Minorities and was chairman of the Zionist Executive (1925–33).

Mount of Olives: Hill east of Jerusalem. It has three summits, of which one is known as Mt. Scopus and is the site of the original campus of the Hebrew University. It was associated with the messianic period and after Second Temple times was a major goal of Jewish pilgrims. At the foot of the mountain is the Garden of Gethsemane, where various churches were constructed. The M. of O. was also the Jewish necropolis from the First Temple times. The Jewish cemetery, desecrated under Jordanian rule (1948–67), was restored after the Six-Day War in 1967.

Mount Scopus see **Mount of Olives**

Mountain Jews see **Caucasus**

mourning (*avelut*): In ancient times, m. customs included rending the garments, wearing sackcloth and ashes, sitting on the ground, and putting earth on the head. There were also professional weepers, generally women. The rabbis determined periods of official m. according to certain biblical indications. M. begins after the BURIAL, at which the mourner rends his clothes. The mourner stays at home for a week (SHIVAH) and is visited by his acquaintances. The day of burial and one hour of the 7th day are counted as full days in reckoning the 7 days of m. From the 7th to the 30th day (SHELOSHIM), the mourner is not allowed to shave or to put on fresh clothes. The mourner recites KADDISH for 11 months for parents and for 30 days for other relatives. It is also recited each year on the anniversary of the death. It became customary to kindle a mourning light during the *shivah* and on the anniversary (*yahrzeit*). M. rites are not observed on Sabbaths and festivals, and a *shivah* is terminated by the advent of a festival.

Mukachevo (Munkacs): City in Ukrainian SSR; formerly in Hungary and Czechoslovakia. Jews lived there from the 17th cent., and a community was organized in 1741. It became a center of the strict Orthodoxy and bitter anti-Zionism of the Shapira dynasty of Hasidic rabbis. Before World War II, M. had 15,000 Jaws (50% of the population) but nearly all perished in the Holocaust. The Jewish population was estimated at 1,000 to 2,000 in 1973.

muktzeh ("set aside"): Objects that are forbidden to be moved on Sabbaths and festivals. Anything used for everyday work may not be used on these occasions.

Mülhausen, Yom Tov Lipmann (14th–15th cent.): Scholar and anti-Christian polemicist. He was rabbi in Prague, Cracow, and Erfurt. In 1389 he was forced to take part in a DISPUTATION with an apostate; he was arrested and released, but 80 other Jews were put to death. In his *Sepher ha-Nitzahon*, he wrote about this and other disputations.

Müller, Hermann Joseph (1890–1967): US geneticist, professor at Indiana University. In 1946, he won the Nobel Prize for Physiology and Medicine for his demonstration that hereditary changes or mutations are induced by X-rays.

Muni, Paul (1895–1967): US-actor, born Muni Weissenfreund. After appearing in vaudeville and with the New York Yiddish Art Theater, he made his name in films, appearing in many character roles. He was acclaimed for his performances as Emile Zola and Louis Pasteur (the latter won him an Academy Award), and in *The Good Earth* and *The Last Angry Man*. He appeared on the Broadway stage in *Inherit the Wind*, in which he portrayed the lawyer Clarence Darrow.

Munich: West German town, the capital of Bavaria. A community existed there from the 13th cent. Many of the Jews were engaged in moneylending. A series of persecutions marked their history, and in 1350 all the Jews were annihilated. They returned in 1375, and after more persecutions were banished in 1450, not returning again until the 18th cent. A synagogue was opened in 1824. In the 20th cent., M. was a center of anti-Semitism, and it was the early focus of the Nazi movement. About 10,000 Jews lived there in 1933, but the community came to an end during World War II. In 1973, 3,611 Jews were living there. In 1972, M. was the scene of the murder of 11 Israeli athletes during the Olympic Games.

Munk, Salomon (1803–1867): French Orientalist. He worked in the Oriental department of the Bibliothèque Nationale, devoting himself to the study of medieval Judeo-Arabic literature. His works include the French translation of Maimonides' *Guide*. It was he who discovered that IBN GABIROL was the author of *Fons Vitae*. From 1864 he was professor of Hebrew at the Collège de France. M. accompanied Crémieux on his journey, with Sir Moses Montefiore, to the Middle East in connection with the 1840 DAMASCUS AFFAIR.

Munkacs see **Mukachevo**

murder: Willful m. is a capital crime, although Hebrew law demands meticulous proof before the extreme penalty is imposed. The law against m. is presupposed from the Creation (cf. CAIN) and was enjoined on Noah (Gen. 9:6). In a few cases, justifiable homicide is recognized—for example, in self-defense. Where the m. is not premeditated, the killer in biblical times had to flee to a CITY OF REFUGE to escape the wrath of the next of kin, who had legal right to take personal revenge. The death penalty for m. was carried out by the sword. If the crime was proved but the death penalty could not be imposed for some reason, the penalty was then lengthy imprisonment.

Musaph ("Additional Sacrifice," "Additional Service"): Service recited on those days when the Bible prescribed additional offerings in the Temple, viz., Sabbaths, New Moons, the three Pilgrim Festivals, the New Year, and the Day of Atonement. It is usually read immediately after *Shaḥarit*. It consists of the AMIDAH (read by the congregation and repeated by the reader), and is generally concluded with EN K-ELOHENU and ALENU. The *amidah* on the Day of Atonement is lengthy and includes a description of the Temple service.

Musar Movement: Pietistic movement founded in mid-19th cent. Lithuania by Israel SALANTER. It stressed the emotional and spiritual character of study, devoting at least half an hour a day to the study of ethical literature (*musar*). The movement had its opponents in yeshivah circles, who feared it would interfere with talmudic studies. However, it generally became influential in most Lithuanian and US yeshivot, and lectures were given by a spiritual guide, or *mashgiaḥ*.

music: The only specific "Jewish" instrument from ancient times is the SHOPHAR (ram's horn), which was used more for cultic than musical purposes. Musical activity is frequently mentioned in the Bible. David was traditionally the first to organize musical life; he himself is mentioned as having been a skilled player on the lyre. M. became an integral feature of the Temple service through the levitical choirs, a chorus of at least 12 singers with an accompanying orchestra. After the destruction of the Second Temple, instrumental m. was no longer performed, partly out of mourning, partly because of its connection with pagan religions. The liturgical song retained its character, and early Christian Church m. was strongly influenced by Jewish usage. The Reading of the Law came to be regarded as characteristic of Jewish m., and a system of notation was devised and added to the Bible text. In the Middle Ages, a number of Jewish scholars wrote treatises on m. There are great differences between Jewish communities, who were all considerably influenced by their environment. The Ashkenazim were influenced by Eastern European m., which was absorbed into their cantoral music traditions. The Sephardim brought their m. from Spain (*romanceros*) and were also influenced by Arabic m., the latter characterizing the m. of Oriental communities. Jews have always participated in the musical life of their host countries. In the 16th–17th cent., Jews were active in musical life in Italy, the Netherlands, England, and the US. In the 19th cent., largely as a result of the Reform movement, Jewish written m. became widespread, and leading cantors in Europe published synagogal m. At the same time, Jews began to enter general musical life in disproportionate numbers; since then, they have been extremely prominent as performers. Jewish composers also achieved international reputations; of these, Ernest BLOCH, in particular, was influenced by Jewish musical traditions. In Israel too, there was intense musical activity —both composition and performance. Israeli composers often tried consciously to synthesize Western and Eastern traditions, and there also emerged a popular folk music, drawing on many different musical traditions.

*Mussolini, Benito (1883–1945): Italian Fascist dictator. His early rule and policy were in no way anti-Semitic, and, in fact, Jews were among his collaborators. However, in the late 1930s he had to fall in with the demands of his ally, Hitler, and enacted anti-Semitic legislation aimed at reducing the participation of Jews in public life. Nevertheless, even during World War II, he refused to follow the worst excesses of the Nazis, until after 1943, when his puppet regime toed faithfully the Nazi line.

Myers, Myer (1723–1795): US silversmith. He was born in New York, where he was prominent in Jewish and general communal activities and in Freemasonry. During the Revolutionary War, he fled from the British occupation, living in Norwalk, Conn., and Philadelphia. His work includes the first objects made in the US for Jewish ritual purposes, some of which are still in use.

mysticism see **Kabbalah**

Nabateans: Ancient Semitic people, originally from the Arabian peninsula, who conquered Edom in the 6th cent. BCE, making their capital at Petra. They developed the caravan trade and established cities (e.g., Avedat, Mamshit) and agricultural settlements throughout the Negev. They were very powerful in the 1st cent. BCE and 1st cent. CE. They were annexed by the Romans in 106 CE, but kept up their culture until the Byzantine period. The remains of their towns and agriculture have been uncovered in modern excavations (e.g., by Nelson Glueck).

Nablus see **Shechem**

Naboth (9th cent. BCE): Citizen of the town of Jezreel. His vineyard adjoined that of King Ahab, who coveted it but could not obtain it legally. At the urging of his wife Jezebel, he fabricated an accusation against N., leading to his death. Ahab obtained the land but was severely rebuked by the prophet Elijah.

nagid ("prince," "chief"): Title used for the leader of the Jewish community in many Muslim and some Christian countries. The position was generally recognized officially. It probably originated in 10th-cent. Egypt, where the office was held from the 13th cent. by the descendants of Maimonides, and it appears also in N. Africa, Yemen, and Spain. In modern Hebrew, the term is applied to heads of certain institutions (e.g., the Bank of Israel).

NAHAL. Acronym of Noar Halutzi Lohem ("Fighting Pioneer Youth"), a unit of the Israeli defense forces combining soldiering with pioneering. N. groups are assigned to villages where—under army discipline—they train in agriculture. The N. group joins a frontier village or sets up a new one, often in areas dangerous for civilian settlement.

Nahalal: First MOSHAV OVEDIM in Israel. Founded in 1921 in the Valley of Jezreel, its concentric layout was designed by Richard Kauffman. Its population was 1,043 in 1972.

Nahariyyah: City on the northern coast of Israel, founded in 1934 by German immigrants. It developed an agricultural economy and became a popular resort. The population has been estimated at 27,900 (1974).

Nahman of Bratzlav (1772–1811): Hasidic rabbi. A great-grandson of the BAAL SHEM TOV, he regarded himself as the only true interpreter of his ancestor's doctrines. He lived in Tiberias in 1798–99, then returned to the Ukraine, living subsequently in Bratzlav and Uman. He stressed simple faith and prayer, and developed the concept of the TZADDIK. He is best remembered for his parables. His followers, who still maintain synagogues in Israel and elsewhere, did not appoint any successor out of reverence for his memory.

Nahmanides (Moses ben Nahman; also known as **Ramban)** (1194–1270): Spanish communal leader, talmudist, kabbalist, and Bible commentator. He was rabbi of Gerona and regarded as the spiritual leader of Spanish Jewry. In 1263, he was compelled by King James of Aragon to conduct a public dispute with the apostate Pablo Christiani. Accounts of this DISPUTATION of Barcelona have been preserved from both sides. It lasted 4 days, with N. conducting himself with courage and distinction. He also tactfully replied to a missionary address by the king. After the disputation, the king made him a gift of money, but his position vis-à-vis the Church officials was so precarious that he had to flee Spain. He went to Palestine and lived in Acre, where he reorganized the Jewish settlement. N. raised talmudic study to a new level, and his novellae were the first important compositions in this genre. His best-known work is his commentary on the Pentateuch, which, as well as showing philological insight, treated the subject from philosophical, theological, and kabbalistic standpoints.

Nahum: Seventh of the Minor Prophets. He prophesied in Judah toward the end of the 7th cent. BCE, foretelling the destruction of Nineveh (which occurred in 612 BCE). The Book of N., containing 3 chapters, is marked by its picturesque and vivid style.

Najara, Israel ben Moses (c. 1555–c. 1625): Palestinian rabbi, kabbalist, and poet. He lived in Safed and Gaza. The outstanding Jewish poet of his time, he wrote sacred and secular works in Hebrew and Aramaic. Hundreds of his religious poems are known, many having passed into the liturgy.

nakdanim ("punctuators"): Scholars who between the 9th and 14th cent. accented and punctuated biblical manuscripts and provided them with the masoretic apparatus. They lived in Muslim lands as well as in Western Europe.

Namier, Sir Lewis Bernstein (1888–1960): Historian and Zionist. Born in Poland, he moved to England in 1908. He was professor of modern history at the University of Manchester from 1931. He was also political secretary to the Zionist Executive of the Jewish Agency (1927–31). His works on modern history were ex-tremely influential. On his marriage in 1947, he converted to Anglicanism.

Naomi: Wife of Elimelech of Bethlehem, who emigrated with her husband and two sons to Moab during a famine (Ruth 1:1–2). When all three died, she returned with her daughter-in-law RUTH to Bethlehem, and encouraged her to marry Boaz.

*Napoleon Bonaparte (1769–1821): French emperor. His attempt to conquer the Middle East in 1799 was thwarted by the British navy at Acre. In 1806, he convened an Assembly of Jewish Notables in Paris, in order to clarify the relations between the Jews and the state. The delegates decided that Judaism consisted of an unchangeable religious element and a political aspect which was adjustable. These conclusions were confirmed by a SANHEDRIN convoked by N. the following year. As a result, a central Jewish communal organization was established.

Nashim ("Women"): Third order of the MISHNAH, comprising the tractates YEVAMOT, KETUBBOT, NEDARIM, SOTAH, GITTIN, and KEDUSHIN. All have *gemara* in both Talmuds. The subject matter relates to marriage, divorce, and marital relations.

nasi: ("prince"): Biblical term for person of importance; in talmudic times, the presiding officer of the Great SANHEDRIN who was the spiritual, and at times also the political, head of the Jewish people. Together with the AV BET DIN, the n. constituted the ZUGOT. From the 2nd cent., the n., now always a descendant of Hillel, was recognized by the Romans as the head of the Jewish community in Palestine (the Patriarch). Various *nesiim* made far-reaching innovations in Jewish law. Outside Palestine, the term was often used among Sephardim for the head of the community. It is also used for the president of the State of Israel.

Nasi, Gracia Mendes (c. 1510–1569): Stateswoman of Marrano origin. Of Portuguese birth, she married Francisco Mendes, a banker; when he died, she went to Antwerp, from there to Italy (Venice and Ferrara), and then to Constantinople. A woman of great wealth, she became the leader of Turkish Jewry, devoting herself to improving the welfare of the Jews and assisting Marranos. In reaction to the burning of 26 Marranos, she organized a boycott of the port of Ancona.

Nasi, Joseph (c. 1524–1579): Statesman in Turkey; nephew and son-in-law of Gracia NASI. Born a Marrano in Portugal, he went with his aunt to Antwerp in 1537. In 1554 he joined her in Constantinople. He was a favorite of Selim, and when the latter became sultan, N. became one of the most powerful persons at court. He was named duke of Naxos and received a lease on the Tiberias area, which he tried to establish as an independent Jewish center, basing its economy on the cultivation of silkworms. His widow established a Hebrew printing press at Constantinople.

Nathan ben Jehiel of Rome (1035–c. 1110): Hebrew lexicographer in Italy. He headed the Rome Yeshivah and built a fine synagogue for the community. He compiled the pioneering lexicon *Arukh*, covering the meaning and etymology of terms in the Talmud and Midrash. This was widely circulated, and a modern 12-volume scholarly edition was published (1878–92) by Alexander KOHUT.

Nathan of Gaza (c. 1643–1680): Sabbetaian leader. Convinced in a vision of the messianic mission of SHABBETAI TZEVI, he became the latter's "prophet" and wrote tracts and letters to Diaspora communities proclaiming the advent of the Messiah. His faith did not waver even after Shabbetai Tzevi's apostasy. He lived his last years in the Balkans, developing and propounding the Sabbetaian theology.

National Council of Jewish Women: US national organization founded in 1893. Its program combines social action and local service, with activities in both the Jewish and general community. It has assisted new immigrants to the US and promoted educational projects in Israel. It has over 100,000 members.

National Jewish Community Relations Advisory Council (NCRAC): US organization founded in 1944, to coordinate Jewish communal agencies throughout the US. It represents 9 national organizations and 81 local community-relations councils.

National Jewish Welfare Board: US organization, founded in 1917, coordinating Jewish community centers and YMHAs and servicing Jewish military personnel. It was responsible for the Jewish chaplaincy service in both world wars and the Korean and Vietnam wars and cared for the welfare of Jewish soldiers on active duty or in veterans' hospitals. The Jewish community centers under its auspices conduct programs of recreation, culture, and education to serve all age groups. They originated in Jewish literary societies founded in the 1840s. The first YMHA (in Baltimore) was founded in 1854. The NJWB maintains a lecture bureau and also sponsors the Jewish Book Council and Jewish Music Council.

National Religious Party: Israel religious political party, known from its Hebrew acronym as Mafdal, founded in 1956 through a merger of MIZRACHI and HA-POEL HA-MIZRAHI. It has remained a partner in almost all government coalitions, initially with the labor parties and from 1977 with LIKKUD. For its parliamentary strength, see KNESSET.

Navon, Yitzhak (1921–): Fifth president of Israel. Born in Jerusalem, he served in various positions in the foreign ministry and prime minister's office before being elected to the Knesset in 1965, first on the Rafi ticket, later for the Israel Labor Party. Among other positions he was deputy speaker and chairman of the Zionist General Council. He was elected president of Israel in 1978.

Nazareth: Town in Galilee, Israel. A Jewish village, it is not mentioned in the Hebrew Bible but figures prominently in the New Testament as the home town of Jesus. Its growing importance from the 4th cent. was largely connected with its reverence by Christians, and the Church of the Annunciation. It became part of Israel in 1948, and has kept an all-Arab population numbering 36,400 in 1974. The neighboring Jewish settlement of Upper N. was founded in 1957 and in 1974 numbered 18,300.

Nazir: Fourth tractate of the MISHNAH order of *Nashim*, with *gemara* in both Talmuds. It discusses the laws of the NAZIRITE.

nazirite: Ascetic person who vows not to partake of the products of the vine or strong drink, not to cut his hair, and not to come close to dead bodies, even of his closest relatives. If no period of time is specified, the vow is held to be binding for 30 days. Special sacrifices were prescribed at the conclusion of this period, or in case of pollution. Lifetime naziriteship was also possible (as in the case of SAMSON). The biblical rules are given in Num. 6. Nazirites were rare after the destruction of the Temple, although they are known up to the present.

Nazism see **Holocaust**

Nebo: Mountain at the edge of the Mountains of Moab, overlooking the Dead Sea and the Promised Land.

On one of its peaks, Moses died (Deut. 34:1–3).

Nebraska: US state. Jews began to settle there soon after N. became a territory in 1854. The first Jews were merchants. From the 1880s, Russian Jews arrived, many sent there by the Industrial Removal Office. In 1976, N. had 8,345 Jews, mostly businessmen or professional workers. The largest community was in Omaha (6,500).

*Nebuchadnezzar: (c. 630–562 BCE): Ruler of Babylonia, who reigned 605–562. He defeated the Egyptians at the battle of Carchemish in 605 BCE. In 598 BCE, after Judah revolted, he invaded it and exiled the king Jehoiachin and 10,000 captives. He placed on the throne his own choice, Zedekiah, but when the latter rebelled in 586 BCE, N. returned to Judah, captured Jerusalem, destroyed the city, and carried off a large part of the population into captivity. There are stories about N. in the Book of Daniel.

Nedarim ("Vows"): Third tractate of the MISHNAH order of *Nashim*, with *gemara* in both Talmuds. It discusses the laws of vows.

Negaim ("Plagues"): Third tractate of the MISHNAH order of *Toharot*, with no *gemara* in either Talmud.

It discusses the laws of ritual cleanliness and leprosy.

Negbah: Israeli kubbutz, affiliated with Ha Kibbutz ha-Meuhad movement. It is situated in the northern Negev, where it was founded in 1939. In the 1948 War of Independence, its defense was decisive in stemming the Egyptian invasion.

Negev: Southern area of Israel covering 4,600 square miles, about half of the country. It is desert land with an annual rainfall of a maximum of 10 inches. The northern area is cultivable and has been considerably developed since 1948. The central section is only cultivable in parts; its main features are three huge cirques. The southern Negev is complete desert and continues down to the Gulf of Elath. Its copper mines were exploited in ancient times and again in recent years. Other mineral deposits have been discovered and mined in the N.

Nehardea: City in Babylonia. It had an important Jewish community in Second Temple times. In the talmudic period, its academy was best known in the period of the *amora* SAMUEL. It was also the seat of the EXILARCH. After the destruction of the city in 259, the academy moved to PUMBEDITA. Fa-

mous scholars lived in N. subsequently, but it never reattained its previous prominence.

Nehemiah (5th cent. BCE): Governor of Judah. He was appointed by the Persian king Artaxerxes, whom he had served as cupbearer. Despite opposition by the SAMARITANS, he rebuilt the walls of Jerusalem and worked with EZRA in reforming the Jewish community in Jerusalem—opposing mixed marriages, reorganizing the Temple services, promoting Sabbath observance, and establishing order. The chronology of the activities of N. and Ezra remains uncertain. The Book of N. (originally combined with the Book of Ezra) is in the Hagiographa section of the Bible.

Nehunyah ben ha-Kanah (1st cent. CE): TANNA. A noted halakhist, he was highly regarded by kabbalists, who attributed various mystical works to him.

neilah ("closing"): Final service on the Day of Atonement. N. was originally a prayer on fast days, recited at sunset as the Temple gates were shut. However, on the Day of Atonement, the name applies to the closing of the gates of heaven. It is recited with solemnity and concludes as night falls. It incorporates *Ashrei* and the AMIDAH (which is repeated before the open ark), and concludes with the *Shema*, other verses, and the sounding of a single blast of the *shophar*. The *tallit* is worn at n., as it is at other services of the Day of Atonement.

ner tamid ("eternal lamp"): Light, which was a permanent feature of the sanctuary in the wilderness and in the Temple. It was part of the candelabrum and was serviced by the priests. Since the synagogue was called "a small sanctuary," it became customary, though not obligatory, to have a perpetual lamp in front of the ark. (In Eastern Europe, however, it was generally placed in a stone niche in a wall.)

Nes Tziyyonah: Town in central Israel near Tel Aviv. It was one of the first modern settlements in the country, founded by BILU immigrants in 1883. In 1974, it had 12,600 inhabitants.

Netanyah: City in central Israel, on the Sharon Coast. Founded in 1929, it was called after Nathan STRAUS. Its economy was first based on citrus plantations, but the town developed in other ways, notably as a resort. From World War II, it was a center of the diamond-polishing industry. The population, as of 1974, was 79,500.

Netherlands see **Holland**

nethinim: Servants in the Temple cult. Traditionally they were first the conquered Gibeonites and were assigned by David to the Levites to aid them in menial tasks. They went with the Jews in the Babylonian Exile and returned with them, but were regarded as inferior, and intermarriage with them was forbidden. They were still known in talmudic times.

Neuman, Abraham Aaron (1890–1970): US historian and educator. He was a rabbi in Philadelphia and professor of history at Dropsie College and its president, 1941–66. He wrote *The Jews in Spain* and was joint editor of the *Jewish Quarterly Review*.

Neumann, Emanuel (1893–): US Zionist leader. He was president of the Zionist Organization of America (1947–49, 1956–60), and a member of the Zionist Executive in Jerusalem (1931–39, 1946–47). From 1951, he was a member of the Jewish Agency Executive, and for several years was chairman of its New York Executive.

Neutra, Richard Joseph (1892–1970): US architect. He was born in Vienna and introduced the International Style to the US, where he lived from 1923. He was best known for the private homes he designed, such as the Tremaine house in Santa Barbara, Calif.

Nevada: US state. Jews first went there in the gold rush of 1859 and the silver rush of 1862. A congregation was founded in Virginia City in 1862. Later the numbers declined, and few newcomers went to N. in the early 1900s, but after World War II the Jewish community grew in Las Vegas, which is now by far the larger of the two communities in the state, with 9,000 Jews as against 380 in Reno. Altogether there were 9,380 Jews in N. in 1975.

Nevelson, Louise (1900–): US sculptor. Born in Russia, she went to the US as a child. In the early 1930s she worked with the Mexican artist Diego Rivera. She produced abstract sculptures and geometrical formats, and also worked in plastics. She is noted for intricate wooden constructions consisting of multiple boxlike shelves.

New Brunswick see **Maritime Provinces**

New Hampshire: US state. Individual Jews were living there at the end of the 17th cent. but they remained few in number until the end of the 19th cent., when congregations were founded in Berlin and Manchester. In 1976, 4,580 Jews lived in N.H., of whom 1,800 were in Manchester.

New Haven: US city in Connecticut. Jews lived there from 1758, with the first community established by German Jews in the late 1840s. In 1976 it had 20,000 Jews.

New Jersey: US state. Although religious tolerance was granted in 1665, no Jewish communities were established until the middle of the 19th cent., and the first community was founded in Newark in 1848. Large numbers of Jews arrived from Eastern Europe from the 1880s, and a number of Jewish agricultural settlements were founded. The Jewish population rose rapidly after World War II, partly as a result of the general prosperity and partly because many Jews working in New York prefer to live in the N.J. suburbs. 429,850 Jews were living there in 1976, in many towns and with a strong communal organization.

New Mexico: US state. Jews of German origin played an important part in the development of the territory from the mid-19th cent. The first congregation was founded in Las Vegas in 1884. After World War II a community was founded in Los Alamos, mostly composed of scientists. In 1976, there were 6,245 Jews, of whom 4,500 lived in Albuquerque.

new moon (rosh hodesh): The beginning of the Hebrew month. In biblical times it was celebrated as a holiday,- with appropriate offerings. Subsequently it was not observed but was marked by liturgical additions (the recitation of Half-*Hallel*, the Additional Service, etc.) Elaborate arrangements were made in the talmudic period for announcing the date of the n.m. to Jewish communities throughout the Middle East. When its appearance had been confirmed by witnesses before the Sanhedrin, a chain of bonfires from hilltop to hilltop carried the news to distant communities. Fasting and mourning are forbidden on the n.m. (which lasts 2 days when the preceding month has 30 days). A special blessing in anticipation of the new month is recited in the synagogue on the preceding Sabbath. This announces the date of the forthcoming month and prays for blessings.

New Testament: The Christian holy scriptures, differentiating them from what the Christians call the Old Testament, i.e., the Jewish Bible. Written in Greek (but often based on an Aramaic original), its canon was determined in the 2nd

cent. CE. It reflects the antagonism of the early Christians toward the Jews of their time. The Dead Sea Scrolls have shown that much of the teaching formerly regarded as of Hellenistic origin was in fact drawn from Jewish sectarian thought.

New Year: Four different New Years are enumerated in the MISNAH (*Rosh ha-Shanah* 1:1). Nisan 1 begins the year for dating regnal years, festivals, and months; Elul 1 for tithing cattle; Tishri 1 for civil purposes; and Shevat 15 is the NEW YEAR FOR TREES.

New Year for Trees (Tu bi-Shevat, i.e., 15th day of Shevat): Originally the age of a tree for purposes of tithing was reckoned from that date, but there was no religious significance. From the 17th cent., partly under kabbalistic influences, a special ritual developed especially among Oriental Jews, who ate 15 different kinds of fruit to the accompaniment of readings from sacred literature. In modern Israel, it has become an Arbor Day marked by tree-planting ceremonies.

New York: US state. The first Jews in North America settled in New York City in 1654, and by the end of that century Jewish traders were working along the Hudson River. Early communities were founded at Wawarsing (1837), Albany (1838), and Syracuse (1839). Many other communities came into being in the course of the 19th cent., while in the early 20th cent. Jews were working as farmers in the state. The massive population of Eastern European Jews who settled in New York City from the 1880s began to move to suburbs farther upstate after World War I and especially after World War II. A popular resort area developed in the Catskill Mountains. In 1976 there were 2,150,515 Jews in the state, and apart from New York City, the largest communities were Buffalo (22,250), Rochester (21,500), Albany (13,500), and Syracuse (11,000). 11.9% of the population of the state is Jewish, by far the highest proportion in all the US.

New York City: US city. The first group of Jews to settle were Sephardim who arrived in 1654 from Brazil, acquiring the right to remain despite the objections of the governor, Peter Stuyvesant. A synagogue existed as early as 1695; this later became the Sephardi Shearith Israel. The next was the Ashkenazi B'nai Jeshurun, founded in 1825. Naturalization became possible in 1727, and from 1740 Jews could have full citizenship. The number of Jews was about 1% of the total.

Immigration grew from the 1820s and by 1847 there were 15,000 Jews, and 40,000 in 1860. The Reform Congregation Emanu-el was organized in 1845. At this time most of the immigrants came from Central Europe; in the 1880s, the mass influx came from Eastern Europe. In 1880, there were 60,000 Jews; in 1914, 1,500,000. Many of the Jews lived on the Lower East Side, to which they transferred the way of life they had known in Europe. Many worked in sweatshops and their language was Yiddish. In the early 20th cent. N.Y.C. was the center of a thriving Jewish culture, and Jews played a key role in the emerging labor movement. Efforts at organizing the community failed. After World War II, the numbers of Jews in the city dropped, due to the cessation of immigration and the tendency to move out to the suburbs. The estimated Jewish population for greater New York is over 2,000,000 (1975)— by far the largest Jewish community of any today, or of any in history.

New Zealand: Jews lived there from the 1830s. The Auckland community was founded in 1840 and that of Wellington in 1843. Originally most of the Jews came from England, but later they arrived from Eastern and

Central Europe. Jews have been prominent in public life, and Sir Julius VOGEL was prime minister. The Jewish population was estimated at 4,500 in 1976, of whom 2,000 lived in Auckland and 2,000 in Wellington.

Newark: US city, in New Jersey. Jews lived there from 1844, and the first synagogue was built in 1858. About 20,000 Jews were living there in the early 20th cent. Their numbers increased greatly, many living in N. and working in New York. In 1976, Essex County (in which N. is situated) had almost 100,000 Jews.

Newfoundland see **Maritime Provinces**

Newman, Paul (1925–): U.S. actor. His successes have included *Exodus*, *Butch Cassidy and the Sundance Kid*, and *The Sting* (the latter two in a smooth partnership with Robert Redford).

Newport: US city in Rhode Island. This was one of the earliest Jewish settlements in the US, and in 1677, Jews originating from Barbados purchased a cemetery there. Touro synagogue was dedicated in 1763, and in 1946 was named a national shrine. The community disintegrated during the British occupation. It was reorganized in 1893 and has 1,200 members (1975).

Nezikin ("Damages"): Fourth order in the MISHNAH and Talmud dealing with civil law, especially monetary matters and damages. It contains ten tractates: BAVA KAMMA, BAVA METZIA, BAVA BATRA (these three were originally a single tractate called N.), SANHEDRIN, MAKKOT, SHEVUOT, EDUYYOT, AVODAH ZARAH, AVOT, and HORAYOT. All except *Avot* and *Eduyyot* have *gemara* in both Talmuds.

Nicaragua: Jews have been living there from the early 1930s. 200 Jews, of European origin, lived in the country in 1975, almost all in Managua, the capital city, which has had a synagogue since 1964.

Nicholas: Russian czars. *Nicholas I* reigned in 1825–55: he endeavored to stimulate Jewish assimilation by police methods. He initiated compulsory military service for Jews (the CANTONIST system) in 1827. In 1844 he abolished the Jewish communities and set up Jewish government schools, which taught secular as well as religious subjects. *Nicholas II*, who ruled 1894–1917, was anti-Semitic, as were his advisers. His reign was marked by cruel pogroms and by the BEILIS trial, all with government connivance. During his rule hundreds of thousands of Jews left Russia.

Nichols, Mike (1931–): US theater and film director. Early in his career he toured in cabaret with Elaine May. He has directed many Broadway hits (including several by Neil Simon), and his films include *The Graduate*, *Catch-22*, and *Who's Afraid of Virginia Woolf?*

Niddah ("Menstruous Woman"): Seventh tractate in the MISHNAH order of *Toharot*, with *gemara* in both Talmuds. It deals with laws governing the ritual uncleanness of a woman as a result of passing through her menstrual period.

Nieto, David (1654–1728): Rabbi, physician, and philosopher. He studied medicine in Padua but became a rabbi in Leghorn. In 1702 he was appointed *haham* in London. He was a philosopher, poet, and mathematician, writing in Italian, Hebrew, and Spanish. He strongly opposed Shabbetai Tzevi.

Niger, Samuel (Samuel Charney) (1883–1955): Yiddish literary critic; brother of the poet Daniel Charney. He started his career in Russia, but after a narrow escape from being shot during a pogrom in Vilna in 1919, he came to New York. He was literary editor of *Der Tog* and published critical studies.

niggun ("melody"): Traditional tune to which a prayer is chanted. It was prominent among Hasidim, who often sang wordless melody repeatedly.

night prayer (*keriat shema al ha-mittah*): Special prayer consisting of a prayer for repose, the first paragraph of the SHEMA, Psalms 92 and 93, the *Hashkivenu* prayer, biblical verses, and *Adon Olam*.

NILI (initials of "The Strength of Israel will not lie," I Sam. 15:29): Jewish underground intelligence organization in Palestine during World War I, aimed at assisting the British against the Turks. Its leader was Aaron AARONSOHN. Some of the Jewish population opposed its activities, fearing the repercussions it could have on the community as a whole. The Turks obtained proof of espionage and captured many of its members, executing some of them.

Nirenberg, Marshall Warren (1927–): US biochemist. In 1968, he was awarded the Nobel Prize for Medicine and Physiology for laying the groundwork for the solution of the genetic code and its function in protein synthesis.

Nisan: First month of the Jewish religious year: 7th of the civil. It has 30 days and its zodiac sign is the lamb. In ancient times its name was ABIB. N. 1 was the New Year of Kings, from which the regnal dates were reckoned. Passover starts on the 15th of the month. N. is regarded as festive, and public mourning is avoided, with TAHANUM omitted from the daily prayers.

Nishmat ("Breath of"): Opening word of doxology recited at the end of the PE-SUKE DE-ZIMRA on Sabbaths and festivals. It is ancient, and is mentioned in the Talmud.

Nissim, Isaac (1896–): Sephardi Rabbi. He was born in Baghdad and lived in Jerusalem, where he served as chief rabbi, 1955–72. N. wrote and edited volumes of responsa.

Nister, Der see **Kahanovitz, Phinehas**

Noachide Laws see **Laws of Noah**

Noah: Chief figure in the biblical FLOOD story (Gen. 6ff.); son of Lamech. He was saved from the destruction that overtook the rest of mankind because of his righteousness. At God's behest, he built an ark which held his family and specimens of all living species. They floated on the flood waters and were saved. Mankind descended from him through his three sons, Shem, Ham, and Japheth.

Noah, Mordecai Manual (1785–1851): US diplomat, editor, and playwright. He entered politics in his native Philadelphia and was US consul to Tunis 1813–15, sheriff of New York County, a newspaper publisher, and a popular playwright. He prepared a plan to settle Jews on Grand Island in the Niagara River near Buffalo, which he called Ararat. The proposal drew a great deal of attention but no settlers arrived.

Nobel Prize winners (Jewish):

	Date awarded
Physics	
Michelson, Albert Abraham	1907
Lipmann, Gabriel	1908
Einstein, Albert	1921
Bohr, Niels	1922
Franck, James	1925
Hertz, Gustav	1925
Stern, Otto	1943
Rabi, Isidor Isaac	1944
Bloch, Felix	1952
Born, Max	1954
Segre, Emilio	1959
Glaser, Donald A.	1960
Hofstadter, Richard	1961
Landau, Lev	1962
Feyman, Richard P.	1965
Schwinger, Julian	1965
Gell-Mann, Murray	1969
Gabor, Dennis	1971
Josephson, Brian	1973
Miltelson, Benjamin R.	1975
Medicine and Physiology	
Metchnikoff, Elie	1908
Ehrlich, Paul	1909
Barany, Robert	1914
Meyerhof, Otto	1922
Landsteiner, Karl	1930

Physics	Date awarded	Literature	Date awarded
Warburg, Otto		Heyse, Paul J. L. von	1910
Heinrich	1931	Bergson, Henri Louis	1927
Loewi, Otto	1936	Pasternak, Boris	1958
Erlanger, Joseph	1944	Agnon, Shemuel	
Chain, Sir Ernst Boris	1945	Yoseph	1966
Muller, Hermann		Sachs, Nelly	1966
Joseph	1946	Bellow, Saul	1976
Reichstein Tadeusz	1950	Economics	
Waksmann, Selman		Samuelson, Paul	1970
Abraham	1952	Kuznets, Simon	1971
Lipmann, Fritz Albert	1953	Arrow, Kenneth Joseph	1972
Krebs, Sir Hans Adolf	1953	Kantorovich, Leonid	1975
Lederberg, Joshua	1958	Friedman, Milton	1976
Kornberg, Arthur	1959		
Bloch, Konrad	1964		
Jacob, François	1965		
Lwoff, André	1965		
Wald, George	1967		
Nirenberg,			
Marshall W.	1968		
Luria, Salvador	1969		
Katz, Sir Bernard	1970		
Axelrod, Julius	1970		
Edelman, Gerald	1972		
Baltimore, David	1975		
Temin, Howard Martin	1975		
Blumberg, Baruch S.	1976		
Yalow, Rosalyn	1977		
Chemistry			
Bayer, Adolf			
J. F. W. von	1905		
Moissan, Henri	1906		
Wallach, Otto	1910		
Willstätter, Richard	1915		
Haber, Fritz	1918		
Hevesy, George			
Charles von	1943		
Calvin, Melvin	1961		
Perutz, Max Ferdinand	1962		
Stein, William	1972		
Peace			
Asser, Tobias Michael			
Carel	1911		
Fried, Alfred Hermann	1911		
Cassin, René	1968		
Kissinger, Henry	1973		

Nordau (Sudfeld), Max (1849–1923): Philosopher and Zionist leader. Born in Budapest, he was a physician in Paris from 1880 but also entered journalism. His *Conventional Lies of Our Civilization* appeared in 1883 and ran into over 70 editions and was translated into 15 languages. His other books and novels were successful; his plays less so. He joined HERZL at the beginning of the Zionist movement, participating in all Zionist Congresses, where his addresses were a highlight. He drafted the 1897 Basle Program. He was a political Zionist, opposing the policy of settling Palestine on a large scale before political rights were obtained. He spent World War I in Spain, but he returned to France in 1921. During his last years, his activist views led to dissension between him and the official Zionist leadership.

North Africa see **Africa, North**

North Carolina: US state. Jews were welcomed in N.C. in its 1668 constitution, but two centuries elapsed before they were permitted to hold public office. The first congregation was established in Wilmington in 1867, and the number of Jews grew after the beginning of the 20th cent. In 1976, there were 10,810 Jews, of whom 2,800 lived in Charlotte.

North Dakota: US state. Attempts to settle Jews on the land in the 1880s did not last long. A congregation was established in Grand Forks in 1892 and in Fargo in 1896. They remain the only two communities in the state, which had 1,445 Jews in 1976.

Norway: A few Jews strayed there in the 17th-18th cent., and then only temporarily. They were allowed to settle with full civil rights after 1851. At the beginning of World War II there were 1,800 Jews in N., including 200 German refugees. Many of these were killed by the Nazis during the war. The Jewish population in 1976 was about 900, mostly in Oslo with 120 in Trondheim.

Norwich: English town. Jews lived there in the Middle Ages, when it was the scene of the first recorded BLOOD LIBEL in Europe, concerning a boy named William. It was a significant Jewish community, consisting mostly of financiers. Between the 1290 expulsion and the 18th cent., no Jews lived there. A small community (170 in 1976) has existed since 1750.

Nossig, Alfred (1864-1943): Author, sculptor, and musician. Born in Lvov, he lived much of his life in Berlin. He was among the founders of an institute for the study of Jewish statistics and an organization for Jewish art. An active Zionist, his individualist views brought him into conflict with Herzl. N. wrote poems, plays, and literary criticism. He was shot by members of the Jewish underground in the Warsaw ghetto when they became convinced that N. was collaborating with the Nazis.

Notarikon: Representation of a word or phrase by a single letter, usually the initial. It was also a method of interpreting words by taking each component letter as the initial for other words. It was used in rabbinical and homiletical interpretation, as well as in Kabbalah.

Nova Scotia see **Maritime Provinces**

novellae (ḥiddushim): Commentaries on the Talmud and rabbinic literature that extract new facts on theories from the text. Until the 16th cent., they were based on sober analysis, but from that date the Polish method of PILPUL often made the writing of n. an exercise in hairsplitting casuistry. The emphasis was now often on saying something "novel" instead of simple elucidation. Many volumes of n. have been published.

Novi Israel (Russ. "New Israel"): Jewish-Christian group founded in Odessa in 1881 by Jacob Priluker to join Reform Judaism with Greek Orthodox dissenters. It recognized the Pentateuch while dismissing the Talmud, observed the Sabbath on Sunday, and rejected circumcision and dietary laws. In 1883 it merged with the Spiritual Biblical Brotherhood group formed by Jacob GORDIN. The sect ceased to exist in 1885.

Numbers: Fourth book of the Pentateuch (*Be-Midbar*, which is the first main word). It tells the story of the Israelites in the wilderness, from the departure from Mt. Sinai to the 40th year after the approach to the Holy Land. Most of its legislative sections supplement or expand the laws given in Exodus and Leviticus.

numerus clausus (Lat. "closed number"): Limitations imposed on persons of certain groups, especially Jews, on their participation in specific vocations, and in their acceptance to institutions of higher learning (both as students and as teachers). This was usual in Czarist Europe and became common in Eastern Europe between the two wars and subsequently in the USSR. Similar restrictions were sometimes tacitly applied at US universities.

numismatics see **coins**

nun (נ): Fourteenth letter of the Hebrew alphabet. Numerical value: 50. Pronounced *n*.

Nuremberg: German city, Jews settled there from the 12th cent., living mainly from moneylending in the Middle Ages. A synagogue was consecrated in 1296. They were massacred during the Rindfleisch outbreaks (1298) and the Black Death (1349). Protection of the Jews was used by the king and municipality for extortion. Church persecution culminated in an expulsion in 1499. A community was reestablished only in 1857. 9,000 Jews lived there before the Nazi period, when N. was one of the main centers of National Socialism. No Jews were left by 1942. In 1970, 290 Jews were living there.

nusah: Differing liturgical rites of various communities and groups. It may also refer to the musical mode to which the liturgy is sung.

Nuzi: Ancient city in Iraq. The town was inhabited by Hurrians, and excavations have revealed important discoveries, especially 4,000 tablets throwing light on the Bible and the biblical period.

Oath more Judaico, Special form of oath imposed on Jews during and after the Middle Ages. It was generally taken over a Scroll of the Law but was often accompanied by degrading circumstances such as standing on a sow's skin. The special Jewish oath was abolished in France in 1846 and in Germany during the 19th cent.; in Eastern Europe it was abolished somewhat later.

Obadiah: Fourth of the Minor Prophets. The shortest book of the Bible is called by his name and contains only one chapter foretelling the downfall of Edom. Its date is uncertain but is generally put at the period following the destruction of Jerusalem in 586 BCE.

Obadiah of Bertinoro (c. 1450–before 1516): Italian scholar. He left Italy for Palestine in 1485, and his descriptions of the journey and of Palestine are a major source of information on Jewish life at the time. In Jerusalem he was recognized as an outstanding authority, and he founded a yeshivah. He was the author of a commentary on the Mishnah, which became standard and was printed in almost all editions.

Ochs, Adolph Simon (1858–1935): US newspaper publisher. After successfully revitalizing the Chattanooga *Times*, he became the publisher of the New York *Times*, which he developed into a paper of international importance. He was succeeded by his son-in-law Arthur Hays Sulzberger.

Odel (Adel) (18th cent.): Only daughter of the BAAL SHEM TOV; mother of the *tzaddikim* BARUCH OF MEDZIBOZSH, and MOSES ḤAYYIM, EPHRAIM OF SUDILKOW. In Ḥasidic tradition, she is the ideal of noble womanhood.

Odessa: Port in Ukrainian SSR. Jews, mainly from Poland and Lithuania, lived there from the late 18th cent, playing an important role in its economic development. It had a wide network of Jewish schools. Many of the seminal figures of modern Hebrew literature lived there, and it was important in the Haskalah and in Zionism. Pogroms occurred frequently throughout the 19th and early 20th cent., and there was active Jewish self-defense. About 180,000 Jews were living there in 1941; many escaped but nearly all the 90,000 who remained were killed by the Germans. A new Jewish community was refounded after the war and numbered 117,000 in 1970.

Odets, Clifford (1906–1963): US playwright. His early plays were experimental, including *Waiting for Lefty* and *Awake and Sing,* expressing the hardships of the 1930s. His later successes included *Golden Boy* and *The Country Girl,* as well as numerous film scripts.

Offenbach,   Jacques (1819–1880): French composer. The son of a cantor in Cologne, O. lived in France from the age of 14, and became conductor of the Théâtre Française. He wrote over a hundred operettas, some of them—notably *Tales of Hoffmann*—winning lasting popularity.

Ohio: US state. The first congregation was organized in 1824 in Cincinnati, which remained the largest Jewish center throughout the 19th cent. Other early congregations were founded in Columbus (1838), Cleveland (1839), Dayton (1842), and Akron (1920). The Jewish population grew rapidly from the 1880s to the 1920s but since then has remained steady. The largest communities in 1976 were Cleveland (80,000), Cincinnati (30,000), Columbus 14,000), Toledo (7,500), Akron (6,500), and Dayton (6,000), bringing the total Jewish population to 161,350.

Oholot ("Tents"): Second tractate in the MISHNAH order of *Toharot,* with no *gemara* in either Talmud. It deals with the ritual impurity caused by a corpse.

Oistrakh, David (1908–1974): Russian violinist. He studied in Odessa and became professor at the Moscow State Conservatory in 1939 and director of its violin department in 1950. He won international renown, and the leading Soviet composers wrote works for him. His son *Igor* (1932–) has also a considerable reputation as a violinist.

Oklahoma: US state. Communities sprang up in the late 19th and early 20th cent., congregations being founded in Oklahoma City (1903), Ardmore (1907), Muskogee (1905), and Tulsa (1914). In 1976 there were 6,060 Jews in O., of whom 2,500 were in Tulsa and 1,500 in Oklahoma City.

olam ha-zeh, olam ha-ba ("this world, next world"): Talmudic terms, the former referring to the material world and the latter to the hereafter.

Old Testament see **Bible**

Olivetti: Italian family of industrialists. The firm was founded by *Camillo O.* (1868–1945), who introduced the production of typewriters. His son *Adriano O.* developed the firm and diversified its products.

omer ("sheaf"): An offering of the first sheaf cut in the barley harvest brought to the Temple on the second day of Passover. Only after sacrifice was made was it permitted to eat of the grain. Seven weeks are counted from the day of the offering, and the 50th day is the festival of SHAVUOT. The period of Counting the O. (Sephirat ha-Omer) is one of

semi-mourning for reasons that are obscure but which may be connected with the BAR KOKHBA events. During this time marriages may not be solemnized, except on LAG BA-OMER. The announcement of each day of the period is made in the course of the Evening Service, after an appropriate blessing has been recited.

Omri: King of Israel who reigned 882–871 BCE. He founded and pursued so vigorous a foreign policy that the Assyrians called the Kingdom of Israel after him for the rest of its history (I Kings 16).

oneg Shabbat ("Sabbath delight"): Name derived from the Bible (Is. 58:13) and applied to a Saturday-afternoon gathering —in modern times, especially those gatherings held for cultural purposes. The custom of the "third Sabbath meal" (*seudah shelishit*) eaten on this occasion was developed by the Ḥasidim, and its modern form was introduced into Palestine by Bialik.

Onkelos (1st or 2nd cent. CE): Translator of the Pentateuch into Aramaic (TARGUM O.). According to the Talmud, he was a proselyte. He has frequently been confused with AQUILA and some modern scholars believe that the Aramaic translation in fact emanated from Babylonia.

Ontario: Canadian province. Individual Jews were in the region from the early period of British settlement. The first synagogue was opened in 1856 in Toronto, which remained the main Jewish community and since the 1960s has also attracted Jews from Montreal. Jews settled throughout the province in many small towns and agricultural areas, but most of these communities disappeared after World War II. In 1971 the Jewish population was 135,190, with 110,-000 in Toronto, 7,500 in Ottawa, 4,000 in Hamilton, and 2,500 in Windsor.

Opatoshu, Joseph (1886–1954): Yiddish novelist and short-story writer. Born in Poland, he lived in the US from 1907, writing regularly for the Yiddish daily *Der Tog*. O. was one of the first Yiddish writers to describe American Jewish life. His historical novels were translated into many languages.

Ophel: Southern extremity of the eastern or Temple hill in Jerusalem. The name has been applied by archeologists to refer to the whole eastern hill of Old Jerusalem, including David's City.

Oppenheim (**Oppenheimer**), David (1664–1736): Rabbi and book collector; nephew of Samuel Oppenheimer. He was rabbi first of Moravia and then of Bohemia. His famous collection of books and manuscripts was purchased by Oxford's Bodleian Library.

Oppenheim, Moritz Daniel (1799–1882): German painter. His first pictures were largely on themes derived from the Old and New Testaments, but his later paintings depicted Jewish family life and customs.

Oppenheimer, Sir Ernest (1880–1957): S. African financier. He started his career at Kimberley and was an outstanding figure in the diamond business, becoming chairman of De Beers' Consolidated Mines. He was baptized. His son *Harry Frederick O.* (1908–　) has also been a leading figure in S. African economic life.

Oppenheimer, Franz (1864–1943): Political economist and sociologist. He was professor at Frankfort University until the Nazis came to power, when he went to the US. He influenced cooperative agriculture in Palestine, and the Merhavyah cooperative settlement, founded in 1911, was based on his ideas.

Oppenheimer, J. Robert (1904–1967): US physicist. He was professor of physics at the University of California and at the California Institute of Technology,

1929–47. During World War II he was in charge of the construction of the first atomic bomb. He was chairman of the US Atomic Energy Commission until 1954, when he was suspended because of his association with Communists in the late 1930s. The hearings on this subject were a *cause célèbre*. From 1947 to 1966 he was director of the Institute of Advanced Study at Princeton.

Oppenheimer, Joseph Suss (Jud Suss c. 1698–1738): Court Jew and financier in Germany. Appointed by the duke of Württemburg as his finance minister, he was so influential as to be the virtual ruler, earning him many enemies. After the death of the duke, he and other Stuttgart Jews were arrested. O. was tried, and subsequently hanged, on a charge of embezzling state incomes. He refused to be baptized in order to save himself.

Oppenheimer (Oppenheim), Samuel (1630–1703): Military contractor, financier, and court Jew in Austria. A favorite of Emperor Leopold I, whom he helped finance, he was the first Jew allowed to resettle in Vienna after the expulsion of 1670. As imperial war purveyor, he financed the government in various wars and was employed on diplomatic missions. He supported the poor and was a benefactor of Jewish scholarship.

Oral Law see **Law, Oral**

ordination (semikhah, "placing" [of hands]): In rabbinic law, the formal transmission of judicial authority. Traditionally Moses was ordained by God and Joshua by Moses (Num. 27:18). The master transmits authority by the laying on of hands. Thus the chain of authority was carried down from generation to generation (see *Avot* 1:1). Only a person duly ordained could ordain another. Any ordained scholar may ordain others. In ancient times, true ordination could be conferred only in Palestine. Consequently, when the Palestinian center virtually disappeared, the chain of o. came to an end. An attempt to revive it in the 16th cent. by Jacob BERAB evoked violent opposition, and the undertaking had to be abandoned. A form of o. was established in Europe in the 14th cent. The *semikhah* given to a modern rabbi, although called o., is different from the ancient form; it involves neither the laying on of hands nor the conferring of the special judicial authority that prevailed in talmudic times. It is rather the *hattarat horaah* ("permission to teach"), which confers competence to serve as a rabbi.

Oregon: US state. Jews

first arrived in the gold rush in the mid-19th cent., and a congregation was founded in Portland in 1858. In 1976, there were 8,685 Jews in Oregon, the only large community being in Portland, wtih 7,800 Jews.

organ: The introduction of the o. into the Sabbath synagogue service became a controversial issue between the Orthodox and the Reform movement in the 19th cent. The Orthodox opposition was based on the ban of playing musical instruments on the Sabbath, the prohibition on instrumental music in worship after the destruction of the Temple, and the association with "the customs of the gentiles." The o. became usual in Reform and some Conservative services. It is also found in many Italian and French synagogues. In the West, it came to be used for wedding and other weekday services, even in Orthodox congregations.

orlah ("uncircumcised"): (1) Fruit of young trees during the first three years of their producing, when it is prohibited to use the fruit. (2) Name of tenth tractate in the MISHNAH order of *Zeraim*, which deals with the laws of o. It has *gemara* in the Palestinian Talmud only.

Orloff, Hannah (1888–1968): Sculptor. Born in the Ukraine, she moved to Palestine at the age of 16 and to Paris at 22. She realistically sculpted portraits, animals, and other subjects.

Ormandy, Eugene (1899–): US conductor. Born in Budapest, he moved to the US in 1920. He conducted the Minneapolis Symphony Orchestra from 1931 to 1936, and thereafter he remained with the Philadelphia Orchestra, which, under his baton, was one of the outstanding orchestras in the US.

orphans: The Bible is greatly concerned with the upkeep of o. (Deut. 14:29; 24:19ff.). They are exempt from tax, and their property is regarded as sacred. The care of o. was always a principal object of Jewish charity, and special organizations called *giddul yetomim* ("upbringing of o.") were established to look after them. From the 19th cent., orphanages were set up in the larger communities.

ORT: Initials of Obshchestvo Rasprostraneniya Truda ("Society for Manual Work"), a worldwide organization to develop vocational training among Jews. It was founded in 1880 in Russia, where it initially worked on a small scale. After World War I the ORT network expanded throughout Europe and eventually spread to Arab lands and to Israel. Its head office is in Geneva.

Orthodoxy: Modern designation for the strictly traditional section of Jewry. The term is borrowed from Christian usage and was first applied by the Reform Jews somewhat disparagingly. Though widely diversified among its various groupings, its adherents all share a belief in the Divine revelation at Sinai and in the immutability of the Law decreed there. They reject any departures from traditional practice that cannot be justified and explained within the traditional framework. O. also challenges the dichotomy between ethical and ceremonial precepts. It has exhibited a reluctance to work with the non-Orthodox, and some Orthodox Jews have been concerned even more with opposing non-O. than in opposing non-Judaism. The relationship has become particularly strained in Israel. The Orthodox do not recognize non-Orthodox marriages, divorces, and conversions. To distinguish the modern type of O., developed by S. R. HIRSCH and A. HILDESHEIMER, from the ghetto-type of O., the term Neo-O. was coined.

OSE see **OZE.**

Ostia: Port near Rome, Italy. The ruin of a synagogue discovered there in 1961 dates from the first cent. CE and is the oldest known synagogue in Western Europe.

ostracon: Ancient inscribed potsherd. It was a common writing material in antiquity. Many have been found in Israeli excavations, bringing information on ancient Jewish life as well as on Hebrew epigraphy.

Ostropoler, Hirsch (18th cent.): Yiddish jester to the Hasidic rabbi Baruch of Medzibozh. His tales and witticisms became proverbial.

Othniel: First judge in Israel. He commanded the army that defeated the king of Aram-Naharaim, who had been oppressing the Israelites for 8 years (Judg. 3:8–11).

Ottawa: Capital of Canada. Jews began to settle there toward the end of the 19th cent. and the first synagogue was established in 1892. There are now 6 synagogues, a Jewish Community Council, and Jewish day schools. 6,000 Jews lived there in 1976.

Ottolenghi, Giuseppe (1838–1904): Italian soldier. He fought in the war against Austria. He was professor of military history, a senator, and, in 1902–03, minister of war.

Ottoman Empire see **Turkey.**

Oxford: City in England. Jews lived there in the

medieval period. In modern times, a Jewish community has existed only since 1840. Jews entered the university in 1854. The Jewish population was 600 in 1975.

OZE: Acronym for the Russian Obshchestvo Zdravookhranenia Evreyev ("Society for the Protection of the Health of the Jews"), an organization for medical and sanitary care among the Jews. Founded in 1912, it was originally concerned with the Jews of Eastern Europe, but later extended to various other parts of the Jewish world, including North Africa, Latin America, and Israel.

Ozick, Cynthia (1928–): US critic. She has published volumes of short stories (*The Pagan Rabbi*), and her writings deeply identify with current Jewish problems and the State of Israel.

Pale of Settlement: The territory to which Jewish right of residence was confined under the czar. For the most part it was limited to former Polish territory. Exemptions were given only to Jews who fell into special categories, such as high school graduates, wealthy merchants, skilled artisans, and ex-CANTONISTS. The declared object was to remove Jewish influence over Russians. If Jews were found outside its limits, their fate was determined by the local ruler. The system was instituted in 1791 and was abolished in effect in 1915 (legally, in March 1917).

Palestine: One of the names of the Land of Israel, originally used for the Land of the PHILISTINES. The name was used for the Roman province of the region. It was not an official name for many centuries until the time of the British Mandate.

Palestine Jewish Colonization Association see **Pica.**

Palestine Liberation Organization (PLO): Coordinating body mainly representing Palestinian refugee guerrilla groups. The largest group is Al-Fatah, whose leader, Yasir Arafat, has been chairman since 1968. Other groups represented include the Syrian-backed Al Saiqa and the Marxist Popular Front for the Liberation of Palestine, the latter led by George Habash. It is committed to dissolving the State of Israel, primarily by the use of armed force. The groups represented have carried out frequent acts of terror against Israeli civilian targets.

Palestine Office: Zionist institution established in Jaffa in 1908 and headed by Arthur Ruppin. It was the central agency for Zionist settlement activities.

Palestine Partition: Various plans were prepared during the latter period of the British Mandate for dividing Palestine into autonomous areas. A proposal of this nature was first advanced in 1937 by the Peel Commission, set up by the British government. It met with opposition in various quarters and came to nothing. In 1946 the Jewish Agency Executive agreed to negotiate on the basis of partition. In 1947, a majority of the United Nations Special Committee on Palestine put forward its plan for the partition of the country, which was accepted by the United Nations and came into operation on May 15, 1948, despite the armed opposition of the Arab states. The changes effected as a result of the fighting were incorporated into the armistice agreements signed in 1949 between Israel and her neighbors.

Palestine Talmud see **Talmud**

Palmah: Abbreviation for *peluggot mahatz* ("assault companies"), the striking force of the Haganah. It was established in 1941, and operated underground until 1948, when it became part of the Israeli army. Its commanders were Yitzhak SADEH (1941–43) and Yigal ALLON (1943–48). The P. was first established to aid the British in the event of Axis armies reaching Palestine. When that threat passed, it continued to exist as an underground force. In the 1945–48 period it concentrated on the organization of "illegal" immigration.

Panama: Jews who came in the early 19th cent. were assimilated. The first permanent settlers were Sephardim who arrived from the Caribbean in the mid-19th cent., and the first community was founded in 1876. Other groups came from Middle Eastern countries and from Eastern Europe. In 1976 there were 2,000 Jews, of whom 60% were Sephardim. The largest settlements are in Panama City (1,500) and Colón (500).

Paraguay: Jews who came in the late 19th cent. were assimilated. Individual Jews arrived before World War I, and a community was founded in 1917. The first group was from Palestine; later groups were of Polish, German, or Sephardi origin. Many moved on to Argentina. In 1976, 1,200 Jews were living there, almost all in Asunción. Of these, 95% are Ashkenazim. P. is reputedly a hideaway for a number of Nazi war criminals, including the Auschwitz doctor, Mengele.

Parah ("Cow"): Fourth tractate of the MISHNAH order of *Toharot*, dealing with the law of the RED HEIFER (Num. 19). It has no *gemara* in either Talmud.

parashah ("section"): (1) A section of the Bible dealing with a single topic. (2) Weekly portion of the Torah (SIDRA) read in the synagogue.

pardes ("garden," "paradise"): (1) Esoteric doctrines and speculations. (2) Mnemonic indicating four types of biblical exegesis—*peshat* (literal), *remez* (allegorical, often philosophical), *derash* (homiletic), and *sod* (mystical).

Paris: Capital city of FRANCE. Jews lived there in the 6th cent., and a settlement existed from the 10th cent. There was a RITUAL MURDER charge in 1179, an expulsion in 1182, and a return in 1198. In 1240, the Talmud was burned following a public disputation. The Jews of P., like those of the rest of France, were expelled in 1306 and finally banished in 1394. Thereafter very few Jews lived in the city until the 18th cent. The first syna-

gogue was established in 1788. After the Revolution, there was a considerable influx. In 1880 about 40,000 Jews lived there to be augmented by arrivals from Eastern Europe, and after 1933 from Germany. By 1939 there were about 150,000 Jews in the city, with a chief rabbi, many synagogues, and the central offices of all French Jewish institutions. Many left during World War II, and 45,000 were deported to their deaths. After the war, survivors from the rest of Europe arrived, as did immigrants from North Africa, so that in 1976, about 300,000 Jews lived in P.

parnas: The lay head of a Jewish congregation. Originally the p. combined religious and secular functions, but in the course of time a professional religious leadership emerged, and the p. was the lay leader.

parokhet: Curtain in front of the ark in Ashkenazi synagogues. The first p. was in the sanctuary in the wilderness and was made by Bezalel (Exod. 26:31).

partisans: Guerrilla movements in World War II. Many Jews participated in the partisan movement in various lands. In certain areas Jewish units were organized. In general, Jews worked within the national partisan movement, but even there anti-Semitism was encountered. In Eastern Europe, which was the main center for Jewish p., Jews often organized family camps in the forests to protect Jews who had escaped from the towns.

Partos, Ödön (1907–1977): Israeli musician. He was born in Hungary and settled in Tel Aviv. He led the viola section of the Israel Philharmonic Orchestra in 1938 and directed the Tel Aviv Music Conservatoire. His compositions were influenced by Near Eastern music.

parveh (Yiddish): Foods that are neither meat nor milk and may therefore be eaten with either, in accordance with the Jewish dietary laws.

paschal lamb see **Passover**

Passover (Pesah): Spring festival, first of the three Pilgrim Festivals. It begins on Nisan 15 and lasts for 7 days in Israel and in Reform circles, 8 days elsewhere. P. has a double origin—one historical, commemorating the Exodus from Egypt, and the other agricultural, marking the festival of the barley harvest. Alternative names for P. are the Festival of Freedom and the Festival of Unleavened Bread (which is its biblical name, marking the fact that consumption of leavened food is forbidden during its duration). The first and last day (outside Israel, the first

2 and last 2) are celebrated as full holidays; the intermediate days being Hol ha-Moed. In Temple times, the paschal lamb was slaughtered on the eve of P. and eaten on the first night. The successor to this is the SEDER service, held in the home on the first night (2 nights outside Israel), at which the HAGGADAH is recited. Full HALLEL is recited in the Morning Prayer on the first day (outside Israel, 2 days), and half HALLEL for the other days. A prayer for dew is inserted into the Additional Service on the first day. Ashkenazim read the *Song of Songs* on the intermediate Sabbath. The laws of the festival are discussed in the talmudic tractate *Pesahim*. The coincidence of P. with Easter led in the Middle Ages to the linking of the RITUAL MURDER accusation with this festival, which thereby became a time of fear. The SAMARITANS still sacrifice a paschal lamb at the P. celebrations on Mt. Gerizim near Nablus (Shechem).

Passover, second (*Pesah sheni*): Alternate Passover sacrifice, offered a month after P. on Iyyar 14 by those who had been unable to offer the original sacrifices through ritual impurity, or unavoidable absence from Jerusalem. It is marked today by the omission of supplicatory prayer (*taḥanun*) in the synagogue service.

Pasternak, Leonid Osipovich P. (1862–1945), Russian artist. His compositions include portraits, drawings, and watercolors. He left Russia in 1921 for Paris and lived his last years in Oxford. His son *Boris Leonidovich P.* (1890–1960), Russian author, wrote lyrical poems and translations of Shakespeare, Goethe, etc. He was awarded the Nobel Prize for Literature for the novel *Dr. Zhivago*, but refused to receive it. P. was baptized.

Patria: Ship which sank in Haifa Bay after being blown up by members of the Jewish underground in 1940. On board were 1,771 "illegal" immigrants, 202 immigrants and 50 members of the crew and police lost their lives.

patriarch see **nasi**

patriarchs (*avot*): The founding fathers of the Jewish peple: Abraham, Isaac, and Jacob. Their history is recorded in the Book of Genesis.

Pauker, Ana (1890–1960): Rumanian Communist. She became a Communist in the early 1920s and was imprisoned from 1936 to 1941. In 1947 she became Rumanian foreign minister, but she was arrested in 1952.

Paul (d. 65 CE): The "apostle to the gentiles." Originally a Jew named Saul from Tarsus in Asia Minor, he studied for some time with the patriarch Gamaliel I but was more familiar with Hellenism than with Palestinian Judaism. He wrote in Greek and drew his biblical sources from the Septuagint. At first he was an enthusiastic supporter of the Pharisees and a violent opponent of the Christians, but after a visionary experience on the road to Damascus, he was converted to the new Christian sect. He embarked on a missionary journey to Asia Minor and was largely responsible for Christianity becoming a world faith. Hc also evolved its theology, according to which the Divine promises to the Jews had been fulfilled and were to be replaced. Hence, unlike Jesus, he was prepared to abrogate Jewish law. Much of his thinking had its roots in Jewish thought, including the teachings of thc Dead Sea Sect.

paytan see **piyyut**

pe (פ): Seventeenth letter of the Hebrew alphabet. Numerical value: 80. Pronounced as *f* or, when punctuated with a *dagesh*, as *p*. It also is one of the letters to have a special final form (ף).

peace offering (*shelamim*): A sacrifice in the form of cattle or sheep offered as a votive offering, a freewill offering, on Shavuot, and other occasions. Certain portions were offered up; part went to the priests; and the remainder to the worshipers, who ate it in a communal meal.

Peah ("Corner"): Second tractate of the MISHNAH order of *Zeraim,* with *gemara* in the Palestinian Talmud only. It deals with the law that gleanings for the poor should be left at the corners of fields that were being harvested.

Peerce, Jan (1907–   ): US tenor. He appeared as soloist in concerts, with orchestras, and at the Metropolitan Opera. He also gave recitals of Jewish liturgical music and often conducted services.

Pekah: King of Israel, who ruled 734–732 BCE. He succeeded Pekahiah, whom he murdered in Samaria (II Kings 15:25). Together with Aram, he organized an anti-Assyrian alliance and attacked Judah, which invoked help from Assyria. As a result of the Assyrian intervention, Israel lost territory and citizens were deported. P. was murdered by Hoshea, who succeeded him.

Pekahiah: King of Israel, who ruled 736–734 BCE. Son and successor of Menahem, his brief reign was unsuccessful, and he was assassinated by a military group headed by Pekah.

Pekiin: Village in Upper Galilee. According to tradition, R. Simeon ben Yoḥai and his son hid there in a cave from the Romans for 13 years. According to local belief, Jewish residence there has been uninterrupted since Second Temple times.

Pennsylvania: US state. Jews of Sephardi origin were living in southeast P. before the end of the 17th cent. They were later joined by Jews of Central European origin, and there was a Jewish cemetery in Lancaster in 1747. Permanent Jewish settlement in Philadelphia dates from 1737, but a congregation was not formally established until the latter part of the century. Throughout the 18th cent., Jews spread throughout most of the state apart from western P., where significant settlement began only in the mid-19th cent. At first Jews lived in nearly all the small towns, but in the 20th cent. the tendency was to concentrate in the large towns. In 1976, the total Jewish population in the state was 496,650. Philadelphia remained the largest Jewish community, with 350,000 Jews, followed by Pittsburgh with 51,000.

Pentateuch see **Torah**
Pentecost see **Shavuot**
People(s) of the Book: Name given in the Koran to

the Jews and Christians, whose religions were drawn from the Scriptures. In the course of time, the phrase was applied especially to the Jews.

peot ("corners"): Sidelocks grown by Orthodox Jews in accordance with an interpretation of the biblical ban on removing the hair at the corners of the head (Lev. 19:27). It is customary among Ḥasidim and Orthodox Yemenites to let these grow completely uncut.

Perelman, Sidney Joseph (1904–1979): US humorous author. A regular contributor to *The New Yorker* magazine. His many published volumes include *Crazy Like a Fox* and *The Best of Perelman*. He also wrote for stage and screen.

Peretz, Isaac Leib (1852–1915): Yiddish writer. He started his career by writing works in Hebrew and Polish but changed to Yiddish in order to reach a wider audience. He worked in Warsaw as an employee in the Jewish Communal Bureau. He achieved wide popularity in the 1890s with his Ḥasidic Tales and other works, and in the early 1900s wrote a number of plays. He was the focus of the Yiddish literary movement and greatly influenced other Yiddish writers, echoing in his writings the miseries and hopes of the ordinary Jew.

Persia (Iran): The first connection with Jews came in the 6th cent. BCE, when Cyrus of P. conquered Babylonia and allowed the exiled Jews to return to Zion. For the next two centuries most Jews were under Persian rule —including, for a considerable time, those in the Land of Israel. The background to the Book of Esther is that Jews lived throughout the Persian Empire. Their position fluctuated, but there were persecutions under Zoroastrian rule. The Arab conquest in the 7th cent. meant that the situation of the Jews was similar to that in the rest of the caliphate. Among the Jews, sects in P. obtained support, such as that of Abu Issa Al-Isfahani in the 8th cent. and Karaism from the 9th cent., as well as the messianic movement of David Alroy. From the 16th cent., P. was under Shi'ite rule, and the Jews suffered persecution and discrimination. At the same time there was a creative life and Judeo-Persian literature developed. The Jewish community at Meshed was forced to convert to Islam in 1839, living for several generations as outward Muslims while secretly continuing to observe Judaism.

Many fled to other countries in western Asia. The general situation was depressed. At the end of the 19th cent., the ALLIANCE ISRAÉLITE UNIVERSELLE began to develop an educational network in P., and in the 20th cent. there was a normalization in the situation of the Jews. There was a tendency towards centralization in Teheran, and although there was still much poverty, there was a general rise in the condition of the Jews. By 1970, 53,000 Jews had left for Israel. The 1976 Jewish population was 80,000, of whom 50,000 were in Teheran, 8,000 in Shiraz, 4,000 in Isfahan and Abadan, and 3,000 in Hamadan; very few were left in rural areas.

Persky, Daniel (1887–1962): US Hebrew writer and editor. Born in Russia, he settled in 1906 in New York, where he taught Hebrew. He wrote a regular column in the weekly *Ha-Doar*, and was prominent in Hebrew-speaking circles in New York.

Peru: Marranos from Portugal helped to develop the country in the 16th cent., but the Inquisition persecuted them in the 17th cent. The modern community was founded after 1870 with settlers from Central Europe and North Africa. In 1976 there were 6,000 Jews, of whom 70% were Ashkenazim, 30% Sephardim. Nearly all the Jews live in Lima.

Perutz, Max Ferdinand (1914–): Biochemist. Born in Austria, he went to Cambridge, England, in 1936. He shared the 1962 Nobel Prize for Chemistry for his discovery of the molecular structure of hemoglobin and of myoglobin.

Pesah see **Passover**

Peshahim ("Paschal Lamb"): Third tractate in the MISHNAH order of *Moed*, with *gemara* in both Talmuds. It deals with the laws of Passover.

peshat: The literal meaning of the biblical text, as distinct from *derash*, the homiletic interpretation.

pesher ("explanation"): Name given to a number of biblical commentaries discovered among the Dead Sea Scrolls. *Pesharim* on various biblical texts have been discovered, interpreting them according to the theology of the Sect.

Peshitta: The Syriac version of the Bible (including the New Testament). P. means "simple" and it is so called because it was rendered directly from the Hebrew. Most of it is of Jewish origin and was made in the 1st to 2nd cent. CE. By the 3rd cent. it was the Bible of Syriac-speaking Christians.

Pesikta de-Rav Kahana

("Section of Rabbi Kahana"): Homiletic Midrash for holidays and special Sabbaths, probably dating from the 5th cent. CE. It was written in Palestine. The origin of the name is uncertain.

Pesikta Rabbati ("The Great Section"): Midrash comprising homilies for the holidays and special Sabbaths. It was probably compiled in Palestine in the 6th–7th cents. CE.

Pesuke de-Zimra ("Verses of Song"): Collection of hymns recited daily at the beginning of the Morning Service. The main components are Psalms 145–50 and Exod. 15. On Sabbaths and festivals, further readings are added. No *minyan* is required for their recitation.

Petah Tikvah: Israeli city. It was founded in 1883, after a previous attempt in 1878 had failed, and soon became a center of citriculture. Later it developed into an industrial center, eventually becoming part of the Tel Aviv urban area. Its population in 1971 was 87,200.

Pethahiah of Regensburg (12th cent.): German traveler. From 1175 he traveled through Poland, Russia, Armenia, Babylonia, Syria, and Palestine. The account of his journey, written down by Judah he-Hasid and others, is a classic of Jewish travel literature.

*Petliura, Simon (1879–1926): Ukrainian nationalist leader. Forces under his command in 1919–20 massacred over 16,000 Jews. P. was assassinated in Paris by Shalom Schwartzbard.

Pfefferkorn, Johannes Joseph (1469–after 1521): Apostate and agitator against the Jews. He was a butcher in Moravia but, after being convicted of burglary, went to Germany, where he was baptized at Cologne in c. 1504. He became virulently anti-Jewish and wrote anti-Jewish tractates. Maximilian appointed him to examine Jewish books and confiscate those that were anti-Christian. Six months later, the emperor was persuaded by the intervention of Christian humanists headed by Reuchlin to reverse his decision. There ensued a violent dispute between Reuchlin and P. Reuchlin was condemned by the Pope, but the attempt to confiscate Jewish books did not succeed.

pharaoh: Title given to kings of Egypt during the early dynasties. Several pharaohs are mentioned in the Bible.

Pharisees: One of the three main Jewish sects prior to 70 CE. They probably grew out of the Hasideans. They are distinguished from the other sects by their meticulous observance of the Oral Law. Although themselves a comparatively restricted group, they directed their activity to the masses, whom they sought to influence according to traditional doctrines. The P. kept themselves in separate groups, observed the rules of purity, and endeavored to extend their influence in Temple circles, which were dominated by their great rivals, the SADDUCEES. In their theology, the P. maintained a belief in the immortality of the soul and the resurrection of the body. Scribes of the P. conducted prayers in the synagogues and expounded the Scriptures. It has been suggested that the basis of the antagonism between the P. and the Sadducees was social. The P. were generally more lenient in their interpretations, and their reliance on the Oral Law gave their interpretations a more dynamic quality. The Pharisee tradition became the norm for later rabbinic Judaism. Because of the tendentious references in the New Testament, the term P. acquired an undeserved pejorative connotation.

Phasael (d. 40 BCE): Elder brother of Herod. He was a discreet and moderate governor of Jerusalem. When imprisoned by the Parthians, he committed suicide. Herod built the Tower of P. in the wall of Jerusalem, and this can still be seen as the basis of the "Tower of David."

Philadelphia: US city, in Pennsylvania. The first Jewish settlers arrived in 1737, and the oldest congregation, the Sephardi Mikveh Israel, was officially organized by 1773. A second congregation, Rodeph Shalom, was founded by German Jews in 1802. Jews from Eastern Europe poured in from the 1880s, and from 12,000 Jews in 1880, the community grew to 200,000 by 1915. P. is the seat of Dropsie University, Graetz College, and the Jewish Publication Society of America. The Jewish population was estimated at 350,000 in 1976, with over 100 congregations.

Philip (d. 34 CE): Son of Herod. In his father's will, he was appointed tetrarch, with territories in Transjordan. He was a good and just ruler. He married his niece SALOME.

Philippines: A number of Marranos lived there in the 16th and 17th cent. The modern community dates from the later 19th cent. Russian Jews came after World War I, and a synagogue was built in 1924. During World War II the Jewish community was deported or interned but was reestablished in 1945. In 1976 there were 200 Jews, almost all in Manila.

Philippson: German family of scholars and financiers. *Ludwig P.* (1811–1889), rabbi and author, officiated in Magdeburg. He believed in limited Reform, initiated several rabbinical conferences, and published a German translation of the Bible. His son *Martin P.* (1846–1916) was professor of history at Brussels University, of which he was appointed rector in 1890, but had to resign because he was a German. He returned to Germany and devoted himself to Jewish communal affairs. His brother *Franz P.* (1852–1929), a banker, was president of ICA from 1919. Another brother, *Alfred P.* (1864–1954), was professor of geography in Bonn. He survived deportation to Theresienstadt in World War II.

Philipson, David (1862–1949): US Reform rabbi. Born in Indiana, he was rabbi in Cincinnati from 1888 and a leading figure in the "classic" Reform movement in the US. He taught at Hebrew Union College and wrote on the Reform movement and on Jewish history.

Philistines: People of non-Semitic (probably Aegean) origin who settled in Palestine. Their main settlement was along the southern coastal plain, where they had five major cities— Gaza, Ascalon, Ashdod, Ekron, and Gath—and from there they moved inland. The invading Israelites at first found it impossible to dislodge them. It was only in the reign of David that they were pushed back to the coast. Thereafter they declined in significance and were no longer a threat. Their name, however, was preserved both in the name PALESTINE and in the familiar unfair application to a person devoid of any artistic sense.

Philo (c. 20 BCE–50 CE): Jewish philosopher in Alexandria, called Philo Judaeus by the Church fathers. Few details of his life are known, except that he headed a delegation of Alexandrian Jews to Rome in 40. His entire milieu was Hellenistic, and his thought is permeated with Greek philosophy, in particular that of Plato. He himself wrote allegorical commentaries on the Bible in a Platonic spirit. All his writings, including ethical treatises and a historical work, are in Greek. His major philosophical contribution is the doctrine of the *logos* radiating between God and the world. P.'s ideas were long forgotten in Jewish circles but played an important role in Christian patristic philosophy and in Neoplatonism.

philosophy: P. among Jews appears as a result of contact with other cultures, as an attempt to harmonize Judaism with contemporary thought (Neoplatonism, Aristotelianism, post-Kantian idealism, Existentialism, etc.). Indigenous Jewish thought did not express itself according to philosophical and theological systems and tended to be far more pragmatic. Philosophic thinking was first manifested in a Jewish framework in a Hellenistic context, the outstanding exponent being PHILO. However, the real flowering of Jewish p. came in the Medieval world out of the contact with Greco-Arab thought. The first great medieval Jewish philosopher was SAADIAH GAON, who introduced the main elements of the Arab Kalam school into Jewish p. The first Jewish philosopher in Europe, Solomon IBN GABIROL, was the outstanding exponent of Neoplatonism, which was current at the time and influenced various Jewish thinkers. BAHYA IBN PAKUDA drew on Kalam elements, but his major work concentrates more on ethical than metaphysical problems. JUDAH HA-LEVI wrote a philosophical work that was often critical of p. but largely followed Neoplatonic thought. Aristotelianism thereafter gradually became the dominant trend, first in Abraham IBN DAUD and reaching its climax in the most important work of medieval Jewish p., MAIMONIDES' *Guide of the Perplexed*. Maimonides' work caused great controversy, but eventually the pro-Maimonidists won out. Other medieval Aristotelians included LEVI BEN GERSHOM, HASDAI CRESCAS, and Joseph ALBO. From the 15th cent. there was little significant Jewish philosophical writing, except in Italy and Holland. It re-emerged in Central Europe with the emancipation, beginning with Moses MENDELSSOHN. Other outstanding names in 19th-cent. Germany included Solomon MAIMON, Nahman KROCHMAL, and Hermann COHEN, the last heading the school of Neo-Kantism and later devoting himself to Jewish thought. The modern existential trend had its leading Jewish philosopher in Franz ROSENZWEIG. The modern nationalist movement also produced philosophers, notably AHAD HA-AM. Martin BUBER, who spent the last part of his life in Israel, wrote on general Jewish p. Like the first Jewish philosopher, Philo, Buber had an impact on Christian religious thinking.

Phinehas: Priest; grandson of AARON. He succeeded his father, Eleazar, in the high priesthood. His action in killing an Israelite who had brought a Midianite woman into the encampment (Num. 25) was highly praised.

Phoenicians: Ancient Semitic seafaring people living in Phoenicia along the Syrian-Lebanese coast north of Mount Carmel. Their best-known centers were the ports of Sidon and Tyre. Their language was similar to Hebrew, and their alphabet was used by the ancient Hebrews. The Bible mentions frequent relations between P. and the Israelites, such as Solomon's agreement with Hiram of Tyre and Ahab's marriage with the Sidonian princess Jezebel, who endeavored to introduce Baal worship. The relations between the two has been illuminated also by the discovery of Ugaritic documents, which have thrown great light on Phoenician religion and civilization.

phylacteries see **tephillin**

Piatigorsky, Gregor (1903–1976): Cellist. Born in Moscow, he appeared at the Bolshoi Theater in Moscow in 1917–21, and the Berlin Philharmonic in 1924–28. In 1929, he settled in the US, where he taught at the Curtis Institute in Philadelphia and at Boston University.

PICA: Initials of Palestine Jewish Colonization Association, a society for Jewish settlement founded in Palestine by Baron Edmond de Rothschild after World War I to take over from ICA (JEWISH COLONIZATION ASSOCIATION) in administering settlements. In 1957, it was terminated and its property transferred to the State of Israel.

*****Pico della Mirandola, Giovanni** (1463–1494): Renaissance Italian humanist, philosopher, and student of Kabbalah. He studied with Jewish kabbalists and scholars and reached the conclusion that the basis of the truth of Christianity could be found in the Kabbalah. He was a pioneer in academic oriental studies.

Picon, Molly (1898–): Actress. Before World War II she was a popular Yiddish-speaking star of Polish stage and screen (*Yiddl mitn Fidl*). She was also a star and a popular entertainer in the New York theater, speaking both Yiddish and English.

pidyon ha-ben see **firstborn, redemption of**

pig: An animal forbidden to Jews as food (Lev. 11:7), it became the object of special abhorrence. It was even not called by name but referred to as "the other thing" (*davar aḥer*). In Israel, pig breeding is forbidden, except in non-Jewish areas of settlement.

Pijade, Mosa (1890–1957): Yugoslav politician. He was imprisoned for Communist activities from 1925 to 1939, during which time he translated Marx's *Kapital*. In World War II he was with Tito in the partisans. Afterward he was president of the Serbian Republic and chairman of the National Assembly.

pilgrimage: According to the Bible, pilgrimages had to be made to the Temple in Jerusalem on the occasion of the three Pilgrim Festivals, namely Passover, Weeks, and Tabernacles. Pilgrims were supposed to offer a special burnt offering on the occasion. The custom was popular, and after the split in the kingdom, rival shrines were established at Bethel as a counterattraction. The custom reached its peak in Second Temple times, when it was observed also by Jews who lived outside Palestine. After the destruction of the Temple, Jews throughout the ages tried to make pilgrimages to the Holy Land to see the hallowed sites and graves. The custom of p. has been revived in modern Israel, and Israeli Jews, particularly those from Oriental countries, make a point of visiting Jerusalem during the pilgrim festivals.

pilpul (from *pilpel,* "pepper"): Process of dialectical reasoning applied to the study of the Oral Law. This casuistic method, introduced by Jacob POLLAK, was prevalent in Poland from the 16th cent. It played an important role in Eastern European scholarship, although opposed by certain rabbis.

pinkas: Record book of Jewish community. Such records have proved of great value to modern historical research.

Pinsker, Simhah P. (1801–1864): Russian Hebraist and archeologist. He wrote on the Karaites and Karaite literature and made a study of the Babylonian system of Hebrew vocalization. His son *Judah Loeb (Leon) P.* (1821–1891) was a forerunner of political Zionism. A physician in Odessa, at first he strongly supported assimilation. But his views changed as a result of the 1881 pogroms, and the following year he published his *Auto-Emancipation,* which argued that Jews must be a nation with their own territory. Later he felt that Palestine should be that territory, and he joined the Hovevei Zion movement, of which he was elected president at the

Kattowitz Conference in 1884.

Pinski, David (1872–1959): Yiddish author. Born in Russia, he settled in the US in 1899 and from 1849 lived in Haifa. In the US he edited Yiddish newspapers and was active in Jewish cultural work. P. was a popular playwright, author of *Der Oitzer* and *The Eternal Jew*. His novels include *The House of Noah Eden*, which had an American-Jewish setting.

Pinter, Harold (1930–): British playwright. He was one of the most influential playwrights of the post-World War II period. His plays include *The Birthday Party*, *The Caretaker*, *The Homecoming*, and *Old Times*. He wrote a number of films directed by Joseph Losey (*Accident*, *The Go-Between*, *The Servant*).

Pirke Avot see **Avot**

Pirke de-Rabbi Eliezer: Midrash on early part of the Bible pseudepigraphically ascribed to R. Eliezer ben Hyrcanus, whose life is told in the first chapter. The work has in fact been dated to the 8th cent.

Pissaro, Camille P. (1830–1903), French Impressionist painter. His early work was influenced by the Barbizon School, his later, by the Impressionists. He was also influenced by pointillism, achieving light effects by broken color. All his sons became painters, including *Lucien* (1883–1944), who settled in England and was an Impressionist painter and typographer.

Pittsburgh: US city in Pennsylvania. Individual Jews settled there in the early 18th cent., but the first congregation dates from 1845. P. was the venue of the 1885 conference of Reform rabbis, who formulated the "P. Platform." There are now 51,000 Jews there.

pittum ha-ketoret ("the ingredients of the incense"): *Baraita* (*Ker.* 6a) describes the different types of incense offering in the Temple (Exod. 30:34–38). It is recited at the end of the Morning Service (among Sephardim, prior to the Afternoon Service).

piyyut: Synagogal poetry. It originated in Palestine, c. 5th cent. CE. The outstanding early *paytanim* (composers of *p.*) were Yose ben Yose, Yannai, Eleazar Kallir, and Phinehas. Their compositions were made for festival services. Later *paytanim* wrote in Babylonia and Western Europe. Israel Davidson, in his *Thesaurus of Medieval Hebrew Poetry*, lists 35,000 poems of p. type and 3,000 *paytanim* and poets. Many have been discovered in the Cairo *genizah*. Classes of p. are named according to their place in the prayer book; they include *yotzer* (in the first morning blessing before the *Shema*); *Ophan* (in the middle of the same blessing); *Zulat* (in the *Emet ve-Yatziv* prayer after the *Shema*); and *Kerovah* (in the first three blessings of the *Amidah*). P. are mainly recited on the Day of Atonement, when *selihot* poems are also read. P. is often written with an initial alphabetic acrostic to aid memorization. The creative flowering of this genre continued until the 18th cent. In modern times their use has been diminished both in order to shorten the service and because of the difficulty of their language.

Plagues, the Ten: Punishments inflicted by God on the Egyptians in order to force Pharaoh to release the Israelites from bondage. They were: (1) the Nile waters turned to blood; (2) frogs; (3) lice; (4) flies; (5) pestilence; (6) boils; (7) hail; (8) locusts; (9) darkness; (10) the killing of the firstborn (Exod. 7:14–12–34).

Poalei Agudat Israel ("AGUDAT ISRAEL Workers"): Orthodox religious labor movement founded in Lodz in 1922 as an affiliate of Agudat Israel. It is independent of its parent body and has joined Israeli coalition governments without Agudat Israel. It has two kibbutzim, several moshavim, and an affiliated youth movement, Ezra.

Poalei Zion ("Workers of Zion"): Socialist Zionist movement. The first such groups were founded at the beginning of the 20th cent., the main influences being Nahman Syrkin and Ber Borochov. A World Union was founded in 1907. The movement was a major stream within the World Zionist Organization. Inside Israel it formed a political party, with several splits and reunions, centering around the Mapai, Mapam, and Ahdut Avodah parties and, most recently, the Israel Labor Party.

Podhoretz, Norman (1930–): US author and editor. From 1960 he edited the magazine *Commentary*, making it an influential journal on the US Jewish intellectual scene. He has published essays and an autobiography, *Making It*.

Podolia: Region in Ukraine. The oldest community dates from the early 16th cent. Many were killed in the 1648 Chmielnicki uprising. Revived later in the century, it was the scene of strong Sabbetaian support and a center of Hasidism. Its Jews suffered severely in the pogroms after World War I.

Most of the community was killed in World War II. Several thousand Jews still live in the region.

pogrom: Anti-Jewish riot. The term is especially applied to the organized attacks on Jews in Russia from the early 1880s.

Poland: Jews lived there from the 9th cent. Little is known about the earliest Jews, but the real migration of Jews from the West started in the Crusader period. Charters of protection were issued in the 13th and 14th cents., guaranteeing Jews freedom of trade and transit as well as religion. But the growing power of the Church in time nullified most of the privileges accorded the Jews. There were RITUAL MURDER libels, charges of DESECRATION OF THE HOST, attacks, and legal restrictions (including confinement to special quarters). P. became a great and influential center of talmudic scholarship. The autonomous life of the community was directed by the COUNCIL OF THE FOUR LANDS. The Jewish reliance on the nobility made them suspect to the peasants, who joined the Cossacks under Chmielnicki in 1648–49 in extensive massacres of the Jews. Many were also killed in the Cossack Haidamak uprisings of 1768. The despair

of Polish Jewry at that period proved a fertile ground for mystical speculation, and the strong impact of SHABBETAI TZEVI had its followup in P. in the movement of Jacob FRANK. In the 18th cent. this atmosphere also engendered the rapid success of Hasidism. With the partitions of P., most of its Jews came under Russian rule. Jews were active in the Polish independence movement in the 19th cent. Strong anti-Semitism developed in the course of that century and continued to be reflected in official policies after P. gained its independence following World War I. Nevertheless P. was the great center of the Jewish people, with over 3,000,000 Jews living there in 1939. Under the Nazis, this community was almost entirely wiped out in the HOLOCAUST. They were herded into ghettos, subjected to mass shootings, and eventually transported to extermination camps (many in P.) to be gassed. After the war, most of those who had escaped and survived tried to leave the country, especially after a pogrom in Kielce in 1946. Those who remained were often strongly identified with the Communist regime. However, even the Jewish Communists were subjected to anti-Semitic purges in

1968–69, when most of the remaining Jews left. Only about 6,000 are still there.

Polanski, Roman (1933–): Film director. He started his career in Poland, where his films such as *A Knife in the Water* won international recognition. Later he went to Hollywood, where he specialized in the macabre, as in *Rosemary's Baby*.

Popper, Sir Karl Raimund (1902–): Philosopher. Born in Austria, he taught in New Zealand, 1937–45, and from 1945 at the London School of Economics. He holds that scientific theories can be accepted only provisionally and can be regarded as valid only as long as they are being subjected to fresh tests. His books include *The Logic of Discovery* and *The Open Society and its Enemies*.

Portugal: Jews lived there from at least the 4th cent. and when it was under Arab rule. After the Christian conquest, conditions were prosperous and many Jews had prominent positions at court. The community was well organized and headed by a chief rabbi (*arrabi mor*). After the expulsion from Spain in 1492, many of the refugees fled to neighboring P., but four years later Manoel II ordered the expulsion of all Jews. Instead of expelling them, he seized most of them and had almost the entire community forcibly baptized (1497). A large Marrano community was thereby created which was subsequently persecuted by the Inquisition, introduced in the 16th cent. Many Marranos fled from P., in order to return to Judaism (e.g., in Holland). Some Jews settled in P. at the end of the 18th cent., but freedom of worship was reestablished only in 1910. Some Marranos were found in northern P., and attempts were made to bring them back to Judaism, but little came of it. In 1976 P. had 600 Jews, mostly in Lisbon.

Potiphar: Chief of Pharaoh's bodyguard who bought Joseph from the Midianites and placed him in charge of his household. When Potiphar's wife "framed" Joseph, P. had him imprisoned (Gen. 37:36; 39:1).

Potofsky, Jacob Samuel (1894–): US labor leader. He was born in the Ukraine and went to the US in 1908, becoming a key figure in the Amalgamated Clothing Workers Union, of which he became president in 1946.

Prague: Capital of Czechoslovakia. Jews were living there in the 10th cent., and a community was in existence in the 11th cent.

From the early 13th cent. they had a Jewish quarter (the *Judenstadt*) with communal institutions and the Altneuschul synagogue and cemetery, which still remain and are among the oldest monuments in Europe. They suffered frequent persecution, including expulsion in the 14th-15th cent. Jews were exiled in 1745–48. The golden age of P. Jewry was from the 16th to 18th cent., when the community was an outstanding center of Jewish learning, its rabbis including JUDAH LÖW BEN BEZALEL (the creator of the legendary GOLEM). The Jews received equal rights in 1848, and in 1852 the ghetto was abolished. Under independent Czechoslovakia between the two world wars, the community flourished, and Jews participated disproportionately in all aspects of cultural life. The Nazis liquidated P. Jewry; the 56,000 Jews in the city in 1939 were nearly all exterminated by the end of the war. Subsequently a new community was established, numbering 3,000 in 1973.

prayer: The Bible contains many individual prayers, and most of the Psalms are prayers. The institution of set formulas, however, is attributed to the post-exilic Men of the Great Synagogue. Prayer became fixed at three regular daily prayers (corresponding to three sacrifices in Temple times), with an additional prayer on Sabbaths and festivals and a fifth prayer on the Day of Atonement. Each of these services centered around the recitation of the AMIDAH. Many additions were made over the centuries, and the recitation of the *Shema* with the concomitant blessings was added to the Morning and Evening Services. While praying, the congregation turns toward Jerusalem, and those in Jerusalem to the Temple site. Prayer was originally led in the synagogue by a member of the community (*sheliah tzibbur*), but later a class of professional prayer leaders (*hazzan*) emerged. The book containing the prayers is a SIDDUR: the festival prayer book is the MAHZOR. Differences grew up between prayer rites in different regions. P. may be in public or on one's own, although certain prayers can only be said in a congregation of ten males (MINYAN).

press: The earliest Jewish newspaper was the Spanish *Gazeta de Amsterdam*, which appeared in 1672; it was followed by the Yiddish *Kurant*, also in Amsterdam, in 1686–87. Other Yiddish and rabbinical journals appeared in the 18th cent., and in 1784 the literary monthly *Ha-Measseph* was founded by Moses MENDELSSOHN. Periodicals in the modern sense appeared in many places in Europe throughout the 19th cent. The oldest surviving Jewish periodical is the *Jewish Chronicle*, appearing in London since 1841. Yiddish newspapers appeared from the mid-19th cent. The Hebrew p. developed in Palestine and later in Europe from the mid-19th cent. with the publication of weeklies devoted to news and literary compositions. It is in Israel that the Hebrew p. is now centered. Europe ceased to be a major center of the Jewish p. in World War II. Nearly half of the Jewish papers are now in Israel, with a quarter of these in Yiddish, but the Yiddish p. is declining.

Pressburg see **Bratislava**

Previn, André (1929–): Musician. Born in Berlin, he was brought up in Paris and lived in the US from 1939. He made his name as a jazz and classical pianist and composed music for many films. He conducted the Houston Symphony Orchestra and the London Symphony Orchestra.

priestly blessing (*birkat-ha-kohanim*): Benediction recited by priests as prescribed in Num. 6:24–26. It was recited daily in the Temple and subsequently in the synagogue when it was introduced into the AMIDAH of the Morning and Additional Services. It is recited by the priests in the congregation on festivals and the Day of Atonement, but in Israel the priests say it daily. Before reciting the blessing the priests have their hands washed by Levites and remove their shoes. The ceremony has been abolished in Reform services but its blessing is said by the rabbi; in Conservative congregations, it is optional.

priests and priesthood: The male descendants of AARON, from the tribe of Levi, were designated as priests with hereditary functions as mediators between man and God. The priests were not allowed to possess land but received 24 priestly privileges, such as sacrifices, tithes, first fruits, redemption money for firstborn, etc. They devoted themselves to teaching and officiating in the Temple. The high priest was also charged with divination through the URIM AND THUMMIM. Priestly service required meticulous observance of the laws of ritual purity. There were also strict laws regarding those whom they were permitted to marry—laws still valid for their descendants. In Second Temple times, the wealthy and aristocratic priests joined the Sadducees. In post-Temple times the p. (*kohan*) is granted precedence in certain ritual matters, such as being called to the Reading of the Torah and the recital of grace after meals.

Prinz, Joachim (1902–): Rabbi. He officiated in Berlin until 1937, when he went to the US and became a rabbi in Newark. P. was president of the American Jewish Congress in 1958–66.

procurator: Roman official, governor of Jude under the Roman emperors 6–66 CE. They had the status of governors but were subordinate to the Roman legate in Syria. Their usual residence was in Caesarea. On Jewish festivals, they lived in Jerusalem.

prophets and prophecy: Prophets in the Jewish tradition were essentially inspired individuals chosen by God to convey His message to men and to give guidance for the future. Their work differed from prophecy among other ancient peoples in that the prophet was first and foremost a messenger of monotheism and morality. As the Israelites believed they were Divinely chosen, prophecy was confined to their number, although on occasion a heathen could be inspired (e.g., BALAAM). MOSES was regarded as a prophet in a class apart. The p. who suc-

ceeded him were religious leaders guiding the nation in times of stress (e.g., DEBORAH, SAMUEL). Under the monarchy, a prime task of the prophet was to guide the king and keep him on the correct religious and moral path. This included sharp opposition to any manifestation of paganism (ELIJAH, ELISHA). From the 8th cent., there emerged the literary p., whose prophecies were committed to writing and incorporated in the "Prophets" (Neviim) section of the Bible. The first were AMOS and HOSEA, and the outstanding ones were ISAIAH, JEREMIAH, and EZEKIEL. During the early Second Temple period, prophecy had its final flowering with HAGGAI, ZECHARIAH, and MELACHI. Thereafter, according to the rabbis, "the spirit of prophecy departed from Israel" (*Sot.* 48b). The prophets often foresaw national disaster and urged the people and its leaders to change their ways. At times, it appears they stressed that mere ritual was a mockery without proper ethical behavior, this led to the view that prophetic Judaism was even a rival of the Judaism of the priests, although in fact, the prophets do not decry ritual as such. The p. also gave visions concerning the End of Days and the ultimate triumph of the word of God through His people, Israel.

prosbul (abbr. of Gk. "before the assembly of counselors"): Legal formula annulling the release of debts in the Sabbatical year. As all bans are canceled by the Sabbatical Year, they became increasingly difficult to obtain as the Sabbatical Year drew near. To avoid hardship, HILLEL devised the p., by which the creditor makes over the debt to the court; it is thereby not canceled, as the annulment applies only to private loans.

proselytes: Converts to Judaism have been known since Bible times. The rabbis distinguished two types: (1) the half-proselyte (*ger toshav*) who undertook some of the basic principles (but not the ritual), and (2) the full proselyte (*ger tzedek*), converting out of pure love for Judaism, who accepted all its laws and ceremonies. In the course of time, only the second type was accepted. Special praise was given to converts, and they are the subject of a special blessing in the AMIDAH. Sincerity of motive is an essential prerequisite, and rabbis are instructed initially to dissuade potential converts so as to assure themselves of their sincerity. Conversion implies a ritual bath and, for men, circumcision. In Second Temple times, Judaism was an actively proselytizing religion. The Edomites were forcibly converted, while Jewish missionaries traveled through the classical world. However, anti-Jewish legislation, especially by Christian emperors, made proselytization dangerous, and on occasion, the dangers involved even evoked a negative attitude to converts. Conversion to Judaism was decreed a criminal offense. Jews therefore ceased to attempt to convert. A notable conversion movement in the Middle Ages was that of the Khazars. It is only in the 20th cent. that there has again been a considerable number of converts, especially in the US. Some of these result from a sincere conversion to the Jewish faith; others are often connected with marriage to a Jewish partner. Some of the strict laws of conversion have been relaxed under Reform auspices. The convert ranks as a full member of the Jewish people; the only disability is a ban on a priest marrying a female proselyte.

Proskauer, Joseph Meyer (1877–1971): US jurist and communal leader. He was a justice in the New York Supreme Court (1923) and president of the American Jewish Committee (1943–49).

Protestantism: Religious movement originating with the Reformation and "protesting" the authority of the Catholic Church. Hopes of early Protestant leaders that their form of CHRISTIANITY would attract Jews were soon shown to be unfounded (and in some cases, such as LUTHER, there were violent anti-Jewish reactions). Some forms of P. remained hostile to Jews; others, often strongly influenced by the Hebrew Bible (as in Holland and Britain), were extremely tolerant. However, the fundamentalism of P. involved the hope for the conversion of the Jews, and many of these churches undertook missionary activities. After World War II, Protestant churches participated in the Jewish-Christian dialogue, but sharp differences often remained.

Protocols of the Elders of Zion see "Elders of Zion"

Proust, Marcel (1871–1922): French author. A half-Jew, raised as a Catholic, he was strongly influenced by his Jewish mother and his many Jewish acquaintances. His great work À la Recherche du temps perdu contains a number of major Jewish characters, notably Charles Swann.

Provence: Ancient province of France on the Mediterranean. Jews lived there at least from the 1st cent. CE. Early settlements included Arles and Marseilles.

By the 14th cent., there were many communities in P., which was an outstanding center of Jewish scholarship, religious and secular. The situation deteriorated when P. was annexed by the French crown in 1481, and expulsions ensued (except in the COMTAT VENAISSON under papal rule). In the 18th cent. Jews returned to P., but —apart from Marseilles— communities were only refounded with the North African immigration in the 1950s and 1960s.

Proverbs, Book of (*Sepher Mishle*): Second book in the Hagiographa section of the Bible. It belongs to the WISDOM LITERATURE genre. Its 31 chapters contain collections of didactic aphorisms, generally of an optimistic nature. The opening of the book ascribes its authorship to Solomon, but this does not apply to the entire book; the Talmud placed its redaction in the period of the Great Assembly.

Prussia: Former German kingdom. The modern community dates from 1671, when Jews expelled from Austria were admitted. A synagogue was permitted in BERLIN in 1712. Frederick the Great removed commercial restrictions. In the aftermath of the French Revolution, conditions improved. In

1812, almost all disabilities on Jews were removed. After 1871, the history of Prussian Jewry becomes part of that of the Jews of GERMANY.

Psalms (*Tehillim*): First work in the Hagiographa section of the Bible. It contains 150 sacred poems, divided into 5 books (1–41; 42–72; 73–89; 90–106; 107–150). The collection is traditionally associated with King David, who is indicated as author in 74 p. Certain other authors are mentioned for some individual p. Some of the p. are alphabetic acrostics; others have refrains. Apparently some were recited by the congregation, others by the individual. Early biblical criticisms assigned a post-Exilic date to the composition of the book, but later scholarship—influenced by increased knowledge of Near Eastern literature—regards the work as pre-Exilic, and at least some of the p. are dated to David's time. By Second Temple times, the book was used in the synagogue, where it has continued to feature prominently in the liturgy. It has also played a major part in the liturgy of the Christian Church. In general the p. have had a widespread religious and literary influence.

Psalms of Solomon: Pseudepigraphical collection of 18 psalms attributed to King Solomon. They were in fact written 70–40 BCE. Extant only in a Greek version, their original languages are Hebrew or Aramaic. The format is of the general eschatological literature of that period.

Pseudepigrapha see **Apocrypha**

Pulitzer, Joseph (1847–1911): Newspaper publisher. Son of a Jewish father, he was born in Hungary and went to the US in 1864. He owned the St. Louis *Post-Dispatch* from 1878, and the New York *World* from 1883. He endowed the Columbia University School of Journalism and the Pulitzer Prizes for journalism and other writings.

Pumbedita: City in northern Babylonia on the Euphrates. For eight centuries it was the seat of an important ACADEMY, rivaled only by that of SURA. It was founded by Judah ben Ezekiel in 259. It continued the tradition of NEHARDEA, playing a major role in the formulation of the Babylonian Talmud. In the 9th cent. it was transferred to Baghdad, where is was of great importance under SHERIRA and HAI. It closed with the latter's death in 1038.

punishment: The following types of p. are provided for in Jewish law: (1) death by stoning, burning, beheading, or strangulation; (2) *karet* (opinions differ as to whether this means premature death or childlessness); (3) death at the hands of Heaven; (4) banishment; (5) corporal punishment; (6) fines; (7) servitude; (8) imprisonment; and (9) excommunication. In biblical times, the penalty for inadvertent manslaughter was exile to a city of refuge. Capital punishment ceased to be inflicted by Jewish courts in Second Temple times. Corporal punishment is applicable where biblical laws are transgressed. Offenses against property are punishable only by imposition of fines. Personal injury requires financial restitution. A minor is not liable for any p.

Purim: Festival instituted according to the Book of ESTHER—to celebrate the deliverance of the Jews of the Persian Empire from destruction at the hands of Haman, the vizier of King Ahasuerus, through the intervention of the king's Jewish consort, Esther. It is related that the Jews were due to be killed on Adar 13, but on that date their enemies were routed, and the following day, Adar 14, was observed as the day of deliverance and subsequently as the date of P. As the deliverance in the walled city of Shushan occurred a day later, P. is observed a day later in places that were ancient walled cities (e.g., Jerusalem) and is known as Shushan P. The Book of Esther is read in the Synagogue at the Evening and Morning Services. The *Al ha-Nissim* prayer is recited in the AMIDAH and the grace after meals. Other P. customs are the carnival and dressing in costume; the sending of gifts; and the Purim meal, when inebriation is encouraged. From the Middle Ages, it became customary to present plays on P. in Europe; the usual theme was the Book of Esther, but earlier Bible stories were also dramatized. In a leap year, P. is observed in Second Adar. The laws of P. are discussed in the tractate MEGILLAH. In many communities, special Purims were observed to mark the anniversary of local deliverance from dangers.

purity ritual: Ritual purity and impurity are basic concepts in ancient Judaism. A thing that is pure can be ritually defiled in various ways, such as contact with a dead body, seminal emission, or with a menstruant woman. Rites of purification include ritual bathing in some cases; sacrifices in others; and the ritual of the RED HEIFER in others. Persons in a state of impurity must not touch holy objects or enter the Temple precincts. Ritual purity connected with the Temple have not been operative since its destruction.

Quebec: Canadian province. Jews were excluded from Q. under the French, and arrived only under the British. In 1881, there were less than 1,000 Jews in the province, but there was a rapid rise thereafter, with Montreal being the focus of Jewish settlement. In 1971, there were 115,990 Jews there, with 113,000 in Montreal. In the framework of the province's educational system, young Jews tended to attend Protestant-sponsored schools or latterly, Jewish Day schools, and were among the English-speaking population. Jews from North Africa who settled there in the 1960s constituted an exception, as French was their native tongue.

Queen of Sheba: Ruler from southern Arabia who visited Solomon (I Kings 10:1–10). See SHEBA.

Qumran: Region on northwest shore of Dead Sea where the DEAD SEA SCROLLS were found in caves in the hillside. Subsequent excavations revealed remains of a large building, presumably occupied by members of the sect responsible for the Scrolls. It was occupied until 68 CE. A nearby cemetery was also discovered.

Rabbanites: Jews who accept the rabbinical interpretation of Jewish law. The name was given to them in the Middle Ages by their opponents, the KARAITES.

Rabbath Ammon (Rabbah): Ancient city in Transjordan, called Philadelphia in the Hellenistic period; today it is Amman, the capital of Jordan. A city of the AMMONITES, it was captured by David (II Sam. 11–12), but after his death, it was again independent. In Roman times, it was a city of the DECAPOLIS. Jews lived there in biblical and Second Temple times.

Rabbenu Tam see **Jacob ben Meir Tam**

rabbi ("my master", "teacher": Title originally used for sages but later for any person qualified to give decisions on Jewish law. From the 1st to the 5th cent. CE, it was used only in Palestine (in Babylonia, the corresponding title was *rav*). In medieval times, the r. had considerable power in the community. The concept of a salaried r. dates only from the 15th cent. (although the *dayyan*, or judge, was salaried much earlier). Some rabbis achieved an international reputation, and their authority spread far beyond their congregations. In some countries, the appointment of a r. had to be confirmed by the civil authorities. The main duties of the r. were to decide legal questions within the scope of Jewish law, supervise religious institutions, and, in many cases, also to head a talmudical college. With emancipation, the r. in the Western world was expected to have also a secular education, and RABBINICAL SEMINARIES were established. There was a shift in functions; now the r. was expected to preach regularly, conduct pastoral duties, and also be a Jewish representative vis-à-vis non-Jews.

Rabbi see **Judah ha-Nasi**

Rabbinical Alliance of America (Iggud ha-Rabbanim): Association of Orthodox rabbis founded in 1944. Its membership numbers 250.

Rabbinical Assembly of America: The rabbinical arm of the Conservative movement. Organized in 1901, it has over 900 members, primarily in the US and Canada. It places rabbis in synagogues, has various committees (law, family, etc.), and publishes the quarterly *Conservative Judaism*.

Rabbinical Council of America: Organization of Orthodox rabbis in North America. It was founded in 1923 by the more modern English-speaking rabbis who were dissatisfied with the framework of the Union of Orthodox Rabbis, which was dominated by the Yiddish-speaking Eastern European element. It has 900 members.

Rabbinical Seminaries: In the conditions of emancipation in the 19th cent., there emerged the need for training rabbis to meet the new conditions which were not being met by the traditional yeshivot. This required a secular education as well as a broader spectrum of Jewish subjects. Such seminaries were therefore founded in Europe and the US. The first was the Instituto Rabbinico, founded in Padua in 1829. Two years later the Seminaire Israélite was founded at Metz. Important seminaries were founded in Berlin and Breslau in Germany, in Austria, Hungary, England, and so on. In the US the Reform HEBREW UNION COLLEGE was established in Cincinnati in 1875; the Conservative JEWISH THEOLOGICAL SEMINARY in New York in 1886; the Orthodox Rabbi Isaac Elchanan Theological Seminary (later part of YESHIVA UNIVERSITY) in New York in 1896; the Reform JEWISH INSTITUTE OF RELIGION in New York in 1928 (later merged with the Hebrew Union College); and the Reconstructionist Rabbinical College in Philadelphia in 1970.

Rabi, Isador Isaac (1898–): US physicist. He was professor of physics at Columbia University, New York, from 1937 and chairman of the general advisory committee of the US Atomic

Energy Committee from 1953. He was awarded the 1944 Nobel Prize in Physics for his research in molecular beams.

Rabin, Yitzhak (1922–): Israeli soldier and statesman. He served in the Palmaḥ, in various positions in the Israeli army, and in 1964 as chief of staff. In this capacity he commanded the Israel forces in the 1967 Six-Day War. From 1968 to 1973 he was Israel's ambassador to the US. He was prime minister of Israel, 1974–77.

Rachel: Matriarch of the Jewish people, favorite wife of JACOB. She was the daughter of LABAN and lived at Aram-Naharaim. Jacob worked for Laban for fourteen years in order to marry her. She was the mother of Jacob and Benjamin, dying in childbirth. Her traditional tomb near Bethlehem has been a site for Jewish pilgrimage. The domed building over it was built in the 18th cent.

Rachel (Rachel Bluwstein) (1890–1931): Hebrew poet. Born in Russia, she went to Palestine in 1909 and settled by Lake Kinneret, the subject of her best-known poem. She wrote simple, nostalgic poems.

Rachel (stage name of Eliza Rachel Felix; 1821–1858): French actress. The oustanding tragedienne of her time, she played in the Comédie Française and achieved fame, notably in the French classics, such as the works of Corneille and Racine.

Radanites: Jewish merchant travelers who in the 9th cent. journeyed between France and China. They went via various trade routes which covered Europe, North Africa, and Asia.

Radek, Karl (1885–c. 1939): Russian Communist. He accompanied Lenin on his famous journey from Switzerland in 1917 and from 1922 was an official of the Communist International. He was expelled from the Communist Party in 1927 but was readmitted following recantation in 1930. In 1937, he was arrested and imprisoned and was not heard of again.

rain, prayer for: Petition recited in the Additional Service on Shemini Atzeret. In many congregations, the cantor clothes himself in white for this service. Liturgical poets wrote special compositions for this occasion. A brief petition for rain (MASHIV HA-RUAḤ) is inserted into the AMIDAH during the winter.

RAKAḤ (Hebrew initials for "New Communist List"): Israeli Communist Party. R. supports Russian policy in the Middle East, and it derives most of its support from Israeli Arabs. See KNESSET.

Rakosi, Matyas (1892–1971): Hungarian Communist politician. He took part in Béla Kun's 1919 Communist republic, and became secretary of the Comintern in 1920. He was imprisoned in 1933, freed in 1940, was in the USSR during World War II, and returned to Hungary in 1945, serving as secretary of the Hungarian Communist Party until 1956 and, for a time, premier of Hungary. In 1963 he was expelled from the Communist Party.

Ralbag see **Levi ben Gershom**

Ramat Gan: Town in Israel. Founded in 1921, it developed into the 4th city of the country, bordering Tel Aviv. It has various industries and the Diamond Bourse, and also numerous public gardens, including the National Park. Its population in 1974 was 120,000.

Ramat ha-Golan see **Golan**

Ramat Rachel: Israeli kibbutz on outskirts of Jerusalem. It was founded in 1921 by a group of the Gedud ha-Avodah, and moved to its present site in 1926. Its resistance during the 1948 War of Independence was decisive in protecting Jewish Jerusalem. Excavations on the site have uncovered a palace from the period of the kingdom, which has been identified with the biblical Beth ha-Kerem.

Rambam see **Moses ben Maimon**

Ramban see **Moses ben Nahman**

Ramhal see **Luzzatto, Moses Hayyim**

Ramleh: Israeli city, east of Tel Aviv. Founded by the Arabs in 716, it became the capital of Palestine. Its Jewish community dispersed under the Crusaders. In 1948 it was occupied by Israeli forces, and many immigrants settled there in the following years. The population in 1974 was 36,300.

Ran see **Gerondi, Rabbenu Nissim**

Rapoport, Solomon Judah Leib (1790–1867): Scholar, called Shir. Born in Galicia, he served as rabbi in Tarnopol and Prague. R. was a pioneer of the WISSENSCHAFT movement, and he made many contributions to scholarship. His researches covered many subjects in Jewish history and culture.

Rashba see **Adret, Solomon ben Meir**

Rashbam see **Samuel ben Meir**

Rashbash see **Duran, Solomon ben Simeon**

Rashbatz see **Duran, Simeon ben Tzemah**

Rashi (R. Solomon Yitzhaki) (1040–1105): French biblical and rabbinical commentator. He studied in Mainz and Worms, and then returned to his native Troyes, where he founded his own academy. Rashi's two great works are his commentary on the Bible and his commentary on the Babylonian Talmud, both of which revolutionized Jewish study. They were the indispensable guides for all future students and were printed in nearly all editions of the Bible and Talmud. The commentary is brief and lucid, presenting the rational meaning of the text. Occasionally R. gives the French equivalent (*laaz*) of words in order to explain them. His Bible commentary was translated into Latin and also influenced Christian exegesis.

Rasminsky, Louis (1908–): Canadian economist. In 1955 he was appointed deputy governor and in 1961 governor of the Bank of Canada.

Rathenau, Walter (1867–1922): German statesman and philosopher. In 1915 he succeeded his father *Emil* (1838–1915) as head of the big German electrical corporation AEG. In 1921 he became minister of reconstruction in the German government, and in 1922 foreign minister. He was assassinated by right-wing extremists. He wrote philosophy and politics.

Rav see **Rabbi**

Rav (Abba Arikha) (3rd cent.): Babylonian AMORA who was ordained by JUDAH HA-NASI. He founded the academy of SURA. He and his colleague Samuel of the Nehardea Academy laid the foundations of the Babylonian Talmud. Where their opinions differ, those of R. are accepted in instances of ritual law.

Rava (d. 352): Babylonian AMORA. His discussions with his colleague ABBAYE are reported on most pages of the Talmud. Where they differed, R.'s views were accepted (except in 6 instances). He founded an academy at MAḤOZA, and after Abbaye's death, R. was the undisputed authority in Babylonia.

Reading of the Law see **Law, Reading of the**

Reading, Marquess of (Rufus Daniel Isaacs) (1869–1935): English jurist and statesman. He was a Liberal member of parliament, solicitor-general (1910), attorney-general (1910), and lord chief justice (1913). In 1918 he was ambassador to the US and in 1921–26 viceroy of India. In 1931 he was foreign secretary. He is the only English Jew to have been made a Marquess. His son, the 2nd marquess *Gerald Rufus Isaacs* (1889–1960), was minister of state for foreign affairs, 1953–57. His wife *Eva* (1896–1973), daughter of Alfred MOND, was chairman of the British Section of the World Jewish Congress.

rebbe: Term used for Ḥasidic leaders, spiritual guides, and teachers. It is a Yiddish form of "rabbi."

Rebekah: Matriarch of the Jewish people; wife of ISAAC; mother of ESAU and JACOB. As a result of her kindness, Abraham's servant invited her to return with him to be a bride to Abraham's son (Gen. 24). After many years of barrenness, she gave birth to twin boys. When these grew up, she supported the younger, Jacob, in his rivalry with the elder Esau.

Reconstructionism: Religious movement founded in 1934 in the US by Mordecai M. KAPLAN. It is intensely Zionist but at the same time believes that the Jewish people everywhere should be dedicated to a spiritual nationalism, with its center in Israel and an ongoing Diaspora. Religion must be organically related to the advance of human knowledge, and Jews should have freedom and variety to work out their religious practices. God is the power in the universe that impels or helps the Jew to achieve salvation or make the most of his life. Torah must include ethical culture, ritual enrichment, and aesthetic creativity. Judaism is a religious civilization. The liturgy is similar to that of the Conservatives, with appropriate supplementary texts. The movement has developed the Society for the Advancement of Judaism in New York, a rabbinical seminary in Philadelphia (founded 1967), and several synagogues elsewhere; it publishes a magazine called *Reconstructionist*.

red heifer (*parah adummah*): Sacrifice connected with the purification ritual for persons who have become ritually impure through contact with a corpse (Num. 19). The sacrificed animal was a r.h., which was without blemish and had never been yoked. Its carcass was buried and the ashes mixed with water; by sprinkling this "water of purification," ritual purity could be regained. The rabbis considered that the implied symbolism was probably beyond human comprehension.

Red Shield of David see **Magen David Adom**

Redak see **Kimḥi, David**

Reform Judaism: Religious trend advocating modification of Orthodox tradition in accordance with the requirements of contemporary life and thought. It began in early-19th-cent. Germany in reaction to the new situation of the Jew resulting from the emancipation. Early innovations included shorter services, use of the organ, and vernacular sermons. Some of the rabbis went to extremes and advocated complete severance from talmudic restrictions. The belief in a personal Messiah was relinquished, as was the hope of a return to Zion. Practices such as the dietary laws and covering the head during services were looked on as outmoded. The movement was adopted in the US, the first such congregation being at Charleston, S.C. In the latter part of the century the Reform movement organized the UNION OF AMERICAN HEBREW CONGREGATIONS, the HEBREW UNION COLLEGE, and the CENTRAL CONFERENCE OF AMERICAN RABBIS. The policy of US Reform was formulated in 1885 as the Pittsburgh Platform. In the 20th cent., many of the more extreme doctrines were modified, and a further formulation made in 1937 (the Columbus Platform) urged, rather than discouraged, the use of Hebrew, putting more emphasis on the traditional ceremonies and customs. Most marked was the change in attitude to Zionism. The initial opposition gradually disappeared, and the last vestiges disappeared with the Six-Day War. In the US there are over a million adherents in some 550 Reform temples.

Reformation: Many of the early reformers turned to the Old Testament in their struggle with Rome, and this involved an efflorescence of Hebrew studies in Europe. Luther initially hoped that he could win Jews over to his Reformed Christianity, but when this failed he gave vent to a vicious anti-Semitism. The R. had little initial effect on the Jews, but many Protestant countries excluded Jews. It was only in the course of time that a more benevolent attitude developed toward Jews in Protestant lands.

refuge, cities of see **cities of refuge**

Rehoboam: King of Judah, who ruled in 928–911 BCE. He was the son of Solomon and his successor. However, when he refused to accept demands to lower taxation, shortly after his accession, dissidents under JEROBOAM broke away and established the northern kingdom of Israel. During R.'s reign, the country was invaded and plundered by the Egyptian pharaoh Shishak.

Reḥovot: Town in central Israel, founded in 1890 by settlers from the First Aliyah. Its main economy was citriculture and, later, industry. Chaim WEIZMANN made his home in R. and established there the Daniel Sieff Institute (later the WEIZMANN INSTITUTE). The Agriculture Faculty of the Hebrew University is also in R., which had a 1974 population of 46,400.

Reichstein, Tadeusz (1897–): Swiss chemist. He was born in Poland and lived in Zurich from 1908. He headed the organic chemistry department of the University of Basle from 1946. He made the first total synthesis of a vitamin and was awarded the 1950 Nobel Prize for Medicine and Physiology for work on the suprarenal glands.

Reines, Isaac Jacob (1839–1915): Rabbi and founder of Mizrahi. He served as rabbi in Lithuanian communities and established yeshivot which incorporated secular studies. A leading member of Hibbat Zion, he became associated with Herzl and founded the religious Zionist movement Mizrahi in 1901 despite opposition from many Orthodox rabbis.

Reinhardt, Max (1873–1943): German stage producer and director. A major influence, he was responsible for innovations in design and production. From 1934 he lived in the US.

Rejoicing of the Law see **Simhat Torah**

Rema see **Isserles, Moses**

Remak see **Cordovero, Moses ben Jacob**

rending of clothes (*keriah*): The practice of rending garments as a sign for mourning is mentioned in the Bible (Gen. 37:29). In Jewish tradition, a person who is mourning a close relative makes a rent of a hand's breadth in depth in his clothes. If the mourning is for parents, it is never completely resewn. Orthodox Jews also rend their garments (1) when beholding the Temple site for the first time; (2) for a Scroll of the Law which has been burned, and (3) upon receiving news of a Jewish tragedy.

reparations and restitution: Monies paid after World War II to the victims or their heirs. The Federal German Republic agreed in 1952 to pay $735,000,000 reparations to Israel over a period of 12 years in compensation for the material damage caused to Jews for whom there were no heirs. A further $110,000,000 was paid to the CONFERENCE ON JEWISH MATERIAL CLAIMS AGAINST GERMANY. The agreement was fully kept and played an important role in developing Israel's economy at a crucial period. East Germany refused to discuss making reparations. Restitution was paid by the West German government also to individuals who suffered as a result of the Nazi regime. The question of restitution also arose in other countries where Jews suffered from anti-Semitic legislation. Generally speaking, elsewhere the attempts to obtain restitution were unsuccessful except in Austria, and the results there were only partially successful.

repentance (*teshuvah*): The Jewish concept of r. is a return to God and to the right path. Man was created with an evil inclination, to which r. is the antidote. The Day of Atonement fast brings pardon for sins, where there is r. It is believed that at this period God seals the fate of all individuals for the forthcoming year and r. —together with prayer and charity—can avert an unfavorable decision made by God. But sins committed against a fellow man can be atoned only after full restitution, reconciliation, and forgiveness. R. is a major theme of Jewish moralists and of the Musar Movement.

resh (ר): Twentieth letter of the Hebrew alphabet. Numerical value: 200. Pronounced as *r*.

resh galuta see **exilarch**

resh kallah ("head of the *kallah*"). Sage who preached publicly in the Babylonian academies. Initially he preached only at the *kallah* assemblies but later all the year round.

responsa: Answers to questions on halakhic subjects sent by rabbinic authorities to questioners. The term is generally used to cover replies from the gaonic period to the present time. About half a million r. have appeared in print, and efforts are being made now to index the vast corpus of material. The r. first became important when replies to questions received by the *gaonim* became a practical guide to custom and tradition throughout the Jewish world. The r. are a valuable source of information. For example, they contain much social and economic information, and one responsum from Amram Gaon constitutes in fact the first text of the prayer book. The impact of the r. was strongly marked in the standard codifications of Jewish law.

resurrection (*tehiyyat hametim*): The teaching that at some future period the bodies of the dead will be revived. Among Jews, such a belief began to develop toward the end of the biblical period, possibly under Persian influence. By the end of the Second Temple period it had become a basic belief among the Pharisees (but not among the Sadducees). The rabbis often connected r. with the messianic era, and Maimonides incorporated it as one of the Thirteen Principles of Faith, although his various pronouncements on the subject are ambivalent. Most Orthodox thinkers took it literally, but Reform Judaism has denied the literal interpretation and revised the liturgy accordingly. Other circles have tended to identify it with the immortality of the soul.

Retribution, Divine: Belief in D.R. implies the punishment of the wicked and the reward of the righteous in this world or the hereafter. It is related to the belief in Divine Justice. The Bible interprets Reward and Punishment in a this-world context, leading to the great dilemma uttered by Job. The rabbis tended increasingly to see Reward and Punishment in a next-world, or eschatological, context. They also developed the concept of vicarious suffering to account for the sufferings of the righteous. Medieval philosophers followed the rabbinical viewpoint, but many modern thinkers have endeavored to rationalize the concept.

Reuben: Eldest son of JACOB and LEAH. He tried to frustrate his brothers' evil designs against JOSEPH (Gen. 37). When Jacob learned that R. had had a relationship with his concubine Bilhah, he deprived him of his firstborn rights (Gen. 48–9). When the Israelites reached Canaan, the territory of the tribe of R. was in Transjordan. Although little is heard of it, it retained its identity and was one of the Ten Tribes exiled to Assyria after 721 BCE.

Reuveni, David (c. 1500– c. 1538): Adventurer. He came from the East, claiming to be an emissary of the Lost Ten Tribes and a forerunner of the Messiah. He was received by the Pope, who gave him letters to the king of Portugal. Here he joined up with Solomon MOLCHO. The two of them went to the Imperial Diet in Ratisbon to bring his plans before Charles V. R. was taken to Spain in chains and put to death in an *auto-da-fé*.

Revel, Bernard (1885– 1940): US Orthodox educator and scholar. Born in Lithuania, he went to the US in 1906. From 1915 he headed the Isaac Elchanan Yeshiva in New York, and in 1928 he founded Yeshiva College.

revelation: The act by which God manifests Him-

self to man. In the Bible
God is said to have appeared
to patriarchs and prophets.
The highest type of r. is the
Mosaic Law revealed at Sinai.
After the time of Moses, the
effect of r. was to increase
knowledge of the Law re-
ceived but never to change or
supplement it. In the talmudic period, a Divine voice
(BAT KOL) was said to have
issued forth on occasions to
indicate legal decisions. Reform theologians and rational
thinkers described r. as a sub-
jective experience or as a
continuous process throughout history; for Orthodox
Jews, however, r. ceased with
the end of the biblical period.

**Revisionist Zionists (Ha-
Tzohar)**: Movement founded
by Vladimir Jabotinsky in
1925. It advocated the establishment of a Jewish state on
both sides of the Jordan,
criticizing official Zionist policies for their timidity. It
split into two groups in 1933,
one founding the Jewish
State Party, which remained
within the world Zionist organization, and the other
being the R. who seceded
and established the New
Zionist Organization, which
existed until they returned to
the framework of the WZO
in 1946. From the Revisionist section of the Haganah
came the underground groups
IRGUN TZEVAI LEUMI and
LOHAME HERUT ISRAEL. Po-

litically, the successor of the
R. was the Herut party. The
affiliated youth movement is
BETAR.

Revue des Études Juives:
Scholarly Jewish journal appearing quarterly in Paris between 1880 and 1940 and ir-
regularly since World War
II.

**Reward and Punish-
ment see Retribution, Divine**

Rhode Island: US state.
The liberal religious laws of
R.I. encouraged early Jewish settlement and Dutch
Jews from Curaçao arrived
there already in 1658. The
famous Touro Synagogue in
Newport was dedicated in
1763. The community in
Providence was not founded
till 1855. In 1976, there
were 22,000 Jews in R.I.,
most of whom lived in Providence.

Rhodes: Greek Island in
the Aegean. Jews lived there
in the classical period, and
again from the 7th cent.
Spanish refugees settled there
after the expulsion from
Spain, and it became an important Sephardi center.
After 1912 the Italians endeavored to make R. a cultural center, and a rabbinical
college was established. Some
4,000 Jews lived there in
1937. Some succeeded in
leaving before the war; the
rest were deported to their
deaths in Auschwitz by the

Germans. Few Jews live there now.

Rhodesia: Jews were among the white pioneers in the country. Communities were organized in Bulawayo in 1894 and Salisbury in 1895. The central body is the Rhodesian Jewish Board of Deputies. There were 5,500 Jews there at the end of the 1960s, but in recent years their numbers have diminished. Most of the Jews are in Salisbury and Bulawayo.

Ribash see **Isaac ben Sheshet**

Ribicoff, Abraham A. (1919–): US statesman. He was a democratic member of Congress, 1949–52; governor of Connecticut, 1955–60; secretary of health, education and welfare under President Kennedy, 1961–62; and senator from Connecticut from 1962.

Ricardo, David (1772–1823): British economist. Member of a Sephardi family, he left the Jewish community after marrying a non-Jew. He was a Radical member of parliament in 1819–23. He was one of the founders of the science of political economy, and his book *Principles of Political Economy and Taxation* was of fundamental influence.

Rice, Elmer Leopold (1892–1967): US expressionist playwright. His plays included *The Adding Machine,* *Street Scene,* and *Dream Girl,* and he also wrote novels.

Richler, Mordecai (1931–): Canadian novelist. Born in Montreal, he moved to London in 1954. Many of his writings deal with Jewish life in Montreal. His novels include *The Apprenticeship of Duddy Kravitz, St. Urbain's Horsemen,* and *Cocksure.*

Rickover, Hyman George (1900–): US admiral, chief of the Naval Reactors Branch of the Atomic Energy Commission and assistant chief for nuclear propulsion of the US Navy's Bureau of Ships. He directed the planning and construction of the world's first atomic-powered ship, the submarine *Nautilus.*

Riesser, Gabriel (1806–1863): German advocate of Jewish emancipation. He was not allowed to practice as a lawyer because he was a Jew, and hence devoted himself to Jewish political and civil emancipation. This emancipation began in some states in the 1830s, and R. was admitted to the bar in 1843. In 1848 he was elected to the parliament at Frankfort, of which he was made vice-president. He was one of the deputation which offered the German crown to Frederick William IV. In 1859, he became the first Jewish judge in Germany.

Rif see **Alfasi, Isaac**

Riga: Capital of LATVIA. Only individual Jews lived there until the late 18th cent. Their numbers increased in the 19th cent., although their position was not fully legalized until 1893. Under Latvian independence (1918–40) there was a rich educational and cultural life. 40,000 Jews were living there at the time of the German occupation. A ghetto was established and the Jews (including the historian S. DUBNOW) were murdered. After the war the community was reestablished, and in 1969, 38,000 Jews were living there, many of whom subsequently emigrated to Israel.

rimmonim ("pomegranates"): Silver or gold adornments placed on top of rollers of Scrolls of the Law. They were originally made in the shape of pomegranates, and so were called r. among the Sephardim.

Rindfleisch Massacres: Anti-Jewish massacres in southern and central Germany in 1298 when 146 Jewish communities were annihilated. The massacres were instigated and led by a Bavarian knight, Rindfleisch.

Ringelblum, Emanuel (1900–1944): Historian. In World War II, he was confined in the Warsaw Ghetto, where he began a collection of documentary evidence dealing with the Holocaust. He himself was killed, but after the war, parts of the archives were recovered. They constitute a major source for Holocaust history.

Rio de Janeiro: City in Brazil. Small numbers of Marranos, mostly from Portugal, settled there from the 16th cent. but assimilated with the local population. Open Jewish settlement began in the early 19th cent., and Jews of Moroccan origin established a communal organization in 1846. There is now a Jewish population of 50,000.

rishon le-Zion ("first of Zion," from Is. 41:27): Title given to Sephardi head of rabbis in Israel, since the 17th cent.

Rishon-le-Zion: City in central Israel. It was founded in 1882 by Bilu pioneers—one of the first settlements in the modern period. The settlers were saved from bankruptcy by Baron Edmond de ROTHSCHILD. The production of grapes and wine became the economic mainstay. Later, industries were established. The population in 1974 was 63,400.

rishonim ("first [authorities]"): Older rabbinical authorities (as contrasted with the later authorities, the *aharonim*). The date of differentiation is now usually placed at the mid-15th cent.

ritual murder see blood libel

ritual purity see purity, ritual

Rivers, Larry (1923–): US painter. His early work was as an abstract expressionist, which he later adapted to popular imagery and commercial advertisements.

Robbins, Jerome (1918–): US choreographer. His choreography for Broadway musicals (*West Side Story, Fiddler on the Roof*) as well as films had great success and influence. He created ballets for such leading companies as American Ballet Theater and the New York City Ballet, which have become standard additions to the American dance repertory.

Robinson, Edward G. (Emanuel Goldenberg; 1893–1973): US actor. After a stage career, he moved to Hollywood, where he had a long and successful career playing gangster roles and character parts. In 1973, he was awarded a special Oscar.

Rodgers, Richard (1902–): US composer of musical comedies. He collaborated with the lyricist Lorenz Hart in many successes (*The Boys from Syracuse, Pal Joey*) and then from 1943 with Oscar Hammerstein II (*Oklahoma, South Pacific, The King and I, The Sound of Music*).

Many of his songs have won permanent popularity.

Romberg,   Sigmund (1887–1951):   Composer. Born in Hungary, he went to the US in 1909. His popular operettas included *The Student Prince, The Desert Song,* and *New Moon.*

Rome: Capital of Italy. Its Jewish community is probably one of the oldest in the world, with an unbroken history of over 2,000 years. In the classical period, there was a well-established Jewish settlement there, of which information is known from Classical literature and from the Jewish CATACOMBS. Even when the city became Christian, the Popes protected Jewish worship in R. although often subjecting the Jews to degradation. In the Middle Ages, R. was prosperous and the home of distinguished scholars. In the late 15th cent. the community was augmented by Spanish refugees. The situation changed with the Counter Reformation, and the ghetto was instituted in the 16th cent., together with other humiliations (badge, censorship, forced baptism, burning of the Talmud in 1553, etc.). The ghetto was abolished only in the latter 19th cent. The Jews were emancipated when R. became the capital of Italy in 1870. During World War II, some 2,000

Jews were deported by the Germans to their deaths. In 1978 there were 15,000 Jews in R.

Romm: Vilna family of printers of Hebrew books. In the late 19th cent. the imprint of "the widow and brothers Romm" is found on many Hebrew books, including the standard edition of the Talmud. The family continued its activity until 1940.

Rosenberg, Ethel (1918–1953) and **Julius** (1920–1953): Convicted spies whose execution aroused a storm of protest. They were charged with delivering US atomic-bomb secrets to the USSR and were the first civilians to be executed for espionage in the US. The case continues to provoke controversy.

Rosenblatt, Joseph (1882–1933): Cantor and composer. He was born in Russia, officiated in Europe, and from 1912 in the US. His concerts and recordings made him world-famous, and his voice was heard in the first talking film, *The Jazz Singer*.

Rosenfeld, Morris (1862–1923): Yiddish poet. He left his native Poland in 1882, and, after a period in London and Amsterdam, settled in New York in 1886. He wrote poems of labor, and became known as the "poet of the sweatshop." His works were very popular.

Rosenheim, Jacob (1870–1965): Orthodox leader. Born in Frankfort. He edited the organ of German Orthodoxy *Der Israelit*. He was a founder, president, and ideologist of the AGUDAT ISRAEL movement. From 1940 he lived in the US, and later in Israel.

Rosenwald: US family. *Julius R.* (1862–1932) joined the Chicago mail-order firm of Sears, Roebuck and was its president from 1910 to 1925. He established a foundation largely used for Negro rural education. Other beneficiaries of his philanthropy included the University of Chicago, YMCAs, YWCAs, and Jewish causes. His eldest son, *Lessing Julius R.* (1891–   ), succeeded him as chairman of Sears, Roebuck. He was strongly anti-Zionist and was the first president of the American Council for Judaism. Another son, *William R.* (1903–   ), is a philanthropist and a Jewish communal worker, heading the United Jewish Appeal.

Rosenzweig, Franz (1886–1929): German philosopher and theologian. Born into an assimilated family, his religious interests took him to the verge of baptism, but he decided to examine Judaism. His experience of an Orthodox Day of Atonement brought him to accept Judaism and to devote his life to its study and teaching. In 1920 he founded the *Freies Jüdisches Lehrhaus* in Frankfort as part of his work for Jewish education. Together with Martin Buber, he embarked on a German translation of the Bible. In his latter years he suffered from paralysis, but he continued to work, although almost unable to communicate. His outstanding work, *The Star of Redemption*, was written while he was a soldier during World War I. It anticipated some of the characteristic positions of existentialist philosophy and has been influential among many Jewish religious thinkers, especially in Germany and the US. His writings on Judaism and Christianity had an impact on interfaith relations, particularly after World War II.

Rosh see **Asher ben Jehiel**

Rosh ha-Shanah ("Beginning of the Year"): The Jewish New Year, observed as a two-day holiday at the beginning of the month of Tishri, and ushering in Ten Days of Penitence. According to Jewish tradition, this is the annual period on which man's fate for the forthcoming year is Divinely determined. The *shophar* (ram's horn) is sounded at all prayers (except on the Sabbath). A solemn ritual is recited with the worshipers (or at least the cantor) dressed in white. The ceremony of TASHLIKH is held on the afternoon of the first day. Among the customs is the eating of a new fruit dipped in honey "for a sweet year."

Rosh ha-Shanah: Eighth tractate in the MISHNAH order of *Moed*, with *gemara* in both Talmuds. It deals with the laws for the New Year festival.

rosh hodesh see **new moon**

Rosh Pinnah: Israeli village in northern Israel. Founded in 1878, it was abandoned in 1880 but refounded in 1882 by First Aliyah pioneers; later it was supported by Baron de ROTHSCHILD. It developed slowly, with its 1977 population reaching 830.

Rossi, Azariah ben Moses Dei (c. 1511–c. 1578): Jewish scholar in Italy, called Min ha-Adummim. His *Meor Enayim*, one of the earliest Jewish scholarly works, investigates critically Jewish history and literature in the Classical Period. He translated the Letter of Aristeas and "discovered" Philo for the Jewish reader.

Rosten, Leo Calvin (1908–): US writer. Under the pseudonym Leonard Q. Ross, he created the humorous character of Hyman Kaplan, describing a new American's experiences learning English in a New York night school. His other works included *Captain Newman, M.D., The Joys of Yiddish,* and an anthology of Jewish quotations.

Roth, Cecil (1899–1970): Historian. He taught at Oxford from 1939 until 1964, when he settled in Jerusalem. He wrote on many Jewish subjects, including histories of English and Italian Jewry. He was the author of popular works, biographies, and studies in Jewish art. R. was editor-in-chief of the *Encyclopedia Judaica.* His brother *Leon* (1896–1963), philosopher, taught at the Hebrew University, of which he was rector in 1940–43. He wrote on Jewish thought, Judaism, and philosophy and translated philosophical classics into Hebrew.

Roth, Henry (1906–): US novelist. He wrote *Call It Sleep* on immigrant life in New York's East Side. This appeared in 1934 but did not reach success until 25 years had passed. R. thereafter devoted himself to waterfowl farming in Maine.

Roth, Philip Milton (1933–): US novelist. His first success was a volume of short stories titled *Goodbye, Columbus,* which won the National Book Award. His best-known works include the novels *Portnoy's Complaint* and *The Professor of Desire.*

Rothschild: Family famed for its activity in the financial world. It originated in Frankfort-on-Main and took its name from the "red shield" sign over their house. Its founder was *Mayer Amschel R.* (1744–1812), who was court agent to the ruler of Hesse-Cassel and himself entered commerce and banking. His sons moved to various parts of Europe but remained in close business association. The English house was started by *Nathan Mayer R.* (1777–1836), who was a leading figure in the London Stock Exchange during the Napoleonic Wars. His son *Lionel R.* (1808–1879) provided funds for Disraeli's purchase of the Suez Canal shares in 1875 and was the first Jew in the British parliament. He was the accepted head of English Jewry. His son, *Nathaniel, Lord R.* (1840–1915), was the first Jewish peer (1885) and was also a leader of the Anglo-Jewish community. *Walter, 2nd Lord R.* (1868–1937) was a zoologist and recipient of the BALFOUR DECLARATION. *Nathaniel Mayer Victor, 3rd Lord R.* (1910–), is a biologist and was chairman of the British Agricultural Research Council and director of the British Cabinet's "Think Tank," 1970–75. In France, the branch was founded by Mayer Amschel's fifth son *James R.* (1792–1868). One of his sons was *Baron Edmond de R.* (1845–1934), who played a major role in financing early Jewish settlement in modern Palestine. In the 1880s when the settlers faced a severe crisis he came to their rescue, establishing the early moshavot and backing their economy. This was done through officials whom he sent to Palestine and whose activities often led to clashes with the settlers. In 1900, R. transferred the supervision of the settlement to ICA (later PICA). He himself visited the country five times (the last time in 1925), and the local population called him "the Baron" or "the father of the yishuv." His son *James de R.* (1878–1957) moved to England, where he was a Liberal member of Parliament. He left a bequest for the building of the Knesset in Jerusalem. Members of the R. family still play a leading role in French Jewish life. Other branches of the firm were in Vienna and Naples as well as Frankfort. The wealth of the R. became a favorite subject of Jewish folklore.

Rubinstein, Artur (1887–   ): Pianist: He was born in Poland and lived in the US from 1940. Throughout his long career, he has been rec-ognized as one of the world's greatest pianists.

Rubinstein, Helena (1871–1965): Cosmetician. Born in Poland, she lived in Australia and then went to Britain, where she founded her cosmetic company. From 1914, she lived in New York.

Ruby (Rubinstein), Jack (1911–1967): Dallas nightclub owner who killed Lee Harvey Oswald, murderer of President Kennedy. He shot him in a police station in revenge for Kennedy's murder. R. was sentenced to death but died before his appeal was heard.

Rumania: The first Jews in the region came in the 2nd cent. CE. Little is known about them for many centuries. Immigrants came from Hungary in the 14th cent., from Spain in the 16th cent., and from Poland in the 17th cent. They received legal status in the 17th cent. In the 19th cent. they suffered from discriminatory legislation, and from 1866, anti-Semitism became part of Rumanian policy. Hasidism was strong in the country. There was large Jewish emigration early in the 20th cent. Attempts were made in the Versailles Peace Treaty to safeguard Jewish rights in R., but anti-Jewish activities continued. At the outbreak of World War II, there were 800,000 Jews in R., but 350,-

000 were murdered by the Germans, often with Rumanian cooperation. From 1948 to 1952, many of the survivors emigrated to Israel. Then, after a difficult period, they were again allowed out in the later 1950s. Jewish communal life was permitted inside R., and from the mid-1950s, the official attitude was more tolerant. After the Six-Day War it was the only Eastern European country to maintain relations with Israel. In 1976 there were 60,-000 Jews in R., with an active communal and religious life.

Ruppin, Arthur (1876–1943): Zionist, economist, and sociologist. He directed the Jewish Statistical Bureau in Berlin in 1903–07. He went to Palestine in 1907 and established the Palestine Office of the Zionist Organization in Jaffa. In this capacity he played an important role in the development of Jewish settlements. From 1922 he directed the Zionist Executive's settlement department. He was a pioneer in the sociological study of world Jewry, on which he wrote books and lectured at the Hebrew University.

Russia: Jews lived in certain areas of R. in classical times, notably in the Crimea. It was in southern R. that the KHAZAR nobility became Jewish. Jews were in Kiev in the 12th cent. The Tartar invasion of the 13th cent. destroyed Jewish settlements. In the 15th cent. Jews are again heard of as merchants and physicians. In 1667 the Jews of the eastern Ukraine were expelled on its annexation to R. Cossack invaders carried out terrible atrocities against Polish Jewry in the 17th cent. Several expulsion orders were issued in the 18th cent., and Jews were not allowed to settle permanently. The situation changed as a result of the 1772 partition of POLAND, which brought 20,000 Jews into R., while the later partitions brought their numbers to a million. In the 19th cent., the great majority of the Jews of the world lived under the hostile rule of the czars. In 1786 their areas of residence were restricted, and this later developed into the PALE OF SETTLEMENT. A series of cruel enactments was passed, including enforced military service (the CANTONISTS). There were periods of comparative liberalization, but the harsh reaction to the assassination of Alexander II led to officially inspired POGROMS, and the discriminatory MAY LAWS. Large numbers of Jews now began to leave for the West. Among the Jews of R. there was an intense ferment, expressed in socialist and Zionist groups and participation in the revolutionary movement. There was Jewish participation in the Dumas, but this was succeeded by further reaction, as shown by the BEILIS blood-libel trial. Despite all the problems, intense Jewish cultural life developed (e.g., in Odessa, which was the center of the Hebrew literary revival). Russian Jews suffered in World War I and were the targets of pogroms by the White armies in the ensuing civil war. However, they welcomed the February 1917 Revolution, which immediately abolished all discriminatory anti-Jewish legislation. Jews were prominent in the early stage of the Bolshevik Revolution, and Lenin strongly opposed anti-Semitism. However, under this regime Jewish religious life (like any other religious life) was suppressed, and non-Communist Jewish institutions were abolished. An attempt by the Soviet government to establish an autonomous Jewish region in BIRO-BIDJAN failed. In World War II, Jews who were trapped in the areas occupied by the Nazis were killed, except for the comparatively few who managed to hide or join the partisans. The Soviet government established the Jewish Anti-Fascist Committee to mobilize world Jewry's support. After the war, Stalin pursued a bitter anti-Semitic policy, aiming at the elimination of all traces of Jewish culture. Leading Jewish intellectuals were murdered, and countless numbers of Jews were exiled. Stalin's death apparently saved the Jews from an even more terrible disaster. His successors canceled the rule of terror but continued to repress Jewish culture, with certain small exceptions resulting from external pressures. The Six-Day War made a profound impression on Soviet Jewry, and they began to pressure for the right to emigrate. From 1970, numbers of Russian Jews were permitted to leave for Israel (although many went elsewhere). At the same time the USSR maintained a bitterly anti-Israel campaign wherever possible and remained solidly behind the Arabs. In the 1969 census 2,151,000 persons declared themselves as Jews in the USSR.

Rutenberg, Pinhas (1879–1942): Engineer, industrialist, and Zionist leader. He took part in the social revolutionary movement in Russia but opposed the Bolsheviks. He settled in Palestine in 1919, receiving the concession for the generation of electricity from the Jordan river, and founded the Palestine Electric Company. In 1929–30, and in

1939 he was chairman of the Vaad Leumi.

Ruth: Moabitess, heroine of the Book of R. She married Mahlon of Bethlehem and after her husband's death, insisted on returning with her mother-in-law, Naomi, identifying with her people and her God. She wed Boaz and was the ancestress of David. The Book of Ruth is in the Hagiographa section of the Bible.

Saadyah ben Joseph (882–942): GAON and scholar. Born in Egypt, he was appointed *gaon* of Sura (although he was deposed between 930 and 936 because of a dispute with the exilarch). S. wrote a number of classic works in different fields, including an Arabic translation of the Bible; the philosophic *Emunot ve-Deot*, one of the earliest works of Jewish medieval philosophy; a compilation of the prayer book; a Hebrew lexicon (*Egron*); and a grammar. Some of his works were directed against the KARAITES and other sectarians.

Sabbath (*Shabbat*): Weekly day of rest observed from sunset on Friday until nightfall Saturday. Jewish tradition connected it with the Divine day of rest during the week of Creation, and the relevant verses of Genesis form part of the sanctification of the S. (KIDDUSH) with which the day is ushered in in the synagogue and the home. It is also called a sign of the covenant with God and a remembrance of the Exodus. The observance of the S. day is one of the Ten Commandments. Jewish law elaborated 39 categories of work which are forbidden on the S. It has been regarded by Jews as a day of physical rest and spiritual uplift, marked by home observance and synagogue attendance. The housewife lights S. candles to inaugurate the day, and another home ceremony, the HAVDALAH prayer, concludes it. Although the laws of the S. must be strictly observed, they may be overruled if a life is at stake. Circumcisions are also performed on the S. if it coincides with the 8th day after birth.

Sabbath, the Great (*Shabbat ha-Gadol*): Sabbath preceding Passover, during which a special *haftarah* is read. Traditionally this is one of the two days of the year on which a homiletical discourse was given in the synagogue (the other was the Sabbath before the Day of Atonement).

Sabbaths, special: Four Sabbaths in the spring season are named after the extra reading from the Pentateuch, which replaces the regular *maphtir*. These are Shekalim (on Adar 1 or the preceding Sabbath), when Exod. 30: 11–16 is read to commemorate the annual half-shekel tax collected in temple times during Adar; Zakhor (Sabbath before Purim), when Deut. 25:17–19 is read to commemorate the command to obliterate Amalek (with whom Haman was homiletically connected); Parah (Sabbath before Ha-Hodesh), when Num. 9:1–22 is read, dealing with the RED HEIFER as a reminder to be ritually pure for Passover; and Ha-Hodesh (on Nisan 1 or preceding Sabbath), when Exod. 12:1–20 is read as a reminder that Passover is approaching.

sabbatical year (*shemittah*): The seventh year, when the land must lie fallow. A respite from agricultural work is ordered once in seven years (Lev. 25:3ff). Any crops that come up during that year are left for the poor. At the end of the year all debts are remitted. The year following seven such sabbatical years—i.e., each 50 years— slaves are liberated, land bought over the last 50 years is returned to its original owner, and land is not cultivated. This is called Jubilee (the English word derives from the Hebrew *yovel*). The Israeli chief rabbinate solved the problem of the *shemittah* year by selling land to non-Jews, but the more extreme Orthodox do not recognize this. 1979–80 is a sabbatical year; the next will be 1986–87.

Sabbetaians see **Shabbetai Tzevi**

Sabin, Albert Bruce (1906–): US scientist. He was born in Poland and lived in the US from 1921. He developed an orally administered vaccine against polio, which went into mass use in 1961. From 1969 to 1972 he was president of the Weizmann Institute of Science in Rehovot, Israel.

sabora see **savoraim**

Sachar, Abram Leon (1899–): US educator and historian. He was national director of the Hillel Foundations, 1933–48, and then president (1968, chancellor) of Brandeis University, which he helped to found. His works include a one-volume Jewish history. His son *Howard Morley S.* (1928–) is professor of Middle Eastern history at George Washington Univ., Washington, D.C., and author of *The Course of Modern Jewish History* and *History of Israel*.

Sachs, Nelly (1891–1970): Poet. Born in Berlin, she lived in Sweden from 1940. From then on her German verse dealt with the theme of the Holocaust. In 1966 she (together with S. Y. Agnon) was awarded the Nobel Prize for Literature.

sacrifice: An offering to God. S. of animals is mentioned in the story of Cain and Abel and again with Noah and the patriarchs. The Canaanites offered humans, but the story of the Binding of Isaac indicates God's displeasure with human sacrifice. Originally no animals were slaughtered. except for s. The Israelites did not dispense with sacrifice but gave it a monotheistic emphasis and centered it in the Temple. Apart from animal s., there were meal offerings, guilt offerings, animal tithes, paschal lambs, etc. Some of these were congregational offerings; others were offered by the individual (after the unwitting commitment of a transgression, or on specified occasions such as the festivals). A basic part of the ritual was the pouring of the blood on or near the altar. The priests received certain offerings or parts thereof; others were consumed by the sacrificer. Before a sin offering, the sacrificer put his hand on the animal and confessed his transgression. A daily burnt offering was sacrificed by the priests every morning and evening. All s. ceased after the destruction of the Second Temple, and prayer was regarded as a substitute. The Orthodox pray for the reinstitution of the sacrificial system, but this has been omitted in the Reform liturgy.

Sadducees (*Tzedukim*): Sect of the later Second Temple period. It attracted the aristocratic and priestly elements and was strongly opposed by the PHARISEES. Tensions between the two even led to massacres and civil war. The S. were distinguished from the Pharisees in their social class and also in their religious doctrines. They did not believe in resurrection, the immortality of the soul, or the existence of angels. They rejected the authority of the Oral Law and lacked the flexibility of the Pharisaic interpretation. There were also differences in many rituals and ceremonies. Their whole authority was connected with the Temple cult, and with the destruction of the Temple, the S. ceased to exist.

Safdie, Moshe (1938–): Israeli architect. He gained fame as designer of the Habitat housing project in Montreal and of the master plans for the 1967 World Fair. He has designed various projects in and around the reconstructed Jewish quarter of the Old City of Jerusalem.

Safed (**Tzefat**): Town in Galilee. It became the center of important religious and literary activity in the 16th cent. Under the impact of Isaac LURIA, his disciples, and other famous kabbalists such as Joseph CARO and Moses CORDOVERO, it was the focus of Jewish mystical study. Great talmudic and rabbinical scholars also lived there, and together with Jerusalem, Hebron, and Tiberias it was one of the four Holy Cities of the Land of Israel. It was the scene of the attempt by Jacob BERAB to revive the institution of OR-DINATION. It suffered from a general decline in the 18th and 19th cent., including epidemics and earthquakes, of which the most serious occurred in 1837. In 1948 the majority of the inhabitants were Arabs, but they fled and the town was subsequently developed as a resort and as an artists' center. The population in 1977 was 14,200.

St. Louis: US city in Missouri. Jews lived there from 1807, and the first congregation was organized in 1837. The population increased with an influx of Eastern European Jews in the 1880s, and by 1976 60,000 Jews were living there.

St. Petersburg see **Leningrad**

Sakel, Manfred (1900–1957): Psychiatrist. He was born in Austria and settled in New York in 1936. He developed insulin-shock treatment for schizophrenia.

Salanter, Israel (1810–1883): Founder of the MUSAR MOVEMENT. His real name was Israel Lipkin, but he became known as S. after the town of Salant, where he studied. He lived in Lithuania and for a time led a wandering life. He established Musar houses where people would retire to examine their conscience and study ethical literature. Under the influence of S. and his disciples, ethical courses became part of the curriculum of many Lithuanian yeshivot.

Salinger, Jerome David (1912–): US novelist. His

Catcher in the Rye achieved great popularity, especially among the younger generation. He also wrote two volumes about the Jewish Glass family, starting with *Franny and Zooey*.

Salk, Jonas Edward (1914–): US virologist. He was professor of bacteriology at the University of Pittsburgh, 1949–61, and from 1961 headed the Institute for Biological Research at the University of California. He developed the Salk vaccine used against several strains of the polio virus.

Salome (**Shelom-Zion**) (1st cent. CE): Daughter of Herod Philip and Herodias. She is popularly identified with the "daughter of Herodias" mentioned in the New Testament as responsible for the execution of John the Baptist by Herod Antipas. A different account of John's death is given by Josephus. S. married her uncle, the tetrarch Philip.

Salome Alexandra (**Shelom-Zion**) (139–67 BCE): Queen of Judea in 76–67 BCE. She succeeded her husband ALEXANDER YANNAI and reversed his hostile policy toward the Pharisees. Her reign was a period of comparative peace and prosperity.

Salomon, Haym (1740–1785): US financier and patriot. Of Polish birth, he went to the US about 1775. In the Revolutionary War he supported the patriots and became broker to the Office of Finance. His financial acumen and assistance greatly helped the republic in its early years.

Salomons, Sir David (1797–1873): English public figure. He was the first Jew to be alderman, sheriff, and lord mayor of London. He was elected to the House of Commons in 1851, but because he would not take the Christological oath, was ejected; he was seated only in 1859. S. participated in the development of the joint stock banking system in England.

Salonica (**Thessaloniki**): Greek port. Alexandrian Jews arrived in 140 BCE and the community was visited by the apostle Paul. Persecutions occurred under the Byzantines and Latin Empire. It developed in the 13th–14th cent., with refugee immigrants from Europe, and especially from the 15th cent. with the arrival of Spanish refugees and Marranos. The Spanish-speaking newcomers became the dominant element in the community. There were 40 different communities, each reflecting a different geographical origin. A Hebrew printing press was established in 1515, and S. was a thriving center of cultural life and the home of many distinguished scholars. SHABBETAI TZEVI won many adherents here, and the sect of the Dönmeh was largely concentrated in S. Some 80,000 Jews lived there early in the 20th cent., when the Jews constituted such a preponderant element in the docks that the port closed on the Sabbath. The interchange of populations between Greece and Turkey after World War I led to a drop in the Jewish population and the emigration of the Donmeh. Many Jews left for Palestine and America before World War II, and those that remained were sent to death camps by the Germans. Only 1,092 Jews remained in 1973.

Salten, Felix (1869–1947): Austrian novelist; in US from 1938 and in Switzerland after the war. He wrote novels, dramas, and essays but is best remembered for his animal tale *Bambi*.

Salvador: Jews arrived in the 19th cent., but the main immigration was in the 1920s, with Jews arriving from Central and Eastern Europe. 310 Jews lived there in 1976, nearly all in the capital, San Salvador.

Samael: Prince of demons or angel of death identified with Satan. His wife is Lilith.

Samaria (*Shomron*): Capital of the Kingdom of Israel founded c. 880 BCE by Omri. Excavations have uncovered remains of Israelite and Roman palaces, a theater, etc. Ahab built there an "ivory palace." It was taken by Sargon II of Assyria in 722–21 BCE, who resettled it with Cutheans. These assimilated to the local population and from them emerged the Samaritans. S. was destroyed by John Hyrcanus, then reestablished by Pompey. Herod renamed it Sebaste in honor of Augustus and also rebuilt and extended it. It declined in Byzantine times, was destroyed by the Persians, and became a bishopric under the Crusaders.

Samaritans (*Shomeronim*): Descendants of the tribes of Ephraim and Manasseh intermingled with non-Jewish colonists, centered around Samaria. At the time of Nehemiah, the S. tried to obtain influence in Jerusalem and to hinder Nehemiah's plans. When this failed, they built their own temple on Mt. Gerizim near Shechem. This was destroyed by John Hyrcanus in 128 BCE but rebuilt by the Romans as a reward for help received by the S. This was destroyed by the emperor Zeno in 486 CE. when the S. suffered terrible massacre. Thereafter they diminished, although there were Samaritan centers in various places throughout the Middle East. Under Muslim rule they were persecuted and declined. The group now numbers some 480, of whom 230 live in Holon and the remainder in Shechem (Nablus). They have a high priest and sacrifice a paschal lamb every Passover on Mt. Gerizim. Their Scripture is the Pentateuch, with certain variants, such as the singling out of Mt. Gerizim as the place chosen by God for worship. They observe biblical festivals. The rabbis regard the S. as non-Jews for purposes of marriage. Talmudic law on the attitude to the S. is in the tractate KUTIM. The language of the S. is biblical Hebrew, and its pronunciation is probably very ancient. Their script is a variant of ancient Hebrew. They have a literature including the *Defter* ("Liturgy") in Samaritan Aramaic. Their most precious possession is the ancient Samaritan Pentateuch, which goes back to a very early original; the manuscript now treasured by them dates from the 12th cent.

Sambatyon: Legendary river. According to tradition, the Lost Ten Tribes dwell across the river. It has a mighty torrent of stones, not water, which cannot be crossed; it rests on the Sabbath, but on that day one is not allowed to cross. Belief in this river was widespread, and in the Middle ages the search for the Tribes often began with the search for the S.

samekh (ס): Fifteenth letter of the Hebrew alphabet. Numerical value: 60. Pronounced *s*.

Samson: Judge in Israel, renowned for his physical strength, which he used in spectacular acts against the Philistines. Eventually the secret of his strength, which lay in his unshorn locks, was prised from him by his mistress Delilah, who betrayed him to the Philistines. They took him, then blinded and imprisoned him. Finally brought before them at a feast in Gaza, he brought down the building, killing the Philistines and himself.

Samuel (11th cent. BCE): Israelite prophet and last of the judges. Dedicated before his birth to a Nazirite life at the sanctuary, he was raised by ELI. After the defeat of the Israelites by the Philistines at Aphek and the death of Eli and his sons, S. directed the religious life of the Israelites. His headquarters were in Ramah. In response to popular pressure, he anointed Saul as king but later, disillusioned with Saul, anointed David as his successor.

Samuel, Book of: Third book of the Former Prophets section of the Bible. It relates the history of the Israelites from the conquest under

Joshua to the last days of David. Much attention is given to the lives of Saul and David. In Hebrew tradition it was one work, but following the Septuagint, it is now divided into two.

Samuel (Mar Samuel) (c. 165–257): Babylonian AMORA, head of the academy in his native NEHARDEA. His halakhic discussions with his colleague RAV are prominently featured in the Talmud. He was also a physician and an astronomer.

Samuel ben Meir (c. 1080–c. 1174): French rabbi, called Rashbam. A grandson of RASHI, he was also a commentator on the Bible and Talmud. In those parts of the Talmud on which Rashi did not write a commentary, S.'s commentary is customarily printed.

Samuel ibn Nagrela (993–1056): Spanish statesman and scholar, called Samuel ha-Nagid. He became vizier to the ruler of Granada, and even commanded his armies in battle. He patronized Jewish learning and himself was a poet and author of grammatical works, halakhic writings, and an introduction to the Talmud. He was succeeded by his son JEHOSEPH, who was assassinated in 1066.

Samuel, Herbert Louis, Viscount (1870–1963): British statesman and philosopher. He entered Parliament in 1902 and held office in various Liberal governments from 1906. In 1909 he became the first professing Jew to become a member of the British Cabinet. During World War I, he played an important role in the negotiations leading up to the BALFOUR DECLARATION. In 1920 he was sent as the first British HIGH COMMISSIONER to Palestine. From 1931, he led the Liberal Party, first in the House of Commons and then in the House of Lords. S. was president of the Royal Institute of Philosophy and wrote philosophical works.

Samuel, Sir Marcus see **Bearsted**

Samuel, Maurice (1895–1972): US author. Born in Rumania, he was raised in Manchester, England, and lived in the US from 1914. He became the foremost interpreter of Yiddish culture in English, through books on Peretz, Sholem Aleichem, and others. He also wrote books on Israel, anti-Semitism, the Bible, and the Beilis case. S. was a gifted orator and a popular broadcaster.

Samuelson, Paul Anthony (1915–): US economist; professor at MIT. He was awarded the 1970 Nobel Prize for Economics. His main studies are on economic theory and econometrics.

San Francisco: US city in California. Jews arrived before the mid-19th cent., and the community developed, although not with the speed or to the extent of that in Los Angeles. Jews played a prominent role in the general growth of the city. In 1976, 75,000 Jews lived there.

San Nicandro: Village in southern Italy where 23 peasant families adopted Judaism after one of their number experienced a "vision." The group went to Israel in 1949 but eventually split up.

Sana: Capital of YEMEN. An ancient and influential Jewish community lived there, the largest in the country. Until 1678 the Jews lived in their own quarter; later they moved to a special suburb. 156,000 Jews left for Israel in 1949–50 and c. 150 remained in the early 1970s.

Sanballat (5th cent. BCE): A leading opponent of Nehemiah, who tried to prevent the building of Jerusalem. S., who was governor of Samaria, had accomplices in Jerusalem, where his son-in-law was high priest.

sanctification see **kiddush**

Sandak: The man who holds the baby on his knees while the circumcision ceremony is being performed.

Sanhedrin: Assembly of 71 elders which was the supreme political, religious, and judicial authority. During the latter part of the Second Temple period, it met in the Temple precincts. There were lesser courts of 23 members, known as Small Sanhedrins. The Great S. was headed by the NASI and AV BET DIN. Its duties included decisions on the calendar and rulings on doubtful points of law. After the destruction of the Temple, the S. continued to meet in other rabbinical centers in the country up to c. 425 CE.

Sanhedrin: Fourth tractate in the MISHNAH order of *Nezikin,* with *gemara* in both Talmuds. It deals with the authority of all kinds of law courts, legal procedure, and capital punishment.

Sanhedrin, French: Assembly with 71 members (in imitation of the ancient Sanhedrin) convened by Napoleon in 1807 to ratify decisions of the Assembly of Notables which had met the previous year. It prescribed conformity with the civil law of the state provided it did not contradict Jewish law.

Santangel, Luis de (d. 1498): Marrano controller of the royal household of Aragon. He introduced Christopher Columbus to Queen Isabella and lent him money to finance his voyage. Columbus sent him the first letter detailing his discovery.

Sao Paolo: Largest city in Brazil. Some Marranos lived there in the 16th cent.

The Jewish community was founded in the latter 19th cent. A thriving Jewish life exists there, with Jewish schools and social institutions. The Jewish population was 65,000 in 1976.

Sapir, Pinhas (1906–1975): Israeli politician. Born in Poland, he went to Palestine in 1929. He was a key figure in economic policy, serving as minister of commerce and industry, 1955–64; and minister of finance, 1963–74. In 1974–75 he was chairman of the Zionist Executive and Jewish Agency.

Sapir (Saphir) Yaakov S. (1822–1885): Traveler. He left Palestine in 1858 on a fund-raising journey, which took him as far as Australia, and which lasted almost five years. His account in *Even Sappir* is a classic of Jewish travel literature. His grandson *Yoseph S.* (1902–1972) was a citriculturist in Israel. He was mayor of Petah Tikvah, 1940–51, Liberal (later Gahal) member of Knesset, and served in various Israel cabinets.

Saragossa: City in Spain, capital of Aragon. An important community lived there in the Muslim period, which continued to flourish after the Christian conquest. After the 1391 massacres it became a Marrano center. The community came to an end with the expulsion of 1492.

Sarah: Matriarch of the Jewish people; wife of ABRAHAM. Her name was originally Sarai and she married Abraham (her relative) before they left Haran. Barren for many years, she gave Abraham her handmaid HAGAR as his concubine. But subsequently S. gave birth, in her old age, to ISAAC. She died at the age of 127 and was buried in the Cave of Machpelah.

Sardis: Ancient town in Turkey, possibly the biblical Sepharad (Obad. 1:20). It had a prosperous Jewish community in Roman times, and its large synagogue dating back about 2,000 years was discovered in 1962. The community ended in the 7th cent.

Sarnoff, David (1891–1972): US broadcasting pioneer. As a wireless operator, he received the first news of the sinking of the *Titanic* in 1912. He founded the National Broadcasting Company in 1926 and became president of the Radio Corporation of America (RCA) in 1930. His son *Robert S.* (1918–   ) was president of RCA, 1965–75.

Saskatchewan: Canadian province. Jews settled in various farm schemes from the latter part of the 19th cent. and a number of agricultural Jewish settlements were founded, under the auspices of the JEWISH COLONIZATION ASSOCIATION. They thrived for several decades but declined from the 1930s, and few Jews remain on the land. In 1971 there were 2,200 Jews in S.

Sassoon: Family of Iraqi origin which was distinguished in Asia and in England. *David S.* (1792–1864) lived in Bombay, built up a widespread business, and was a noted philanthropist. His son *Sir Abodullah* (later *Albert*) *S.* (1818–1896) settled in England and with his brothers became a noted figure in English society in the circle of Edward VII. Other outstanding members included *Sir Philip S.* (1888–1939), undersecretary for air in the British government; *Siegfried Sassoon* (1886–1967), poet, novelist, and author of *Memoirs of a Foxhunting Man*; and *David Solomon S.* (1880–1942), who collected an important library with many Hebrew and Samaritan manuscripts.

Satan: In the Bible, an angel, with the function of acting as accuser (cf. Book of Job). Later he developed into a hostile spirit, and eventually into the prince of the demons. In post-biblical literature, he is identified with the angel of death.

Saudi Arabia see **Arabia**

Saul (11th cent. BCE): First king of Israel, reigned c. 1029–1005 BCE. He belonged to the tribe of Benjamin and was chosen king by the prophet SAMUEL in response to popular clamor for such an appointment. He soon scored brilliant victories over hostile peoples, but there was a break between him and Samuel, who anointed David to succeed him. Saul, who at first admired David and gave him his daughter as wife, eventually grew extremely jealous, to the point of seeking to kill him. He himself lost his life, together with his son Jonathan, after being defeated by the Philistines in a battle on Mt. Gilboa.

Savoraim ("expositors"): Scholars and heads of the Babylonian academies in the period following the *amoraim* and preceding that of the *geonim*—roughly, the 6th to 7th cent. They expounded obscure passages in the Talmud and added certain explanatory notes on the text.

Saxony: German state. Jews were there from the 10th cent., and until the late 12th cent. their position was satisfactory. However, they suffered during the Crusader period and during the Black Death, and were expelled in the 15th cent. They were not permitted to reside there again until the 19th cent. Civil rights were finally achieved in 1888. The community of 20,000 was destroyed by the Nazis. S. is now in East Germany; there are communities in Leipzig, Dresden, and Karl-Marx-Stadt.

sayings of the fathers see **avot**

Schapira, Hermann Tzevi (1840–1898): Mathematician and Zionist. He was professor of mathematics at Heidelberg. At the First Zionist Congress in 1897 it was he who proposed the foundation of a Hebrew University; he also inaugurated the idea of the Jewish National Fund.

Schatz, Boris (1866–1932): Sculptor and painter. Born in Lithuania, he founded the Royal Academy of Art at Sofia. In 1906 he went to Jerusalem to found the Bezalel School of Arts and Crafts, which he directed until his death. S. played a pioneering and influential role in the development of art in Israel.

Schechter, Solomon (1850–1915): Scholar and theologian. Born in Rumania, he went to England in 1882, and in 1890 was appointed lecturer in Talmud at Cambridge. In 1896–97 he went to Cairo and, having identified the Cairo genizah, brought back vast quantities of manuscripts to Cambridge, some of which he published (Hebrew original of Ecclesiasticus, the Damascus Documents). In 1901 he went to New York as president of the Jewish Theological Seminary (popularly known as the "Schechter Seminary"), which he developed, together with associated institutions such as the United Synagogue, into the center of Conservative Judaism. He himself played a large part in working out the ideology of the new movement.

Schiff, Jacob Henry (1847–1920): US financier and philanthropist, of German birth. He headed the banking house of Kuhn, Loeb and Co. He was the unofficial lay leader of US Jewry and was active in many organizations (a founder of the American Jewish Committee, for example). He liberally supported many, including the Jewish Theological Seminary, Jewish Publication Society [the Schiff Classics], the Montefiore Hospital, the Henry St. Settlement, etc. Although not a political Zionist, he supported the rebuilding of Palestine.

Schiper, Ignacy (1884–1943): Polish historian. He wrote on Jewish economic history and on all aspects of Polish Jewish history. He was a founder of Poalei Zion and was active in Polish political life, sitting in the Seym 1922–27. From 1939 he was confined in the Warsaw ghetto, until sent to his death in a concentration camp.

Schnabel, Artur (1882–1951): Pianist. He was born in Moravia, and lived in the US from 1938. He was regarded internationally as one of the outstanding pianists of his day, specializing in the classical masters, especially Beethoven. He was also a composer.

Schnitzer, Eduard see **Emin Pasha**

Schnitzler, Arthur (1862–1931): Austrian author. He was originally a doctor, and his medical background is often reflected in his writings. His plays and novels are marked by a brilliant style, humor, and naturalism. Some deal with Jewish topics.

Schocken, Salman (1877–1959): Publisher; also founder of a chain of department stores in Germany. From 1927 he published German and Hebrew books, eventually extending his activity to the US and Israel. He founded the Institute for the Study of Hebrew Poetry and acquired a collection of rare books (the S. Library, in Jerusalem). After 1934 he lived in Palestine and the US. He was active in Zionist causes (e.g. the Hebrew University). His son *Gustav Gershom S.* (1902–) edited HA-ARETZ from 1937. For a time he was a Progressive member of the Knesset.

Schoffman, Gershon (1880–1972): Hebrew novelist. Born in White Russia, he worked in Galicia and Austria before settling in Israel in 1938. His main work consists of short sketches and essays.

Scholem, Gershom Gerhard (1897–): Authority on Jewish mysticism. Born in Germany, he joined the Hebrew University in Jerusalem in 1923. He was president of the Israel Academy of Arts and Sciences. His researches inaugurated a new era in the study of Kabbalah, placing it on a scientific basis and demonstrating its place within Jewish historical tradition. His writings include *Major Trends in Jewish Mysticism* and *Shabbetai Tzevi*.

Schönberg, Arnold (1874–1951): Composer. He was born in Vienna and taught in various places in Europe before going to the US in 1933. He had left Judaism but returned to it after the advent of Hitler. S. was one of the outstanding innovators in modern music through his atonal techniques. He wrote operas, symphonies, and chamber music.

Schwartz, Joseph J. (1899–1975): US communal leader. From 1939 he worked for the American Joint Distribution Committee and played an important role in saving Jews during the war and helping them in its aftermath. He was executive vice-chairman of the UJA in

1951–55, and from 1955 to 1970, he was vice-president of the Israel Bond Organization.

Schwartz, Maurice (1890–1960): US Yiddish actor. In 1918 he founded the Jewish Art Theater in New York, which performed until 1950. As actor, producer, and director, he was a commanding figure in the Yiddish theater.

Schwartz-Bart, André (1928–): French novelist. His family was killed in the Holocaust, and he fought with the French *maquis*. The subject of his first and best-known book, *The Last of the Just*, is Jewish martyrdom down the ages. With his West Indian wife, he wrote on the history of the West Indies.

Schwarzbard, Shalom (1886–1938): Yiddish poet in Russia. After World War I, he was a member of the Red Guards fighting PETLURA. In 1926 he shot Petlura in Paris in revenge for the anti-Jewish pogroms he had instigated and in which S. had lost many relatives. He was tried and acquitted.

Science of Judaism see **Wissenschaft des Judentums**

Scotland: Jews were in Edinburgh and Glasgow in the 17th cent., but communities were founded only later—Edinburgh in 1816 and Glasgow in 1823. The latter grew considerably from the end of the 19th cent. and has 13,000 Jews, but Edinburgh remained small and has only 1,100 Jews. Small communities also exist in Aberdeen, Ayr, and Dundee. Altogether there were 15,000 Jews in S. in 1976.

scribe (*sopher*): In the Bible the s. was a high administrative function but in the Second Temple period it came to mean the literate man engaged in the interpretation of the Torah and the transmission of the Oral Law. They are therefore considered the precursors of the PHARISEES. EZRA is called the Scribe, and the class of scribes was active for the next two centuries. However, information on their activities is meager. The New Testament mentions them with the "Pharisees." Eventually the term was limited to penmen writing Torah scrolls and the like.

Scroll of Law (*Sepher Torah*): Manuscript of the Pentateuch used for synagogue readings (see LAW, READING OF). A scribe writes it on strips of specially treated vellum, according to well-defined regulations (codified in the tractate *Sopherim*). Among Oriental Jews it is kept in a wooden or metal box (*tik*); among Ashkenazim, it is covered with a mantle (*me'il*) and ornamented with various decorations (breastplate, finials, etc.). Up to three scrolls are taken out for the Torah reading; on SIMHAT TORAH all scrolls are taken out of the ARK in which they are kept. The Scrolls are treated with reverence, and should one be dropped inadvertently, the entire congregation is required to fast.

Scrolls, Five: The five short biblical books of the Hagiographa read on special occasions in the Jewish year: SONG OF SONGS on Passover, RUTH on the Feast of the Weeks, LAMENTATIONS on Av 9, ECCLESIASTES on Tabernacles, and ESTHER on Purim.

Sea of Galilee (Lake Kinneret): Freshwater lake formed by Jordan River, 65 m. north of Dead Sea. It is 14 m. by 8 m. and is 696 ft. below sea level. In ancient times it was known as the Sea of Chinnereth and as the Lake of Gennesaret. In Christian eyes it received special significance as a center of activities of Jesus and his disciples. In modern times, Jewish settlements were founded along its banks, starting with Deganyah in 1909. According to the 1949 Armistice Agreement, the lake was under Israeli sovereignty, but a large section of the eastern bank was controlled by Syria. It was the scene of considerable tension until 1967. The Israeli National Water Carrier pumps water from the lake to the Negev.

Sebaste see Samaria

Seder ("Order"): Ritual around the table in the home on the first two nights of PASSOVER (in Israel, on the first night). The HAGGADAH is recited and a festive meal is eaten.

Seder Olam ("Order of the World"): Name given to two early historical works. *Seder Olam Rabbah* summarizes Jewish history up to the 2nd cent. CE; and *Seder Olam Zuta* (dating from the 8th cent.) contains similar contents.

Segal, George (1924–): US sculptor. He is best known for his life-size plastic casts of people placed in an environmental setting.

Segrè, Emilio Gino (1905–): Physicist; member of a distinguished Italian Jewish family. He taught at the University of California at Berkeley and worked on the discovery of plutonium 239, used for the first atomic explosion. He won the 1949 Nobel Prize for Physics for discovery of the antiproton.

Seixas, Gershom Mendes (1746–1816): First native-born minister in the US. He served Congregation Shearith Israel in New York for fifty years. When the British took

New York in 1776, he went to Philadelphia and founded a congregation there. S. participated in Washington's inauguration in 1789.

selah: Word of uncertain derivation found 71 times in the Book of Psalms. It has been translated as "forever" but may be a musical indication.

Seleucids: Dynasty of Hellenistic Syrian rulers founded by Seleucus Nicator, one of Alexander the Great's generals. Relations between the S. and the Jews deteriorated during the rule of ANTIOCHUS IV EPIPHANES, which led to the Hasmonean revolt. Jews finally succeeded in throwing off the S. rule in Palestine in 128 BCE.

selihot ("penitential prayers"; lit. "forgivenesses"): Type of PIYYUT requesting forgiveness for sins. Originally composed (especially in the 12th–13th cents.) for the Day of Atonement and other fast days, they were later written for other services. They are founded on the THIRTEEN ATTRIBUTES (Exod. 34:6–7), a confession, and appropriate biblical verses, and were incorporated in the framework of the *amidah*. From the Middle Ages, the s. became closely connected with the Penitential Period, concluding with the Day of Atonement. A special service of s. is recited at or before dawn. The Sephardim begin these special s. services from Elul 1; the Ashkenazim from the week before Rosh ha-Shanah.

Semag see **Moses ben Jacob of Coucy**

Semak see **Isaac ben Joseph of Corbeil**

semikhah see **ordination**

Sephardi(m): Descendants of Jews who lived in Spain and Portugal until the expulsions in the later 15th cent. Sepharad, mentioned in Obadiah 1:20, was probably Asia Minor (SARDIS?). After the expulsion from Spain, the refugees settled mostly in Mediterranean lands. They became the dominant element in many of these communities. They brought their own customs, language (LADINO), music, etc. There were differences in synagogue rites which were especially marked where Sephardim lived in proximity to Ashkenazim: the Sephardi rite derived from Babylonian usage, and the Ashkenazi from Palestinian. Marranos established Sephardi communities in Northern Europe and the Western Hemisphere. Today the non-Ashkenazi community (including "Oriental" Jews, who, strictly speaking, are not Sephardim) now number 17% of world Jewry but over 50% of the Jews in Israel.

Sepher Torah see **Scroll of Law**

Sepher Yetzirah ("Book of Creation"): Brief text of ancient origin and great influence in development of Jewish mystic tradition. Probably written between the 3rd and 6th cent. in Palestine or Babylonia, it identifies the elements of creation in the first 10 numerals and the 22 letters of the Hebrew alphabet.

sephirot ("numbers"): Term used in Kabbalah (from the 12th cent.) for the 10 emanations through which the Divine manifests Itself. The concept derives from Neoplatonic and Gnostic thought.

Sepphoris (Tzippori): Town in central Galilee. In late Second Temple times, it was the chief city of Galilee, and the seat of the patriarchate and the Sanhedrin from the time of Judah ha-Nasi until the time of his grandson Judah II. It was a Jewish city under the Byzantines and was the focus of a Jewish revolt in the mid-4th cent.

Septuagint (Lat. "The Seventy"): Greek translation of the Bible, so named because according to legend the Pentateuch section was translated by 72 scholars. It grew out of the requirements of the Hellenized Jewish population of ancient Egypt. At first the Greek renditions were probably oral; later a written translation emerged. The Pentateuch was translated in the 3rd cent. BCE. The entire translation was completed before the Christian Era.

seraphim: Celestial beings mentioned in the Bible (Is. 6:2), where they are described as six-winged creatures. In later writings, they appear as one of the 10 top orders of angels.

Serkes, Joel ben Samuel (1561–1640): Rabbi in Poland and Lithuania, known as the Bah from the initials of his book, *Bayit Ḥadash*, a commentary on Jacob ben Asheis' *Arbaah Turim*. His glosses on the Talmud have been printed in most subsequent editions of the Talmud.

Serkin, Rudolf (1903–): Pianist. He was born in Bohemia, and made his debut in the US in 1933. From 1939 he headed the piano faculty at the Curtis Institute of Music in Philadelphia, and in 1968 he became its director. He has toured extensively.

seven benedictions (*sheva berakhot*): Blessings recited at the wedding ceremony. They are of ancient origin and are mentioned in the Talmud. During the week after the marriage they are recited during grace after every meal at which there is a *minyan*.

Seville: Spanish city. Jews lived in the region in the Visigothic period, and there was a strong community there under Muslim and later under Christian rule. In 1391 it was the scene of massacres, following which many Marranos lived there. The Inquisition began its activities in S. in 1480, and its Jews were expelled in 1483.

shaatnez: Cloth containing a mixture of wool and flax which Jews are forbidden to wear (Lev. 19:19; Deut. 22:11). The rabbis held that the reason for this commandment is beyond human comprehension.

shabbat see **sabbath**

Shabbat ("Sabbath"): First tractate in MISHNAH order of *Moed*, with *gemara* in both Talmuds. It deals with the laws of the Sabbath.

Shabbazi, Shalom (17th cent.): Outstanding Yemenite poet. He wrote hundreds of religious and secular poems in Hebrew and Arabic, sometimes using both languages in the same poem. Many of his *piyyutim* have been incorporated in the Yemenite liturgy. They often show a kabbalistic influence. His grave in Taiz, which was a site of pilgrimages for both Jews and Muslims was destroyed by the Yemenite authorities in 1977.

Shabbetai ben Meir ha-Kohen (1621–1662): East-ern European talmudist. He was known as Shakh after the initials of his book *Siphte Kohen*, an exposition of the *Yoreh Deah* section of Joseph Caro's code *Shulḥan Arukh*.

Shabbetai Tzevi (1626–1676): Pseudo-messiah; central figure of the Sabbetaian movement. Born in Smyrna, he devoted himself to talmudic and kabbalistic studies and practiced asceticism. When he was 22 he began to make mystical revelations, hinting at his messianic calling. The opposition of the Smyrna rabbis led him to travel throughout the Middle East, where he won widespread support from the masses. In 1665 he met NATHAN OF GAZA, who influenced him to proclaim himself as the messiah. When he went back to Turkey he received an ecstatic welcome, and the messianic ferment affected Jewish communities in all parts of the world. He publicly proclaimed himself as Messiah in 1665 in Smyrna. The following year he went to Constantinople to claim his kingdom from the sultan. He was arrested and put in prison, where he was allowed considerable freedom and continued to stir up messianic expectations. However, when his life was in danger he accepted apostasy to Islam. This led to confusion among his followers, but there were those who rationalized it within the framework of his doctrines and continued to believe in his mission. This group—the DÖNMEH—have continued to exist, mostly in Turkey, until modern times. S.T. was imprisoned in a small village in Albania and died in obscurity.

Shaddai: Name of God, often found in the Bible and generally translated into English as "almighty." It is displayed on the *mezuzah*.

shadkhan: Marriage broker. The s., known from the early Middle Ages, fulfilled an important social function in the Jewish community, down to modern times. It was a highly regarded occupation, and famous rabbis were proud to engage in it.

Shaffer, Peter (1926–): English playwright. He has written many successful plays, including *Five-Finger Exercise, The Royal Hunt of the Sun* (about the conquest of Peru), and *Equus*. His twin brother *Anthony* also wrote popular plays, including *Sleuth*.

Shaharit: Morning Service, recited daily before the first quarter of the day has passed. Historically it was a substitute for the dawn sacrifice (TAMID). Tradition has ascribed its institution to Abraham. It starts with benedictions of praise; biblical and rabbinic verses; the PESUKEI DE-ZIMRA; the SHEMA and its benedictions; the AMIDAH, which in congregational prayer is repeated by the reader; and TAḤANUN. On Mondays and Thursdays as well as Sabbaths and festivals, there are readings from the Torah. The concluding prayers include ALENU and the mourners' KADDISH. On new moons and festivals, HALLEL is recited. The prayer shawl is worn for *s.*, and on weekdays the phylacteries are put on.

Shahn, Ben (1898–1969): US artist. His paintings have a photographic realism and are often concerned with social issues. He designed murals at Radio City and the Federal Security Building.

shaliaḥ (*meshullaḥ*): Emissary of rabbinical academies and Jewish communities in Eretz Israel to Jewish communities elsewhere to collect funds for their upkeep. Those sent from the four Holy Cities of Palestine (Jerusalem, Hebron, Tiberias, Safed) were called *shadar*. In modern times, the name is given to emissaries sent from Israel to organize education, collect funds, etc.

Shallum: (1) King of Israel, 747 BCE. He slew Zechariah and seized the throne, but after five months he in turn was killed by Menahem, who succeeded him (II Kings 15:10–14). (2) See JEHOAHAZ.

Shalom aleikhem ("Peace unto you"): Customary greeting, generally abbreviated to *Shalom*. Also opening words of hymn welcoming the Sabbath angels, recited on return from synagogue on Friday evenings.

Shalomzion, Alexandra see **Salome**

Shammai (c. 50 BCE– c. 30 CE): Palestinian rabbi; he and HILLEL forming the last of the ZUGOT. He was vice-president of the Sanhedrin. He is described as of severe character, in contrast to the gentleness of Hillel. Like Hillel, he established a school, Bet Shammai, known for its more stringent interpretations of the law than those of Bet Hillel.

shammash: (1) Synagogue official, with varying functions in different eras and places. (2) The extra candle used for lighting the Hanukkah lights.

Shanghai: Port and city in China. In the mid-19th cent., Sephardim largely of Iraqi origin (notably members of the SASSOON family) established themselves there and were important in international commerce. Three synagogues were in existence from the early 20th cent. After 1917, Russian Jews ar-

rived. Refugees from Europe found haven there during World War II, when there were 25,000 Jews. Although there were restrictions by the Japanese, the community survived the war and subsequently re-emigrated. The community ended after the Communists took over China.

Shapira, Moshe Hayyim (1902–1970): Israeli religious politician. Born in White Russia, he was a founder in 1919 of the Mizrahi youth movement. In 1925 he settled in Palestine. From 1935 he was a member of the Jewish Agency Executive. A representative of Ha-Poel ha-Mizrahi (later the National Religious Party) in the Knesset, he served in nearly all Israeli governments until his death.

Shapp, Milton J. (1912–): US politician. In 1970, he was elected governor of Pennsylvania.

Sharett (Shertok), **Moshe** (1894–1965): Israeli public figure. Born in the Ukraine, he went to Palestine in 1906. In 1933, he succeeded Hayyim Arlosoroff as head of the Jewish Agency's Political Department. From 1948 he was foreign minister of Israel, and in 1953–55 served as prime minister. Then he was foreign minister again but resigned in 1956 as a result of differences with

David Ben-Gurion. From 1961 he headed the Jewish Agency Executive.

Sharm el-Sheikh: Bay and settlement at southern end of Sinai Peninsula. Strategically placed, it was fortified by the Egyptians but was captured by the Israeli army in the Sinai Campaign and the Six-Day War. After 1967, it was developed by Israel as a tourist site (Ophira).

Sharon: Central part of Israel's coastal plain. Although fertile and densely inhabited in olden times, it was neglected in the Middle Ages and became the site of malarial swamps. After World War I, Jewish settlers drained the swamps and resettled the entire area, which is now a center of citriculture.

Shas: Abbreviation of *Shishah Sedarim*—"Six Orders" (of the Mishnah). It became especially widespread as referring to the Talmud, after the Church censors forbade the use of the word "Talmud" in the 16th cent.

shaving: The Bible forbids rounding the corners of the head (removing hair from the temples) or destroying corners of the beard (Lev. 19:27). Talmudic tradition forbids the removal of the hair with a knife or razor but allows a depilatory (in modern times, the rabbis permit an electric razor). S. is forbidden on holidays (including Sabbaths) and during periods of personal and public mourning.

Shavuot ("Weeks"): The second of the Pilgrim Festivals; also called Pentecost because it falls on the 50th day after Passover. Its Hebrew name derives from the fact that it occurs after the counting of 7 full weeks from the second day of Passover (the Counting of the OMER). It was a harvest festival at which barley was offered up in the Temple, as well as first fruits (hence another name, "Feast of the First Fruits"). It was also associated with the date of the Revelation of Mt. Sinai and is also called "Festival of the Giving of the Law." It falls on Sivan 6 and is observed for 2 days (in Israel and among Reform Jews, for one day). Under kabbalistic influence, it became customary to hold a midnight reading of the sacred literature (*tikkun hatzot*). The Ten Commandments and the Book of Ruth are read in the synagogue during the festival.

Shaw, Irwin (1913–): US novelist and playwright. He made his name with the play *Bury the Dead* and the novel *The Young Lions* set in World War II. Later successes have included *The Troubled Air*, *Rich Man*,

Poor Man and *Beggarman, Thief.*

Shazar (**Rubashov**), **Shneour Zalman** (1890–1974): Third president of Israel. Educated in a Ḥabad environment in Russia, he lived for a time in Germany, and settled in Palestine in 1924. Here he played a prominent role in the labor movement and edited the labor daily newspaper *Davar*. He sat in the Knesset on behalf of Mapai and was minister of education and culture in 1949–50. Later he was a member of the Jewish Agency Executive. In 1963 he was elected to succeed Yitzhak Ben-Zvi as president of Israel and was re-elected for a 2nd 5-year term in 1968. He did extensive research in various aspects of Jewish studies. His wife *Rachel* (*née* Katznelson; 1888–1975) was a leader of the women's labor movement in Palestine.

Sheba, Queen of: Ruler of Sabea in southern Arabia who journeyed to Jerusalem to visit Solomon, apparently on a trade mission, and tested his wisdom (I Kings 10). The story of her visit is the subject of many Jewish and Muslim legends. The former Ethiopian royal house claims descent from the union of the Queen and Solomon.

Shechem (**Nablus**): Town in Samaria, situated between Mt. Ebal and Mt. Gerizim. It was an ancient town predating the Israelite invasion. It is mentioned in several contexts in the Bible, including as the burial place of Joseph. It has always been the religious center of the Samaritans (who still venerate Mt. Gerizim as their most holy site). In 72 Vespasian founded the nearby city of Neapolis (the modern Nablus), which remained an important city, with a bishopric from 314. In 1967, it had 44,000 inhabitants, the great majority of them Muslims.

shehitah: Ritual slaughter of animals or birds in accordance with Jewish law. The windpipe and gullet of animals have to be cut by a sharp instrument according to prescribed rules by a trained slaughterer (*shoḥet*).

sheitel: Wig worn by Orthodox Jewish women to cover their hair after marriage (although among Oriental groups and some Ḥasidic sects, the hair is customarily covered by a kerchief). The Talmud forbids married women to expose their hair in the streets, and the use of the s. to prevent this developed from the 15th cent.

Shekalim ("Shekels"): Fourth tractate of the Mishnah order of *Moed*, with *gemara* in the Palestinian Talmud only. It deals with the annual half-shekel tax to the Second Temple.

shekel: A unit of weight which became a monetary unit from the time of the Maccabees. A half-shekel was paid by all numbered in the census in the wilderness to the upkeep of the Sanctuary (Exod. 30:13–15), and a similar tax was collected in Second Temple times. The Zionist Movement revived the concept in modern times and gave the name to a small annual contribution which was collected from members of the movement.

Shekhinah: Divine Presence. Used by the rabbis to indicate the manifestation of the Divine Presence in the life of man or in Creation. It represents the immanence of God in the world.

sheliah tzibbur ("messenger of the community"): The person who leads the congregation in prayer. It is now frequently applied to the *hazzan* and is often abbreviated to *shatz*.

sheloshim ("thirty"): Thirty days of MOURNING after the death of a close relative. It is customary for men not to shave during this period.

Shem: Son of Noah; eponymous ancestor of the Semitic people.

Shema Yisrael ("Hear O Israel"): The Jewish confession of faith, based on Deut. 6:4. The full passage (Deut. 6:4–9; 11:13–21; Num. 15:37–41) is read every morning and evening, and the first part is also said before going to sleep. The first verse is also recited on other occasions, including the conclusion of the Day of Atonement and on the deathbed. It was also the last statement of Jewish martyrs.

Shemaiah (1st cent. BCE): President (*nasi*) of the Sanhedrin; together with Avtalyon, the fourth of the ZUGOT. According to a Talmudic tradition both were descended from converts.

shemini atzeret ("eighth day of solemn assembly"; cf. Lev. 23:36): Last 2 days (in Israel and among Reform congregations, last day) of the Festival of Tabernacles; regarded by the rabbis as a separate festival. In Israel SIMHAT TORAH is observed on the same day; in the Diaspora on the 2nd day. It is a full holiday when *Hallel* and the Additional Service are recited. A prayer for RAIN is read during the Additional Service. Among Ashkenazim, the *yizkor* memorial prayer is said.

shemittah see **sabbatical year**

Shemoneh Esreh see **amidah**

Shemot see **Exodus**

Sheol: The abode of the dead, according to the

Bible. It is situated far below the earth and is especially the dwelling of the wicked. It came to be synonymous with hell.

Sherira (c. 906–1006): GAON of Pumbedita, 968–998. Under his leadership, the prestige of the academy, whose influence had been declining, was restored. His responsa were highly authoritative. One of them contains an important account of the development of rabbinical tradition.

sheva berakhot see **seven benedictions**

Shevat: Eleventh month of the religious calendar and 5th of the civil. Zodiac sign is the water carrier. It has 30 days. The 15th of the month is the NEW YEAR FOR TREES. It corresponds to January–February.

Sheviit ("Seventh Year"): Fifth tractate of the MISH-NAH order of *Zeraim* with *gemara* in the Palestinian Talmud only. It deals with problems of the sabbatical year.

Shevuot ("Oaths"): Sixth tractate of the MISH-NAH order of *Nezikin,* with *gemara* in both Talmuds. It deals with different types of oaths.

shewbread: Temple offering. Twelve loaves (corresponding to the twelve tribes) placed each Sabbath on the golden table in the sanctuary in the Temple. They remained until the next Sabbath. A small part was burned on the altar and the rest were consumed by the priests.

Shield of David see **Magen David**

Shiloh: Capital of the Israelites under the Judges, north of Jerusalem. The Tabernacle was erected there in the time of Joshua. The town was destroyed by the Philistines, who captured the ark after the battle of Aphek (c. 1050 BCE).

Shimoni (Shimonovitz), David (1886–1956): Hebrew poet. Born in Russia, he lived in Palestine from 1921. He wrote idylls about the landscape of Eretz Israel and the struggles of the early settlers.

shin see **sin**

Shinwell, Emanuel, Lord (1884–   ): English politician. A Labor member of parliament from 1932, he was minister of fuel (1945–7), minister of war (1947–50), and minister of defense (1950–51).

Shir ha-Kavod ("Hymn of Glory"; also known after its first words as *Anim Zemirot*): Alphabetic acrostic recited in the Ashkenazi rite responsively at the end of the Morning Service and the Sabbath Additional Service. It is often read by a small boy, with the congregation reading the responses. It dates from about the 11th cent.

shirayim ("remainders"): The leftovers of the food eaten by the Ḥasidic *rebbe*. His followers believe that these have received special sanctification, and they struggle to obtain some for themselves.

shivah ("seven"): Seven days of MOURNING commencing immediately after the burial of a close relative. The mourner remains at home (except for the Sabbath, when he visits the synagogue) and is visited by relatives and friends. He sits on the floor or on a low stool and prayers are recited in the home.

Shlonsky, Abraham (1900–1973): Hebrew poet and translator. Born in the Ukraine, he settled in Palestine in 1921—initially building roads—and became one of the country's leading literary figures. S. translated many classics (Shakespeare, Pushkin, etc.) into Hebrew.

Shneersohn: Ḥasidic dynasty, disseminating the ḤABAD school of Ḥasidism. It was founded by SHNEOUR ZALMAN OF LYADY, who was succeeded by Dov Ber of Liubavich. One of his descendants, *Joseph Isaac S.* (d. 1950), left the USSR, after a period of imprisonment, and settled in New York. His successor, *Menahem Mendel S.* (1902–   ), has developed the influence of the Liuba-vich movement and has established an educational network in various parts of the world.

Shneour Zalman of Lyady (1745–1813): Founder of the ḤABAD school of Ḥasidism. As a young boy he was a brilliant talmudic student, but was attracted to Ḥasadism by Dov BER OF MEZHIRICH, who urged him to prepare a revised edition of the *Shulḥan Arukh*, which S. did when he was 25. He became the ideologist of Ḥasidism, and from 1777 was one of the movement's leaders. He was involved in bitter polemics with the Vilna Gaon and the Mitnaggedim. Following false accusations, he was twice imprisoned by the Russians in St. Petersburg. From 1804 he lived in Lyady. When Napoleon's army approached, he fled to the interior of Russia and died on the journey. He developed his own system of mystical theology. His best-known work, *Likkutei Ama-rim*—better known as the TANYA—was regarded by his followers as the fundamental text of Ḥasidic spirituality.

Shneour, Zalman (1887–1959): Hebrew and Yiddish author. He left his native White Russia and lived in Europe and, from 1941, in the US. He made his home in Israel from 1951. His poems are sensual. He wrote stories about Jewish life in Eastern Europe under Czarist rule and in the Holocaust.

Shnorrer: A professional beggar.

shohet: A person trained and qualified to practice ritual (SHEḤITAH). Such a person must also be a pious Jew.

Sholem (Sholom) Aleichem (1859–1916): Yiddish novelist and humorist; his real name was Shalom Rabinowitz. He lived most of his life in Russia, but traveled in Europe and spent his last years in the US. He is the most popular of the Yiddish writers. His stories have become classics and have been translated into various languages; they have been adapted for the stage, screen, and—in *Fiddler on the Roof* —as a musical. He created a world of folk characters, such as Menachem Mendel and Tevye the Milkman, and imaginary places in Eastern Europe, such as the town of Kasrilevke.

shophar: Ram's horn sounded on ceremonial occasions such as the proclamation of the JUBILEE or anointing a king (I Kings 1:34). It is now almost entirely confined to synagogue use and is sounded during the month of Elul and during the ensuing Ten Days of Penitence, notably on Rosh ha-Shanah (unless falling on a Sabbath).

The use of the s. is derived from the story of the binding of Isaac and the ram caught by its horn in a thicket.

shtadlan: Representative of Jewish community who interceded with royalty and other top dignitaries on behalf of Jewish communities or individuals. He was generally noted for his wealth, eloquence, or connections.

Shulḥan Arukh see **Caro, Joseph**

Shushan Purim see **Purim**

Siberia: Geographic name for Asiatic RSFSR. Jews were exiled there in the 17th cent., and Jewish prisoners founded the first communities in the early 19th cent. Jews were forbidden to go there to join exiled relatives. Many Jews were among the political prisoners exiled to S. in the late 19th and early 20th cent. Under the Soviets Jewish settlement increased, due to the BIRO-BIDJAN scheme, to industralization, and the move to S. during World War II. 57,654 Jews were living there in 1959.

Sicarii: Patriot extremists in late Second Temple period (6–73), so-called from curved dagger (*sica*) they concealed in their clothes. They played a prominent role in the fraternal internecine strife that weakened the defenders of Jerusalem while they were besieged by the Romans in 66 ff. One of their leaders was ELEAZAR BEN JAIR, defender of MASADA.

Sicily: Mediterranean island. Jews lived there in Roman times, and there is a report of a synagogue in the 6th cent. The community flourished under the Arabs (9th–11th cent.). Jewish population was large in the later Middle Ages and prospered under the Normans. From the late 14th cent. their chief judge, who was appointed by the king, was known as the *dienchelele*. When the country came under Spanish rule this influenced policy toward Jews, who suffered forced conversions and massacres in 1392. The 37,000 Jews of S. were expelled in 1492. Subsequent Jewish settlement was tiny.

sick, visiting of (*bikkur holim*): A major Jewish religious duty. The commandment was stressed by the rabbis, and special associations were established for the purpose.

siddur ("order"): Ashkenazi term for daily prayer book.

sidrah ("arrangement"): Weekly portion of Pentateuch read in the synagogue on Sabbath mornings (with shorter excerpts in the Morning Service on Mondays and Thursdays). The Pentateuch is divided into 54 *sidrot*, which are read in the course of a year. (In the old Pentateuch custom, there were 175 such portions read over 3 years, the triennial cycle.)

Sieff, Israel Moses, Baron (1889–1972): British Zionist and industrialist. Together with his brother-in-law Simon MARKS, he headed the chain store Marks and Spencer. They were associated in Zionist work and collaborated closely with Chaim Weizmann. He founded the Daniel Sieff Research Institute at Reḥovot. His wife *Rebecca* (1890–1966) founded WIZO and was its president.

Silesia: Region of Central Europe. Jews lived there from the 12th cent., and many engaged in moneylending and trade. The largest community was in BRESLAU. Over the centuries the Jews were subject to frequent expulsions. The community increased from the 18th cent. Over 15,000 were living there in 1939, most of whom were killed by the Nazis. After World War II some 50,000 Jews returned to the area, but most subsequently left.

Sills, Beverly (born Belle Silverman; 1929–): US soprano. She debuted in 1947 with the Philadelphia Civic Opera. By the late 1960s, she was acclaimed as one of the world's outstanding singers.

Siloam (**Shiloaḥ**): A

pool in Jerusalem connected to the GIHON spring by a tunnel made by Hezekiah (II Kings 20:20). An inscription was discovered along the tunnel from the time of its construction (the original is in a museum in Istambul).

Silver, Abba Hillel (1893–1963): US Reform rabbi, Zionist leader, and orator. From 1917 he was rabbi of Congregation Tifereth Israel (The Temple), Cleveland. He headed many US Zionist organizations. As chairman of the American section of the Jewish Agency, he presented the case for an independent Jewish state at the UN sessions in 1947. His writings include *Messianic Speculation in Ancient Israel* and *Where Judaism Differed*.

Silverman, Samuel Sydney (1895–1968): British politician. He was a Labor member of Parliament from 1935 and achieved the abolition of capital punishment in Britain.

Simeon: Second son of Jacob and Leah. Avenging his sister Dinah, he dealt harshly with the citizens of Shechem, for which he was condemned by his father. After the conquest of Canaan, the tribe received territory in the Negev (Josh. 19).

Simeon ben Gamaliel: (1) Patriarch (*nasi*) in 1st cent. CE. In 66 he was a leader in the early stages of the revolt against Rome. (2)

Patriarch in 2nd cent. CE. During the persecutions following the Bar Kokhba rebellion, he was in hiding. Subsequently he was appointed patriarch of the Sanhedrin at Usha in Galilee. He was the father of JUDAH HA-NASI.

Simeon ben Lakish (3rd cent.): Palestinian AMORA, called Resh Lakish. Originally a gladiator, he was influenced by R. Johanan bar Nappaha to devote himself to religious studies. He became R. Johanan's deputy (and brother-in-law), and their legal discussions are a major element in the Palestinian Talmud.

Simeon ben Shetaḥ (1st cent. BCE): Scholar and president of the SANHEDRIN. A leader of the Pharisees during the reign of Alexander Yannai and Salome Alexandra (who was Simeon's sister), he helped them to increase their influence during his sister's reign. He and Judah ben Tabbai were the third of the ZUGOT. He laid the foundation for elementary education for Jewish children.

Simeon bar Yoḥai (2nd cent. CE): TANNA; pupil of R. Akiva. He conducted a school at Tekoa in Upper Galilee, where his pupils included Judah ha-Nasi. The halakhic Midrashim *Siphrei* and *Mekhilta* evolved from the teachings of his academy. Because of his hostility to the Roman authorities, he and his son Eleazar had to go into hiding and hid in a cave for 12 years. Many legends emerged from this period, and kabbalists believed that S. wrote the ZOHAR during this time. The date of his death, LAG BA' OMER, became a popular feast, centered around his traditional tomb at MERON.

Simhat Torah ("Rejoicing of the Law"): Name given in the Diaspora to the 2nd day of SHEMINI ATZERET; in Israel it is an additional name for that festival. It is a holiday marking the annual cycle of readings of the Pentateuch in the synagogue. On this occasion, the reading of Deuteronomy is completed and that of Genesis commenced, to the accompaniment of much festivity. All male worshipers are called up to the reading. The festival originated in the medieval period.

Simon, Neil (1927–): US playwright. He has written a series of successful Broadway hits, many of which were subsequently filmed. These include *Barefoot in the Park*, *The Odd Couple*, and *Plaza Suite*.

Simon the Hasmonean (d. 134 BCE): Second son of Mattathias. In 142 BCE he succeeded his brother Jonathan as high priest and as ruler and had great successes in completing the ex-

pulsion of the Syrians. He was murdered in Jericho by his son-in-law, Ptolemy, who wanted to succeed him.

sin (ש): Twenty-first letter of the Hebrew alphabet. Numerical value: 300. In printed script, if dotted on the left (שׂ), it is pronounced *sin*; if on the right (שׁ), *sh* (*shin*).

sin offering (*hattat*): Propitiatory sacrifice brought in atonement for a sin committed inadvertently. It was also offered after childbirth and leprosy. It consisted of an animal or a bird.

Sinai: Peninsula between Israel and Egypt. Site of mountain where Moses received the Torah. The peninsula throughout history has been a wilderness inhabited by Bedouin. It was captured by Israel from Egypt in the S. Campaign but was returned shortly after. It was again captured by them in the Six-Day War. The exact location of Mt. S. is uncertain but there is a traditional site at Jebel Musa (i.e., the "mountain of Moses"), where the monastery of St. Catherine's was built in the Byzantine period.

Sinai Campaign: War between Israel and Egypt, October 29–November 5, 1956. It followed an alliance designed against Israel and signed by Egypt, Jordan, and Syria, accompanied by threats against Israel, continuing incursion of terrorist gangs, and the Egyptian build-up of armor in the Sinai Desert. In a series of daring operations, the Israeli troops conquered the entire peninsula, stopping 10 miles short of the Suez Canal in accordance with an ultimatum from Britain and France (with whom the operation had been discussed in advance), then went down to Sharm el-Sheikh and occupied the Gaza Strip. Large quantities of Russian-manufactured munitions were taken as well as nearly 6,000 prisoners. Israeli losses were 171 dead and 700 wounded. On November 2, the British and French endeavored to intervene along the Canal area. They had to desist under American and Russian pressure. Pressure was brought on Israel to withdraw, and she gave up all territories occupied by March 1957 in return for certain undertakings. The S. C. opened the Gulf of Elath to Israel shipping and led to a drop in anti-Israel activities for several years.

Singapore: Jews lived there from the mid-19th cent.; the first synagogue was built in 1878 and the second in 1904. Jews from Baghdad, India, and England settled there. The first chief minister when S. achieved independence in 1955 was David MARSHALL. There were 500 Jews in 1976.

Singer: *Isaac Bashevis S.* (1904–   ), Yiddish novelist, was born in Poland and went to the US in 1935. His novels, in English translation, incorporated mystical and erotic elements. They included *The Family Moskat, Gimpel the Fool,* and *The Manor.* His brother *Israel Joshua S.* (1893–1944), Yiddish novelist, lived in the US from 1933. His outstanding works were the epic novels *The Brothers Ashkenazi* and *Yoshe Kalb.*

Siphra ("Book"): Tannaitic halakhic Midrash to Leviticus; probably compiled in Palestine in the 4th cent.

Siphre: Tannaitic halakhic Midrash to Numbers and Deuteronomy; probably compiled in Palestine in the late 4th cent.

Sivan: Ninth month of the Jewish civil year and 3rd of the religious year. Its zodiac sign is Scales, and it has 30 days. The Feast of Weeks occurs on the 6th (outside Israel, also on the 7th).

Six-Day War: War between Israel and Egypt, Syria, and Jordan, June 5–10, 1967. It followed a long period of tension caused by tension inside Israel and border attacks, notably from Syria. From May 15, President Nasser of Egypt moved a large force into the Sinai Peninsula. He demanded (and obtained) the withdrawal of the UN Emergency Force from the Gaza Strip and declared the Gulf of Elath closed to Israel shipping. Other Arab states made similar preparation and were gripped by war fever. In a pre-emptive move, Israel struck and within 3 hours destroyed 300 Egyptian planes, mostly on the ground. Other attacks decimated the Jordanian and Syrian air forces. In 3 days, the entire Sinai peninsula was occupied. The Jordanians opened fire and attacked in the Jerusalem area on the first morning. In 3 days, the entire West Bank, including the Old City of Jerusalem, was in Israeli hands. Israel then moved the bulk of its forces northward and in three more days the Golan Heights had been stormed and captured from the Syrians. The Arabs suffered 15,000 casualties; Israel's losses were 777 killed, 2,186 wounded. The subsequent debate in the UN was lengthy, and after several months a resolution was passed, but no agreement could be reached on its execution and the territory occupied by Israel remained in its hands. The period of the Six-Day War witnessed a remarkable upsurge of sentiment and pro-Israel identification among the Jews of the world.

siyyum ("termination"): Festive ceremony held on completion of writing of Pentateuch scroll or of the study of a tractate of the Talmud. In the latter case, it has been customary since Talmudic times to hold a special meal. This is often timed to coincide with the Fast of the Firstborn, where it supersedes the fast.

slavery: Slavery was a recognized institution in the ancient world, and was incorporated as part of Jewish law, which made provisions for its humane application. One Israelite could become slave of another only for a limited period and had to be freed with the advent of the SABBATICAL YEAR, with compensation. Non-Jewish slaves were regarded as semi-proselytes and were subject to Jewish law (including the Sabbath rest). An emancipated slave could become a full proselyte and could then marry a Jewess. In the course of history, Jews were active in the slave trade under certain circumstances. Supreme efforts were made by all Jewish communities to redeem any Jews in danger of being sold into slavery. Jews were prominent in the Western Hemisphere in the struggle for abolition, although there were those who opposed it.

Slobodka Yeshivah: Rabbinical academy in Kovno,

founded in 1882, dedicated to the ideals of the MUSAR MOVEMENT. In 1924 some of its students founded a yeshivah in Hebron, but after the 1929 riots moved to Jerusalem (under the name Hebron Yeshivah). After World War II, the original yeshivah (closed 1941) was reopened in Bene Berak in Israel.

Slovakia: Region of Czechoslovakia; previously of Hungary. Jews lived there from the 13th cent. Pressburg (Bratislava) was an important Jewish community by the 14th cent. Anti-Semitic outbursts occurred in the latter 19th cent. The community prospered under Czech rule between the two world wars. Some 100,000 Jews were living there in 1939; over 60,000 were sent to the death camps. After World War II many Jews lived there, but most left. About 9,000 Jews were living there in 1968.

Smolenskin,   Peretz (1842–1885): Hebrew novelist and editor. After years of wandering, he lived in Vienna from 1868, when he founded the Hebrew monthly HA-SHAHAR which became the central organ of Hebrew literary activities and Jewish national thought. His own novels and articles were widely circulated and very influential. In his last years he joined the Hibbat Zion movement.

Smyrna see **Izmir**

Sobibor: Nazi extermination camp in Poland. It was in operation 1942–43, in which time 250,000 victims were killed, mostly from eastern Poland and the USSR.

Sobeloff, Simon Ernest (1894–1973): US jurist. He was US solicitor-general from 1954 until 1956, when he was appointed judge of the Circuit Court of Appeals.

Sodom (*Sedom*): Ancient city in the Jordan plain where LOT and his family settled. The city was destroyed by "fire and brimstone"—along with the other cities of the plain—and became a byword for wickedness (Gen. 19). The site of ancient S. is uncertain. In modern times, the name has been given to the southern end of the Dead Sea where the potash works are situated.

Sokolow, Nahum (1859–1936): Zionist leader and one of the chief creators of Hebrew journalism. He edited the newspaper *Ha-Tzephirah* in Poland. He was general secretary of the World Zionist Organization in 1906–09, editing its journal *Die Welt* and establishing its Hebrew weekly *Ha-Olam*. During World War I, he played a major role in Western capitals in the negotiations culminating in the Balfour Declaration. During the Paris

Peace Conference, he was president of the Committee of Jewish Delegations. He played a leading role in post-war Zionism and was president of the World Zionist Organization in 1931–35. He wrote a standard *History of Zionism, 1600–1918*.

Solomon: King of Israel, c. 961–c. 920 BCE. His mother, Bathsheba, maneuvered his accession to the throne even before the death of his father, David. After consolidating his position, he built the TEMPLE in Jerusalem, which had been projected by his father. He built up the country, constructing a harbor on the Red Sea, developing smelting furnaces for copper and iron in the Negev, and achieving a reputation for wisdom which became proverbial. His territory was extensive, ranging from Egypt to the Euphrates. However, the extravagance and the imposition of forced labor sowed the seeds of the collapse and breakup that occurred early in the reign of S.'s successor. In Jewish tradition, a number of works—canonical and otherwise—were ascribed to S.'s authorship, notably Proverbs, Song of Songs, and Ecclesiastes.

Solomon ben Adret see **Adret**

Solomon, Vabian Louis (1853–1908): Australian

statesman and industrialist. He was prime minister of South Australia in 1899 and a member of the convention that framed the federal constitution.

Soloveichik: Distinguished family of talmudists. These included *Joseph bär S.* (1820–1892), who headed the Volozhin yeshivah and was rabbi in Slutzk and Brest-Litovsk. His son *Hayyim* (1853–1918) taught at Volozhin and succeeded his father at Brest-Litovsk. His method of talmudic study was highly influential. *Joseph Dov S.* (1903–) lived in Boston from 1932, taught at Yeshiva University, and is the outstanding Orthodox authority in the US.

Soncino: Italian family who pioneered in Hebrew printing, initially in the small Italian town of S. The press was established in 1484. The first generations worked in various Italian towns, from 1526 in Turkey, and from 1557 in Cairo. Nearly half the known Italian INCUNABULA were printed by members of the family.

Song of Degrees: Superscription of fifteen psalms (120–134). It has been suggested that the meaning is that they were sung either while ascending to Jerusalem or to the Temple area.

Song of Songs (Song of

Solomon; Canticles) (*Shir ha-Shirim*): Biblical book; first of the five scrolls in the Hagiographa. It contains love poems, traditionally attributed to Solomon. Scholars differ as to its dating but suggest it was edited c. 5th cent. BCE. It has been described as a dialogue or drama; as a collection of bridal songs; and as an allegory, with the Talmud interpreting it as a dialogue between God and Israel, and Christian tradition as a dialogue between Jesus and the Church. It is read in the synagogue on Passover and by Sephardim every Sabbath.

sopher see **scribe**

Sopher (Schreiber), **Moses** (1762–1839): Hungarian rabbinical authority and Orthodox Jewish leader; son-in-law of Akiva EGER. From 1803, rabbi in Pressburg, where he established a famous and large yeshivah. He was generally known as Ḥatam Sopher after his 7-volume collection of responsa and novellae. He was a leading opponent of the Reform movement.

Sotah ("Errant Wife"): Fifth tractate in the MISHNAH order of *Nashim*, with *gemara* in both Talmuds. It contains the laws dealing with a married woman suspected of adultery (Num. 5:11–31) and with the laws of the RED HEIFER (Deut. 20:2–9; 21: 1–9).

South Africa see **Africa, South**

South Carolina: US state. The liberal attitude of the authorities encouraged Jewish settlement, and a congregation was founded in Charleston in 1749. The first Reform congregation in the US was established there in 1824. At that time Charleston's 700 Jews constituted the largest Jewish community in the US. Jews settled in Columbia from the late 18th cent., but the Jewish population of the state was never large. In 1976 it numbered 8,065, with 3,000 in Charleston and 2,500 in Columbia.

South Dakota: US state. Jews settled in the territory in the late 19th cent., but their numbers were always small and in 1976 totaled 500.

Soutine, Chaim (1894–1943): Painter. Born in Lithuania, he settled in Paris in 1913 and joined the School of Paris. His expressionistic work included portraits, landscapes, and still lifes.

Soyer: Family of US painters. *Raphael S.* (1899–) has produced many murals and other paintings in a mood of stark realism. His twin brother *Moses S.* (1899–1974) and his brother *Isaac S.* (1907–) paint in similar styles, often on topical themes taken from the life of the working and lower-middle classes.

Spain: Jews probably arrived in Roman times, and Jewish tombstones have been found from the third century CE. Jews were initially well treated by the Visigoths, but after these turned to Catholicism, the Jewish situation deteriorated. In the 7th cent. the practice of Judaism was forbidden. The Arab invasion of 711 brought relief, and for the next centuries the Jewish communities prospered and flourished, economically and culturally (known as the "Golden Age"). Some Jews rose to high rank. The invasion of the Almohades in 1136 led to an intolerant interlude when Judaism was again proscribed. In the growing Christian parts of the country, the Jews were generally living in toleration and maintaining their affluence and cultural achievements. The 12th cent. saw much less toleration, under various Christian influences. The following century, the Dominicans initiated activities aimed at converting the Jews. Anti-Jewish feeling reached a climax in 1391 with a wave of massacres throughout the country. Many Jews accepted Christianity to save their lives, but a large number continued to observe Judaism in secret (they were known as New Christians, MARRANOS, or Conversos). In order to ferret out these heretics the INQUISITION was introduced in 1478. This in turn encouraged activities against those Jews who remained openly Jewish, culminating in the order of expulsion in 1492, by edict of Ferdinand and Isabella. The exiles went mostly to Portugal and to Mediterranean lands. The Marranos remained in the country, where they and their descendants continued to be hounded by the Inquisition, down to the 18th cent. A few Jews began living in S. in the latter 19th cent., and laws prohibiting synagogues were abolished in 1909. Small congregations now exist, especially in Madrid and Barcelona, and in 1976, there were 9,000 Jews in the country.

Spektor, Isaac Elhanan (1817–1896): Lithuanian rabbi; officiated from 1864 in Kovno, where he founded a famous yeshivah. From an early age, he was the outstanding talmudic authority in Russia and issued responsa to many communities. His rulings were generally lenient, especially concerning *agunot*. S. supported the Ḥovevei Zion movement.

Speyer (Spire): Town in the Rhineland. Jews lived there from the 11th cent.

when they received privileges and were protected by the bishop. Closely connected with Mainz and Worms, it was a focus of Jewish scholarship. The community was destroyed at the time of the Black Death (1349). Refugees returned but were repeatedly banished. The modern community of 264 (1933) perished in the Holocaust, and no new community was constituted.

Spinoza, Benedict (Baruch) (1632–1677): Dutch philosopher of a Portuguese Marrano family that had escaped to Amsterdam. He had a Jewish education and a good knowledge of medieval Jewish philosophy. His religious views were regarded as heretical by the Sephardi community, which excommunicated him in 1656. In 1660, he left Amsterdam, and earned his living polishing lenses. His *Theologico-Political Treatise* expanded his political philosophy and was the forerunner of biblical higher criticism. His *Ethics* proved one of the most influential works of western European thought; it is a metaphysics of pantheism, applying Euclidean methods to demonstrate his metaphysical concept of the universe, with ethical corollaries.

Spire see **Speyer**

Spitz, Mark (1950–): US swimmer. In the 1968 Olympics he won 4 gold medals and in the 1972 Olympics achieved the record feat of winning 7 gold medals.

sport: There is no special evidence of s. among the Jews until a late period. Hellenism made an appeal to certain classes, and a gymnasium was constructed in Jerusalem in 174 BCE in which youths participated in the nude. Life in ghettos precluded much sporting activity, although from time to time there is mention of Jews having participated in sports. From the 18th cent. Jews are heard about in boxing, such as the English pugilist Daniel MENDOZA. By the time of the first Olympic Games in 1896, a number of Jews were among the medal winners, and have continued to win their share, up to Mark SPITZ's unprecedented 7 medals at the 1972 Munich Olympics. At the end of the 19th cent. a federation of Jewish sporting societies was formed which later developed into the MACCABI movement. A leading Jewish sports club was Ha-Koah in Vienna. Among famous Jewish sportsmen are the boxing champions Benny Leonard, Max Baer, and Barney Ross; Richard Savitt and Tom Okker in tennis; the Abrahams brothers in athletics; Hank Greenberg and Sandy Koufax in baseball; Nat Holman in basketball; Richard Bergmann and Victor Barna in table tennis. Many Jews have been prominent in CHESS and in bridge. Israel sports organizations include Maccabi, Hapoel (under the auspices of the worker's movement), Betar (of Ḥerut) and Elitzur (religious). Israeli teams participate regularly in international tournaments, and have had successes in basketball, soccer, chess, and bridge.

Sprinzak, Yoseph (1885–1959): Israeli labor leader and first speaker of the Knesset. Born in Moscow, he went to Palestine in 1908 and was among the founders of the Histadrut and of Mapai. From 1949 he was a Mapai representative in the Knesset and as its first speaker (until his death) played an important part in the development of its traditions.

stamps: In Palestine, the first post office was established in 1852 by the European powers. Turkey set up post offices in the 1860s. Under the British Mandate, stamps had Hebrew, English, and Arabic lettering. The Jewish People's Administration issued provisional stamps early in May 1948, and the first stamps of the State appeared on May 16 (Doar Ivri). Israeli stamps have been in wide demand and are a popular subject for collec-

tions. New ones are issued for the New Year, for Independence Day, and for special occasions. Another popular branch of philately is Judaica, the collection of stamps with Jewish themes. There are associations of Judaica collectors who also publish their own journal.

Star of David see **Magen David**

Steiger, Rod (1925–): US actor. A star of stage, TV, and movies, he won an Oscar for his performance in *In the Heat of Night*. His other successes included *On the Waterfront* and *The Pawnbroker*.

Stein, Gertrude (1874–1946): US writer. From 1903 she lived in Paris, where her salon and patronage influenced many writers and artists (e.g. Hemingway). She wrote in a repetitious, impressionistic style. Her works include stories, poems, operas, and autobiographical works.

Stein, William Howard (1911–): US biochemist; from 1938 at Rockefeller Univ., New York. He was awarded the 1972 Nobel Prize for Chemistry for his work on chemical reactions which constitute the concept of life and living organisms.

Steinberg, Isaac Nahman (1888–1957): Politician and writer. A member of the Russian Socialist Revolutionary Party, he was commissar for law in Lenin's first government, in 1917–18, but left Russia in 1923 and went to Europe and to New York in 1943. He became a proponent of TERRITORIALISM and founded the Freeland League, advocating Jewish colonization in countries other than Israel.

Steinberg, Milton (1903–1950): US Conservative rabbi. He was rabbi of the Park Avenue Synagogue in New York. His books on Judaism were influential, and he was a popular lecturer and teacher. He wrote a novel about the life of Elisha ben Avuyah.

Steinberg, Saul (1914–): US artist. Born in Rumania, he went to the US in 1942. An original cartoonist, several albums of his works have been published.

Steinhardt, Jakob (1887–1968): Painter and printmaker. He was born in Poland and lived in Jerusalem from 1933. He headed the Bezalel Art School, 1953–57. Most of his work, on Jewish and Israeli themes, are woodcuts.

Steinitz, William (1836–1900): Chess master. He was the first world chess master (1866–94). Born in Prague, he lived in London from the 1860s and spent his last years in New York. He wrote on chess.

Steinschneider, Moritz (1816–1907): Scholar, who lived most of his life in Berlin. He is the outstanding figure in Jewish bibliography, in which he produced a prolific output displaying remarkable erudition. His works include catalogues of Hebrew books and manuscripts in various libraries (including the Bodleian, Oxford), Judeo-Arabic literature, Jewish scientific literature, Jewish medieval translators, Hebrew typography, etc. He founded and edited the periodical *Hebraische Bibliographie*, 1858–82.

Stern, Avraham (1907–1942): Palestinian underground leader. He was born in Poland and went to Palestine in 1925. He left the Irgun Tzevai Leumi because of its suspension of anti-British attacks during World War II and formed the LOḤAME ḤERUT ISRAEL (also known as the Stern Group). It carried out anti-British acts of sabotage. He was killed by British policemen. His "underground" name was Yair.

Stern, Isaac (1920–): US violinist. He made his debut with the San Francisco Symphony when he was 11. He established an international reputation based on a wide command of the violin repertoire. He appeared frequently in Israel and headed the American-Israel Cultural Fund.

Stern, Lina Solomonovna (1878–1968): Russian

physiologist and biologist, born in Lithuania. In 1939 she was the first woman to be admitted as a full member of the Soviet Academy of Sciences. Her research was in endocrinology and the chemical and physiological bases of nervous activity.

Stern, Otto (1888–1969): Physicist. He taught in Germany until Hitler came to power, when he went to the US and was professor at the Carnegie Institute of Technology in Pittsburgh. In 1943 he was awarded a Nobel Prize in Physics for discovery of the magnetic momentum of protons and for work on the molecular beam method of the study of molecular properties.

Stern, William (1871–1938): Psychologist. He taught at Hamburg from 1897, but when Hitler came to power went to the US and taught at Duke University in North Carolina. His *Psychology of Early Childhood* became a classic study. It was S. who introduced the idea of an intelligence quotient (IQ) and founded personalistic psychology.

Stieglitz, Alfred (1864–1946): US photographer and exhibitor. He was a pioneer in promoting photography as an art. He edited a photography magazine and opened a famous gallery in New York.

Stone, Richard (1928–): US politician. He was elected to the Florida Senate in 1967 and was Florida secretary of state from 1971 until elected to the US Senate on the Democratic ticket in 1974.

Strasbourg: City in Alsace, France. Jews were living there from the end of the 12th cent. and suffered during the third Crusade. The Jews lived mainly as moneylenders. There was a fierce massacre in 1349 in which 2,000 Jews died. Jews returned in 1369 and were expelled in 1388. They continued to live in the city from the late 18th cent. After World War II, the community (numbering 12,000 in 1976) had one of the most active cultural and educational programs in Europe.

Straus: US family of merchants, industrialists, and philanthropists. *Isidor S.* (1845–1912), born in Bavaria, acquired ownership of the famous New York department store Macy's by 1896, and the family has been associated with it since. He was a member of Congress, 1894–95. His son *Jesse Isidor* (1872–1936) was ambassador to France, 1933–36. Isidor's brother *Nathan S.* (1848–1931) was New York parks commissioner in 1889–93. Deeply interested in public health, he campaigned for compulsory pasteurization of milk and distributed such milk to the poor of New York. He gave much of his fortune to health projects in Palestine, where the town of Netanyah was named for him. His brother *Oscar Solomon S.* (1850–1926) was minister to Turkey (1887–89, 1898–1900, 1909–1910). The first Jew in a US Cabinet, he was secretary of commerce and labor under President Theodore Roosevelt. Among his many Jewish activities, he was president of the American Jewish Historical Society, 1892–98, and was a founder of the American Jewish Committee. Nathan's son *Nathan S.* (1889–1961) headed the US Housing Authority, 1937–42.

Straus, Leo (1899–1973): Philosopher. He taught in Germany until the Nazi period, when he went to the US, where he was professor at the New School for Social Research until 1949; he then went to the University of Chicago. His main field was political philosophy, and he wrote studies of Spinoza, Maimonides, and Judah ha-Levi.

Straus, Oscar (1870–1954): Austrian composer. His best-known works are operettas, including *A Waltz Dream, The Chocolate Soldier,* and *The Last Waltz.*

Strauss, Lewis Lichtenstein (1896–1974): US government official and banker.

During World War II, he was special assistant to James Forrestal, undersecretary of the navy, and was appointed a rear admiral in 1945. He was a member of the US Atomic Energy Commission in 1946–50 and chairman in 1953–58. In 1959 he was named secretary of commerce, but his appointment was not confirmed by the Senate. He was president of Temple Emanu-El, New York.

*Streicher, Julius (1885–1946): Nazi anti-Semite. He edited the crude anti-Jewish paper *Der Stürmer,* which published obscene anti-Semitism, 1923–45. S. played a key role in Nazi policy toward the Jews. He was executed after condemnation by the International Military Tribunal at Nuremburg.

Streisand, Barbra (1944–   ): US singer and actress. She made a great success in 1964 in her Broadway appearance in *Funny Girl,* a musical biography of Fanny BRICE. Later she won an Academy Award for the film version. She has continued to appear in successful films such as *Hello, Dolly, On a Clear Day You Can See Forever,* and *A Star is Born.*

Stricker, Robert, (1879–1944): Zionist, active in his native Moravia and later in Austria. In 1933, he was a founder of the Jewish State Party. He founded and edited the only German-language Jewish daily *Wiener Morgenzeitung*. He refused to leave Austria in 1938 and died in Auschwitz.

Struma: Ship carrying 769 "illegal" immigrants from Rumania to Palestine in 1941. Refused entry by the British, they were turned back to Rumania, despite the fact that Rumania was pursuing a pro-Nazi policy. The ship sank in the Black Sea and all but one of the refugees were drowned.

Subbotniki ("Sabbatarians"): Russian Sabbatarians with strong Jewish influence. Some of its followers accepted only the Old Testament but not the New. Its history goes back to the 15th cent. It was persecuted by the Russian government and Orthodox Church until the early 20th cent. Before 1917 it had tens of thousands of adherents, some of whom became Jews and settled in Palestine.

Subcarpathian Ruthenia: Part of Ukrainian SSR. Jews lived there from the 17th cent. The community was greatly influenced by Hasidism. Between the world wars their conditions under Czech rule improved, but World War II brought tragedy, and few of the 100,000 Jews survived the war. In 1971, 13,000 Jews lived in the region.

sukkah ("tabernacle"): Temporary booth set up for the Feast of Sukkot (Lev. 23:42). It is a center of hospitality during the festival, and all meals are eaten there. Booths probably played a part in ancient harvest festivals, hence their association with this festival. In Jewish tradition, they were associated with the temporary structures established by the Israelites in the wilderness. The roof of the s. is covered with cut vegetation and must be open to the sky.

Sukkah: Sixth tractate in the MISNAH order of *Moed*, with *gemara* in both Talmuds. It deals with the laws of the Feast of Tabernacles.

Sukkot: The fall festival of Tabernacles, last of the three annual pilgrim-festivals, a harvest festival, also known as the Feast of the Ingathering. It commences on Tishri 15 and lasts for 7 days; the 8th day (and 9th in the Diaspora), SHEMINI ATZERET, being a separate holiday. Work is prohibited on the first day (2 days in the Diaspora) and on Shemini Atzeret. The intermediate days (including HOSHANA RABBAH on the 7th day) are ḤOL HA-MOED. Special characteristics are the dwelling in the SUKKAH and the taking of the FOUR SPECIES and carrying them in procession around the synagogue. In Second Temple times, this was also the occasion for the Water-Drawing Festival. *Hallel* and the Additional Service are recited on each day. The Book of Ecclesiastes is read in the Synagogue.

Sulzberger: US family. Its members include *Arthur Hays S.* (1891–1968), president and publisher of the *New York Times;* and *Mayer S.* (1843–1923), jurist and communal leader, judge of the Court of Common Pleas in Philadelphia, and first president of the American Jewish Committee.

Sulzer, Solomon (1804–1891): Austrian cantor and pioneer of modern liturgical music. From 1826 he was *ḥazzan* in Vienna. His compositions were influenced by general music trends of his time and were influential in Central Europe and among Western Jewry.

Sun, Blessing of the: Ceremonial blessing, recited once every 28 years (1953–1981) on the first Wednesday of Nisan when the sun enters a new cycle (and is therefore supposed to stand on the same spot where it was at creation).

Sura: City in southern Babylonia, site of one of the leading academies, founded by Rav in 219. It was in S. that the Babylonian Talmud was compiled by R. Ashi and Ravina in the 4th–5th cent. Its heads had the title GAON

from the late 6th cent.; its best-known *goan* was Saadiah. In the 10th cent. the academy transferred to Baghdad and merged with its great rival, PUMBEDITA.

Surinam (Dutch Guiana): Jews arrived from Brazil from 1639. In the 17th–18th cent., it became the largest Jewish community in the Western hemisphere. Its members were active in all aspects of economic and social life, under Dutch rule. For economic reasons it declined in the 19th cent. There were 500 Jews in S. in 1976, with an old synagogue.

Susanna and the Elders: Apocryphal work telling how two corrupt Jewish elders schemed against the pure Susanna and were foiled by the wise judge Daniel. It was originally written in Hebrew or Greek and dates from the 2nd or 1st cent. BCE.

Süsskind von Trimberg (c. 1200–1250): German minstrel (minnesinger). Six of his poems, in Middle High German, have been preserved and are the sole medieval German poems on Jewish themes.

Sutzkever, Abraham (1913–): Yiddish poet. Born in White Russia, he was a founder of the Young Vilna group of poets. He was in the Vilna ghetto in World War II, and escaped to join the partisans. In 1947 he went to

Palestine, where he edits the Yiddish literary quarterly *Die Goldene Keit*.

Svevo, Italo (Ettore Schmitz) (1861–1928): Italian novelist living in Trieste, where all his works are set. His psychological novels, of which *The Conscience of Zeno* is outstanding, have been of influence in European literature, notably on his friend James Joyce.

Sweden: Jews were allowed to settle there from the 18th cent. Most disabilities were finally removed beginning in 1853. About 3,000 refugees from Germany arrived in the 1930s, and many more arrived during World War II, most subsequently leaving. 15,000 Jews were living there in 1976.

Switzerland: Jews were living in Basle in the 13th cent. The community grew, but massacres were perpetrated there during the Black Death period (1349). Subsequent settlement was intermittent, and the Jews were "permanently excluded" in 1622. Most cantons retained this exclusion until the 18th cent. Restrictions were gradually removed from 1861. Since 1893, ritual slaughter has been forbidden ("on humanitarian grounds") and Jews have had to import kosher meat. 25,000 Jewish refugees were taken in by neutral S. during World War II, but the country was criticized for not having done more. The 1976 Jewish population is 27,000.

Sydney: Australian city. Jews from England settled there with the first convicts in the early 19th cent., and the first congregation was formed in 1832. The community grew in the 19th cent. with immigrants from England and Germany, then from Eastern Europe from the 1880s and from Central and Eastern Europe after 1945. The 28,000 Jews (1976) have 19 synagogues (one Reform).

synagogue (*bet hakneset*): Leading religious institution in Judaism. Its exact origin is unknown. It is generally believed to have emerged not later than the Babylonian Exile. Synagogues were in existence in Second Temple times, the large one at Alexandria being particularly famous. They were also in existence in Palestine (early examples having been excavated at Masada and Herodium). The New Testament also evidences synagogues both in Galilee and in the classical world. Their importance grew after the destruction of the Temple, when they became the focal point of Judaism (the rabbis applied to them the term "little sanctuary" in Ezek. 11:15–16). Excavations have revealed that many of these synagogues were elaborately decorated, with striking mosaics and murals. From the 3rd cent. women—previously seated separately on the same level—were accommodated in a special upper gallery. The Ark of the Covenant, initially portable, became a permanent fixture in the eastern wall, which was the focus of the s. In front of the ark it became customary to burn a perpetual light. When the Roman Empire was Christianized, many synagogues were destroyed, some were turned into churches, and further construction was forbidden. Restrictions were also placed on s. building in the Muslim world. From the Middle Ages, the s. as place of prayer and study was the center of Jewish life. Many of them had adjacent communal institutions. The oldest surviving s. still in use is the Altneushul in Prague (14th cent.). Many Polish synagogues were built as fortresses so as to be more easily defended against mob attack. Many Eastern European synagogues were built of wood. The 19th-cent. Reform movement introduced an organ, moved the reader's platform from the center to the east, and had mixed seating for men and women. In modern times, in the US, the s. (or

"temple") complex has been developed as a community center.

Synagogue Council of America: Organization founded in 1926 to present a united Jewish front in activities involving public relations and relations with non-Jewish organizations. Its membership includes Orthodox, Conservative, and Reform synagogues.

Synagogue, the Great see **Great Assembly**

Syria: Ancient ARAM. In Second Temple times there was a Jewish population, notably at Antioch. There were few Jews there in Talmudic times, but their numbers grew under the Arabs. Jews were traders and bankers and S. was a center of scholarship. After the 15th cent. Jews from Spain took over the leadership. The 1840 DAMASCUS AFFAIR was a blood libel which had international repercussions. After World War II, Jews began emigrating, and their numbers dropped from 15,000 in 1947 to 3,000 in 1977. From the period of the establishment of the State of Israel, they were subject to continual persecution and discrimination. S. maintained an attitude of intense enmity toward Israel and frequently took the lead in acts of hostility.

Syrkin, Nachman (1868–1924): Zionist socialist ideologist. He was born in White Russia but lived for a time in Germany. He took part in the First Zionist Congress, then supported the UGANDA PROJECT and TERRITORIALISM from 1905 to 1909. From 1907 he lived in New York and in 1909 joined the Poalei Zion movement, becoming one of its leading theoreticians. His daughter *Marie* (1899–) taught English Literature at Brandis University, was a member of the Jewish Agency Executive, and wrote extensively on Israel and Zionist themes (including biographies of Hannah Szenes and Golda Meir).

Szenes, Hannah (1921–1944): Palestine poet and Haganah heroine. Born in Budapest, she went to Palestine in 1939 and joined kibbutz Sedot Yam. During World War II she volunteered to be parachuted behind the Nazi lines. She was captured, tried in Budapest, and executed. S. wrote Hebrew poetry, including the poem "Blessed Is the Match."

Szigeti, Joseph (1892–1973): Violinist. Born in Hungary, he taught in Geneva from 1917 to 1924 and in 1926 settled in the US. He was one of the best-known violinists on the international circuit.

Szold: US family. *Ben-jamin S.* (1829–1902), rabbi and scholar, was born in Hungary and in 1858 went to the US, where he served Congregation Oheb Shalom in Baltimore for over 40 years. His daughter *Henrietta S.* (1860–1945) was the first woman to study at the Jewish Theological Seminary. She was secretary of the Jewish Publication Society of America 1892–1916 and edited the *American Jewish Year Book.* In 1912 she organized and was the first president of HADASSAH, the Women's Zionist Organization of America, and in 1918 organized the dispatch of the American Zionist Medical Unit to Palestine, where she herself settled. She was a member of the Zionist Executive from 1927, heading the office department for health and education. After the Nazis came to power she directed YOUTH ALIYAH and was responsible for rescuing thousands of Jewish children from Nazi Europe.

Szyk, Arthur (1894–1951): Illustrator. Born in Lodz, he studied in Paris and settled in the US in 1940. He was noted for his stylized caricatures and anti-Nazi drawings. He illustrated the Passover Haggadah and the Israeli and US Declarations of Independence.

Taanit ("Fast Day"): Ninth tractate in the MISH-NAH order of *Moed*, with *gemara* in both Babylonian and Palestinian Talmuds. It deals with fast days decreed because of drought.

tabernacle (*mishkan*): Portable sanctuary constructed in the Wilderness (Exod. 26–7). Its chief designers were BEZALEL and Oholiab. Its most sacred section was the Holy of Holies containing the Ark of the Covenant. It was incorporated in the TEMPLE (I Kings 8:4).

Tabernacles see Sukkot

Tablets of the Law see Commandments, Ten

Tabor: Mountain (1,750 ft.) in the Jezreel Valley. It was the place where Barak gathered his army before defeating the forces of Sisera (Judg. 4). In Christian tradition, it is the site of Jesus' transfiguration, and churches have been on the mount since Byzantine times.

tahanun ("supplication"): Petition for grace and forgiveness said daily except on Sabbaths, festivals, days of joy, Av 9, and in houses of mourning. Originally recited in an attitude of prostration, it is known as *nephilat appayim* ("falling on the face"); it is still customary to lean the face on the arm during its recitation. The present wording dates from the gaonic period.

takkanah: Ordinance promulgated for public welfare or for strengthening religious and moral life and supplementing the law of the Torah. The *t.* goes back to antiquity, and some are ascribed to Moses and Ezra. Those instituted in the talmudic period cover many aspects of life. To R. Gershom Me'or Ha-Golah is ascribed the *t.* forbidding bigamy, which came to be accepted by all Ashkenazi communities.

tallit: Prayer shawl with fringes at each corner. It is worn by male worshipers at Morning Services throughout the Day of Atonement and on Av 9 at the Afternoon instead of the Morning Service. It is usually white, with a black or blue stripe and made of wool, cotton or silk. See also TZITZIT.

talmid hakham ("disciple of the wise"): Rabbinic term for a scholar.

Talmud ("Learning"): Comprehensive term for the MISHNAH with either of the two great commentaries (GEMARA) on it—the Palestinian (incorrectly the Jerusalem) T. and the Babylonian T. It is a cumulative compilation of centuries of discussions in the rabbinic academies of Palestine and Babylonia. It is traditionally based on the ORAL LAW transmitted at Mt. Sinai. It consists of laws from the Mishnah with the discussion on each one, together with many digressions, sometimes of legal content (HALAKHAH) and sometimes of a narrative nature (AGGADAH). The redaction of the Palestinian T. was com-

pleted in Tiberias c. 400 CE under pressure of growing persecution. It tended to be ignored in early Jewish study, and most commentaries on it date from the 18th cent. or after. It was the Babylonian T. which emerged as the most influential book in Judaism next to the Bible—indeed, under certain circumstances it eclipsed the Bible as the object of Jewish study. The foundations were laid by RAV and SAMUEL, and its redaction was accomplished by R. ASHI and RAVINA, c. 500. There are differences in the surviving books on which *gemara* exists in the two Talmuds. The main language of the Talmud is Aramaic. The Babylonian T. is four times the size of the Palestinian. The Talmud became the source of Jewish law, and its study has been the basis of Jewish religious life. Many commentaries were written on the Babylonian Talmud. The most accepted and influential was that of RASHI, together with the further elucidations provided by his school (TOSAPHOT). From time to time, the T. was attacked by the Christian Church and, after a disputation in Paris, 24 cartloads of Talmud manuscripts were burned in 1242. This example was copied in Italy and Eastern Europe.

Talmud Torah ("Study

of the Torah"); Term applied to Jewish religious study, regarded by the rabbis as one of the most desirable occupations. The phrase was then applied to the teaching of Torah to children, and eventually was applied to the place where education, particularly of an elementary nature, was provided.

Tam, Jacob ben Meir see **Jacob ben Meir**

Tamid: Ninth tractate in the MISHNAH order of *Kodashim*, with *gemara* in the Babylonian Talmud only. It deals with the laws of the daily morning and evening offering (*tamid*) and touches on many details of Temple organization and the sacrificial rite.

Tammuz: Fourth month of the religious, 10th of the civil year; corresponding with June-July. It has 29 days, and its zodiac sign is the crab. The 17th of the month is a fast commemorating the breaching of the walls of Jerusalem by Nebuchadnezzar. This begins the THREE WEEKS of mourning culminating on Av 9.

Tanakh: Initial letters of Torah, Neviim, and Ketuvim (Pentateuch, Prophets, Hagiographa). Usual Hebrew name for the Jewish Bible.

Tanhuma: Name given to various Midrashic compilations. The oldest is also known as *Yelammedenu* from

the characteristic opening phrase in each sermon. Most of the discourses refer to the opening verse of the week's Torah reading (according to the Triennial Cycle). The work was probably edited about the 5th cent.

tanna ("one who studies and teaches"): Rabbinic authority from the period of Hillel and Shammai down to the time of Judah ha-Nasi (1st cent. BCE–end of 2nd cent. CE). Their teachings are found in the Mishnah, *baraita*, and halakhic Midrashim. Later the term was applied to the "reciter" of the Mishnah texts in every academy.

Tanya (Aram. "There Is a Teaching"): Ḥasidic classic by SHNEOUR ZALMAN OF LYADY, the founder of the Ḥabad school. It first appeared in 1797 as *Likkutei Amarim*. It is studied daily by Ḥabad Ḥasidim.

Targum (Aram. "Translation"): The Aramaic translation of the Bible. In the Second Temple period an Aramaic translation was added verse by verse in the course of the public Bible readings so that they would be comprehensible to the listeners. Eventually the translations were committed to writing. There are three Pentateuch Targums: T. ONKELOS; T. Jonathan; and T. Yerushalmi. The T. to the Prophets is called after Jonathan ben

Uzziel. There is no authorized T. for the Hagiographa, but those that exist are often Midrashic. The Targums represent ancient traditions and have been extensively used by scholars for the understanding of the Bible text.

tashlikh ("thou shalt cast"): Ceremony "to cast sins into the sea" practiced on the first day of Rosh ha-Shanah (or on the second day when the first is a Sabbath), when Orthodox Jews reciting the Afternoon Service visit a river or a seashore or some place of water and recite biblical verses concerning sin, repentance, and forgiveness. The prayers derive chiefly from Micah 7:10–20. The ritual seems to have originated in 14th-cent. Germany and spread to Oriental and Sephardi Jews.

tav (ת): Twenty-second and last letter of the alphabet. Numerical value 400. Pronounced as *s* by Ashkenazim, *t* by Sephardim, or *th* (originally) when without a *dagesh* (ת) and as *t* with one (תּ).

Taz see **David Ben Samuel ha-Levi**

Tchernikhowsky, Saul (1875–1943): Hebrew poet. He was an army doctor in Russia in World War I. From 1922 to 1931 he lived in Berlin, and then in Tel Aviv. One of the outstanding modern Hebrew poets, his work covered many forms of poetry (idylls, love poems, etc.) as well as translations of Homer, other ancient classics, and modern poets. He admired Hellenism and introduced sensual elements to Hebrew verse. T. was an influential linguistic innovator.

Tchernowitz, Chaim (1871–1949): Talmudic scholar. He founded a yeshivah at Odessa. In 1923 he went to the US and taught at the Jewish Institute of Religion, New York. In 1940 he founded the Hebrew monthly *Bitzaron,* which he edited until his death. He wrote works of talmudic scholarship and on the development of halakhah under the pseudonym Rav Tzair ("Young Rabbi").

Technion: Israel Institute of Technology; engineering university in Haifa, founded in 1912 on the initiative of the Hilfsverein der deutschen Juden. In anticipation of the institute's opening, there was a bitter struggle over the language of teaching, its sponsors proposing German and the *yishuv* demanding Hebrew. World War I intervened, and by the time the T. was opened in 1924, Hebrew was unquestionedly selected as the language of instruction. It moved to a 300-acre campus on Mt. Carmel in 1954. In 1974 there were over 8,000 students and 15,000 studying in extension courses. The teaching staff exceeds 1,000.

Teheran see **Iran**

Tel Aviv: Israel's largest city; on the central coastal plain. Founded in 1909 as Ahuzat Bayit, a garden suburb of JAFFA. In 1921 it received the status of a town, and its first mayor was Meir DIZENGOFF. At the time of the 1936 Arab riots, a harbor was built (it was closed in 1965). In 1948, Jaffa surrendered to Jewish forces and its Arabs abandoned the town. It became a united city (T. A.-Jaffa) in the new State, the independence of which was proclaimed in the T. A. Museum. T. A. is the commercial and entertainment center of the country. It is the home of all major Hebrew newspapers, T. A. University the T. A., Haaretz, and Diaspora museums, etc. Its 1974 pop. was 357,600, but it stands at the center of an urban area which is the country's major population concentration.

Tel Aviv University: University founded in 1956 as a municipal institution, becoming autonomous from 1962. In 1974 it had 11,100 students and an academic staff of 1,900.

Tel el Amarna see **Amarna**

Tel Hai: Settlement in northern Israel founded in 1918. It was the scene of a famous defense against Arab attack in 1920, when Joseph TRUMPELDOR was killed.

Teller, Edward (1908–): Physicist. He was born in Budapest and settled in the US in 1935, teaching at the universities of Washington, Chicago, and California. He worked on atomic fission and was known as the "father of the hydrogen bomb."

Tels (Telsiai): Lithuanian town noted for its yeshivah, which was founded in 1875. It flourished until closed by the Soviets in 1940. The following year it was reestablished in Cleveland.

Temple: The center of Jewish national worship in Jerusalem from the time of Solomon until the 1st cent. CE. Planned by David and built by Solomon on Mt. Moriah in Jerusalem, the First T. stood until its destruction by Nebuchadnezzar in 586 BCE. It contained a hall, shrine, and inner sanctum. The holy of holies, in which was placed the ark, was entered solely by the HIGH PRIEST, and then only on the Day of Atonement. SACRIFICES were brought to the court and offered by the priests who were the permanent servants of the T. Worshipers would especially come on the occasion of the three PILGRIM FESTIVALS. The Second T. was first constructed in 538–515 BCE. It was reconstructed on several occasions in the ensuing centuries, most notably by Herod. Detailed information is available on the Herodian T. from the Talmud, from Josephus, and from remains and excavations (e.g., the western and southern walls of the T. compound). In the siege of Jerusalem (66–70), it served as a center of military activity and was destroyed by Roman soldiers in the year 70. The event was regarded as a national tragedy by the Jews. Thereafter, wherever they were, they turned in prayer to the T. site. A pagan T. was built there by the Romans, and in the 7th cent. the Muslims constructed the Mosque of Omar (or the Dome of the Rock) with the Al-Aksa mosque also on the T. mount. During Crusader times, these were used by the Crusaders but subsequently were again turned to Muslim sacred use.

Temurah ("Exchange"): Sixth tractate in the MISHNAH order of *Kodashim* with *gemara* in the Babylonian Talmud only. It deals with the regulations concerning the exchange of an animal consecrated for sacrifice (*temurah*) (Lev. 27:10, 33).

Ten Commandments see **Commandments, Ten**

Ten Days of Penitence (*Aseret Yeme Teshuvah*): Penitential period beginning with the New Year and lasting until the Day of Atonement (=Tishri 1 10). According to the rabbis, this is the annual period when God judges the fate of all men for the following year. Hence the entire period became one of penitence. Penitential prayers (*selihot*) are recited and a number of special petitions inserted into the regular prayers, while the *amidah* is followed by the recitation of *Avinu Malkenu*. Before the Day of Atonement, it became customary to give money to charity, to visit the cemetery, and, among Oriental Jews, to undergo flagellation.

ten martyrs (*asarah harugei malkhut*): Ten sages put to death by the Romans after the Bar Kokhba rebellion. According to rabbinic tradition, they were executed for defying the edict forbidding the teaching of Torah. The identification of the 10 differs in various traditions: they include Akiva, Ishmael ben Elisha, and Hanina ben Teradyon.

Tennessee: US state. The first Jewish settlers came in the late 1830s, the oldest communities being founded in Memphis and Nashville, both in 1853. One of the most recent communities in the state is at Oak Ridge, largely consisting of scientists. In 1976, there were 17,360

Jews, of whom 9,000 were in Memphis, 3,700 in Nashville, and 2,250 in Chattanooga.

Tenuat ha-Moshavim ("The Moshav Movement"): Movement of smallholders' settlement (MOSHAV OVEDIM) in Israel. It had 242 villages in 1976, with a population of 90,000.

tephillin ("phylactenes): Two black leather boxes worn by adult male Jews at morning prayer (originally worn all day). One is worn on the forehead, the other on the arm, and they are affixed by black leather straps. They contain portions of the Pentateuch written on parchment.

Territorialism: Movement established by former Zionists to seek and establish an autonomous Jewish community on any suitable territory. When the 1905 Zionist Congress rejected the East African Project and all other potential projects outside Palestine, Israel ZANGWILL set up the Jewish Territorial Organization (ITO), finding support from non-Zionists as well as some ex-Zionists. Various possibilities were investigated in the following years, but the movement was unable to endorse any of them. After the Balfour Declaration, some of the Territorialists returned to Zionism, and the organization was disbanded in 1925. There were some successor groups (e.g., the Freeland

League), but none made any headway.

Terumot ("Heave Offerings"): Sixth tractate of the MISHNAH order *Zeraim* with *gemara* in the Jerusalem Talmud only. It deals with the laws of the heave offering (Lev. 22:1–14) which Israelites and Levites allocated to the priests.

tet (ט): Ninth letter of the Hebrew alphabet. Numerical value: 9. Pronounced *t*.

Tetrarch: Title given by Romans to rulers of provinces in Judea and Syria. The rank was lower than a king but the t. had the authority of a king, subject to his obligations to the Roman emperor.

Tevet: Tenth month of the religious year and fourth in the civil calendar. It has 29 days, and its zodiac sign is Capricorn. Its first 2–3 days conclude the festival of HA-NUKKAH and T. 10 is a fast day on the anniversary of the start of Nebuchadnezzar's siege of Jerusalem.

Tevul Yom: ("One Who Has Bathed That Day"): Tenth tractate of the order *Tohorot* in the MISHNAH with no *gemara* in either Talmud. It deals with problems related to the law (Lev. 15:7–18, 22: 6–7) that a person who is ritually unclean remains so until sunset, even if he immerses himself ritually during the day.

Texas: US state. Individual Jews arrived from the 1820s, and the oldest congregations were founded in Houston (1850), Galveston (1858), Brownsville (1870), and Dallas (1871). At the beginning of the 20th cent., the Galveston Plan attracted 20,000 Jewish immigrants to settle in the southwest, and this led to the establishment of many new communities. In 1976, the Jewish population was 69,255, the largest communities being in Houston (24,000), Dallas (20,000), San Antonio (6,500), and El Paso (5,000).

Thailand: A few refugees from Soviet Russia settled in Bangkok in the 1920s and were joined by 120 refugees from the Nazis in the 1930s. Most left after World War II. A synagogue and community center were opened in 1966, but the community remains tiny.

Therapeutae: Jewish ascetic sect, living near Alexandria in 1st cent. CE. Nothing is known of their origin and fate. They resembled the ESSENES and spent their time in prayer and study.

Theresienstadt (Terezin): Czech town where the Nazis established a ghetto to which 150,000 Jews were deported, 1941–45. 33,000 of these Jews died in T., 88,000 were sent to extermination camps (half of them to Auschwitz), and only 11,000 survived until liberation.

thirteen attributes (*middot*): The Divine attributes of mercy enumerated in Exod. 34:6–7. "The Lord, The Lord, God, merciful and gracious, long-suffering and abundant in goodness and truth," etc. They are of great importance in the liturgy, especially in *selihot* prayers and on the Day of Atonement.

Thirteen Principles of the Faith: Customary designation for Maimonides' formulation of the dogmas of Judaism (in the Mishnah commentary on tractate *Sanhedrin*). These are: (1) the existence of God; (2) the unity of God; (3–4) the incorporeality and eternity of God; (5) only He may be worshiped; (6–7) the Law is revealed through the prophets, of whom Moses is the chief; (8–9) the Law, which is immutable, was given at Sinai; (10) God's omniscience; (11) Divine retribution; (12–13) belief in the Messiah and Resurrection. The prose and rhyme version (YIGDAL) were incorporated in the prayer book.

Thomashefsky, Boris (1868–1939): Actor and director. Born in the Ukraine, he went to the US in 1881 and was long a romantic lead in the New York Yiddish theater. His grandson Michael

Tilson Thomas (1946–) is conductor of the Boston Orchestra.

Tibbon see **Ibn Tibbon**

Tiberias: City on the western shore of the Sea of Galilee, founded by Herod Antipas in 14–18 CE and named for the emperor Tiberius. After the destruction of Jerusalem, it became the main Jewish city in the country. It was the seat of the Sanhedrin from the 2nd cent., and the Palestine Talmud was mostly assembled there. It was a main center too for the MASORETES from the 7th cent. In the Middle Ages, it declined and became a small fishing village. An attempt made by Joseph Nasi to establish it as a Jewish city failed, but it was rebuilt in the 18th cent. It was regarded (with Jerusalem, Safed, and Hebron) as one of the four holy cities. In the 20th cent. its hot springs were developed, and after 1948, many newcomers settled there and the area of the town increased. In 1974 its population was 25,200.

Tiberius Julius Alexander (1st cent. CE): Roman procurator; son of the wealthy Alexandrian Alexander Lysimachus, who was a brother of the philosopher PHILO. He was in Roman service from his youth and served as Roman procurator of Judea (46–48). In 66, Nero appointed him prefect of Egypt. He was second-in-command to TITUS in the siege of Jerusalem (70).

tikkun ("repair"): Prayers and readings for special occasions, instituted by the kabbalists. These include *T. Hatzot*, midnight prayers, originating in circles around Isaac LURIA: *T. Lel Shavuot*, all-night readings on the Festival of Pentecost; and *T. Hoshana Rabbah*, readings on the night of Hoshana Rabbah. Various rites observed *tikkunim* on other occasions. The term *t.* was also used in kabbalistic circles for the "repair" that man can effect of a spiritual catastrophe by virtue of his prayer and right conduct.

tikkun sopherim ("scribal correction"): Eighteen changes in the biblical text made by the SCRIBES. Their object was to avoid anthropomorphism. The term was also used for an unpointed text of the Pentateuch used in preparation of the Reading of the Law.

Tisha be'Av see **Av, Ninth of**

Tishri: First month of the Jewish civil and 7th of the religious year. Holidays falling during this month are Rosh ha-Shanah (1st–2nd); Day of Atonement (10th); Sukkot (15th–21st); Shemini Atzeret-Simhat Torah (22nd; in the Diaspora 22nd–23rd). T.

3 is the Fast of Gedaliah, and the 1st–10th, the Ten Days of Penitence. The month has 30 days and its Zodiac sign is the Scales.

Tiszaeszlar: Hungarian town, scene of a BLOOD LIBEL in 1882. Anti-Semitic agitators charged 15 Jews with killing a Christian girl for ritual purposes. Throughout Hungary there were widespread attacks on Jews. After a long imprisonment, the prisoners were eventually acquitted, but the verdict led to further waves of anti-Semitism.

tithe (*maaser*): The tenth part of one's income, set aside for a specific purpose. In ancient times a t. of the produce was set aside for religious purposes. The first t. was given to the Levites; and in Second Temple times also went to the priests. A second t. was taken by the owner himself to Jerusalem in the 1st, 2nd, 4th, and 5th year of the sabbatical cycle. In the 3rd and 6th years, this was replaced by a t. to the poor. A t. of animals was also taken in and offered as a sacrifice.

***Titus** (40–81): Roman emperor, 79–81. After being active in the conquest of Galilee, he took over command from his father, VESPASIAN, of the Roman army in Judea in 70 and directed the siege and destruction of Jerusalem. Jewish tradition calls him "T. the wicked." For several years he had a romance with the Judean princess Berenice. The Arch of T. erected in Rome was in honor of the Judean victory of Vespasian and T. The present structure is not the original and dates from the reign of Domitian (81–96). It depicts T.'s triumphal procession in Rome, bearing the sacred vessels taken from the Temple in Jerusalem.

Tobiads: Influential Judean family in Second Temple times. They supported the Hellenizing movement and were influential in Jerusalem until the time of the Maccabean victory, after which they disappeared.

Tobit, Book of: Book of Apocrypha of uncertain authorship apparently dating from the Persian period. The righteous T. regains his sight by magical means thanks to the help of the angel Raphael. The theme is of righteousness rewarded.

Tog, Der ("The Day"): New York Yiddish daily newspaper established in 1914. In 1954 it merged with the *Morgen-Journal*, and the joint paper ended in 1971.

tohorah ("purification"): Ceremony of washing the dead before burial. It is carried out by members of the HEVRAH KADDISHA, who place the corpse in an upright position and pour water over it.

Tohorot: ("Cleannesses") Sixth and last order of the MISHNAH. T. deals with ritual uncleanliness, and all 12 tractates (none with *gemara*, except *Niddah*) deal with impurity. The 5th tractate is also called *T*. It deals with lesser degrees of impurity.

Toledo: City in Spain, ancient capital of Castile. Its Jewish community is the oldest in Spain and under the Visigoths was the most important in Spain. It flourished under Muslim rule, and was a Karaite center. Equal rights were granted under Christian rule after 1085. In the 14th cent. it had 9 synagogues, and 2 of these are still standing. Intellectual life flourished and T. was an outstanding cultural center. The community was hit hard by the 1391 massacres and thereafter was a Marrano center. The Inquisition was active in T. from 1486. The Jews left with the expulsion from Spain in 1492.

Tomb of Rachel see **Rachel**

Tombs of the Kings: Jerusalem tomb dating from Second Temple times. It was discovered in the 19th cent. and was at first thought to be the tomb of the ancient kings mentioned in the Bible. It was, however, subsequently identified as the tomb of Queen HELENA of Adiabene, whose sarcophagus was found there.

tombstones: In Palestine, the Jewish tomb-caves and catacombs usually did not have t., but there are examples throughout the biblical and Second Temple periods. The general custom of erecting tombstones over graves is of comparatively recent origin among Jews. Among Sephardim the stones are laid flat; the Ashkenazi custom is to place them vertically. They are usually consecrated within a year of the burial (in Israel, within a month). Inscriptions are a regular feature from the 1st cent. BCE. These are mostly in Hebrew but the use of other languages is frequent. They are also decorated with the familiar Jewish symbols.

Topol, Chaim (1935–): Israeli actor. He first appeared with the army troupes. He then acted with the Haifa Municipal Theater and appeared in Israeli films (*Sallaḥ Shabbati*). His international reputation was made with his appearance as Tevye in *Fiddler on the Roof* in London and in the film version.

Torah ("Teaching"): The Pentateuch, traditionally given to Moses on Mt. Sinai (the Written Law) together with a verbal exposition (the Oral Law). It came to mean the sum totality of Jewish law and guidance as imported to Israel by Divine revelation. The T. is seen as the source of Jewish life, and its study is the *summum bonum*. The word is often used also for a Scroll of the Law (*Sepher T.*).

Torah ornaments: The Scroll of the Law is adorned with ornaments (differing in various rites and traditions). The Ashkenazim and Western Sephardim drape the scroll in a mantle (*meil*) of costly material. Other ornaments include the band (*mappah*); a crown (*keter*) with finials (*rimmonim*) placed on top of the rollers; a breastplate; and a pointer (*yad*). Among Oriental Sephardim, the scroll is kept in a metal or wooden case (*tik*).

Torah, Reading of the see **Law, Reading of the**

Torah va-Avodah ("Torah and Labor"): Confederation of pioneer youth groups within the Mizrachi movement devoted to the concept of religious labor.

Toronto: City in Ontario, Canada. Organized Jewish life began in 1849, and the first synagogue (Holy Blossom, originally Orthodox but later Reform) was established in 1856. The Jewish community grew in the later 19th cent. and developed rapidly after World War II. It has a very strong communal life. In 1976, there were 110,000 Jews in T.

Torquenada, Thomas de (1420–1498): First head of the Spanish Inquisition. A Dominican, he was appointed inquisitor general in 1483. He was largely responsible for the order expelling the Jews from Spain in 1492.

Torres, Luis de (15th cent.): Spanish interpreter to Columbus on his first expedition. He was baptized shortly before the expedition sailed and was the only person of Jewish birth on the boats. He was the first European to set foot in America and eventually set up his own rule in Cuba.

Tortosa: City in Spain. Jews lived there in the early Christian cents., and it was a center of Jewish learning in the 10th–11th cent. It was the scene in 1413–14 of a noted DISPUTATION forced on representatives of Spanish Jewry by the anti-Pope Benedict XIII. It lasted 21 months, during which time considerable pressure was exerted on Spanish Jewry to convert. Many did so, and subsequently the T. community lost its importance.

tosaphot ("additions"): Collection of explanatory notes on the Babylonian Talmud by French and German scholars of the 12th–14th cent. They are printed in the outer column of all Talmud editions. At first they supplemented Rashi's commentary but later developed their own approach. Unlike Rashi, whose commentary is running, the t. relate only to selected points and problems. The tosaphists (i.e., authors of *t.*) originated in the family of Rashi and his school. 300 tosaphists are quoted.

Tosephta ("Addition"): A collection of tannaitic *beraitot*. It is often parallel to the Mishnah and provides alternative readings. It is divided into the same 6 "orders" as the Mishnah. Various theories have been advanced as to the relation between the T. and the Mishnah. The paragraphs of the T. are called BARAITA.

Touro, Judah (1775–1854): US philanthropist. He was born in Newport, Rhode Island, and settled in New Orleans in 1801, being badly injured in the Battle of New Orleans in 1815. The historic synagogue in Newport is named after him. His will made bequests to many Jewish institutions, including a grant to the Jewish poor in Palestine.

Tower of Babel see **Babel, Tower of**

translators: The great period of Jewish t. was in the Middle Ages, and one of its main centers was southern France. In the 12th–14th cent. Jews played a key role as t., especially from Arabic to Latin (sometimes with Hebrew as intermediary language) and were largely responsible for the transmission of Greek science and thought (which had been preserved by Arabic authors) to Christian Europe. Jews also assisted Christian scholars in translating from Arabic to Latin. There was also considerable translation into Hebrew (e.g., of the medieval Jewish philosophical classics, most of which were written in Arabic).

Transylvania: Rumanian province. Sephardi Jews from Turkey settled there in the 15th cent. The first community was in Alba Iulia. By the mid-19th cent., 15,000 Jews were living in T., many originating from Poland. Anti-Semitism spread between the world wars and the Jews suffered during World War II, when almost all the 150,000 Jews in northern T. were deported to their death. Jews returned there after the war but community life was now weak. 15,000 Jews were living there in 1955, but half of these had left by the early 1970s.

Treblinka: One of the largest Nazi extermination camps, north of Warsaw. In 1942–43, 750,000 Jews from 13 countries were killed there, including over 200,000 deported from the Warsaw ghetto. The camp was destroyed and bodies were cremated by the Germans in Nov. 1943.

Trent: Town in northern Italy. In 1475 its small Jewish community was expelled following a BLOOD LIBEL charge. The alleged victim, a child called Simon, was beatified and his relics were venerated in the cathedral until 1965, when the Catholic Church declared the accusation to have been false.

Trepper, Leopold (1904–): Intelligence agent, born in Poland. During World War II, he established in Western Europe a widespread spy network for the USSR, known as the "Red Orchestra." After the war, he was imprisoned in Russia. After his release, he went to Poland and, after a long struggle, was allowed to emigrate to Israel.

trespass offering (*asham*): Offering brought by an individual for trespasses committed intentionally or unintentionally. The offering was a 2-year-old ram which was eaten by the priests.

Treves see **Trier**

Tribes, Lost Ten: The tribes which formed the Kingdom of Israel were conquered by the Assyrians in 721 BCE and the majority of their numbers were deported to Assyria. There they soon assimilated and lost their separate identity. Their disappearance was never accepted by the rest of the Jews, especially in view of prophecies linking the final redemption with the reunification of the entire Jewish people. The Midrash attributes several dwelling places to them, and fantastic reports concerning them gained currency for many centuries. Numerous peoples claimed descent from them (from the British to the Japanese), but these claims are unhistorical.

Tribes, the Twelve: The Israelites were divided into 12 clans traditionally descended from the 12 sons of Jacob. Levi received the priestly office and the tribe of Joseph was divided into two— Ephraim and Manasseh. The land of Canaan was divided by Joshua among the tribes, with Reuben, Gad, and half the tribe of Manasseh receiving territory in Transjordan. The tribes seldom came together as a unit according to the stories from the Book of Judges. They were united under the rules of Saul, David, and Solomon, but there was a further split with ten tribes constituting the northern Kingdom of Israel and the others the southern Kingdom of Judah.

Trier (Treves): W. German city. Jews lived there from the 11th cent. and were under the authority of the bishop. In 1096, during the First Crusade, they underwent persecutions and forced baptisms, but the community was soon refounded. It was again expelled in the 1349 Black Death outbreaks and in 1418. Equal rights granted during the French occupation in 1794 were acknowledged by the Prussians only in 1850. In 1933 there were 800 Jews. That community ended during the war. In 1971, 75 Jews were living there.

Tripolitania: North African country, now part of LIBYA. Jews were there at least from the 3rd cent. BCE. The numbers grew under the Romans, coming from the East, Palestine, and Egypt, and some of the local Ben Berber tribes adopted Judaism. Further growth occurred under the Muslims and after the expulsion from Spain in 1492. Jews occupied key positions in commercial life. The community suffered from Germans in World War II and from Arab attacks in the aftermath of the war, with a serious pogrom breaking out in 1945, when over 20,000 Jews were living there, mostly in the city of Tripoli. There was extensive emigration to Israel, speeded by establishment of the independent state of Libya. The remaining Jews left after hostile acts following the 1967 Six-Day War.

Trotsky (Bronstein), Lev Davidovich (1879–1940): Russian revolutionary and Bolshevik leader. He lived in exile for much of his life before the 1917 Revolution. He then returned to Russia, joined the Bolsheviks, and was commissar for foreign affairs and chief negotiator of the Brest-Litovsk treaty with Germany. T. then became commissar for war and the navy, organizing the Red Army and directing its successful struggle against external and internal enemies. After Lenin's death, he differed with Stalin, and was expelled from the party in 1927 and exiled from the USSR in 1929. He lived in various countries before finally settling in Mexico, where he was assassinated, possibly at Stalin's instigation.

Trumpeldor, Joseph (1880–1920): Zionist socialist leader. He studied dentistry and volunteered for the Russian army during the war with Japan in 1904–05, in which he lost an arm. He was made one of the few Jewish officers in the czarist army. In 1912 he went to Palestine. During World War I he formed the ZION MULE CORPS in Egypt and later helped Jabotinsky to form the Jewish Legion. After the war, he was a leading figure in Jewish labor circles in Palestine and established the HeHalutz movement in Russia.

He organized the defense of exposed Jewish villages in Galilee and was killed in defending Tel Hai against Arab attackers.

Tschlenow, Jehiel (1863–1918): Russian Zionist leader and physician. He was among the TZIYYONE ZION leaders who opposed the UGANDA SCHEME in 1904. At the Helsingfors Conference in 1906, he proposed widespread land purchase in Eretz Israel.

Tu bi-Shevat see **New Year for Trees**

Tuchman, Barbara Wertheim (1912–): US historian; granddaughter of Henry MORGENTHAU. Her historical works (for which she twice won the Pulitzer Prize) include *Bible and Sword, The Guns of August,* and *The Proud Tower.*

Tucker, Richard (1916– 1975): US singer and cantor. He started his career in a synagogue choir, then became a cantor in Brooklyn. From 1944 he appeared at the Metropolitan Opera, becoming one of its leading lyric tenors.

Tucker, Sophie (1889– 1966): US entertainer, known from nightclub and stage appearances as "the last of the red-hot mommas." Her best-known song was "My Yiddishe Momme."

Tunisia: Although there are legends of Jewish settlement from earlier times, concrete evidence dates from Roman times. Their position continued usually good after the Arab conquest when Kairouan was the site of an outstanding yeshivah. The period of rule by the Almohades (from 1146) brought terror to the community, but under their successors conditions were again tolerable. Spanish refugees who settled there in the 15th century transformed the nature of the community. T. became a French protectorate in 1881, and Jews could acquire French citizenship from 1910. The community suffered from the Vichy and German regimes during World War II, and from Arabization subsequently. From 1948 there was a growing emigration to France and Israel, and the number of Jews dropped from 67,000 in 1959 to 8,000 in 1973.

Tunkel, Joseph (1881– 1949): Yiddish humorist who wrote under the pseudonym Der Tunkeler. Born in White Russia, he edited satirical weeklies in the US from 1906–10, in Warsaw from 1910 to 1939, and in the US again from 1940.

Tur-Sinai (Torczyner), Naphtali Herz (Harry) (1886–1973): Hebrew philologist and Bible scholar. Born in Lemberg, he taught in Vienna and Berlin (1919–23), and was professor of Hebrew at the Hebrew University from 1933. He was the first president of the ACADEMY OF THE HEBREW LANGUAGE. He participated in a German translation of the Bible, edited the LACHISH LETTERS, and was responsible for completing the lexicon of Eliezer BEN-YEHUDA.

Turkey: For earlier period, see BYZANTIUM. In the 15th-16th cent. the sultans were generous in admitting Jewish refugees, notably those from Spain and Portugal who became the dominant element in the community. CONSTANTINOPLE, ADRIANOPLE, IZMIR, and SALONICA were among the largest, most flourishing Jewish centers in the world, noted for their culture. Jews played a leading role at court (Joseph NASI, Solomon ASHKENAZI). Famous rabbis headed yeshivot, and printing presses poured out Hebrew books. The Jews of T. supported SHABBETAI TZEVI, and his failure led to the beginning of their spiritual decline. His followers, the DÖNMEH, continued to exist in T. At the beginning of the 10th cent. the community was still the 3rd largest in the world but had declined inwardly. Subsequent developments weakened it further, and it suffered as a result of the nationalism which dominated the country. Half the community emigrated to Israel after 1948, and 30,000 remained in 1976, with 22,-000 in Istanbul (Constantinople) and 2,500 in Izmir.

Tuwim, Julian (1894–1953): Polish lyric poet. He headed the Skamander group (so-called from their monthly periodical), which sought to produce a new poetic language appropriate to the modern experience. During World War II, he lived in the US and Brazil.

tzaddik ("righteous man"): A person outstanding for his faith and piety; an ideal of moral and religious perfection. In HASIDISM, it was applied to the Hasidic rabbi, who was a charismatic individual, seen as intermediary between God and man, and was accordingly accorded utmost reverence by his followers. Many *tzaddikim* adopted luxurious modes of living, although others continued to live simply. The fanatic devotion of the Hasid to his *t.* widened the gap with the MATNAGGEDIM and was a cause of the deterioration in Hasidism in the 19th century. (See LAMED VAV.)

tzade (צ): Eighteenth letter of the Hebrew alphabet. Numerical value: 90. Originally pronounced *ss*; later, in many communities, as *tz*. Written צ and ץ at the end of a word.

Tzeire Zion ("Young Men of Zion"): Socialist Zionist movement. Groups began to emerge throughout Russia from 1903. It devoted itself to practical activities and after World War I formed the background of HE-ḤALUTZ. In 1920, part formed the Zionist Socialist Party and another factor helped to establish Hitaḥdut.

Tz'enah u-Re'enah see **Ashkenazi, Jacob**

Tzeva Haganah le-Israel (abbr. Tzahal, "Israel Defense Army"): Israeli army. It was established on May 26, 1948, as the successor to the HA-GANAH. Despite a critical shortage of arms, it defeated the invading Arab armies in the WAR OF INDEPENDENCE. After the war it was carefully organized, expanded, and equipped to meet the continuous challenges posed by a long frontier and unremitting hostility. It is partly regular and partly conscripted. Men and women are called up at the age of 18 (men for 3 years, women for 2) and remain on reserve duty for many years (men until 55). Land, sea, and air forces are not independent but are part of the army command. The general staff is headed by a chief of staff who is subordi-nate to the minister of defense. Apart from military training, the army operates an extensive educational program. The Israeli army has been in full action in the 1956 SINAI CAMPAIGN, the 1967 SIX-DAY WAR, and the 1973 YOM KIPPUR WAR; in addition it has conducted the fight along the borders and against infiltrators and saboteurs.

tzidduk ha-din ("justification of [Divine] justice"): The Jewish burial service which incorporates verses "justifying God's judgment."

tzimtzum see **Kabbalah**

tzitzit ("fringes"): Fringes appended to each of the four corners of a garment (Deut. 22:12). Originally male Jews wore such a garment at all times but today a special one (*arba kanphot*, "four corners," or *tallit katan*, "small *tallit*") is worn during the day by observant Jews beneath their outer garments. They include a "shade of blue" in accordance with Num. 15:38. A blessing is recited when putting on the *t.*

Tziyyone Zion ("Zionists of Zion): Group of Zionists, mainly from Russia, who strongly opposed the Uganda Scheme in 1904 and strongly opposed TERRITORIALISM.

Uganda Scheme: Offer of territory in East Africa (then in Uganda, today part of Kenya) made in 1903 by the British colonial secretary, Joseph Chamberlain, to Herzl for Jewish settlement. At first Herzl was interested in the offer, but under pressure from Russian Zionists, who would accept only Palestine, and after an unfavorable report by an investigating commission, the scheme was dropped.

Ugarit: Ancient city in Syria; modern Ras Shamra. The discovery beginning in 1929 of clay tablets written in a cuneiform alphabet has deeply affected the study of Canaanite mythology and its bearing upon biblical scholarship. They have thrown light on the literary and cultural background of the Bible.

Ukraine: Soviet republic. Jews lived in parts of the U. in the period of the KHAZARS. The main influx began in the 16th cent. The major massacres during the CHMIELNICKI and HAIDAMAK uprisings did not stop Jewish migration to the U. The Frankist and Hasidic movements originated there, as did various seminal Zionist movements (Hibbat Zion, Bilu). Its strong tradition of anti-Semitism has remained in the 20th cent. Many Jews left after World War I. Attempts were made to found Jewish agricultural colonies there, and in 1930 there were 90,000 Jewish agriculturists. Before World War II half of Russia's 3,000,000 Jews were in the U., but these either fled or were murdered in 1941–42. There have been further manifestations of anti-Semitism since the war. In 1970, there were 770,000 Jews.

Uktzin ("Stalks"): Twelfth tractate in the MISHNAH order of *Toharot*, with no *gemara* in either Talmud. It deals with the problems of ritual impurity connected with stalks, husks, or kernels.

Union of American Hebrew Congregations: Organization representing the REFORM congregations and their members in the US. It was founded by Isaac Mayer WISE in 1873 and was the earliest Jewish congregational federation in the country. Headquarters are in New York City, and various Reform religious organizations are affiliated.

Union of Orthodox Jewish Congregations of America: US organization of Orthodox synagogues founded in 1898. It has an affiliation of 1,500 congregations. It is responsible for a *kashrut* certification service whose symbol is a U within a circle.

Union of Orthodox Rabbis of US and Canada: Organization of Orthodox rabbis, founded in 1902. About 660 rabbis are members.

Union of Sephardic Congregations: US Sephardi organization founded in 1929. It services Sephardi congregations throughout the country.

Union of Soviet Socialist Republics see Russia

United Hias Service see Hias

United Israel Appeal: US Zionist fund-raising organization founded as the United Palestine Appeal in 1927. In 1937 it merged with other fund-raising agencies to found the UNITED JEWISH APPEAL.

United Jewish Appeal (UJA): US organization founded in 1939 by the UNITED ISRAEL APPEAL and the AMERICAN JOINT DISTRIBUTION COMMITTEE with the NATIONAL REFUGEE SERVICE as beneficiary. It is the largest annual fund-raising campaign in the US. Its proceeds are divided among local communal needs, Israel, and relief and assistance for Jews in need throughout the world.

United States: Jewish settlement dates from 1654 with the arrival in New Amsterdam (now New York) of 23 Jews from Brazil. Gradually they obtained various rights and before long were joined by other Jews from Europe, and spread along the Eastern Seaboard. Most of the early Jews were Sephardim, but by the 19th cent., Central and East European Jews constituted the majority. By 1776, 2,500 Jews were living in North America. The Declaration of Independence and other decrees enacted before and during the Revolution gave Jews equality, but in some areas, restrictions remained into the 19th cent. The 19th cent. saw immigration from Central Europe, while the Jews of the US expanded across the continent to the Pacific. By the time of the American Civil War—in which Jews fought on both sides—there were 150,000 Jews in the US. The entire character of American Jewry was changed as a result of the mass immigration from Eastern Europe following the 1881 pogroms. Between then and 1914, over 2,000,000 Jews arrived in the US. The majority went to the big cities (especially New York), where they initially lived in conditions of severe overcrowding and worked long hours for minimal pay in sweatshops. They played a central role in the development of trade unions, while the older-established Jews were prominent in business and finance. Alongside the Reform and Conservative movements, Orthodoxy grew rapidly. Yiddish was the language of the first generation, richly expressed in the press and literature. By World War I, US organizations had been founded to implement the participation of US Jews in world Jewish affairs. These ranged from the American Joint Distribution Committee, which succored Jews the world over, to various Zionist organizations which helped to win US support for the 1917 Balfour Declaration. From the 1920s the uncomfortable growth of anti-Semitism led to the formation of various defense agencies. US Jews played a large part in both world wars in all branches of the armed services. They were also active in events leading to the establishment of the State of Israel and generous in their material support through the United Jewish Appeal, the Israel Bond Drive, and other charitable organizations. In the postwar period, the third generation of most American Jewish families was thoroughly integrated into American life and society, and over 80% of young Jews studied at universities. One of the main problems facing the community was that of assimilation, expressed most vividly in the rising rate of intermarriage. The total number of American Jews is estimated at approaching 6,000,000, although its rate of increase was less than that of the rest of the community.

United Synagogue: Association of Ashkenazi synagogues in London, established in 1870. It has about 80 synagogues, to which 100,000 members are affiliated. It is the principal supporter of the British chief rabbinate and the London *bet din.*

United Synagogue of America: Association of Conservative synagogues. Founded in 1913 by Solomon SCHECHTER, it has over 800 affiliated synagogues in the US and Canada. In 1957, it organized the World Council of Synagogues representing Conservative congregations throughout the world.

Unterman, Isser Yehudah (1886–1976): Rabbi. He was born in White Russia. After serving in Lithuanian communities and as communal rabbi of Liverpool (1924), he became chief rabbi of Tel Aviv in 1946. From 1964 to 1972 he was Ashkenazi chief rabbi of Israel.

urim and thummim: Divine Oracle in Bible times. They were apparently lot-casting objects attached to the high priest's breastplate. They were used until the reign of Solomon.

Uris, Leon (1924–): US author. He made his name with his novel about World War II, *Battle Cry.* His novel about the establishment of Israel, *Exodus,* was a best seller and a successful film. Other books include *Topaz, Mila 18* (about the Warsaw ghetto), and *Trinity* (about Ireland).

Uruguay: Jews began to arrive only at the very end of the 19th cent. Nearly all its 50,000 Jews live in Montevideo. Three-quarters are of European origin. There is also a Sephardi community.

ushpizin ("guests"): Seven visitors (Abraham, Isaac, Jacob, Joseph, Moses, Aaron, David) who, according to a mystical tradition, are welcomed to the *sukkah* in each home during the 7 nights of the Feast of Tabernacles.

Usque, Samuel (16th cent.): Historian; lived in Ferrara, Italy. He wrote in Portuguese *Concolaçam as tribulaçoens de Israel,* a survey of Jewish history, meant to encourage Marranos to return to Judaism.

Ussishkin, Menahem Mendel (1863–1941): Zionist leader. A dominating figure in Russian Zionism, he rallied to the support of Herzl and was Hebrew secretary of the First Zionist Congress in 1897. On a visit to Palestine in 1903, he laid the groundwork of the teachers' association. To fight the UGANDA SCHEME, he organized the TZIYYONE ZION. He settled in Palestine in 1919. From 1923 he headed the Jewish NATIONAL FUND, and on his initiative, large tracts of land were purchased in the Jezreel Valley, the Hepher Plain, Haifa Bay, and other sites.

Utah: US state. Jews lived in Salt Lake City from the 1880s, and the Mormons provided them with places of worship. The first non-Mormon governor of the state was Simon BAMBERGER (1917–1921). The number of Jews in Utah remained small and in 1976 numbered 2,160, nearly all of them in Salt Lake City.

Uzziah (Azariah): King of Judah, who ruled c. 785–c. 734 BCE. He waged successful campaigns against Philistia and Arabia, exacted tribute from the Ammonites, formed a coalition that opposed Assyria, and rebuilt the Red Sea port of Elath. In his latter years, he was stricken with leprosy and appointed his son JOTHAM as co-regent.

Vaad Arba Aratzot see Council of Four Lands

Vaad ha-Lashon ha-Ivrit ("Hebrew Language Committee"): Committee established in Jerusalem in 1890 to determine Hebrew terminology and usage. In 1953, it became the ACADEMY OF HEBREW LANGUAGE.

Vaad Leummi ("National Council"): National council of Palestinian Jewry during the period of the British Mandate. Its 36 members were chosen by general election.

Vakhnakht ("watchnight"): Home celebration held on first Sabbath eve after birth of a male child. Watch would be kept over the child (originally to protect him from demons).

Vancouver: Canadian city. Jews settled there from the mid-19th cent. A congregation was founded in 1895. After World War II, the community grew with the general development of the West Coast. About 8,000 Jews were there in 1976.

Vatican Council: The second Vatican Council meeting in Rome (1962–65) dealt, on the initiative of Pope John XXIII, with the attitude of the Catholic Church to Judaism. A declaration was formulated by Cardinal Bea, and the Secretariat for Christian Unity aimed at improving relations between the Catholic Church and the Jewish people and condemning the tradition that the Jewish people should be held responsible for the death of Jesus.

vav (ו): Sixth letter of the Hebrew alphabet. Numerical value: 6. Originally pronounced *w* but now pronounced *v*. It is also a long vowel representing *oo* (וּ) or long *o* (וֹ).

Va-Yikra see **Leviticus**

Veil, Simone (1927–): French public official. During World War II she was deported by the Germans. Subsequently she was a high official in the Ministry of Justice. In 1974 she was appointed minister of health.

Venezuela: Jews first went to Corro in the 1820s. Those Jews who settled in the 19th cent. were largely assimilated. Jews came from N. Africa and (after 1934) Germany. In 1976 there were 15,000 Jews, more than half of them in Caracas.

Venice: Italian city. Jews were first mentioned in the 10th cent. and a Jewish quarter in 1090. From 1394 the Jews had to wear special badges. In 1516 the Jews were segregated in the area near the New Foundary (Ghetto Nuovo, from which the term GHETTO derived). V. was an important Jewish cultural center throughout the Renaissance period. The community declined in the 17th cent. The French Revolutionary Forces broke down the ghetto gates in 1797 and granted emancipation to the community. Final emancipa-

tion was achieved in 1866. Only one of the five historical synagogues is now regularly used for services. About 800 Jews were living in V. in 1973.

Vermont: US state. Although individual Jews lived there previously, the first community, in Poultney, was established only after the Civil War. The number of Jews in the state was never large and in 1976 totaled 1,855, of whom 1,225 lived in Burlington.

*****Vespasian** (9–79): Roman emperor who ruled in 69–79 CE. In 67 Nero appointed him commander of the Roman army to subdue the revolt in Judea. By 68 he had conquered Galilee and Transjordan and was preparing to attack Jerusalem. On Nero's death he was summoned to Rome and left the completion of the conquest, including the subjugation of Jerusalem, to his son TITUS.

Vienna: Capital of Austria. Jews first settled there in the 12th cent. and received a charter of privileges in 1238. Many scholars lived there in medieval times. A Jewish quarter was instituted at the end of the 13th cent. In 1421 the Jews were massacred or expelled (Ger. *Wiener Geserah*). A small number of Jews lived there in the 16th cent., and a community was reestablished in the early 17th cent. Jews came from Hungary, Galicia, Bukovina, etc. Equal rights were received in 1867. Many Jews were prominent in the political, economic, cultural, and scientific life of the city, which was a center of Jewish study and scholarship. Anti-Semitism spread from the 1880s, notably under the burgomeister Karl Lueger. Over 180,000 Jews were living there at the time of the 1938 Anschluss. 100,000 escaped before the war; others were killed during the war. A community was founded again after the war, numbering 9,000 in 1976.

Vilna: Capital of Lithuanian SSR. A community was first organized in 1568 and received a charter in 1633. From the 18th cent. it developed as a major Jewish center known as the "Jerusalem of Lithuania." The dominating figure was the Vilna Gaon, Elijah Ben Solomon Zalman, who led the community and the opposition to the young Hasidic movement. It was a center of Haskalah and of printing and later of Zionism and the Bund. Between the two World Wars it was the headquarters of YIVO. 64,000 Jews were living there in the 1930s. In World War II, the Germans established ghettos and killed the Jews. After the war, some Jews returned, and 16,000 were living there in 1970, but many subsequently emigrated.

Vilna Gaon see **Elijah Ben Solomon**

Vinchevsky,   Morris (1856–1932): Yiddish author. Born in Lithuania, he lived in Western Europe before reaching New York in 1894. He conveyed his Socialist ideas in essays and poems that appeared in Yiddish periodicals.

Virginia: US state. A Jew is mentioned there in 1658 and other individual Jews throughout the 18th cent., but the first congregation was established in Richmond in the 1780s. Other communities were founded in the 19th cent., and many Jews went to live in V. during the world wars in connection with the military bases that were established there. In 1976, it had 58,245 Jewish inhabitants, the largest communities being in Richmond, Norfolk, and Alexandria.

Vital Hayyim Ben Joseph (1542–1620): Kabbalist. He was a pupil of Isaac Luria in Safed and after Luria's death was the chief exponent of his teachings. He lived in Jerusalem from 1577 to 1585 and from c. 1598 in Damascus.

Vogel, David (1891–1944): Hebrew poet. He was born in Russia, lived in Vienna and Paris, and died in a concentration camp. His poetry is considered the forerunner of Hebrew modernism.

Vogel, Sir Julius (1835–1899): New Zealand statesman. Born in England, he entered New Zealand political life and was prime minister in 1873–75 and 1876. Subsequently he was New Zealand agent-general in London.

Volhynia: Province of northwestern Ukraine. Jews were there in the 13th cent., and it was a center of scholarship until the Chmielnicki massacres of 1648–9, which decimated the community. The following cent. it was a Hasidic center, but Haskalah was also strong there in the 19th cent. Its c. 300,000 Jews were annihilated in World War II.

Volozhin: Town in White Russia noted for its Etz Hayyim yeshivah founded in 1802 by HAYYIM OF V. It was headed by R. Naohtali Tzevi Judah Berlin from 1853 until it was closed on order of the authorities in 1892. It existed on a smaller scale from 1899 until World War II.

Volynov, Boris (1934–):Russian cosmonaut. He was commander of the spaceship *Soyuz 5* which participated in the first space linkup (1969) and was in *Soyuz 21* in 1976.

vows: A vow can be made to God to perform a deed or to abstain from something which is allowed. The Bible did not allow for the voiding of a vow (Num. 30: 1–16) but the rabbis went into details to find reasons for absolution (notably in the Talmudic tractate NEDARIM). Vows should be avoided altogether if possible. Those of children have no validity, while a husband has certain powers to annul those of his wife. A competent *bet din* may also absolve the vower.

Vulgate: Latin translation of the Bible by the Church Father JEROME, made in Palestine from the Greek. It was, until the 20th cent., the authoritative text of the Catholic Church.

W

Wailing Wall see Western Wall

Waksman, Selman Avraham (1888–1973): US microbiologist. He taught at Rutgers University and headed its Institute of Microbiology. He won the 1952 Nobel Prize for Physiology and Medicine for his work as co-discoverer of the antibiotic streptomycin.

Wald, George (1906–): US biologist and biochemist; professor at Harvard. He discovered the presence of vitamin A in the human eye, and for his work on the biochemistry of vision was awarded a 1967 Nobel Prize for Medicine and Physiology.

Wales: The Jewish community in Swansea dates from the mid-18th cent. In the 19th cent. communities were established at a number of mining centers (Cardiff, Merthyr Tydfil, Tredegar). There was some anti-Jewish rioting in the 1911 strikes. In recent years many of the small communities have ceased to exist, and 3,500 of W.'s 4,300 Jews live in Cardiff.

Wallach, Otto (1847–1931): German organic chemist, professor in Berlin and Gottingen. He received the Nobel Prize for his work in alicyclic compounds.

Walter, Bruno (1876–1962): Conductor. He conducted in Germany and Austria (where he was assistant to Gustav MAHLER) until forced to leave by the Nazis. He then settled in the US, where he conducted the NBC Symphony and the Metropolitan Opera. From 1941, he was a regular conductor with the New York Philharmonic Orchestra.

Wandering Jew: Figure in Christian legend (named Ahasuerus), condemned to everlasting wandering for reviling Jesus during his last journey while carrying the cross. His punishment was to last until Jesus should return to earth. The legend was originally not directly connected with a Jew. It first appears in writing in Bologna in the 13th cent. It has taken various literary forms.

Wannsee Conference: Conference held on Jan. 20, 1942, in the Berlin suburb of Wannsee at which details for the extermination of European Jewry were worked out.

War of Independence, Israel: War between Jews and Arabs, 1947–49. Immediately after the November 29, 1947, UN decision to partition Palestine into Jewish and Arab states, Palestinian Arabs, reinforced by guerrilla units ("Arab Liberation Army"), opened hostilities to prevent implementation of the UN resolution. In March 1948, the Jewish population became the object of terrorist attacks, and Jewish Jerusalem was cut off. In April, a Haganah attack resulted in a number of places falling into Jewish hands. The second phase began after the withdrawal of the British completed on May 15. Armies from Jordan, Syria, Lebanon, Iraq, and Egypt, and a token force from Saudi Arabia, invaded the country and recorded considerable early advances, including the overrunning of the Ezion bloc of settlements by the Jordanians. Parts of Jerusalem, including the Old City, were also in Arab hands, but attempts to overrun the New City failed. Elsewhere the Arab advance was stemmed, and eventually pushed back. The siege of Jerusalem was broken. A truce made under the auspices of the UN on June 11 ended by July 8, and now there was a major change in military superiority, with the Israeli army winning a number of important victories on all fronts. A second cease-fire order on July 19 was broken by a week of fighting in October, by which time Israel occupied upper Galilee and the northern Negev. Finally in December-January, the entire Negev (except the Gaza Strip) was cleared of Arab troops. A series of Armistice agreements was signed with all the invading countries (excluding Iraq and Saudi Arabia) between February and July 1949. Although these were intended to be only the first step toward a more permanent peace settlement, no further progress in that direction was obtained.

Warburg: Family originating in Germany with distinguished members in the US, many in the banking field. *Aby Moritz W.* (1866–1929) was a German art historian and founder of the W. Library, now in London. *Otto W.* (1859–1938), botanist and Zionist leader, was a professor in Berlin and president of the World Zionist Organization 1911–20. From 1920 he headed the Jewish Agency's experimental station at Rehovot and taught at the Hebrew University. *Otto Heinrich W.* (1883–1970), a German biochemist (who was baptized), received the Nobel Prize in 1931 for discoveries made in the fields of respiration and fermentation. He remained in Germany throughout the Nazi period. The outstanding member of the family in the US was *Felix Moritz W.* (1871–1937), banker and Jewish communal leader. He was chairman of the American Joint Distribution Committee, 1914–32, a founder of the Palestine Economic Corporation, and a member of the enlarged Jewish Agency in 1929. He was a noted philanthropist to general and Jewish causes. His brother *Paul Moritz W.* (1868–1932), banker, helped to establish the Federal Reserve Board in 1913. Felix's son *Edward Mortimer Morris W.*

(1908–   ) was chairman of the Joint Distribution Committee, 1941–66, and of the United Jewish Appeal, 1950–55.

Warner: Four brothers who formed the motion-picture company bearing their name. They were: *Harry Morris W.* (1881–1958), *Albert W.* (1883–1967), *Samuel L. W.* (1887–1927), and *Jack Lemand W.* (1892–   ).

Warsaw: Capital of PO-LAND. Jews lived there from the late 14th cent. They were expelled in 1483 and excluded in 1527. Jews were living there in the 18th cent., and their numbers grew in the 19th cent. By the end of the 19th cent. a third of the population was Jewish. Full rights were received in 1862. Jews participated in the national uprisings against Russia. It was one of the world's great centers of Jewish scholarly and cultural life. By 1939 there were over 370,000 Jews. In World War II they were crowded by the Germans into a ghetto, together with deportees from elsewhere in Poland—almost 500,000. The terrible living conditions led to a high rate of starvation and disease, claiming 100,000 lives. In 1942, 300,000 Jews were sent from the ghetto to the Treblinka death camp. When the deportations reached their final stages, a desperate armed revolt broke out (April-June 1943), and Jews fought house-to-house battles with the Nazi troops (the "Battle of the Warsaw Ghetto") before being finally wiped out. 56,000 were killed in the revolt period. The ghetto was demolished. After the war a monument was erected there. Jews returned to W. after the war, but waves of emigration to Israel reduced their numbers, and by 1976 only 5,000 were left.

Washington: US state. Jews arrived in the 1860s, and several communities were established in the latter part of the 19th cent. In 1976, there were 15,890 Jews, of whom 13,000 lived in Seattle.

Washington, D.C.: Capital of the US. Jewish settlement dates from the 1840s, with the first congregation organized in 1852. Many Jews were among the business, and, later, the civil-service communities. In 1976, 112,500 Jews were living in greater W.

Wasserman, August von (1866–1925): German immunologist and bacteriologist. He was professor at Berlin University. In 1907 he discovered a sero-diagnosis of syphilis known as the W. reaction.

Wassermann, Jakob (1873–1924): German novelist. His best-known works include *Caspar Hauser, Christian Wahnschaffe,* and *The Mauritius Affair.* Jews are fre-

quently portrayed in his works.

Water-Drawing, Festival of the (Simhat Bet ha-Shoevah): Water libation ceremony, observed in Second Temple times during the intermediate days of the Feast of Tabernacles.

Weber, Max (1881–1961): US painter, printmaker, and sculptor. He was born in Russia and lived in New York from 1891. His works are to be found in many American galleries. During the last decades of his life, he painted many pictures on Jewish subjects, especially Hasidic themes.

wedding see **marriage**

Weeks, Feast of see **Shavuot**

Weil, Simone (1909–1943): French mystic and social philosopher. To identify with the workers, she worked in a car factory and then participated in the Spanish Civil War. She escaped from the Germans in World War II and died in England. She rejected Judaism and was drawn to Catholicism, although critical of some of the Church's teachings.

Weill, Kurt (1900–1950): Composer in Germany, who wrote several musical dramas, notably with Berthold Brecht (*The Threepenny Opera, The Rise and Fall of Mahagonny*), with great success. In the US from 1935, he wrote the music for Broadway musicals and films, including *Lady in the Dark, One Touch of Venus,* and *Lost in the Stars.* His best-known songs include "Mack the Knife" and "September Song."

Weinreich, Max W. (1894–1969), Yiddish linguist. He was a founder of Yivo in Vilna and its research director, also after its transfer to New York, in 1939. He wrote on Yiddish language and literature. His son *Uriel W.* (1925–1967), also a distinguished Yiddish linguist, taught at Columbia University and published a Yiddish-English dictionary and the *Language and Culture Atlas of Ashkenazic Jewry.*

Weisgal, Meyer Wolf (1894–1977): Zionist. He was born in Poland and went to the US in 1905. He was secretary of the Zionist Organization of America and edited *The New Palestine.* He was deeply devoted to Chaim Weizmann and served as his American representative. He settled in Israel in 1949 as chairman of the executive council of the Weizmann Institute for Science, for which he raised large sums of money and of which he was president in 1966–69 and chancellor 1970–77. He wrote an autobiography, *So Far.*

Weiss, Isaac Hirsch (1815–1905): Historian of the Oral Law. From 1864, he taught at the Vienna Bet ha-Midrash. He published editions of *Siphra* and *Mekhilta.* His major work was the 5-volume *Dor Dor ve-Doreshav,* a history of the Oral Law down to the Middle Ages, dealing with the development of both halakhah and aggadah.

Weizman, Ezer (1924–): Israeli soldier and politician, nephew of Chaim Weizmann. He fought in the Royal Air Force in World War II and was a pioneer of the Israel Air Force, being appointed the commander-in-chief in 1958. When the Likkud government came to power in 1977, W. was appointed minister of defense.

Weizmann, Chaim (1874–1952): Zionist, scientist, and first president of the State of Israel. Born at Motol near Pinsk, Russia, he studied at German and Swiss universities, and in 1904 was appointed lecturer in biological chemistry at Manchester University, where his discoveries helped the British War effort. He was active in the Zionist movement, from its foundations, but was critical of Herzl and was a founder of the Democratic Faction. He strongly opposed the Uganda Scheme. He took the leading role in the negotiations that culminated in the 1917 BALFOUR DECLARATION. The following year he headed the Zionist Commission in Palestine and was elected president of the World Zionist Organization, a position he held until 1946 (except for 1931–35). His policy was based on faith in Britain, and he led Zionist support for the Allied war effort in World War II. He was, however, disappointed with Britain's policy after the war. He left London and lived largely in his home at Rehovot in Palestine, where he pursued scientific research. He was elected first president of the State of Israel in May 1948. W.'s personal influence was decisive at many crucial moments in Zionist history. His autobiography is *Trial and Error*.

Weizmann Institute of Science: Israeli institution for scientific research. It developed out of the Daniel Sieff Institute opened in Rehovot in 1934, headed by Chaim WEIZMANN. The W.I. was dedicated in 1949. Its activities center around research in the natural sciences, including the biosciences, mathematics, computers, desalination, and hydrology. Its staff consists of 400 scientists and 1,000 technical and administrative workers. The graduate school has 500 students. Associated with the Institute is Yad Chaim Weizmann, a memorial foundation developing projects connected with Weizmann.

*Wellhausen, Julius (1844–1918): German Semitic and Bible scholar. He put forward the Documentary Theory of the origin of the early books of the Bible. Although more moderate tendencies subsequently predominated, many of W.'s theories continue to find scholarly acceptance.

Welt, Die: Zionist weekly which became the official journal of the World Zionist Organization; published 1897–1914. Its first editor was HERZL. There were also Hebrew and Yiddish editions.

Werfel, Franz (1890–1945): Poet, playwright, and novelist in Germany. Born in Prague, he lived in Austria and later in the US. His novels include *The Forty Days of Musa Dagh* and *The Song of Bernadette*. His play *Jacobowsky and the Colonel* was also made into a popular film.

Wertheimer, Max (1880–1943): Founder of Gestalt psychology. Born in Prague, he lived in Germany until 1933, when he went to the New School of Social Research, New York.

Wesker, Arnold (1932–): English playwright. His socialist-oriented plays often deal with Jewish elements. They include *Chicken Soup with Barley, Roots,* and *Chips with Everything.*

Wessely, Naphtali Herz (1725–1805): Haskalah poet and educator in Germany. He wrote the commentary on Leviticus in Mendelssohn's German Bible translation. His proposal for a Jewish educational system in a Haskalah spirit aroused Orthodox opposition. His *Shire Tipheret,* an epic portrayal of the Book of Exodus, was a pioneer attempt to express modern forms of literary composition in Hebrew.

West, Nathanael (1903–1940): US writer. He lived in New York but spent his last years in Hollywood, scene of his *Day of the Locust.* His other well-known work is *Miss Lonelyhearts.* He and his wife were killed in an automobile accident.

West Indies: After the Portuguese reconquered Brazil, in 1654, Jewish refugees went to Curaçao and Barbados. Communities also sprang up in Surinam and Jamaica. Jews in French possessions were expelled in 1683. The Jews played a leading role in establishing the sugar industry and in other commercial developments. The community declined in the 19th cent., with many of the Jews leaving for the US and Britain. After World War I, and especially after 1933, Jews arrived in Cuba, Puerto Rico, and other islands.

West Virginia: US state. The first congregations were established in Wheeling in 1849 and Charleston in 1873. The number of Jews in the state was never large and fell from a maximum of 6,000 in 1956 to 4,120 in 1976, of whom 1,120 lived in Charleston.

Western (WAILING) Wall (*Kotel Maaravi*): The W. W. of the Temple compound as constructed by Herod. It remained undestroyed after the fall of Jerusalem and became the most sacred focus of Jewish pilgrimage. The part of the W. W. that has always been exposed contains three sections, of which the bottom layers are Herodian; a further 60 feet lies underground. Since 1967, excavations have traced the W. W. along its length running under the present Old City of Jerusalem. The W. W. was the cause of disputes between Jews and Arabs which led to widespread rioting in 1929. It came under Jewish sovereignty in 1967, since which time it has attracted many visitors and has been the site of many ceremonies. Excavations conducted in the area by B. Mazar (also along the southern wall) have uncovered many remains from various eras, including the time of the First Temple.

White Paper: Statement of policy issued by the British government. Several of these were important in the development of the British Mandate over Palestine. The Churchill W.P. of 1922 excluded Transjordania from the area to which the Balfour Declaration applied. The Passfield W.P. of 1930 contained anti-Zionist recommendations which were soon canceled by the British government. The 1939 W.P. issued by Colonial Secretary Malcolm MacDonald restricted Jewish immigration and the sale of land to Jews. It was the main source of contention between Jews and the British government in ensuing years.

White Russia (Belorussia): Soviet republic. Jewish traders visited the area in the 14th cent., and settlement dates from the 16th cent. Despite hardships and massacres, the Jewish population grew steadily. It was a center of Jewish scholarship and also of Hasidism (especially Habad), Haskalah, and Labor Zionism. During World War II, most Jews in the region were killed by the Germans. Jews returned there after the war, and in 1970 their number was estimated at 48,000.

whole offering (holocaust) (*kalil*): Sacrifice in which the whole animal was burned on the altar; applied, in particular, to the meal offering (Lev. 6:15–6).

Wiener, Norbert (1894–1964): US mathematician; son of *Leo Wiener* (1862–1939), Yiddish and Slavic scholar. Norbert W. was a child prodigy and received a Harvard doctorate at age 18. He taught at the Massachusetts Institute of Technology. He created (and named) the science of cybernetics, dealing with computers.

Wiesel, Elie (1928–   ): Author. Born in Hungary, he survived Auschwitz and went to Paris and later to New York. At first a journalist, he turned to writing novels. His early work (*The Gates of the Forest, Night*) dealt with the Holocaust period. Later works were about Soviet Jewry (*Jews of Silence*), Hasidism (*Souls on Fire*), and Israel (*Beggar in Jerusalem*).

wigs: Although wigs were fashionable in talmudic times, the religious obligation for a married woman to wear a wig (*sheitel*) and never to expose her hair in public dates from the 15th cent.

Wilder, Billy (1905–   ): Film director. Born in Vienna, he worked in German films before going to Hollywood in 1934. He received six Oscars and his successes included *Some Like It Hot* and *The Apartment*.

Wilensky, Sir Roy (1907–): Rhodesian trade unionist and statesman. His father was Jewish and his mother non-Jewish, but W. is a professing Jew. In his early days he was a professional boxing champion and railway engine driver. He entered politics and was named to the "Northern Rhodesia Executive Council." When the Central African Federation was founded in 1953, he became its deputy premier, and from 1956 until its break-up in 1963, was its premier.

Willstatter, Richard (1872–1942): German organic chemist. He was professor at Munich until 1925, when he resigned on account of anti-Semitic pressure; he spent his last years in Switzerland. He was awarded the Nobel Prize in 1915 for his work on plant pigments, especially chlorophyll. He also showed that enzymes are chemical substances.

Winchell, Walter (1897–1972): US journalist. He wrote a satirical gossip column in the New York *Mirror* 1929–69 which was widely syndicated. He also broadcast over radio and television.

wine: In early times, w. was a regular beverage, although it was forbidden to imbibe to excess. It was used in sacrifices and in Jewish ceremonies such as KIDDUSH and HAVDALAH. On the festival of Purim, it was permitted to drink considerably. The drinking of w. belonging to non-Jews was strictly forbidden by the early rabbis. Wine-growing was practiced by Jews throughout the ages and in modern Israel (notably at Zikhron Yaakov and Rishon-le-Zion). Jews were also prominent in the wine and liquor trade, especially in eastern Europe.

***Wingate, Charles Orde** (1903–1944): British soldier and Zionist. Stationed in the British army in Palestine during the Arab terror campaign of 1936–9, he formed a unit of Haganah fighters to counter the Arab attacks (Special Night Squads). Many of the military heroes of the State of Israel received their first training under W.

Winnipeg: Canadian town. Jews were there from the late 1870s, and several synagogues were founded in the 1880s. The community grew rapidly from the late 19th cent. with E. European immigration. In 1976 there were 18,500 Jews.

Wisconsin: US state. Jews were among the early pioneers in the state, the first-known Jewish settler being a fur trader who came in 1794. The major influx was from Central Europe after 1880. The first congregation, mainly composed of traders, was founded in Milwaukee in 1847, and one was founded in La Crosse in 1857. In 1976 there were 32,070 Jews in W., the largest communities being in Milwaukee (23,000) and Madison (3,700).

Wisdom Literature: Term applied to a literary tradition in late biblical books (Proverbs, Job, Ecclesiastes, etc.) which contain practical aphorisms pertaining to the right life. In post-Exilic literature, wisdom is identified with knowledge of the Torah and is eulogized in apocryphal and other works (Ben Sira, Wisdom of Solomon, etc.).

Wisdom of Solomon: Book in Apocrypha. It portrays the nature and rewards of wisdom and belongs to the WISDOM LITERATURE. Attributed to Solomon, it was in fact written originally in Greek, possibly by an Alexandrian Jew. Its date is uncertain.

Wise, Isaac Mayer (1819–1900): US Reform rabbi. Born in Bohemia, he went to the US in 1846. W. was rabbi in Albany and in 1854 went to Cincinnati, where he pioneered Reform practice. He founded the English weekly *The Israelite* and the German-language *Die Deborah* and edited both. He published a Reform prayer book, *Minhag America*. In 1873, he formed the UNION OF AMERICAN CONGREGA-

TIONS; in 1875 he founded the HEBREW UNION COLLEGE, of which he was president until his death; and in 1889 he organized the CENTRAL CONFERENCE OF AMERICAN RABBIS.

Wise, Stephen Samuel (1874–1949): US reform rabbi, Zionist, and communal leader. After serving as rabbi in New York and Portland, Oregon, he founded the Free Synagogue in New York (1907) based on the principle of the freedom of the pulpit. He established the JEWISH INSTITUTE OF RELIGION in 1922 to train Reform rabbis. W. was a founder and the first secretary of the Federation of American Zionists and held leadership positions in the Zionist movement, both in the US and internationally. He was a founder of the American Jewish Congress and, for many years, its president. W. was active on behalf of organized labor and in New York municipal affairs.

Wissenschaft des Judentums (Ger. "Science of Judaism"): Term coined in 1823 by Leopold ZUNZ to develop Jewish scholarship on scientific lines. Zunz, together with A. GEIGER, was its founder. It was strongest in Central Europe, although there were manifestations in Galicia and elsewhere throughout the continent. It led to many scholarly periodicals and publications, and also to the founding of the modern type of rabbinical seminary. It was the forerunner of the "Jewish Studies" developed in the 20th cent.

WIZO: Abbreviation of Women's International Zionist Organization, an organization of women Zionists founded in London in 1920 and active in 50 countries. At first it had headquarters in London and Palestine but from 1948 its headquarters have been in Tel Aviv. It is a worldwide movement, but does not operate in the US, where the parallel organization is Hadassah (in Canada the women's Zionist movement called Hadassah is affiliated with W.). It has 250,000 members, of whom 90,000 are in Israel. Its practical work in Israel includes child care and vocational and agricultural training.

Wolffsohn, David (1856–1914): Zionist leader. Born in Lithuania, he became a timber merchant in Cologne. An early Zionist and close colleague of Herzl, he was the chief figure in the establishment of the JEWISH COLONIAL TRUST, which he directed. He accompanied Herzl on his 1898 Palestine visit and succeeded him as president of the World Zionist Organization—an office he held until 1911.

Wolfson, Harry Austryn (1887–1974): Scholar of philosophy. Born in White Russia, he went to the US in 1903. He taught Hebrew literature and philosophy at Harvard, 1915–58 (professor 1925). He wrote studies on Jewish and general philosophy (Philo, Hasdai Crescas, Spinoza, Church Fathers, Averroes).

Wolfson, Sir Isaac (1897–): British businessman and philanthropist. He headed the Great Universal Stores chain group and bought out many other companies. He financed Wolfson Colleges in Oxford and Cambridge, established the W. Foundation, and made many generous grants in Britain and Israel. W. was president of the UNITED SYNAGOGUE.

Women's International Zionist Organization see **WIZO**

Woodbine: Village in New Jersey, US, established in 1891 as a center of Jewish agricultural settlement by the Baron de Hirsch Fund. In 1903 it was the first all-Jewish municipality in the US. It failed as an agricultural settlement of E. European Jews, and industry became its source of livelihood. Non-Jews settled there and the Jewish population declined, numbering 140 in 1968.

Workmen's   Circle

(Yiddish Arbeiter Ring): Jewish fraternal order in the US and Canada, with 64,000 members in 421 branches (of which about a quarter are English-speaking; the others, Yiddish. It was organized in 1900 and was active in trade unions with a large Jewish membership. It runs a network of Jewish seminar schools, stressing the Yiddish language.

World Hebrew Union see **Berit Ivrit Olamit**

World Jewish Congress: Association of representative Jewish organizations and communities from all parts of the world. It was founded in 1936 to succeed the COMITÉ DES DÉLÉGATION JUIVES. Over 60 countries are represented, including E. European communities. It seeks to protect Jewish rights and interests in all lands. It has headquarters in Israel, Britain, and the US. Its first president was Stephen WISE, who was succeeded by Nahum GOLDMANN and Philip KLUTZNICK (from 1977).

World Union for Progressive Judaism: Root organization of Reform Jewish groups throughout the world. Founded in 1926, it has affiliated groups in 26 countries, with rabbinical seminars in London, Paris, and the US.

World Zionist Organization see **Jewish Agency, Zionism**

Worms: City in W. Germany. Jews were living there in the late 10th cent., and a synagogue was inaugurated in 1034. In 1074, the emperor rewarded the Jews for their loyalty by exempting them from taxes, and a charter of privileges was granted in 1090. However, the community was destroyed in the First Crusade and again in the Black Death. Many famous scholars (such as Baruch ben Meir and his son Meir of Ruthenburg) taught in W., and Rashi studied there. It was closely connected with the communities of Mainz and Speyer (see SHUM). The community underwent many vicissitudes. Its famous old synagogue with the "Rasli chapel" was burned by the Nazis in 1938 and reconstructed after the war. About 1,000 Jews were living there in 1933: only 50 in 1970.

Wouk, Herman (1915–): US author. He made his name with his novel of World War II, *The Caine Mutiny*. Subsequent successes included *Marjorie Morningstar* and *Winds of War*.

Written Law (Torah She-bi-khtav): Law given to Moses on Mt. Sinai. Originally it referred to the Pentateuch (the Torah) but later it was used for the entire Bible. It contrasts with Oral Law.

Wroclaw see **Breslau**

Wyoming: US state. Jews arrived in W. in 1867, and there was an influx as a result of the 1876 gold rush. A synagogue was first established in 1915 in Cheyenne. The number of Jews was never large; in 1976 there were 345.

Y

aaleh ve-yavo ("May [our remembrance] ascend and come"): Prayer recited in each *amidah* on new moons and festivals and in the grace after meals on those occasions. It is mentioned in the Talmud, and the style reflects the early *paytanim*.

yad ("hand"): A pointer, usually of silver, used as a guide in reading the Scroll of the Law.

Yad va-Shem ("Monument and Memorial"): Martyrs' and Heroes' Commemoration Authority in Jerusalem for the remembrance of the martyrs of the Holocaust. It was established in 1953 on Memorial Hill (next to Mt. Herzl) in Jerusalem. There is a memorial shrine, museum, archive, and library. Studies on the Holocaust are published under its auspices.

Yadaim ("Hands"): Eleventh tractate in the talmudic order of *Tohorot*. It has no *gemara* in either Talmud. It deals with rabbinic enactments concerning the washing of hands and their ritual impurity.

Yadin, Yigael (1917–): Israeli soldier, archeologist, and politician; son of E. L. SUKENIK. He was chief of operations during the Israel War of Independence and chief of staff of the Israeli army in 1949–52. He then resumed his archeological career, becoming professor at the Hebrew University. Y. excavated at Hazor and Masada and in the Judean Desert, and published studies on these expeditions as well as on many aspects of the Dead Sea Scrolls and the Bar Kokhba Letters. In 1976 he established the Democratic Movement for Change, which in 1977 joined the government coalition with Y. as deputy premier.

yahrzeit (Yiddish from Ger. "year-time"): Anniversary of the death of a near relative. The *y.* light, which burns for 24 hours, is lit and KADDISH is recited by the mourner in the synagogue.

Yalow, Rosalyn (1921–): US medical researcher. She was awarded a Nobel Prize in 1977 for devising a biological analytical technique (radioimmunoassay) for tracing minute substances in blood and tissue.

Yamin Noraim ("Days of Awe"): Term applied to the New Year and Day of Atonement and the intermediate period, constituting the Ten Days of Penitence, the traditional period of Divine judgment.

Yannai (5th-6th cent.?): Liturgical poet in Palestine. Biographical details are unknown. He wrote *kerovot* for each weekly Torah reading. His *piyyutim* were discovered only during the 19th-20th cent., especially in the Cairo Genizah.

Yannai, Alexander see **Alexander, Yannai**

Yarkon: River in Israel flowing into the Mediterran-

ean in northern Tel Aviv. It rises at Rosh ha-Ayin and its length is 16 miles. In ancient times a port stood on its northern bank. Since 1955, half of its waters have been diverted to the Negev for irrigation purposes.

Yarmuk: Longest river in Transjordan; running into the Jordan. It drops a total of over 2,750 ft., and this was utilized from the early 1920s in the hydroelectric plant set up at its confluence with the Jordan at Naharayim. This power plant was on the border between Jordan and Israel and has been unused since 1948.

Yeb see **Elephantine**

Yehoash (pen name of Solomon Bloomgarden; 1872–1927): Yiddish writer and translator. Born in Lithuania, from 1890 he lived in the US, spending many of his early years there in a home for consumptives. He wrote a great variety of works (poems, plays, stories, etc.) but is best known for his Yiddish translation of the Bible.

Yekum purkan (Aram. "May salvation . . . be granted"): Two Aramaic prayers recited in the Ashkenazi ritual on Sabbath before the Additional Service. One is for the welfare of students and teachers in the academies of Palestine and Babylonia, the other for the local community. They were composed in the gaonic period.

Yelammedenu see **Tanḥuma**

Yellin, David (1864–1941): Hebraist and educationist in Jerusalem. He founded and was principal of a teachers' college and president of the Teachers' Association. He was prominent in the revival of the Hebrew language. Active in many aspects of the work of the *yishuv*, he headed the Vaad Leumi (1920–28) and was deputy mayor of Jerusalem. His literary research centered on medieval Hebrew poetry.

Yemen: Its Jews claim that their ancestors arrived in biblical times. A Jewish population on a sizable scale is known from the pre-Islamic era. They made converts among the local inhabitants, of whom the best known was Dhu Nawas. After the rise of Islam, the Jews in Y. received protection and freedom of religion in return for payment of taxes, but their status was inferior and they suffered various discriminations. In the course of time, the study of the Kabbalah became popular, and there were distinguished scholars and liturgical poets. They were prone to messianic fervor. Many worked as artisans, especially as silversmiths and goldsmiths. Emigration to Palestine began in the late 19th cent., and by 1948, 18,000 Yemenite Jews had settled in the country; nearly all the remaining 46,000 went to Israel in 1949–50 in a specially organized exodus code-named Operation Magic Carpet, when they were flown from Aden. About 2,000 emigrated subsequently and only a few hundred remain.

Yeshiva University: Institution of higher learning under religious auspices in New York. It originated in the Etz Chaim Yeshivah founded in 1886 and the Isaac Elhanan Theological Seminary founded in 1897. The two merged in 1915, added Yeshiva College in 1928, and became Y.U. in 1945. Its college for women —Stern College—opened in 1954. It has over 7,000 students and many divisions, some in Judaica, others in general studies, including the Albert Einstein School of Medicine.

yeshivah: Oldest institution for higher talmudic learning in Judaism. For earlier periods see ACADEMY. After flourishing in Babylonia from the 2nd cent., it was introduced in S. France in the 10th cent. and in Spain, and spread to Central and Eastern Europe. Its modern growth dates from the foundation of the yeshivah at Volozhin in 1803. Other famous yeshivot in E. Europe include Tels, Slobodka, and Mir. Many of these transferred to US and Israel, which are now the major centers of y. study.

Yetzirah, Book of see **Sepher Yetzirah**

Yevamot ("Levirates"): First tractate in the MISHNAH order of *Nashim*, with *gemara* in both Talmuds. It deals with the laws of levirate marriage and the ceremony of *halitzah*.

Yevsektzia (Russ. abbr. "Jewish Section"): Jewish section of Russian Communist Party's propaganda department. It was active between 1918 and 1930. It initiated territorial schemes in the Crimea and BIROBIDJAN. It published the Yiddish daily *Emes*. Y. was responsible for the liquidation of Jewish organizations, etc. Its leaders were themselves killed during the 1936–38 purges.

Yiddish: Language, mainly of medieval German origin, widespread among Ashkenazi Jews from the Middle Ages until recently. It began in the 10th cent. in the Rhine region. There is a considerable admixture of Hebrew as well as words from the country in which it is used. The history of the language divided into Old Y. (1250–1500), Middle Y. (1500–1700), and Modern Y. (from 1700). There were many dialect variations according to region. It is written in Hebrew letters. In 1939 there were 10,000,000 to 12,000,000 speakers, but the Holocaust and the abandonment of the language by younger generations have greatly reduced the spoken and written use of the language. A rich literature developed through the ages, reaching its zenith in the late 19th and early 20th cent. with the writings of Mendele Mokher Seforim, Y.L. Peretz, and Sholem Aleichem. Y. press and theater also flourished, but these have sharply declined since 1939.

Yigdal ("May He Be Magnified"): Hymn sung at the conclusion of Sabbath and festival Evening Services; among Ashkenazim, also before the daily Morning Service. It is a poetic rendering of Maimonides' Thirteen Principles of the Faith. Its authorship has been ascribed to the 14th-cent. Daniel ben Judah of Rome.

yishuv: The Jewish community of Israel.

Yivo (Yiddish abbr. for Yiddisher Visenshaftlikher Institut, "Institute for Jewish Research"): Institute founded in Vilna in 1925, particularly for the study of Yiddish and Yiddish-speaking Jewry. During World War II, its main center was transferred to New York. It publishes various monographs and periodicals.

Yizhar S. see **Smilansky, Yizhar**

Yizkor ("He shall remember"): Opening word of memorial prayer commemorating the dead, recited for close relatives, recited in Ashkenazi communities on the last days of the three Pilgrim Festivals and on the Day of Atonement.

yod (ˈ): Tenth letter of the Hebrew alphabet. Numerical value: 10. Pronounced *y*; also used as vowel letter.

Yom Atzmaut see **Independence Day, Israel**

Yom Kippur see **Atonement, Day of**

Yom Kippur Katan ("Minor Day of Atonement"): Eve of new month which was a day of fast among the pious from the 16th cent. The custom originated in kabbalistic circles.

Yom Kippur War: War fought between Israel and the Arab states from October 6 to October 25, 1973. During Yom Kippur, Egyptian and Syrian armies launched attacks on Israeli positions, scoring initial successes. The Egyptians crossed the Suez Canal and captured the forward Israeli positions (the Bar-Lev line). Israel's first counterattacks on this front were unsuccessful, owing to the efficacy of Russian rocket weapons (Sam–6) and antitank weapons used by the Egyptians. Meanwhile the Syrians advanced a consider-able distance into the Golan Heights, but they were held and driven back past the lines from which they had started, despite reinforcements they received from Iraq, Jordan, and other states. Arab arms losses were replaced by the USSR, and Israel was the recipient of a massive arms lift from the US. On October 16, Israel crossed the Suez Canal and attacked the Egyptian forces from the rear, cutting off a sizable part of the Egyptian army and reaching the edges of the city of Suez. It was only when the Arabs were threatened with defeat that serious international efforts were made to stop the fighting. The US secretary of state, Henry Kissinger, flew to Moscow, and as a result of an agreement reached there, the UN passed a cease-fire resolution which was eventually implemented. Early in 1974, disengagement agreements were negotiated by Kissinger between Israel and Egypt and between Israel and Syria. In the former, Israel released the surrounded Egyptian army and evacuated the western bank of the Suez Canal, and in the latter it withdrew from the Syrian territories occupied in the course of the fighting. Israel lost over 2,600 men in the fighting. During the war, the Arabs for the first time used the oil weapon—threat of withdrawal of oil resources—to win widespread international support. The disappointment felt inside Israel as a result of the initial setbacks and the change in the international climate led to widespread unrest and dissatisfaction inside the country, culminating in changes in the political and military leadership.

yom tov see **festival**

Yoma ("The Day"): Fifth tractate of the MISHNAH order of *Moed*, with *gemara* in both Talmuds. It deals with the service of the high priest in the Temple on the Day of Atonement and concludes with laws of the fast.

Yose ben Yose (c. 4th–5th cent.): The earliest-known liturgical poet (*paytan*); probably lived in Palestine. Some of his *piyyutim* have been incorporated into the Sephardi liturgy on the Day of Atonement. Many of his compositions were discovered in the *genizah*.

Yosef, Ovadiah (1920–): Rabbi. He was born in Baghdad but was taken to Jerusalem as a child. For a time he was deputy chief rabbi of Egypt. In 1968 he was appointed Sephardi chief rabbi of Tel Aviv–Jaffa, and in 1972, Sephardi chief rabbi of Israel.

yotzer ("createth"): First of the two benedictions recited prior to the *Shema* in the Morning Service. It praises God "who restores light every morning." It is also used as a name for all the special hymns added to the *Shema* blessings on Sabbaths and festivals.

Young Israel: US organization representing over 100 Orthodox synagogues. It has branches throughout the US, and its activities included an Institute for Adult Jewish Studies and an employment bureau for Sabbath observers.

Young Judea: US Zionist youth organization; originally under the auspices of the Zionist Organization of America, later of Hadassah. Now called Ha-Shahar.

Youth Aliya (Aliyyat ha-Noar): Zionist organization for the transfer of children and young persons to Israel for their education. It was founded in 1933 by Recha Freyer. Under the direction of Henrietta Szold, it was responsible for rescuing many children from Nazi Europe. By May 1948, 31,000 children had been absorbed. By 1970, another 218,000 had been educated at Y.A. youth villages and educational establishments. Much of its budget is met by HADASSAH and other women's Zionist groups.

Yudghanites: Jewish sect founded in the 8th cent. by Yudghan of Hamadan, who maintained that he was a prophet. He taught a spiritual and mystic interpretation of the Torah. A small number of Y. were still to be found in Isfahan in the mid-10th cent.

Yugoslavia: Jews were living in the area now known as Y. in Roman times. There were communities in the medieval period, and these were considerably augmented by refugees from Spain in the late 15th cent. Under Ottoman rule the Jews generally fared well; but under the Christians, they suffered. Their situation improved with the 1878 Treaty of Berlin. In World War II, the Germans carried out large-scale deportations and massacres. Jews were active with the partisans. Most of those who survived left for Israel in 1948, and in 1976 7,500 remained.

Yulee (Levy), David (1810–1886): US politician. He was the first Jew to sit in the Senate, representing Florida, 1845–51 and 1855–61.

Z

Zacuto, Abraham ben Samuel (1452–c. 1515): Spanish astronomer and Hebrew author. He was the first to make a metal astrolabe, and his astronomical tables were used by Columbus. He taught astronomy at Salamanca and Saragossa. After the expulsion from Spain, he went to Portugal (where he became court astronomer and was consulted by Vasco da Gama), and after the expulsion from Portugal in 1497, to Tunis. Here he completed *Sepher Yuḥasin*, on the historical development of the Oral Law.

Zadok: Priest in the time of David. He established a dynasty which held the high priesthood until Hasmonean times.

Zambia: Jews were pioneers in the country (then Northern Rhodesia) and helped to develop its copper mining. 400 Jews lived there in 1976.

Zamenhof, Ludwig Lazarus (1859–1917): Philologist and creator of Esperanto. An ophthalmologist in Warsaw, he published in 1887 his proposal for a simple international language.

Zangwill, Israel (1864–1926): English author. His novels and stories dealing with Jewish life in the East End of London (e.g., *Children of the Ghetto*) were extremely popular. He also wrote plays (*Melting Pot*), verse translations of Jewish liturgy, and other works. He was an early follower of Herzl, but after the rejection of the UGANDA SCHEME, he left the Zionist movement and founded the Jewish Territorial Organization, which sought (unsuccessfully) to find alternatives to Palestine as places for autonomous Jewish settlement.

Zavim ("Sufferers from Flux"): Ninth tractate in the MISHNAH order of *Tohorot*, with no *gemara* in either Talmud. It deals with ritual impurity of a person with a running issue (probably gonorrhea).

zayin (ז): Seventh letter of the Hebrew alphabet. Numerical value: 7. Pronounced *z*.

Zealots: Group of Jewish militant nationalists in 1st cent. C.E. It stemmed from the anti-Roman activities of Judah the Galilean in 6 C.E. The Z. played a key role in the revolt against Rome in 66 CE. They sought to intimidate other groups in Jerusalem, causing civil war. Under their leader John of Gischala, they controlled the city when the siege began in 70. Their final stand was at MASADA under Eleazar ben Jair.

Zebulun: Sixth son of JACOB and LEAH. The tribe of Z. was one of the strongest in northern Israel. Its territory included the Valley of Jezreel, and the tribe was associated with trade. The plain between Haifa and Acre is known as the Plain of Z., al-though this name is historically unwarranted.

Zechariah (d. 743 BCE): King of Israel, the son of JEROBOAM II. After a six-month reign he was assassinated by Shallum, thereby ending the dynasty of Jehu.

Zechariah (6th cent. BCE): Prophet; lived at the time of the return from the Babylonian Exile. Like his contemporary HAGGAI, he urged the immediate rebuilding of the Temple. The book of his prophecies is the 11th in the Minor Prophets section of the Bible. The latter part is eschatological in character and attributed by many scholars to a different authorship.

Zedekiah (Mattaniah): Last king of Judah, who ruled 597–586 BCE, the son of JOSIAH. He was appointed by Nebuchadnezzar, king of Babylonia, but despite the warnings of Jeremiah went over to Egypt. As a result Nebuchadnezzar reinvaded Israel and captured Jerusalem. Z. was captured and his sons were murdered in front of him; he was blinded and sent in chains to Babylonia, where he died.

Zederbaum, Alexander (pseudonym Erez; 1816–1893): Journalist. He founded and edited *Ha-Melitz* (1860), the first Hebrew weekly in Russia, as well as its Yiddish supplement *Kol Mevasser*.

Zeitlin, Hillel (1872–1943): Philosopher and Yiddish journalist. At first a Zionist, he became a Territorialist under the shock of the Kishivne pogroms, which also led him to return to religion. He wrote initially in Hebrew but from 1906 mostly in Yiddish. Z., who lived much of his life in Vilna, is regarded as the leading proponent of Hasidic thought in modern Yiddish literature and translated the Zohar into Hebrew. He died during deportation to an extermination camp.

Zeitlin, Solomon (1892–1976): Historian. Born in Russia, he settled in the US in 1915 and taught at Dropsie College, Philadelphia, from 1921. He edited the *Jewish Quarterly Review* and wrote many works on the Second Temple period. He assigned a medieval date to the Dead Sea Scrolls.

zekuhut avot ("merit of the fathers"): Doctrine that the pious deeds of the parents bring blessing also for their progeny. This applies in particular to the merits of the Three Patriarchs.

zemirot ("songs"): Sabbath table hymns. The custom, although recorded earlier, was especially developed in the 16th cent. by the kabbalists, who were responsible for composing many z. The Hasidim have a large repertoire, in particular for Sabbath afternoon meals. The term z. is also used among Sephardim, Italian Jews, and Yemenites for the PESUKEI DE-ZIMRA.

Zephaniah (7th cent. BCE): Ninth of the 12 Minor Prophets; of royal descent. He was a contemporary of Jeremiah. His prophecies were largely directed to the aristocracy and were uttered in the early part of the reign of Josiah. He foresees the coming of the Day of the Lord when the evil will be punished and the righteous rewarded.

Zeraim ("Seeds"): First order of the MISHNAH, consisting of 11 tractates, dealing with agricultural legislation.

Zerubbabel (6th cent. BCE): Leader of the Jewish exiles returning from Babylonia. He was a grandson of King Jehoiachin and of Davidic descent. He was appointed governor of Judah under Darius I (521 BCE). The work of rebuilding the Temple started under him, but it had to be suspended, and there is no indication whether he was present at its completion.

Zevahim ("Sacrifices"): First tractate in the MISHNAH order of *Kodashim*, with *gemara* in the Babylonian Talmud only. Its subject matter is the slaughter of animals and birds for sacrifice in the Temple.

Zhitlowsky, Chaim (1865–1943): Philosopher of the Yiddish culture movement. He was a noted figure in the Russian Socialist-Revolutionary Party, the Bund, and the Territorialists. He lived outside Russia from 1888 to 1905 and from 1908 he made his home in New York. In his last years, he was strongly pro-Soviet.

Ziegfeld, Florenz (1869–1932): US theatrical producer, known for the annual musical revues Z. *Follies*, presented from 1907.

Zikhron Yaakov: Israeli village on Mt. Carmel, founded in 1882 by newcomers from Rumania. It was assisted in its early days by Baron Edmond de ROTHSCHILD and developed as a center of wine production. The remains of Baron de Rothschild and his wife were interred nearby (at Ramat haNadiv) in 1955. The population in 1972 was 4,726.

Zim: Israel shipping company founded 1949. It has extensive cargo services but has cut down its former large passenger fleet. Its head offices are in Haifa.

Zimra, David ben Solomon ibn Avi (1479–1573): Halakhic authority and kabbalist, known as Radbaz. Born in Spain, he was chief rabbi

of Egyptian Jewry for 40 years, and then was *dayyan* in Safed for 20 years. He left over 3,000 responsa as well as a commentary on Maimonides' *Mishneh Torah* and kabbalistic works.

Zimri (d. 885 BCE): King of Israel. Captain of chariots for ELAH, he murdered the king and seized the throne, but was deposed by Omri and committed suicide after a 7-day reign.

Zinoviev, Gregori Vevsevevich (1883–1936): Russian Communist leader and advocate of world revolution. He was an active Bolshevik from 1903 and a noted orator. An intimate of Lenin, he traveled with him in 1917 in the sealed train. He was the main architect of the Comintern in 1919 and one of the troika who ruled Russia after Lenin's death. In the 1936 purges, he was charged, convicted of plotting against the state, and subsequently shot.

Zion: The original Mt. Z. was probably to the southeast of Jerusalem, although its exact identification is disputed. The present Mt. Z. has been so called only since the Middle Ages. It contains an ancient tomb popularly identified as the tomb of King David, as well as the Dormition Abbey with the site associated by Christians with the Last Supper. Recent excavations have shown the remains of Herod's palace. Z. is also a poetical name for Jerusalem.

Zion Mule Corps: Detachment of 650 men for mule transport in British army during part of World War I. It was founded in Egypt in 1915 on the initiative of TRUMPELDOR and JABOTINSKY. It fought in the Gallipoli campaign and was disbanded in 1916.

Zionism: Movement whose goal is the return of the Jewish people to the Land of Israel. Jewish life in the Diaspora has always been characterized in prayers, messianic movements, and constant ALIYAH. In the late 19th cent. the HIBBAT ZION movement, especially in Eastern Europe, began to crystallize the concept, which became an effective instrument under Theodor HERZL, who established the World Zionist Organization at the First Zionist Congress in 1897. On this occasion the policy of the movement was spelled out in the BASLE PROGRAM. It proceeded to establish the JEWISH COLONIAL TRUST as its financial arm. The movement in its early stages was divided among political Zionists (stressing the obtaining of political rights), practical Zionists (stressing the implementation of settlement in Palestine), religious Zionists, and cultural Zionists (the last stressing Israel as a spiritual center of inspiration). The movement was centered in Europe and during and after World War I achieved its first great political success with the recognition of a Jewish National Home by the League of Nations. After the war, Z. operated through the JEWISH AGENCY with the KEREN HAYESOD as its financial instrument. It worked for the implementation of the British Mandate, for the encouragement of immigration, and through the national Zionist movements for fundraising and education. With the establishment of the State of Israel in 1948, some of the functions of the Zionist Movement were taken over by the State, but Zionist leadership remained responsible for the organization and financing of immigration, of immigrant absorption (until 1970), of initial agricultural settlement, and of educational and information work throughout the world. The supreme institution is the ZIONIST CONGRESS, and ideological differences are expressed through the Zionist parties.

Zionist Commission: Commission appointed by the British government in 1918 and sent to Palestine to advise on matters related to Jews. It was headed initially by Chaim WEIZMANN. In 1921 its functions were transferred to the Zionist Executive in Palestine.

Zionist Congresses: Supreme institution of the Zionist Movement. The first such gathering was held in 1897 at Basle. Since 1951 they have been held in Jerusalem. Participants are elected according to parties with voting open to Zionists who purchase a SHEKEL.

Zionist Organization of America (ZOA): US organization founded in 1898 and affiliated with the World Confederation of General Zionists. It conducts Zionist Activities in the US and supports projects in Israel.

Zipporah: Wife of Moses and daughter of Jethro. She bore Moses two sons, Gershom and Eliezer. She saved the life of one of her sons by circumcising him (Exod. 4:24–6).

Zohar ("Splendor"): Central work of the KABBALAH. It is a commentary on the Pentateuch and certain books of the Hagiographa. It attributes its origin to R. SIMEON BEN YOHAI but it is now generally agreed that it originated with the 13th-cent. Spanish kabbalist Moses de LEON, who incorporated earlier material. The work is written in Aramaic. It became extremely influential, espe-

cially in the period following the expulsion from Spain.

*Zola, Emile (1840–1902): French novelist. He was an outstanding defendant of Dreyfus, and his article *J'accuse,* which indicted the persecuters of Dreyfus, appeared on the front page of Clemenceau's paper *L'Aurore.* Zola himself was forced to flee to England for a while.

zugot ("pairs"): Pairs of scholars transmitting the Oral tradition in the period preceding the *tannaim.* They are listed in *Avot,* the first being the *nasi* (head of the Sanhedrin) and the second his deputy (*av bet din*). They were: Yose ben Yoezer and Yose ben Johanan; Joshua ben Perahiah and Nittai the Arbelite; Judah ben Tabbai and Simeon ben Shetah; Shemaiah and Avtalion; Hillel and Shammai.

Zunser, Eliakum (1836–1913): Yiddish poet. His popular songs, originally recited on festive occasions, received wide circulation. He left Eastern Europe for New York in 1889.

Zunz, Leopold (1794–1886): German historian; founder of WISSENSCHAFT DES JUDENTUMS. He laid down the program for the movement and published works of outstanding scholarship. His best-known study was his history of Jewish homiletics,

Gottesdienstliche Vorträge der Juden. His other scholarly works covered most fields of Jewish scholarship, notably Midrash and liturgy.

Zweig, Arnold (1887–1968): German author. During the Nazi period he lived in Haifa, but he returned to East Germany after World War II, where he was president of the Academy of Arts. His best-known work was his war novel *The Case of Sergeant Grischa,* published in 1927.

Zweig, Stefan (1881–1942): Austrian writer. He wrote novels, essays, dramas, and a series of literary and historical biographies. His fiction included *Beware of Pity.* His autobiography, *The World of Yesterday,* appeared after he and his wife committed suicide in Brazil, to which they had fled after the Nazi accession to power.

CECIL ROTH

Cecil Roth was born in London in 1899 and educated at Oxford. Among his many books are *History of the Marranos, History of the Jews in England, The Jews in the Renaissance* and *A Short History of the Jewish People*. His death has deprived the world of one of its foremost Jewish scholars.